D0855166

Woman and Man in Paul

Overcoming a Misunderstanding

Norbert Baumert, S.J.

translated by
Patrick Madigan, S.J.
and
Linda M. Maloney

A Michael Glazier Book
THE LITURGICAL PRESS
Collegeville, Minnesota

A Michael Glazier Book published by The Liturgical Press

Cover design by David Manahan, O.S.B. Detail; St. Cecilia with Sts. Paul, John, Augustine and Mary Magdalene; oil painting by Raphael, ca. 1513–16; Pinacoteca, Bologna.

This book was originally published in German by Echter Würzburg under the title *Frau und Mann bei Paulus: Überwindung eines Missverständnisses.*

© 1996 by The Order of St. Benedict, Inc., Collegeville, Minnesota. All rights reserved. No part of this book may be reproduced in any form or by any means, electronic or mechanical, including photocopying, recording, taping, or any retrieval system, without the written permission of The Liturgical Press, Collegeville, Minnesota 56321. Printed in the United States of America.

| 1 | 2 | 3 | 4 | 5 | 6 | 7 | 8 |

Library of Congress Cataloging-in-Publication Data

Baumert, Norbert.
    [Frau und Mann bei Paulus. English]
    Woman and man in Paul : overcoming a misunderstanding / Norbert Baumert ; translated by Patrick Madigan and Linda M. Maloney.
        p.   cm.
    "A Michael Glazier book."
    Includes bibliographical references.
    ISBN 0-8146-5055-4
    1. Bible. N.T. Epistles of Paul—Criticism, interpretation, etc. 2. Sex—Biblical teaching. 3. Sex role—Biblical teaching. 4. Marriage—Biblical teaching. 5. Men (Christian theology)--Biblical teaching. 6. Woman (Christian theology)—Biblical teaching. 7. Bible. N.T. Epistles of Paul. I. Title.
BS2655.S49B3813 1996
227'.083053—dc20
95-4795
CIP

Contents

Abbreviations

Abbott	Walter M. Abbott, S.J., ed., *The Documents of Vatican II,* New York: The America Press, 1966
Atf	Baumert, N., *Antifeminismus bei Paulus*
BDR	Blass, F. and A. Debrunner, *Grammatik*
ChuA	Baumert, N., *Charisma und Amt*
DGJ	Baumert, N., *Dem Geist Jesu folgen*
DS	Denzinger, H. and A. Schonmetzer, *Enchiridion Symbolorum, Definitionum et Declarationum de Rebus Fidei et Morum,* 35th ed., New York: Herder, 1974
DV	Vatican II, dogmatic constitution *Dei Verbum* (Revelation), Abbot, 111–128; Flannery, 750–765
EuE	Baumert, N., *Ehelosigkeit und Ehe im Herrn*
EWNT	Balz, H. and G. Schneider, eds., *Exegetisches Wörterbuch zum Neuen Testament*
Flannery	Austin Flannery, O.P., ed., *Vatican Council II: The Conciliar and Post Conciliar Documents,* Collegeville, Minn.: The Liturgical Press, 1975
GdG	Baumert, N., *Gaben des Geistes*
GS	Vatican II, pastoral constitution *Gaudium et Spes* (Church in Modern World), Abbott, 319–331; Flannery, 283–292
LG	Vatican II, dogmatic constitution *Lumen Gentium* (Church), Abbott, 14–96; Flannery, 350–423
Lit	"Literature index" (from the German, *Literaturverzeichnis*)
LThK	Höfer, J. and K. Rahner, eds., *Lexikon für Theologie und Kirche*

| L.-Sc. | Liddell, H. G. and R. Scott, *A Greek-English Lexicon* |
| M.-G. | Menge, H. and O. Guthlin, *Enzyklopädisches Wörterbuch der griechischen und deutschen Sprache* |

Münchener Neues Testament: See under Hainz, J

NA	Nestle, E. and K. Aland, *Novum Testamentum Graece*
OT	Vatican II, decree *Optatam Totius* (Priestly Formation), Abbott, 437–457; Flannery, 707–724
Past.	Pastoral letters
PG	J.-P. Migne, ed., *Patrologia Cursus Completus: Series Graeca,* 161 vols., Paris, 1857–1866
PL	J.-P. Migne, ed., *Patrologia Cursus Completus: Series Latina,* 221 vols., Paris, 1844–1855
RAC	Klausner, Th., ed., *Hausgemeinde und Hauskirche im frühen Christentum*

Rehkopf, F. See under Blass, F. and A. Debrunner

Schrage, W. See under Gerstenberger, E. S. and W. Schrage

s.v.	sub voce = see under the respective term, e.g., in a lexicon
ThWNT	Kittel, G., ed., *Theologisches Wörterbuch zum Neuen Testament*
TRE	Kruse, H. and G. Müller, eds., *Theologische Realenzyklopädie*
Ts	Baumert, N., *Täglich sterben und auferstehen*
UR	Vatican II decree *Unitatis Redintegratio* (Ecumenism), Abbott, 341–366; Flannery, 452–470
UT	Unified Translation
vl./vll.	varia(e) lectio(nes) = different reading(s)
WNT	Bauer, W., *Wörterbuch zum Neuen Testament*

Introduction

What is Paul's position on human sexuality? What does he say about the station of men and women? In his letters do we not detect a hatred of the human body? He frequently takes up sexuality under the title of sin, and the married state seems to come out decidedly in second place in comparison with the celibate state. Further, Paul seems to preach a subordination of women in the family, in society, and in the Christian community. If we add to all this the consequences and uses to which his more striking passages have been put through the ages, we indeed bend under a crushing weight. Too often these texts have formed an obstacle between humankind and God and rendered more difficult humanity's access to the Good News.

But with such an interpretation have we really done justice to Paul? In the following pages a different picture of Paul will be sketched. In this process not only will new light be shed on well-known Pauline statements; in many instances the currently favored translation itself will be subject to interrogation and an alternative understanding uncovered; through this method many of the criticisms leveled against Paul will be killed at their root. Others will be revealed as conditioned by their time period, in such a way that the permanently valid proclamation can be separated from its time-encumbered formulation. We will achieve this through a methodical investigation of the literal meaning of the text as well as through an appropriate hermeneutic, the correct starting points for an interrogation of biblical texts. Both contribute to our grasping what "the writer really intended to say"

(DV 12). In this way the authentic theological authority of the apostle takes on distinctive features.

The result is a genuine liberation. The criterion for "freedom" is naturally not a subjective *Zeitgeist* or the complaints and aspirations of unredeemed humanity, but rather the revelation of God, who engages humanity to the full measure of its nature and "renews them according to the image of the Creator" (Col 3:10). The often twisting path through the textual analysis lands us in a surprising new territory and reveals Paul to be, in the questions here broached, the proclaimer of the freedom of the children of God.

In part "A"—the principal part—seven chapters will present passages from those letters which are generally recognized to be authentically Pauline; part "B" will discuss striking texts from the other letters ascribed traditionally to Paul. Without venturing a judgment on the question of authenticity, this method will enable us to put the principal texts in direct confrontation with thematically related passages from the remaining Pauline corpus. Such a method will allow us to see, on the one hand, how Paul judges in the so-called principal letters, and on the other, if and how the "deutero-Pauline" letters differ from the former on the themes under consideration.[1] Many of the topics treated in part A will turn up again in part B.

Since our investigation is predominantly oriented toward the text, we must be willing to accept such a splintering. The cross-references which appear in the footnotes permit a reading of Paul that is more theme oriented. As a help to this there is a discussion of the biblical view of humanity in part C, which should be read in tandem with the others, especially with the "perspectives" given in the last part. For what are the consequences, if the basic texts must be read in a new and different fashion, for the teaching and life of the Church? Is Galatians 3:28 really a ringing manifesto for the social liberation of the young Christian community? What dogmatic, moral, pastoral, and social consequences should be drawn from the vision presented in parts A through C? In part D I avail myself of these other theological disciplines to reflect on such questions.

---

1. Recently the authenticity of Ephesians has again been defended more strongly; see below, notes 351, 513, 652. There are even voices in favor of the authenticity of the Pastoral Letters; see below, note 401.

The selection and arrangement of passages is done according to content. This is the more simply and naturally achieved in that 1 Corinthians, from which most of the texts are drawn, is not a single, unified letter, but rather consists of distinct and independent units: 1-4; 7; 12-14; 15; 16. Between these we find collections of shorter statements loosely bound together by topic: 5-6 and 8-11. The same holds true for 2 Corinthians. I thus do not agree with the recent tendency, arising principally in Anglo-Saxon countries, to again defend the thesis of the unity of the document.[2] It is much more likely—following Lüdemann's thesis, which puts Paul's first stay in Corinth as well as the Letter to the Thessalonians in the year 41[3]—that the different parts of the letters to the Corinthians appeared over a span of fifteen years (41-55). This hypothesis opens entirely different possibilities for the development of the Corinthian community and for Paul himself. More numerous and longer stays by the apostle in Corinth (also, moreover, in Philippi and Thessalonica) become possible. The reports in Acts shape the life of Paul in a literary fashion, similar to the way Jesus' life is freely handled in the Gospels. The local traditions are probably authentic here, even if, as in Acts 18:1-18, they push together or amalgamate several visits. The divisions between units would be perhaps 18:11-12 and 17-18. In this way new possibilities are opened for the sequence of distinct units in 1 Corinthians. All this would further justify our method, especially the treatment of individual thought-units by themselves.

The key to our new interpretation is supplied predominantly by philological investigations. I have already published one part of the exegetical research in an earlier work,[4] and another part

2. L. L. Belleville, "Continuity or Discontinuity," in *EvQ* 91 (1987) 15-37. Many of the arguments quoted in favor of uniformity could be explained by the ordering intention of the redactor.

3. G. Lüdemann, *Paulus, der Heidenapostel I* (FRLANT 123) (Göttingen, 1980) esp. 173-212. See, however, the questions from D. Slingerland, "Acts 18, 1-17 and Luedemann's Pauline Chronology," *JBL* 109 (1990) 686-690. Indeed, the chronology of all the remaining texts of the New Testament is newly open to question, with a tendency toward an earlier dating and the postulate of an earlier Hebrew or Aramaic version; see K. Faschian, "Neue Studien zur Frage der Entstehung der ntl. Schriften," *WIWei* 53 (1990) 66-72.

4. *Ehelosigkeit und Ehe im Herrn; Eine Neuinterpretation von 1 Kor 7* (fzb 47) (Würzburg, 1984) (abbreviated "EuE"). This constitutes a new

in a later publication.[5] I avail myself frequently of my dissertation (Ts), and other publications.[6] It is the labor of this book to demonstrate how these multifaceted earlier studies belong together and constitute individual stones, so to speak, that must be placed next to one another to fashion a new mosaic of Paul. To the extent that further linguistic investigation is carried out here, it takes place in indented blocks and in reduced type or in the notes,[7] so that the main text may be devoted to the unfolding of the principal theme and remain accessible to readers who cannot handle Greek. Whatever Greek or Hebrew words must nevertheless be referred to are transcribed in the main text in Latin letters. Long quotations and tables are also printed in reduced type.

We will present our results in opposition to the thesis of the so-called German "unified translation" (UT, the German "Ein-

---

interpretation of 1 Cor 7. Chapters A II–IV present the results of this research. Reviews: J. Hainz in *ThPh* 60 (1985) 578f.; J. Murphy-O'Connor in *Revue Biblique* 92 (1985) 462f.; M. Orge in *Ephemerides Mariologicae* (Madrid, 1985) (Spanish); B. Bruns in *Pastoralblatt für die Diözesen Aachen,* etc., 37 (1985) 158f.; M. S. Zimmermann in *Geist und Leben* 58 (1985) 455–459; S. Medala in *Collectanea Theologica* 56 (1986) I 171–173; D. Tomczyk, IV 167–173 (both in Polish); K. N. Papadopoulos in *ΚΡΙΤΙΚΟΝ ΚΑΙ ΒΙΒΛΙΟΓΡΑΦΙΚΟΝ ΔΕΛΤΙΟΝ,* τόμ. *ΝΨ* (1986), τεῦχ. *Γ,* ʼΑΘΗΝΑΙ 1986, σελ. 692–693 (modern Greek). I discuss the observations and criticisms of Murphy-O'Connor and H. Kruse at the appropriate places; see below, notes 55, 82, 190, etc.

5. N. Baumert, *Antifeminismus bei Paulus?* (series: *Forschung zur Bibel* 68 [Würzburg, 1992] abbreviated "Atf"), with the following "individual studies": A: I Gal 3:28; II 1 Cor 11:3-16; III 1 Cor 14:33b-36; IV 1 Thess 4:3-8; V Rom 7:1-6; 1 Cor 5/6; VI 1 Cor 7:10f. (and the Synoptic divorce texts). B: VII Eph 5:15-33; VIII 1 Tim 2; IX 1 Pet 3. C: X ἔνι in Gal 3:28; XI 2 Cor 10:2 and 1 Thess 3:3; XII καιρός (e.g., "Atf I 1 a").

6. See the bibliography. Semantic and syntactic corrections in the interpretation of an author (i.e., St. Paul) can only be justified from an appreciation of the entire work; a new insight into one aspect simultaneously alters the entire picture. Thus my exegetical studies to date are all internally related and mutually support one another; cf. Ts 263–266.

7. **The numbering of the footnotes normally jumps at the beginning of each chapter to the next increment of "50" (thus: 51, 101, 151, etc.). Thus certain numbers are skipped.** References within the book are given by citing the respective chapter (e.g., "see below, A II 2") or a text which is to be found close to a footnote (e.g., footnote 14: see "close to note 219").

heitsübersetzung" translated throughout into English) which presents a greater consensus of contemporary exegetes than would a translation by a single person. Moreover, most of the corrections proposed in this book could stand out in contrast to almost all current Bible translations, for the latter presuppose the same basic understanding of the original text. It is thus not a matter here of stylistic fine points only; readers will notice how great the difference in content is. In the presentations of the texts, on both sides in *italics* are printed any words in which an objective (semantic) change is recommended. Those words printed in **bolder** type are emphasized as a consequence of their **position** in the Greek sentence. Exclamation marks (!) indicate altered punctuation marks, structure, or syntax. Aids to the reader in the form of parentheses and occasional awkward renderings have been presented in order to allow the thought sequence and the field of associations of the original text to appear as clearly as possible. For a fluent reading or reading out loud, one may omit the material between parentheses.

The topic is relevant to our contemporary concerns. Is the community of believers prepared to transform its thinking, to listen to women, to learn from them and to allow them to take on full stature within the Church, so that this voice by which God speaks may also advance to its full distinctness? Exegetical research,[8] feminist literature, scientific conferences, and spiritual retreats have all contributed to the production of this book—although I could not at this point separate or disentangle the complex path of their interaction. At those points where it is primarily a question of translation, I have supplied the most important grounds for my choices.[9] Specialists will regret the omission of a richer bibliography; however, it was my goal here to assimilate exegeti-

8. Although Delling, Niederwimmer, and Neidhart remain firm in interpreting Paul in a manner hostile to the body and to women, the general tendency has for a long time been moving in the direction of correcting this misinterpretation; see, e.g., the works of Neuhäusler, Fitzmyer, Murphy-O'Connor, Thyen, Gerstenberger and Schrage, Schüssler Fiorenza, Brooten, Schnackenburg, Thraede, Dautzenberg, Merklein, Weiser, and others; see the bibliography.

9. The bibliography at the conclusion of this work contains only those works most frequently cited and additions to the bibliography in *EuE* (see

cal results into a wider constellation, so as to make them accessible to a wider public.

below, note 51). Otherwise see the abbreviations in Schwertner, *Theologische Realenzyklopädie,* "Abkürzungsverzeichnis," Berlin 1976 (TRE), and for the authors of antiquity those in WNT and L-Sc. (sometimes more extensive).

Part A

The Principal Pauline Letters

I. Cordial Relations

1. Forceful Language

"God is my witness, how I long for all of you with the heart-felt love[10] of Jesus Christ" (Phil 1:8). This exclamation from the imprisoned apostle shows a man who, with body and soul, heart and mind, has received and passed on to others the love of God. A rigid antifeminism and sexual inhibition do not fit well with such a personality. Then why does the reading of his letters leave behind a divided impression? It is widely recognized now that his sharp distinction between spirit and flesh does not indicate an anthropological, but rather a soteriological dualism: he does not mean a difference between soul and body, but rather that between divine power on the one hand, and human weakness and sin on the other.[11] However, the principal question remains. Before we take on the disputed texts, however, we should first attend carefully to the warm, lively talk of the apostle.

Paul prays for the Philippians (1:9) that their "love should more and more overflow with knowledge and all understanding" (spiritual "aesthesia"), and affirms of the communities in Macedonia that they have not only contributed gold, but "have given their

10. $\Sigma\pi\lambda\acute{\alpha}\gamma\chi\nu\alpha$–literally, the intestines, as the seat of the affections.
11. For the reason Paul uses "flesh" to refer to sin, see below, C 3.

very selves, first to the Lord and then to us" (2 Cor 8:5). He is so personally bound to his communities that he longs to see them, he struggles for them, he trembles if they drift into danger, and "revives" if they "stand firm in the Lord" (1 Thess 2:17–3:10; 2 Cor 7:7-11). He is not only a man of extraordinarily strong feelings, but also disposes of an exceptional freedom in expressing these feelings. His speech again reflects this; Wilamowitz discerned in it an "invigorating lack of form which nevertheless captures and conveys his thoughts and feelings."[12] Paul, who would be "all things to all people" (1 Cor 9:22), manages to "weep with those who are weeping and to laugh with those who are laughing" (Rom 12:15), as well as to urge the communities to embrace and kiss (2 Cor 12:12; Rom 16:16). We should believe him when he says to the Corinthians that he "holds them in his heart" and has "inscribed them in his heart, not with ink, but with the Spirit of the living God" (2 Cor 7:3; 3:2; Phil 1:7). Only lovers speak that way.

In his relation with God all his senses are involved, not only sight and hearing (Gal 1:16; 2 Cor 12:1-5; Rom 10:14-17), but also smell and taste (2 Cor 2:15; 5:2-4[13]). The Spirit of the incarnate Son of God has indeed constituted him as a "new man." Thus he can say: "Imitate me, as I have become an imitator of Christ" (1 Cor 11:1). For "God himself has become resplendent in our hearts" (2 Cor 4:6). This is no gush of sentimental feeling, but rather indicates a "metamorphosis" (Rom 12:3; 2 Cor 3:18) that has become seasoned through much suffering into a "surpassing comfort," so that he may "comfort all those who are in distress." This validation of all his feelings is thus a lively consequence of the fact that Paul already experiences himself as taken up in the resurrected life of Christ (Rom 6:3-11).[14] Also "you have not treated me badly in my trial and you have not spit [me] out, but rather have taken me up like an angel of God, like Jesus Christ" himself (Gal 4:14). For "the power of God comes to completion and shows itself in weakness" (2 Cor 12:9).

---

12. U. v. Wilamowitz-Moellendorff, *Die Griechische Literatur des Altertums* (Berlin, 1907) 159; cf. EuE 15.

13. For details see Ts 172ff. as well as GdG 94-98 and 115f.

14. "Present resurrection" already with Paul in his main letters: Ts 49-60; 90-94; the same for 1 Cor 6:14; see below, around note 219.

Redeemed love is also apparent in the fact that Paul experiences his relationships within the "body of Christ" according to the pattern of all family relationships. As Jesus says: "Whoever does the will of my Father is brother and sister and mother to me" (Mark 3:35), Paul feels himself bound with his communities as his "brothers and sisters." Admittedly—and here a first question comes up—he speaks, following contemporary linguistic custom, exclusively of "brothers." On some occasions he may have in mind those "associations" made up only of men;[15] on other occasions women are naturally also intended to be included in the term, expressly in 1 Thessalonians 5:23: "all of you together."[16] At Romans 16:1 he calls Phoebe "our sister." Concerning his relation with the women among his "coworkers" we will address this question later. Here it is only important to point out that he does not address the community members as though looking down from above, but rather places himself as one brother among them and feels himself supported by them.[17]

Also he does not exercise his fatherly role in a paternalistic fashion; it rather represents for him the inescapable and nontransferable responsibility he bears before God: "I do not write this to shame you, but rather to advise you as my beloved children.[18] For even if you had a thousand teachers in Christ, you would still not have many fathers; for indeed *I* have engendered you in Christ Jesus through the gospel" (1 Cor 4:15). To the Thessalonians he writes that he feels himself "made an orphan by being separated from them for a moment,"[19] but with great longing to see them. "For who, then, is our hope or joy or our crown, if not you?" (1 Thess 2:17-19). Here a man inserts himself with all of his per-

---

15. For "community assembly" in the narrow sense, see also below, A VII 3.

16. This is the way ὁλοτελεῖς should be translated: ChuA 225f.; see below, note 323.

17. Cf. Ts 100-104, 111-113; Phil 1:19 should be read: "through your prayers and provision with the Spirit of Jesus Christ." See Ts 310, 314f. Thus Paul also receives strength from the community. On the question of his coworkers, see below, A VII 4, nos. (4)-(10).

18. Τέκνα = physical children, from τίκτειν = to bear, in contrast to the general παῖς, παῖδες = children, young people, servants, lads (cf. Matt 8:6).

19. Cf. EuE 27: and Atf 432-434.

sonality into the community of salvation through his spiritual authority, but "unprotected" by any authoritative institutional structures. This becomes especially clear through the fact that he also dares to express his spiritual relation to these people through maternal images: "I have spoken to you as one speaks to nurslings in Christ. I gave you milk to drink, not hard food; for you could not tolerate it yet" (1 Cor 3:1f.).

2. "Like a nursing mother": 1 Thessalonians 2:4-8

Unified Translation (UT)		Proposed Translation (PT)
. . . in order to please God, who searches our hearts.	4	We seek to please **God,** who searches our hearts.
You know that we have never attempted to flatter through our language,	5a	As you know, we have never come either with flattery
nor have we acted out of hidden covetousness, as God is a witness.	b	or with a subterfuge for avarice, God is a witness,
Nor have we desired any honors before human beings, either from you or from others, although, as apostles of Christ, we *could have invoked our position.*	6	nor are we seekers of honors from human beings, neither from you nor from others.(!)
	7a	Although as apostles (those sent, official representatives) of Christ, we could have *carried on as important persons (with authority),*
On the contrary, we met you in *friendly fashion:* as a mother cares for her children,	b	did we (rather) behave indeed (!) in a manner suitable to children in your presence—as a (nursing) mother presses her own (physical) children to her heart. (Now he comes to the present:)
thus were we *devoted* to you and	8a	*Accordingly,* even as we are (becoming) *separated* from you,
wished to make you participants	b	we decided **to make you participants**
not only in God's good news, but also in our very life; for you had become very dear to us.	c	not only in God's good news, but also in our own life (soul, heart), because you have become dear (ones) to us.

At 7b: "love for children"; with NA I read νήπιοι and the present tense εὐδοκοῦμεν; however, after v. 6a I place a period (cf. N. Baumert, "'Ομειρόμενοι in 1 Thess 2, 8," *Biblica* 68 [1987] 561). Θάλπω = *fovere,* to have dear, to protect and care for" (Passow s.v.b.); also Eph 5:29. At 8a: Οὕτως consequent: EuE 524ff.—ground for "becoming separated." See again 'Ομειρόμενοι.

One should notice the three parallel members in v. 5/6. Each statement is amplified with a grounding explanation, which we have set off with dashes. However, with v. 7 the thought takes a new turn. According to the UT it would stylistically disturb the rhythm that we have just indicated, and in its content also v. 7 does not fit as a "concession" with regard to what has preceded it. Flattery, avarice, and ambition for honors are definitely negative; on the other hand, Paul considers "coming out with authority" altogether proper! With "invoked our position" the UT introduces a negative connotation and, through "although," gives the impression that Paul considers it thoroughly legitimate "to cultivate honors before humankind." But here that is placed in opposition to "pleasing God"! With the comma before δυνάμενοι and the semicolon before ἀλλά the text editions admittedly suggest a connection between v. 7 and v. 6. They do not venture—which the content more strongly suggests—to construe 7a and b as elements in the same sentence. Still ἀλλά = "(thus) nevertheless" may not only introduce a main clause, after a "conditional introductory clause" (BDR # 448:5: 2 Cor 4:16b; 11:6), but also following a (concessive) participial clause.[20] There is indeed no participle in 2 Cor 13:4 (with vl.) or Col 2:5, but a conditional sense is operative; cf. also 1 Cor 9:2. Verse 7 would then be again parallel to 5/6 providing an afterthought, here set off by dashes.

In the discussion of the purity of his intentions Paul brings himself personally into relation with the community and thus immediately becomes the herald of the gospel. If a man attempts such a discourse before a mixed group of men and women, this testifies not only to a deep tenderness in his sensitivity, but also to an extraordinary inner freedom. It can only be the result of deep internal spiritual experience (otherwise it would be flat and unendurable), but it also shows that the writer has not suppressed manly sentiments like paternal or maternal affection, but rather has integrated them spiritually. He also freely uses sexuality and

20. Cf. Denniston, *Greek Particles* (Oxford, 1966) 11f.: Plato, *Rep.* 383 A.

the erotic as images for his spiritual experiences.[21] It will be made clearer as we look at the three following texts that there is here no excessive sublimation or spiritualization.

3. "To change one's tone of voice": Galatians 4:17-20

UT		PT
These people are concerned with you not with a good in-	17 a	They *woo* you under false pretenses,
tention; they seek to make you disloyal, so that *afterwards* you may take care of them.	b	seeking to *obligate* you to woo them in return.
It *would be* good *if you would always exert* yourselves in my regard with a good intention, and not only when I am with you,	18 a b	However, it *is* good (does me good) anytime *to be wooed* into something good—and not just when I am with you,
with you, my children, for whom I am again suffering the pangs of birth, until Christ takes shape in you.	19 a b	my (physical) children, for whom I am again suffering the pangs of birth, until Christ *has achieved* form in you.
I wish I could be with you now and *speak with you in a different manner;*	20 a	I would like to be with you now and *would prefer to change my tone of voice,* for I am perplexed
for your behavior perplexes me.	b	with you (don't know what to say to you).

At 17b: Not "exclude" or "make disloyal" (UT): about what? about whom? When the word is used in an absolute sense, that is, without an object, it means: to coerce, to "obligate" (M.-G). One should observe the completions, which most translations recommend here, e.g., "from me" (Luther), "afterwards" (UT).

Verses 18 and 19 are composed out of an experience of the mother–child relation. Admittedly Paul expresses it indirectly

21. Halkes, 39, with note 13 refers to Phyllis Trible, *God and the Rhetoric of Sexuality* (Philadelphia, 1978) 200-202: "*rhm*-the woman's womb as an indication of God's compassion. JHWH is described poetically as a God who is pregnant, who cries out in the pangs of birth, who bears a child and nurses it."

and a bit more elegantly than it sounds in the UT. "Birth pangs" is an unusual image for a man; its use says something about the liveliness and inner freedom of Paul. Verse 20: to "change his tone"—like a mother who turns to her baby and speaks to it in an altered pitch; "There, there. . . ." This aspect was not conveyed in the earlier understanding.[22] The commentaries are of the opinion that Paul means that, if he were present, he would find the proper tone more easily. This would make sense in the context, but then the *image* of "changing one's tone" is still not clarified. Otherwise expressed, it is intended in contrast to a written instruction. But then Paul should have said: "I would like to raise my voice" or some such remark. Schlier attempts a reference to "angel voices" (1 Cor 13:1) to say nothing of the idea I found in one commentary: "If only I could make my voice so loud that you could hear it over the distance which separates us." Luther says that Paul could thereby do better justice to each individual to the extent that he "adapts his words for every change of emotion, as needed." But then it should read: "to fit" my tone "again and again—according to the nature of the individual—to transform," or such like. Such commentaries all depart from the context of the situation; this passage and the next are connected by the fact that rivals are seeking to separate Paul from his community. So he also plies them emotionally, fights for them like a mother for her children or like a bridegroom for his fiancée.

4. "I have espoused you to myself": 2 Corinthians 11:1-3

UT		PT
I hope you will *endure a little* *foolishness from me!*	1a	Please, allow me to be foolish for a moment!
But of course you will do this.	b	*Yes, really, indulge me!*
For I *love* you *with* God's *jealousy;*	2a	For I *court you* with the *wooing love* of God;
I have betrothed you *to a single husband,*	b	indeed, I have *betrothed* (bound) *you to myself*

---

22. Like ἀλλάσσειν τὸ εἶδος or ἑαυτόν: to *alter* one's shape, to *take on another (form); cf.* M.-G. s.v.

	UT		**PT**

| | | c | *to give you over* (to) **Christ** as a pure virgin to her only husband. |

<table>
<tr><td>*in order to lead* you as a pure virgin to Christ.</td><td></td><td>c</td><td>*to give you over* (to) **Christ** as a pure virgin to her only husband.</td></tr>
<tr><td>However, I fear,</td><td></td><td>3a</td><td>Still, I fear that *somehow*—</td></tr>
<tr><td>as the serpent once through its duplicity deceived Eve,</td><td></td><td>b</td><td>as the serpent in its cunning duped Eve—</td></tr>
<tr><td>you also in your mind might stray from the upright and pure devotion to Christ.</td><td></td><td>c</td><td>your mind *may be* **seduced** (your conviction, your thoughts be corrupted), away from the simplicity and purity fixed on Christ (away from the uprightness and continence = virgin love, that was directed toward Christ).</td></tr>
</table>

At 1b: 'Aλλὰ καί—"yes indeed, as a matter of fact" as an intensifying or repeating exclamation. For more particulars, cf. Ts 293 with note 545 and p. 313, note 569, with a small correction of Bl.-D. (UT) takes no definite position, since no contradiction is presupposed, which ἀλλά = "but, rather" could remove (one should note the strained explanation in BDR 448.6), and because this particle can indicate not only a contradiction, but also progress, repetition, or incitement. For this reason Bultmann's arguments (ad loc) are unconvincing.

At 2a: Ζηλοῦν with the accusative of persons: to admire, flatter, woo someone; pejorative: flirting (Gal 4:17). More particulars ChuA 211.—"Jealousy" gives the general idea, but in its modern understanding has an excessively negative connotation. M.-G s.v. quote jealousy in the negative sense only for "1.b ß" and prefer for the first meaning: "zeal, eager striving, warm love or protection." On the word order: If the genitive stands in front of the word it modifies, it is emphatic. This pattern also leads to a chiasm.

At 2b: On the emphatic word γάρ cf. Ts 356 and 361 (note). 'Αρμόζεσθαί τινα—to bind someone *to oneself;* one may say of a man that he betroths a woman *to himself.* In the dictionaries to "betroth someone" is cited as an exception, and indeed, only for this verse (Ts 293)!

At 2c: For extensive reasons for this interpretation: Ts 292-295.

At 3a: "In a certain sense, from a certain point of view," thus not completely! One should not suppress this "somehow" in the translation; cf. Ts 392-395. It is related to ὡς = "in a certain fashion," cf. EuE 219-223 and below on 1 Cor 7:29f.

Verse 1a literally: Would that you would indeed tolerate a "moment of foolishness" from me! A conditional imagined as contrary to fact, BDR 359$_2$. Ἀνέχεσθαί τινος—endure someone, as 1b immediately adds; 2 Cor 11:19; Eph 4:2; Col 3:13; Matt 17:17; Luke 9:19, 41; Acts 18:14; "to tolerate something": 2 Tim 4:7; Heb 13:22. But the verb here has no double genitive around it, and μιχρόν τι cannot function as a second object in the accusative (?!), is also not part of an accusative of relationship, but rather indicates the time period, like 2 Cor 11:16. Ἀφροσύνης however describes this short time as a "moment without reason," so to speak, a fit of stupidity. Thus μου is not a simple genitive indicating possession. It does not mean either "my insignificant foolishness"—in that case the article would have to appear twice—or "a little foolishness from me"—for then there would have to be a dative of relation as in the Koiné manuscripts. It also does not mean: "a small amount of my foolishness," because ἀφροσύνης is too far away from the μου and to have this meaning it would have to have an article. The (non-)sense of the final possibility would be: "a paltry amount of foolishness which is proper to me" (?!). With the indefinite article, however, it also does not make sense: "a paltry amount of *one of* my foolishnesses." Accordingly my interpretation in Ts 293, where on this point I followed the conventional interpretation, should be corrected to the proposed sense of "a moment of foolishness."

In verse 3c with μὴ φθαρῇ both the aorist and the passive are important. If your sense "could" deteriorate (UT), it should normally be in the subjunctive present; the aorist subjunctive does not necessarily indicate a previous time, but rather regards the action as a whole, and here in fact as more complexive than ingressive. For immediately afterward (11:4) Paul reproaches them severely: they *are already* corrupted. The passive at a later time could indeed be translated as an intransitive "distance himself," but the authentic passive "to be destroyed," is common throughout (2 Pet 2:12 puts it together with "to be treated badly"); in Paul it corresponds to the active constructions in 1 Cor 3:17. And 2 Cor 7:2 (to lead a person astray or to their destruction) is in our case the active contrast to Eve's being deceived, which from the context clearly means that the community *has been* corrupted by the "super-apostles." The following and somewhat independent ἀπό is thoroughly compatible with such a passive; cf. 1 Thess 2:17; Gal 5:4; obviously also Rom 9:3 and in Gal 1:6 with the middle voice; you have crossed lines as a deserter, "away from" . . . (EuE 416). Thus "to be seduced" is the best translation; one should only notice that ἀπό here means the thing or behavior that a seducer seduces a person *from*.

Here begins the segment that has been called "fool's speech." The catchword "foolishness" (*aphrosynē*—also in 11:16, 17, 19; 12:6, 11) admittedly does not refer to the psychological aspect of having "lost one's senses," but rather the objective condition of being without reason, without insight. "Fool" has too many improper connotations. Paul begins to speak about highly personal things: that he is not below the super-apostles in integrity and loyalty (11:1-5), in knowledge (v. 6), in financial indifference (7-15), in genealogy (16-22), in the marks of an apostle (23-33), and finally in personal revelations (12:1-6). He fully realizes that a "rational" person does not normally speak about such things. Yet: "I dare you." The following verse 1b is thus an imperative! A (correcting) stipulation "You have already done so" (cf. UT) removes the impetus from the entire address, in a certain fashion confines the momentum that Paul has just built up, and is questionable linguistically.

Paul is not entirely comfortable making this speech, for the community itself must have noticed the purity of his motives (2 Cor 3:1; 12:11): a clever and circumspect person *(sōphrōn)* does not speak about such things. One should note: the catchword is not introduced because he is speaking about an intimate relation, but rather because he must now assume the role of being *a witness to himself*—in all the areas that he then goes on to discuss (cf. 2 Cor 1:23; 10:12, 18; cf. John 8:13f.; 5:31-37).

The first area that Paul mentions is, compared with the later ones, the most personal: "My relationship to you is supported and stamped with the courting love of God himself. If I have bound you to myself, I did not do this to obtain a wife for myself, but rather to lead a bride to Christ. He it is who was yearning for you and for whom I won you. Thus my relation to Christ is clear and pure; however, I fear that your relation to him is not such!"

Paul receives the image of the bridal relation of the community to God from the prophets, and he applies it as if it were entirely natural to the relation to Christ. What he is fighting for is the undivided love of the community for Christ. It should be like a wife who is simply and without reservation oriented toward her husband and devotes herself in purity to him alone. Thus he comes to speak about the temptation in the Garden of Eden. Here the important point is not, as in 1 Timothy 2:13f., that the woman was seduced *before* the man[23] (the woman indeed stands here as an image for the community made up of both men and women!), nor any infidelity of a wife to her husband; rather, the point of comparison is that in Eden a *human* deviated from obedience toward *God* (!). In the application admittedly Christ with regard to the community appears in the position of a husband to his wife (not so God to Eve); however, it is God who with (jealous) concern observes the love of the woman whom Paul has led as a bride to Christ. In this way the rhythm of the sentence can be understood: *I long* specifically for *you* with *God's longing* (a chiasm); indeed, I have bound *you to myself,* so as to turn you over, to entrust you as a pure virgin *to Christ* (emphatic position)—thus not to "some other Jesus" or to a "false apostle" (11:4, 13).

So one should mark this distinction: if the negative background for the community is Eve, who deviates from God, and the community remains in the bonds of marriage with Christ, nevertheless the community is not yet called a "second Eve"; but since Paul in other places characterizes Christ as the "last Adam" and the "second man" (1 Cor 15:45-47; cf. Rom 5:12-21), such a thought is a possible logical consequence (cf. 1 Cor 6:17; 11:11f.; Eph 5:29-32; Rev 21:2; 22:17) and corresponds to Romans 7:4, as we shall see in the next segment.

However, such thoughts stand only in the background and will appear in the unfolding of our text; they do not answer the question of its direct message. When Paul "hands over a pure virgin" to the Lord, he is thinking at that point about the inception of a marriage relation of the community with Christ! Although this is not said directly, it is clear that the *image* (!) does not mean a love relationship involving abstinence,[24] but the commencement of a marriage. For the union is regarded in terms of its origin: I have exerted myself to hand over a pure virgin to

23. At any event, this text shows that the *topos* of the "seductress" was familiar to the Paul of the main letters. More on this below, B II 4.

24. My remark in Ts 293 that "the connection between the community and Christ is *pervasively* conceived under the image of the 'virgin' " should thus not be misunderstood in this sense.

Christ, as I guided you to him; and since that time you have been really betrothed to him, matrimonially bound. But have you remained in your love, or have you betrayed your fidelity to him?

On this passage John Chrysostom comments: "Virgins in the world are virgins only before their marriage; here, however, things are different: even those who were not virgins before their marriage become so afterwards." Also Prümm speaks about a "virginity of the soul" and being a "spiritual bride" in the sense that the relation to Christ is itself considered as "virginal."[25] However, thereby the distinction between image and application is not clearly maintained: of course we have to do here with a spiritual communion with Christ, but under the *image* of the marriage union, not of abstinence. The decisive factor in all this is the undivided nature of the devotion. The adjective *hagnos* appears again in verse 3 in the *haplotēs kai hagnotēs,* and can thus stand for matrimonial fidelity (= devotion to *one* husband) (cf. also 2 Cor 7:11; Ignatius, *Eph.* 10:3). Besides that, one should notice that this "purity" was first made possible by the surrender of Jesus on the cross, thus was not proper to the community before. It *became*—before the "marriage"—a "pure virgin," so as to be able to belong entirely to him.

However, who are these rivals who are attempting to seduce the bride/wife? Ultimately it is the "serpent" or Satan (2 Cor 2:11; 11:14; 12:7), but concretely it is "his servants," the "pseudo-apostles" (11:13-15). On whose position are they trespassing? They are not direct rivals of Christ, but of Paul! If they are indeed proclaiming "another Spirit," "another gospel," and "another Jesus" (11:4), this trespasses on the position of the true Messiah/Christ; still, they would thereby be enticing the Corinthians away *from Paul*[26] and seeking to win them *for themselves* (Gal 4:17; 2 Cor 7:7). Gradually it should become clear why, not only on grounds of language[27] but also of content, the image of

25. K. Prümm, *Diakonia Pneumatos I* (Rome, 1967) 600f.

26. This is indeed the basic problem of 2 Cor and especially chs. 10–13—in a similar way, Gal 1:6 and 5:6: You have "run" from *me* (καλέσαντος) (to another party); see EuE 415–417.

27. Compare again above, A I 4, the references "At 2a" and "At 2b."

"best man," here generally assumed, does not fit.[28]

The best man has discharged his duty once he has handed the bride over to the bridegroom. However, Paul is here reflecting on his enduring relation to the community. "I have bound you *to myself,* so as to hand you over *to Christ*"—again and again. A process was initiated with the first handing over at the start of the life of the community that is not yet finished: "After I have led you to him, it is now my duty to watch over this love. So you are and remain irrevocably bound *to me.*" Paul has not broken off this relation after the "handing over." Indeed, in this context he fights for the recognition *of his apostolic status (apostolē),* his commission, and his *permanent* responsibility for this community.

Thus the connection of the community to the apostle and its fidelity to Christ should be thought of as parallel, as though they were on two levels, but not successive, as if Paul was only active while leading the community to Christ and not afterwards, or as if there were two steps *in the relation to Christ itself,* specifically betrothal and marriage.[29] For that reason such a (conventional) interpretation often postpones the "handing over" of the bride until the second coming of Christ,[30] in order to explain the difference between betrothal and marriage. However, the community already belongs entirely to Christ! Verse 4 refers to the fact that

28. Schnackenburg, in Eph (EKK) 256, calls this into question and sees Paul "rather as the bride's father." In this case the relation is even closer; however, the *permanent* responsibility for the community here runs *parallel* to the community's "marriage."

29. Since "husband" and "Christ" obviously refer to the same person, it is linguistically completely inappropriate to subordinate v. 2c to v. 2b. In that case Paul should have said: I have engaged you to Christ in order to present a bride/wife *to him* (!) *as the only* husband (which, however, is not there and would be almost a tautology: "to engage a woman to a man, *so that* she would be presented to him as a wife"!?). However, the reversed sequence—to engage her (to whom?), in order to present her to Christ— would constitute a serious linguistic lapse; in addition a general subject for the sentence is lacking.

30. Something that indeed is quite remarkable—despite apparent parallels (see the commentaries): "to be engaged now, so as *then* to marry." On 2 Cor 4:14, see Ts 94f., 292ff. Cf. also note 160 below.

the community has already become unfaithful. Still as a betrothed person? Still "before the marriage"? No!

This *"betrothal,"* which here refers to a legal, but in no way sexual relation, refers first to the relation between Paul and the community, the resulting marriage on the other hand consists in the relation to Christ. The two occur simultaneously; the second is so closely tied to the first that by breaking with Paul they also break with Christ, who indeed stands behind him (2 Cor 5:20; 13:3). All who would "build further" must do so in concert with Paul—for the simple reason that there is no other foundation than the one he has laid (1 Cor 3:9-17; 4:15). However, any "super-apostles" are in fact "pseudo-apostles" (11:5, 13); they preach "another Jesus" (11:4; Gal 1:6f.). If the twelve apostles may be understood as each the father of a tribe, whose functions thus are not interchangeable, something similar becomes apparent here with regard to the "apostle to the Gentiles" (Gal 2:8f.): "I have betrothed you to myself like a bride as a commission from God, so that you may belong entirely to Christ."

Naturally the objective facts here explode the image, or better: Paul construes the image from the reality at issue. He sees in the concrete situation that he cannot release the community from his responsibility and abandon them to these people without their simultaneously becoming estranged from Christ. He here derives the basic idea behind all of 2 Corinthians from the relation between husband and wife. In so doing he reaches back and takes hold of images from the Old Testament.[31] However, he reshapes the material and superimposes two images.[32] He sees himself bound so tightly to the community that he must protect and support the relation of the community to Christ through its relation to himself, to such an extent that, if the community should bind itself to "other apostles," immediately its relation to Christ would be destroyed. Admittedly *hērmosamēn* is adequately translated as: I have "bound" you to myself; however, the speech patterns

31. Hos 1; 2; Isa 1:21; 50; 54; 62; Jer 2:2; 3; Ezek 16 and 23; Mal 2:10-16. With Hosea this break in the covenant is represented through the prophet's marrying a prostitute (!).

32. It is not uncommon in Paul for one image to pass over into another: 2 Cor 3:14: "the face of Moses" into "writing"; 2 Cor 5:2: "house" into "garment"; see Ts 170.

and images in the context strongly suggest the specific meaning "betroth." A later tradition will speak of the bishop being betrothed/engaged to his community, and will forge the bishop's ring as a symbol for this. It is almost impossible to demonstrate whether an earlier interpretation of our text in the sense here proposed contributed to this development.[33]

The boldness of this image consists in the fact that Paul experiences his relation to the community so deeply that he can characterize it as a "betrothal." Indeed in the progression of the sentence this is the first catchword that strikes us. Naturally it did not arise without a connection to the immediately following image, but is also still authentic in itself. This does not mean that Paul imposes himself in the love that exists between humankind and God; it is rather a sign of how far he sees himself taken over by the Spirit—it is indeed the courting love of God the Father in him that enables and authorizes him to be the protector of their love to Christ through this forceful and personal insertion. He even names their fidelity and dependence upon him "clean, pure, chaste" *(hagnos)* (2 Cor 7:11ff.). It is precisely the betrothal between himself and the community that allows the purity of his service and their virgin love for Christ to correspond and thereby to become a "moving, powerful" word. A man here stands before us who does not hesitate to avail himself of all the power of human love in order to make himself into the transmitter of the saving love of God.

5. Self-giving in Marriage— An Image for a Covenant with God: Romans 7:2-4

In the last example, next to the personal relationships in the community the relation to Christ was already discussed using the image of matrimonial fidelity. The motif can be discovered not only in the very personally stamped 2 Corinthians, but rather also in the more "objective" teaching letter to the Romans. While we are accustomed to see a special (eschatological) symbol in celibacy,

---

33. An association perhaps by Ignatius, *Eph.* 5:1: "You are dependent (upon the bishop) the way the Church depends upon Jesus Christ, and Jesus upon the Father, so that all may harmonize together in unity"—συμφωνᾱ.

in Romans 7:2-4 Paul takes the marriage union as an analogy through which to explain the new covenant.[34]

> [2]*A woman subjected to her husband/betrothed* is bound by the law as long as her husband/betrothed is still living; however, if the man dies, she is **released** from the law concerning her husband/betrothed. [3]Accordingly, while the man lives, she will be called a shameful woman[35] if she unites herself with (or: is united to) another man; however, after he *has died,* she is free from the law, so that she (then) is not "a shameful woman" if she unites herself with (or: is united to) another man. [4]Thus, my brothers, *in what concerns the law* (insofar as your existence stands under the law = is sinful), you also have become *dead through the body of Christ,* so that you might unite yourselves with another, with him who *has risen* from the dead, so that we, *in what concerns God* (= in our spiritual existence), **might bring forth fruit.**

In Romans 6:11f. Paul has described this new existence and drawn the ethical consequences from it. He sees sin and Law on the same plane to such an extent that the power of sin has abused the Law, which is good in itself, and cast humankind thereby into slavery (7:7-12). A person who has lived under the "Law" for a long time has the horror in his or her bones. He or she is tempted not to trust totally the new freedom and to measure everything by the Law and not by grace. For that reason Paul reaches once again for an image. The catchwords for our text, which have appeared earlier, are: "law, dominate (*kyrieuein* 6:13/7:1), die, disempower (*katargeisthai* 6:6/7:2, 6), life, resurrection, bringing forth fruit (6:21f./7:4f.), to be a slave no longer to sin, but to God (6:16, 22/7:6)." These will all be incorporated into the new image, the relation between husband and wife, or will appear in the application of this image. "Binds" *(kyrieuei)*—in 7:1c in a prominent place—resonates with and emphasizes 6:13, that this Law—as an instrument of sin—exercises a tyranny over human-

---

34. There is a more detailed investigation in Atf V; for that reason we supply here no alternative proposed translation to UT. Again, the *italics* indicate variations; **bold** print indicates an emphasis received from a word's position in the sentence.

35. Cf. with this below, D IV 1; the word does not determine whether this will happen as a married person, see what follows; for this concept: Atf VI 2, 211-220.

kind (7:7f.). In the same way a woman who has fallen in love with another man experiences her connection with the man to whom she is "bound" as a chain and his death as a liberation, because she is then free to follow her heart's desire.

Is it so sure that Paul is here thinking of a "wife" (UT)? The "woman standing under a man" *(hypandros)* can just as well refer to an engaged woman.[36] In terms of content that would fit better here. Then Paul would understand the existence of humankind under the Law not simply as a marriage, but only under the perspective that humanity is "bound," but without yet the full love of marriage. Since in ancient times for the most part maidens were betrothed while still in their youth, and love first developed only after they were joined with their husbands, in this waiting period it would more likely be the case that the woman "actually" loves another. Naturally Paul does not regard both the old and the new covenant as of equal worth; one thinks of the "taskmaster" and "steward" in Galatians 3:24 and 4:2. In that case existence under the Law would be an—undesired—engagement, and only the surrender to Christ for the first time the actual marriage with the desired physical union. Certainly the tendency of the statement moves in this direction, although it cannot be rigorously demonstrated that the first contract here means only a betrothal. At least it would then be a marriage not fully achieved.

Someone who thinks and writes like that shows that he does not suffer from sexual repression or disgust with the body, but rather that he finds it quite natural to use sexual union as a symbol for his deepest love.[37] If in the development of this image Paul describes the undesired union as "the flesh" (7:5), this is not intended to oppose a purely spiritual union (with Christ) to a "physical" union.[38] On the contrary, (in the image) *both* relationships are *physically* intended—however, only in the second relation is the complete expression used: "to be united with a man." In 7:3a this expression can only mean sexual union, for it is concerned with a single act of adultery, not about a new (unlawful) mar-

---

36. In our case this is conceived in terms of the process of engagement (she *has become* bound; the meaning of δέω is also suggested here, as in 1 Cor 7:27; see below, AIV 1 and close to note 149; EuE 421–423.

37. Similar to 1 Cor 6:13, 17; see below, A V 1-3.

38. On the integral Semitic anthropology, below C 2.

riage. If the husband dies, however, then such a union (that is, in a new marriage) occasions no scandal. The construction "to belong to one man" (UT) must be understood in this sense. However, at 7:4 this image will then be applied with the same words to the relationship to the resurrected Christ: "to be united with him" = with him "as" a wife is "one" with her husband and then (physically) becomes "fruitful."

Admittedly there remains here the question of what sociological perspective Paul is adopting. Is not the woman the one who is under submission? Does not the acceptance of this image imply the confirmation of a one-sided domination of the man over the woman? Now, with any comparison, the point being compared is the most important, not the material out of which the comparison is fashioned. Paul is naturally a child of his own time, and is not here pondering the propriety of the current laws governing marriage. Nonetheless, the woman is here an image for the better part in humankind (for that not having anything to do with the Law), not the man. Still, we shall treat this question in more detail.

First, we should notice that Paul twice refers to the union of husband and wife in love in order to illustrate simple, undivided love for Christ. This shows that he appreciates sexual union as an expression of deep love and that this expression carries no negative connotations for him, but rather leads directly to "fruitfulness" in the Spirit. He has neither hesitation nor anxiety in speaking about it. That recalls the statements of the Baptist and of Jesus himself (Mark 2:19f. par.; John 3:29). One should only notice that, from the Baptist on, the Old Testament image is so applied that now, instead of "YHWH," Jesus is the bridegroom in whom the archetype comes to fulfillment. This is acceptable for a Jew only if he or she recognizes the same God in both forms of the covenant.

In these last statements the reader has probably thought of Ephesians 5, the classic text in which marriage is regarded as pointing to the union between Christ and the Church. We have explained in the introduction why we will postpone taking up this passage until the second part (B 1). Here we will only point out that the manner of treating this motif in Ephesians 5 fits well without any further commentary in the line of development we have presented thus far; the image is only further unfolded there. In contrast to Romans 7, where the relation of the sexes is only used as material for the comparison, in Ephesians marriage itself is the purpose of the statement, which then simultaneously becomes in its concrete form a real symbol for the new covenant.

II. The Protection of Marriage Against Religious Rigorism: 1 Corinthians 7:1-16

1. Introduction to 1 Corinthians 7: Inquiry about Abstinence

Instead of beginning with 1 Corinthians 7, perhaps some would have preferred to begin with passages in which Paul speaks directly about sexuality, independent of wider symbolic references, so as to avoid the possibility of a spiritualization or sublimation of the topic. However, nowhere does Paul present a systematic anthropology or ethics; he rather speaks of sexuality only in connection with certain questions of community life. Thus in his principal letters—just as in the Gospels—there is no thematic discussion of marriage. What Paul has to say about it is occasioned by an inquiry about abstinence. We are forced therefore to extract his view on sexuality and marriage indirectly from texts whose primary topic is something else. This should not be taken as a sign that Paul repressed such questions, but is rather a consequence of the nature of occasional writings, to which genre letters belong. 1 Corinthians 7 is a *response* to a specific inquiry; indeed, it begins: "On the matter you wrote about." If then we had the letter of inquiry, we would be better able to understand Paul's text! Since we do not, we are forced to reconstruct it "backwards" starting with Paul's letter. What have the Corinthians asked about?

If one peruses the current translations of 1 Corinthians 7 and ignores its *Sitz im Leben,* one receives a divided or contrary impression. According to the heading in the UT, this chapter is about the "order of rank in the community." Is this a comprehensive treatment of this question? We are surprised that Paul begins by discussing "abstinence in marriage" and indeed regards marital sexual relations or even marriage itself as (perhaps only?) a means to avoid sexual perversion. It appears to be a "concession" to human weakness, while celibacy would be the authentic ideal "for all" (7:1, 6f.). But then how, in 7:2-4, can he suggest marriage for *everyone?* And why is he willing to sacrifice the possible salvation of an unbeliever so easily for the assurance of the "peace" of the Christian partner (7:15f.)? Does he not in the end reduce married couples to second-class Christians when he describes celibacy as "better" (7:38) and denies to married couples the possibility of undivided devotion to Christ (7:34f.)? Does there then exist a fundamental opposition and rivalry between love of God and human love? This is only meant as an introduction; many broader problems are also raised by the passage in question.

Since a detailed analysis is already available for this chapter, we will content ourselves here with merely tracing the general sequence of thoughts and presenting the results which were there wrung through great effort.[51] The inquiry from the Corinthians did not run: "Paul, what is your position on marriage and celibacy?," but rather they reported about certain individuals who, out of religious motives, had voiced a wish for abstinence. Thus Paul is not delivering a fundamental tractate on "states of life," but is rather carrying on a pastoral conversation with people who are moved by this concrete question about abstinence. Admittedly, he is carrying it on not with the individual people themselves, but through the intermediary of the community assembly, in which apparently these questions were addressed. For this reason the community had turned to Paul. Therefore the genre to which this chapter belongs would be: "Pastoral Aid for Community Decision in the Form of a Letter."

A living encounter with Christ in the experience of the Spirit brings with it a transformation of one's value system. The Corinthians, who have for the most part come to belief as adults, have *experienced* that they have become "new people." Such a transformation alters profoundly one's relations to God, to one's fellow humans, and to oneself; for that reason such a transformation cannot simply pass over human sexuality without comment. Everything is now seen with different eyes, everything is

---

51. EuE, bibliography; see further documentation there. Since in both works we study 1 Cor 7 in the sequence of the verses, it is not difficult to find the respective passage.

experienced differently, everything is lived differently. This is true for all living Christians, but apparently some in this situation have suddenly experienced the desire for sexual abstinence. It is only a few, and they are not always understood by the others— as is the case today. All too quickly comes the reaction: "That is not normal." However, is the "norm" for the individual only what is ordinary and conventional? Jesus said: "Let anyone accept this who can" (Matt 19:12). Apparently Paul believes that some (!) are experiencing the kingdom of God in this fashion. Married people are thus saying that they would like to remain abstinent for the moment, and single people are experiencing the desire to live out their relation to God in the form of celibacy. That is, their "call" has this distinctive mark to it. Similar things happen in other areas: sometimes a person—an artist, for example— experiences such a creative outburst that he or she ignores everything else, takes almost no time to eat, and also temporarily foregoes sexual relations.

Today as well there are people who, on the basis of a new, strong encounter with the Spirit experience such a powerful change in their entire capacity for love and relationship that out of this the desire for sexual continence grows. In such a situation the decision not to engage in sexual contact is no "ascetical achievement," and also not a psychological repression, but rather the work of the Spirit. However, while in today's Church structure such people could find sympathy and even join a religious order, for Paul's contemporaries this was something entirely new. Married people (7:1-5, 10-16), single people (7:6-9), and engaged people (7:25-40) were asking: "How should we respond to the spiritual impulse toward abstinence?" And thus the community assembly asks the apostle: "Is it proper that they remain abstinent?" *These are the petitioners* to whom Paul is responding! The letter thus reads entirely differently. Clearly Paul discerns that not all have the same degree of spiritual depth and maturity; he is aware of many other motives and circumstances. However, he here initiates a *conversation* with these particular people.

This is the key to the entire text. If on the other hand one ignores this *Sitz im Leben,* and rather—which often occurs when the text is proclaimed in the liturgy—the statements are taken as general counsels for everyone, this can lead to serious misunderstandings. If someone is giving pastoral advice to a person which is tailor-made and specific to this person's situation, one cannot simply shift and apply this advice to other people and circumstances. In the same way we will only correctly understand Paul if we respect the privacy and specificity of his dialogue with these petitioners. It is not everyone who feels him- or herself drawn by the Spirit toward celibacy. Whether or not one can extract from his statements basic principles that can be extended to other circumstances is a matter which must be further examined and justified on its own. Moreover, it will then be very interesting to see what Paul thinks about sexuality and marriage.

2. Reconstruction of the Letter of Inquiry

As an introduction to 1 Corinthians 7 we shall begin with an attempt to formulate the question raised by the letter, as the results of our research permit this. Even though this letter of inquiry was supposedly written in the name of the entire community assembly, most likely it was the leaders (those "who labor among you"— 1 Thess 5:12) who were the authors. Certainly the original was more colorful and more concrete. Here we can only attempt to identify the substance of the questions that would match the responses we have in front of us. A glance over the thematic structure under A IV 4 will make this process clearer.

Conjectured Text of the Letter of Inquiry

The Community Assembly of Corinth sends greetings to Paul, beloved brother in the Lord and apostle of Jesus Christ.

After you departed from us, again and again, both in personal discussions and in our general assembly, the question has come up of how individual members should treat the wish to refrain from sexual relations out of love for the Lord.

First some married men came forward who said that since they have received the Spirit, their sexual desire has greatly diminished; they experience the wish to remain abstinent and sometimes find physical relations with their wives a burden. On the other side several women have complained that their husbands have neglected them. What should we say to them? Is it proper for married men to stay away from their wives? (Response: 7:1-5)

Others who are single, namely, bachelors, widowers, and widows, say to us: "If Paul can live unmarried, then so can we; it must then be a good thing to live that way." You know N. and

N. Their families and the people in the city simply do not understand this, and there is this kind of talk: "What kind of new fashion is this?" Opinions in the community are divided. What do you have to say about this? We realize that you live that way, but is that something for everyone? Some young widows now say they do not wish to remarry, and we ourselves are not sure if this is a good thing. But they also invoke your example. (Response: 7:6-9)

Further, there are couples in the community in which one partner has even expressed the desire to leave the other (and Mrs. N. has already done this?). They say: "We no longer need the institution of marriage and would rather—as many apostles and their co-workers are doing—live by ourselves alone in community with the Lord." They find living together with their partner almost a burden. Their custom in the past has been that, if there are sufficiently serious grounds, a marriage may be dissolved through divorce; this appears to them now as a sufficiently serious ground. (Response: 7:10-11)

And some whose spouses are not believers are now telling us how dangerous such a marriage can be, for their partner is "unclean." What should we say to such people? (Response: 7:12-18)

The people and circumstances are often so different; can one give the same answer to everyone? (It is questionable whether this was raised in the letter. At any event, Paul centers his answer on this.) (7:17-24)

Finally, several engaged individuals have caused us special anxiety by suddenly announcing that they do not wish to marry. How should these young men behave towards their fiancées? Should they break off the engagement? Some have already done this and received on that account furious reproaches from the family, for they have abandoned their fiancées. Further, can they actually sustain such a condition? Others are saying they wish to remain perpetually engaged, but without marrying. This request is met with great resistance both from the parents and families, but also in the community assembly. So much complaint was visited upon one couple (N. and N.) that under the pressure they eventually married (however, the husband is now a bit distressed in his conscience). Several young men are saying that they had already discussed this wish with you and that you encouraged them to carry it out. Others are bringing this wish now before us and asking what they should do. Do you really think that such a thing can go well? Tempers are somewhat on edge about this, and a clarifying word from you would do a lot to help us all. (Response: 7:25-40)

We hope all goes well for you. May the Lord bless you, brother.

3. Abstinence within an Already-Existing Marriage: 1 Corinthians 7:1-5

The various answers will follow in separated segments. The contrast of the two inscriptions above the chapter makes clear the altered orientation of our interpretation.

UT		PT
The Order of Rank in the Community: 7:1-40		*To the Inquiry about Abstinence:* 7:1-40
		1st Part: Responses for married couples, single men and widows: 7:1-16
Christian Marriage: 7:1-7		*Abstinence within an already-existing marriage?* 7:1-5
Now to the inquiry contained in your letter! "It is good for *the* man not to touch *any* woman." (!)	1a b	Taking up the matter you wrote about, (!) *it is good* for a *(married)* man (on occasion) *not to* approach *his* wife (not to touch her);
But because of the danger of fornication each one should *have his own* wife	2a	however, in view of unlawful sexual relations, each man should **maintain** (marital) **communion** *with his wife* ("possess" her),
and each woman should *have her own* husband.	b	and each woman should **maintain** (marital) **communion** *with her* husband.
The husband should carry out his duty with regard to his wife	3a	A husband should carry out his duty with regard to his wife (do what he "owes"),
and likewise the wife with regard to her husband.	b	and likewise the wife with regard to her husband.
It is not the wife who disposes over her body, but her husband.	4a	The wife does not dispose freely over her body (her sexuality), but rather her husband;
In the same way the husband does not dispose freely over his body, but rather the wife.	b	but in the same way the husband also does not dispose freely over his body, but rather his wife.
Do not deprive one another *unless* it be by mutual consent,	5a	Do not cheat one another (do not let one another be

UT	PT
	deprived), *unless possibly by some sort of* agreement (in "symphony") *according to the situation* (occasion),
and then only for a time,	
in order to be free for prayer.	b so as to be free for prayer (so that you may be free for prayer);
Then come back together	c *and* then come back together again,
again, so that Satan may not	d so that, *as a consequence of your* abstinence Satan **does not**
lead you into temptation, in	**lead you into temptation** (so
case you cannot endure it.	that Satan does not indeed **seduce** you because of your not-coming-together).

Questions and Difficulties Present in the Unified Translation: Why does Paul begin the theme of marriage with "abstinence"? Is the (only) reason for contracting marriage to avoid sexual deviance? Does it necessarily follow that he can enjoin marriage as a *necessary duty* for everyone? Does not verse 2 stand in contradiction with verses 1 and 7? There indeed is where the center of controversy lies! But can Paul really mean that it is best not to consummate any marriage? In that case the human race could only have a future if some people ignored this ideal (which "actually" is valid for all)! Has Paul, as a Jew, forgotten Genesis 1:28: "Be fruitful and multiply"? In that case, what kind of image does he have of God and humankind? If married people "dispose" of sexual rights over one another, does this not cheapen the act of giving oneself to the other? After all, this should occur as an expression of mutual love! Or is the other regarded merely as an instrument for the satisfaction of one partner's sexual drive? Why does Paul look upon marital relations as an obstacle to prayer? Further: in this connection how long is "for a time"? Normally a few days go by until the next sexual contact; is that not enough time for prayer? Finally in verse 5: as the reason for "coming together" Paul does not mention mutual love, but rather fear of Satan and his temptation. What abysses are opening before us!

On the Proposed Translation: Before we simply slam shut the Bible in indignation, we should consult the original text. Is verse 1b really a repetition of the Corinthians' inquiry and at the same time an inscription over the entire chapter?[52] In that case they would be asking: "Are any sexual relations allowed (at all)?" (thus Conzelmann). Are we supposed to believe that this young community has really called marriage fundamentally into question? For they are acquainted with the Lord's word forbidding divorce, whereby he invokes the Creator (cf. below 7:10). What is going on here?

Paul had the letter of inquiry lying before him, and also assumes that its contents are well known to his recipients. Thus he begins immediately with the first question.[53] However, this simply questions whether abstinence may be practiced *in marriage* (vv. 3-5!). Thus already in verse 1b, "man and woman" refer to a married couple. This half-verse is not a heading over the entire chapter, rather only an introduction to the first passage. There are *some* men who have withheld themselves from their wives out of religious motives. Paul can appreciate the value of abstinence entered into for spiritual motives (see below), but here he senses a false enthusiasm that would not sufficiently integrate the order of creation into spiritual life. Hence he is speaking to these "pious" men who are tending toward rigorism, when he begins by saying: "It is indeed *honorable* (not: "it is *better*"—Conzelmann) *for* a married man, if he draws back from his wife—for example, if she is not feeling well" (Lev 18:6-23; cf. Ezek 18:6). And so he is addressing these men, perhaps with a certain light humor, on their honor as "gentlemen."

It is not easy to convert people who tend toward religious rigorism to a contrary point of view; for that reason Paul has recourse, as he often does, to a *captatio benevolentiae*. That is, he meets these men where they are: "It is indeed proper for you to draw back, *but* [there is no period here, rather the thought continues] are you also aware that by this step sooner or later you are

52. In that case it would then be more a "claim" of the Corinthians, as Fitzer, *EWNT* III, 331, emphasizes. Paul would then attempt to check this tendency. However, 7:25-40 recommend celibacy (see below). If this sentence were intended in such a fundamental sense, Paul would be involved in a fundamental contradiction. However, in 7:2 he immediately takes up a special case—this in contrast to Moiser, 104f.

53. Fitzer, *EWNT* III, 331 sees in v. 1b another "claim" by the Corinthians.

placing yourselves in danger of sexual deviance? For then you will not want to lose face before your wife, but will be tempted to go to a prostitute or something else.[54] And do you not realize that by this act you might also drive your wife into sexual isolation? That is why the two of you normally ought to maintain marital relations with one another." Thus the phrase "to have a woman" does not mean to marry a woman, but rather to *have relations* with her[55]—as one can also say in English slang "to have a wife." Further, there is no indefinite article "a" there; rather, it emphasizes "one's own" wife. This assumes that the man is already married. Thus, this passage is not mentioning the danger of unchastity as the reason for contracting marriage; verses 1b-5 are rather directed against these "pious" exaggerations within a marriage and in defense of a healthy married life. *If* you are married, then avoid extreme forms of abstinence and conduct yourselves with all simplicity and meekness according to your state in life.

Apparently Paul is here referring to concrete cases which indeed were the occasion for the inquiry. Perhaps the person who brought the letter himself named names. Would it be off the mark if we

54. Fitzer, *EWNT* III, 332 reduces the plural to only "frequent sexual relations with hierodules." However, as we show below, note 208, 1 Cor 6:12-20 is not primarily thinking about temple prostitution. Besides that, Paul is not only reproaching the frequency, but intends it absolutely. And it is also not as if he is here "forbidding unchastity"; rather, his manner of speaking assumes that the Corinthians also regard πορνεία as sinful. Therefore, the only question that remains is how broadly this term should be interpreted. Is Paul here thinking only of "improper sexual relations," or also of other sexual irregularities? On this, see below, A VI 1 and Atf VI 5.

55. And indeed *only* in this sense; that this concerns married people is indicated by the context. In his review article "Pauline Studies," *RB* 92 (1985) 462f., J. Murphy-O'Connor complains that my interpretation is "not all that new." As we will see shortly with Origen and the notes concerning him, on this point it stands upon a good tradition; however, in the last decades this tradition has not been reflected in the commentaries, or has been so mixed up with the question about sexual relations in general that the Pauline pronouncements are viewed as referring to something completely different. Cf. Niederwimmer, 83–91. Lang can also write: "In v. 2 'to have' refers primarily to sexual union; it should not be restricted to marrying or keeping a woman." As a matter of fact, it is not at all concerned with "marrying" because it is directed to people who are already married.

suspect some zealots to lie behind it (cf. 1 Cor 14)? In contrast
to Philippi, probably a greater part of the community members
in Corinth were people whose situation in life in function of their
recent past was somewhat strained.[56] If such people come to believe, they have special personal difficulties until they arrive at a
mature balance. The passage is thus not an abstract discourse on
the essence of marriage, or on the difference between married and
unmarried persons, but rather consists in practical admonitions that
illuminate a difficult situation. In that case the motive "on account
of sins of unchastity" does not express a negative evaluation about
contracting marriage as such, but rather is the sign of a realistic
pastor. Paul warns about overestimating one's own powers and
demands that one not bring one's partner into danger. Now the
whole thing has a different sound.

> Since the question became so painful in the course of time, we
> here give Origen as a witness. He interpreted v. 1 as referring to
> married people. He begins his commentary on ch. 7: "If people
> sin in the sexual area, then they sin in a twofold way: either they
> fall short of the commandments, or else go beyond them.[57] If for
> example we do not administer a state with our best capacity and
> make mistakes through not observing the norms of justice, it comes
> about that, if we *over*step the rule with the intention of doing some-
> thing better, we miss the thing in question. A balanced weight (stand-
> ing in the scales) is something that is neither (too) large nor (too)
> small, but rather balances (with the weight on the other side of the
> scale). With reference to knowledge of how one should live (this
> means): if you are bound to a wife, (if you abstain) then you place
> (too) large a weight on the other side (of the scale); you are not
> taking your wife into account, but are saying: 'I can control myself
> (sexually) and live in a cleaner fashion.' But look, your wife is being
> destroyed because she is not capable of bearing your purity, she,
> on whose account Christ died" (cf. 1 Cor 8:11: Origen thus assumes
> that Paul is speaking about married people).
>
> "Something of this sort was happening in Corinth. There was
> disturbance in the families of the community (in the houses of the

---

56. Cf. Saffrey 362ff. (with reference to 1 Cor 1:26f.): after the resettle-
ment in the year 44 B.C.E., Corinth was filled with many uprooted people,
slaves who had been set free in Italy, but also παλίνπρητοι—slaves who had
been sold numerous times because they were good for very little *(krinagoras)*.

57. Ὑποβαίνοντες τὰς ἐντολὰς ἢ ὑπερβαίνοντες.

brethren), in that, sometimes men, sometimes women, tried to live in abstinence, and would set themselves against the other. The Corinthians wrote the apostle a letter concerning this; and to this letter the apostle writes what is written above" (an allusion to the entire text of 1 Cor 7, which he cited earlier). "He did not sharpen what he said about chastity (= abstinence), nor did he weaken what he said about virginity by giving a preference to marriage—like a good administrator . . .—but rather he maintained more or less throughout the entire chapter his position (tendency) and encouraged abstinence (to hold themselves "clean"). . . . He did not begin with the lesser—indeed he did not do it himself (that is, he entered into no sexual union)—but with the more perfect (namely, with abstinence), in that he said: 'In what concerns the matter about which you have written me: it is good for a man not to touch a woman,' as if to say: I praise those of you who, on the basis of the intention of being clean, have distanced themselves from sexual union with a woman. But take into account not only what concerns yourselves, but also what concerns the woman; for love does not seek its own. Thus because of sins of unchastity, each one should 'have' his wife, and each wife her husband."

To the extent that this text implies a ranking along the lines of: "marital relations = the less," "abstinence = the greater," "I praise you" or "to be clean"; we can detect therein late antiquity's opposition to the body and especially that of Origen, which influenced the entire later view of this text, but which, however, is not proper to Paul. As to what concerns the point we are asking about, however, it is said here with all desirable clarity that the exegete Origen is of the opinion that in verses 1b and 2, Paul is speaking of how the problem of abstinence should be addressed *in an already existing marriage.*[58] If we consider that this Church

---

58. For the text, see Cramer, *Catenae, ad loc* (not in GCS). Similarly Cornely in the *Cursus Sacrae Scripturae,* with many further pieces of evidence from the tradition: "Commercium illegitimum verbis illis non comprehendi, contextus ni fallor evidenter docet. Postquam enim tam gravibus verbis foeda fornicationis turpitudo immediate antea descripta est, nec simplici 'bonum est' eius evitatio commendari nec legitimo coniugum commercio quasi acquiparari potuit. De solis igitur coniugibus Apostolus loquitur, atque ἄνθρωπος et γυνή sicut in reliquo capite ἀνήρ et γυνή solos designat coniuges. Abstinere ab actu coniugali igitur . . . bonum est, qua voce bonitas moralis exprimitur aut saltem utilitas quaedam spiritualis." Ad v. 2: "Erronee interpretes quidam (Thom. Dion. Cai. etc. Mai. Bisp.) de ineundo matrimonio sermonem esse arbitrantur; nam Apostolus rationem tantum indicat, quae plerisque

Father, who was born around 185, could still base his exegesis on many oral traditions—because of the external circumstances, these were especially long-enduring—then we are brought back almost to the time of the apostle himself.

The construction in verse 1 assumes that there are men who are thus abstinent; however, in 2–4 Paul presents the matter from both sides and indicates that in the sexual union both are equal, with the same rights and duties.[59] This type of question might seem strange to us, but it comes up even today if a married person has a conversion or an experience of the Spirit. Under these circumstances the other partner will sometimes say: "The only thing he/she wants to do is pray; he/she no longer pays attention to me." The one partner cannot understand the inner experience of the other. They detect in the other only a change in their behavior and in their criteria of value. For that reason the one who has been "shaken" should not make his or her own experience the only criterion, but should also regard what the other lawfully needs—and what is due the other! Such a deferral to the other will sometimes not be easy.

Gradually we can come to understand why Paul uses the expression "to fulfill one's *duty,* to deliver what one *owes, has promised*"; not because he would like to regard marital relations only as a (necessary) "obligation." How often have women especially been threatened by a stern homily on this sentence never to refuse their husbands? A physical encounter naturally always

---

coniugibus usum contracti iam matrimonii necessarium reddit. Ineptissime igitur antiquiores quidam ex hoc versu deduxerunt, omnibus hominibus matrimonium esse praeceptum atque coelibatum prohiberi (cfr. Lap. etc.). Praeceptum quidem hic habemus, siquidem coniugibus usus matrimonii praecipitur, neque tamen absolute, sed *propter fornicationes;* ubi igitur incontinentiae periculum deest, ibi etiam praeceptum cessat, uti in sequentibus Apostolus accuratius explicat." As further testimony for his own (and our) interpretation Cornely presents, besides Chrysostom: "Theod. Hieron. Herv. Lomb. Gagn. Est. Iust. Lap. Sa. Tirin. Nat. Pic." all the way down to Rückert and Kling. Cf. again above note 55.

59. Lang, 90, writes: "Such a view of marriage, placing husband and wife on equal footing, one finds neither with the Rabbis nor with the Stoic philosophers, not even with the Stoic Musonius, who esteemed marriage very highly." Cf. still, below note 311.

requires an appropriate personal atmosphere. Paul is not here speaking about the marital act in general, but is addressing persons who have withheld themselves from their partners out of "pious" reasons. He must remind such people that they have indeed "promised" their partners a sexual union. Thus, from the way he expresses himself we can extrapolate indirectly which questions he is answering.

"Dispose" should be understood in the same way. It does not imply that one belongs to the other[60] or that one could invoke this "right." Rather it is saying that married persons, in the exercise of their sexual functions—that is the only thing that is here meant by "body"—cannot decide concerning themselves autonomously, but in this matter should always remain open to the partner, in such a way that they "give themselves over" to the other, put themselves at the other's "disposal" or have an obligation to the other. Thus Paul presents not a "right to expect" but rather a "duty to provide," and indeed in each case from the point of view of what the one is prepared to allow the other to do. And the motive: because my partner retains the disposal over me, for that reason I should not autonomously decline—of course only as long as the partner has justified desires and expresses these in a form that is appropriate to the marital union![61]

These obvious presuppositions remain unexpressed! Every statement must be understood within its context. In this way our text aims at cleansing the marital act from all egoism. Marital "surrender" only comes to perfection in its mature form, if one is "with the other," looks away from him/herself toward the other

60. Niederwimmer puts it strongly, 91f.: "Marital relations result in the husband and wife losing the right to dispose over their own bodies; from that time forward they are physically delivered over each to the other. . . . This formulation, strictly interpreted, precludes the modern notion of partnership. The union is in no sense one of free will, but rather one that is primordial and mythological. . . . The myth of the *unio carnalis* is not corrected by a principle of personal freedom." And even if Paul formulates the right of possession "the other way around in favor of the wife, . . . marriage is still understood as the ownership of a person of the opposite sex, or more precisely of his or her body." This position is not shared by the majority of exegetes.

61. In marriage as well, Philo "emphatically rejects passionate sexual relations (*spec. leg.* 3, 9, 113)": Delling, "Geschlechtsverkehr," 820.

—entrusts him or herself to the other—in confidence that the other will not exploit this. Love is only awakened by a love that always offers a (vulnerable) surplus of trust—as Christ does (Eph 5:25). Thus this putting-oneself-at-the-other's-disposal[62] is the direct expression of the voluntary union entered into out of love, through which the partners, in contracting their marriage, have each placed themselves in the other's hands. On the other hand, it does not necessarily follow from this sexual orientation toward the partner that these must always be full sexual relations—only that in the experience of the physical powers of love they must be conscious of wishing to "belong" to their partner.

It is thus a matter of integrity, of the wholeness of the person in oneself and in the relation to the partner. In this inner freedom from oneself sexuality becomes the place of a real coming together, of a "symphony." Paul uses this word in verse 5, admittedly primarily with regard to abstinence. He emphasizes thereby that even a withdrawal from the partner should always be a decision they make *together,* so that even in that they remain *one* and still place themselves at one another's disposal. He warns against either embarking upon such abstinence unilaterally or of going too far with it. For that reason we find the three-

---

62. Bruns, 191f., 194, develops this aspect very thoroughly. Yet the tendency to trace the expression ἐξουσιάζειν back to a Gnostic motto (182, 190: "each may dispose over his or her own body as he or she sees fit") should be resisted; see below notes 203f. It stands in the context of Jewish and Jesus' interpretations of Gen 1:24 (one should also certainly not press this, similarly Bruns, 179). Ἐξουσία is the common word for the power of disposal and does not necessarily imply a (Gnostic) approach. Someone who today either in everyday speech or in spiritual literature speaks of the "Spirit" or the "cosmos" is not necessarily on that account infected with "New Age" thinking or making a pitch for such. Thus here Paul is not combating any Gnostic system, but is simply responding to a tendency, a certain one-sidedness, that can develop naturally out of a certain intensive form of piety; that, and no more. Bruns' observation on p. 190 appears to me to be correct, that it is not right to say that through marriage husband and wife "lose" (Niederwimmer), "hand over" (Wolbert), or "no longer" dispose over (Schrage) the rights to their own bodies. There is nothing in the text to this effect. Because the topic here (which many overlook) is not a general right to disposition over the body, but only as this concerns sexuality, the question arises whether the person *ever* had this right of disposition over his or her sexuality

fold reservation "unless possibly by some sort."[63] However, he recognizes the genuine desire of the petitioner and hopes that the motivation is clear: If you wish to withhold yourselves, then make sure this takes place in unity (*ek symphōnou*—in symphony). Especially at that point there must be a harmony of hearts, otherwise what is intended as glorification of God will lead to harm for the partner! Thus, by *pros kairon* Paul does not have in mind a firmly established time-span;[64] rather, the expression means "as the occasion suggests," or if the circumstances, the dispositions of the partners, and their own spiritual impulses "agree with one another." If such a *kairos* arises in your lives, you may remain abstinent from one another. You should with your spiritually purified feeling and healthy sensitivity notice if such a behavior is in keeping with your mutual understanding. Thus Paul is certainly not thinking of a "time plan" projected much earlier.

"Prayer" is the only motive mentioned for abstinence. Here we should not be thinking of the wedding night of Tobias and Sarah.[65] Whether the partners pray together or alone they should

---

before marriage, or whether it is not rather *through* marriage that this power is for the first time set free, and indeed precisely *through* the fact that another person "may take disposition" over it. In fact, is not a purported "disposition over oneself" in the sexual area opposed to the very *nature* of sexuality? Paul does not state this explicitly; however, it is a justified conclusion, if one frames the question in this fashion.

63. Εἴ μήτι ἄν—"except perhaps maybe": the striking accumulation of particles indicates that Paul's statement is strongly conditioned.

64. The fact that according to rabbinic interpretation such a promise or vow should bind for two or three weeks at the most (Fascher; Delling, "Geschlechtsverkehr," 819f.) only indicates the background. A temporary abstinence *done for religious reasons* is not something completely new, especially in times of *prayer and fasting;* cf. Exod 19:15 (Lamsa, G. M., *Old Testament Light*). However, as we have shown, "according to the situation" is linguistically the more appropriate and also the more accurate translation; see EuE 27f., as well as Atf XII, 408.

65. Tob 8:4-9: After having driven out the demon, the two of them pray on the wedding night precisely as a *preparation* for the marital act. In the morning they are still sleeping even while the father is already digging the grave. Thus, it is not: abstinence for the sake of prayer, but rather prayer for the sake of the union. Thus this text has rather in view the integrity of the sexual communion, about which we have just spoken. "I take this sister

nevertheless be agreed as to the *motivation for their abstinence.*
If this takes place "for a certain occasion" and in freedom, this
can actually bring about a deepening of their personal relationship. Paul is not implying that physical union disturbs the relation to God and hinders prayer; we should remember here that
people are being so filled by a spiritual experience that they would
like to remain turned entirely towards it. The point of departure
is indeed that people experience in themselves the *desire* for abstinence.

Perhaps someone might reply by asking: "But what kind of
spiritual impulse is it that would suppress physical love? Should
it not discover directly in marital self-giving an especially deep
and complete expression? After all, is not marriage a sacrament?"
Now, we saw above in chapter 1 that Paul is well aware of this
symbolic power. At the same time, within the limits of the human
psyche, it is not the case that everything is possible at the same
time and with equal intensity.[66] Our text shows clearly that Paul
does not mystify sexuality. Rather, behind it should stand an
experience that is valid for the spiritual integration of every kind
of human passion. Besides work there should be times of thematic
prayer—even though work can and should be a kind of prayer.
If someone occasionally fasts, that does not imply a devaluation
of eating.[67] In the same way the sexual drive benefits from a "dis-

---

not because of lust—*οὐ διὰ πορνείαν*—(as my wife), but rather in truth."
This presumes that, not only outside marriage, but also when entering into
a marriage or in its consummation one can have impure motives. However,
the text does not suggest that sexual desires are "improper," but rather that
the couple has the desire to "grow old together"; today we would say "until
death does them part." Cf. also H. W. Wolff, 250.

66. Cf. Naphthali 8:8 "There is a time for a man to embrace his wife,
and a time to refrain from embraces for his prayer." Cf. Qoh 3:5.

67. Spiritual sayings are correctly interpreted through spiritual texts. To
that extent it is instructive to see what Ignatius of Loyola (*Spiritual Exercises,* no. 213) has to say concerning the order of meals while one is making
the exercises: "Assuming that the individual is careful not to fall ill, it holds
true that the more the individual abstains from what attracts him, the faster
he will arrive at the medium (!) which he should maintain in food and drink,
and this for two reasons. On the one hand, because by so fostering and dis-
posing himself *(disponendo se),* not infrequently the interior feelings, consolations, and divine inspirations will be experienced, through which the

cipline." It must indeed again and again give way to other things; why not also to prayer?

It is thus not a matter of deprecating sexuality but rather of a hierarchy of values, and especially of the "redemption" of sexual activity. The integration of sexuality into the new life brought about by the Spirit does not happen automatically just because both partners become Christian and what they are doing is "permitted." To fully accomplish marital union "in the name of the Lord" (1 Cor 7:39; cf. 10:31) requires more than that. It does not consist in embellishing this process with spiritual decoration or in "sublimating" it (through renunciation or suppression); it rather consists in bringing its execution so completely before God that this takes place "in the Spirit," without for all that losing the smallest part of its naturalness. On the contrary, only in this way is physical union freed in its deepest essence, that is, to be an ever new and ever deeper expression of love. How does one achieve this? By a careful attentiveness of heart, by an inner sensitivity simultaneously to the Lord and to one's partner,[68] who—correctly understood—can never be rivals. Rather, the two Christian partners together are at the same time the "bride" of the Lord. They become so all the more to the extent that ordinary matters are penetrated by the presence of the Lord. Here there

---

medium is indicated to him that is fitting for him (!). Secondly, because the person performing such abstinence will no longer find within himself sufficient physical power and disposition for the spiritual exercises, he more easily reaches the point of judging what is more suited for his physical maintenance." Transposing this to our question, the second reason would run something like this: If after a certain time abstinence makes a life together more difficult for the other partner, or the tensions in self-restraint become more elevated, then this should be interpreted—besides the spiritual insights—as a natural criterion from which the individual may determine what "suits" him, and what not. For a healthy spiritual life goes hand in hand with a healthy natural sensitivity and judgment.

68. Thus Christ only deepens what is already described in Tob 8:4-9; cf. above, note 65. H. W. Wolff, 259, summarizes the outlook of the Old Testament: "It is always the disturbances in the relationship with God that manifest themselves—in the most varied fashion—in disturbances in the lives of men and women together. In the required exclusivity of love, nothing less than the created gift of love in its totality stands in the balance." Cf. below, close to notes 255, 259, 475, 629.

are many levels of growth and intensity. During this process it is the impulse of the Spirit that must guide the partners; in this way they will experience how through occasional renunciation their marital union gains in depth, because the Lord himself penetrates them more and more with his presence.

Concerning celibacy for the sake of the kingdom, Jesus says: "Let anyone accept this who can" (Matt 19:12). Apparently the Holy Spirit can awaken powers in a person that establish from within a new relation to the world and to the body and which reach even to our spontaneous reactions; as a consequence the celibate can be really "happy" and "fulfilled" in his or her celibacy—without deprecating physical love. On the other hand occasionally a married person "prefers" not to have sexual relations, or more exactly: the new or spiritual person (in them) does not desire it. This is not so uncommon; other experiences also occasionally cause sexual desire to diminish. To that extent "it is good for you" now and then to abstain, as with fasting. It promotes the integration of the entire personality and is thereby "wholesome and proper."[69]

In addition, the Corinthians are beginners in the spiritual life and are in danger of going too far. They must first learn to let go voluntarily of a purely worldly, perhaps strongly instinctual and egoistical pattern of sexual union, before they can reach the Christian "having while in a way not having" (1 Cor 7:29), that is, attain a spiritually integrated sexual life. Paul takes pains to instruct them about the *basic reason for relationship* (with God and the partner) and to protect them from other motives, such as a (still self-centered) religious exaggeration. The more one advances down this path, the less one will pose the formalist question that still strongly judges by external criteria: "Is it proper to abstain, or not?"; rather, through a mature love of God and neighbor one is able to judge what is appropriate at the time. Thus through his remarks Paul is trying to guide the people toward this maturity, so that they will inquire what God is showing them at the time—through the impulse of the Spirit as well as through the disposition of their nature (7:2; 5:9). Thus already there re-

---

69. Perhaps this aspect also enters in. That would then be the other meaning of καλόν with the dative: "helpful, useful, valuable"; see above, note 53; EuE 42.

sounds here the key sentence that comes to expression in the next question in 7:7b, and then from 7:17 until 7:24 constitutes the "objective middle" (Eichkolz) of the entire chapter: "Always in accord with the way God calls you at the time!"

With this *Sitz im Leben* our passage becomes understandable. The apostle knows something about people and their sexuality, but he sees it as one part within the totality of the person. Thus he concludes with the counsel that they should "come together again."[70] For an excessive abstinence can turn into a burden for the relationship. A person may then become unfriendly, surly, and eventually "look down in the dumps"—all of which opens the door to bad things. Besides that, by "temptation" again, as in verse 2, he is thinking perhaps of possible sexual failings, but certainly not only that. It is to be noted that, in our interpretation, the point is no longer that married people "*cannot* be abstinent";[71] *akrāsia* does not mean "the *inability* to be abstinent" —as a moral weakness—but rather refers to the objective fact that they "*practice* abstinence."[72] Such an actual (neutral) abstinence could be the point of attack for the tempter, and for that reason they should come together again.

If on the other hand, by *akrāsia* Paul were thinking of a disorder of the soul or instincts, his advice would be unusual: "Because you cannot control your sexuality, it is better that you enter into marriage than that you visit prostitutes." Even if because

---

70. Ἐπὶ τὸ αὐτὸ εἶναι is a common expression for "to be in one place." Someone suggested to me that this might be indeed the correct interpretation. If one prefers the variant ἦτε, however, the sentence would refer directly to the sexual union, which is not attested. It is different with ἐπὶ τὸ αὐτὸ συνέρχεσθαι, which I prefer. "To come together" does not by itself imply sexual union; the syntactic construction in that case would not mean "to come together in one place," but "for the same thing" = for the previously mentioned purpose, or simply "*for that reason* comes together anew." Such restrained, suggestive discourse is common for sexual matters. Admittedly, the objective situation is not altered by this, since in any case the interpreters see here a request to restore sexual union.

71. Lietzmann interprets v. 1f.: "Virginity is the ethical ideal; the person who cannot preserve it should marry to avoid πορνεία." And Conzelmann: "Incontinence belongs to the essence of married people."

72. Ἀκρασία (with a long ā)—not from κρατεῖν, ἐγκρατεῖν, but from κρᾶσις—mixing (= sexual relations), thus "not mixing."

of weakness a person frequently chooses the lesser of two evils, it would still be a remarkable piece of advice to say: "So as to avoid a greater temptation, give in rather to the lesser." Many readers would come away from a cursory reading with the impression that every case of sexual arousal is a temptation from the devil.[73] Although this is not conveyed by the conventional translation, the impression remains that incontinence (= lack of self-control) "is the nature of married people; otherwise they would have remained single" (Lietzmann). Supposedly Paul would not believe them capable of a longer abstinence. However, in 7:25-40 he expects young engaged couples to be capable of considerably more. How are these compatible? Once more it becomes clear that with these petitioners Paul has before him people who tend to religious exaggeration and have not yet reached spiritual maturity.[74] However, a general instruction for married people would have looked totally different. Naturally it is also true of marital consummation: "No matter what you eat or drink or do, do everything so that God's glory appears therein" (1 Cor 10:31).

4. *"I would wish that all could be celibate"?:*
   1 Corinthians 7:6-9

UT		PT
I say this as a *concession,* not as a command.	6	This (the following) on the other hand I say by way of *agreement* (consent, approval), not as a requirement (order, as what went before);
I could wish that all people *were* (unmarried) as I am.	7a	*naturally* I *agree* (indeed, I have nothing against it) that all men

73. This recurs continually in the literature. Neidhart (246) is of the opinion that Paul "sees sexuality in itself as only a malady" and that "the apostle is lacking in any sense of the positive worth of sexuality." He quotes G. Theissen, 177: what in 7:5 "is meant by Satan's temptations should be clear: sexual fantasies that disrupt our concentration in prayer," or H. Ringeling, *Theologie der Sexualität* (Gütersloh, 1962) 28: "For Paul sexuality is a medium for sin." For a collection of similar quotations, see Moiser, 103f.

74. And in 7:17 (see below, A III 1) he will once again qualify all his concrete suggestions (but not his principles!).

UT		PT
		and women may be as I am, (!)
Indeed, each has *his or her* gift of grace from God,	b	*but* each receives *his or her* **own** gift from **God,**
the one this, the other that.	c	one this, the other that.
(Marriage with pagans— Divorce: 7:8-16)		(!)
To the unmarried and the widowed I say:	8a	*Thus* I say to the *unmarried* men (singles = bachelors, widowers) and widows:
It *is good* if they remain like me.	b	It is *good for them* (advantageous, favorable) if they remain like me;
However, if they cannot live in abstinence, they should marry.	9a	however, if they do not have control over themselves, they should marry.
It is *better* to marry than to be consumed with desire.	b	*For* it is *more favorable* (stronger, more advantageous) to marry than to burn (to become cramped).

The climax of these difficulties comes in verse 7, which is most often related to the first passage. To start with, one asks what the "this" in verse 6 refers to: What does Paul say as a "concession"? That those people mentioned in verses 1-5 may marry? But did he not just say—according to the current interpretation—that they indeed *should* do that? But such a jump backward to verse 2 is very unlikely. Is he supposed to be "permitting" them to *come together* again? But this is what he just counseled them to do! One must be ready to undertake bold thought processes to extract a sense from this passage that is free from contradiction, and must call the following statement to one's aid. But what does verse 7 say? Does it really say: "I would prefer that all could remain celibate; but (unfortunately) God has set things up differently"? Where is Paul flying off to? Is it true that he is now revealing what he actually thinks? The problem does not become any smaller if he continues: It "is" good (objectively? universally? for all the unmarried?) to remain celibate. Once again he has to slow himself down in his enthusiasm: "Admittedly, if you are not up to it, it is better to marry." This leaves an aftertaste: in that case you have chosen the lesser good. The contrast with verse 10 would in that case be very sharp, for there Paul "orders" the exact opposite, that married people remain together.

We have already remarked how important it is to keep the petitioners and their question before our eyes. As in 7:1-5, here also the impression arises that Paul more discourages than encourages. Further, he has the fear that the enthusiasts among his readers could use what he says to pour oil on the fire. For that reason he *begins the new passage* with a qualification: I say this by way of *agreement*.

Five elements go into this interpretation. First, the demonstrative pronoun "this" does not refer to what has gone before, but to what is to follow,[75] namely the advice for those who are unmarried. Therewith we lose the connotation that marriage is a tolerated (lesser) evil. Secondly, by "agree" (not concede!), Paul indicates that he is here answering only those *who themselves* have the desire to remain celibate; only in that situation can he endorse, agree with, or react to, whereas if it were a "requirement," the initiative would lie with Paul. Thus no one who does not feel in themselves this desire should feel themselves addressed in what follows. Third, verse 7 begins not with the subjunctive, but with a clear statement. The verb means not "wish" (UT),[76] but rather

75. In addition to the arguments in EuE 48/51, see: Johannes Capellus (17th cent.) in: *Critici sacri* VII 1045: " 'Hoc' refertur non ad antecedentia, sed ad id, quod sequitur versu octavo" (reference to Joel 1:2; Ps 49:1). "Ideo (Paul) coelibatum non imperare, sed suadere, sed concedere se dicit." Moiser, 107, draws together 1-7 and arrives at the remarkable thesis that Paul "here allows scrupulous married folk to separate." On συμφώνη, our interpretation is exactly in keeping with the evidence presented by Karin Metzler; why, then, does she here claim an "exceptional meaning"?

76. It is significant that the oldest trace of the interpretation "I would prefer that everyone remain unmarried" occurs with Tertullian, that is, with an author who tends to extreme positions and to rigorism, and in the Latin thought-world. Although T. knew Greek well, it remains questionable whether he was apprised of the change in meaning this word specifically had undergone in the previous 150 years (EuE 399-401); Tertullian, *De monog.* 3:1; 3:3, 6; 11:8; *Ad ux.* I 3:6; II 1:4. Jerome, who translates it *volo,* prides himself that he does not go as far as the native Greek-writing Pierius, according to whom precisely by these words Paul is proclaiming or commanding celibacy—κηρύσσει, *Epist.* 38:3/CSEL 54:349.

"to be in agreement,"[77] and thus continues the thought of "agreeing" in verse 6! Besides, after verse 7a there should be no period, but a comma, because 7a and b constitute a simple complex sentence.

With that the meaning of this passage is completely changed! No more is there an unrealizable wish at the end of a section about marriage: "If only all could be celibate," but an *answer* to any such celibates who might be *asking* concerning the possibility of such a celibate life. However, even with them Paul presents celibacy not simply as desirable; instead, he avoids this: "As far as I am concerned, all could remain like me, *but* (!) you should not concentrate on me, rather ask yourselves what gift *God* has given *you!*" Apparently people have asked him: "Can we not live like *you?*" (That is probably the reason for the strange coded expression for "celibate living.") How does a person react who has been asked such a question by another? Can one simply ignore it? Paul tends to be more temperamental: "Of course I have nothing against it if everybody lives as I do" (if I were asked the question)—"*however,* you should not take *me* as your standard, but only what *God* has given you!"[78]

However, this gift is not a *special* spiritual capacity—that is why many commentators emphasize that celibacy only is a charism, and not marriage. The Greek word in Paul means simply *gift* (of grace) and here means neither marriage nor celibacy, but rather refers to the foundation, here one's concrete "nature": Look to see whether you "are like me," whether God has so formed your nature and your relation to God that this lifestyle suits you, or whether God has made you differently. It is true that normally by this word Paul refers to goods of the order of salvation; however, in this situation we cannot exclude the pos-

77. A parallel: In 1 Cor 14:5 Paul is also responding to people who carry a certain practice (praying in tongues) to an extreme: "Indeed, I have nothing against the fact that you all pray in tongues"; not: "I would like" (UT) or "desire"; cf. EuE 407.

78. The fact that he can say in another connection: "Imitate me, just as I have become an imitator of Christ" (1 Cor 11:1) shows only that we must situate every statement in its proper setting. Authentic discipleship is something different from simple imitation, and here Paul is clearly guarding against the latter. In this case, the thought is not "uncharacteristic for Paul" (Moiser, 107).

sibility that he also has in mind goods of creation; *charisma* is not yet with him a limited term, whereas today in theological discourse we use it only for goods of salvation.[79] The focus is naturally the form of the new relation to God that in 7:17-24 Paul will name "calling." However, this can just as much be a call (which is still something different from a gift or a capacity) to marriage or to celibacy! In this sense naturally the call to marriage also is here a gift of the order of salvation.

Whom does Paul then have in mind? By the *agamoi* are here meant only older unmarried *men,* that is, bachelors, and widowers,[80] thus not young men who are not yet of marriageable age. Even in our own time we normally use "singles" only to refer to those who have passed the normal age for marrying. Such people have posed the question *whether they may remain unmarried.* On the woman's side only "widows" are here mentioned; perhaps because in contrast to them, women in advanced age who have until now remained unmarried hardly had any further prospects for marriage; or perhaps only widows were among the petitioners. In any event, Paul is not speaking here to "all the unmarried"; that would be primarily the young! Instead it is the somewhat older persons who are asking such questions. One almost gets the impression that Paul recognizes some people among the petitioners—perhaps some names were mentioned to him of people he knew—who either have not found a partner or who have never dared to enter into marriage, but who nevertheless are not content with their bachelorhood and are now trying to "make a virtue of necessity." The danger too easily arises of giving a religious justification for unresolved human problems.

Besides, one again senses people who are demanding too much of themselves. That is why Paul emphasizes: "Only if they can live it easily and with joy should they live celibate. If on the contrary they suffer under it, chafe against it and become stressed,[81]

---

79. For a full discussion of this word and the history of the notion, see my contributions ChuA; "Sprachregelung" 21–48; there references to various previous works; GdG 145–161. For more, see below, D VI 1.

80. Erasmus reads "widower," as does Moiser, 108.

81. Niederwimmer, 97, understands this as "to be seized by sexual passion . . . that is already the equivalent of πορνεία." But thereby the predisposition itself and the arousal that attends it would already be a sin. Here

then they ought to marry" (imperative). Again we see how Paul sooner dissuades than encourages someone about celibacy. He apparently realizes clearly that the call to a celibate life must be a "gift" of God, and that any human striving toward it is dangerous. Further, he does not assert that celibacy is "good in itself" (he assumes this), but rather asks: Is it well *for you,* is it advantageous *for you,* is it good *for you?* Thus Paul does not weigh celibacy against marriage "in itself," but rather asks what is good and advantageous for each individual. He is thus not proposing a moral evaluation, but rather a "weighing of goods."

Again we have a completely altered picture. We see a wise, experienced pastor in conversation with specific individuals who have come to him expressing a desire for celibacy. Any commentary which would interpret these sentences simply as intended for all single people, and especially as encompassing all young people, would miss its sense completely. For Paul it is so natural that normally young people will get married that during the entire chapter he does not even mention this "normal case." They also have not asked him—naturally!—"whether one may marry." It is just a few betrothed individuals who have inquired whether they may remain unmarried. It is not until verses 25-40, however, that we get an answer to that question. The interpretation that has reigned until now had to struggle with many apparent contradictions. The notion that God could give one gift to some, and another gift to others, for example, stood in apparent contradiction with the demand in verse 2 that everyone should marry. And the notion that Paul exhibited a certain stubbornness with regard to his personal preference, when he knew it did not correspond to the will of God, is revealed, when seen in the light of day, to be nothing but imputation and caricature. That is not the Paul we know.

"the traditional sexual rigorism is heightened into a sexual pessimism." But the simple desire is not here condemned, but "the being-torn-by-it." If the individual affected internally nourishes and cultivates such desires, that would be a sin, and not only "less favorable." As a consequence Paul is here thinking about the case where someone, in spite of strong desires, abtains. However, a person who cannot freely "dismiss" such desires and "give them back to God" in love becomes tense. Thus our translation appears to me to be justified. The excessive sexual impulse in such a case can either be conscious or unconscious.

5. *Divorce of a Spouse for Religious Reasons?:*
   1 Corinthians 7:10-16

THE STRUGGLE BETWEEN MARRIAGE
AND DESIRE: 7:10-11

UT		PT
Not I, but the Lord, commands the married:	10 a	*However* to the married I give instruction—not I, but the Lord,
A wife should not *leave* her husband	b	that a wife should not *separate* from her husband
—if however she leaves him, let her remain unmarried or be reconciled with her husband—	11 a	—however, if in fact she has already *separated* (from him), she *should* (must) either remain unmarried or again bind herself (be reconciled) to her husband—
and a husband may not *divorce* his wife.	b	and that a husband should not *send* his wife *away.*

We have taken these two verses as a unit by themselves. Just
as the UT connected verses 6-7 with the first section "On Marriage," in the same way it put verses 8-16 together under the title
"Marriage with Heathen—Divorce." But the first time we hear
about divorce is in verse 10, and about marriage with heathens
in verse 12, while 8-9 fits neither one of them. Besides that, Paul
is not speaking fundamentally about "divorce." In verses 8-16
he is turning to different groups among the adults in the community: the unmarried, Christian spouses, and the "rest" (v. 12),
namely those married persons whose partners do not belong to
the community. However, that does not mean that the corresponding counsel given at each point is meant for all the married or
unmarried, but *only for those* among this larger group *about
whom Paul's advice has been sought.*

Since until verse 9 the topic has been exclusively abstinence,
either within marriage or from marriage, one has to wonder what
the provocation is for these remarks on divorce. Did the community really inquire about the possibility of divorce? Had they not
been beforehand sufficiently instructed by Paul on Jesus' prohi-

bition against divorce, as most of the commentaries have it?[82] The initial tone does not suggest that he is informing them of this for the first time; on the other hand he would be very severe if he were directing these words to people whose marriage was in trouble and who because of this are at their wits' end, or who are in a desperate condition within their marriage.

The sudden shift from an understanding address to a brusque "I order the married" and the further intensified "not I, but the Lord" suggests to us something else. We shall see more clearly in the mixed marriages of 7:12-16 that religious reasons lie concealed behind the desire for separation. With regard to the entire passage it is a reasonable assumption that even the Christian couples who are addressed in verse 10 are confronted with a similar question. Paul has the letter of inquiry before him and presumes that the community knows its contents. For that reason he can leave out many references which we outsiders would need in order to reach a definitive interpretation. Thus we must draw inferences from the context and from the style of the formulation. "If you (for example, out of a pious desire[83]) suggest that you may simply abandon your partner" (one should notice here who is taking the initiative), "then I *command* here under instruction and in the name of the Lord himself that a wife should not simply walk away from her husband and that a husband should not send his wife away."[84] This sharpens the problematic of 7:1-

---

82. Conzelmann: "One asks oneself: is this elementary principle that is so foreign to ancient society and which was valid for all of early Christianity supposed to have remained unknown in Corinth?" J. Murphy-O'Connor's critique (cf. above note 55) emphasizes that what is given here is no "statement of principle." Certainly here, as our presentation makes clear, it is specific people with a specific inquiry who are addressed, but Paul argues from a general principle. The only question is what that principle was (see the following).

83. In this sense Chrysostom comments, PG 61:154: "Since it happened that divorces occurred because of abstinence (δι᾽ ἐγκράτειαν) and other pretexts or small-minded, petty attitudes, he (Paul) says that it would be better if the beginning (= a certain separation) did not arise at all. However, if it has already occurred, the wife should remain with her husband, if not in a sexual union, at least by not taking up with another man."

84. The formulation is shaped by the prevailing marital law, according to which it is always the husband who "dismisses" ("repudiates" would be

5, since the desire for celibacy now tends to dissolve the marriage entirely. That would explain why Paul becomes so vigorous. Even if those persons concerned have invoked Jesus' words about "those who have left wife and family," still in this context it is apparently not a matter of missionary calling.

In addition, Paul may have had the impression in the cases presented that egoism dressed up as religion is also a factor (cf. 7:25-40), that living together may become difficult if the (Christian!) partner does not have the same interest in abstinence, if thus the "symphony" mentioned in 7:5 is lacking. This suspected motivation cannot be demonstrated in a compelling fashion from the text, but it is further suggested by the fact that in the following section the Christian spouse also wonders whether to send the partner away, and there expressly for "pious" reasons ("uncleanness"). The brevity of the formulation is explained by the fact that the readers themselves had posed the question; the sharpness of tone, however, by the fact that Paul again sees himself compelled to defend marriage against a religious rigorism. With people who are straining under the weight of their marriage, a man who "weeps with those who are weeping" would have spoken differently.

Independent of the motivation, in the background stands the conviction that a Christian may never initiate a divorce. Here Paul stands in the doctrinal tradition of the historical Jesus; it is one of the few places in which he invokes it.[85] Although the UT uses "separate," the Greek words otherwise mean "divorce" and "dismiss (forever)," as they do immediately in 7:12, 13 and 15. Apart from temporary separations, the idea of an enduring, definitive "separation" while the marriage itself continues nominally was

---

too strong here) or from whom the wife "departs" (cf. Atf VI). In Greece a wife could more easily dissolve a marriage on her own initiative than in Judaism.

85. This shows us that with him one may not oppose the exalted Jesus to the earthly Jesus. After all, it is the "earthly" Jesus who died for us. Occasionally 2 Cor 5:16 is interpreted as if Paul wished to emphasize that the earthly Jesus had no importance for him. Bultmann *(Der Zweite Brief an die Korinther)*: "Christ himself cannot be seen in his earthly properties." However, "according to the flesh" is attached adverbially to "recognize"; see Ts 30:34.

up to that time unknown in Jewish and Christian circles; also, it could not be so sharply rejected by Paul, because it would conform to Jesus' (presumed) prohibition against divorce. The Corinthians whose question Paul is answering would have understood the word in the usual Hellenistic sense,[86] that one partner wishes to really dissolve the marriage so as to be able to live celibately and thus set the other free for a new marriage. Against that, however, Paul says: "In accord with the Lord's word, *you* may not 'divorce' *yourself* from your partner."

The main problem in this paragraph lies in verse 11. Does Paul really here give a dispensation from the Lord's word which he has just underlined so emphatically? According to the results of our investigation of the texts in the New Testament dealing with divorce, we must pay special attention to who is playing the active role in a divorce. Jesus' command that "what God has joined together, human beings may not put asunder" says only that no one may *initiate* a divorce; however, if someone does this, the innocent party remains free for a further marriage.[87] That is why Paul is speaking from the viewpoint of the active party; the other—in 7:10f. a Christian partner—is not expressly commanded to remain alone. A further reconciliation is put forward only as *one possibility;* from that we may not conclude that the other *must wait,* but rather that Paul is presuming: "in the case where the partner remained alone." Here, however, he is speaking to the conscience of the *active* party: "*you* may not divorce,"[88] and indeed—in our view—not even out of the desire for abstinence. "For you have given your promise to the other" (7:4)!

Thus Paul is giving no "dispensation," but rather on the one hand is standing on an empirical border: if the marriage has already been dissolved at your own instigation, then in any event

86. On χωρίζεσθαι see EuE 95; Atf VI, 256f.

87. More on this below, D IV 1 and Atf VI. On this point I thus go beyond what I wrote in EuE 63–67.

88. Once again: if Paul from the very outset had meant only a so-called "split between bed and board, with the marriage bond continuing," he then would be forbidding "in the name of the Lord" something that no one had ever extracted from the sayings governing divorce in the Synoptics; and in spite of that, the Church would later have allowed it as a solution in difficult cases!? He can only have meant "divorce"; otherwise he would not have reacted so strongly.

remain alone if your partner has remarried, or attempt to re-invigorate the marriage, in case your partner is still free. Perhaps Paul is thinking throughout this of an actual case in Corinth.[89] Again we must assume that the readers knew more than we, so that the text was understandable to them. At the same time the sentence is framed as a generality, so that Paul is also preparing for the encounter with such a possibility in the future. In what does it consist? In that, *even in spite of the Lord's prohibition,* someone could divorce their partner for human reasons, perhaps simply because their partner did not please them anymore? The "exception" is thinkable only if the motive lies on a different plane, similar to the priority of the faith in 7:12-18. And because this motive appears to have such a strong weight to it, it becomes understandable why Paul challenges the petitioners with the "Lord's command." They would only be able to justify such a divorce if the desire for abstinence came from the same Lord who had given the command: You should not dissolve a marriage. *Then,* however, the person in question (as the active agent in the divorce) must remain celibate (indeed, this was also the reason for the separation) or—in case that is difficult and/or the partner is still free—be reunited with his or her spouse.

One could now object that in such a situation the admonition to remain alone would not be necessary. But is this true? Just as Paul in 7:2, 5, 6f. and 9 (and again in 7:14) reminds the "pious" people of their limits and points out dangers, so here he counsels the woman who leaves (or has left) her husband from a desire for abstinence that she may not later marry another, but rather should also remain true to her resolution, in case she does not again return to her husband. "To be reconciled" does not necessarily mean that the two flew apart in an argument. From the context it is more likely that the separation does not (or did not) take place in a violent fashion, but rather with sympathy or at least toleration of the Christian (!) partner. At the same time the active party has demanded something from the other. Whoever tries to retract always requires a reconciliation both with himself or

---

89. Thus Murphy-O'Connor, "Divorced," 602f. The Greek aorist is sufficiently explained with a relative anteriority (if a solution is accomplished) and then implies universal validity (EuE 65f.), but is at least open for a historical past.

herself—to correct the earlier step—and with the other. One may not load on too much to *katallagēnai;* it refers to *taking up again an interrupted relation* and is used especially for the reestablishment of a (lapsed) marriage.[90] "To bind up again" would also catch the sense. Our interpretation joins seamlessly what has gone before and what is taken up again in what follows, while a general instruction on "indissolubility" would appear too sharp and out of place in this context. Rather, Paul sees very soberly the limits and the dangers of people, especially with "pious" zeal that has not yet run its course, and thus here again protects marriage against religious rigorism.

THE PAULINE "PRIVILEGE OF LOVE"
IN MIXED MARRIAGES: 1 CORINTHIANS 7:12-16

UT		PT
To the rest I say,	12	To the rest, *nevertheless,* I say,
not the Lord:	a	not the Lord:
If a brother has an unbelieving wife and she *is willing to continue* living together with him,	b	if a brother has a wife who is not a believer, and she (for her part) *together with him holds it to be a good thing* (is disposed, has decided with him) to live together with him,
he should not repulse her.	c	he should not send her *away;*
Also, a believing woman should not repulse an unbelieving husband if he *consents* to continue living with her.	13 / a / b	*and if* a woman has a husband who is not a believer, but he regards it as good to live together with her, she should not *send* the man *away.*
For the unbelieving husband is sanctified *through* his wife	14 / a	For the unbelieving husband is **sanctified** *for* the wife (in the eyes of the wife),
and the unbelieving wife is sanctified *through* her believing husband.	b	and the unbelieving wife is **sanctified** *for* the brother.
Otherwise your children *would be* unclean; (!)	c	for indeed, (we all know) your (newborn) children are unclean

90. Just as ἀλλαγῆναι, used with reference to a marriage, means "dismissed," *repudiare;* see Fitzmyer, "Divorce," 213.

UT		PT
		(for the heathen as also for us earlier),
but they are holy.	d	*but now* (for us who are saved) *are* holy.
However, if the unbeliever decides to separate, he should do it.	15 a	If, of course, the **unbeliever** *divorces* (seeks to separate), he or she *should be divorced;*
The brother or sister in such circumstances is not *bound like a slave;*	b	a brother or sister *in such a situation* is not enslaved *(through my words).*
God has called *you to a life in peace.*	c	But **God** has called *us* in **peace** (God has indeed called us in/with peace);
How do you know, wife, *whether you can* save your husband?	16 a	*perhaps,* wife, *you will save* your husband (bring him to Christ the ''savior''),
Or *how do you know,* husband, *whether you* can save your wife?	b	or *perhaps,* husband, *you will save* your wife!

In contrast to verse 10 (''however'') Paul emphasizes here that for the question that follows he cannot fall back on any word of the Lord. Thus in his view there is no statement in the oral tradition concerning marriage with non-Christians. This is understandable, because it only became a problem after Easter. The problem of mixed marriages is naturally well known to the Jews, but here there is a new situation of the marriage of a Christian with a nonbeliever.[91] As a consequence Paul, together with the entire primitive Church, understood the Lord's command not to

91. Since the singles and the married couples in the community were mentioned before, λοιποί can only refer to those Christians who find themselves in a mixed marriage; the systematic categories in 7:8-12 are complete; see above, A II 5. With all three groups the question is one of entering into or dissolving a marriage. Moiser's interpretation, 108f., that Paul in 7:10 is speaking to those who at the time of their conversion were married, but in 7:12f. on the other hand about those who have been dismissed by their pagan spouses, has no foundation in the text. It is much more likely that they are currently living together with a non-Christian.

divorce the marriage partner primarily as advice *for the community of disciples,* not with the same meaning for all people.[92]

What is the question on the table? From the UT one has the impression that it is the *believer* who wishes to continue the marriage, because the unbelieving party is said to "consent"—that would mean to acquiesce in the Christian partner's suggestion or desire that the marriage be continued. But verse 14 makes it clear that the Christian partner is pressing for the *dissolution* of the marriage. And in verses 12-13 the Christian is exhorted not to "send the other away." Thus it was the *Christian* who raised the question to Paul: "*May* I (not: *must* I) send my partner away?" Otherwise Paul would have answered: "You should/can certainly *stay with him or her!*" In verses 12f., however, *syneudokei* does not mean to acquiesce in another's request (UT), but rather to concur with someone else about a (third) matter, to mutually approve or positively validate it. Perhaps Paul is presuming that —following this instruction—the believing party will ask (not necessarily: *request of*) the partner whether or not they intend to continue together;[93] however, the believer is not required to ask, because she or he is not the source of the proposal for divorce.

And why should the Christian be thinking about divorce? The cause must have something to do with being a Christian. He or she is addressed as "sister" or "brother," that is, as a believer; the potential "holiness" of the unbeliever is referred to, and they are reminded of their "call." The thought in this is probably that initially both partners were non-Christians and then, after the marriage, one of them came to believe in Christ. The fundamental question is *not* raised whether a Christian should be allowed to live in marriage with a non-Christian—that must have already been clarified at the baptism of the one partner or, in case he or she was already a Christian before, at the time of the marriage. No, here the problem is one that appeared long *after* the one party's conversion within an already existing marriage. Both the believer's life and also the relation to the partner have been changed through the one's relationship with Christ. The other party senses that the partner loves Christ more than him or her—

---

92. On the reasons and consequences, see below, D IV 4; more in Atf VI 10.

93. Naturally *Οἰκεῖν μετ'* also includes sexual union; cf. also 1 Cor 7:14.

and under the circumstances responds with jealousy. Besides that, it is not easy to accept it when the Christian party develops brotherly and sisterly relations within the community and the spouse remains outside. There are similar tensions today. A wife, for example, may then properly say: "That is not the man I married; he was not nearly so pious."

However, this concerns only the surrounding context of our problem. For first it is the *believing* partner who has a desire to separate. Why? Because these tensions are burdensome? But as long as the non-Christian partner, whom these should bother much more, has made no suggestion about divorce (thus does not experience the tension as strongly as we have depicted it above), the Christian would have no ground for this! So here again it is likely that behind the affair stands a desire in the believing party to be alone, that is, live in abstinence. In this case all the passages from this chapter thus far would indeed be unified under a single topic[94]—"on the matter you have written about" (1 Cor 7:1). We find suggestions for this also in verse 14.

Throughout the entire chapter one has the clear impression that Paul is wrestling with his interlocutors. He senses a tendency from which he is trying to dissuade them. This paragraph must face an argument such as: "But a non-Christian is unclean! Would I not be polluted through such and infiltrated by heathen, demonic influences?" What interest could the Christian parties in such marriages have to bring forward such an argument *now?* Why did they not do so at the time of their conversion? Apparently they now have some particular interest in becoming *free from* this partner. However, Paul attempts to wrest them away from this argument. For[95] a Christian, nothing is any longer unclean (Rom

---

94. Moiser also argues for a "single theme" (104); however, with his statement that there is "really a duty either to renounce marriage or to remain single" (110, 119), he overshoots the mark. The people are rather asking whether continence would be "allowed," or more accurately, how it should be correctly practiced.

95. This is an ethical dative: "in my eyes, according to my view of things = for me." "To this very day in the Jewish ritual the bridegroom says to the bride: for me [!] you shall be sacred" (Schelkle, 88). Naturally the unbeliever is not sanctified through my becoming a Christian, but rather as a consequence of my conversion appears to me in a new light, and I should hold him or her sacred. Speculations as to whether partners receive a sancti-

14:14), for to the Lord belongs the earth and all that is in it (1 Cor 10:26). Thus a Christian regards everything with different eyes, and that includes a sexual relationship with a non-Christian. For both Greek and Jewish tradition, the process of birth entails "uncleanness." Paul argues the same way: "When you were pagans, after the birth the mother had to 'purify' both herself and the child." This took place in the so-called *amphidromos;* they had to bring a sacrifice into a temple and go around the altar with the child. "But you know indeed," Paul continues, "that you no longer have to do that, even if your relatives object to this."

One can imagine how deeply the decision to become a Christian penetrated into the everyday life of people. Paul presumes that the readers know about this new view and have also long since altered their practice after birth. "However, if 'now' even a newborn is no longer unclean *for you,* then neither is your partner, with whom you have created it." Thus the question about the sexual union stands somehow in the background. Paul does not allow them to describe this as unclean, even if it occurs with a heathen![96] In case fear of sexual contact has played a role with

---

fication appropriate to their nature transmitted *through* the Christian, or whether the children do not indeed need to be baptized, are all beside the point; cf. J. C. O'Neill, "1 Corinthians 7:14 and Infant Baptism," in: A. Vanhoye, *L'Apotre Paul* (BEThL LXXIII) (Leuven, 1986) 357–361. "Sacred" in v. 14 is understood as the overcoming of supposed cultic impurity, as both the Greeks and Jews recognize this, not in the personal moral sense in which we understand the word today. Thus, it would be better to say "clean-unclean." For more, see below, A VI 3.

96. In contrast, see what K. Niederwimmer, 85, writes concerning 1 Cor 7:1: "To expect the imminent end of the world and to be free for Christ are hardly the only reasons for Paul's sexual ascesis. . . . Paul's statement conveys not only a distaste for sexual relations in general (and that primarily out of fear of being demonically infected through the sexual act), but along with this an anxiety-filled distaste for women *in genere*. . . . The statement appears to be the result of ritual anxiety before the demonic power of sexuality and specifically of woman; she has a negative taboo." This interpretation is worlds away from our own! It represents an extreme position, and is in no sense the consensus of exegetes. Where do we find the apostle of Christ here? Cf. only 1 Cor 10:23-31. Paul experienced no anxiety about demons. See further EuE 81f. and 63.

the petitioners—perhaps also as a welcome argument for why they should be set free—Paul grants it no ground. One should notice the logical thought sequence from verse 14: from one principle recognized by the petitioner—and independent from the current question—about the "cleanness" of a newborn, Paul concludes to what he wishes to prove: the cleanness = permission for contact with the marital sexual partner. Thereby is the probability very high that also with our question, as with the previous one, the Christian partner's wish for abstinence played a role, to which Paul now rebuts only the specific arguments.

"However, if the *nonbeliever* divorces"—in that case the brother or sister is not *slavishly bound.* By what? Much speculation goes in the direction that in that case the Christian party should not regard *the marriage* as a yoke of slavery—which once again would afford us a "deep insight" into how Paul regards marriage. In fact, we find this mentality in later commentators, but Paul is thinking of something else. He does not say: "If *you* can no longer bear your unbelieving partner, and if the marriage has become a torture *to you,* then *you* can go," but rather: If your *partner,* even though *you* are ready, will not continue, then "he or she should be divorced,"[97] which means: then the Chris-

---

97. Χωριζέσθω is an imperative. The usual rendering (he or she may separate himself or herself), which I still carried over in EuE 68 and 83, would have been better expressed through a subjunctive. Here we have again one of the numerous Pauline word plays (cf. EuE 575 under "Sprache"), a switch from the middle to the passive meaning. This passive is frequently encountered; see L.-Sc. s.v. I.II.III and Passow with many citations; κεχωρισμένη is normally used for a divorced woman, in the sense of a person who *has received* a divorce (less often: who has herself divorced; cf. Atf VI 10). Paul also makes use of the passive in a different connection: Philemon 15; cf. further Hebrews 7:26 and perhaps Acts 18:2. Thus the imperative after the conditional sentence "if he or she divorces" (or perhaps: seeks to divorce; a present *de conatu*) means: he or she *should* become divorced! This is a command—but to whom? Certainly not to the nonbeliever, in accord with the motto: if he is going anyway, let him go (?!), but is rather directed to the believer: in that case, also, as far as you are concerned, the nonbeliever should be divorced, which means that from your side you should consent to the divorce and not be of the opinion that, on my advice (!) you should prevent it by all means. One should bear in mind that divorce did not take place, as with us, through a civil process, but was settled within families

tian parties *should* go along with the separation and give their consent without having a bad conscience. "In that case *you* are not bound!" By what? By the "slavery of marriage"? Paul presumes that his readers know that "the Lord" does not bind them in a mixed marriage with the same bonds as two disciples. Thus they realize that they dispose of the possibility of divorcing. However, he himself had advised them to remain as they are if possible. Thus they are "not bound" *by his advice!* And why "slavish" bonds? They should not make out of his counsel an "enslaving law" (a Pauline topic!) and hold themselves to it in a slavishly literal fashion, but rather weigh the situation and in freedom decide what is good before God and corresponds to love. Thus Paul does not put forward his advice in an absolute fashion. We shall see this (cf. 7:12) immediately in 7:17 and even more often. They should indeed hold the possibility open for the non-Christian, but also not oppress them with their desire for reconciliation nor run around after them. It is a question of developing a sensitivity for what is appropriate.

"But God has called us in peace!" Here every word is important. Even if the nonbeliever wishes to divorce, still *God* (in emphasized position) *has called* (in our being Christian) *us* (that is, all Christians) *in peace*. Shalom—peace—does not mean something like a still, motionless condition, but rather refers to union in a relationship, the mutual being with one another of two persons (cf. Rom 5:1; 1 Cor 10:11; Eph 2:14-17; 4:3). It is *God's* intention that the greatest possible union develop between humans. This is grounded *in general* in our call by Christ. That is why here the preferred reading is "us." "Since *our* call as Christians is oriented overall toward peace, *you* can easily draw the proper conclusion from that with regard to your marriage situation: the nonbeliever may leave, and in that case you should release him or her. However, from your side at least attempt to preserve the marriage; for *God's* love, which is given to us through our call, aims in this direction and also gives you the strength[98] for it."

---

by the partners themselves. Thus it is a matter here, as with συνευδοκεῖ in v. 12f., of the negotiation phase, for which the believer now receives a directive through the imperative. What follows also fits with this interpretation.

98. Καλεῖν ἐν is not the same as καλεῖν εἰς. Behind this stands the Hebrew "*b*," in the sense of an instrumental "through, under, by means of" peace

"Perhaps"[99] you can even "save" your partner. It is not as though the Christian was now the savior of the other party, and also not as if the latter, if he or she abandons the Christian, would go to hell, but it is rather a matter of the saving community of Christians on earth, of *ekklēsia*/community. Perhaps you may bring the other into a saving relation to Christ. How God today and after our death judges and deals with those who have never known and accepted Jesus is discussed elsewhere (cf. Rom 2:14; 1 Cor 5:13). *Here* the topic is only that of access to the community of the redeemed during our lifetime.

We have deliberately translated *chōrizesthai* as "divorce" because this word, as we saw already in verse 10, normally means this and because here certainly more than a "separation" is being discussed. Rather, through his response Paul makes us aware that in the primitive Church marriage with a non-Christian was not considered indissoluble. At least he gives us here some information on this question and is not making some exception from the "stricter" command of the Lord. How could he ever bring himself to say: "The Lord does not allow this, but *I* give you permission"? But verse 12 is not construed that way. A closer inspection discloses that Paul is throwing his own authority onto the scales

---

(EuE 84). The God of peace has so worked our calling as to establish in us the attitude of peace. This specific meaning of "calling" parallels exactly the progression καλεῖν-κλῆσις that is presented in 7:17-24, as we shall see immediately.

99. In the official edition of the German Unified Translation, a note pointed out that v. 16 could also be translated with "perhaps" in the manner suggested here. However, as in most translations, this was not incorporated into the text proper, because it did not fit in well with the context. For if one interprets "bound like a slave" to refer to the marriage bond, and interprets v. 15c to mean that God will not require a Christian to assume any excessive burden, but rather the Christian's "peace of mind" has priority, then one must come to the conclusion that the interior peace and balance are indeed more important than rescuing the other. However, Paul's thought moves in a different direction. S. Kubo, "1 Cor 7:16: Optimistic or Pessimistic?" *TS* 24 (1978) 539-544, only returns to a "pessimistic" or more accurately "uncertain" conclusion because he speculates that vv. 12-14 and 15-16 are addressed to two different audiences. However, the different direction taken in 15 a/b comes from Paul's point of view, not from that of those addressed.

to encourage them *to stay* in the marriage: "*I* say to you, if the nonbeliever is prepared to remain, then do not send him or her away (even though you are not bound to stay with him or her by the Lord's command)." This is the "privilege" that Paul gives here and which he spends the rest of the section grounding and defending. It then also becomes more comprehensible why in verse 15 he relativizes *his own advice:* "Do not follow this slavishly, like a 'law'; at the same time recognize that God's call should move us in the direction of the preservation of a marriage. And that is the reason I *advise* you to persevere in a mixed marriage, in spite of the possibility of divorce."

If we choose to use the word "privilege" in this context, we now see that we are speaking about the *privilege of love* in a mixed marriage. On the other hand, the way the term Pauline privilege is used in canon law, namely the claim that a marriage with an unbaptized person may be dissolved in favor of the faith of the Christian party, can indeed invoke this passage, since it shows that the early Church considered such marriages capable of being dissolved. However, this should not be seen as either an exception to a generally valid command by the Lord, nor as a special privilege that Paul is asserting "in virtue of his full authority as an apostle."[100]

III. One's Personal Call as the Criterion: 1 Corinthians 7:17-24

Now follows a second major part of the seventh chapter in which Paul comes to speak about the principle underlying everything. It has been called a "digression"; however, this section is on the contrary the very core of the chapter.[101] It consists of a basic proposition that is repeated three times (17a, 20, 24), and

100. Admittedly this misunderstanding can only with some difficulty be cleared up through the linguistic conventions. For further reflections on canon law, see below, D IV 5 and 6; also EuE 88-98; Atf VI 10. Schürmann, 429, speaks rather of an *exemplum Paulinum,* and correctly emphasizes that *in favorem fidei* is a questionable terminology.

101. Similar to 1 Cor 13 between 12 and 14. Moiser, 105, 110. The paragraph provides the basis for the apostle's responses.

which in between is explained twice by an example. Examples of what? Of the ongoing question to be decided concerning abstinence! First we must understand the statements in themselves, and then gradually make ourselves aware of what role they have in the entire chapter.

1. "Each as God calls him or her": 1 Corinthians 7:17a

UT		PT
God's call and the *condition* of those called: 7:17-24		The *center* of the chapter: 7:17-24. The core sentence repeated three times: 17a, 20, 24
For the rest each one should so live as the Lord has assigned *it* to them, *as* God's call has struck them.	17 a	But (still) **each one** should lead his or her life as **the Lord** has imparted it to them, as **God** has called them.

When the Christian couple asked Paul about abstinence, Paul reminded them of the Lord's command (although in v. 11 he also did not rule out as impossible a life in separation; on the other hand, to the Christian partner in a mixed marriage *he* had *himself* given the "advice" that they should remain in the marriage, even though at the same time he had indicated that they should not make a "law" out of his counsel. He knows his community and with this letter has concrete individuals in mind. At the same time he knows that some Christians are allowed "to leave their wives" for the Lord's sake (Luke 18:28f.). Was not the early community thinking of such apostles when they transmitted these words of the Lord? Naturally, God remains the *Lord of marriage* as well as *of celibacy* (7:6-9). That is the reason Paul now sets down a strong oppositional term: *Still* each person must in the final analysis consider how the Lord himself is leading him or her. Thus Paul will not convert all his suggestions from 7:1-16 into an absolute criterion.

The UT misses this transition. As for its title, it is indeed *technically* correct to distinguish between God's call and a specific lifestyle; however, terminologically in verse 20 the "call" *(klēsis)* is exactly what the UT translates by "condition." Thereby the main problem of 7:17-24 becomes immediately graspable. There is something wrong here! In verse 17a this view already has the consequence that the UT distinguishes between God's "call" and the condition *in which* ("as'") this call has found the individual.

However, by an emphatic positioning of the subject—in Greek at the end of the sentence—Paul intends to emphasize that it is *God,* and not himself with his counsel, who is the final criterion for each individual. However, God establishes this criterion through God's call! Thus a person should live in the manner that this *call* demands of them, as it *"has struck"* them—not as it is usually translated: "they should remain in the *condition,* in the *position,* or in the profession in which the call *found* them" (cf. 7:20). What is determinative is definitely not the previous condition, but what is new, and the condition becomes "assigned" through the call. Therein "assign/measure out" and "call" are objectively synonymous; both words refer to a gift of the new order of salvation. The "God of Measure" allocates to each person his or her own "portion" (7:7; cf. also 2 Cor 10:13; Rom 12:3), and each person should shape his or her life according to this portion; *peripatein* is a dynamic word and does not mean an unbudging maintenance of an initial position.

Thus it is important to Paul that individuals should not blindly follow Paul's own advice, but rather finally decide for themselves in spiritual responsibility before God. In that way it could come about that someone might *"still"* dissolve their marriage for the Lord's sake, decide to stay in abstinence within a marriage, remain married or celibate. It would then be an authentic decision made responsibly, after having weighed this advice, and no longer simply an "imitation" or the taking over in complete dependency of an apostolic standard or "counsel." In addition to the generally applicable orientation—something like the "call in peace" in verse 15b—the individual must consider how his or her own spiritual impulses and the counsel of the apostles are to be realized under individual conditions and what his or her personal limitations might be, but also where the "strengths" he or she has been given by God lie. So the final authority to decide on all these questions, including those concerning marriage and celibacy, rests with the individual Christian.

2. The Example of Circumcision:
   1 Corinthians 7:17b-20

UT		PT
This is my instruction for all communities.	17 b	*And thus* (therefore, correspondingly) I *direct* (!) in all communities: (!)
If someone who is circumcised is called, he should *remain* circumcised.	18	if someone who is circumcised is called, he should *not* try to *reverse* it ("not cover it");
If someone who is uncircumcised is called, he should not have himself circumcised.	b	if someone is called who is uncircumcised, he should not have himself circumcised.
The important thing is not whether one is circumcised or not,	19	Circumcision *counts for nothing,* being uncircumcised *counts for nothing,*
but rather observing God's commands.	b	rather, following **God's** instructions (is what is important, is all).
Each should remain in the *condition* in which God's call has found him.	20 a b	To the **call** (of God) *that he or she has received* **to that** each person should remain fixed (orient oneself, shape one's life thereby).

One could derive an initial impression that Paul is laying down very precise instructions and principles. This impression is strengthened in the UT by the demonstrative pronoun "this" in verse 17b, which picks up the thought from the previous sentence, that each person should *remain* in the way of life in which God's call came to them. This appears to be—quite logically—carried further in the statement of verse 18: "If you were circumcised, then *remain* circumcised." Indeed, *houtos* at the beginning of verse 17b is a particle indicating consequence (the conjunction is *kai,* the verse is leading into the one that follows, thus the full colon at the end of 17b), and the word "remain" is not present! The latter is nothing but the English version (UT) of "not cover" = "remain" circumcised. Paul rather intends to say: in accord with the principle just mentioned in verse 17a, I also direct other things in the communities, for example the question of circumcision: it is not important for a Christian whether one is circumcised or uncircumcised (as also neither marriage or celibacy), but rather the new call in which God gives us "instructions." Paul intends thereby the general rules for conduct *(entolai)* in the gospels, as well as individual instructions that each person experiences as part of his or her call. The latter instructions build in a certain way on the former and are embedded in them. However, they are not simply identical! Thus the chief point of the example is not the "remaining" in circumcision, but rather the *relativizing* of the whole matter (placing it in context or relation) in view of the call.

The whole traditional interpretation clamps down on verse 20. Here "remain" appears once again to be underlined, and given the previous example that could only mean: "remain either circumcised or uncircumcised." Thus it is a matter of the initial situation in which the call *came upon* him, or even of the "condition" *in which* the call struck him. Indeed, "remain" seems to play a central role also in the next verses: to "remain" a slave. Thus the logic of the text seems to commend the conventional interpretation.

However, *klēsis,* which here is translated—but not before modern times—by "condition," means literally "call/vocation" and otherwise with Paul always stands for the divine call through Christ. In the Greek text this root, including the verbs, appears in the short section 7:17-24 nine times and otherwise always has the meaning of a divine call. Thus, with what right can we give to the substantive in 7:20 a meaning which stands in contradiction to the other references, namely something which precedes the "call" and cannot be touched or altered by it? Linguistically a difficulty was seen in the expression *"remain in* the call." One could indeed only construe this physically: to remain in the *condition* in which one was at the time of the call. However, the formula is here intended in an ethical sense: to remain in the call, to "stick to" to the call, to orient oneself toward the call, similar to "abiding in love" in John 15:9. Then verse 20 says: Each should discover a standard for such decisions as circumcision/noncircumcision, marriage/celibacy, abstinence/marital relations in his or her personal call from God! This is the criterion to which people should orient themselves.

The logical "trap" which the commentators fell into lay first of all in verse 18, where they assumed that Paul has spoken about "remaining" with circumcision. If verse 20 is then seen as a way of summarizing and applying the first example, then here also "remaining" should carry over this sense. However, this is precisely the "trap": Should Paul really hold fast in verses 18 and 20 as an immovable reality, on whose preservation he places great value, to what in verse 19 he twice very emphatically characterizes with "nothing" (the UT with "not" is here too mild)? In verse 19 God's instructions are certainly the determining factor; then how in verse 20 does it suddenly switch to the context under which one hears these instructions? The "logic" of the passage forces us to see the "divine instructions" and the "call" in the same perspective. From the objective point of view Paul indeed intends to *relativize* the importance of being circumcised or uncircumcised; if a circumcised person has a foreskin sewn on again (to give expression in some way as a Christian to his "freedom from the Law"; Hellenistic Jews often had this done to fit into the wider society) or a Gentile man undergoes not only baptism but also circumcision (we are thinking of the problem that comes to full expression in Galatians, but also in 2 Cor 11:18-22), they thereby give these signs excessive importance. These would then displace both God's "instructions" and their "call." Thus "remaining" with either circumcision or lack thereof = not changing one's condition, is in this case a *consequence* of a life lived in the call. Thereby "remain" here has a completely different positional value than the "remain in the call" of verse 20. Here it should be seen as "relative" to the call. Besides that, in verse 18b of the original text the word *menein*/remain does not appear!

There may certainly be cases in which, perhaps out of consideration for a Jewish sensibility, one could circumcise a Christian just as Paul also allows, without scruples, Jewish Christians to have their sons circumcised.[102] The only requirement is that they not misunderstand this as a means of salvation, nor demand it of uncircumcised Christians! To that extent the statement in Acts 16:3 that Paul had Timothy circumcised does not constitute a contradiction to our passage, but is rather an expression of the same point of view. Precisely *because* circumcision "counts for nothing" can one—with a correct interpretation—also on occasion undergo circumcision (Gal 2:3). This "counting for noth-

---

102. This could also be implied in Gal 2:9.

ing" naturally constitutes a rhetorical emphasis, and does not deny that both the law and circumcision have been a way God has acted toward God's people. But these now become unimportant in comparison with the call in Christ. For that reason one must now "remain fixed" on *this,* the calling.

3. Is It Preferable to "Remain" a Slave?: 1 Corinthians 7:21-23

UT		PT
If you were a slave when you were called, that should not *depress* you;	21 a	If you were called as a slave, *don't think about it* (don't be concerned about it);
even if you can now become free, *prefer to continue living as a slave.*	b	*however,* if you *are really able* to become free (are really in a position to free yourself), rather, *make use of it.*
For anyone who is called in the Lord *as* a slave	22	For the *slave called in the* Lord
is one set free by the Lord.	a	is one **set free by the Lord!**
In the same way one called *as* a free person is now a slave to Christ	b	In a similar way a free person (who is) called becomes **a slave of Christ.**
You have been bought at a great price.	23 a	Your freedom has been bought (with a cash payment, by Christ) (for God);
Do not make yourselves into slaves to human beings!	b	do not become slaves to *human beings.*

"Remaining" has haunted the following example as well, although the word only appears in the concluding verse 24. However, objectively speaking it seemed present in the "prefer to continue living as a slave" (UT); Wilckens: "remain nevertheless all the more (in your condition)." We have already seen the "logic" that seems to force such a translation. At the same time, both translations register that there are also grounds for the interpretation: "seize rather the opportunity (to become free)." Now, not only *can* one so translate it (linguistically it is clearer), but one *must* do so, because of the "context" (UT, note.), following the same "logic" as before. Thus Paul does not intend to absolutize the condition in which one stood when one was called, but on the contrary intends to make the call itself the standard by which all other matters are judged—including the question of abstinence or marital union! The triad of contrasts—"Jew–Greek, slave–free, man–woman" is a familiar constellation.

Specifically, Paul here clarifies the question of sexual relations using two as examples: "Whether Jew or Gentile—what is decisive is the call by Christ"; "whether slave or free—you are in Christ" (1 Cor 12:13). Both stand in service of the statement: whether celibacy or marital union—it must always be *imparted by God* and only as such receives its worth.[103] With this it is clear that Paul does not here intend to extend the condition of slavery, just as before he was not recommending either circumcision or the absence thereof.

However, the relativization begins with the fact that he makes it clear to those who are slaves—and the Corinthian community is supposed to have had many slaves, both male and female (Chloe? 1 Cor 1:11, 26ff.)—that their ultimate worth, or the lack thereof, is not determined by that condition. "Don't bother yourself with that," which means: "Don't go around in a disturbed state thinking that your salvation depends upon it." The translation "that should not depress you" introduces a soothing tone, either in the sense: "even if it is difficult, be of good spirits" or—which would be worse: "Don't take it so hard, don't let your sorrow overcome you." But Paul is no Stoic philosopher preaching an impassivity of emotion *(ataraxia)* in every life situation, but rather a man who is thoroughly aware of "distress" and suffers because of it *(thlipsis* is a key word with him). So he will not forbid the slave to "groan" about his fate (cf. 2 Cor 5:24; Rom 8:22f.). No, he will rather *relativize* the status of being a slave (22a). "See to it that your thoughts do not perpetually revolve around this fact so that you thereby become once again enslaved to your (factual condition) of being a slave." But does this mean that the slave may "do" nothing in order to free himself or herself? Here the interpreters go separate ways.

The principal stream among the commentators sees Paul advising the slave if possible not to accept an offer to be set free.

103. Thus objectively this is an authentic parallel to Gal 3:28; see below D I 2 and 3, around notes 517–519, and Atf I 4.

At the same time there is a small but stubborn contrary current that flows from the time of the Fathers down to Luther and into the present—sometimes with a broad consensus—that interprets verse 21b in the sense of "rather try to become free," with various nuances. Our research came to this result:[104] here Paul is thinking primarily that a slave, by engaging in various projects (saving money, proper behavior, good service, etc.) can contribute something to his or her eventual liberation. If there exists such a possibility, "put it to good use. Do not miss this opportunity, but rather 'get busy' (cf. v. 21a) about this possibility of becoming free." "Rather" indicates that one could also, with right, forego these opportunities, for example if one was too old or lacked self-confidence, or if freedom would make excessive demands upon one. For after all, there was no social security in those days! It also occasionally happened that, practically speaking, a slave was treated like a son in the house (cf. Deut 15:16; Exod 21:5) and saw no advantage to being set free. Most commentators, however, concentrate on the possibility that freedom was sooner or later *offered* to the slave, either through a general amnesty, the fact that a fixed term had run its course (at the latest after twenty years most slaves were freed), or through the benevolence of their masters. In that case the slave *would have to* accept freedom sooner or later anyway and thus had no choice. For that reason it is unlikely that Paul is thinking of these cases (or at least not only of these). The expression "rather take advantage of it" is indeed meant in the active sense. It is important that Paul encourages slaves to exploit their "chance for freedom."[105]

The justification for this runs: "For a person who, while a slave, was called in the Lord, is set free by the Lord" (also UT). It is not that one is "called *to be* a slave in the Lord," also not that one's condition of slavery is raised "in the Lord" to a calling (one could misinterpret many commentators in this sense), but rather: A person who was a slave at the time of conversion has experi-

104. It is not possible even to summarize the numerous semantic and syntactic reflections here; for this, see EuE 114–151.

105. This is the title of P. Trummer's contribution in *Bib.* 56 (1975) 344–368: "Die Chance der Freiheit." In a similar direction: S. S. Bartchy, *First-Century Slavery and the Interpretation of 1 Cor 7:21,* SBL Dissertation Series 11 (Missoula, 1973).

enced with that call a liberation at the spiritual level. If among humankind one must still discharge the duties of a slave, one should realize that in Christ one has found true freedom and the full worth of one's person. And if this may first occur on the spiritual plane, it naturally has consequences for one's total self-esteem and personal conduct. Thus verse 22a is first of all a reason for 21b (specifically, to place oneself within the context of the opportunity for freedom): "The fact that you are free in Christ argues that you should also take advantage of the legal possibilities; for the interior and exterior should match one another." However, the verse also grounds verse 21a: "You have been set free in Christ, so you should not busy yourself with your servitude, for your freedom in Christ is greater."[106]

All this is addressed primarily at the level of individual ethics. The institution of slavery as such is not here under scrutiny, but also *not simply accepted as something intended by the will of God!*[107] If in general Paul does not develop any social program,[108] then why should he dismember the social structure precisely at this, its weakest point, and indeed in the reverse direction, in that he removes from the weakest their last possibility of pulling themselves up—something that everyone else is doing? In any event, the tendency that we have detected in his statements moves in the direction of freedom.[109] Besides Philemon[110] and Ignatius, *Letter to Polycarp* 4:3 our thesis is also supported by the fact that there is scarcely any indication in the tradition of anyone placing an obstacle to the freeing of a slave by invoking this text, or of slaves who declined such an offer being celebrated as heroes.

---

106. This does not constitute a contradiction, for in 21a one should not be preoccupied with one's condition as a slave. However, to the extent that an *opportunity for freedom* presents itself, one should "rather" attend to it; in other words, one should be looking, not backwards, but forwards.

107. In the patristic era the Church did not invoke this passage to justify slavery, as is sometimes maintained. Although Chrysostom interprets this verse in the sense of "remaining a slave," he still characterizes slavery as an "injustice that is a consequence of sin": Ritter, 88f., with many examples; especially PG 61:353f. For 1 Cor 7:21, see PG 61.

108. For further reflections on this, see below, D I 1-3.

109. Schlatter, 136, makes this clear from the context.

110. Compare this with below, note 528.

The supposedly "deeper theological" reasons for the other interpretation are also not valid. We would suddenly encounter here a rigorism that would stand in contradiction to what we have previously seen in this chapter. With reference to the "condition," that would mean: "If you are set on something, then choose rather the more difficult, even if you have other possibilities."[111] For the main theme this would mean: "Even if you are 'burning,' (7:9) stay rather in the celibacy you have undertaken previously." With regard to marriage, it at least fits for the passage about mixed marriages (7:12-16): "Even if you find this marriage a form of slavery,[112] it is better to remain in it—even though the Lord grants you the opportunity for divorce." And in looking ahead to 7:35: "If I am encouraging you to celibacy, I intend it only for your good; even if you should discover it to be a 'chain' and should have other possibilities, still remain with it and think only of what kind of value it is to be undisturbed by the Lord" (?!). When seen in the full light of day, as regards both the context and the content, the current interpretation is absurd.

If Paul is arguing for the greatest possible freedom, that in no way means that he would not support the slave who has to remain a slave; on the contrary, he would do so, and indeed with a view towards the greater freedom which has already been achieved. Salvation through Christ consists in the fact that he takes from us many human burdens, and on the other hand that he *at the same time* strengthens us through his power to carry whatever cannot be removed. Imprisonment and suffering are consequences of sin and in no sense a value. Any mystification of suffering that would exalt pain as a way to reach more glory is as foreign to the apostle as a mysticism of sin which would say "sin, so that grace may more abound" (Rom 6:1). The same goes for the so-called "humility" which would deliberately or unconsciously exalt lowliness into a virtue; if one seeks the least, it is not because one is guided by a greater joy and love for the Lord, but ultimately by contempt,[113] indifference, and lack of love for

111. For a fundamental treatment of this, see below, D V 3.

112. Occasionally in fact reference is made here to 1 Cor 7:15, as L. Schottroff, 103.

113. In order to produce a meaningful statement from 1 Cor 7:21, many authors argue on the basis of Paul's reservations with regard to the world,

"worldly" values, and shows nothing of "gratitude for their portion" (1 Cor 10:30).

In all this there is finally hidden a hankering for achievement and a subtle rigorism which is foreign to Paul, even when it might sound "pious." The conscious sharing of another's everyday burden and of Christ's death (Gal 6:2; Phil 1:29; 2 Cor 4:10f.; Col 1:24) is something completely different. A voluntary "sacrifice" and "penance" are only Christian if they are produced out of such love.

Through our interpretation the rug is pulled out from under every rigidity and every "social conservatism," but also any morbid penitential thinking or the intention to discover in this text a means by which to achieve domination over the passions. Although John Chrysostom on the whole sketches a healthy picture, spiritual freedom for him still consists too much in "domination over the passions," so that the gift-nature of the new dignity no longer appears in its full Pauline sense. Here gradually a Hellenistic hostility toward the body pushes out a Jewish sense of the integrity of salvation. It begins with the fact that here one may take the option to remain a slave as the more pious course—a view that perdures down to our own day.

What consequences this has for many decisions regarding celibacy are obvious when Sickenberger writes: Paul "clearly can

---

which are more or less correct insights, but in the wrong place. This concern is fully preserved by "don't concern yourself with this" (21a), precisely in the sense that worldly burdens *cannot pose an obstacle* to salvation. However, the fact that something "does not harm" me does not exclude the possibility that its opposite could be "of greater use" to me. Cf. again above, note 106. In 21b the discussion is about what consequences salvation brings about, and how "the earth, which belongs to the Lord" (1 Cor 10:26), can serve this salvation. For that reason one should not speak of a "Pauline posture that is turned entirely inwards and is indifferent to everything exterior" (Bachmann), or say that "civil freedom has no value within the Church" (Conzelmann). In that case it would also not be health that Jesus restored in an exemplary fashion, or so many other things for which one may "petition" (Phil 4:6). But our example stands in the context of a discussion of sexual conduct. Even if marriage and celibacy should be "relativized," they are still a place where "God should be glorified" (1 Cor 6:12-20).

only have given out the advice to remain a slave if he presumes a moral value in it equal to that of virginity." However, for the latter "moral value" is not the criterion, but whether one can "take it well," namely God's gift (7:7b, 9, 35, 37), and whether it "is good for you" (7:8, 26, 28c, 32, 38, 40). In the same way, becoming free is here judged from whether one is "up to it." Others (Origen, Jerome) see in the option to remain a slave an allusion to marriage. Would that then make marriage the morally greater thing to do, and not a lower? Neither the one nor the other. Morally seen—and in our case that must also mean: spiritually and as seen by God—both the option to become free and to remain a slave are "relative," that is, to be seen in relation to the call, in any case in such a way that under otherwise equal conditions, freedom is closer to the call ("rather"). All this is contained in the correct estimation of the justification contained in 22a.

We have placed verse 22b in parentheses. It is an aside included to complete the example of slavery from the other side, before the main theme (that of slaves) is continued in verse 23. Paul had begun in verse 21: "If you are called as a slave, do not concern yourself about it." He could have added as a reason: "for you have been set free by the Lord." And then to that would have fit: "On the other hand, if you are called as free, you are a slave to Christ." That would have corresponded to the examples of circumcision and lack of circumcision. However, because with the example of slaves the possibility of being set free is important to the apostle (we see how this thrust immediately explodes the chain of thought), the main thought takes the other direction, as we discover, and thereby the reference to the reverse situation becomes a kind of appendage. The intention, however, is still clear: while the slave experiences the encounter with Christ as something like being set free and one's self-esteem is raised through it, the free person—as a general category—experiences in the encounter with Christ (for the first time?) that he or she indeed has a *Lord*. Thus, while the slave learns freedom and independence in Christ, the bourgeois is led thereby to humility.[114]

114. Misdirected is the suggestion (cf. Cornely and Barrett to that verse) that in their calling slaves would be freer at least on the spiritual level, and free persons would now be slaves on the spiritual level, so that as a result

Fully developed, the latter means: analogous to the fact that his or her fate no longer holds the slave fast, free persons, who now no longer belong to themselves, in the same way no longer dispose in a lordly fashion *over the use of their civic freedom,* but must now, as "slaves of Christ," negotiate from spiritual slavery all *secular* "free" decisions (those that remain free psychologically and with regard to the civil law). Before Christ they are no longer spiritually autonomous in the use of their civic freedom; that civic freedom has changed, in analogy to the change that took place with the slave through his or her call—independently of whether the latter has the possibility of being set free or not. God governs in every form of life and also takes—through God's call and the human response—just as much possession of the personal power of disposal as, in the trusting acceptance of this call, God enters into the human need of the slave, strengthening and raising the slave immediately in his or her specific burden. Thus if someone asks: "How should I deal with my pre-Christian cultic membership, how with my being a slave, and how with my being born free?," that person must judge each of these situations by their relation to the call received. In the same way: "Take the sexual situation and relations in which you stand as a given; they cannot impair your salvation. Whether you are married or not, whether you 'burn' (v. 9), whether you stand under external compulsion or 'have peace in your heart' (v. 36f.), place this in relation to your call and deal with it from there!"

Verse 22 probably echoes the idea that the slave, through the call, has become free not only in relation to God, but is also psychologically freer with regard to other people. Thus he or she treats the earthly lord differently, specifically as "one set free in the Lord," even if he or she remains a slave. The change is not only internal and (hidden in grace) somehow ontological, but also even appears in external matters and is thus also perceptible in

---

they are somewhat alike; each is in one sense a slave and in another sense free. And beyond that, the freed person is supposedly yet further dependent, if now on Christ. However, this totally misses the point of the comparison. "To be a slave in Christ" is something totally different from the civil state of slavery! In fact, it bespeaks a deeper freedom! Paul is a master of wordplay; precisely for that reason one should be careful before attributing to him such objective mistakes.

action and in psycho-social matters. The two levels, of which we have now spoken several times, are thereby clearly distinguished without being distinct in practice.

This integral effect of the salvation offered in the call now also opens up the meaning of verse 23: while indeed in the picture of being bought free all Christians are *intended,* still the *picture* attaches to the first mentioned group: we were *all* "slaves" of sin and our freedom for God was bought by Christ. Then what does this mean: "Do not become slaves of humankind"? Paul is not speaking against party leaders in the community, nor about the "slavery of marriage" (Origen), nor does he mean that free persons should not sell themselves into civil slavery (cf. 1 Clement 55:2). Rather he takes up again—after the parenthetical remark on free persons—the example of slavery: "Take advantage of the possibility to become free and, since you belong to Christ, do not enter into a voluntary dependency on mortals; that would show a lack of independence or a false dependency on the secular lords, which does not correspond to your freedom in Christ." This is strong support for our interpretation of 21b.

As a second possibility, verse 23 can also be a justification for 21a: "Even if you must remain a slave: do not forget your freedom in Christ, but rather, in spite of external unfreedom, avoid the typical slavish faults of fear of other people and lip service."[115] This kind of behavior comes from the fact that the slave, at root, is not reconciled with his or her fate and consequently, by sacrificing dignity seeks to curry favor among other people. "For that reason 'Do not become' slaves before humankind, but rather serve your human lords as slaves who have the awareness of having been set free in Christ." Thus the imagistic language fits here as well, even if the main point now lies more in the spiritual realm and in this sense is meant to be "figurative."

Finally, verse 23, which indeed constitutes the conclusion of this complex of examples (21-23), may also be applied in a figura-

---

115. This is thus the counterpart to the rejected $\pi\varrho o\sigma\omega\pi o\lambda\eta\mu\psi\iota\alpha$ = "partiality," in Col 3:25. God also does not accept "flattery" by a slave who does evil—and obviously, as this word is used in Eph 6:9, to be bribed or manipulated by a "master" who commits injustice (Lev 19:15). Cf. Ts 426: The tendency of such household rules goes in the direction of raising the self-consciousness of a slave!

tive sense to free persons. Admittedly this is less contained in the meaning of the words than in the matter intended. Free persons are in danger in another way of becoming "slaves to humankind," in that they want to "please people" (Gal 1:10; 4; 9; 17). As a consequence, such an application is indeed legitimate, although not directly expressed. Imagistic language indeed always refers beyond itself to a more complex reality.

4. Remaining with the Call: 1 Corinthians 7:24

UT	PT
Brothers and sisters, each one should remain before God *in the condition in which* God's call *found* him or her.	24 *In that which* (in which) he or she was called, brothers and sisters, each one should remain with God (linger therein with God, sojourn in God's presence, orient oneself toward God).

In the concluding specification of the "key sentence" the topic is again *kaleisthai en:* "to be called in," and *menein en:* "to remain." With the first, as in 7:20, it is not the circumstances that are intended, "in which" we were called by God, but rather the quality and the atmosphere of the call, "with" which we were called. And likewise the "remaining": *Keep yourself* (in the call with which you were called) *with God* (the position of emphasis). The addition of "with God" makes unambiguously clear that also in 7:20 "remain" has reference to the *divine* call, and not to a human condition. This "holding fast" in a moral sense, and not a physical "abiding in one's condition" (UT), is the semantic key to the entire passage, which now is summarized. Thereby call *(klēsis)* clearly means the *spiritual* originality of the individual. In the first example personal reminiscences of the apostle could have played a part. The one who had been a fanatic for the Law had to learn in the encounter with Christ that all of one's fulfillment of the Law was "human work," and now learned to distinguish between "human pronouncements" and "following the commands of God." In the same way now for those for whom circumcision (here a catchword for a certain attitude) was so important, the "call" becomes a passage to *God's authentic command,* which "draws one into trust." On the other side, a pagan who is chained to many gods and demons experiences the call as a liberation from the fear of demons and as a new union with God, who has led the pagan forth from these cultic chains.

There is something ultimately correct in the thought "according to the situation," but it cannot be extended: "*therein* (namely, in this situation) one should remain," rather: "according to the situation the *call* met one differently, and *therein,* in this call, he or she should remain." It is not the case that the situation changes the call, but the call changes the situation; however, *God modifies* God's call in view of the different situations of humans,[116] and indeed always in such a way that they are led out *of their specific constraint,* thus directly changing their condition. From the human side the call cannot be simply derived from their previous situation, and it is more than just a "change of scene" from what went before. One should only think of the prophets, or of Paul himself; their call went far beyond simply being a corrective to the earlier paths of their lives. In any case the call is never something merely conservational, but rather always something that changes, to the extent that it "redeems." However, precisely because it decisively *changes persons in relation* to their current situation, it thereby bestows upon the same things a new positional value, either in the sense that they "count for nothing" (v. 19), that they "cannot hinder" the call (v. 21a), or that the person should seize them because they can "help him or her to live in accordance with the call—that is, in freedom" (v. 21b) and now become the place of their "service" (v. 22b).[117]

It is nowhere a matter of pure interiority, but rather of a shaping of the entire life space from the center outwards. On the other hand it is not directly a matter of one's "condition," of abiding or changing as such, but rather again that the call may come to

---

116. Obviously the authors continually try to emphasize this aspect of the matter; cf. Merklein 245f.; however, they cannot plausibly draw it from the text itself. This becomes blatantly obvious in Neuhäusler, 59.

117. Objectively this again corresponds to a text of the *Exercises* (cf. above, note 67), Ignatius of Loyola, *Spiritual Exercises,* no. 23: "The person is created for the praise of the Lord our God, . . . other things are to help him achieve this goal. It follows that the person should make use of these to the extent that they help him towards this goal, and should free himself from them to the extent that they hinder him from attaining it."

expression. For that reason *each one* must remain by *his or her own center* (vv. 17 and 24)![118] It is thus not as Neuhäusler views it:[119] "The call and its content coincide if a grown Gentile or Jew, a married person or celibate, takes up the faith. Thus the moment of becoming a believer is determinative for the style of charism that one will possess." In that case a single person who became Christian could not marry—not to mention the case of children or young people. It is rather the case that Paul intends to bring the Corinthians no longer to view abstinence as in itself bringing salvation and to absolutize it. The community had no doctrines, but simply trends, with consequences of which they may not be fully aware. At first there are always submerged, vital interests present, which only later elaborate a theory, not the other way around. For one turns to theory if one discovers one that one likes. In any case, in the community there was no "ascetic faction."

Perhaps the intensity of the tendency toward abstinence is also a kind of response by the newly converted to an insecure sexual environment or also to their own past lives; perhaps it has its roots in a lack of religious self-reliance or in the temptation to try to "secure" the new life through abstinence or to guarantee it for oneself. Paul places his emphasis on an attempt to relativize the importance of abstinence and to defend marriage. And yet at the center of the inquiry he perceives that in the community a new relation, or call to Christ, has been awakened. It is a gift *(charisma)* of God and is worth protecting against alienation because it can only be understood and lived in a very individual and personal relation to God. This emerges more clearly in the third part of 1 Corinthians 7.

---

118. This may be easily extended to other situations: each person's encounter with Christ will differ as a function of its point of departure: the sick differently from the healthy, the poor differently from the wealthy, those confident by nature differently from a person with a low self-estimate, etc. Similarly the call—colored by the point of departure—retains its individuality as God's *answer* to a person's situation, so that the call does not absolutize the situation to which the call comes, but rather takes a position with regard to it. Only to that extent does the "situation" enter into the reality of the calling, but it is not itself the κλῆσις.

119. Neuhäusler, "Ruf Gottes," 59.

IV. On Celibacy for an Engaged Couple:
1 Corinthians 7:25-40

The third part of 1 Corinthians 7 brings an answer to the question of young people who are or were engaged and seek the path of abstinence. If in the first part the concern was more for the protection of marriage against a religious rigorism, now the tendency is to *encourage* the petitioners to celibacy, to point out the particular difficulties of marriage, as well as to offer help for them.[141] Correspondingly, Paul here is addressing younger people, while at 7:6-9 his audience was somewhat older ("singles").

The extent of the problems with this third part is apparent. The very title in the UT (see below) is a surprise. Paul does not speak of "marriage and virginity" for the first time; this was already the topic of the first part. However, if he is speaking about "virgins," why does he return in verses 27 and 29b again to married people, and in verses 39f. to widows? Is he jumping around in his thinking? And does the motive for celibacy really consist, as it is usually taken to be, in the "shortness of the time"? Then how are the reasons of "affliction" and "the affairs of the Lord" bound up with that? Finally, in verse 32b the topic of "anxiety" shifts from objective distress to subjective wrong attitudes. The whole thing culminates in the reproach that a married person "is preoccupied with this world," is thus "divided" between Christ and his or her partner, and as a consequence remains always a second-class Christian. If a young man who is trying to live celibately "cannot master himself," then he should marry—although it would be better to be celibate! This is the unadorned result of the traditional interpretation.[142]

1. A Much Disputed Question:
1 Corinthians 7:25-27

UT	**PT**
Marriage and virginity: 7:25-38	On *"Virgins":* 7:25-40
As for what concerns the ques- 25	Concerning *"the virgins"* (fiancées)

---

141. Moiser regards these two basic tendencies similarly, 113.
142. Cf. again the letter with the questions of the community, see above, A II 2. Moiser brings together in a narrow space even more difficulties.

UT		PT
tion about *celibacy,* I have received no command from the Lord,	a	I do not possess any **command** from the Lord,
I give you *only a piece of advice,* as one whom the Lord made worthy of trust by his mercy.	b	however, I offer an opinion (as a remark), since I received mercy from the Lord, so as to be worthy of trust (to be given a position of trust).
I think *it is good because of the impending* crisis, *indeed it is good for a person to be this way.*	26	I believe now the following *is, in light of the present* (current) crisis, *correct, because* it is good for a *man* (it becomes him) *to the extent it is that way* (it is with himself and his fiancée as you write): (!)

A STRIKINGLY BROAD INTRODUCTION: 1 CORINTHIANS 7:25-26

Even more clearly than in 7:12 Paul now emphasizes that he has no "command" from the Lord. If this were a matter of the general question about celibacy, then there would at least be one "word" of the Lord (Matt 19:12). Did the apostle not know about this? This is scarcely likely, and the same is true of Jesus' urging, "to leave wife and family" or "to hate them" (Luke 18:29; 14:26). Then why, in taking up this question, does he invoke only his own authority and, in contrast to 7:12f., not even give "advice," but rather refer indirectly and very cautiously to his "own opinion"?[143]

It is a matter of the special question about engaged young men who now, after their betrothal, feel a wish to remain celibate. Thus we find here again a clear connection with the topic of "abstinence." As we see from 7:37, *parthenos* here means "fiancée": or our colloquial "his girl." It is not intended to refer to all maidens of marriageable age, as Schlatter believes, but rather only to certain ones "about whom" Paul has been asked—the same ones who will be discussed until 7:40.

---

143. I have explained in EuE 167 why "advice" (UT) is not to the point. Besides that, the word "opinion" recurs again in 7:40 and thereby forms an *inclusio* for this part. For what this means for discussion of "state of the counsels," see below, D V 5 and D VI 5.

The question appears sensitive and hotly debated in the community, for Paul refers here and in verse 40 to his spiritual authority.[144] Against whom does he bring this into play? Evidently against those who will have difficulties accepting what he is now going to say, for which, however, some young men have apparently expressed a wish. Paul thus takes up the concern of young Christians with a specific call—against those who are more skeptical and to which group belong especially fathers and leaders. With all caution and knowing the subtleties of the problems at issue, he again emphasizes in verse 26 that he is giving his "opinion," that what follows is directed only for the petitioners. The extremely complicated grammatical construction suggests that he is formulating his thoughts very carefully, so as to leave no room for misinterpretation. Further, the long introduction shows that he only slowly dares to move into his presentation.

The end of verse 26 brings the decisive reservation: "to the extent that it is that way with the petitioners"—that is, that the young man after his betrothal feels the desire for a life of abstinence and that the fiancée evidently feels a similar desire. Then similarly, as in 7:1, "it is good for a man"[145] addresses his honor as a man; the petitioner is considering whether the way of abstinence "is honorable to him." The impression arises from this and from verse 28b that the desire for abstinence is also voiced by the fiancée. If she requests it of him, then it is "honorable for him" to accede to the wish; indeed, she has much less possibility than a man to remain "alone" in her social circumstance. On the other hand, the translation "it is favorable for him" can easily have an egoistical coloring and would not correspond to the principle of mutual agreement which we find throughout the entire chapter. Also, the parallel responses to the questions in 7:28-34 and 36-40 let us conclude to the similar interests of the fiancée, even though because

144. This is therefore an *"inclusio"* in both form and content; see the previous note; thus it forms a framework around the third part.

145. Not: for "a person" (UT); here, as in 7:1, ἄνθρωπος means specifically "man" in contrast to woman, as a sexual partner: EuE 40-42, 170. Besides that the thought builds a parallel between the beginning of the first and third parts (7:1 and 7:25) with a different nuance in each case of καλόν; see above, note 69.

of the legal situation many verses are formulated in terms of the male.

It would be strange if *only* men experienced such a desire. They have posed a question "concerning their betrothed," and that means at least that they also are asking from the perspective of their engaged partners something as to how they should conduct themselves, if *the latter* would like to remain celibate. The entire rest of the chapter shows that Paul gives the women a share in this decision and does not talk past them. If the desire came exclusively from the male side, it would not have been impossible to break off the engagement. The advice "do not try to release yourselves," indeed presumes that the fiancée is at least positive toward celibacy (v. 36). The explosive power of the question thus lies in the fact that in Paul's opinion, in spite of the wishes for abstinence, the engagement should not be broken off. But first: "If the presuppositions are as you have presented them in the question, then the following principle in verse 27 is good and honorable (advantageous) for such a man." This complicated introduction will only be understood if one has clearly grasped the problem. It was obvious to the readers; for us, however, it can only be deduced from the later verses.

THE PRINCIPAL THEME IN 1 CORINTHIANS 7:26a: "THE IMPENDING CRISIS"

The knot becomes tangled as soon as the theme that Paul explains only later is mentioned, but the "crisis" (*anagkē* = constriction, cramped space) must fit together with the "affliction" *(thlipsis)* in verse 28c. When we join this with the "shortness of the time" in verse 29 and the "this world is passing away" of verse 31, the logic appears unmistakable: Paul is thinking about the particular afflictions which will immediately precede the second coming of Christ, which is expected in the near future; and this would be a plausible reason for not marrying. But still, is this the motive of the young people who are petitioning him? The construction does not give the impression that Paul is here picking up one of their catchwords; "crisis" is rather one of Paul's themes. And however we twist and apply *enhestōsan* it does not mean a trouble that "is approaching" or only "threatens," but rather a "distress" which is "present" and "current." The meaning of the words allows no other possibility![146]

Since besides that, according to our explanation 7:29 no longer speaks about the "shortness of the time," and 7:32 says nothing about the "world passing away," we may venture an entirely new line of thought. What is meant is not distress as a warning of an ultimately uncertain time of the second coming and the later (?) "passing away of the world," but rather *the current distress of the Christian in this world!* The theme of "estrangement" is common in Paul and the early Church, and it will be thoroughly spelled out in 7:29-32. Anyone who has found Christ and received his Holy Spirit clearly feels the difference between the new and the old, the inner and the outer person, between "this world" and the "new creation," the affliction ("confinement") in this world and the consolation that comes from God.[147] This contrast is felt more strongly by someone who has experienced the new life more profoundly and at the same time is tied up in a pagan environment that is alien to the gospel, or merely in a secular environment.

We shall consider when we look at 7:29ff. whether in all this an (un-Christian) flight from the world is present. Here it is sufficient that Paul sees in the common Christian tension between the new and the old *eons* a reason not to discourage young engaged couples from their wish for abstinence, but rather—cautiously and making distinctions—to support them in this. Even if he is the first to employ this catchword, it shows his empathy for the petitioners whose situation he here brings to expression—also against the "skeptics." We may confidently believe that *he* knew what was

146. Cf. only Rom 8:38. Thus, for example, Diodorus of Tarsus on Rom 12:6-8 (Staab, 106): Prophecy is primarily the revelation of hidden facts, εἴτε τῶν μελλόντων, εἴτε τῶν παλαιῶν, εἴτε τῶν ἐνεστώτων καὶ λανθανόντων; cf. Ritter, 33. Chrysostom is thinking here not about the final crisis, but of the labors and difficulties of the condition of marriage: *De virgin.* 42, 47, 49; cf. Ritter, 67. Here I would make a distinction: the present "difficulties of the time" (in general, 7:26) take a particularly strong form in marriage (7:29b). Moiser also, 105, 111, speaks of the "present distress."

147. Thus pressure and distress proceed from the "world," are experienced in our worldly existence, and receive the character of a special burden through the fact that one's spiritual home lies elsewhere: Rom 12:2; 1 Cor 1:18-31; 4:9; 7:28-32; 2 Cor 1:3-7; 5:6-8 (Ts 222–226); Gal 4:26; Phil 1:23f.; 3:20; further, see EuE 547, index "Fremdheit," as well as below, C 4.

going on, even if we must have recourse to deductions from the indications given. Finally, we must say a word about the twice-mentioned *kalon* in verse 26. This appears to be another word-play, since the moral judgment in verse 26a (it is right) is justified with a reference to the fact that it is "honorable" (and favorable?).[148]

THE INSTRUCTION FOR THE PETITIONERS: 1 CORINTHIANS 7:27

UT		PT
If you are bound to a woman [wife], do not attempt to be free;	27 a	If you are (through *betrothal*) bound to a woman [wife], do not seek to be set free (make no effort to be released);
if you are without a wife, do not seek one.	b	if you have *freed* yourself from a woman [wife], do not seek a woman [wife].

At 27b: In EuE 173f. and 425 I was careful to understand λέλυσαι as a reflexive medium, also for the reason that in the synoptic divorce sayings it is generally understood in the passive. However, my doubts are now resolved; see below at 396f. as well as Atf VI, I. It is actually the past tense of "seek no solution." In turn, this is a further support for ἀπολελυμένη = those who have freed *themselves*.

The apostle is addressing a very specific audience: engaged people who wish to live celibately. The usual interpretation, that Paul is again speaking in the first place to married people, fits neither with the title "About the Virgins," nor with the fact that for the question of divorce, he has "no instruction from the Lord" (cf. 7:11). The sentence indeed connects directly with the "if this is the way it is." Further, the choice of words suggests our interpretation.[149]

---

148. See again above note 69 and note 145.

149. With the breaking off of an engagement the bridegroom had to go to those legally responsible for the woman (the father or brothers) and "petition" for the dissolution, must "seek" it from them, while a married man could unilaterally issue a letter of divorce. Further, δέδεσαι fits better for engagement—as in Rom 7:2 (Atf V 1); EuE 178.

Paul is presuming that the petitioners are considering the possibility of a "separation." His "opinion" on this is: *"Do not yourself initiate a separation!"* However, verse 27b does not simply mean "if you are free" (would he recommend celibacy to all unmarried people? cf. 7:9), but "if you have freed yourself"—naturally not from a marriage (on this 7:10f.), but from an engagement. However, why should a young man not look for another fiancée? Everything becomes understandable if he is addressing petitioners who would indeed like to live celibately. But why does he then say to them: "Do not seek a woman"? Well, it could be the case that his family is putting pressure upon him. It could also be that he has first separated himself from his fiancée out of a certain rigorism (contrary to Paul's opinion expressed in v. 27a), but now hears that one can continue the betrothal relation in a permanent fashion. So he might think, in spite of his desire for celibacy, of entering (again) into an engagement. While up to now it has only been a matter of a "simple betrothal," something like a "spiritual betrothal" now might be brought under consideration, which Paul would still not advise. In 7:37 we will come back to this question. However, in no sense does Paul here give a general instruction that unmarried people should not marry (cf. 28a)!

The maxim set out in the style of a diatribe on stoic virtues presumes several things: (a) The difference in age at the time of the wedding was often considerable: the man up to thirty, the woman around eighteen years, with the Jews often even younger.[150] (b) The engagement often took place many years before[151] and was contracted by the bridegroom and the father or the brother of a girl who often was not yet fully of age (age of majority was 12 1/2). (c) This was the valid legal contract which could only be fulfilled through marriage. For that reason a betrothal in ancient times carried a stronger legal obligation with it than today and was not as easy to break off. (d) There were no official marriage registers, so betrothal and marriage arrangements were entirely in

150. Cf. EuE 175f. Besides her lack of independence before the law, this situation also contributed to women's difficulty, at least psychologically, in reaching a condition of equality. See below, D I 4.

151. In Judaism the "normal time between engagement and drawing up the marriage contract, and the wedding and setting up a household was one year," Str-B. II, 394; cf. Kruse, 95.

the hands of the families who often exerted strong psychological and social pressure. (e) Since at the time many Christians stood isolated within their (still pagan) extended families, the *ekklēsia/* public assembly of God took on partly the role of a human support system. However, the "law" naturally remained with the families. Not only for the bride, but even for the bridegroom, the actual sphere of free decision-making was therefore more limited than today. For that reason also Paul counsels the young men who ask him not to break off their engagement, but also not to seek a new relationship, *if* they are nurturing a call toward celibacy within themselves.

The motive is thus not that "one should not change anything," as is often said with reference to 7:17, 20, 24, and certainly not a contempt for sexual relations. The picture is completely corrupted by such insinuations, and there remains no room for an authentic spiritual call to celibacy: for the gleam of virginal love of Christ that grows out of an inner relation to him, without for that reason devaluing human love and physical self-giving (Matt 19:11 and 12d). The very fact that Paul credits the engaged couple with having an enduring relation to one another shows that he does not discount human relationships or build a taboo around them. He regards them as carrying in themselves no threat to the personal relationship to Christ.

All this Paul will explain in verses 35-38. First, however, he points out the limits of his maxims, so that no one will falsely interpret his "opinion." First is the case where they cannot maintain his principle and after a period reverse themselves and marry (7:28-34). This is formulated from the perspective of the partner who abandons the principle on his own initiative. Then in 7:35-38 the question is again raised, this time from the perspective of the female who feels too much is demanded of her, until finally in 7:37 Paul reaches the goal of the case of two engaged people who remain celibate "in symphony."

For the design of the entire chapter the result is: Paul has deliberately postponed the question from the engaged people. Their condition puts them in a certain sense between the two groups named in the first part: married and single. Everything that he now says to the engaged presumes the fundamental principles mentioned above, namely:

(1) that he only intends this for those people who feel a call and are convinced that they can maintain the way of celibacy with a certain joy and lightness (for if they burn, they then should marry);

(2) that in all these questions, in analogy with married people, complete agreement with the partner is naturally presumed; that means that the fiancée is prepared to go the same way;

(3) that after looking at all the circumstances each person must discover his or her ultimate orientation from the *call* with which God has called *him or her* (7:17-24). These foundations are scarcely mentioned; however, if they are not observed, the following text will appear bizarre.

2. And If Nevertheless They Get Married?: 1 Corinthians 7:28-34

IS MARRIAGE "NO SIN"?: 1 CORINTHIANS 7:28a-c

UT		PT
However, if you marry, then you do not sin;	28 a	If, however, *as a matter of fact* you marry, *you will not have sinned* (I do not say that you have sinned),
and if a virgin marries, then she *also* does not sin.	b	and *also the* virgin (fiancée), if she marries, *will not have sinned;*
Admittedly such people will not escape *earthly distresses;* (!)	c	however, such people will experience an affliction *through the flesh* (still such people have to take into account an additional burden because of the "world").

Was Paul aware that in 7:26 and 27b (as already in 7:1) he appears to have turned the sentence from Genesis 2:18: "it is not good for a human being to be alone" on its head? For now it is indeed good to be alone! However, on the other hand neither his nor the Corinthians' question went so far as to suggest that the "not being alone" of married people was suddenly a sin (of course not!), but only how a person in Christ grows into a completely new constellation of relationships and a new way of evaluating personal relations. Thus, like everything before, verse 28a is also directed to specific petitioners.[152] Here it is young men who are engaged and in this situation feel a desire for celibacy. They seem to have a twofold question: (1) *For my own part,* how should *I* handle this desire? (2) How should I handle the relationship *with my fiancée?* Should I break off with her?[153] Should I attempt to inspire her to my way of thinking? Would we be able to sustain this together? What do the families say? What does the community say?

Paul's answer is directed to the level of conscience: "If you, who at first have the desire and intention to remain celibate, nevertheless marry later, the question could arise in you whether you have offended against the 'call' of God you believed you previously received?" Paul distinguishes: If you nevertheless marry, "then I do not say that you have made a mistake."[154] Here people are honestly seeking to discover what in the concrete circumstance God's will may be for them; and to that belongs, next to the "desire" and after a time of reflection, also the realization that power and joy in it remain and the circumstances provide a good opportunity for such a step (7:35-38). If in 7:17-24 Paul has so clearly emphasized the individual's judgment of conscience, he will not here put it down again, but rather only underlines his opinion that a change need not necessarily constitute an infidelity. He thereby has regard for the consciences of those who have changed their intention (not: vow), and means to protect them from qualms of conscience. Again he looks at the question from the perspective of both partners (v. 28b), although it has been raised by the men. (Is this an indirect suggestion that women did not dare to ask questions publicly?) Naturally "the" virgin here refers to the fiancée in the pair being talked about (the anaphorical article), and not generally: "If *a* virgin marries, then she also does not sin" (UT). The Corinthians have neither raised such a general question, nor

152. On their situation see the letter with the questions of the community, above, A II 2.

153. The advice: "Do not seek to free yourself" presumes that the bride has similar thoughts, but obviously is still searching; cf. above, close to note 145.

154. A complicated variation of a conditional sentence: a future condition followed by a future aorist without an implicit subjective expectation; see EuE 187. Thus not: "in neither way do you sin"—for example, because celibacy is only a "counsel" anyway; such a divine invitation can carry an obligation (7:17); see below, D V 5.

by his answer does Paul have such a fundamental vindication of marriage in mind. Naturally it is no sin for a girl to marry.

The qualification in 7:28c goes in another direction. "Burdens of the flesh"[155] does not mean that the marriage is somehow "carnal" (sinful) (for a Christian it grows out of a *charism*): "flesh" also does not mean sexual temptations, but rather relates to the "confinement" in verse 26: The confinement and estrangement experienced by all Christians in common in this world will be *more strongly* experienced by married people, for they (must) insert themselves more forcefully in the objective relations of the still unredeemed "world." Those people who had considered celibacy before will feel this contrast between spirit and flesh—a characteristic Pauline theme—especially clearly. For such people the definitive entrance into a marriage signifies, in contrast to what they had previously sought, an additional burden "through the world." However Paul intends by this reference not to deter them from marrying—he has just assured them that such a step could be in accordance with God's will—he means only to make them conscious of the specific burdens this brings with it, so that they will not later be surprised. They should be able to take this step in authentic freedom with a full knowledge of its implications.[156] However, so that they may not be depressed by this argument and for that reason slide again into a certain unfreedom, Paul immediately shows them how they can *still,* in spite of these extra afflictions through the flesh, remain in the freedom of God's children.

EXPECTATION OF THE "IMMINENT COMING OF THE LORD" AND "LIVING AS IF"?: 1 CORINTHIANS 7:28c-32a

UT	PT
. . . however, I would *like to spare you (these afflictions).*	28 *Well,* I am *being careful of* you d (I treat *you* with great respect and care);

155. Not "for" the flesh, EuE 191–196. Naturally the outer person (see below, close to note 466) is the place where the pain will be experienced, but here we have a *dativus instrumentalis;* it signifies the realm through which the person is attacked. Thus "flesh" is synonymous with "world" in v. 31b.

156. Paul clarifies what he means specifically by affliction in 7:29-31. We will come back to that at the end of the next passage.

<table>
<tr><td colspan="3" align="center">**UT**</td><td colspan="2" align="center">**PT**</td></tr>
</table>

UT		PT
For I am saying to you,	29	*in this sense then I say,* (thus also
brothers and sisters:	a	mean) brothers and sisters:
the time is short.	b	*the moment is at hand,* (the
		striker is armed) (!)
For that reason, *whoever has* a	c	as a consequence, *if they live*
wife, *should so behave* in the		*with wives (when they have*
future *as if he had none,*		*relations with them), they*
		should in some sense (some-
		how) not live with them,
whoever weeps,	30	*if they* are weeping, *in some way*
as if he were not weeping	a	they should not weep,
whoever rejoices,	b	*if they* are rejoicing, they
as if he were not rejoicing		should in a certain sense *really*
		not rejoice,
whoever buys, as if he were not	c	*if they are in business, they*
a man of means,		*should not,* so to speak, settle
		down,
whoever makes use of the world,	31	*and if they use* the world,
as if he derived no profit from it	a	in a sense *they should not exploit*
for the form of this world *is*	b	it. For *the way* of this world is
passing away.		absorbing (imprisoning); (!)
I *would wish,* however, that	32	but, **I would** rather **see** you
you *could be* without cares.	a	without cares.

The problematic of these paragraphs is familiar. Following the usual interpretation it appears that Paul, by reference to the "worldly distress," is placing those people willing to marry under pressure to reach a decision. That again seemed to fit well with 7:7: "I would wish that all were celibate" (UT). In the same way now he would be pressuring them by saying that indeed *he* would gladly spare them such efforts, and he would justify his subjective wish for them by an objective reference to the shortness of the time—until the second coming. As a consequence it would be easier and better not to marry.

However, the current interpretation of this text has already displayed a logical hiatus in the translation common up until now. For, according to verse 29a, Paul is not recommending celibacy, but rather addresses the following sentences to people who—in spite of everything—are getting married! Thus he would be saying to them: "But even if you choose the more difficult (marriage), it does not help you much. For even then you must 'live as if you were not married' etc."; and in 32a he would finish: "If it were my decision, I would gladly free you from all these cares by having you remain celibate." Here finally would come the recommendation for celibacy—indirectly—that is commonly imputed to 29b. However, if we had so construed the argument, it would have been logical to say: "Look at the married people, how difficult they have it." But Paul does not say that.

However, verses 29b-31 do not refer directly to the difficulties of marriage in order to dissuade possible candidates from venturing in. Rather, these verses are directed at engaged people who, after attempting abstinence now wish to marry, in order to help them to the necessary detachment. In the usual interpretation of 7:28-32, the (strange) "logic" would run as follows: "If you had remained celibate, all these spiritual (ascetic) strivings would not be necessary for you; rather, remain without all these cares," namely *without the efforts of such a detachment.* Admittedly one tends to supply: "without the worldly cares of marriage"; however, that is not what was spoken about before. There are too many breaks in the logic.

The theme of the "shortness of the time" also seems to contradict this line of thought. If the distress is *only* for a short time, that should reduce its weight and more *easily* justify contracting a marriage! Indeed, in Mark 13:20 the shortness constitutes a *help for* married people; however, Paul seems to view the shortness as an intensification or as an exasperating factor *against* contracting a marriage. The two themes of "affliction" and "the shortness of the time" must be fully distinguished from one another, in order to point them in the same direction: a) You will experience affliction, b) besides that (where do we find such a word?) it is no longer worth it simply on the basis of the shortness of time. The fact that in that case the affliction would also be shorter, is not noticed. Is it also no longer "worth it" "to laugh or to weep"? This is a strange logic. In any case in verses 32b-34 celibacy is again characterized by the fact that it spares one from a certain form of "cares about the things of this world" (similar to the way the "affliction" seems smaller according to 7:28), and it is not motivated by the approaching end.

But in 28d-31a Paul responds to the problem that he had raised in 28c: "By marrying you will have to undertake an additional burden; however, I know how to protect you." Thus he now formulates a defense against this burden. If their personal call, in spite of an initial attempt, does not in fact lead to celibacy but to marriage, then like a "father" he will help them to bear up under this. So on the one hand he helps them with the dangers of an unfriendly environment, and at the same time to remain conscious of their true home.

In this regard verse 29b does not speak of any (too short?) *period of time; kairos* rather means here "the critical situation, the disadvantageous occasion, the danger" and echos "distress" and "affliction" from 26, 28c. Thus: "the danger that you may come to feel more clearly your estrangement in this world lies in ambush."[157] For that reason, conduct yourselves "in some sense as if not possessing" *(hōs mē)*. Not: "as if" you were not indeed together with your wife—that would ultimately show contempt for another person and for secular reality—but rather: "if you have communion with her, at the same time *'in some sense' do not have communion,"* that means: "Always remain in the yet deeper communion that you have found with Christ. If you live this way, you will notice that then these two relationships do not disturb, much less exclude one another, but that the relation with Christ supports the marital relationship." The latter thus becomes endurable (is protected, saved) only if the first is alive. Finally, in verse 31 *schēma* does not mean "form," but rather "conduct,"[158] and *paragein* does not mean "pass away," but rather "to take (spiritually) captive."[159]

---

157. Καιρός συνεσταλμένος—the (threatening) situation is "ready for action, is in place"; see above, note 147 and below, D V 1. For more details, see EuE 208–212; 431–439; Atf VIII 1 and XII. Perhaps it goes together with the image of girding up one's loins. N. Brox refers with regard to 1 Pet 1:13 (EKK 74) to the "apparent metaphor": "Because one tied at the waist the long or widely-cut gown to go out or for work, this gesture of girdling would serve as a general image for being ready."

158. EuE 231–236; further, Atf VIII 1; one also thinks of the stoic σχέσις.

159. EuE 228–231; A. Vögtle, *Das Neue Testament und die Zukunft des Kosmos* (Düsseldorf, 1970) 91f., interprets this in our sense. In Latin, Horace, *Ode I* 2:25-30; 4:1-46. Further indications: BDR no. 198.3 (end); Theod. M on 1 Cor 12:10 (Staab, 192); ἐπιορκιστῶν σχήματι—in the fashion of the exorcists. Dio Cassius 69, 26.5ff.; Stob IV 7.61: παρασχηματίζεσθαι—to change his behavior; cf. Rom 12:2.

To again make clear the line of thought, we present here a paraphrase of the entire section. One should notice therein the five areas: relations with partners, sorrow, joy, work, and possessions. We will return later to discuss how the life of celibates would be affected in these areas.

> *Paraphrase:* Well, I have compassion for you (for my part I do not leave you in trouble but rather lend a helping hand in your difficult situation, handle you carefully and with respect, shelter and protect you); and in this regard it is my view (from this perspective I interpret what is coming), brothers and sisters: "the occasion is ready to pounce" (the unfavorable situation which afflicts, burdens, and in addition distresses you through the flesh, is coming soon; the danger is waiting in ambush); as a consequence they (who after initial attempts at celibacy have finally decided to marry), insofar as they have sexual communion with their wives, should in a certain sense not have such communion; (just as) if they are weeping, in a certain sense they should not weep; (as also) if they are rejoicing, they should in a certain sense not rejoice; (as also) people who have business in the market should in a certain way not make themselves at home there (not establish themselves there); (finally) as those who use the world for their purposes, they in a certain sense should not exploit it. For the style and manner in which the things and persons of this world work upon you leads you into dependency (the world ensnares and takes possession through the demands and calls which continually emanate from it, and in this way causes affliction and distress); however, it is my wish that you remain without cares ("I would like to do" = it gives me pleasure and joy for you to remain free from this suction, from the excessive afflictions of this entrapment—specifically through the "somehow not").

It now becomes clearer: Paul is not thinking here of some sort of *immediate* afflictions accompanying a soon-expected end to the world,[160] but rather of the *tension-filled relation to the world*

160. On other grounds, Schnackenburg, Hierzenberger, and Schürmann also offer reservations against the conventional thesis of the "expectation of the imminent second coming in the NT"; see EuE 210, note 355; A. Vögtle (see previous note), and idem, *Offenbarungsgeschehen und Wirkungsgeschichte* (Freiburg, 1985) 33; H. Giesen, "Eschatologie II," M. Görg and B. Lang, *Neues Bibellexikon* (Benziger: Cologne, since 1988) with an expanded bibliography.

which the Christian must endure *day after day*. Anyone who has been touched by the Holy Spirit and lives in the spirit of Jesus feels with each step how foreign the "world" is. This begins in one's dealings with the "goods of this world" and the experience of one's own weakness, continues in the lack of understanding in one's own family, among one's friends and coworkers, and in the sociopolitical realm, and can even lead to hostility and serious persecution. Paul knows only too well this "affliction" from his own life; and he understands that it will eventually be visited upon all Christians.

According to Paul, married people are especially hard hit by this. Why? Probably because, with the demands of the family and the allegiance to another person, they have an extra burden to carry, which can from time to time make it more difficult to follow the call of the Spirit (at the very least, they feel all the more strongly the contrast to the unredeemed world), or because under distress and persecution they always carry at the same time an additional burden of human responsibility for their partner and family. The problems are for them in a certain way more acute or "closer to the skin." Thus anyone who, in regard to the new situation of a committed Christian existence would prefer to remain unmarried has it "easier" (for his or her spiritual existence) and can justify such a step. In contrast to Christians of the Middle Ages, for Jews and for the early Christian community the question was more whether a person *was permitted* to attempt celibacy (if it is imposed on someone, that is a different case). That is why Paul says that "because of the current distress" it is morally permissible *for Christians* to remain celibate—specifically, if the person affected feels the call (7:17-24) and can obey it in inner freedom and joy (7:9) as well as without external pressure (7:36).

Admittedly, someone who, after a first consideration and attempt is finally unable to carry through with celibacy should not be bothered by false guilt, for with a call God also gives the power and the joy for it and creates the appropriate external conditions. "Thus, if you do not feel this power, but rather another call, namely that toward marriage (7:7), then follow it with all your heart, so as thereby also 'to please the Lord.' For the call to marriage is also a *charism* and proceeds from the gift of the Spirit. However, so as to give you a little protection against that 'affliction' of which I have just spoken, I mention one thing to you:

Retain the basic motivation on whose account celibacy appeared attractive to you—namely, 'to please the Lord'—also in your marriage. Since in the realm of marriage the world threatens you all the more, and more furiously grabs out after you, protect yourselves by a spiritual distance; do not let the world take possession of you. Rather, even while married, live in a certain fashion as though not; in that way the 'world' will not be able to possess you."

With this we are at the central thoughts of our verses. It would be a misunderstanding of this text to think that Paul is here demanding from married people an especially heroic achievement, a sort of ascetical acrobatics, that, namely, they should not find joy in anything that comes with their marriage, but should "always act as if" it were not there; that indeed, they may not even once in a while weep with their whole heart, but rather must then so comport themselves "as if they were not weeping." This "as if" is a rather clumsy translation in English. It promotes the view that Christians should not take the world seriously, but should rather always regard even their marital union ultimately with a little skepticism. However, Paul is referring to something quite different. He means *to help those who marry, to protect them against that particular "distress."* Thus, he does not mean to *warn* against God's creation or certainly against the marital partner, but rather to offer a defense precisely against those unfriendly powers in the world which are attempting to enslave (spiritual) people. Against this undertow that threatens people and takes away their freedom, against this hostility from the side of an *unredeemed* world, Christians may protect themselves by not allowing it to affect them interiorly, that is, "while having, in a certain sense not having." To that extent they are exercising the same attitude to which celibates give symbolic expression by their external situation.

In practice this means: "Don't let yourself be taken prisoner by any joy that comes to you from this world, but rather measure it against the joy that Christ has and continues to work. Only to the extent that you are supported and stamped with such joy will your 'laughter' be free, while without this center all laughter will constrict you in relation to your deepest freedom and will thereby destroy true joy." Thus Paul does not mean to embitter all earthly joys for us, but rather to liberate them to their true reality. The same is true for sorrow. Paul is not forbidding us to feel sorrow and, if the need arises, to weep and to complain (Rom 12:15; 2 Cor 7:9f.), but rather intends to say: "Do not be so overcome by (worldly!) sorrow that it obscures your view of Christ. Rather, measure all suffering of the body and soul by the cross of Christ, by his redeeming death. Then the standard of our measure is changed, and our worldly suffering is relativized. Besides that, you recognize that Christ is helping you carry your affliction, and thus the burdens are shifted. Thereby sadness has lost its threatening, destructive character. If you are engaged professionally, then do not make yourself at home in it,[161] and if you must preoccupy yourself with some affairs in this world, do not exhaustively appropriate the goods of this world,[162] as if your salvation lay therein, but always retain within yourself a free space (in Christ); then nothing in this world can oppress you, because nothing 'can separate you from the love of Christ' (Rom 8:39). So in your trafficking with the world, learn in some way *while having, not to have.*"

However, what does this mean for the marital union, and why does Paul speak about this relation to the world, which indeed concerns all Christians, in connection with marriage? Not because the sexual relation would necessarily draw married people away from Christ, but rather because in this context Paul is speaking to people who intend to marry, and because he would like to offer them help. Like every other area, marital union is also a place in which for the Christian salvation should take place. The relation to one's partner may also be lived in either a "secular" or "spiritual" way. In its unredeemed shape it has always something of egoism or subtle desire about it, and only matures into a pure love through being connected to the one who is Love

161. With ἀγοράζοντες it is not yet a question of purchase and possession, but rather that a person becomes absorbed in work: "is busy in the market-place" and "settles down there." These images should be retained.

162. Here for the first time one's attitude to possessions is taken up. The sharp "in a sense not use the world" is naturally not intended in an ecological sense; the person becomes a prisoner if he or she so exploits possessions as to extract the full amount from this world. However, the stewardship of nature is a command that can be deduced from this, one that lies in the intention of the creator and is also part of Paul's viewpoint (1 Cor 10:26, 30f.).

itself. The fact that Paul goes on to four further realms next to it does not mean that celibates may no longer cry and laugh, work and own (Paul himself is a "worker-priest"), but only means to emphasize that all these areas work upon married folk in a stronger and more oppressive fashion.[163] Naturally, the priority of the relation with God is not given unconditionally to the celibate, who of course lives in the dimensions of this world. He or she also has to make strenuous efforts to maintain this priority; it is only that Paul believes that in these areas such a person's "inner person" has it "somewhat easier." And although here he is also thinking directly of married folk who have first intended to live celibate lives, the underlying principle naturally also applies in the appropriate degree to all married people and similarly to all celibates.

Verse 31b provides a summary reason for the preceding verses and shows what is at stake: From the "way of this world" comes a riptide; if you naively allow yourself to be sucked into this set of relations, you are caught more quickly than you suspect. In the language of the gospels, this would be the warning to be awake and sober (cf. Rom 13:11-14; 1 Thess 5:1-11; Eph 5:14-17). Anyone who sees here (as happens not uncommonly) a contempt for the world[164] has not noticed that this point concerns the fundamental soteriological issues of Pauline theology and of the entire New Testament, not the relationship with God's good "creation." A person without Christ lives under the slavery of sin and is not able to redeem himself or herself. And this curse lies not only upon the person, but also upon the entire "world."[165] That is why Paul warns about the clutches of the unredeemed "world" (both in us and around us), about the suction that inhabits human relationships, objects, and social situations, and from which we

163. Perhaps the reader is wondering where this comparative lies in the text. Paul speaks unequivocally of "distress" in an absolute way, i.e., without any further explication; however, no one will seriously consider that he means to say that the celibate lifestyle is "completely" free from "distress" or "care"; thus what we have here is an intensification.

164. On this see below, close to note 460 (soteriological dualism); D I 2; D V 1.

165. With this it is important to keep in mind that κόσμος is frequently used especially for the "human world," sinful humanity; see only 1 Cor 7:33f.; however, in this context topics such as ownership and work are also included.

can only be rescued "in Christ"—specifically, by "in a certain manner not having."

At the conclusion there is not a wish contrary to fact (UT)—as in 7:7, here the indicative is used—but rather Paul stresses that he "rejoices," that he "is happy to see it," if the petitioners are "without cares." However, this does not mean here that they would do better not to marry, but rather that such burdens will not have the effect of "cares" if in their marriage they maintain this ultimate critical distance to the world and thereby are at home with the Lord. For in this way these married people will achieve an inner freedom and lightness that grows out of the relationship with Christ. With the word "care," from the Greek root *-mer,* there begins here a daring wordplay whose extravagances have unfortunately not been noticed, and which on that account has led to the worst possible misunderstandings.

DIVIDED BETWEEN ONE'S SPOUSE AND CHRIST?: 1 CORINTHIANS 7:32b-34

UT		PT
An unmarried man *occupies himself with the Lord's things; he desires to* please the Lord.	32 b	An unmarried man *occupies himself with the Lord's wishes* (is busy about the Lord's interests), (namely), with how he might please the Lord;
A married man *occupies himself with the things* of the world; *he desires* to please his wife.	33	*however, to the extent that (inasmuch as) he is married, he is* occupied with the world's *interests* (namely here), how to please his **wife** (!)
Thus he is divided.	34 a	—and is torn (divided between the many things of the world).
However, an unmarried woman and a virgin *occupy themselves with* the Lord's *things,*	b	*And* an unmarried woman as well as a virgin (also a finacée who remains celibate) *occupies herself with the* Lord's *wishes,* (that means)
to be holy in body and spirit	c	namely, to be holy in body and spirit;
A married woman is occupied with the world's *things; she*	d	*however, to the extent that (inasmuch as) she has* married,

UT	PT
desires to please her husband.	she is occupied with the world's *interests,* (namely) *how she* might please her husband (and is preoccupied).

According to our interpretation there has so far been no talk about the "time until the second coming." At least from this point on, also according to general agreement, the talk is only about the *present* immanent tension in being a Christian, the distinctive features of marriage and celibacy for the Lord.[166] Still, at this point protest escalates against the apostle, for he seems to suggest that an undivided love for Christ is impossible for married people! For one naturally interprets verse 34a: "He is divided between Christ and his wife." With that Paul consigns the married person to a condition where the unavoidable cares which they take on with marriage automatically become a "preoccupation" with the world, something which does not please God, or at least not as much (as the actions of the unmarried); he or she seeks now "to please human beings"[167] instead of God.

The context is again crucial. Paul has helped the engaged who after an initial attempt at a celibate life have gone on to marry to preserve the spiritual foundation in their marriage. He now once again makes clear to them the presuppositions on which this "in a certain manner not having" rests; he provides what we may call a clarification of ideas. Thus the two categories "the unmarried" and "if he has married" are here used in an abstract sense (for example "unmarried as such"): "If we carefully ex-

166. Merklein attempts (250f.) to tone down the outrageousness of the statement by saying that this statement may only be understood against the background of the expectation of the imminent second coming. However, even if the distress were especially great and the time especially short, the statement would still maintain that a married person is "divided" in consequence of his or her *status,* and not because of the shortness of time!

167. Gal 1:10f. In *De virgin.* 27 Chrysostom remarks, cf. Ritter 67, that according to Paul's words marriage is rather a disgrace. Although he continually attempts to retrieve its honor, he does not do justice to these texts. He is too deeply caught up in Greek dualism, in addition to a late antique disdain for the body.

amine each state, they show the following characteristics," or "*inasmuch as*[168] someone is living celibate for the Lord's sake, *to that extent* he or she is oriented toward the Lord's interests." That is the motive for this style of life; otherwise it would not be "celibacy for the Lord." Thus the status description stands here for the respective nature of the two states—which naturally unite in themselves simultaneously a relation both to God and to the world.

Clearly there are many celibates who live in this condition for other reasons, and also some who, after having undertaken to live celibately "for the Lord," may lose this motivation. But in that case they would have become untrue to what is specific or distinctive about this style of life. *As a "celibate"* (as Paul is here using the term) on the contrary one is *per definitionem* directed toward the Lord's wishes. On the other hand, a person who, after such a beginning has gone on to marry, enters then a different field of relations. *As a married person* it is his or her duty (and indeed, one given by God, naturally!) to occupy themselves with worldly interests (which are the unavoidable context of their existence) and to focus upon their spouse, to cultivate their togetherness as a personal relationship: "to please one another." This is what is distinctive about their new condition. This is not given to them as a reproach, but only to make them once more aware that they are thereby engaged in a new way in this world. There is also present here no contempt for God's creation; Paul is merely reminding us that this creation is currently a world that stands under sin and on which as a consequence God's curse still lies, so that it is difficult "to earn one's bread" (Gen 3:17ff.). It is equally clear that celibates also must make their way in this "world." So what Paul intends to say is the following: "This is the condition of our existence; but if you marry, it is yours *in stronger proportion and in a new way.*" In the interests of pre-

---

168. On the specifying function of the article, especially with participials, see Ts 401–409. For 1 Cor 11:7 we refer to Closen, who gives numerous examples of such conceptually contrasted positions, which still do not exclude the subjects concerned from the other point of view; see Atf II 4 (Gen 6:2: sons of God = men; daughters of humanity = women). In this case "real" engagement with the world and with God applies to both, although one is presented as an example in one case, and the other in the other.

cision we Westerners would have added a "more"[169] and in such a case would prefer to work with abstract concepts, something like "the distinctive characteristic of married life is a stronger engagement with the demands of secular reality"; however, the Semite prefers to express such things in a concrete fashion, through images intended to typify the condition as such.[170]

The reproving undertone which one detects here is also encouraged by the fact that *merimnān* is usually translated by "to be anxious." Although it is to the celibates' honor that they "be anxious" for the Lord, the concern and effort of married people are directed "to the world" and "to one's wife." By this, not only is the object of care presented as something of comparatively less value, but at the same time one is warned against letting one's heart agonize over such objects: "A Christian should in fact have no 'cares' (Phil 4:6), but the married person still does. It may be that they cannot avoid it; nevertheless, it represents a defeat." However, the Greek word here (in the accusative) contains no negative connotations; "to busy oneself with," not "to be anxious or fret over."[171] Both "occupy themselves"—according to Paul—*to the extent that* their condition of life has a distinctive character (and only to that extent), with different types of objects: the celibate "with the Lord," the married person "with the world and the spouse." This hardly precludes that celibates, *to the extent that* they are people in this world, must also have to occupy themselves with this world, and that the married, *to the extent that* they are Christians, naturally also seek to please the Lord; only that what is characteristic of each, that in which they are distinguished, lies in the different objects of their activity. Why does Paul so emphasize this? Because he tries to deduce what is characteristic of the activity from what is characteristic of the various

169. Cf. above, note 163.

170. See again above, note 168.

171. Delling, "Eheleben," 696, cites a papyrus from the third century B.C. (BGU 1463, 4f.): "The purpose of marriage is described as a τά τινος φρονεῖν καὶ νοεῖν." Thus also μεριμνᾶν: "think," not "worry." Schelkle, 86, correctly translates 1 Cor 7:32 with Clement of Alexandria (*Strom.* 3:88, 2/PG 8:1189A): "Is it not possible also for a married person, together with the partner, to have the Lord's affairs 'in mind' "? Cf. again above, close to note 166f.

objects of that activity. One could almost translate it this way: while the celibate person *may (is permitted to)* occupy himself or herself with the Lord, the married person *must (is compelled to)* occupy himself or herself with the world and the spouse. The first (activity) is, in itself, lovely and "simple," fulfilling and satisfying; the second, *in itself,* is multiple and fatiguing, a hardship and a continual irritation. It will become immediately clearer in verse 7:35 that, in practice, Paul believes that both groups in fact occupy themselves with both kinds of object. However, here he intends to compare the two activities in themselves; he does so by contrasting a representative of each.

We are now coming finally to the highpoint of the wordplay. For the root of the word "divided," which follows here, sounds the same as the beginning of the root for "to busy oneself" *(me-mer-istai, mer-im-nan).* Paul of course realizes the different meanings of the words but he here executes an elegant wordplay, which we may imitate as follows: "The married man *occupies* himself with the world and his wife, and becomes *pre-occupied;* he *exerts* himself on their account, and becomes *exhausted;* he *tears* at the things of this world, and is *torn apart* by them." Since the things of this world are so various, he is "pulled this way and that" between them, is splintered and heavily burdened. At this point "affliction" and "distress" from 7:26, 28c reappear. However, the distress arises not from being split between Christ and one's partner, but rather that one is divided *by the multifarious things of this world.* However, those who are celibate for the sake of the Lord and the "virgin" (fiancée) occupy themselves *as such* with the Lord's interests and thereby experience a peace that is not of this world. They experience "simplicity" and completeness in busying themselves with the "one thing necessary" and in their dedication to the "One." And that means "to be holy in body and spirit," with one's entire being, to be in all one's dimensions[172] entirely God's property (= to be holy to God).

172. Here, similarly to 1 Thess 5:23, anthropological categories are set next to one another so that "spirit" does not mean redeemed existence, but rather: the "Holy" Spirit should encompass a person's "body and soul." Thus, this should not be understood in the sense of Greek dualism, but in that of Semitic integralism; see below, C 2 and 4.

Thus verses 33 and 34 only wish to emphasize that the one who is occupied with "this world" is "divided" and "torn apart" among the diverse claims and objects. For Paul that is no obstacle to the further claim that she or he of course belongs "entirely" to Christ! It is only that the Christian must be aware of this double fact if he or she nevertheless decides to marry; for if this person is overcome by the danger—whether it be due to individual egoism or the inability to escape the egoism of the partner—this can bring much "distress" with it. Paul would like to preserve his young readers from this by giving them this advice: In this situation act as "in some way not having," do not allow yourself to be totally determined by the relationship to your partner, but rather measure everything according to this relationship which was alive in you when you inquired about a life of celibacy. To the extent that even while married you seek in the first place "to please Christ," you are also living in your marriage "in a certain way as if not married," you are protected against such an enslaving power in yourself and in your partner and discover therein the ability to love your partner "in the Lord" (7:7 and 40). By preserving the Lord a place at the center of your existence even after your marriage, you yourself are preserved from any such self-glorification or adulation of your partner and thereby remain free for a full human married love.

"While having, in a certain measure not having" thus becomes the principal image for Christian marriage. And so that a Christian may thereby better understand this attitude that involves a spiritual attitude to all creation, Paul illustrates it for them by considering the external situation of the celibate: just as this person *in fact* has no partner, so every married person "in a certain sense" should have no partner, so that both—married and celibate—may stand in the same basic attitude before God: to belong primarily and in undivided fashion to the Lord.[173] It is thus clear that—according to this text—the married Christian indeed occupies himself or herself both with the spouse *and with God.*

173. Is then the condition of "being holy," that was promised to all the people of the covenant (Deut 26:18f.), and now holds in a stronger fashion for all baptized, inaccessible to married people (7:34c)? Cf. below, close to notes 268 and 274; Atf IV 6 (end).

In the same way Paul realizes that even those who live celibately also occupy themselves with the things of this world and thus are in no way free from false attachments to the world; they are also "oppressed" and must be on the lookout. The examples in verses 30f. make it clear that these concern everybody: the celibate also laughs and cries, is on the job in the marketplace and profits from the world. And occasionally he or she also experiences beyond that the natural human longing for a partner. Still, nothing from that will damage his or her life in the Spirit if he or she keeps in mind that his or her true life and true riches lie elsewhere (2 Cor 6:9f.). By concentrating on the Lord and his love, he or she achieves automatically a freedom and lightness in relations with people and things to which, if he or she were to lose his grip on Christ, he or she would become shackled. This becomes symbolically visible in freedom from a marital partner—something the married person lives "though having, in a certain measure not having."

Thus the deepest core of the statements in this section is not that Paul is digging a deep trench between the married and un-married, but rather that he is stressing a common basic attitude in them both, since the celibates in their external actions and the married by *in a certain way* "not having" are both primarily bound to the Lord in the Holy Spirit. Paul presumes that *those he is addressing* understand this, since they have first expressed a desire to live as celibates. He wishes to help these people to incorporate the shape of their original longing and love for Christ (for "him alone") even into their marriage. At the same time this also expresses indirectly that every Christian who marries or in-tends to marry must understand in their heart what "celibacy for the Lord" means, because thereby a fundamental attitude com-mon to all Christians is expressed: to belong primarily and in an undivided fashion to the Lord, whether it be by simply "not having," or by "in a certain sense not having."

MARRIAGE AND CELIBACY AS SPIRITUAL REALITIES

What at first appeared the ultimate hostility to marriage now proves to be a text of great spiritual depth. We would like to go into it a bit deeper. Starting from the situation of the petitioners Paul here comes indirectly to speak about a principle of the spiri-

tual life, a basic tension in which every Christian lives: the inter-
penetration of the divine and the secular. This problematic of the
basic Christian attitude is by nature difficult to express in words.
In any case "in a certain fashion not having" *(hōs mē)* does not
constitute a psychologizing, an "ethicizing," or a retreat into pure
interiority; rather, what is at issue is an integral orientation of
the Christian who has her or his root and center in God and only
with some difficulty is able to describe her or his relation to the
concrete details of this world. We here come upon a basic theme
in Pauline theology that is treated in his letters in many variations: the co-existence of two worlds or the existence of the new
eon within the old. In 2 Corinthians 5 we found a similar remarkable contrast: body/visible shape in contrast to the Lord,[174] an
equally dissimilar pair as here world/wife/husband and Lord,
or in 1 Corinthians 6:13 body and Lord. The "Lord" here is
not a spiritualistic dimension of human existence, but rather is
the actually present, concealed, but vital reality of Jesus' resurrection which makes Christians into Christians.[175]

The basic thrust of our section was: a man who relates to his
wife as "in a certain way not having" discovers thereby the Lord
(kyrios) in her. He thereby achieves "celibacy" in his marriage
and also avoids the divided condition of a purely secular marriage relationship, because he lives out of his charism (7:7). It is
only that, in comparison with his previous life of celibacy, he now
has a portion that is more difficult[176] for the inner man, that of

174. Ts 222–232. I translate 2 Cor 5:6-9: "Thus we are continually full
of courage; we know that we are still estranged from the Lord, to the extent
that we have our home in the body—for by our faith, our (Christian) life
is determined, not by the visible form (of this world)—and we are therefore
confident and have decided to emigrate from the body and to make our home
with the Lord. For that reason we seek—whether at home or abroad—to
find our honor in doing what is pleasing to him."

175. Cf. Ts 49–60; 89–96. Further, Phil 1:20f., Ts 311 and 316; 1 Cor 6:14;
see below, close to notes 202, 214 and 219. For more details, below, C 3
and C 4 (2).

176. It would be an unacceptable simplification to extend this to all married people or celibates, since it depends in each case on a person's vocation.
Paul is thinking here of two stages that follow one another in particular individuals, specifically those who posed the questions, and similarly in 7:38b;
see below, A IV 3.

living in greater tension, but he adopts therein the same basic Christian attitude. On the other hand Paul is naturally fully aware that the celibate person also possesses the principle of "flesh" within himself or herself and for that reason is not released from the grip of this world. It would be misleading to attribute to him the position that through celibacy as such one is freed from the world and its cares. The text thus presumes that a Christian in either lifestyle has both principles in herself or himself and moves within both spheres: Spirit/Lord and flesh/world. However, since it is Paul's intention to aid people, who "nevertheless marry," with what is specific in their new situation, he characterizes what is typical in the spiritual life by invoking the living conditions of those who are celibate (for the Lord), described from the outside, and what is typical of "life in this world" in the living conditions of the married, again described from the outside, without taking into consideration whether they are Christian.

An explication of the text should also uncover its unexpressed background. Thus, while *directly* this section is addressed to married people (although it is popularly regarded as the *Magna Carta* for religious [celibate] life), *indirectly* something is also said about the meaning of Christian celibate existence—but *only* indirectly. The task for those who are "celibate for the Lord" consists in giving visible expression to what in fact constitutes the essence of *every* Christian—a statement that has commonly (and correctly) been made, but now through our analysis has been given a more secure exegetical foundation. It thus becomes clear: not only are celibates a symbolic proclamation of a *future* condition (Mark 12:25 *par.*), but primarily a sign for what constitutes the *present* existence of Christians (to please the Lord). In turn, married people are also a sign for that kind of existence that is "in the world, yet not of the world" (John 16:33; 17:11), or in Paul's language: for the fact that, although being "in an alien land"[177] we nevertheless are truly at home (Phil 3:20). Through such symbolism married folk protect people living a celibate life from esoteric beliefs, an excessive spiritualism, and arrogance, and especially from misperceiving their life style as a "state of per-

---

177. 2 Cor 5:6-9, see Ts 222–244 and EuE 574, "Fremdheit" in the index.

fection,"[178] as if the striving for perfection was only proper to this lifestyle *in contrast to the married state*. If the striving for perfection is said to characterize the one state, this must be understood "positively, but not exclusively," that is, without excluding others, i.e., married people. Indeed, we also saw that Paul appreciates marriage as an image for our relation with Christ, that is, "symbolically."[179] Thus the two states are referred to one another, for only together do they make up "Christ" (1 Cor 12:12).

In discussing the "activity" of the celibates Paul is thinking neither of monks with their heads bowed in contemplation, nor of the full-time pastoral coworkers in community service (they are engaged people!), but rather he clearly has in mind people who are continuing in the middle of their familial and professional environments and there carry out their usual work. "To occupy oneself with the Lord's interests" thus does not mean something like "pious exercises and contemplative meditations," but rather concerns the *way* in which tasks affect a human being and how he or she carries them out, whether in the married state or in celibacy (Rom 14:6-8; 1 Cor 10:26). Finally what matters is the object of our love. It is for that reason that indeed even the married Christian can live "as in a certain fashion not having." This matter is relevant in the context not on account of its religious-moral aspect, but only from a consideration of how a

---

178. A term that one should avoid because it does much damage. Thereby the vocation to marriage is too easily denigrated and excessive demands stirred up in celibates, which leads finally to hypocrisy. What is specific to this condition is not "complete discipleship" (this is proper to being a Christian as such), but rather a "specific symbolic manifestation of discipleship." More on this below, D V 5. This was well understood at the beginnings of Christianity. Thus Ignatius, *Pol.* 5:2 is simultaneously a commentary on this point: "If someone for the honor of the Lord's flesh (εἰς τιμὴν τῆς σαρκὸς τοῦ κυρίου) can remain in continence, he should do so without becoming vain. If he takes pride in it, he has lost his way, and if he aspires to be more esteemed than the bishop" (apparently the latter at this time did not live a celibate life) "he has become corrupt. It is seemly, however, for men and women who marry to enter into union with the agreement of the bishop, so that the marriage takes place to the glory of the Lord, and not from lust. Let all things be done to the glory of God."

179. In Latin: sacramentally (!); on this matter, see above, A I 4 and 5.

particular lifestyle affects the individual, similar to the way 7:35 proposes as its goal to shape a life in Christ into its least burdensome form.

To that extent behind our text there stands the conviction that the petitioner who is about to marry takes on an *additional* burden: while before his marriage he or she could go up more directly to the Lord with a willingness to please that was already fixed on the Lord, as a married person he or she must carry out a new process of integration in which the legitimate "being pleasing to one person" must integrate itself deeply into one's personal relation with Christ (as "in a certain way not"). By any account, this is a painful and "demanding" process. It is of course understood that even as a celibate one would have to undergo a similar process of integration along the path to salvation, but here that is not thematized, for Paul is speaking to those who "nevertheless" have chosen to marry. Whether for an individual this or the other way is the one by which he or she will be more concretely pleasing to the Lord can only be answered by considering the particular call. This distinction, which is thematized in 7:17-24, is not explicitly discussed in 7:32-34; nevertheless, it stands in the background. Thus it is not that the two Christian (!) states are compared as to their worth or content; rather, it is merely said: if a person detects the possibility of celibacy in himself or herself, *for that person*—under otherwise equal conditions and purely considered in itself—the path of marriage is *more fatiguing and more painful* than the other path (however, such persons can protect themselves from these burdens by "in a certain way not having") and *not* that celibacy constitutes "a higher stage of relationship to God" (Conzelmann).

Thus, once the apodictic statements are "relativized" and located in their limited intentionality and in relation to their context, the "pleasing" emerges all the more clearly from the subsoil beneath the text. It demonstrates that Paul regards personal relation as the center of marriage and of celibacy; in this discussion, he begins with marriage. Evidently Paul's discourse was prompted by a parallel he recognized between the relation of the partners in marriage and the relation of a Christian to Christ. From the partner's desire to please in marriage he takes the *terminology* for the relation of Christians to Christ (here first shown in the "case" of the celibates, but then for all). *With regard to the subject matter,* however, Paul begins with the unmarried. The "desire-to-please-Him" is not here understood as "service" or "work" for the Body of Christ, the Church (as it is in 2 Cor 4:5; 1 Cor 15:10f.), but rather takes its meaning entirely from this kind of personal relationship: the desire to please the Lord, to be beautiful for him as a wife is for her husband.[180] What people attempt in their inter-human secular existence is experienced in the spiritual realm in a deeper and more satisfying manner. Again we see: it is not a matter of specific activities, but rather to please the Lord precisely in *our dealings with* the world. This personal aspect becomes clearest if dealing with the world consists in dealing with one's wife. Even there it is true that it is *within* a personal human relationship that simultaneously and typically one's personal relationship with Christ is realized. And that means: *As* a married person to live "married, in a certain fashion unmarried." This makes us spiritually free and thereby "carefree." Ignatius of Loyola advises: "No longer love any created object in itself, but only in its creator and Lord."[181]

We are now in a position to give an answer to the question of how far this text may be applied to *all* married people, and not only to those petitioners who experience celibacy as a real possibility for themselves, and for whom the answer was first formulated. It is like being present at a pastoral conference where one is merely a spectator, not a partner in the discussion: after one has listened to how the pastor has counseled these people about their situation, one may take this or the other thing heard and apply it to one's own situation, so as to derive benefit for oneself. However, one is only in a position to correctly transpose what one has heard if, on the one hand, he or she has accurately evaluated the situation of those seeking advice, and on the other, has correctly seized upon the general principles that support the pastor's particular advice. At the same time one must be aware that the same pastor, when dealing with other people, might formulate an answer (even to the same problem) somewhat differently.

180. Cf. above, A I 4 and 5; thereby we have here even an indirect objective parallel to Eph 5:22-29; see below, B I 1.3.

181. Ignatius of Loyola, *Spiritual Exercises,* no. 316. It is precisely about this "distanced relation to creation" that above, close to note 172, we were speaking: "while having, in a certain sense not having."

Thus, when married people wish to understand this text correctly, they must realize at the beginning that Paul is speaking to people who feel a desire in themselves for celibacy. To people who have no such desire, Paul would have spoken entirely differently. Nevertheless, the general principle lying behind this is that every Christian must discover and animate within him- or herself precisely the same attitude of wishing to be totally pleasing to the Lord, undividedly and without qualification. Out of the experience of such a complete and unconditioned love for the Lord they will then achieve an understanding of celibate living, and thereby find a way to live also in their own situation "in a certain way not having," or seeking to please one's spouse "in the Lord" (7:39). This is a lifelong process. Access to our text thus requires a love of the Lord that understands this kind of life with him. However, as we have said, if Paul had been giving marriage instruction, he would certainly have spoken differently (cf. 1 Cor 6:19; Eph 5:22-33).

After the reception of the Spirit marriage is no longer the same thing it was before; and for that reason a Christian can in general correctly live marriage only as "in a certain way celibate." For to the extent that it is built on the *charism,* the "call" of the Lord (to marriage) and is thus formed "in the Lord" (7:1-16, 39), it changes its essence, it is to a certain extent transformed (Rom 12:2) and redeemed. This is painful, for marriage like every other human relationship and activity does not already have this quality in itself at the beginning, but rather in normal people carries psychologically within itself a total claim that seeks to capture the spiritual person (1 Cor 2:14f.) and thereby burdens it. In itself it carries the risk that one will appropriate the other, or that the latter will subordinate him- or herself to the other in servitude. This "pull" or "suction" comes from the "world," it lies in the nature of things and is only overcome if, even as married, one lives "in a certain way unmarried." This implies no devaluation of sexuality; it applies equally to every other field of relations: joy and sorrow, profession and use of worldly things—they each have the tendency to raise themselves into absolutes. For that reason a person must maintain a distance with regard to all of them. One must not allow these values to become norms, but rather must always measure them against another norm; this is the process of redemption. An indirect confirmation of this reflection comes in verses 33f., as also in 7:29c, where marriage is considered in its secular, unredeemed structure. It is not implied that marriage is something evil, but rather that as a secular reality it brings a distinctive onus with it; and from this onus Paul would like to spare and protect married people through the "in a certain fashion not."

Thus the relation to one's partner is transformed from a *totality* to a healthy *relativity*. The concept of wishing to please people is not thereby destroyed, but rather integrated within the relation to Christ, and this means: it is liberated into its true, and hence *relative* nature. To profile this more sharply, in verses 32b and 34b/c Paul presents to the married people how the relation of wishing to please has worked itself out in his celibacy. The contours are indeed somewhat sharply delineated, perhaps also linguistically not sufficiently clearly articulated, so that one could easily misunderstand them. Psychologically, behind them stands the conviction that Christ grabs hold of people even in their capacity for human love in new ways—as up until now no religion and not even the "Old Covenant" has done. Certainly the Jew who was faithful to the Law wanted to live in a way that was pleasing to God. However, if a Christian, grasped by the Spirit, wishes "to please the Lord," that also brings something new with it that *has something to do with God's incarnation as a human being:* a new directness, humanness, and physicality of the desire for God (7:34c), which puts the love relation to humans in question in a new way, so as to integrate it in a deeper fashion. Is not the principal commandment to love the Lord with one's whole heart and with all one's strength brought thereby to its "fulfillment"?

Here we can draw help from the Old Testament concept of undividedness *(tamīm),* which probably stands behind Matthew 5:48: "to be perfect" means not to run on two tracks or in two directions, but rather to live with an undivided heart. With Paul simplicity is first of all an indication of correct orientation (Rom 12:8; 2 Cor 8:2; 9:11, 13), however in Ephesians 6:5 and Colossians 3:22 it is also the sign of proper obedience. In 2 Corinthians 11:3 it characterizes, as we saw above (A14), the attitude of marital fidelity and devotion to Christ. In comparison with our passage the "cunning"—there, by the way, understood as temptation to sin—reminds us of the fact that the world "takes prisoner''; and "pure virgin'' = fiancée echoes the "holy'' of 7:34 *(hagnē–hagía)*. It is to be noticed that in 2 Corinthians 11:3 this is an attitude for *all* Christians. Thus there "undividedness'' is not understood as the overcoming of a split between Christ and the world that supposedly comes with one "state'' or the other, but rather as referring to the orientation to Christ that is imposed on all Christians.

Thus the not-being-divided that stands behind 7:32 should not be too hastily understood as a meditative recollection and retirement, but rather primarily means the collectedness of the heart in attention and love that should be common both to the "working apostle'' or the married person in the middle of the "world.'' Thus this text contains more for the spirituality of the Christian in the world than perhaps one at first suspects. Of course one can draw a straight line from the preservation against splintering (7:34a) to the "simplicitas'' of the "monk''; however, one should notice that Paul is not thinking of such specifications—he is not considering any state of life—but rather of the fundamental attitude that should also serve married people as a model. It is a continuation and a deepening of the Old Testament's "simplicity, which finally is nothing else but the holiness and perfect righteousness of a life oriented to God.'' This "basic form of every virtue'' means "to give one's whole heart to God and to deal generously from the heart in one's relations to one's fellow human beings''; it is "to be free from all ulterior motive,'' "faithful to Christ, belonging to him with one's entire will'' as well as "unpretentious humility and uprightness.''[182] All this is a specific feature of the basic attitude of all Christians; the celibate gives only one form of symbolic expression to this general Christian attitude.

The trouble begins as soon as one starts, not with this basic orientation, but from an external "monastic'' lifestyle, in order to determine one's understanding of complete dedication, unfor-

---

182. H. Bacht, "Einfalt'' in RAC IV 826–828. In addition one may also point out that "being one and undivided'' are also divine attributes in Greek thinking, while multiplicity is seen as a sign of imperfection. Admittedly, behind this stands the distinction between matter and spirit, which Paul, as a Jew, does not fully accept; cf. below, C 2-4. Bacht clearly shows how closely this is related to the Stoic tradition.

tunately frequently invoking this text. Then it is scarcely possible to describe credibly the lives of married Christians as examples of total dedication to Christ; rather, beneath the surface the spirituality of the religious orders becomes the hidden norm of Christian piety, with which the ideal of the perfection of a "Christian in the world" can scarcely compete. However, "in a certain manner not having" does not specify any particular life situation as the norm, but rather gives first priority to the heart, a basic posture which Paul is convinced is proper also to married people filled with the Spirit. Philippians 3:13 is relevant here: "Because I strain forward for the 'one,' I leave everything 'else' behind me." Clearly Paul does not believe that there are Christians who "next to" the One have (unfortunately) also an "other" task. Anyone who "separates" here is already not divided between Christ and the world—for strictly speaking there is no such thing, cf. Luke 16:13—but already has fallen victim to the world.

The counsel that this "desire to please the Lord"—following 2 Corinthians 5:9 one would almost like to say: whether it be not having, or in a certain fashion not having—can only be a-chieved through a perpetual emigration (2 Cor 5:8) involving an ever-deeper freeing of self from the "entanglements"[183] of this world, is found again and again in the spiritual tradition, in many variations, often with similar terminology, without revealing any connection with this text. Gregory the Great compares his exhausting service as the Bishop of Rome with the recollected life he could previously enjoy in the monastery:[184] "However, if one's spirit is split and torn apart and forced to deal with so many[185]

183. This is the undertone of παράγειν in 7:31b: "to ensnare," etc., EuE 464f.; Ts 236–241.

184. Gregory, *Hom. in Ez.* I 11:4.5-6/CCL 142, 170–172. Liturgy of the Hours: II, second reading from 3rd of Sept. Year II (German: Heft 7, 236ff.).

185. With Paul as well at 7:33f., it is a question of the multiplicity of this world. On Luke 10:41 (Martha, you are busy with many things), see EuE 485f. as well as 500–504 on this general topic. The consequences for Matt 6:25-34 are considerable; see EuE 490–498. The notion of "splintering" into many pieces, in contrast to remaining "one," returns continually in spiritual instruction, e.g., Cassian, *Coll.* 1:5f. or the "Centuria of the Monks Kallistus and Ignatius," *Das Herzensgebet. Mystik und Yoga der Ostkirche,* ed. A. Rosenberg (Munich, 1957) 47: "Those should keep quiet

important things, then how can it pull itself back in order to collect itself to prepare a sermon?'' Gregory sees that in these many-sided contacts he himself makes many mistakes and ''lies prostrate.'' ''However, the Creator and Redeemer of the human race has the power to give me, unworthy as I am, a superior manner of life and the ability to preach, since *out of love for him* I do not spare myself in the presentation *of his words.*'' There is a parallel with 1 Corinthians 7: one is inevitably torn apart in one's contact with the world; however, in one's simultaneous turning to the Lord this is outweighed by his power and the love of him, so that despite the actual tasks, one lives and works ''in a certain manner not having,'' that is, like a ''monk or hermit.''

Ignatius of Loyola justifies his advice that the exercitant should withdraw for the spiritual exercises from her usual living conditions on the grounds that the exercitant should ''spend her time in retirement and not direct her understanding in a divided fashion on many things, but rather place her entire attention on *one single thing,* namely the service of her Creator.''[186] This does not mean that otherwise she would be divided *between Christ and the world;* for if it is not possible for her to get away, she may still make the exercises. Analogous with this there is in all spiritual

---

who maintain that, in the middle of distractions one could preserve peace of soul; avoid contact with such scatterbrains.'' As with Gregory, it is here also a matter of a spiritual posture; however, here it appears possible only through a dismissal of the outside world. What strikes us is the manner of speech. Similarly on p. 52: ''When the Spirit will be taken out of the splintering of the world . . . into the unified vision of the coming transformation.'' P. 53: ''If he goes out into multifarious thoughts and external things, then he becomes—against his will—once again divided.'' And p. 56: ''The whole horizon of our eyes and the curiosity about what is visible and graspable in nature is suited to dividing and splintering the spirit, indeed even to dispersing it and reducing it to wandering.'' On the other hand, Basil says: ''A spirit that does not disperse itself with externals nor is seduced by the senses into the world, enters into itself'' (Cf. 2 Cor 4:18 and 5:7; Ts 138f., 227–233). It is always a question of being divided among the things of this world, not of a division between the world and God! As I have said, that would already constitute a turning away from the Lord. This is evidently based on spiritual experiences which Paul also was familiar with.

186. Ignatius of Loyola, *Spiritual Exercises,* no. 20.

activity the problem of "con-centration." L. Tersteegen prays: "Make me simple, interior, secluded, soft, and still in your peace," and a woman in prayer hears the words:[187] "What do you choose? Your own dispersal and exhaustion—or me, your Lord and Father? You can choose my love *and* the house of dispersion, of cares." In all this it is a matter of a shift in the center of gravity, a transformation of the person's values: of the world which I *displace* from the center, and of him whom I *install at* the center. Similar experiences must have led Paul to these formulations.

3. If They Would Like to Remain Celibate:
1 Corinthians 7:35-40

Again we divide the text at an unusual place. As long as verse 35 contains a conclusion, it works as a pacifier: "If I present the disadvantages of marriage to you, I am only doing it for your own good. For you can serve God 'in the proper way and undisturbed' only as celibates." This would be to intensify a tendency which has always caused a lot of difficulties and which in the meantime we have demonstrated to be without foundation. In addition one asks oneself: How can Paul say "to their profit" that "the married man concerns himself with the things of the world," etc.? Such a statement about the nature of a thing cannot be used for any possible "purpose." For this reason one "surmises" from the context that Paul is delivering indirectly a counsel for celibacy. However, this is said nowhere directly. In fact, the formula fits better as something Paul would suggest as a recommendation. But then either verse 35 must refer back to 32a, 28c, and 27, *or* the demonstrative again concerns—as in 7:6—*what follows.*

If we read the text in this way, then we have before us, as in 7:6f. and 7:25f., again a somewhat longer introduction to the paragraph which then follows, in which both parts work together much more succinctly and mutually interpret one another. The succinctness is intensified through the fact that verses 39f. belong under the same major thought. For Paul is now beginning the final topic which had been left open: if at first he provided aid

187. The source is a personal sharing.

to those engaged people who, after an initial attempt at celibacy, ultimately married, to help them support the extra burden, now he returns to address those who remain celibate. He intends now to explain more fully the "opinion" he has referred to already in 7:25 and expressed in verse 27, and at the same time realizes that this opinion will not be easily understood by all; in verses 35 and 36 he returns to the point that they should only remain celibate if both are up to it and can do so in complete freedom. A consideration of the female partner is now more prominent (v. 36). Only in verse 37, after much preparation, does Paul disclose his long-awaited position. He has not made it easy for himself—or for us!

CHOOSE ACCORDING TO WHERE YOU ARE MORE COMFORTABLY WITH THE LORD: 1 CORINTHIANS 7:35

UT	PT
I say *this for your* profit,	35 The *following*
	a I say *according to* what is profitable *for you,*
not to lay a chain upon you,	b for I do not intend to lay a chain (noose) upon you,
but rather so that thereby you may always be able *to serve* the Lord *in a proper way and undisturbed.*	c but (I am speaking) according to what is *in accord with a noble lifestyle* (superior sensibility) *and so that you* may remain *solidly in communion with the* Lord *without (excessive) strain.*

> *Paraphrase of 35c:* . . . but rather I take as a norm[188] being-well-mannered and "sitting-well-with-the-Lord without heroic effort," which means: according to what (a) a proper mode of life, excellent morals, and a noble bearing suggest to you, and (b) in which you can remain with the Lord relatively comfortably, sit at his feet, without it being too difficult for you.

Where does the thought of the "chain" come from? Up until now it has been construed this way: if I counsel you to celibacy, I am only trying to help you to the proper service of the Lord

---

188. On this meaning of πρός, besides EuE 276, see also: ChuA 220; "Begriffsgeschichte," notes 9, 15f., 40, 58, 61 with the text.

and I do not intend to "shackle" you (through marriage? through celibacy?). This relation had to be established by seeking beyond the immediately *preceding* verses. It must be construed differently if it looks *forward* to the following verses. In the latter case Paul is taking up the last open problem and intends finally to offer an exhortation on celibacy to those who *have not* married. In that case, however, the chain could not possibly be celibacy and of course not marriage, but rather his own *counsel* to celibacy, just as in 7:15 he had emphasized that they should not be "slavishly bound" by his recommendation (to remain in a mixed marriage). Thereby it is very important for him that this decision by engaged people for celibacy take place with maximal inner freedom and, indeed, a certain ease. The criterion for such a decision should be: what is to your "profit," "what good morals and propriety suggest to you,"[189] and "where you feel in good communion with the Lord without great effort," where you could, so to speak, sit more lightly at his feet.

Thereby the counsel in 37f. to celibacy is again (!) relativized; in fact, verse 36 indicates once again the justification and even the duty to contract a marriage. Hence in verse 35c the basic criterion for *both* possibilities is open. In the one case—verse 36— it will be easier if you marry, either because otherwise too great a demand will be made upon you, or the circumstances will make the celibate lifestyle too hard for you; in the other case, on the contrary (v. 37), you can maintain a celibate lifestyle and therein discover a relation with Christ that *for you* is more attractive.[190]

189. One would almost like to translate εὔσχημον as: what is "chic"; thus Duden: "chic: Swiss for advantageous dealing." That meaning is also not absent. The word has something to do with style. Choose that which in your situation is more elegant.

190. Kruse, 109, takes offense at my interpretation, as if thereby I were propagating a "Christianity without the cross," and it "would be unnecessary to inquire about a motivation." Now, it is a central point of Paul's theology that the life in Christ implies a path through death, as I have thoroughly demonstrated in my dissertation "Tägliche sterben und auferstehen" (Ts). This is something that each person is called to, and especially every Christian, and which Paul wholeheartedly supports; cf. 2 Cor 5:5. The question is only what a person should choose, where he or she has to make a decision. A free renunciation for the kingdom can only be based on a call (cf. 1 Cor 9:1-18). So everything depends upon whether the individual is

It thereby becomes clear that Paul does not regard celibacy as an absolute value, but only "relatively," in relation to the conditions mentioned.[191] Basically this introduction only becomes comprehensible when one has understood the concern of the following verses. For that reason at the conclusion one should read through them again carefully.

ONLY IF YOUR (FEMALE) PARTNER DESIRES IT: 1 CORINTHIANS 7:36-38

UT		PT
A person who in relation to his virgin *believes* his conduct is *improper,*	36 a	*Thus* if someone is *convinced* it would be unfair ("stingy") to his fiancée to be celibate, *in case*

---

called to this by God. And to determine this precisely, Paul provides in this chapter various aids. In this, one's natural situation and cimcumstances play no small role (7:9, 35f.). Obviously such a path may imply great sacrifice (1 Cor 9:25-27); however, it then takes place always in the context of a determination of the greater value (Phil 1:18-26; 3:7-16) and through a love and power bestowed by God. But I am not of the opinion that the impulse to Christian celibacy is "charismatic, yet still probably inborn," but that what is at issue is a special grace in the order of salvation (see above, A II 4) which has its basis in the individual call through Christ and which can certainly contrast with a powerful sexual desire. An authentic calling frequently "contradicts" a person's natural inclinations. However, if someone—in spite of the presence of such contradictions in themselves—comes in Christ to an interior freedom and peace, and the external circumstances permit it, then he or she can make such a sacrifice (v. 37). This precisely does not mean that a person may "overtax" him- or herself. A greater humility lies in recognizing one's own limitations. How easily so-called idealism becomes pride and self-aggrandizement. Such renunciation becomes a cramp that is no longer a witness to God's kingdom. For Paul it is here a question of freedom: not one's own achievement in accord with the law, but rather a gift bestowed on the person by God, whether it be to celibacy or to marriage. For more, see below, close to note 707; D V 3 and 5; further close to notes 773-775.

191. Indeed, this is specifically emphasized by many authors on the basis of the entire Pauline theology; cf. Merklein 248-251; however, it is now made understandable on the basis of this text. Balch's results on similarities with Stoicism now fit in better: "Paul's terms are, that marriage makes some Christians anxious and distracted, while celibacy makes others anxious and distracted" (436).

UT		PT
if *his* desire for her is *too* strong,	b	she is seized by a strong desire (for marriage),
he should do what necessity compels *him, if so it must be;*	c	*and* (if) *in accordance with this what she desires takes place,*
he does not sin; they should marry.	d	he should do it; he does not sin (!), they should marry.
However, the person who *remains fixed* in his heart	37	On the other hand someone who
	a	in his heart *has become peaceful and undisturbed,*
because he has control over himself and is not delivered over to his desire,	b	*without standing under necessity, rather having* (complete) *freedom in what concerns his wish* (for celibacy),
thus the person who has decided in his heart to leave his virgin untouched, acts *correctly.*	c	*and thus* (as a consequence for him personally) *has reached a decision* in his heart to preserve his fiancée, *certainly does something good thereby.*
The person who marries his virgin, acts *correctly;*	38	*Thus (on the one head)* the one
	a	who marries his fiancée, does *well;*
and yet the one who does not marry her, acts *better.*	b	*(on the other hand)* the one who does not marry her, *acts more favorably* (more profitably, more strongly, happier).

We saw already in 7:26f. that, although the inquiry seems to come from men, Paul has not forgotten the moral and psychological situation of their partners. The key word here is "she." As throughout the entire chapter Paul has presented responses mostly for men and for women, he now turns to speak directly of the fiancée. Although legally she is still a dependent of her father or brother or through her engagement now comes under the patronage of her betrothed—she is henceforth one who "stands under a man" *(hypandros)*—in spite of that in Paul's eyes in the question of contracting the marriage and of marital relations she has an equal rank with the man. Thus the bridegroom may not do something that contradicts the wishes of his fiancée. We might ask: why does the bridegroom not simply release her, if he wants to remain celibate? This, perhaps, would constitute a disappointment for the fiancée. If she had no sympathetic understanding for his desire, she could come to regard Christ as a rival. Thus this section is probably about women who (at least in the beginning) desire the same thing (cf. above at v. 27). However, under the conditions that prevailed in those days it was simply more difficult to break off an engagement.

Paul's position is thus far from any fanaticism or rigorism regarding vocations. Otherwise expressed: In calling people God pays attention to the legitimate concerns of all those involved. Specifically: "The obligation to your fiancée has such a priority that you should sooner marry her than for the sake of your abstinence (against her will) release her!" Verse 27 had said "Do not break off the relationship." Thus if at first the two of you attempt the path of celibacy together, but after a while your fiancée notices that she is not up to it—perhaps because, out of youthful enthusiasm, she has agreed to something which, in more mature years, she now sees she is not able to carry out—then it would not be "noble and excellent" for the bridegroom to leave her hanging or to send her away. Rather it is now his moral duty (!) to marry her and therewith to give up his deeper preference, to live a life of abstinence. In that case it is "no sin," that is, no violation of his call (nor is there any suggestion that marriage in itself could be a sin: 7:28). Thus Paul is saying: "You are now standing at a dividing line, specifically before the fact that your partner does *not* have this call, and for that reason *you may* act against *your* earlier choice." We can see by the way he compares these goods how high Paul sets the human obligation taken on when one enters into an engagement.[192] *He* then "must" (imperative) do what *she* wishes: *they* (the two of them) should marry.

Still, somebody who does not stand under such an obligation coming from outside, whether it be from the fiancée or from the pressure of relatives, and also has found for himself peace and freedom and assurance in the Lord—we recognize the work of the Spirit and the Spirit's call through this interior clarity!—such a person "would certainly do well[193] to preserve his fiancée," that is, not to enter into a marital union with her. At last what the question in 7:25 was all about, and what evidently caused much

---

192. However, it becomes clear that we are not speaking about a vow of celibacy! More on this below, D VI 2.

193. This is not an imperative, but a modal future: EuE, note 494.

head-shaking among members of the community, is clearly named. There is no less consternation today and indeed in the entire history of interpretation; therefore, for a long time people thought Paul was here speaking about a father who was pondering whether he should marry off his daughter or not. But there is no foundation for such an interpretation.[194] Rather here as in 7:25-34 it is about engaged people.

But still, how does Paul think that this should be put into practice? Are both to stay in the houses of their parents? Are they to move into *his* parents' house or *her* parents' house? Are they to live in the same house, perhaps all by themselves? This last would be a preliminary step toward what later would be called a "Josephite marriage," and which in the first centuries was rather common.[195] Still, in our case the decision for abstinence occurs *after* the engagement, while in a "Josephite marriage" such an agreement was reached before the legal bonds were drawn up. Paul is presuming that it is here a case of people who do not have to control themselves with great difficulty, but rather who experience themselves as so personally bound to Christ that they are able to dispense with marital relations. This does not mean that it will not occasionally be difficult for them. However, from their spiritual center they do not "wish" it. The later Church will regulate such vocations through forms of religious orders. At the beginning, however, this possibility did not exist. Paul here opens for the petitioners a way, a possibility, in the midst of their life circumstances, to follow this call.

Is this a problem that seems strange to us today? What in the early Church was possible can even today not be treated lightly. The forms of religious life have become questionable in our own day, especially for women. Is it possible to shape something new? A natural presupposition is the clear empowerment through the

194. Ὑπέραχμος then is translated as "overripe, beyond the age of marriage"—something, however, that comes for every woman. And why would not the attitude of those affected become part of the discussion?

195. For more details, EuE 322f. as well as 47 and 104. Kruse, 95ff., concludes, probably correctly, from Luke 1:34 that Mary already desired to live in continence with her betrothed before the announcement from the angel. In 7:36-38 admittedly a "Josephite marriage" is not meant, but rather a permanent "engagement."

Spirit (vocation) and human physical-psychological health ("without strain": vv. 7, 9). For that reason it is important to point out how again and again in this chapter Paul sets limits when he suspects human or spiritual immaturity. Perhaps that is the reason it took him so long—until the end of the chapter—to come to the point.

Verse 38 recapitulates. There is no general rule: "marrying is good, not marrying is better," but rather (a) anyone from the *petitioners under the conditions specified* who enters into marriage with *his fiancée,* acts properly. There is no fault in that; for how could a person who out of love for his fiancée abandons his heart's desire (for abstinence) appear the less thereby in God's eyes? (b) People, however, who *of themselves and for the reasons mentioned* do not marry, "act more strongly." It is not socially or morally "better" (UT), but rather more advantageous, more favorable. This judgment is dependent upon the spiritual motivation: for people *who are so called* this is "easier" for the "inner person," for their spiritual existence, and should be accompanied by great joy, even if it means at the same time hardship for the "outer person."[196]

Normally we approach this topic from the other side: for the outer person, marrying is "easier" and celibacy is harder—without noticing that, *if someone has the appropriate calling* (cf. "in this condition": v. 26), it is indeed more favorable and even easier to be able to follow the vocation. For such people marriage would constitute a renunciation; it would be, as long as the vocation is alive in them and they have not suppressed their spiritual existence, the more difficult (v. 36)! One only gains insight into the whole passage if one recognizes the different ways in which the Holy Spirit can work, how it can change human beings, and what powers it is able to awaken in them. Paul is aware that not everyone has a calling in this direction—that is why he makes so many distinctions—however, he is counting on the fact that everyone can at least understand it so far as to extend space and freedom to such people in the community. For indeed the letter is directed to the community assembly.

One can almost omit looking any further at the Unified Translation; in fact, it only repeats what most all the commentaries say.

196. On this Pauline terminology, see below, C 4 (2) and (3).

However, once one has thought through this possible new solution, one sees how twisted and peculiar this old interpretation is. After celibacy has been forcefully recommended down to verse 35 (!), verse 36 abruptly begins: "However, if anyone believes himself to act improperly with regard to his virgin, . . ." Thus this counsel to celibacy would be qualified in the following way: "Indeed, I only wish that you be entirely with the Lord; however, if you are not able to do it, then you are (not only allowed, but even) *obligated* to marry." Simplified, this would mean: then you *may not* "serve the Lord in an undivided way," but rather you must relinquish such intimacy and "divide" yourself. Who would be convinced by this? It would exercise a powerful moral pressure. Besides that, it is nowhere directly indicated at what point Paul turns from those who "nonetheless marry" toward a new group. This is postulated in 7:32a: "I would nevertheless (!) prefer that you be without cares (= unmarried)." Yet the turn to a new group first comes with verse 35, as we have shown and as fits the entire thrust of this chapter. This is the group of those who "are not seeking to break off" (7:27) and also are not marrying, but rather as engaged people are attempting the path of abstinence.

Thus, with "*aschēmonein* = to behave improperly," suddenly a problem would appear that is difficult to fit into the context and whose content also is shocking. It seems to return in the *hyperakmos,* the "strong desire," that is attributed to the man. If an engaged man can only with great difficulty control himself sexually and is afraid of one day imposing himself on his fiancée—then he should (may?) do what his impulses are pushing him towards. Is he then simply to give in to irresistible impulses? But according to 7:9 in that case it is supposed to be the *stronger* thing to marry. Besides that, *opheilei* refers to a *moral obligation;* thus it cannot be something like this: since it is no sin to marry, he can do so without scruple. The linguistic harshness can still be detected in the very syntax of the UT. As far as the content goes, however, this would constitute a surprising devaluation of marriage and a condescending manner of taking care of the sexual impulses of those who cannot otherwise master them.

Even more crass would be this disdain contained in verses 37f.: However, if someone is able to summon the moral force and has himself "under control," and is *not* "delivered over to his instinct" (like the person named in v. 37?), then the decision for abstinence is the "better." When one hears this, one automatically thinks of a morally higher status; however, the word has no moral connotation. Then in 7:9, would marriage really be the morally higher? Certainly it is better, and under some circumstances also morally superior, to "burning," but Paul is not thinking here primarily of morality. He does not intend to say to the man who perhaps is attempting a celibate life with great difficulty that this is a sin, but rather to show him with regard to what is so hard for him (thus something that for him is weaker, unprofitable), how he should make his decision: "Choose what, *for you,* is possible without great strain." The "stronger" then coincides with what is "good *for* him" (7:1, 8, 26, 35) and will find its highpoint in the "happier" of v. 40. Not, however: Whoever marries his virgin acts correctly (rightly), but whoever does not marry her acts "more correctly" (= more rightly?). Thus we must distinguish: "Good" in 38a *(kalōs)* has of course a moral accent, for it "justifies" the marriage of the person affected; "stronger" on the other hand (*kreisson*—a different word family) connotes that this will be more favorable for him—which its moral legitimacy presumes rather than justifies.

THE FREEDOM OF AN ENGAGED WOMAN AFTER HER PARTNER'S DEATH: 1 CORINTHIANS 7:39-40

UT		PT
A wife is bound as long as her husband is alive;	39 a	A **woman** (the female part of such an engagement) is bound as long as the man is living.
however if the husband *has died,* she is free to marry anyone she wishes;	b	However, should the man *die,* she then has the freedom to **marry** *anyone* she likes;
only it should take place in the Lord.	c	only it should take place in the Lord.
However, she would be esteemed happier if, following my *advice,* she remains *unmarried*	40 a	Admittedly, she is happier if she remains *in this condition* (unmarried, as she was up until now)—in my *opinion;*
—and I believe that I also have *the* Spirit of God.	b	and *indeed* I believe that I also have God's *Spirit.*

The final difficulty of this chapter lay in the fact that Paul returns now suddenly to questions that were handled long before. For the third time he seems to enjoin the indissolubility of marriage, although according to the traditional interpretation it is striking that in verse 27 he does not defend it with the same acuity. Does he now intend once again to exhort the *wife* especially? But already in verse 10 she was the one who was first admonished. Does she especially need this? There had been no inquiry as to whether a widow could marry, but only if she could remain celibate (v. 8). Thus why this strange addition at the conclusion of the chapter? Has Paul lost the thread of his thought? Is this a postscript in which he again invokes his "advice" (cf. v. 25) for another group, specifically after the "virgins," now to the "widows"? However, these were already included in the reference at 7:34b. Have perhaps some married women asked him what they should do in the event their husbands die? This is all highly improbable.

It is more likely that "woman" here means the woman in a relationship of engagement, which is already the topic of discussion. A clear presumption (7:27, 37f.) is that the two of them will remain engaged for the rest of their lives. If Paul in this context considers the death of the man, then he is probably projecting (at least unconsciously) a fairly long time interval, which incidentally argues against the thesis of his expectation of an imminent second coming. But then why does he not refer to her as a "virgin," as before? Now *parthenos* (cf. our "*Fräulein*/miss/maiden") can only be used for a young woman; in Greece there was no category for an "old maid." After a certain age only the general gender indication "woman" is possible. Thus: a *woman* (the place at the front of the sentence gives this word emphasis) is bound so long as "her" man—that is, her betrothed—lives.[197] If the two of them have at one point decided upon a celibate relationship (which presumes that the woman has agreed to this), this does not imply any vow, but rather a mutual promise; in common legal practice, however, a fiancée continues to have a relationship with her "husband." She is and remains someone

---

197. There is the same terminology in Deut 22:24 and Matt 1:19f.; Str.-B II 393f.: "A betrothed woman is called the man's 'wife.' " After his death, however, she is a "widow from the time of her engagement."

who "stands under this man"—*hypandros,* and thus cannot in conscience simply separate from him. She must either marry him (v. 36) or carry through in a celibate relationship with him. Legally she is "bound" through the engagement (as in v. 27).

That Paul is thinking of a bond through a common promise *before God* remains questionable. In any case he is of the opinion that this form of celibacy is only obligatory for the fiancée as long as *this* man lives. It thus becomes understandable why Paul now stresses that after his death she is free. For a widow this would be clear; for an engaged woman, however, who had chosen the path of celibacy, this remained a real question. As in verse 28 (a and b) and 36d, there stands behind the question again the thought that perhaps she might thereby be "sinning" against a *call from God,* in the event she chooses to marry. A promise to a man is only valid for the length of that man's life. Once again Paul puts great emphasis upon the interior freedom of the decision for celibacy. Only afterwards does he add: Admittedly, if she *remains in this condition,*[198] she is happier. Thereby once again Paul is giving an interpretation of his understanding of "stronger" in verse 38. Since until now she has lived a celibate life and has the possibility to carry it further, that will mean for her greater happiness—which presupposes that she has already known and experienced such "happiness" in her life up to now. This is redeemed love. Naturally Paul is presuming that she can keep on with it "without strain" (vv. 9, 36) and "without distress" (v. 37). This concessiveness adds confirmation to our interpretation of verse 35, which one may now want to reread.

Finally, the addition of verse 40b affords us once again a glimpse into the personal psychology of the writer. He has wrestled together with his community in order to lay before them a difficult "opinion" on a sensitive topic. He made sure to distinguish between the Lord's statements and his own counsels, and numerous times qualified and nuanced his own statements in function of what God reveals to the individual. He now underlines this once more: this is *my opinion.* He is not giving a simple "advice" to remain celibate (v. 37d contains no imperative!), but says only

---

198. As up until now she "was"; for a widow in the full sense, this would not be accurate, but would have to be interpreted: "as she *became* after the death of her husband": however, this is not what is written.

what he under certain assumptions would consider stronger and happier; however, he keeps himself back from applying any pressure for the condition of celibacy.

If Paul invokes his own authority, he does so on the one hand to warn people against going too far, and on the other hand to create space for those so called against pressure from society and also from the community. It is apparently in the latter that those intended by the final comment are to be found: thus not so much the petitioners, who indeed desired abstinence and were grateful that Paul would confirm them in this, but rather the "clever" and indeed also the "skeptical" men of the community assembly, who here naturally have a word to contribute, and who did not always bring sympathetic understanding to the young people. To these he says: "And indeed I believe that I also have God's Spirit"—and not just you! If we catch here a slightly aggressive undertone, this is not meant to offend, but is said more in solicitation: "Try to accept this, even if you yourselves could not fully achieve it. I invoke for this my spiritual authority (as in v. 25), to create a place in the community for as many as God has called." We almost could say: "Do not extinguish the Spirit."

4. The Structure of 1 Corinthians 7

In conclusion a glance at the thematic construction[199] of this chapter can support our interpretation. The unifying thread is the inquiry concerning abstinence. If in 7:10-16 the discussion was generally about divorce, that would not only break the train of development, it would also be a strange question to raise, in that the Corinthians must have known Jesus' position on divorce. Indeed, Paul presupposes in 7:10 that they are familiar with the Lord's words; he only reinforces them. However, if he is presuming as an audience throughout the entire chapter, as we believe he is, people who, out of a spiritual motivation, have experienced a desire for abstinence, then the tone of the letter, among other things, becomes comprehensible. The third part would then be

199. For the formal structure, which is only manifest in the original text, see EuE 332–335.

entirely a response to engaged people who have raised *this* question, while the second part introduces the fundamental principle, the "objective center" which directly connects marriage and celibacy, and "adapts" or "relativizes" it to each person's individual call.

Secondary Emphases or Tendencies

(1) Verses 27-28 speak with regard to the petitioners themselves (men, from 28b also women), in each case with regard to the one who experiences a strong interest in this direction and is inquiring about it, while 36-38 are concerned with the point of view of his partner. The same points would be valid for a woman, but this is not stated, most probably because a man has priority before the law. In the same way 39f. could be repeated with regard to the man.

(2) No young people are envisaged in the first part, only married or unmarried people who are above the normal age of marrying ("singles"); on the other hand, the third part addresses the engaged, thus younger people, however only such who might have raised such a question, and thus not young people in general!

(3) The first part displays a strong tendency to warn against unreflective zeal and to protect marriage; the third part, in contrast, with a circumspect introduction and a clear indication of limits, encourages celibacy.

(4) Paul really does not address the question of what has today become the "normal situation" regarding Christian celibacy, namely that young people from a very early age have to ask themselves whether they shall remain celibate. Would he not be especially cautious here?

(5) At the same time, all the questions and answers can be understood out of the new experience of the Spirit (1 Cor 2-4; 12-14; Gal 3:1-5) and do not require for their clarification either an "ascetic school" or a "gnostic teaching."[200]

V. *"The Body for the Lord and the Lord for the Body":* *1 Corinthians 6:12-20*

After the chapter on abstinence we shall read the text which immediately precedes it: against trafficking with prostitutes. Why

---

200. More details on this in EuE 345–347 and 573f., index: "Askese" and "Gnosis"; Thraede, 101f.; Thyen, 119. One should notice that the term *ascesis* in exegesis, especially of Protestant outlook, is used differently than it is in Catholic spirituality, where it has a positive connotation. On this see Wolbert, 172–202.

in this sequence? First of all for reasons of content. In a book like this, sexuality should not be first treated under "sin." On the other hand, because the text's *reasoning* gives us our clearest statement on sexuality as such. This will be understood more easily after the prejudices about 1 Corinthians 7 have been cleared up. But then why do these warnings appear in this letter *ahead of* this chapter? This could be adequately explained if there had been a redactor at work[201] who grouped together three transgressions in the community in chs. 5–6 and then added the independent block 1 Corinthians 7, because the last things handled in 6:12-20 were questions of sexual life. In any event, this text addresses an entirely different situation from that in chapter 7.

1. The Misunderstanding of "Freedom"

The discussion now has to do with people who have gone to the other extreme. They interpret their freedom in Christ as sexual liberation, something like a "sexual revolution."[202]

> *The Text of 1 Corinthians 6:12-20*
> [12]"All things are lawful for me"—but not: "all things are beneficial." "Everything *stands at my disposal*"—but not: "I stand *at someone else's disposal*." [13]Food is for the stomach, the stomach for food (proportioned to one another); God indeed makes the one *harmless* and the other (removes the harmful potential from each). Still the body is not for intercourse with prostitutes, but for the Lord, and the Lord for the body (he is related to the body). [14]However, God (the Father) has raised up the Lord *and* has *also* truly **raised** us up through his Power (his Spirit). [15]Do you not realize that your bodies (you in your physicality) are members **of Christ**? Am I now to deliberately seize Christ's members (impose myself upon them, "steal" them) and make them into the members of a prostitute? Such a thing should never happen! [16]Or do you not know that whoever joins himself with a prostitute becomes one **body** (with her)? "For" it says (scripture says), "the two (become) one (single) **flesh**." [17]On the other hand whoever joins himself (attaches himself) to the Lord is one **spirit** (with him)! [18]Guard

---

201. Cf. above, introduction.
202. For a comparison of the text to the UT and a more detailed justification for our translation, see Atf V 2.

yourselves against intercourse with prostitutes. Every other sin
—whatever a person does—lies outside the body; however, whoever traffics with a prostitute sins against his own body. [19]Or do
you not realize that your body is the temple of the Holy Spirit
dwelling within you, which you have received **from God,** and that
you do not belong to yourselves? [202] That is, you **have been bought
for a price** (through a **cash payment,** specifically with Christ's
blood). Therefore **glorify** God in your body (let God's brilliance
shine out in your body)!

"All things are lawful"—is this a declaration of freedom emanating from a "wave of gnosis" (otherwise not perceptible at
this period) that was sweeping over the community at this time?[203]
If this came from a foreign source, Paul would give it such a positive tone. Is such a claim not rather a misunderstanding of his
own proclamation of our new freedom in Christ?[204] Now more
than ever we know what it means when we say that "the whole
earth belongs to the Lord" and that God "has put all things"
at human disposal" (Ps 8:7; cf. 1 Cor 15:27f.; Gen 1:28f.), for
"everything is yours" (1 Cor 3:22). On the one hand this freedom aroused opposition, especially among Jewish Christians, but
was accepted by others, perhaps more by certain Gentile Christians. This is in the first instance a normal phenomenon in religious psychology whose ground lies primarily in the makeup of
different characters and which can be observed even today on
occasions of outbreaks of new spiritual movements.

A forceful and towering personality such as Paul's was, in its
"height, breadth, and depth," simply too much for some people
to comprehend, so that it is not surprising if lesser spirits simply
misunderstood him. Since he most probably in his oral preach-

203. Thyen also rejects this: 119; more on this in Atf V 2 and EuE 574
(index).

204. According to Bruns, 183, this thesis cannot be from Paul. However,
even Schmithals, 219, is of the opinion "that Paul accepts this slogan." The
fact that the same word appears in 10:23 strongly suggests that 10:23–11:1
belongs to the same letter, perhaps, in fact, in close proximity to our passage. The "reduplication" of topics from 1 Cor 10 in 8:1-13, as well as the
completely different direction in the preceding passage 10:14-22, are further
indications that parts of different letters have been set together in a new way
in 1 Cor; cf. above, Introduction.

ing also gave a sharp point to his teaching (e.g., "circumcision
is nothing"—"meat sacrificed to gods is nothing," 1 Cor 3:21;
7:19; 10:19; cf. also 6:18), his pronouncements are open to such
misinterpretation. Many people need more "rails" to give direction to their lives. On the other hand, the question arises as to
how seriously the thesis of verse 12a was advocated by the Corinthians. Is it not a common occurrence that people misuse quite
comprehensible statements by applying them incorrectly, so as
thereby to have an excuse to justify themselves? Did the Corinthians seriously believe that if they would ask him this question
he would say "yes"?

Our text is directed toward certain (!) people who are misusing
their "freedom." This is already the background of verse 12a:
even if everything, including sexuality, is put at your disposal,
still everything must be used at its proper time (Qoheleth 3) and
in its proper place (1 Cor 7:29-31), it must be "for the glory of
God" (10:31) and be guided by "love," "otherwise it is in vain."
(13:3).[205] In the same way verse 12b: "Everything is at my disposal," but this should not result in someone having disposition
over me, specifically someone who has no right to it, a prostitute. A comparison with 1 Corinthians 7:4 shows that the statement there is not envisaging the same situation as here. The two
texts do not contradict one another but rather both presume
that in sexual relations one person "disposes"[206] over the other,
and, as concerns relations with a prostitute, this can lead to a
dependency which—in contrast to the marital union—is not compatible with belonging to Christ.

The strongly theological, and not merely moral argumentation
indicates that on this point Christianity sets forth new standards.
Just as in the questions of divorce and adultery Jesus set up new
limits and demanded a pure intention, so here Paul directs this

205. Compare again Ignatius of Loyola, *Spiritual Exercises,* no. 23: Other
things (besides the human being) "have been created for humankind to help
them to attain the goal for which they have been created." For that reason
one should make use of them to the extent they aid one towards this, and
distance oneself from them to the extent they hinder one from this. For the
same passage in a different context, see above, note 116.

206. Cf. above, around note 60; another variation of ἐξουσία: 1 Cor 11:10;
see below, after note 310.

"radicalization" onto familiarity with prostitutes. Thereby he extends one of the emphases coming from the prophets.[207] Because in the Hellenistic world visiting prostitutes was excused as a gentleman's peccadillo, this temptation must have been great especially at the beginning, and Paul's energetic intervention becomes understandable. Whether it be Jewish or Gentile Christians, whether it concerns temple prostitutes[208] or others, still in every case it is a matter of unredeemed sexual desire that is seeking to camouflage itself theologically.

"Food for the stomach and the stomach for food; certainly God does not make one harmful to the other" (v. 13). One may notice how in what follows about questions of "food" Paul rescues the application of his (!) fundamental declaration of freedom, so as to return to the crucial point in the question of sexual matters: their deficiency in love for the Lord. Behind this stands the "freedom" Paul has declared in what concerns food offered to idols (1 Cor 10:23-33). As Jesus calmed any anxieties in his Jewish hearers that certain dishes might be harmful (Mark 7:1-7), in the same way Paul has freed Christians coming out of paganism from the anxiety that animals whose flesh has been offered to the gods or which had merely been slaughtered in their name and whose meat had been sold publicly or was given to them by friends could do them *harm*. So Paul's main point here is not "transitoriness" (Conzelmann)—does the "stomach" pass away, and not the body?—but rather the powerlessness of the gods and the earthly elements (1 Cor 10:26; 8:4f.; Gal 4:3f.). The removal of such anxiety leads directly to "freedom" (Gal 5:1). By contrast, "what is transitory" is overcome through "what is not transitory" (1 Cor 15:50-54; 2 Cor 4:18, etc.); but that is not the point here. Since 1 Corinthians 7:31 does not speak any more of passing away, comparisons from this perspective are without foundation.[209]

207. Hauck/Schulz, πόρνη κτλ. in: TDNT VI 579-595, here 585f.

208. It cannot be maintained that here Paul is thinking only of temple prostitution: Atf V 2.

209. Cf. above, close to notes 159f. In our interpretation, there the discussion is about the *real* pull of the "world," whereas here on the other hand, it is about a *supposed* negative result; admittedly, both are overcome through Christ.

A correlative text, 1 Corinthians 8:8, makes this point clearly: "Food (offered to idols) does not subject us to the (heathen!) god; if we do not eat them, we suffer no loss (because of the god), and if we eat them, we derive no gain (from the god)."[210] Thus, you must use a different criterion (such as love) to decide whether you will eat it or not; however, you need not have any scruple over the matter. Paul is here playing upon the fact that in the cultic meals of the pagans, anxiety often plays a role; "If I do not participate in this meal, *this* god will become angry at me." Christians could become concerned in this way: "If I now eat again at the meal, I come once again into contact with this divinity, with that god, and 'deliver myself over to him'; he could now hurt me for revenge, because I have abandoned him." For this reason they prefer to avoid all contact with him—as a consequence of their former habit (8:7), following which they ate it precisely *as* sacrificial food. They have not yet truly grasped that they are only "so-called gods," and that "nothing in the world" can be "an image of the gods" (8:4f.). However, Jewish Christians also show anxiety concerning flesh offered to the gods, even if their Gentile fellow Christians consume it.

Thus, whether it is a matter of heathen cult meals or foods that for either Jew or Gentile are "unclean," it must constantly be repeated that such things "cannot harm" a Christian, and *for that reason* are permitted. On the other hand there is no argument presented in either 1 Corinthians 6 or 8 that some foods could benefit us, either with God or with idols. Besides that, the verb in 1 Corinthians 6:13b does not mean "to cause to pass away," and the future tense shows a certain pronouncement about something valid in the present. In this passage this means: God will *most certainly* remove the threatening power from the objects in question; God *necessarily* makes the stomach and the foods that are in it *harmless*. God does not punish the stomach of a person who has eaten such things, nor does God bestow

210. Thus differently from the conventual understanding: see Ts 289–292. For all that, in 1 Cor 10:20, the phrase "what they offer, they offer to demons, and not to (the one) God," is not rejecting the idea that the sacrifices could have been offered to the true God, but that they are offered to a (pagan) god (their image of god is "nothing": 10:20a); they are offered rather to demons who, in contrast to the "gods," are indeed a reality.

magical powers on those dishes, as has been imputed. Thus this event does not mark either the end of the world or of one's life, but now merely takes place in the lives of Christians.

2. Sexuality and Resurrection

A further confirmation for the interpretation "to make ineffective" lies in the distinction: unclean food/unclean sexuality. While the first cannot hurt our physical body, the path to the prostitute constitutes a disrespect and damage[211] to the new reality of the resurrection in which we are already living. Now no longer are two worldly realities (like stomach and food) proportionate to one another; rather, since the incarnation the body (the person) of a human being is oriented with his or her love towards the Lord, and for that reason the question of personal, physical surrender now reaches another dimension. Verse 13c, which has no predicate, most likely refers to a relationship.[212] Thus we are not here on the biological level, but rather that of personal membership: relation to Christ, our "Savior," whom God has raised from the dead. But like Jesus, God has also raised *us* from among the dead through the power of the divine Spirit[213] and thereby transformed us into "members" of his body. For the "body of Christ" is not a body in the physical order, neither of an individual nor of a society such as the family or the state, but rather it is a body that is built up (1 Cor 12:13) through the "power" of the "Spirit who awakens from the dead" (cf. Rom 1:4); and this is the condition of the members, too.

Thus Paul is speaking in a certain manner of the collective resurrected body in this world. This resolves the many difficulties

211. Indeed, it does not take place "in the Lord": 1 Cor 7:2—5:9, 10, 14, 29, 35, 39; see above, II–IV.

212. "Belong" is not a good translation; the Lord does not "belong" to the body; he takes up a relation to it.

213. Fuchs, 188, says correctly that δύναμις means the πνεῦμα ζωοποιοῦν, cf. 2 Cor 3:6; see 1 Cor 6:17. For that reason as well I prefer as predicate the past form ἐξήγειρεν, B vl; more on this in Atf V 2. That the Paul of the main letters is already speaking of a "present resurrection" (here and now) with Christ, I show in Ts 51–55; 263–266; for 2 Cor 4:14: Ts 89–94; Phil 3:11: Ts 391f.; Rom 6:4f.: Ts 53.

exegetes have here about Paul claiming to have a vision into the future.[214] Thus v. 14 contains the key assertion of the argumentation: Because you *have been* raised up and made members of the "resurrected One" (it is indeed not the earthly body, but the raised body), it would contradict the most intimate nature of your being a Christian to join this existence with a prostitute. To emphasize it one more time: not because it is a sexual act (otherwise Paul would have to forbid sexual union to all married people), but rather because it is a misuse of sexuality and thereby a sinful act, the expression of an injury to our love relation to Christ. For you are now "one spirit" with him and your body is a "temple of the Holy Spirit." Are these not Pauline synonyms for our present rebirth in Christ, which baptism has initiated (Rom 6:5)?

It is surprising that Paul does not here, as he does in 1 Corinthians 7:2 and 5, refer to the offense against one's spouse—a portion of those addressed are doubtless married men—but rather places the prostitute in opposition to the "Lord." He thereby goes immediately to the root of the matter: "In faith and baptism you have become one with the Lord; how can you now betray this relation of love?" This shows indirectly on the one hand how natural it is for him to represent the relation to Christ with the image of physical surrender (Rom 7:4), and on the other, how much, when he thinks of sexuality (and he does so positively), he thinks of a *love* relationship—one which here, however, is the betrayal of another love. Thus for Paul, "to belong to the resurrected body of Christ" is no mere dispassionate observation concerning a fixed and unchangeable manner of existence, but rather primarily is a relational concept: to be "one" in the "spirit" with him, to belong entirely to him in simplicity like a betrothed (2 Cor 11:3). If anyone disturbs this, they destroy that which is

214. Cf. only Fuchs, 188f., 191; Conzelmann on v. 14f.: the "enthusiastic anticipation of the resurrection" had as a consequence "the devaluation of the body to an earthly object." However, how is the doctrine of the resurrection *of the body* supposed to explain such a "devaluation" of the body? Conzelmann, further: "Out of the eschatological hope . . . there results a *present* belonging to Christ." However, it is the other way around: because we already belong to him, we therefore have such a hope for the future (1 Thess 4:13f.).

both the highest and the most delicate: the love between God and humanity. Of course one can say that every sin destroys this love; yet it has a special quality if love is injured under the form of love.

The peculiar contrast between "stomach" and "body" does not constitute a difference on the same level, between part and whole—otherwise how could Paul say that the stomach is made harmless, while the body is not?—but rather more between two aspects of human existence and ways of acting: the one has to do with biological eating, the other with personal dedication. "Body" here means "person,"[215] more exactly human beings in their physical love relationship or "humans with regard to their sexuality." Sexuality thus belongs in a special way to each as a person. Thus one could also translate it: The stomach for food, *sexuality* for—not prostitutes, rather the Lord! For it is one's sexual dimension that comes to the fore in dealing with prostitutes. Then "The Lord for the body" also means that Christ (as the bridegroom) is oriented to human sexuality and turns himself lovingly toward humans. Sexuality is changed through being taken up in the resurrection and transformed in a new way into a relation with Christ. This is not meant in an abstract, sublimated, metaphorical, or "purely spiritual" (= nonphysical) sense; rather, in a *truly spiritual* way; that means: in such a way that the Holy Spirit dwells in the body as its temple (v. 14) and penetrates even to the body's sexual dimension and activities.

The formulation may thus be applied to both married and unmarried people: with the unmarried their sexuality's relatedness to Christ shows itself through their acceptance of this dimension to their existence and in their foregoing of its employment; with the married by the appropriate completion of marital sexual union; for both, however, their sexuality has previously been integrated into a living relation to Christ (1 Cor 7). It is thus not excluded from the relation as something "unspiritual"; rather, as a consequence of the resurrection it is redeemed and transformed (at least a beginning is made, as with the entire person). What is central is that persons find in Christ their complete lover, their deepest "Thou," the purest relation of trust and love, one

215. It is recommended that the reader consult now at the latest the sections explaining semitic anthropology; see below, part C, here especially C 3.

that is not possible with another human being (Rom 5:5; 7:3; 8:35ff.; Gal 2:20). The person should want to "please" him (cf. 2 Cor 5:9 and our commentary on 1 Cor 7:32-34). This love that surpasses and penetrates everything makes it possible on the one hand to accept in complete freedom one's sexual dimension as a gift from the Creator, and on the other to use it by the power of the Spirit not in an autonomous fashion, but rather as the expression of the love of God: whether this be in refraining (married folk also have to practice this from time to time, as well as those who are "not yet" married), or whether it be in a marital union "in the Lord."

"The Lord for the body and the body for the Lord" may thus be taken as a brief slogan for sexuality integrated in the love of God, which belongs to the nature of every Christian. This constitutes neither suppression nor spiritualization nor mystification, but rather a freedom of the spirit which only the Spirit of God can bestow and which of course ripens only slowly in the life of each individual Christian. It is thus not simply a naive lack of development (a so-called "childlike innocence"), but rather a mature humanity and Christianity (childlikeness as a gift of grace). Paul merely indicates this here. However, his language is clear enough; for, as many commentaries emphasize, the phrase "your bodies" in verse 15 refers back to the personal pronoun in verse 14: God has raised *us* Christians (in general), and thus your bodies (that means again: "you" inclusive of your sexuality) are "members of Christ." However, you *may not* make these into members of a prostitute.

3. "Corporality—the Goal of All God's Paths"

"Member of a prostitute, one flesh with her"—another aspect of "body" thereby comes to expression, specifically the unity of many members (1 Cor 12:12-27), however in the special sense of the unity of man and woman. Paul underlines this "unity" with the quotation from Genesis 2:24, which also allows him to add a little wordplay: while "they become one flesh" is used in the original text in a positive anthropological way (thus not in the sense of sin), and thereby the marital union—before original sin— is presented as a deep, encompassing unity, Paul here certainly also intends to say: it now has become a union in "weakness." When it takes place with a prostitute, however, this becomes a union "in sin."[216] Thus Paul exploits the twofold meaning of "flesh" in order to communicate through a clever wink at the "wise reader" (one hears through the text the quotation marks) that "flesh" applied to intercourse with prostitutes contains, theologically speaking, at the same time something negative: this kind of union damages our love relationship with the Lord! In that case human sexual union is not taking place "in the Spirit."[217] However, whoever "joins with the Lord," becomes "one *spirit*" with him. We find here again one of Paul's favorite devices, the theological application of a pair of categories: it is not the Greek opposition between body and soul/spirit, but rather that between "union with a prostitute" and "union with the Lord." It thus is not various parts of a person that condition the quality of the possible union, but rather in every case it is a matter of a person's entire humanity. Thus naturally in the relation to the Lord the body is included; for from verse 13c onward the subject is the "body." Thus, whoever joins with the Lord (also) becomes in his or her physicality and sexuality "one spirit" with him.[218] It thereby becomes clear from within that intercourse with a prostitute is not compatible with this (v. 18a).

Verse 18b must be understood from such a spiritual experience: "Every other sin lies outside the body." This verse taxes the commentators. The word *sōma*/body is used in a third nuance beside "sexuality" and "body of Christ." Certainly there are sins which appear to be "purely mental or spiritual," such as envy or pride. But that would be a characteristic Greek distinction. Does Paul intend here perhaps to exclude sexual sins of *thought* (Matt 5:28), as if these were not "in the body"? And what about assault, murder, or self-mutilation? Are they somehow outside the

216. Again: here the reader must be aware of what is said below in part C.

217. Schiwy, 147: "The Septuagint's rendering through σάρξ is welcomed by Paul, for the life-giving unity of the partners in the body given by God becomes, in case of immorality, in fact a death-bringing unity in the flesh that wars against God."

218. Conzelmann, 135: "In itself one would expect: 'A person who unites with the Lord is *one body* with him.' In fact, this thought is the objective presupposition; ἐν πνεῦμα then explains of what type this one body is."

body? Thus it cannot be a matter of *this* distinction (soul/body). To "commit" *(poiein)* a sin means to carry it out, whether it be in external action or in thought.

However, every process is specified through its object, that toward which it is oriented. Since Paul emphasizes in 18c one's "own" body, the preceding *toward* must stand in opposition to it: every other sin is somehow *external,* specifically external to one's *own body.* Thereby *sōma*/body cannot have only the sense of the personal pronoun. In a certain sense every sin is of course a violation of oneself. Our verse clearly brings an "ad hoc argument" (similarly Conzelmann), specifically adapted to this question. If we tone down the rhetorical flourish, we could say: other sins (whether all or many) are directed toward things "outside my *own* body"; their content and object are persons or objects outside my Christian (!) existence, to the extent that it is bodily.

Thus verse 18 it no longer concerns the collective "body of Christ" (in this sense every sin places the perpetrator outside the body of Christ), but rather the individual body, still indeed that *of a Christian.* Naturally this statement may be applied in a wider sense to every person; here, however, Paul is thinking about the body *of a Christian,* as the foundation in verse 19 as well as verses 14-17 show. In verse 17 also, being "one spirit with Christ" referred to the unity of the individual with Christ. Paul is arguing not with reference to our creation, but to our redemption. Thereby human sexuality becomes newly integrated by Christ, taken up into a more profound totality. Otherwise Christ would not be the Savior of the whole human being; and redemption does not mean inhibition and suppression, but rather liberation and fulfillment. Thereby the entire sexual dimension of humankind with its deep roots in the soul is sanctified in Christ, and through his Spirit fitted into a divine relation. Traffic with a prostitute, however, goes against this redeemed "body," and thus against the authentic nature of redeemed humankind, against God's new creation in us[219]—the already present *reality of his resurrection* in the "members of his body" (1 Cor 6:14f.). Such

219. 2 Cor 5:17; Gal 6:15. In Phil 2:13 Paul recalls, with specific reference to the richness of the life entrusted to us (as here immediately in v. 19f.): it is *God's* gifts and *God's* powers that govern there. For more details, see N. Baumert, "Wirket euer Heil mit Furcht und Zittern?" *GuL* 52 (1979) 1–9.

a person sins against the full reality of his own Christian existence.[220]

Paul then mentions five key words that specify the concept of "body":

(1) The body participates in the *resurrection.* While it is true that "the entire person" rises, still the power of the resurrection becomes especially clear in that element in which the Fall was most clearly evident. Not only for Greeks, but also for the Jews resurrection is something physical. In neither culture does one speak of a "resurrection of the soul," rather of its "continued existence," or with the Greeks of its "immortality." Thus "body"

---

220. The danger here is not an excessively individual understanding of salvation, for which Neidhart, 249, criticizes the apostle: "If 1 Cor 6:18 is accepted, then love is not the highest gift; rather the charism which shines more brilliantly than all the others is the freedom from sexual needs, the complete extinction of the sexual fire, the unruffled placidity of a virgin body." Here a loving renunciation is confused with freedom from needs, pride over an unviolated body with the undivided offering of one's heart (2 Cor 11:3), and no distinction is made between a natural desire and a cramping up that is always the manifestation of an unmastered desire (this is how 1 Cor 7:9 should be understood). It is equally misleading to say: "(Paul's) renunciation is ego-centric: because thereby the man's own body is rendered unclean. The prostitute as a person does not even enter the field of view of theological consideration. . . . Apparently at the lowest level of his thinking, there where sexuality comes up, the command to love is no longer the fundamental axiom." First of all, the notion of "levels" to his thinking does not come from Paul, and secondly we have noticed that the equal position of man and woman in the marriage relationship is a basic axiom of 1 Cor 7. Further, Paul is not a person who, in contrast to Jesus, would look down upon marginal groups (1 Cor 1:26-29; 4:9-13; 6:11!; 9:19-23). How, then, would this "worker-priest" have spoken with slaves and whores (the latter were often slaves who were forced into this role), when he led so many of them to Christ? However, here he is speaking to Christian men who have forgotten that their bodies belong to someone else since their conversion! The letter is an occasional writing and does not attempt to treat systematically the nature of prostitution, just as 1 Cor 7 is not a systematic treatment of marriage. One rather detects in the phrases something of the Stoic axioms: "A man who sexually encounters hetaera, sins against himself" (Musonius 65:4ff.), and "with all his unclean dealings a man stains the god in his own breast" (Epictetus II 8:13); similarly perhaps *Jub.* 30:2, 6, see Hauck/Schulz, TDNT VI 583, 587, 588.

is here seen as the "place" of personal self-realization in which one becomes completely oneself. In this perspective "resurrection" then connotes the final step of the realization of redemption, the last step of the achievement of salvation, because here the Holy Spirit transforms the person in an *encompassing,* complete sense. For Paul the "body" is on the one hand the place of humanity's enslavement to sin, in which it becomes manifest that humankind is delivered over to sin (to that extent, anthropologically speaking, the human spirit is more the human self: 1 Cor 2:11a); on the other hand, salvation means precisely that the "Holy Spirit" penetrates the person's body (beginning with the spirit) and thereby breaks the enslavement, so that now in a new way the body lives more and more (= is raised up) by the Spirit of God.

(2) That this body is *a member of Christ,* and "one *pneuma/spirit*" with him, means that a human is penetrated even in the dimension of his or her powerlessness, so to speak at the weakest point, by life in the resurrection. For that reason particular respect is needed here because here the person is most vulnerable (cf. 1 Cor 12:22f.).

(3) *Temple* of the already "indwelling" Holy (!) Spirit (Rom 8:11; 1 Cor 3:17) describes the same reality through an alternative image. Through this and the following category it becomes clear that "holiness" is language closely connected with "body."[221]

(4) Even the catchword *property,* introduced in 19d and 20a, refers to physicality. It is a basic category to which in Judaism the mutual exclusivity of marriage belongs (cf. 7:4f.), but even more the relation to God (Deut 7:6). For that reason every other incorporation and every disposition to another power is a sin against God's property, and to that extent an act of spiritual adultery. "Do not then injure Jesus' loving surrender on the cross through the selfishness of an autonomous disposition over that which he has 'acquired.'"

(5) As a final characteristic of the Pauline category of the body is its use for the *totality.* Even though he does not mention it expressly, we should especially emphasize this catchword from his Semitic anthropology. For the body is not opposed to the soul

---

221. Cf. 1 Cor 7:34; see above, note 173; 1 Thess 4:3-8; see below, close to note 268; further, Atf IV (towards the end).

in a dualistic manner, but rather refers to the person in a thorough and complete sense. Precisely for this reason is the body the "place" of the spirit.

Thus it is not that "v. 18 seems like an insertion in the text" (Conzelmann; Baltensweiler is similar); rather, it works like a convex lens and focuses the vital point of the entire section (like 7:17-24). It is not a "rational foundation between the pneumatic emphases in vs. 17 and 19" (Conzelmann), but rather illustrates exactly what "pneumatic" means: that specifically the gift of the Spirit also includes one's body, and this means the entire person; and in this specificity achieves its ultimate clarity. The famous saying of Oettinger that "Physicality is the goal of all God's paths" is formulated in a thoroughly Pauline spirit.

However, the concluding clause in verse 20 echoes once again the "summary" already given in verse 19: "So *glorify* God in your body"—or, as one could also say: *Make God glorious* in your body, allow God's brilliance to come to incandescence in your person.[222] One should notice the forward positioning of the predicate, which provides emphasis. *Glorify* God, and do not dishonor God! However "*In* your body" (not: "through it," as a means, rather in it as a place) means, according the context, here as at the beginning of this passage, sexuality. Allow the love and glorious freedom of the children of God to shine through your sexual conduct; give God glory, and not shame!

It would be scarcely possible to give clearer expression to the fact that our redemption in Christ is complete than by the fact that, in the context of sexual actions, Paul speaks of the fact that our body is a member of Christ, which means that the love of Christ permeates even human sexuality. Thus what is specific to corporeality is finally the totality = completeness[223] of salva-

222. In 2 Cor 4:15 as well the point is made that "grace overflows into the divine glory" = shines through me; see Ts 99, 102ff.; or in Phil 1:20, that Christ "will be exalted in my body" = in my person; Ts 112 and 311, 315. It is seriously to be pondered whether this is not also the case in 1 Cor 10:31, where indeed the same problem is present: "Do everything so that God's brilliance may shine forth" = do everything so that God's glory shines through it. $\Delta\delta\xi\alpha$ would then come closer to being a *nomen actionis* (shining forth) and objectively would lie in the same direction as $\delta\sigma\xi\acute{\alpha}\zeta\epsilon\iota\nu$.

223. Similarly G. Fitzer, 32: "For Paul sexual activity apparently has such a personal meaning that it cannot be separated from the whole person. The

tion, and for that reason the "sin against one's own body" has a *unique quality*. Paul does not say that it is the most serious, but rather that it is especially repulsive, because the body is "holy." Today we would rather say: relations with a prostitute are in a special way an offense against one's own worth. Thus it is not contempt for the body or sexual inhibition that stands behind this passage, but on the contrary a high esteem for the body and a boldness about love: the redeemed new person who in all faculties and sensibilities is penetrated by God and aligned toward God. Moreover, such a perspective on sexuality fits thoroughly with our construal of chapter 7, and no longer constitutes an opposition to Ephesians 5.

VI. The Most Serious Sin?

In 1 Corinthians 6:18 we learn that fornication ("unchastity") has a specific, distinctive baseness. So far we have avoided this term. Conzelmann is of the opinion that Paul is here relying upon "a Jewish way of speaking that designates lewdness as the worst sin (Proverbs 6:25ff.)." But we must contest the reference to Proverbs 6. That chapter primarily treats various other problems, and in the catalogue of offenses that immediately precedes it (Prov 6:6-19), sexual sins are not directly named, even if "feet that hurry to run to evil" *could* refer to such sins (6:18). Besides this, there the concern is only about "adultery" = relations with a married person. This is worse than stealing (6:30f.), because "jealousy arouses a husband's fury; and he shows no restraint when he takes revenge" (v. 34). The reflections move primarily on the plane of human wisdom; from this perspective, traffic with a prostitute is "less evil":[251] "for a prostitute's fee is only a loaf of bread" (6:26); the "command of the father, of the mother, of the teacher" (5:1; 6:20), on the other hand, which

---

πορνεύων sins against his own body, that is, against the wholeness of the person, in which the body is not excluded. . . . With Paul this is apparently an injury to the personal wholeness that tends toward being an *imago dei*."

251. Proverbs 6:24, 29; cf. Deut 22:22 with 22:28f. and 23:18f.; Hauck/Schulz TDNT VI 584f.

warns against adultery, concentrates primarily on the negative *consequences.* Of course the author's opinion is that this is also wrong in itself and before God (6:16), but it is not said there that God reacts in the same way as humans.

It has often been pointed out that the sixth and ninth commandments are not listed first (Exod 20:14, 17). In the Pentateuch the requirements touching order in one's sexual life always appear in the midst of many other prescriptions; in the general rule of Qumran (1 QS IV:9-11), sexual offenses appear at the beginning of the second half of the catalogue of offenses. Admittedly adulterous relations with a married woman are punished by death (according to Deuteronomy 22, also with the death of the man), and in late Judaism it is one of the three great sins (worshipping idols, murder, adultery). But does *porneia* have the same weight? What does it mean? Let us get an overview of the terminology here.

1. Standards and Categories of Sexual Morality

Ethical standards were propagated in certain categories and formulas. Since in other languages words with exactly the same meaning are practically never available, translation inevitably brings with it larger or smaller discrepancies.[252] The translator may be aware of this, but they are practically never perceived by the reader or listener. With regard to our question, the following is relevant:[253]

> *Porneia,* usually translated as unchastity, does not refer to every sort of sexual irregularity, but only *forbidden* sexual relations, normally between a man and a woman, occasionally also homosexual. Originally applied to love "for sale" (root: *pimpremi—* sell), by the time of the New Testament it had for a long time no longer been restricted to this context. It always refers to an external action, with regard to sins of thought in relation to such a physical act. However, the word does not refer to an individual trespass with regard to one's own sexuality, and thus is not ap-

252. I have worked out something of the sort with χάρισμα; see ChuA and *Sprachregelung.*

253. Here again I give only the results of the investigation: Atf V 4 and VI 2-5.

propriate for the many psychic problems which accompany sexual maturation. Since sexual relations between near relations were perceived as improper, incest is also referred to as *porneia.*

Moicheia, which we normally render by "adultery," in Greek refers primarily to *every sort of "free" sexual activity* (taking place outside of a bonded relationship, but not for money) *between a man and a woman*—similar to the fundamental Hebrew word *na'ap.* Thus the sixth commandment should be translated: "Thou shalt not have any dishonorable sexual relations (= those occurring outside a permanent bond)" or "Thou shalt not violate or rape another."[254] It was clear to Jews what this word meant; however, we have to extricate its meaning from the constellation of the texts before us. Not every sort of forbidden act had the same weight; in the legal texts the only case punished is the one where a man disturbs another's marriage, not his infidelity to his own wife. However, the word may also be applied in a situation where the legal institution of marriage is not being damaged. The earlier formulation "thou shalt not practice unchastity" was *as a translation* too broad; however, "thou shalt not commit adultery" (UT) is too narrow.

To the extent that *aselgeia* means sexual *licentiousness and intemperance,* it places the accent on the excessive, exaggerated manner and thus may also be used to refer to legitimate sexual contact or masturbation. It does not refer to any specific act as such, such as masturbation.

Akatharsia—uncleanness—also does not refer to specific acts; starting from cultic uncleanness it can, along with many other words, refer to *every sort* of sexual impurity; of itself it adds no semantic specification and for that reason contributes no new content. The term can and may also include the environment and perimeter, but does not of itself indicate what is morally out of order in the sexual area. A command only applies to what the hearer/reader knows from elsewhere is not allowed. In no sense is the genital sphere in itself characterized as "unclean."

The English word "unchastity" is broader than all these terms and is often rendered specific through the context. In a loose sense it refers to practically the whole scale of sexual sins. For that reason it is not ideal as a translation; however, there is no other word available.

---

254. On this word, see below, note 614 and D IV 1, as well as Atf V 4; for the objective consequences, see below, D III and IV. On the special situation of an engaged couple, see below, close to notes 609f.

In the nine *catalogues of vices* that appear in the Pauline and deutero-Pauline letters, sexual transgressions are placed first four times (1 Cor 5:9; 6:9; Gal 5:19; 1 Tim 1:9) and in the middle of a group three times (Rom 13:3; Eph 5:3; Col 3:5-9); in 2 Corinthians 12:20f. they appear among the fundamental sins, and similarly in Romans 1, where they are no longer mentioned in the actual "catalogue." Although this sequence can usually be explained from the context, many people still have the impression that Paul wishes to emphasize especially the rejection of sexual sins. May we conclude from the texts therefore that Paul suffered from an unhealthy attitude toward sexuality? Is this perhaps his personal "Achilles' heel"?

There is another explanation. In the two long "lists" in Galatians 5, *porneia* stands at the head of the catalogue of offenses, while love stands at the head of the catalogue of the virtues. In Ephesians 5:2 and Colossians 3:14 also they stand in contrapuntal relationship. Further, one may regard 1 Corinthians 13:4-6 as the mirror image of a catalogue of offenses (cf. 1 Cor 12; 14). Persons who see the nature of a Christian entirely in terms of love for God and for their fellow mortals—for a Jew, a deepening of Deuteronomy 6:5 and Leviticus 19:18; see Matthew 22:37ff.— would clearly be especially sensitive when the human power for love is led astray. Although it is true that in the only catalogue of offenses in the Gospels, at Matthew 15:19, sexual sins do not appear at the beginning, in the parallel passage at Mark 7:21 they do appear in the explanation of "bad thoughts."

Not for nothing do the prophets fight over the love of this people under the image of the marriage vows and adultery, and are especially upset over sacred prostitution. Theologically and spiritually Paul is certainly in the same tradition. And if we must concede that "Thou shalt have no impure sexual relations" is a correct translation for the sixth commandment, this naturally implicitly contains the demand that one avoid all irregular sexual activity, just as "Thou shalt not kill" is meant to include related activities (Matt 5:22). The only question is, what should we understand by sexual impurity and irregular sexual activity? Just as "sexual licentiousness [is] a consequence of the abnegation of the true God,"[255] in the same way love for God becomes especially

255. Hauck/Schulz, TDNT 6:588, with reference to Wis 14:24-26. See below, close to note 475 and D III 2 (5).

visible in the purity of one's sexual life and human relations. Thus sexuality in its entire range has a special function as a signal; it is a kind of indicator of the purity of one's love. "Where your treasure is, there will your heart also be" (Matt 6:21).

2. *Idol Worship and Self-Dishonor as Root Sins: Romans 1*

This connection becomes most clear probably in the extended analysis of human nature: the Gentiles (Rom 1:18-32) and Jews (1:32c–3:8) have both sinned, each in their own way (3:9-20). Before Paul begins in 1:29ff. a conventional, but here especially multiform catalogue of offenses—under the title of "All that is Unlawful" 1:29—he uncovers the basic structure of sin: humanity's refusal to worship God has as a consequence that God abandons humanity to itself. The ultimate reason is not a lack of knowledge—"What can be known about God is plain to them" (v. 19)[256]—but rather the conscious refusal of gratitude and honor, which instead they gave to idols (vv. 21-23). "Therefore God gave them up in the lusts of their hearts to impurity, to the degrading of their bodies (their persons, the full form of their natures)" (v. 24). Because they did not honor God, as a punishment God allowed them to dishonor themselves. Thus uncleanness is here directly defined as that which destroys a person's honor and worth, or "human nature," the form of their being (*sōma*/body, cf. 1 Cor 6:18). To it belong naturally not only sexual misdeeds but also everything that does not come out of pure love (cf. Rom 14:23). This fundamental pronouncement is now repeated and deepened into two concentric circles: 1:25-27 and 28-32.

Romans 1:25-27: Again Paul begins by saying that, instead of the Creator, they worshiped the creation; again the talk is of "substitution" (as in 1:23) and the reason for this is no lack of awareness, but rather a deliberate "lie"; and again God (!) responds by delivering over humans to their "degrading passions."

---

256. Cf. 1 Cor 8:1-3; Phil 1:9f. Wibbing illustrates the difference between the intellectualism of Greek ethics and the Pauline reverence before "the holy God." "If Paul borrows terms like ἀρετή and ἐγκράτεια from his surrounding thought-world, he understands them as requirements of love" (119f.).

What in verse 24 is collectively called "uncleanness" (= an impure conscience, egoism as impairing the fundamental orientation to reverence and love), is at verse 26f. illustrated by an example from the area of sexual behavior: "Their women 'exchanged' natural intercourse for unnatural." That which they practice in their turning away from God and in their worship of idols, they now repeat with themselves. And in like manner the men. Paul shares with the Judaism of his time the conviction that homosexuality is "against nature,"[257] as well as that the sin of the (non-Jewish) "peoples" shows itself therein in a special way. Evidently Paul would like to use an example in which it will become clear that the refusal to worship God leads to a dishonoring of oneself and a disrespect of one's fellow humans. One could also illustrate this by showing the self-destructive effect of envy, of greed, or of aggression; however, the power of misdirected love seems to him to show especially clearly and forcefully the perversion of the basic commandment. He is not deliberately "wallowing" in dirt, but rather is going directly to the center of the basic structure of human sin: the destruction of one's own nature.[258]

257. To what extent this judgment is only "material" for his basic theological pronouncement, or is itself a considered statement, we will consider further in our systematic section; see below, D III 2 (4). We cannot evade the fact that Paul considers it objectively a sin (cf. 1 Cor 6:9c), although *here* in Rom 1 it is regarded more as a punishment. He is thus also presuming that these people at their deepest level are not happy, even if they will not admit it to themselves and to those around them. An important aspect here is the strength of the disordered affections; at Rom 6:16 he will speak of "slaves of sin."

258. Here Paul lies in a direct line with Gen 6:2, where the dominance of sin, which had the flood as a consequence, is also represented by sexual aberration (not in sexual relations and generation as such; see Gen 5). Closen, 27, understands by the "sons of God" not some "lecherous angels," but rather *men,* which is surely correct. "As *humankind* (in general) increased, the *men* (among them) noticed. . . ."; cf. Closen, 22, 25, 157–171, 179f. P. 163: "The indication of the deepest intimacy with God ('sons of God': Gen 6:1-4) is thus reserved for the point in Genesis where the most precipitous fall through the most material sin, humankind's 'becoming flesh,' is reported." Even if we would prefer to say "special embodiment" of sin rather than "material," and if "flesh" should not be restricted exclusively to sexuality, the thought remains that sexual aberration stands as a symbol

Paul's description of this as "against nature" implies that he regards normal relations between men and woman as fundamentally good (a commentary on 1 Cor 7:1f.). It is also presupposed that sexual relations "in accord with nature," that is, those between a man and a woman, require a meaningful order and receive it through marriage. Since Paul is speaking in a typological fashion, it is not his purpose here to present people who commit homosexual acts as the greater sinners, but rather to use this physical "perversion" of human nature as an easily understandable illustration of the general principle he has established in verse 24. He also does not intend to say that all pagans are homosexuals. If today we would mention drugs, assault, and abortion—the last also a result of an unhealthy sexuality—to show by these indicators where mortals without God are led, this would also not implicitly contain a judgment about the individuals concerned. Paul, a pastor in a harbor town, does not here get on his high horse in order to bring down denunciations upon the heads of such people; on the contrary, he is offering the Good News to them— even to them! However, what in practice is happening among them he interprets as a punishment sent from God that works itself out in them as an example for the whole society. Humanity in its entirety is guilty in many ways; these phenomena are only named because what is unhealthy and evil in sin can be easily seen in them. Paul here stands thereby in the tradition of Hellenistic Judaism, which saw "lewdness as a direct outcome of idol worship."[259]

However, in Romans 1:28-32, the second repetition, sexual sins no longer appear, apparently because this area has already been covered by the striking example. Paul is not himself fixated upon sexual sins, nor are they in themselves the most serious. However, they are powerful signs: they are an indication that reverence and love for God have not (yet) shaped the entire personality, and that a person has not yet passed from egoism to love; that in response to the question: "To whom does your heart belong?"

---

for sin in general. For the connection with the fall from God, see Closen, 181; Augustine, *Civ. Dei* 15:2/CSEL 406, 109. On Closen also above, note 168, and below, note 644 as well as Atf II 4.

259. E. Schweizer, "Gottesgerechtigkeit," 426, 469f., refers to Wis 14:12, 30; *Ep. Jer.* 43; 1 QS 4:11-14; see *Hen.* 10:6; *Test. Dan.* 5:5-7 among others. Cf. below, note 475.

one has not yet placed God in the first position, that, indeed, this person often has no real love for God and does not consider it all that important. Christians today fail through this same "half-heartedness," just as many Jews did in the time of Jesus. On the other hand: if with regard to sexual life a person will not let him- or herself be "lectured to" by anyone—not even by God—then that person has not yet seriously considered that God is waiting for his or her love.

Paul is not speaking a psychologically sophisticated language, and also not taking into account the various subjective situations and conditions of individual people. However, he knows what he is talking about and can also differentiate, as we saw in 1 Corinthians 7. He also realizes that all the sins that he enumerates have various steps and degrees of intensity in their realization. He is certainly not ignoring these differences, but is rather confronting people through their "physical" deeds. The language of Jesus is the same. Starting from this objective orientation, we can consider what subjective attitudes are necessary if human beings are to so orient themselves with their entire personality on the love of God that their sexuality also locates itself from *that* perspective. This will always be a step toward health, toward naturalness, and toward inner freedom.

3. Exclusion from the Community:
1 Corinthians 5:1-13

Let us look now at two texts that assume a position on a specific case. 1 Corinthians 5 seems especially severe, for there the threat is to exclude someone "guilty of unchastity" from the community. Why does Paul react so strongly? What has the offender done that he should be "delivered over to Satan"? Do we not detect here a strong feeling against these sins? Is this perhaps one more indication that Paul considers them the most serious?[260]

> *The Text of 1 Corinthians 5:1-5 and 9-11:*
> [1]To top it off, there is talk of incest among you, and indeed of a kind of incest that has never taken place among the (other, pagan)

---

260. On the following text, see my article in Atf V 3, with the comparison to the UT; here again I give only the results.

"peoples"—(!) that someone has taken a wife of his father's. ²And you are arrogant and have not even *criticized* (it) very much, so that the person who perpetrated this deed would have been *put out* from your midst? ³In any case I naturally—although absent in body, present in what concerns the spirit—*as someone present* (in spirit) have already *made a judgment over* the person who has so acted, *in the name* of the Lord Jesus, ⁴whereby your and my spirits *endowed with* the power of our Lord Jesus have gathered together, ⁵to hand over that person who is of such a sort to Satan *for* a destruction of the flesh, so that on the day of the Lord the spirit may be saved. . . . I *had* **written** you in my letter to have nothing to do with lewd people (who practice impure sexual relations) (that means) ¹⁰not *completely* (totally) with the lewd people of this world and the greedy and predatory and idol-worshipping people, since you would (then) have to withdraw from the world. ¹¹But indeed I *did* write you not to associate with one who calls himself a brother and is a lewd person (e.g., one who commits incest) or greedy or an idol worshipper or a slanderer or a drunkard or a robber, (that is) *thereby,* that you not so much as eat together with such a person!

What do we have before us? The incestuous marriage—commonly translated as lewdness[261]—between a man and "a wife" of his father is not a marriage with his mother, but *perhaps* with his stepmother; thereby it is not said that she had brought him up. It is more likely that she was a later sexual partner of the father. In any case Paul is convinced that not only Jews (Deut 23:1; 27:20; Lev 18:1, 8, 18), but even the liberal Greeks are shocked at this "incest." Thus it is not just a case of his own heightened sensitivity. And yet at the same time: why so severe a verdict of exclusion? Paul sees a simultaneous sin by the community if it so openly permits such conduct in its midst. This brings up the social dimension of guilt. It works to "infect" the whole, like "yeast" (5:7f.). It is not that someone would soon imitate this extreme case, but rather the general point that thereby sexual irregularities might come to be considered of small importance, and indifference would take hold. However, the community does not seem to have appreciated the significance of the misdeed. It does not understand that thereby its status as a com-

261. Probably similar to *porneia* in Acts 15:28f. and Matt 5:32; 19:9; see Atf VI 7.

munity of Christ is called into question. For once again we are at the "nerve" of what it means to be a Christian: the presentation of our specific relation of love to Christ is thereby injured. For that reason there stands in the middle portion of chapter five—it is constructed like a palindrome, in a way similar to chapter seven: A B A'—a reference to Christ's surrender in love on the cross.

We must distinguish among three elements: the act of the community, of the "Satan," and of God with regard to this person. The proclamation of excommunication is naturally an event within history. But for what purpose then do they "hand over" the person concerned to Satan? The destruction of his flesh does not mean that Satan will kill him, but rather that on earth—as with the righteous man Job—Satan may test and burden him more severely, because the person no longer enjoys the protection of the body of Christ. Further, the "salvation of his spirit" does not refer to a further existence in heaven, but rather to a reversal that takes place in this world. For a person can only be "saved" to the extent that in freedom he attaches himself to the "Savior," not as though it was the automatic consequence of any empirical "destruction" or of physical death. The new possibility of conversion is rather a new offer of grace from God to this person, a "day of the Lord" in this time,[262] which the apostle hopes will be at some point bestowed upon the condemned—just as an addict comes only after suffering greatly to a healthier awareness and the possibility of a new beginning. Only on the "Last Day" will it become apparent what was decided in the previous "days of the Lord."

This interpretation of the text depends heavily upon the way Paul here contrasts "flesh" and "spirit." It is not the distinction between (mortal) "bodies" and (immortal) "souls," for otherwise the resurrection of the body would be abandoned. Rather we find here the typical Pauline *soteriological dualism.*[263] The defective existence that is a consequence of sin (expressed in Greek terms: "in body and soul") should experience affliction and loss

262. I thus understand "day of the Lord" at this point in a more open way; cf. Atf V 3.
263. To understand this correctly, the reader again must read part C, especially C 3 and 4.

so that the "spirit" may be saved, that is, that its new existence in Christ may *not* perish. The individual concerned indeed belongs actively to the community and for that reason should, as one who is still marked by the *pneuma* of Christ, be saved. Thus Paul is wrestling for the *Christian existence* of this person, so that "on the day of grace" it will be rescued for him. The hoped-for return is aided by the fact that the "outer person"—now in the sense of his physical weakness (with body and soul)—experiences a death. The difference from 2 Corinthians 4:16: Paul voluntarily accepts such a "death of the outer person,"[264] while it is *inflicted* upon this other man. Thus in 1 Corinthians 5:5 the term "flesh" shifts from "sinful" to "weak" existence, while "spirit," perhaps approaching the anthropological term "vitality," here refers to the converted new existence. This corresponds to the fact that Paul in the immediate context, when he uses the term "spirit" in discussing himself, means the existence brought about in himself through the Holy Spirit (cf. the liturgical greeting: "and with your spirit"), whereas for its opposite now he does not choose "flesh" (that would rather mean: sinful existence), but rather "body": *to the extent* that he is a weak, physical man, limited in space and time.

As soon as we attempt to ponder the practical consequences here, we again recognize in Paul a realistic spiritual counselor. He expressly emphasizes that he is only concerned that *within the community* a distance be maintained by the fact that no one should "so much as" eat with the individual under discussion. This "so much as" indicates that "not eating together" is naturally not the only form, but a sort of extreme limit. On the one hand it excludes any closer contacts, but on the other hand allows certain social contacts—with this person, as with the "sinners" outside the community. They should not separate themselves "entirely" from sinners, that is, *only up to a certain point*. Without doubt an exclusion within the community is more difficult to maintain than one towards those on the outside. In spite of the unavoidable contacts, however, the individual concerned should feel the internal distance and not receive the impression

---

264. One should notice that this "corruption" is a progressive transformation of the sinful-mortal existence; cf. Ts 117–129; similar remarks apply here.

that his behavior is approved of—a problem that is especially acute in families. Thus the individual is not so-to-speak stricken from the rolls of the community; he remains a member, but one disapproved or "shunned." It is more an exclusion from the realm of spiritual protection than from that of the juridical boundaries, similar to being *"under interdict"* during the Middle Ages.

Touching the next point naturally Paul does not intend that the community should direct this "judgment" over an *action* also against the *person himself* (1 Cor 4:3f.; Rom 2). Thus the word "judge" must continually be interpreted from the context, here as also in Romans 14. Our text of course provides not the slightest justification for an inquisition or persecution of heretics. If "Satan" may harm the brother in the spiritually unprotected realm, even through "accidents" or similar things, this does not mean that Christians should lay a hand upon him or otherwise cause something to happen to him. However, according to the outlook of late Judaism, the role of "Satan" consists—similarly in Job (1:12)—in "testing" people under God's restrictive permission, whether this be so that the person may not be disturbed by this (1 Thess 2:18) and that his or her true character may come to light in the "tormenting" (2 Cor 12:7), or whether it be that the person be thereby converted: 1 Corinthians 5:5.

Once the events in the community and Paul's attitude have been made comprehensible, the question returns of why he reacts so strongly to a sexual infraction. In the center of this chapter, verses 7-8, stands the reference to the surrender *in love* of Jesus on the cross (as in 1 Cor 6:19). Possibly Paul is reacting emotionally here, not because he had something against sexuality, but because, if it is disfigured, human capacity to love becomes distorted. We see here the sensitivity of a loving heart acting somewhat like a mirror of "God's jealousy" (2 Cor 11:2).

4. Impurity During Courtship:
1 Thessalonians 4:1-8

Again Paul takes a position in a concrete case of unacceptable sexual behavior, and here it is certainly not a matter of "sex for sale." Thus the term *porneia* in verse 3 must have a wider meaning. It is disputed whether the expression "to acquire one's *skeuos,''* which is difficult to translate, means to acquire "one's own *body*" or "to win one's *wife.''* The word "to acquire" must then be stretched so broadly as to include the use of one's own sexuality, a new wooing in each case of the sexual affections of the marital partner, or the settlement of a marriage. At the same time *"to win her as a support''* means "to find a bride," to "win" her. Just as in 1 Thessalonians 4:10f. and 13 concrete cases from the community's life are considered, so also in 4:3-8 Paul is responding to a specific case: someone has apparently had sexual relations with an unmarried woman who already belonged—perhaps through engagement—to another, as a way to bind her to himself. Thus the entire passage is not about three themes often thought to be its subject (general lewdness, the nature of the marital relations, one brother defrauding another in business affairs, or similar things. cf. UT), but rather is the response to a single problem.[265] In the following text Paul is presuming that both the person himself as well as the community regard the conduct in question as *porneia.*

	UT		**PT**
For the rest, brothers, we ask and exhort you in the name of Jesus the Lord		1a	For the rest, brothers, we ask and exhort you in the Lord Jesus
You have learned from us how you should live to be pleasing to God		b	*that,* as you have received from us, how you should shape your life and be pleasing to God
and you do live that way;		c	—as you in fact live—
become therein even more perfect!		d	(that) you seek therein to grow further ("to become luxuriant").
You also know what exhortations we gave you as commissioned by Jesus, the Lord.		2	You know well what instructions (commands) we gave you through the Lord Jesus (invoking him, through his person).

265. Again, here only the results are reported. The special study announced in EuE 5 appeared for the first time in R. F. Collins, *The Thessalonian Correspondence* (BEThL LXXXVIII) 316-339: "Brautwerbung—das einheitliche Thema von 1 Thess 4:3-8," now also in Atf: IV. Since I did not there present my translation and the UT in contrasting columns, it follows here. On τὸ μή Witherington, 65, produces similar reflections, but he falters with the global concept.

UT		PT
For this is what God wishes: your holiness.	3a	According to this (following these instructions) it is indeed God's will—your holiness!—
This means that you should avoid lewdness, that each of you learn to have relations with his wife in a wholesome and respectful manner, not in passionate desire like the heathen who do not know God	b 4 5	*that* you hold yourselves back from unacceptable sexual relations, that each one of you know how to *win* his wife (his "support") in holiness and honor, —not in passionate desire like (in fact) the peoples who do not know God—
and that no one exceed his *rights* and *deceive* his brother in *business affairs,*	6a	*so that thereby* (in this process of courting) he does not mistreat his brother (to whom the fiancée already belonged) *and* defraud him (with regard to the fiancée),
for the Lord avenges all such things, as we *have already* said and showed you For God did not call us to live uncleanly, rather *to be* holy.	b c 7	because God avenges all such deeds, as we *had in fact* openly said and demonstrated to you. For it is not the case that God had called us *with* (on the basis of and with the consequence of) uncleanness, but *in* holiness.
Whoever rejects *this,* thus does not reject merely a man (the *apostle!*), but rather God who bestows upon you his holy spirit.	8a b	*For that reason,* whoever pushes someone aside, he pushes not a man (the *brother, rival*), but rather God, who directly gives **you** (and even this brother) his holy spirit.

It happens often enough today, as it did then, that someone steals away a man's intended, even in a small community. An especially effective way to do this is by having sexual relations with the woman in question. It thus does not require any wild imagination to conceive how such a situation could arise.[266] Verse 3a

266. Added to this is the fact that at that time the engagement was concluded through the κύριος, so that the bride did not always have an immediate love relationship with her betrothed; cf. above, A I 5 and A IV 1.

names the unifying catchword, which reappears in verse 8b as a framing device:[267] "holiness." It appears as a refrain also in 4:4 and 4:7; the word has, especially in contrast to "lewdness" and "uncleanness," a special connection with the physical,[268] which through the "holy" spirit (4:8) has become a temple (1 Cor 6:19! cf. 3:16f.). Holiness can be realized in the proper use of sexuality just as much as in the celibate life dedicated to God (1 Cor 7:14 and 34c). Thus because a Christian belongs with his or her entire nature, including the body and sexuality, to God, one should not profane one's body. An offense in this area is serious, not because sexuality is something dangerous or shameful, but because it *has been sanctified.*

Once the text has thereby been sufficiently clarified as a unit, it offers us some further material related to our question concerning Paul's understanding of sexual morality. Let us inquire one more time about *porneia.* The occasion for its coming up again is an inadmissable sexual relation[269] with another's fiancée. The general "instructions" to which Paul refers in 4:2 naturally did not contain the explicit injunction: "Don't steal another's fiancée"! What does Paul have in mind, if he here warns us against the danger of *porneia* (4:3b)? Not how a man deals with his own sexuality—as though Paul were here issuing a warning against masturbation;[270] also not that a husband in *his sexual relations* should behave "in holiness and honor,"[271] but rather that a man seeking a wife should not break into another relationship.

267. R. F. Collins, 424, brings this out clearly.

268. Cf. 1 Cor 7:14, 34 and 1 Cor 6; see above, notes 95, 173, 221; Atf VI toward the end. Also Procksch, the article "ἅγιος" in TDNT I 101, 110, sees in holiness more a "responsible morality" than "moral action," since the word, in spite of pronounced personalization in the New Testament, never lost its connection with the corporal and cultic, and thereby has the Christian way of being in view. The old Jewish marriage law is found in the tractate *qidduschim*—holiness!

269. Nevertheless, μοιχεία need not stand here; see Lövestam, 20f.; cf. above, A VI 1 and Atf VI 5.

270. No reference can be produced for such a meaning for πορνεία; see above, A VI 1 and Atf VI 5.

271. Lack of self-control would be formulated differently. It is also no longer a parallel to 1 Cor 7:2, as Collins, 426f., assumes, although there precisely—in contrast to 1 Thess 4—*marital* relations are what is being talked

The chief reason for this restriction is that the woman in question has already been promised to another through engagement (there was scarcely such a thing as "free love" before marriage).

To the extent that the context of this interpretation is attended to, individual conduct with one's own sexuality is not the topic, but rather the conditions attending relations between a man and a woman. For it goes without saying that where a sexual act is not allowed, everything that could lead to this should be similarly evaluated (Matt 5:28). Thus by *porneia* Paul is thinking neither of improper erotic experiences nor of a mental or experiential degeneration of the sexual instinct, but rather of specific relations. For this reason also we must be reluctant to translate *porneia* in this general command as "lewdness," lest we think thereby merely of passion in sexual relations. The Greek word is not commonly used in a pronouncement about the *style and manner* of the sexual act *in marriage*. For these reasons also we should reject the interpretation "to have relations in a respectful way" (UT).

Then why in 4:5 does there appear "not in passionate desire"? Could not this after all point in the direction of "having relations in an unbridled fashion"? But this would not fit with the *porneia* in verse 3, which rejects a specific objective act, and not just the style and manner. On the other hand, *epithymia*—which Paul always uses in a negative sense (Rom 7:7)—refers to uncontrolled *desire*, a "sinful *appetite*" or *"covetousness," degenerate instincts,* and not the objective elements of a sexual relation. Since according to our interpretation of 1 Thessalonians 4, it is a matter of a specific sexual act, here it is not the passionate style of the relation, but rather the *motivation* for such an act that is under discussion. This young man's desire is "covetous" because he is allowing himself to be stimulated by an (in itself) natural affection for this woman and is placing himself above the objective boundaries established by the brother. Thus "covetous" here refers not to the intensity of a legitimate[272] act, but rather to the motivation prompting an unrighteous act.

---

about! And κτᾱσθαι does not mean "possess," but "acquire"; cf. Witherington, 67. On this matter, see Atf IV 3.

272. H. Ulonska, "Christen und Heiden; die paulinische Paränese in 1 Thess 4:3-8," *ThZ* (Basel) 43 (1987) 216f., writes that Paul "has rejected

Kyrios in the quote from Psalm 94:2 (93:1) in verse 6b refers in the Septuagint to YHWH, the Lord. Since Paul usually uses *kyrios* to refer to Jesus Christ, H. Ulonska concludes that he here "confusingly . . . associates Christ with thoughts of revenge with reference to sexuality," and asks whether Paul "is aware of this improper application."[273] But, apart from the fact that here *kyrios* probably means "God" (see vv. 3 and 5), this is the same "Lord" who gives his Holy Spirit! It would be dangerous to shove the notion of vengefulness onto the God of the Old Covenant, and to exclude it entirely from the image of Christ and God in the New Testament (1 Thess 2:16; Matt 25:41; Rev 6:17). The *avenging God* does not appear here to "terrify" people about their sexuality, but rather is intended as a help for them to take seriously the commands and not to go astray carelessly in this matter. The entire passage is stamped by the effort to make the individual in question aware of the extent and consequences of his act, and thereby to rouse careless people and lead them to an awareness of their personal responsibility.

The *avenging God* no more suppresses sexuality as such than does the sixth commandment. It would be disastrous to so dis-

---

passionate desire between men and women" and intends therewith that "the erotic-sexual element of powerful desire" should be eliminated. However, he thereby falls into the same fatal confusion as Neidhart (see above, note 220), whom he quotes with agreement. And when U. continues that "passionate desire is for Paul in no sense neutral; rather, it finds its way into other areas: sufferings, breakdown, distress, beatings . . .," those would be substitute activities, the consequences of sexual repression. However Paul is an extremely sensitive person in all areas. His sexual desire does not show itself through compensatory activities, but dissolves through a deep love of Christ into a free desire "to be pleasing to the Lord." This willingness to bestow something in love—thus in this perspective, to "die"—is the basic structure of his spiritual life, and may be discerned in many aspects of his life. Suspicions concerning "sexual anxiety in Paul" (the reference is from H. J. Thilo, "Paulus und die Geschichte einer Entwicklung psychoanalytisch gesehen," *Wege zum Menschen* 37/1985, 2–14) rather raise questions about the psychoanalyst himself, whether he recognizes *what is specific to spiritual experiences,* is familiar with them from within, and as a consequence is in a position to set such phenomena in their proper relationship.

273. Ulonska (see previous note), 217. A study on κύριος in Paul is in preparation.

tort the saving love of Jesus, as if he ultimately retracts all of his prescriptions. Precisely because he takes the commandments seriously and therewith our sins, he gives himself up to death for us. This is a fundamental conviction of Pauline theology. Wibbing correctly points out that the vice lists in Paul, as in early Judaism, appear in a judicial context.[274] The fact that here the talk is of "avenging" fits also with that. However, as for what concerns the evaluation of marriage, it follows from the exhortation to "win your fiancée in holiness and honor" that Paul naturally views entrance into marriage—and consequently thus also marital relations—as something good and intended by God. In this sense our text reinforces 1 Corinthians 7:1-5,[275] although it is about a different "case."

5. Shame: 1 Corinthians 12:20-26

UT		PT
Thus there are many members, but only **one** body	20	Now, there (are) *indeed* many members, but still (they make up) **one** body.
The eye may not say to the hand: I have no need of you.	21 a	But the eye cannot say to the hand: "I don't need you,"
The head cannot say to the feet: I don't need you.	b	nor the head to the feet: "I don't need you";
On the contrary, it is precisely the members of the body which	22	rather the seemingly *lesser* (apparently in a weaker posi-

274. Wibbing, 114–117. But since for Paul the eschaton has already begun, the image of the judgment is transferred in part into the present; cf. above, A VI 3. Thus, although in 1 Cor 5:7 and 6:20, in order to warn against sexual offenses, Paul refers to the gift of Jesus' love on the cross (on which indeed God's judgment took place!), *here* he motivates directly with the *judgment* (cf. 1 Cor 5:12f.; 6:9; 6:7f.; Rom 1:32). This is no "misuse" (Ulonska, above, note 272). Spiritually it is rather to be understood as Ignatius of Loyola in the first week of the *Exercises* presents the "Consideration of Hell," with the justification that, if love does not suffice as a motive, a person may at least be kept from sin by fear.

275. Cf. again 1 Cor 7:2, see above, close to note 55. Admittedly I can now no longer agree with Collins, 426f., in seeing in 1 Thess 4 an "exhortation to marriage"; it is only an exhortation to purity in seeking a wife.

UT		PT
appear *weaker* that we cannot do without.		tion) members of the body are **necessary,**
Those which we regard as less *noble*	23 a	*as well as* the (members that) we consider to be of *less worth* (in a secondary position)
we accord all the more *honor,*	b	—to them we accord a greater *value* (to these we extend more considerate *attention*)—
and our *unseemly* parts	c	*as also to* our *shameful* (members)
we treat with more *decorum* (!)	d	—they *have* a *greater shyness* (a more pronounced sense of shame, so that they conceal, and thereby protect themselves);
while the *decorous* have no need of *such.*	24	on the other hand, our *non-shameful* (members) have *no need* (our—in a figurative sense—"more confident" members need no special attention or protected place).
But God has so *fashioned* the body	b	Yes (in fact) **God** has *mixed* the **body** together (an ordered plurality),
that he gave more *honor* to the *least* member,	c	by giving a greater *value* to the *more needy,*
so that no division *may arise* in the body,	25 a	so that no *conflict* (no disintegration) *might rule* in the body,
rather that *all* the members in *harmony may care for one another.*	b	but rather that the **members** might *feel that they share a common* interest.
For that reason, if **one** member suffers, all the others suffer *with it;*	26	*Hence,* if one member suffers, all the members suffer *together* (because of or for the same thing),
if a member is honored, all the others rejoice *with it.*	b	if one member is honored, all the members rejoice *with one another* (over this honor, knowing themselves to be honored thereby).

At 24b: Not "but" (UT); ἀλλά is used "in a more free way" in a "transition," "if the discourse is suddenly broken off and turns in a new direction." K.-G. II 286, 8; here with a turn to God's

activity that confirms what went before. At 26a: "Hence" rather than "and thus," consequent καί.

From the talk about "dishonorable" and "indecent members" (Conzelmann), which we today attempt to render differently (UT), our suspicion again crops up about a hostility to sexuality. However, after some grammatical and semantic corrections, this text also appears in a different light.[276] First of all, in verse 12f. Paul presents the comparison "human body—body of Christ," and then extends the imagery from two perspectives: from the point of view of those members who have a low self-esteem and who believe they are "losers" (14-19),[277] and from the perspective of those who appear to have done better and who are in danger of setting themselves above the others (20-24). There then follows in 25/26 a description of the goal: this is so that the body may be capable of living and acting. Finally in verse 27 begins the application of this image to "you as the body of Christ" (27-30).

It perhaps does not fit our perceptions that the hand is a "weaker" member compared with the eye, or that the feet are "weaker" compared with the head (UT). In any case Paul presumes that the eye and the head are "more important and of higher value"; and that the others are to that extent in a "secondary" position. He surely has in mind people in the community who appear to have more or less valuable talents. They should not feel themselves either superior or inferior, but rather learn something from the body's members. These realize that the members which appear "less" are "necessary."[278] Paul does not say "*more* necessary." If he or she has to, a person can live without

276. More details in EuE 485, here with some improvements for 12:22-25.

277. However, in v. 18 it is not the case that "the development of the image is interrupted," nor in v. 19 that "the differentiation is strikingly" emphasized (Conzelmann). It is rather the case that Paul is constantly speaking from the point of view of the Creator, and in v. 18 summarizes the intention of the Creator, something which, after the second half of the image in v. 24 is repeated like a refrain. Specifically, verses 12:12, 18, 24, 27 are the joints in this text, in which v. 27 introduces the application. Just as v. 14 introduces the first image, v. 19 introduces the second.

278. This is how ἀσθενέστερα should be translated; despite its greater physical power, the hand appears in the "weaker" position with regard to the more highly qualified eye.

a hand or eyes or feet, but not without a head. In that case are the feet really "necessary" (UT), compared to the head? In the original text it does not say so.[279] Admittedly Paul is not thinking of possible mutilation, but is presuming a healthy person who "needs" all his or her faculties. However, instead of fixing upon which members we classify as "less," we should *rather* concentrate upon their *necessity.*

> This principle is clarified in verse 23f. According to the nuance that one gives the specific terms, one sees behind them one or two types of members. In our view this is not an ascending list ("climax"), but rather a "definite division into categories" (cf. Conzelmann). For here the "necessity" of those members that "appear to be in a weaker position" is justified through *two specific "dependencies."* First, in each case the group in question is described (23a and c), then the behavior is named from which its "necessity" may be deduced (23b as well as 23d with 24). Both groups are placed in the same rank under the title "necessary" by "as well as . . . as also" *(kai . . . kai).* However, the asyndetical (!) reasons, as is often the case with Paul, are best put in parentheses. Finally, the "behavior" in 23b is the behavior of a person toward his or her members, while in 23d it is *behavior by the members themselves!*
>
> A primary reason for the difficulties lies in the fact that attention is not paid to this last-named distinction. Paul is thinking concretely in the first-named group (v. 23a/b) primarily of those he names "less," "hands and feet," in the second group (vv. 23d/24) rather of the private parts and all that we conceal. It is semantically important that the two roots τιμ- and σχημ- are not synonyms; rather the first corresponds to the worth or estimate, the second on the other hand to the realm of shyness or shame. However, in some translations it appears as though the one term leads naturally into the other. However, the unifying titles are ἀσθενέστερα and ἀναγκαῖα. The structure: Those members that appear the less should be viewed as "necessary," *as well as* those that appear of lower value
> —we bestow upon them greater attention

279. Ἀλλὰ πολλῷ μᾶλλον indicates a strong contrast which applies not only to the subject, but to the entire following statement: "But *it is rather* (much more) *the case* that the less important are *necessary:* one says this with more justice about them, than that the superior have no need of them."

as also the shameful parts (are necessary, for:)
—they have a more pronounced feeling of shame.

The necessity of the first group is indicated by the fact that we accord *more* attention to them,[280] bestow upon them greater notice and care, and thereby show that *we* consider them necessary. Paul is certainly linking up with verse 21a here; manicure and pedicure are a part of normal body care, for which even in those days there were salons and the baths. On the other hand the "shameful"[281] members realize in their own sensibility how they should conduct themselves: to protect themselves through concealment. Otherwise they could not carry out their proper function.

280. *Τιμάω* means first of all to assess, from which it is here used in an objective sense: for how "valuable they are considered," or how much "more value is attached to them": *περιτιθέναι τινί τι* is translated: "to bestow or lend something to someone" (M.-G. s.v. I 2); thus, not to "clothe" as with a garment! Because this was translated with "honor," the contrast to the supposedly "dishonorable" or "indecent" members was not seen.

281. This is the best way to render *ἀ-σχήμων;* in Latin, *pudenda.* The word's root means stance, behavior, appearance, constitution. "Without appearance" for us certainly has primarily a negative connotation: unseemly, ugly, improper; *εὐ-σχήμων*, on the other hand, "of good appearance, seemly, becoming" (cf. 1 Cor 7:35; see above, A IV 3). The field of reference is consequently primarily that of the aesthetic, public, and communicable. Therefore, if certain regions of the body are denominated *ἀ-σχήμονα* (probably all regions that are normally kept covered, and in the ancient world and in the Orient the sensitivity is rather stronger here than in the contemporary West), this implies no denial of the beauty of the human body—the Greeks were not prudish in these matters, and Paul avails himself of the current Greek expressions—rather, as our context shows, these members are viewed in contrast to those which are *εὐ-σχήμονα:* those which, like the head and the hands, move with complete freedom. The word play with *εὐσχημοσύνη* in the sense of shyness is obvious: the *εὐσχήμονα* have no need of *εὐσχημοσύνη*, that is, they require no special modesty or concealment with clothing. It is clearly a question of modesty. However, the Greek privative "*a*" becomes in English "in-decent," (Kürzinger) or "dis-honorable" (Conzelmann), with a negative valuation that the Greek does not have. The sense is well captured by "private" or "bashful" (something that in itself is *not* public, but which still has a positive connotation). It is specifically these members that "have" a feeling for what is proper; therefore, by *εὐσχημοσύνη* a spontaneous reaction is intended! Now the terms fit with one another, and no hostility to the body is expressed. The manner in which Paul introduces this comparison

They realize almost of themselves their need for protection—even when "we" on occasion do not realize it. They are, so to speak, automatically bashful, of their very nature, and that is an indication that they are very necessary. They "take care of" themselves as though all by themselves for the sake of the whole and for their special service. Both groups appear to be in a "weaker" position, but they are more "necessary" than "weak." One only has to look at the matter from the right angle.

Thus, in contrast to the preceding verse 21, in 23b no longer is the conduct of one group of members to another described, but rather that of the person as a whole toward individual members: *We* do them honor. Then in verse 23d this point of view is abandoned (so we cannot say: "we treat them" UT); rather, the behavior of individual members themselves is examined.[282] That is, although on the one hand *we* at first display greater attention to the less noticed members, the "bashful" members on the other hand *have of themselves* a greater feeling of shame. It is as though it lies in their very nature not to *wish* to show themselves openly.

To suspect this to be sexual repression would be to miss the main point. Paul is making no theological pronouncement about the feeling of shame, but is only *using* it as an illustration. It is as natural for him as for his audience[283] that they regard these members as in a "weaker" position compared with the others,

---

and the entire context manifest this sufficiently. The fact that private parts are covered does not indicate that they are dishonorable, but rather have received "from God value and esteem" (12:24; cf. Gen 3:21). And thereby they maintain their dignity.

282. Which naturally presupposes that "we" conduct ourselves in our members. But it is primarily a natural reaction of the members themselves. Weiss is correct: "they are already that way"; cf. Conzelmann, note 32. This need not be a stoic tendency, nor a "compensation" by which they receive "more" honor, but means only that *they themselves* have "a greater" modesty. The UT translation that *we* "treat" them in this way is not present in the text. Also, ἔχειν does not mean "to receive."

283. The image of the body is frequently invoked. Admittedly, comparisons specifically for this part are lacking in the material cited by Conzelmann. Has Paul simply added the private sphere as an independent part? In any case, the openness with which he does this speaks against the suggestion of sexual inhibition.

"who have no need of this." It is also not an indication of psychological inhibition, for shame is an essential human protection device to preserve for intimacy a space of trust and of personal love. Naturally these borders shift with the times and the culture, but humankind always develops a sensitivity for respect and personal worth and for what "is fitting." Paul here spontaneously invokes this area to give a graphic example of how the *body* constitutes a unity, and how therein each member naturally knows and accepts its own place. From that the members of Christ's body should learn something, both the "strong" and the "weak," those manifest in public and those hidden. Let us examine a little more of the psychological and theological background.

The theme that behind fallen humankind's feeling of shame lies the problematic of a distorted identity is another topic. Scarcely anyone emphasizes as clearly as Paul that through sin humankind has become disturbed and wounded in its deepest nature; he also indicates that in Gen 3:7–11:21 (cf. 2:25) this disorder is presented under the image of shame. To that extent shame does indeed have something to do with "embarrassing." For before this "they were naked and were not ashamed." After the Fall they were ashamed and hid themselves until *God* covered them—as a protection for their now fallen nature! A modern permissiveness which forgets this only shows thereby its depravity and self-righteousness. In any case, the cause for this concealment is not a contempt for the body, but rather sin as humanity's free act. Thus, what we have here is not an anthropological, but rather precisely the typical Pauline *soteriological dualism.*[284] Deep roots in the Old Testament indicate that sin—which consisted not in the sexual relations of the first humans, but rather in pride, the wish to be equal to God through "knowledge"—expresses itself in the feeling of shame: shame before one another (Gen 3:7) and shame before God (3:8ff.)—in that sequence. Thus the fracture in our interhuman relations points to a source in a deeper fracture in the relations between God and humankind.

However, that does not keep Adam—from the perspective of the author—from "knowing his wife" (4:1) and naming her "Eve, the mother of all the living." In their punishment the two are not required to give up sexual relations; however, all the areas of human life, inclusive of sexuality, are *burdened* thereby (3:16f.). Also along

284. Cf. above, close to note 263, and below, C 3 and 4.

"the path to one another" there grow up "thorns and thistles."
Thus God does not remove from humankind the shame which
broke out after their sin; however, God does overcome the "rip"
that runs through its nature, at least to the extent that God "covers"
humankind. Further, people who clothe themselves act according
to God's intention: they thereby protect the "delicate" members.
Shame is an indication of the humility of fallen humankind, while
shamelessness is a sign of arrogance.[285] Thus it is not surprising
that precisely in sexuality's capacity for shame Paul sees a specially
vulnerable region of humanity, a weak point where the tempter
can make the attack. Lapses in this region appear to him to be
in a special manner a signal of disorder in one's love for God and
love of neighbor. For that reason he reacts here rather powerfully, not "allergically," but rather "sensitively," perhaps also
"tenderly." A person who loves someone feels any shadow of a
disturbance in the relationship with the beloved as a sorrow. However, in 1 Cor 12:23 that constitutes only the background for what
is for Paul the obvious fact that humans have "bashful parts."[286]
The point of the comparison is simply that members with different relations to publicity and communication still belong without
difficulty to one another and work together in harmony.

Paul takes up again the overcoming of shame—admittedly in
another area of communication—in 2 Cor 3:1–5:10. Unlike Moses
he uses no "veil" to conceal himself from the community, for here
everyone, apostle and community alike, "regards in a mirror with
uncovered faces the glory of God" (3:18)—specifically, each sees
in the face of the other God's brilliance—so that both the community for the apostle, and the apostle for the community, becomes a mirror for God. Thereby both apostle and community
are the same sort of thing, they are "all reformed according to
the same pattern,"[287] so that no longer, as in the Old Covenant,
is there a fundamental difference between messenger and God's
people. See 2 Cor 4:1: "For that reason . . . we do not allow ourselves to become vexed (we do not become disgruntled), but have
renounced bashful concealment." Thus Paul does not withdraw

285. Cf. Zeph 3:3-5; Sir 4:21; 10, 10, 24f.; 41:16; Dan 9:7. One should
read the relevant portions of the Concordance.

286. Not "im-modest"; those that are "not-modest" are rather the other
members; see 1 Cor 12:24.

287. That thereby both of them are transformed "into the form *of Christ*"
is the objective foundation of this text, although it is not directly stated; cf.
Ts 341.

exasperated to his sulking corner, and does not use, like Moses—for whom it was proper—a veil, but rather "recommends himself through the revelation of the truth"; here that means: the truth concerning the gospel as well as the truth about himself. Therein flames forth his hidden "glory" *(doxa)* which is only perceptible in the spirit. "The hiddenness of shame" (4:2) thus refers to the shyness of the personal realm of intimacy that Paul here overcomes. Thus it is not: "We have renounced all disgraceful deceitfulness,"[288] as if earlier he had behaved that way, or that Moses had been "deceitful." Even if here the Greek word is *aischyne,* and not as in 1 Cor 12:23 *a(eu)schemosyne,* in both cases it is a matter not of disgrace, but of shame.

When the expressions from 1 Corinthians 12:23 are once made comprehensible through the normal feeling of shame, a further correction which we have carried out in verse 25 follows naturally, so that the overall development may be yet clearer: *merimnān* with the accusative does not mean that the members *"care for* one another" (UT)—previously there has been no discussion of this—but that *"they attend to the same thing in each other's interest,"* they occupy themselves with the same thing.[289] Eyes and hands, head and feet, are oriented toward the same business;

288. Thus the UT. For a justification and further context, see Ts 333–342. For the psychological aspect, see also Theissen 120–160, as well as 180: " 'The veil' symbolizes a border between the conscious and the unconscious." The contradiction that Theissen establishes here with regard to 1 Cor 11 will be resolved in our next chapter; see below, A VII 2. Only: in 2 Cor 3f. the "veil" is obviously an *image,* it is intended *figuratively;* for Israel and Paul it is no longer a matter, as with Moses, of removing a real veil, whereas in 1 Cor 11 one has always supposed a physical veil.

289. For more details, see EuE 482–485. There I still rendered ὑπέρ by "in each other's place, in order to avoid 'for one another,' " because the object of μεριμνᾶν is certainly τὸ αὐτό and not the other member. Taking one another's place would mean that the one assumes the problems of the other. However, in both cases it would have to say that the "one" member cares for "the others." If *all* the members are occupied ὑπὲρ ἀλλήλων, a better interpretation would be: "in the interests of" (Schwyzer II 521). In that case *all* would be conducting themselves for the benefit of *all the others:* in the interests *of one another,* and thus not one in the interests *of one other,* but rather in the interests of oneself *and* the others, specifically, in the common orientation that they all have—*and not in their own interests.*

otherwise the body would not be able to live. The eye sees a fruit, the feet walk toward it, the hand reaches out for it, the mouth eats it, etc. Only in the cooperation of the members can the body continue to exist, specifically when they pursue *together* the same business, the same affair, and the same goal. It is similar with the community: the individual member should not regard the other members, but rather the one God who is active in all of them, the one Lord whom they serve, the one Spirit which leads and harmonizes them (1 Cor 12:4-6), as well as the one service with which they are commissioned. For "*God* has mixed the *body* together" (12:24), God has arranged different kinds of *parts* ("members") together into *a single whole.*

In this way they can only survive if they do not degenerate into rivalry one with another, but rather concentrate *together* on the actual manner of life that has been given to them: "If one member suffers, all the members suffer with one another"; this means, then *they all* bear the pain together. And "if one member is honored, all the members rejoice with one another," which means that all the members then know that *this* honor applies to them all, and they rejoice—not "on account of the member that has been honored," rather over the *honor* that through the one member now extends to *all.* They do not conceive an ambition to achieve each its own distinction. And it is the same way with sorrow: it is of little use if one member feels sorry for another and has "compassion" for it. If a member of the body feels pain, the others do not turn to it attentively, rather they all feel the *same pain* with it.[290] They are thus not oriented toward that member, rather they suffer the *pain* with it, carry the same burden; they stand together, either to fulfill the demand or to fend off attack. Their activity is thus objectively directed toward the actual task before them, and *each carries out its own job in this regard,* each in its own way, as is appropriate to that member's function.

---

290. Admittedly this is close to the idea that in that case the healthy organs also care "for the sick" organs, or the stomach for the body, etc.; however, this would have to be expressed differently (see the previous note), and is also not the main problem. If one "exalts itself over the others," the correction for this does not consist in its caring for the others (perhaps still from a superior position, or "in spite of" its lower position?), but rather

In the same way God has compounded the "community" into the body of Christ; God has not given the same task to everyone, but rather has posed to them as members a common commission, to which they must continually be attentive, to see whether what they are doing really contributes to the life and completion of the whole (ch. 14). If not, it must give way within the community; one should then forego initiatives that for the moment are not accepted or positively validated by the others (14:19, 28-32). No one will attempt to wrest another's "role" for himself or herself, but rather "all concern themselves in the interests of one another with the same common task" (12:25).

If thus everyone in their own way and according to their function carries out the life processes, and carry together the joys as well as the sorrows, then the "weaker" and "more lowly" members will no longer have any inferiority feelings, and the "bashful" are no longer tempted to behave like the others (*for them, that would be shameless*); rather, they naturally accept their concealed location, without envying the others their exposed position. The differentiation in unity thus also becomes clear in that we honor those members which appear less important; and those that are hidden due to their natural shyness do not at all desire the public exposure of the others. For it is *God* who has so arranged it; it is still the same Spirit who is active in all of them, and the same Lord whom they all serve (12:4-6, 13, 18, 24, 27).

Working backwards, one may now apply the pronouncements about the body of Christ again to the human body that has become disordered by sin (although the discussion in 1 Corinthians 12 does not do this, for here the body is regarded positively as a model): God's Spirit overcomes the division and tension (cf. 12:25) that is the experience of sinful humans as a whole, also including their sexual situation. The Holy Spirit helps us toward an integration and an identity, so that members in a weaker position lose any feelings of inferiority; the head no longer disdains them, any spiritualistic "contempt for the body" is overcome, and the shameful parts know themselves to be honored in their contribution to the entire body, without thereby having to abandon their concealed or intimate position.

---

that it *gives up* the comparison with the others and directs itself to their common project.

VII. Women in the Community

While the regulations concerning sexuality are more or less the same for men and women, other texts take up in particular the behavior of women within the framework of the newly established Christian "assembly." One most likely thinks first of the commands about keeping quiet and wearing a veil in church: 1 Corinthians 11 and 14. Yet how are the statements: "yes to prophetic utterances" but "no to speaking in the community" compatible? And how do these fit into the overall picture of the principal Pauline letters? Must we dismiss 1 Corinthians 14:34-35 as perhaps a "gloss" by a post-Pauline hand? Is this likely on the basis of an overview of the Pauline letters which adduces a whole sequence of further indications on the place of women in the community? All these positions have been defended.

1. Base Line of the Contemporary Discussion

Each age reads the Bible with its own eyes. The numerous other, for the most part, positive references to women in the Pauline letters were for a long time largely ignored; they seemed to fit without difficulty into both the social-patriarchal, as well as the ecclesial-hierarchical viewpoint, and an elevated estimate of women is thoroughly compatible with this understanding. For instance, it would be a distortion to depict the Middle Ages as merely a period of oppression and in every era there were important women. In the first centuries no one took offense when in Romans 16:1 a woman is called a "deacon" (Vulgate: *in ministerio ecclesiae*) and in Romans 16:7 a woman is grouped with the "apostles." People realized that she did not belong to the "Twelve," and that consequently the term apostle had to be taken here in a broader sense. John Chrysostom considered the notion of a female apostle not at all impossible. When female deacons are referred to in the *Didascalia* in the fourth century,[301] contemporaries realized what this concretely meant. Nowhere is there any

---

301. Not "deaconesses" in the sense of charity workers, but helpers in the instruction and baptism of women; but also not female baptizers! Thraede, 99: "Aid and help with baptism were already traditional functions of Jewish women."

trace of a discussion about whether women should have access across the board to the same functions as male deacons.

In the contemporary literature, which has, indeed, thoroughly examined this history, up until now I have not found any evidence of a serious discussion at any period on whether women had or should have access to the priesthood.[302] It is common to explain this with the fact that the Church and theological writing are for the most part dominated by men, but it would be too simple to attribute this merely to either a conscious or perhaps unconscious repressive mechanism. Was not this topic of interest to women? Catherine of Siena and Teresa of Avila may have used sharp words to criticize the leadership style of the men guiding the Church in their day, but are there indications that they thought women should also have access to these positions?

Whether no one thought such things, or simply dared not express them, the fact is that it took until the twentieth century for this question to receive a serious discussion. Up to that point all the relevant passages in the New Testament were read by all the denominations in such a way as to seem more or less compatible with the prevailing view of the Church. There was of course a high estimate of women in the New Testament, but it was restricted to those functions which, in the life of the Church throughout the centuries, were accorded to women. This goes so far that, despite an existing discussion tending to a contrary position, in Romans 16:7 Lietzmann prefers the masculine form Junias "in view of the following statements (title 'apostle')"; Käsemann and Schlier in their commentaries, as well as the UT, do not mention the possibility of a female name; Aland also places the corresponding masculine locution in the text. Phoebe encounters the same fate; she is still often referred to as simply a "deaconess," "hostess" (Zink), or "servant" (UT, the Munich NT).

But how far one is thus understanding the objective basis correctly, or rather, without admitting it, simply allowing one's "obvious" convictions, really "prejudices," to slip in is an open question. Is it just that people were too lazy to discuss the change in the corresponding terms? The role of women in the Church seems fixed. However, since in our examination of 1 Corinthians 7, we came to significant results that are contrary in the received

302. More on this below, D II and D II 11.

interpretation, we should be open to new ideas on this topic as well. At the same time, because the interest that is guiding our research lies in examining the position of women, we should be careful not to let this interest color the historical-critical material. We shall distinguish clearly between what the texts say in themselves, and what may be extracted from them by further hermeneutical reflections. We will take up this last part chiefly in part D.

Against the traditional consensus, a position has gradually formed which today attributes to the women of the first generation in the Church a far wider competence than before was credited. What opened the way for this interpretation was, among other things, the theses that Ephesians/Colossians as well as 2 Thessalonians and the Pastoral Letters were not written by Paul; in fact, some of them must be dated very much later.[303] The more these letters and also Acts appear to be distanced from the main letters, the more is one inclined to place a deep trench between them, with one result being that a text like 1 Corinthians 14:33b-36 may be excluded as inauthentic; on the other hand, statements like Galatians 3:28 or Romans 16:1, 7 may be read so strongly as implying "equality" that the household codes and the Pastoral Letters can only seem a "decline." One is then in possession in the text itself of new evidence for *Frühkatholizismus,* and is therefore inclined to elevate at least the early Paul to a height which he—unfortunately—was not himself able to maintain; for there then remains, for example, the annoying passage in 1 Corinthians 11:2-16, which some remove for this very reason. There was indisputably a historical decline in this question until far into the following centuries; however, are the contrasting images of life within the first century from contemporary exegesis historically accurate? In this book we can only follow up one lead on this question, but at the same time situate it within the larger framework of the entire New Testament corpus.

Research into the role of women in the early Church has brought together many new and important observations.[304] For

---

303. Cf. above, Introduction.

304. Here we have especially in mind (consult the bibliography) the works of Kalsbach, Stendahl, Boucher, Thraede, Thyen, Brooten, G. Lohfink,

simplicity's sake we will first present two contrasting positions, and then, after an examination of the text, attempt to reach a conclusion.

Elisabeth Schüssler Fiorenza speaks of a "Lukan silence" about women in the early Church. "Nowhere in his work does Luke picture women as missionaries and preachers. Rather he stresses that women . . . support or oppose Paul's missionary work." By contrast, in Paul himself women appear "not merely as rich patronesses of the Christian missionary movement but as prominent leaders and missionaries who—in their own right— toiled for the gospel. These women were engaged in missionary and church leadership activity both before Paul and independently of Paul. Without question they were equal and sometimes even superior to Paul in their work for the gospel" (p. 161). The dispute mentioned in Acts 6:1 was about the fact that the Hellenistic women "in the daily service" were not given access to the liturgical function of breaking the bread.[305] The fact that Acts ignores the role of women as missionaries and leaders in the (house) churches is a sign of the "androcentric character" of this work, whereas in fact women functioned as leaders both among the itinerant missionaries and in the house churches.

The practice of "missionary partners" in the Jesus movement was taken over by the Christian missionary movement and "permitted an equality between men and women in the labor of the missions"—whether as married couples or in an ascetic society made up of men and women. Only the five *men* mentioned were subordinate to Paul, while the female coworkers whose names are known were not "helpers" or "assistants," but worked with him "on an equal basis." Phoebe's tasks were not limited to those

---

Klauck *(Hauskirche)*, Schüssler Fiorenza *(Memory)*, Halkes, Dautzenberg, L. Schottroff, Weiser and Kruse.

305. E. Schüssler-Fiorenza 165f.; for further details, 167–175. One wonders how this became different through the choice of seven male deacons; was this something Jewish women would normally have done, and more besides? Kruse, 111: " 'Table service' does not mean preparation of food or service at table (that was something the widows themselves could do), but rather the provision and distribution of resources. Only for that were seven men necessary." Whether to that number the wives and children left by the apostles and other disciples also belonged is worthy of reflection.

prescribed for women by the surrounding culture; rather, she was the "official teacher and missionary in the church at Cenchreae . . . entrusted with preaching and tending churches." If Paul does not call her an "apostle," this is to avoid the possibility that she might be regarded as "an apostle of the church at Cenchreae," for such people had only a limited commission. The common practice was for missionaries to be sent out in twos, although Paul's custom was unusual in that he only took male coworkers with him (1 Cor 9:5). An echo of this practice of "missionary partners" is found in the "Acts of Paul and Thecla." (However, this would constitute an exception to the Pauline custom.) According to W. Ramsay, Thecla is "the model of the female Christian teacher, preacher, and baptizer; her story was invoked at the beginning of the second century to justify the rights of women to teach and baptize." Admittedly one notices that even in this work in its present form, a male writer could not allow a woman to function "as an itinerant missionary who preaches the gospel."

As for what concerns the house communities, according to Schüssler Fiorenza these gave women the opportunity for preaching and for liturgical worship, including both social and Eucharistic table service. She rejects the distinction between "private and public spheres" to the extent that in the house churches the "public sphere was *in* the house and not outside [it]." And since in the general assembly of all the house churches of a city as a "union of equals" women exercised leadership roles, this would cause tension with the "traditional patriarchal household structures."

To Theissen's thesis that the "Christian missionary movement . . . was not in conflict with its society but was [as a love patriarchy] well integrated into it," Schüssler Fiorenza counters that the "model" for the young Church was not the patriarchal family, but rather the "egalitarian community structures of private collegia or cultic associations." In short, "women were among the most prominent missionaries and leaders in the early Christian movement. They were apostles and ministers like Paul, and some were his coworkers. They were teachers, preachers, and competitors in the race for the gospel. They founded house churches and . . . their authority and ministry were neither restricted to women and children, nor exercised only in specific feminine roles and functions" (pp. 183f.).

Similarly, Luise Schottroff writes: "Phoebe, Prisca, and Junia had similarly international roles as evangelists, just as Paul himself did. . . . Paul did not see himself as the main bearer of the early Christian mission but as one among many . . . and he viewed himself that way—not as the boss of a host of coworkers with unique significance for the gospel."[306]

These are substantial claims erected upon a modest material basis. On the other hand, one is reminded that, at that time, there were indeed "specific female roles and functions"; it must then be demonstrated that women also took over "specific male functions."

S. L. Love reads the same texts completely differently. He places them within the "macrosociological perspective" of an urban lifestyle within the framework of an agrarian culture. In such a context the role of women may be summarized under three aspects: care for the household, bearing children, and meeting private, in contrast to public, behavioral expectations. In such cultures, "equality and freedom" are "social anachronisms." The "subordinate status of women was accepted without question in Jewish, Greek, and Roman society." Language was "father-centered," as were family trees; "heads of households" were males whose dominant position was patent in the conversion of entire families ("houses"); the Church as household or family of God was synonymous with kingdom, nation, city, and temple. "Subordination to authority" was a "characteristic feature of household structure and conduct." If occasionally "women functioned as leaders of Second Testament households," that was by way of exception (we shall return to this): most probably we are dealing here with wealthy widows—these two factors would explain the situation. Finally, the household code was also father-centered. As for motherhood, Love refers to 1 Tim 2:15 and 5:14; the impulse to celibacy in this kind of cultural environment was "irregular."

Finally, Love lays particular emphasis on the distinction between public and private behavior models: woman's sphere is the private realm of the home, while the public sphere belonged

---

306. L. Schottroff, 95ff. [37–38 of English]; for a response, see below, A VII 4 (4)-(6) and A VII 5.

to men. Love finds this principle fully maintained in Acts, the Pastoral letters, and 1 Peter, but also in 1 Corinthians 11 and 14. While he concedes that, because of the esteem for celibacy (1 Cor 7:34-40), there were in Corinth a disproportionately large number of unmarried women—according to our research, really only a few—still, even in this situation "a woman usually is in a direct subordinate relationship to a man." I would like to add to this: and even if a wealthy woman had a greater influence than a poor man, and a widow or unmarried woman could have a greater significance in the community than an ordinary male, nevertheless within the family sphere these women would of course retain their specific feminine positions and assume neither there nor in society roles that were appropriate for men. All this is opposed to the position of Schüssler Fiorenza.

Besides this, along with Trompf (213), Love insists that leadership patterns "in all known ancient Mediterranean cultures reflect male dominance." Even if the "church experience at Corinth may reflect the dialectical social tension current in Greco-Roman culture"—where there were emancipatory impulses—"practices which blurred the public/private sexual role distinctions needed to give way to the more widespread existing cultural demands. The social readiness was not there" Also with regard to 1 Corinthians 11 and 14, Love believes that "social customs ultimately prevailed." Thus the New Testament as well gives "a consistent witness to the separation of public and private role behavior for women." Even if, in the latest discussion by Scroggs, Schüssler Fiorenza, and others, the claim is made with reference to Gal 3:28 that "an equal status for women is evident in the earliest stages of the church's life (Jesus and Paul), manifest in their public participation with men," their contribution must still be classified as similar to the service by the women around Jesus (Luke 8:1-3).

If on occasion women enjoyed special freedoms, perhaps as the leaders of house communities (did they really have such?) it corresponded to the broader sphere belonging to women of the upper classes; however, with regard to married women, this should be seen as a reflection of the status of their husbands—even if publicly Aquila retreats behind his wife Priscilla. Philippians 4:2-3 is also evidence of the fact that women "carried out their work in collaboration with men; there is no discussion of any specific public duties." Even if a prophetess is accepted as bearing divine revelation, she remains socially and ecclesially restricted in her role and does not take on a "leadership function." Thus according to Love the changes in relationships in the New Testament —love and mutual submission—were carried forward within a context of the limits set by an agrarian social order. He finds no rift between the principal Pauline and the so-called deutero-Pauline letters.

We should be just as cautious about drawing a line between Judaism and Christianity. Often a Judaism that was antagonistic to women was made to function as the dark background to make the (social!) liberation of early Christianity more brilliant. In opposition to this, Madeleine Boucher maintains (52–55) that an equality between men and women "was first taught in Judaism." "There seems to have been little if any difference in the status of women [in Judaism and Christianity]." Luise Schottroff adopts a similar position (98–99). To the extent that it touches social behavior, this is from the outset the more probable; the impact of the Christian message upon social structures is indeed no sudden event. Further, Jesus lies in fact within the tradition of a woman-friendly wing within Judaism. Exceptional personalities at all times have distanced themselves from mechanisms of social oppression.

The key to this conclusion in Love's most recent work is, in concert with the entire recent discussion, an attention to the macrosociological structure of society. As a matter of fact, neither Jesus nor Paul took it as their immediate goal to change social structures, but rather, within their historical framework to proclaim the unconditional love of God, the forgiveness of sins, and a new empowerment through the Spirit of God. If our contemporary social and political conclusions are too quickly linked with this message, or even substituted for it, we will be exposed to the same critique with which one could reproach the prince-bishops of the Middle Ages, or a missionary activity carried out for purely political reasons. God is the God of history; God respects the laws of historical development without for all that declaring any given stage of historical development completely good, or attempting to arrest history at that level.[307] Let us then examine the texts thoroughly to see what pronouncements they do in fact make,

---

307. In that sense K. Rahner, 296–299; see below, D II 2.

and further, what conclusions may be deduced from them, and which not.

2. The Veil as a Sign of Subordination?: 1 Corinthians 11:3-16

How much struggle has this text occasioned! Frequently barriers have been thrown up against women by invoking this text as an excuse, or else they were obliged, at the extreme, to fix a piece of paper on their heads when they entered a church, should they not have a scarf with them. As with our previous text, 1 Corinthians 12:23, here it seems also to be basically about "shame." Indeed, women must even protect themselves from lecherous angels! Or is the veil rather an indication that they stand under some man's authority? Since the term also applies to unmarried women and to widows, it must have been a matter of general familial or rather communitarian (and not only marital) subordination. In any case, woman appears to be only a *reflection of man,* and not an *image of God* in her own right, as the man is. For she is indeed fashioned "for" man, who is her superior (how does this fit with "re-flection"?). This is justified not only from creation, but also from the relation to Christ. Admittedly, tensions in the text indicate that Paul himself is not sure of his argumentation. Thus in verse 13 he appears simply to dismiss all earlier biblical observations, invokes "nature" in an unusual way, and finally concludes in verse 16 with a somewhat gruff authoritarian defense. In a previous work *(Antifeminismus bei Paulus II),* we have explored in detail all these questions; here we will only give a short presentation of the results.

The background to the apostle's exhortation is the fact that occasionally in the midst of the prayer assembly a woman who was praying or speaking a prophetic word would loosen her hair. This would have a powerful effect. With the Greeks it was not unknown for prophets and prophetesses, perhaps as a way to break the tension of the ecstatic experience or to underline the importance of their prophetic roles, to sometimes loosen their hair and gesticulate in an animated fashion, so that their hair would sweep rather impressively across their faces and necks. Paul criticizes this practice in *both men and women* (!); however, since men at this time only seldom wore their hair long, he describes their misconduct differently: lack of self-control and pomposity may show itself with a male if he "preoccupies himself with his head." On the other hand, women at that time customarily wore their hair long; it was, at least with a married woman, braided or piled high on her head. Thus, normally a woman's head was "covered" by her hair (not her "hair covered with a veil"). This expression would not fit the male situation since he did not wear his hair in a pompadour. Moreover, at all times there are some men who no longer have any hair to "cover" their heads; thereby a speaker who has more or less hair, or long or short hair, may still adopt a powerful stance or make a dramatic impression.

Since gesticulation with the head while at prayer or prophetic speech is at all times out of place, it becomes questionable whether Paul here, as is often suspected, is thinking at all about the social position of women, since braided hair is a sign of a married woman. Also, the comparison with "those who have been shorn" does not allow us to conclude to a provocation of the men, but rather highlights the unattractive aspect of an unkempt woman (*aischron* = ugly), which also damages her reputation. At that point she is no longer *doxa*—"beauty and splendor." In fact, the occasion for Paul's remarks seems to have been misconduct by *women,* since the men do not receive any such reprimand, although such behavior would be equally reprehensible in them.

The affective reaction of the apostle is interesting, as is also the way in which, in authentic rabbinical fashion, he tries to justify his position in a biblical and theological fashion. Because it is about a woman's "head," he seeks out biblical and theological passages in which this catchword appears, and plays with two associated meanings which we may best capture in English by *head* (physiological, organic) and *source* (an interpersonal relationship). In Greek, however, the same word, *kephalē,* is used for both. This word does not mean "leader," implying a superior position, but rather indicates a relation to one's origin (as: the spring is the "head" [source] of the river). Paul is here thinking of the second account of creation (Gen 2:21f.). He is also presuming that in questions concerning this type of behavior his audience would feel the same way as he, and would therefore both understand and accept his argumentation. He himself grew up in a Greek-speaking environment and knows well what people in such a cultural sphere would feel to be proper or improper. Further, we are not here talking about all women, but only of a few who in his opinion lack a sense of tact.

The text[308] (1 Cor 11:3-16): [3]But I want you to understand that Christ is the head of each man; the man, however, is the head of a woman, and God is the head of Christ. [4]Just as any man who, while praying or prophesying, *makes motions with his head,* dishonors **his** head (namely Christ), [5]in the same way a woman who while praying (out loud) or in prophetic speech (in the assembly) *loosens her hair,* dishonors **her** head (namely, the man); it is indeed the same as if she had been shorn. [6]That is, if a women *does not cover her head* (with her hair), she should indeed cut off her hair. However, if it is unattractive (disfiguring[309]) for a woman to cut her hair (shorter) or to shave her head, then she should *have her head covered* (with her hair arrangement).

[7]As you know, a man is not required to *keep his head covered,* since he is the image and radiance (manifestation, visible brilliance) of God; however, the woman is the radiance ("brilliance" and glory) of the man. [8]Indeed, the man *is* (exists) not from the woman (the masculine from the feminine nature), but rather the woman from the man (the feminine from the masculine); [9]it is also known that a man was not **created** *because of* the woman, but rather a woman *because of* the man. [10]For that reason a woman is obliged *to keep her head under control,* because of (the presence of) the angels.

[11]Moreover, neither (is) woman *without man* nor man without woman **in the Lord**; [12]for just as the woman (Eve) **out of** the man (Adam), so also the man (Christ) **through** the woman—the whole, however, from **God.**

[13]Judge for yourselves! Is it proper that a woman *with her hair loosened* (in public) should pray to God? [14]Nature *also* does *not* teach you that it is disgraceful (a disparagement) for a man *to let his hair hang long,* [15]but *on the other hand* it is beautiful (an

308. For the contrast to UT, see Atf II, 54ff.; here we present a smoother, more readable text, with the usual emphases; cf. above, after note 7.

309. This seems to be more correct than what we said in our first edition (cf. also Atf 105, note 189). Jerome criticizes some so-called "virgins" for letting their hair fall down under a carelessly-knotted band (more a sign of disorder than of sex appeal); and he reads 1 Cor 11:14 in this way: "men wear their hair in long curls"; cf. J. Steinmann, *Hieronymus—Ausleger der Bibel* (Cologne, 1961) 126.

embellishment) for women to do the same; for the hair is given (to all!) *as a cover* (for protection).

[16]Moreover, if someone disputes this: **we** do not have such a custom, nor do the communities of God.

As we see, this passage now falls together and has a clear development. Let us examine the text one more time. Verse 3: that "head" here indicates a relation to one's origin is obvious, both from the semantic material and in the relation of Christ, the Son, to the Father, as well in the genealogy from Genesis 2:21 (v. 9). From this verse 8 derives "being from the man" —also a relation of origin. It is developed in a different way in verse 12, so that the "without" in verse 11 also must have in mind the actual *descent* (similar to Eph 1:10, 22; 4:16). Finally this development is confirmed through the counterpart "radiance" (v. 8). On the other hand, here there is certainly no "relation of dominance," in that the Father does not "dominate" Christ (who voluntarily subjects himself to him, 1 Cor 15:28).

One question remains, and that is: in what sense is Christ the origin of the man? Since the thought here is progressing typologically, Christ is seen as a sort of "second Adam" and thus as in a special way the fundamental model for the man. But in that case would not women have their fundamental model in Eve, and subsequently in a new way in the mother of the Messiah? Precisely such an interpretation is hinted at indirectly in verses 9 and 11, but is not developed at least with the words "head" and "radiance," for these terms have already been reserved for the relationship between the partners. Thus Paul is not here interested in women in their relation to some sort of "mother of the species"; thus he only uses the catchword "head" for the comparison of the man with Christ. This builds an associative background for the entire argument. Paul places this sequence at the beginning of his answer (v. 3), because he intends to say more later concerning the woman's "head." Thus the admonition for behavior derived from this thought sequence runs: "Each one should regulate his or her behavior in a manner appropriate to the origin."

Now, verses 4-6 offer no more difficulties as far as their content, in that a preoccupation with the hair as a matter of fact is not appropriate and should be criticized in both women *and in men.* This is not evidence for any antipathy against women, but rather should be understood and applied to the situation. However, the justification is different—and this again requires an explanation. Paul reproaches any such conspicuous behavior in a man by referring him to his relation to Christ, in a woman by referring her to her relation to her man, since in each case the catchword "head" suggests this relation to him! And he is indeed thinking not primarily of a *married* woman, but rather has in mind all, including unmarried women, since the following reflection does not actually begin with marriage, but rather with the basic relationship of the sexes, archetypically represented by Adam and Eve. Is that the reason that Paul thinks of woman as transmitted from God *through* the man? Does Paul then believe that woman has her origin in Christ only through the "mediation" of the man?

Verse 7 appears at first to confirm this suspicion. Still, it does not say: "the man *should not cover* his head" (UT). How could one otherwise reconcile such a command with the head coverings of the priests in the Temple or the men's prayer shawls? Perhaps the law was not yet in effect which obliged men to wear the Kippa in the synagogue; however, as we saw, as regards women, this discussion is not about an extra head covering, but rather about covering the head with *the hair!* And *to that* is the male "not obligated." *Katakalyptesthai tēn kephalēn* retains this meaning in different contexts, and so also here. Moreover, the other norm for men is grounded not through their similarity to Christ, but through their origin in God. They are indeed the "image and glory" of God. "Image" means the same as visible form in which what is invisible "discloses" and renders something of itself sensible; *doxa* moreover also lies in a genealogical tradition: the man is (in pure analogy) the expression, manifestation, and visible form of the invisible God, as though transparent to God's "radiance."

Is then the woman *not* a locus of God's revelation? Why is she only the "radiance of *a man*"? Does Paul deliberately intend here to oppose Genesis 1:27 by saying that the woman is *not* an "image of God"? One notices that he does *not* say that she is an "image" of the man. Thus, in the continuation of this comparison in verse 9 he deliberately lets this term drop, since the woman—naturally—is *also* an "image" of God! *Doxa*/radiance on the other hand is the reverse side of the relation to one's origin in one's "head"—which again does not deny that ultimately as an image she is also a radiance of God. At this point the most abstruse and far-fetched ideas are attributed to Paul. But then it is not noticed that he here (in typical rabbinic or "Pauline" fashion!) is "playing" with word and with image associations. In his perspective, woman has an added quality which he especially emphasizes here (Closen speaks of a partial opposition on the basis of a common foundation, for example Israel and humanity: *Sünde,* 172-184; Atf 81): she is (also) the "glory" of the man, and in that sense related to "her head"; she is not the "reflection" of the man (in German, *Abglanz* [UT]), rather in relation to him she is "embellishment, beauty, pride"; further, in relation to creation, she is in a certain sense the "culmination, realization, and highpoint" of humanity, while the man is the "origin." They belong together! If they damage this relationship, they dishonor simultaneously themselves and their partners. We may not be accustomed to this manner of thinking, and it certainly also reflects a patriarchal outlook; but this type of "play" in Hebrew anthropology is far from both chauvinism and from an anxious, narrow dogmatism. We will return to this.

Verses 8 and 9 seek to further justify in a biblical fashion this head-radiance relation as the relationship to one's origin. For at least in the second creation account, there is a *sequence* in the process of creation. This perspective is related to Adam and Eve only in verse 9, where the verb "he was created" is emphasized by being placed toward the front. On the other hand, verse 8 first adds another characterization of the *ongoing, essential relation* between man and woman, which up until now has been the topic of discussion. *Estin* is commonly translated by "comes from" (UT), but this is an expansion (supposedly in accord with the author's intentions); however, this cannot be justified by the semantics of the word.

Thus, let us stick with: "The woman *is* from the man," not the other way around. What can this mean? There is no "radiance, brilliance" in itself, but only as possessed by a subject, which is thus an "origin," but in another sense than through generation. Thus the man "is" a continuous manifestation of God, not only in the act of creation, and the woman is a *permanent* "radiance" of the man. However, *Kabod/doxa* is an extremely personal category: "radiance of a person," importance, worth, and representation of his/her essence (2 Cor 3/4). This category does not imply any temporal succession, but rather a simultaneity of activity and effect, like "lamp" and "illumine," spring and stream (we recall the expression: "the spring is the 'head' of the stream"), head and (not body, but rather) glory. In this way the woman "is from" the man, lives in a certain fashion continually from him and in relation to him; that at least is how the linguistic images formulate it. And from this Paul draws the conclusion: she should not dishonor her "head = origin" by a disordering of her "head."

Moreover, Paul now sees this timeless, essential relation of the two as grounded in the historical and fundamental succession in the act of creation from Adam's "side." Otherwise the "*kai*/also" would not have a proper sense; for only *now,* in verse 9, does a consideration of the process of creation appear! This does not mean that the woman was created "for" him (UT) (how would this fit with the image of "brilliance"?), but rather that *on the basis* of the man she was designed and fashioned by God: flesh of his flesh = of his nature. Paul is concerned about the sequence: the beginning[310] in this perspective is the man, not the woman, and that relationship is irreversible.

Verse 10 presents several riddles. However, *exousia* means neither "veil" nor "sign that she stands under an authority," nor a sign that she has autonomy over her own head, as some have more recently tried to interpret it. *Exousian echein* means: "to maintain control over the head, to hold the head in order"—and not to cast it into disorder by loosening one's hair. Here a circle completes itself in the immanent interpretation of the text. The expression confirms in its own way once again that previously it was a matter of a "lack of control" with regard to the head (and indeed by both men and women, as v. 14 will once again show), and with the woman that this has something to do with the "glory-head relation." One could ground the whole affair much more simply on the natural feelings of propriety, as Paul

---

310. This is what Chrysostom writes: "God gave to all Adam as their single head—μίαν ἅπασιν ἔδωκε κεφαλὴν τὸν Ἀδαμ; then why were not all made from the earth?" PG 61:289. On Witherington, 58: not only a river, but people also may have a "source."

will also do in verse 13; however, the rabbi loves a profound, biblically stamped anthropological metaphor. Can we hold it against a man like Paul who enjoys wordplay—even if this has caused us serious headaches? We will later want to ponder the point that this anthropological model should not without further consideration be transmuted into dogmatic pronouncements.

However, the woman is obligated to a proper comportment for still another reason: no lascivious evil angels lie in wait to see if there will be some "nakedness" here (*aischron* = ugly, unattractive, and hence worthless; but not "sex appeal"); rather, it is the good angels who in a certain sense are the protectors of public order during a worship service. Like Catholic parents who point to the tabernacle as a way to instill appropriate conduct in their children while at church, Jewish parents probably invoked the presence of angels to their children when they brought them with them into the synagogue. One should not misread the unforced style of a Jewish worship service as a sign of irreverence. There are fixed rules of conduct which are the expression of a deep reverence before the Tora and ultimately before the presence of the All Holy One. Indeed, since God's name remains unmentioned, it is entirely appropriate, in questions dealing with external conduct, to refer to the presence of holy *angels,* which moves humans (indirectly) to the necessary reverence *before God.* For that reason a woman should therefore not engage in any improper, theatrical behavior during the worship service, for she thereby ultimately distracts from God, places herself at the center of attention, and in general upsets the reverence before God. That is the reason it reads: "because = on the basis of the angels."

Verses 11-12: Now comes an insertion: Not "nevertheless" (UT), but rather "moreover." Rather casually, to make clear that naturally there are yet more profound things to be said about the relation between man and woman, Paul adds: The two of them are mutually dependent *in the Lord!* However, he does not use this as an argument either for or against the female conduct in question, for indeed to "make an impression with the head" was behavior that concerned *both* of them, and misconduct here was not something specific to the woman. So Paul stands here under no secret pressure, as before was assumed, to compensate for a "devaluation" of the woman. More likely for him, and this directly from his biblical-Jewish background, the equal worth of woman is so taken for granted[311] that it never occurs to him that he might have said something denigrating concerning women.

As in verses 8-9, here we find a gradation: first of all an expression of the nature of the mutual relation of men and women "in Christ" (v. 11), and then the justification through a reference to the prototypes (v. 12). If in the order of creation the woman understands herself as coming from the man, and not the other way around (indeed, his entire argument is built upon this generally accepted head-radiance relationship), now in Christ something new is added. The original relation indeed remains in place (and as a consequence also the specific argument against a woman loosening her hair in church remains in effect), but it is now expanded to a mutuality: In Christ, the *man* does not exist *without the woman!* It is not as though Paul had to weaken his argument; it is rather that the anthropological model he has chosen leads to deeper questions, and that he thereby takes this opportunity to "complete" his model. Perhaps he detected in the one-sided sequence the danger of rendering the male superior. Thus once more: this has nothing to do with the "head argument," nor is it an attempt to call the order of creation into question; rather, from their relation "in the Lord," the perspective of sin and redemption is now added to the picture.

In Christ the man can no longer understand himself as independent from the woman; rather, both live through a mutual give-and-take, as when the entire community is (also) carried through the prayer and prophesying discourse of women. (And because this service is so important, it should not be endangered through irregular behavior.) Thus Paul is himself aware that his communities, to which many women belong, are sustained by *both* his male and female coworkers.[312]

311. See again above, before note 307. Balch summarizes the Stoa thus: "Antipater, Hierocles, and Paul all understand the wife to be 'similar' or even 'equal' (a rare term) to her husband, but inconsistently; all four subordinate her in practice." They thus would hardly have experienced the discrepancy in this way! Similarly Thraede, 119; Boucher, 52f.

312. Cf. Ts 100–114; similarly Schottroff, 95–98, even if she extracts from this a complete "equality"; however, she is correct in saying: "The communities are the decisive carriers of the history of early Christianity, not Paul as a single person." There are sufficient other missionaries among the "nations," completely independent of him.

Once again Paul offers a typological foundation for the (now mutual) relation between man and woman: verse 12. "For just as *the* (!) woman (now with the article, for it is a specific woman) from *the* man (is, namely Eve from Adam), so (is) also *the* man (the new Adam, who now becomes in a new way a type for all his posterity) 'through' the woman (the mother who bore the Messiah/Christ: Gal 4:4; Gen 3:15)." Just as Eve was formed out of Adam,[313] in the same way the "anointed one" came into earthly existence *through* the woman. Thus in his dependency upon the woman Christ is now—according to verse 12—the proto-type for *males*. It would be strange if Paul, as this is usually taken, would be here emphasizing what is obvious, that after Adam all men are born of women; further, this would contribute nothing specific to the new situation "in the Lord."

It is rather the case that through the coming of the Messiah "from a woman"[314] simultaneously the old conflict between the sexes is healed. Paul is aware of this conflict—immediately before Galatians 4:4 stands Galatians 3:28—although in 1 Corinthians 11 it is only indirectly discernible. The "domination" which was a punishment for sin (Gen 3:16) was thus overcome *when "the man" voluntarily subordinated himself below the woman* (in the sense also of Phil 2:7), and thereby provided an ideal for all males.[315] It is not said directly that thereby the mother of the Savior becomes in practice the female counterpart to the new Adam, that is, the new Eve; however, this constitutes the background of the text, for Christ and his mother are here prototypes for the new relation between man and woman.[316]

Perhaps one is tempted to ask again: Then why must the woman still keep her head covered and subordinate herself to the man?

313. Paul thus characterizes the derivative relationship of Eve to Adam through ἐκ. This takes up the διὰ τὸν ἄνδρα of 11:9 that was still operative in the ἐκ γυναικὸς εἶναι (cf. v. 8).

314. We see below, B II 4, that in 1 Tim 2:15 as well the "birth of a child" indicates the appearance of the Messiah from the woman. This is thus a notion that was alive in the early Church; cf. besides Gen 3:15 and Gal 4:4; also with Matt 1:21-23; Luke 1:31; 2:7, 11; 11:27. Also, is the "young woman" of Isa 7:14 supposed to have no significance for Paul?

315. On this, see below concerning Eph 5. Christ as "model": 1 Cor 11:1.

316. Cf. above, A I 4; further, my article: "Jesus Christ—die endgültige Offenbarung Gottes—Biblische Sicht," 55-57.

However, we have just seen that in this context the discussion is not at all about subordination, but only that she, like the man, should conduct herself with reverence while performing spiritually during the worship service. For the rest, in verse 11f. the new relation is added *to,* and does not replace, the former head-radiance relation; formally this is an insertion. Thus the reference to the new dependency of the man upon the woman is not some kind of argument against the command to keep her head under control, but only an anthropological extension of the *ground* for this behavior (a similar command is also given to the man). For "all comes from God": *both* relations to their origin are from God; the new does not cancel the relation set up at the moment of creation, but rather completes it and heals it of the injury inflicted through sin.

Thus Paul is remaining at the same level of wordplay (in v. 12 he is playing with the prepositions) and of anthropological symbolic imagery. Is it possible that Paul noticed that this rabbinical model which appeared to him ideally suited for his exhortation with regard to the "head" could somehow be interpreted as discriminating against women, and is he therefore indicating that, on the level of our worth in Christ, there is no difference? But that would not vitiate his first argument, for the relation set up at creation is indeed retained from beginning to end: "in the Lord" there are now *the both of them!* The man is and remains "head/source"; however, the woman is in a new way "the transmitter of life," and not only for the man's children (cf. Gen 3:20), but also now for the man himself. It goes without saying that such a vision challenges every form of androcentrism and clericalism.

After this insertion which is at the same time the theological highpoint of the entire passage, verses 13-15 return to the specific topic of discussion.[317] If verses 4-6 already suggested that it is a matter of aesthetics and hence of esteem *(aischron),* this topic now returns. The apostle is assuming that men and women in the community are reacting the same way he is, and so would the people concerned, if they would consider the matter closely. It "indeed is not proper"; the Greeks too consider letting down one's hair in an "assembly" to be out of order—although some prophets ignored this. However, it is unattractive, flashy, and is

317. We saw a similar structure (A B A) in 1 Cor 7 and 12-14.

occasionally the object of ridicule. Further, one cannot defend it by invoking "nature" (a large discussion grew up in the ancient world, especially in the Stoa, over the function of hair). Evidently someone in the Corinthian community has defended the (mis-)conduct of a woman's loosening her hair by saying that it is "seemly" in a woman, that it corresponds to her essence and "nature."

In Paul's response to this objection, one may suggest that a small particle has been overlooked, and for that reason people have gotten precisely the wrong impression. Paul is not asking a question;[318] rather, he intends to say: "And nature also teaches you no such thing; neither does it say that for a man it is a disparagement, while for a woman it is an embellishment"—what? Not simply "to wear one's hair long" (UT) (this is not the issue under question, but rather to let it hang loose [if a man had long hair, it was tied]). This was in fact the controversial behavior, and it is here once again criticized—by an argument addressing something that is universally human. This again seems to indicate that the actual occasion was not improper behavior by certain men, but that someone had tried to defend this behavior in certain women as "chic" or "elegant." However, this kind of "honor" is out of place at the worship service, since it detracts from God's honor. This perhaps accounts for the sharp tone. However, the argument referred to stays with the order of nature: whether for man or for woman, hair grows in order to provide *protection*. As affording both shelter and warmth, it is appropriately conceived as a "covering" (whose absence is noticed by those who no longer have any hair). Thus, this is not in the first instance a matter that touches only women, as if they had long hair in place of a veil. To that, one could respond: in that case they would no longer have *any* need for a veil! And does not a man's hair also grow naturally as long? Here we come upon one of the many breaks in the text that previously had to be dealt with because of a reading that inserted the idea: "It is given to her (UT: "to woman") as a covering."[319] However, hair protects *everyone!*

318. A question would have begun: *οὐ, οὐχ(ί)*. *Οὐδέ* introduces a statement.
319. After weighing all the evidence, however, we find that this *(αὐτῇ)* is the worse reading, so that now P⁴⁶, D, F, G and the Koine texts together

It must be conceded that verse 16 concludes rather abruptly. Does this mean that Paul intends it to suppress dissent? It could well be that the impulsive Paul was somewhat irritated (see also v. 6), but this does not necessarily indicate any disparagement for women. It happens easily if one argues with people who understand nothing—whether they are men or women (cf. only 1 Cor 4; frequently in 2 Cor and Galatians). Also, it is only *certain* women who are doing this, and perhaps only *some* men who are defending such conduct (v. 15a). Paul would have probably heard the names, and therefore knew who was involved. Perhaps he had had occasion earlier to tangle with these people. What do we really know for sure? Hence, we must be very careful before we here attribute a sudden authoritarian or chauvinistic statement to Paul, who had built up the "poor and the least esteemed" into a community (1 Cor 20–31), and who in the immediately following text becomes angry over the fact that the rich are shaming the poor (11:22; cf. 12:14), and who exerts himself to be not only a Greek to the Greeks, but—so to speak—to become a sympathetic partner to women. It is not easy for him to invoke the authority he has received from God (1 Cor 4; 7:25, 40; 9; 1 Thess 2), but if it is necessary, he is ready to do so (2 Cor 10–13; Gal 1; 4:13-20).

Perhaps besides this there lies in the background a tension with the Jewish-Christian communities, who could less easily accept such conduct on the part of prophetesses. Paul had a difficult enough time rescuing the authentic kernel of the message of God's grace from the Judaizers. Perhaps this also plays a role in the reference to the "communities of God" (in the plural!), specifically to those from which he brought the "community rule" with him to Greece and before which he continually had to defend his mission. It is as if he wants to say: "It is difficult enough that I must defend the freedom of the gospel and also its necessary inculturation; do not now make it unnecessarily more difficult for me by things that you yourselves consider improper!" It goes without saying that he remains within the sensibility of his Jewish-Hellenistic environment and the patriarchal assumptions of the

---

with the internal arguments, prevail against ℵ, A, and B. Aland recently has set the word in brackets. However, even if one allows it to remain, our thesis still holds, since in that case the hair is still given her "as a covering," and "not for glory." Cf. again above, note 309.

ancient world. However, this coloring remains "material" to his presentation and does not rise to the status of a formal or dogmatic pronouncement. Moreover, objectively speaking the question being debated is not a question of emancipation, for Paul forbids the same thing to men. His goal is to preserve unity among the communities, their proper esteem on the part of the Gentiles (vv. 4-6, 13-15; 1 Cor 5:1; 6:1-6; Phil 4:5; Rom 12:17), and reverence before God.

3. Women Should Keep Quiet? Where?: 1 Corinthians 14:33b-36

As pertains to our topic certainly no text from Paul's authentic letters is more frequently cited—and excoriated! Everyone knows it. Today many women lectors are still disturbed by it— totally apart from the practice of "preaching" by woman pastoral associates. Our research has led us to the conclusion that the Christian "assembly/*ekklēsia*"[320] came together in five different ways:

1. Liturgy of the Word: 1 Corinthians 14:26-33
2. Breaking bread: 1 Corinthians 10:16
3. Common "Agape" meal: 1 Corinthians 11:20-33
4. Instruction—"Bible study": cf. Acts 17:11
5. Debate and Decision: cf. Acts 6:1-5; 15; 20:17-38.

The last is a "community assembly" in the narrow sense, in which discussion would take place and decisions would be made concerning questions of community life; it fits most closely with the term *ekklēsia* emanating from the secular realm—the (originally autonomous) "parliament" of a Greek city-state, as mentioned in Acts 19:39. Thus the choice of this word again reflects the fact that the Christian assembly in the midst of this world understood itself as the "autonomous" people of God, the expanded universal *qāhāl jahwe*. Indeed, such "assemblies" were probably the primary audience for the apostle's letters; these are

320. In Atf III again the corresponding justifications. On this matter, cf. H.-J. Klauck, "Gemeindestrukturen im Ersten Korintherbrief," *BuK* 40 (1985) 9–15; here 12f.

not thought of as some sort of liturgical texts for the worship service (alongside the Torah!?); rather, for the most part they are intended to provoke a discussion and decision. For the Greeks, at such "town meetings" with a discussion and decision agenda, women could not even be present, let alone take part in the discussion. The Hellenistic mystery cults distinguished between so-called executive meetings and the regular cultic assemblies, and probably maintained a similar distinction concerning the participation of women according to the type of meeting it was. However, the Jewish-Christian model, which most certainly did not admit women, was the decisive influence for the Christian community assembly. Thus, given the Hellenistic environment, it would have been a "progressive" step even to allow women to be present during discussions. This certainly is to be attributed to the new brotherhood and sisterhood in Christ, and also to the greater independence of the Hellenistic woman. Another reason undoubtedly was the fact that this type of "assembly" took place in private homes; at the same time, the exclusion of women from male discussions even in their own homes is not unknown—even today.

This clears up immediately the apparent contradiction that would otherwise arise with 1 Corinthians 11, where women indeed may speak. There, however, *praying* out loud and *prophetic* discourse by women is presupposed as a contribution to the worship service, while here the woman seeks "to learn something." This is doubtless just the first step to having a participation in *council deliberations;* however, even the idea of a woman asking questions in "public" is (still) frowned upon, not only in Jewish circles, but also within the Greek sphere.[321] This is what is meant in v. 35b by "talking in the assembly" *(en ekklēsia);* thus *ekklēsia* has three meanings in this text: "community" as corporation (33b), "community assembly" (34a) in the style of our town council (although this at the same time would be a full assembly of the men), and the abstract description "in assembly" = publicly. Thus, according to the universally known "community rule" (cf. 14:36 with 11:36), women are "not permitted" to voice their opinions in *council (= publicly).* The invocation of the "law," however, does not indicate a regression to an un-Pauline legalis-

---

321. Notice this distinction in Love, see above, A VII 1; cf. Atf III 2.

tic consciousness, but rather places as a point of reference beside the universal "sensibility," the Greek rules and the Christian community order, as well as the Jewish *tradition*—as in 1 Corinthians 9:8f. In this case one cannot point to a specific "commandment" in the Scriptures, but only invoke a universal consensus (an unwritten law, so to speak) of Jewish custom. Paul thereby makes extremely clear that here it is not a question of belief nor of a revealed truth concerning the nature of men and women, but only of a human code of conduct that is based on tradition and is thus naturally conditioned by the times, although not because of that without importance for forming conscience.[322]

> *The Text of 1 Corinthians 14:33b-36:* [33b]As in all the communities of the saints, [34]women should keep silent in the *community assemblies;* indeed, they are not permitted (by the existing code) to speak. They should rather submit themselves, as the Jewish *tradition* decrees. [35]However, should they *wish to inform* themselves about something, they should inquire of their men at home; for it is offensive to have a woman *speak her mind in public.* [36]Has the word of God gone out from you, or have only you received it?

Despite the more positive treatment of women in the Christian community (she received in baptism the same "sign of the covenant" as a man: Acts 5:14; 8:12; 16:15), this does not constitute a reversal of the entire social relationship between the sexes. The statement that they should inquire of their men at home does not exclude even the lady of the house herself; en *oikō* would then mean: in the house = in the private atmosphere of the family, not in the "public" assembly (even if in her house). In any case Paul is not here intending to set limits to a basic movement for emancipation, but rather to take the position that currently *certain* women, on the basis of their newfound freedom, have gone too far—and this is even perceived by other women. He is thus not anticipating a universal protest by women, but, as with 11:16, from "some contentious people" (men and women). Here, however, they should first subordinate themselves to the community

---

322. For more details, see below, D VI 4 and the "Conclusion" at the end of this book.

assembly. This implies a subordination to the men only indirectly; and it applies also to unmarried women and to widows.

Today we should like to ask: why does Paul not fundamentally question the entire "code"? Why does he not think through our equality in Christ to its logical conclusion? Evidently the center of gravity for him, as in Jesus' proclamation, does not lie in efforts to change social structures. We will take up this point in part D. However, it must first be said that clearly Paul has understood correctly that God's work of salvation is "historical"; this means that it leaves a person in their situation, so as to allow them to make progress from the interior of their nature outward step by step. For that, however, one must also have a sensitivity to what is both possible and appropriate. Before we attribute a flaw in character to this apostle of freedom, we should perhaps ask ourselves whether this God-possessed man did not possess greater wisdom about how people should be educated; and we should further believe that he knew more about their concrete situation than we do. Approached from this direction, our text, as the sign of a liberalizing tendency in a Pauline community, can provide us indirect information about a general pattern of behavior in the early Church.

Just as, at 1 Corinthians 11, we should not make the foundation of the exhortation concerning the head into a central tenet of faith, so we should not believe that at 1 Corinthians 14:33b-36 an essential code is being proclaimed. Paul only wants to make sure that the women do not do something that will generally be perceived as *aischron*/offensive, similar to loosening their hair while engaging in prophetic speech. And because it is improper and goes against the community order, people who engage in such activity are spiritually immature. Behind all this stands a fundamental principle: if the situation should change, you should do whatever will be perceived as appropriate! Thus, following this same principle, today not only would Paul not be *against* such "participation" by women in discussions, he would rather insist upon it! For otherwise our parish councils would be "unbiblical." It must be admitted that our author is here reacting a bit impulsively, similar to the way he reacted in 1 Corinthians 11; however, this intensity ultimately only argues for Paul as the actual author, although the current location of this passage (in 1 Cor 14) may be the work of a later redactor.

4. *The Remaining Texts from the Principal Pauline Letters*

We shall present the remaining references to women in the community from the principal Pauline letters according to their theme.

(1) If Paul is addressing his *"communities,"* naturally women (and children) are also included, even though he never names them.[323] Granted, occasionally behind the term "brothers" a narrower usage may be operative in which Paul would be really addressing only the men,[324] or perhaps specifically the "community assembly" of men,[325] or else his coworkers.[326] Fine points like this must be deduced from the context and are difficult to define. In the majority of cases we must certainly read such terms in an inclusive sense.[327] This becomes explicit in 2 Corinthians 6:19, where Paul expands 2 Samuel 7:14 to speak of sons "and daughters," similar to Joel 3:1f. (Acts 2:17f.).

(2) From the lists of greetings it becomes clear that Paul had numerous *personal contacts* with women. Besides those who are named in what follows, there are "the mother of Rufus, who has also become a mother to me, Philologus and *Julia,* Nereus and *his sister* and all the saints. Greet one another with a holy kiss!"[328] This testifies to an interior freedom in his relationships with women and his esteem for them; similar to Jesus in the scene

323. Expressly included: "all of you together," 1 Thess 5:23; see ChuA 225f.

324. 1 Cor 7:29: The context is addressing men "about" women.

325. 1 Cor 14:34; are not some forms of address, such as 1 Cor 12:1, meant in this way, even if women are present? However, the ones who bear the responsibility are men.

326. Just as our "brothers" (thus probably 1 Thess 5:14, see ChuA 225f.) including the "female coworkers"; see below, in this chapter: (6). However, the language has a masculine flavor. Schüssler Fiorenza, 180, believes that ἀδελφή in Rom 16:15 is such a "title." But then what would αὐτοῦ stand for? Nevertheless, it remains possible that Paul also understands "sister" in the narrower sense of female coworker, most likely so in 1 Cor 9:5 and Rom 16:1; see below (6); cf. Schüssler Fiorenza, 172.

327. Weiser, 159–164, 168f.; there is also material on the following questions.

328. Rom 16:13-16. From the Pastoral Letters again: "Eubulus, Pudeus, Linus, *Claudia,* and all the brothers send their greetings," 2 Tim 4:21; the "sisters" are also intended.

at Jacob's well (John 4:9, 27), Paul here stretches the otherwise conventional proprieties.

(3) According to 1 Corinthians 11:3-16, in *worship assemblies*— whether in small household communities or also in city worship services (which indeed also took place in houses)—women could pray out loud and offer prophetic contributions. This same point doubtless stands behind 1 Corinthians 14:1-33a. Is it correct to say that "ecstatic and pneumatic experiences" in Judaism had already challenged the "traditional division of the sexual roles in favor of a stronger independence for women"?[329] Posing this question differently: if in the Christian worship service under the influence of the Spirit women did receive a greater significance, did they then take over specifically "male" roles? And to what extent may we say that they then exercised a "leadership function"? Here enters the hypothesis of a "charismatic community model," according to which all functions grew out of a "charismatic understanding of service."[330] If by "charisma" is meant evident talents for service that are distinct from an "office" given to a person for a fixed term and passed along from person to person, then I do not consider it legitimate to exclude the latter from the Pauline community model.[331] Even though much had (not yet) been precisely defined by rules, and forms of service only gradually took shape, Paul clearly defends what later would be called "office," and assumes it first of all in his own case.

For that reason I do not consider it justified to make a leadership role out of a prophetic commission. When the pseudoprophetess Jezebel in Revelation 2:20 is characterized as a "prominent prophet leader" (Schüssler Fiorenza, 164), she may have been a "superior-prophetess," but not a female prophetic "leader." There were also from time to time prophetesses in Judaism (2 Kings 22:14; Neh 6:14; Luke 2:36); but they did not thereby become either queens or priestesses, nor even female elders—just as male prophets did not by that fact become leaders! Neither Miriam nor Debora are typical "prophetesses." The office of prophet at the time of Jesus had been clearly defined, and no one

329. Dautzenberg, "Stellung," 191.
330. Dautzenberg, "Stellung," 186.
331. ChuA 224ff. and "Sprachregelung," 21–23; 33–37, the last as a resumé of five articles, with much more extensive criticisms and proofs.

would confuse it with the office of leadership. This is true even into our own days.[332] Indeed, it is highly dangerous if a prophet does not submit his or her prophecy to examination, but rather presents himself or herself as some kind of leader and attempts to establish the claim (1 Cor 14:29-33; cf. *Didache* 11-15). On the other hand, by its very nature prophecy has to be related to those who bear authority, for often prophets must call the latter to account. Thus from 1 Corinthians 11 there is no path leading to "community leadership," no matter how the latter is shaped.

(4) *To toil in the Lord:* With these words Paul describes his own apostolic work (1 Cor 3:5, 8; 15:10; Gal 4:11; Phil 2:16). In 1 Thessalonians 5:15 and 1 Corinthians 16:16 the participle is used almost like a fixed term for "those in the communities who do the work," thus who should be respected and to whom one should submit oneself. In Romans 16:6 and 12 it is said of Maria, Tryphaena, Tryphosa, and Persis that they have "made great efforts." Should we conclude on this basis that they are "community leaders"? Such a conclusion would have to be reached on the basis of other evidence.[333] If various members each in his or her own way "make great efforts" for the kingdom of God, this does not necessarily imply that the specific characteristics of their activity are the same; further, in light of Philippians 2:3 and the "mutual" submission encouraged by Ephesians 5:21, one must be careful not to immediately associate a leadership structure and the delegation of formal authority with such a "submission" (as in 1 Cor 16:16).

(5) Evodia and Syntyche *"have fought together (synēthlēsan) with me for the gospel"*: Philippians 4:2. Even though the two of them are listed in verse 3 among his "coworkers," no title can

---

332. Trompf, 213, gives a reference to spirit churches in Africa and the Pacific, where a female prophet is accepted without question as the instrument of divine inspiration, without implying any claim at the level of community to the leadership role of the men; this is cited with agreement by Love, 57. This also applies to the entire Pentecostal movement.

333. Πρόστατις does not mean this, in spite of many opposing votes, e.g., Schüssler Fiorenza, 181; Klauck, 31; Heine, 99; however προιστάμενοι with the genitive are those who place *themselves* before someone = who intervene on his or her behalf! "Presider" on the other hand is προεστῶτες; cf. ChuA 216, 225.

be deduced from this.[334] The statement recalls "battles" undergone *together* (!) in Philippi.[335] These could have been religious
quarrels or also physical "persecutions." Also Epaphroditus, in
Philippians 2:25, is described as a "coworker and fellow com-
batant *(systratiōtēs),* and Archippus similarly in Philemon 2. In
2 Corinthians 10:1-5 Paul uses the word for combat more actively
and naturally in an extended sense. In Philippians 4:2, however,
the image switches from that of a soldier's combat to that of an
athlete's competition. Further, the dictionaries indicate that the
corresponding compounds *syn-athlein, syn-agōnizein* refer more
to a supporting than to an equally based fight. For that reason
the text suggests only that there were common struggles for the
spread of the Good News. These forms of expression indicate how
much Paul thinks, works, and feels "in a community way," and
specifically also with women, but on the other hand they do not
permit the conclusion that in this struggle the latter had the same
jobs, or even "offices." It is further correct to say that one may
not conclude that there were private differences between the two
women, but rather struggles in their common "efforts on behalf
of the gospel";[336] but from that it does not follow that these
"missionary women" in the service of the "proclamation . . .
occupied the same status as Paul" (Schüssler Fiorenza, 169f.).
We would need specific evidence to argue that their activity took
place outside the framework of what was accorded to women in
that society.

(6) *Female Coworkers.* The use of this term would seem to raise
the prospects of "equality" with male colleagues especially high.
Unfortunately, this word also does not warrant speaking of "egalitarian community structures" or of an "equal partnership" with
Paul. Schüssler Fiorenza concedes a "subordination" to Paul by
his male coworkers, but she refuses to admit it in the case of (certain) women (169f.). The fact that Priscilla (and Aquila) as well
as many other women spread the gospel before (and independently

---

334. Heine, 97: "female co-fighters for the gospel, thus female missionaries."

335. Hardly a common(?) imprisonment, as Heine, 97, suspects.

336. Phil 1:27 has συναθλοῦντες τῇ πίστει: "work together for the gospel
message entrusted [to us]," and thus that we now no longer live under "law,"
but in the "principle of trust."

of) Paul is clear even from the data concerning his conversion. If then they later "work together with him," this does not necessarily imply an equal footing with the "apostle to the Gentiles."[337] Unwarranted conclusions like this are not helpful for clarifying the historical data. In the same way one must be careful about equivocal expressions such as "missionary and preaching activity." Of course, every Christian should "proclaim" the gospel; however this does not exclude the possibility that people carry out this commission in very different ways. Nothing is achieved by claiming that Paul recognized no "office," for then also *women* could not have occupied such a (nonexistent) "office"; if one defends the role of office, on the other hand, it does not necessarily follow that one may extend this term in the same sense to Paul's male and female coworkers.

What Paul has to say in Galatians 2:7 about his personal commission "to the uncircumcised" cannot immediately be extended to his coworkers. Without subordinating to him all those who work in the same sense (such as those who were already active as missionaries before him or those sent out from Jerusalem— 2 Cor 10:15f.), it is nevertheless true that he has a unique, irreplaceable *apostolē*/mission. This idea does not come first from Luke (Acts 13:2). As open as the "titles of office" may still be, and as open as Paul's attitude was toward other laborers in the "work of God," still Paul clearly sees his own service as a unique and irreplaceable commission,[338] even though it is carried out in solidarity and unity with the entire Church. Thus he, and only he, has responsibility for "his" communities (1 Cor 4:15; 2 Cor and Gal). Paul would have been surprised if one attributed to him—from our modern sensibility—the belief in an equal status for all forms of service. So we must be more strongly aware than

337. The "bias" becomes detectable where Schüssler Fiorenza, 169f., cf. also 183, attempts to explain why Paul does not refer to Phoebe as an "apostle"—although he could have so referred to her. For more details, see below, in what follows.

338. 1 Cor 3:10; 9:1; Ollrog, σύνεργος in EWNT, reduces offices too much to one level, even if we have to reject "servant" of Paul. However one cannot exclude "female companion" and "female helper," also in the sense of a subordinate coworker. Even so, the distinction between σύνεργος θεοῦ and σύνεργός μου should be observed; see Bertram, TDNT VII 874.

in the past that next to Paul there were other independent missionaries, and that even within his sphere of work he recognized completely independent "female coworkers in the labor of God" who were responsible for their own work, but also that the nature of their activity did not fundamentally violate the preexisting social and ecclesial structures.[339] We shall return to this point. Thus if Paul mentions men as coworkers "of God" (1 Cor 3:9; 1 Thess 3:2) or "of himself" (Rom 16:9, 21; 2 Cor 8:23; Phil 2:25), this can designate very different things and need not indicate the same thing in each case. Thus "Greet Prisca and Aquila, my coworkers in Christ Jesus" (Rom 16:3) may have a different quality from: "Evodia and Syntyche, who have fought together with me for the gospel (for the spread of the gospel), together with Clement and my (!) coworkers." Each is appreciated according to his or her own style, and the talents granted to them (1 Cor 3:12; Rom 12:3).

(7) People like to see a special sort of female coworker in 1 Corinthians 9:5: "Do we not have the right to take a believing woman along with us, like the other apostles and the brothers of the Lord and Cephas?" This does not mean a wife, but primarily a helper for personal needs.[340] Schüssler Fiorenza (172, 179) calls this: "to be accompanied by a female co-missionary." But this removes the point from Paul's argument, for his intention is precisely to renounce any *personal* advantage. We certainly cannot exclude the possibility that such a "sister" did collaborate in the missionary labor, but here certainly not in the sense of someone on the same level, but within the framework of the possibilities that society held open for women at that time.

---

339. Thus the thesis of G. Theissen, see above, before note 306, remains intact, that the early Christian missionary movement outside Palestine "did not exist in conflict with society, but rather was well integrated into it"— despite the objections of Schüssler Fiorenza.

340. For proof, see EuE 325–331; whether with other apostles this was occasionally their wife must remain an open issue; it is unlikely, however. Cf. Kruse, 98f.; however, "Paul is not here emphasizing that the apostles are allowed to marry" (Wendland, NTD 7). All the more, he does not at all mean to claim it for himself. This does not fit with 1 Cor 7. For the context, see G. Galitis, "Das Wesen der Freiheit," *Freedom and Love,* L. de Lorenzi (Rome: Benedictina, Bibl. Ecum. Section 6, 1981) 133f.

(8) Romans 16:1 characterizes a *woman as a deacon:* "I commend to you Phoebe, our sister—moreover, deacon of the community in Cenchreae—that you receive her in the Lord, in a way fitting for the saints, and that you support her in whatever she needs; for she herself has been a helper (support) to many, and to me personally."[341] This is certainly not a deaconess in the modern sense of a pure service of charity; "deacon of the community" sounds like something more official and recalls Philippians 1:1. Since also those addressed apparently recognized what was being talked about, this kind of position cannot have been a unique case. Must we not also consider the possibility that, in Philippians 1:1, there were women among the "deacons"? What was their task? Certainly "the service of the word" was also part of it (G. Lohfink 390f.); however, we must be cautious in employing such a phrase with its contemporary, more specific meaning. Without question they introduced many converts to the faith, and probably not only women.[342]

However, does it follow from this that in their "official" area of responsibility they were in all matters placed in an equal position with the men; for example, did they have equal voice in a "parish council"? Until evidence is produced to the contrary, we must assume that they carried out their tasks within the sociocultural framework of the community norms. And there is no indication that this would allow a woman in the course of a worship service not only to proclaim a text from Scripture, but also to present an interpretation of it in the form of a sermon (Luke 4:10, 20f.; Acts 13:15, 42). Nowhere does Scripture report that a woman "preached" (Acts 14:3, 9, 21, 25, etc.). And where in the secular realm is there any testimony concerning a woman functioning as official speaker? Thus "proclamation" by a woman had a different face. This is not mentioned, because it was taken as obvious. The term does not as yet have an "official" stamp. We must thus assume that the early Christians understood by the

341. For justification, see above, note 333; similarly G. Lohfink, 389; Weiser, 172. W.-H. Ollrog, "Die Abfassungsverhältnisse von Röm 16," *Kirche,* D. Lührmann and G. Strecker (FS G. Bornkamm) 221–242 speaks in favor of the originality of the text.

342. Prisca and Aquila worked with Apollos—apparently in personal conversation: Acts 18:26. Cf. however below, B II 3.

same word, *deacon,* a gender-specific differentiation when it was used of a man or a woman.[343] When in 1 Corinthians 3:5, 8 Paul applies the terms "deacon, effort, and coworker" both to himself and to others, it does not follow from this that he places the others on the same level as himself, nor that the term would have the same meaning when applied to women.

(9) The same is true for the title *apostle.* After the works of B. Brooten and G. Lohfink,[344] there can no longer be any doubt that in Romans 16:7 we should read the feminine form Junia: "Greet Andronicus and Junia, my compatriots and my co-prisoners, who are outstanding among the[345] apostles, who were in Christ already before me." When after the first millennium the masculine form established itself, this is doubtless to be explained by the fact that the term "apostle" had become so narrowed in meaning that people no longer believed it could be applied to a woman. But still, that gives us no justification for committing the opposite error, namely, of reading a meaning that only developed later into a term's earlier appearance.

It is clear that Junia does not belong to "the Twelve." If it is not a matter of "being sent out by the community" (2 Cor 8:23), but of an absolute usage, then it apparently refers to someone who has seen the resurrected Jesus (1 Cor 9:1; 15:7). Thus the Fathers do not hesitate to denominate Mary Magdalene an "apostle." Further, all the other women who have encountered the risen Jesus also belong to this category. Could not the terms

343. Thraede, 99, refers to Pliny, *ep* 10.96.8: "Two Christian *ancillae* were tortured; they are called *ministrae*" (thus in the feminine form); behind this there certainly stands διάχονοι; cf. below, note 429; on the later history, below, note 432.

344. Brooten, B., cf. G. Lohfink 391f. In a similar sense Dautzenberg, *Stellung* 184; Heine, 49f. and the commentaries by Wilckens and Pesch. A small correction to Lohfink: according to P. Lampe, "Junia/Junias: Sklavenherkunft im Kreise der vorpaulinischen Apostel (Röm 16:7)" *ZNW* 76 (1985) 132, already from the ninth century all the minuscule *manuscripts* contain the masculine form 'Ιουνιᾶν. Aegidius Romanus around 1300 would then be the first known *commentary* in this sense. The oldest manuscripts, P[46] among others, read 'Ιουλιᾶν, thus clearly a feminine name.

345. Sanday-Headlam, *Romans* (ICC) 423 write: "The passage was apparently so taken by all patristic commentators." Not "most renowned *among* the apostles" (Meyer); cf. Rengstorf, TDNT VII 267f.: EWNT s.v.

"the 500 brothers" and "all the apostles" (1 Cor 15:6-7) also encompass women? "Apostles" have the specific commission to serve as a founding generation by being witnesses to the resurrected Jesus. But do they for that reason have the same competence in all the other important areas? Acts 1:22 differentiates among them; in Galatians 2:8 Paul speaks of Peter's apostolic mission *(apostolē)* to the circumcised and of his own to the uncircumcised (Rom 11:13!). Also, in the introductions to the letters to the Romans and Galatians, Paul apparently means, when he names himself an "apostle of Jesus Christ," his own *particular* mission, for he never includes his coworkers under this term; rather, in 1 Corinthians 1:1 and 2 Corinthians 1:1 he names them separately.

We must then take account of the fact that Paul uses this word that is so central for him in both a narrow (1 Cor 1:1) and a wider sense (1 Cor 15:7). As pertains to our discussion, one may conclude only that Junia—like many other women—belonged indeed to the first witnesses, and thereby occupied a special position in the early Church. This does not imply the "office of apostle" as Paul himself received it, or indeed in the sense of the "Twelve." Thus here as well the woman's role remained within the pattern of the preexisting social structures; she is not elevated to any special *office,* such as, however, Paul does claim both for himself and for Peter. Nevertheless, the practice, which is only mentioned once in each case but certainly happened frequently, of naming a woman a disciple,[346] a deacon, and an apostle, is indeed a sign that the proclamation of the Good News was entrusted to both men and women. However, it would be an exaggeration to conclude from this that in the beginning the functions and tasks were intended for and accessible to both sexes in an identical way, until supposedly—at the latest in the period of so-called "early Catholicism"—the men, through their more powerful social position, re-asserted their dominance. Our modern concern for equality should be advanced through systematic reflection, not on the basis of such (un-)historical "facts."

(10) May we not at least assume a *leadership position* for women in the *house communities?*

---

346. $Μαθηταία$, sc. Tabitha, Acts 9:36.

Romans 16:3-5: "Greet Prisca and Aquila, my coworkers in Christ Jesus, who have stuck out their necks for me—not only I thank them, but also all the communities of the (Gentile) peoples— and the assembly (community) in their house." 1 Corinthians 16:19b: "The assemblies (communities) of Asia greet you; Aquila and Prisca especially greet you in the Lord, with the assembly (community) in their house." Philemon 2: "Paul . . . to Philemon, our friend (beloved) and fellow worker, and to the sister Apphia, and to Archippus, our fellow-fighter (co-soldier), and to the assembly (community) in your house."

It is generally emphasized that Prisca was indeed the more active personality, because most of the time she is named before her husband; it is here a married couple, nevertheless, who receive the community into their own house. It remains unclear whether Apphia is Philemon's wife or a "sister" in the sense of rendering a particular service to the community. Some conclude from 1 Corinthians 1:11—"Chloe's people"—that she also had a house community; others suspect that she may have been a wealthy matron who had male and female slaves in her "house," and perhaps was not even a Christian herself. Or was she perhaps a female slave herself who, in keeping with the social structure of the community, exercised considerable influence? According to Acts 16:15, 40, Lydia, the dealer in purple goods, also had a house community. Finally there is Colossians 4:15, the only place where a woman by herself is named as providing hospitality: "Greet the brothers in Laodicea" (a typical expression, which also includes "sisters.") "and Nympha" (a widow? or has her husband not become a Christian?) "and the assembly in her home."

May one conclude from these references that women possessed "leadership"[347] in their house-assemblies? Certainly in these cases they occupied a privileged position. Schüssler Fiorenza (165f.) assumes that they—and similarly Phoebe the deacon—shared in the distribution of the Eucharistic meal. But such distribution was probably not yet liturgically ritualized. Another question is whether they *presided* at the Eucharistic celebration. According to the Jewish model, originally the father of the house would occupy the presider's chair. In his absence, would the lady of the

347. Πρόστατις in Romans 16:2 is not a female leader; see above, notes 333 and 341.

house have taken his place, or would one of the other males present have been asked? At least if there were "honored guests" present, such a practice was not uncommon among both Jews and Greeks. It might also depend upon how "private" or "public" such an affair was perceived as being. We get some data on who presided at the Eucharistic liturgy only relatively late, and by then there is no question but that men are in the leadership position. Even if in individual cases at the beginning women may have taken over this role, this does not imply any fundamental decision, for the principle still applied that as soon as a house *father* was present, he would take over the role. Otherwise it would be remarkable that there is no trace of any dispute over this matter (one thinks of 1 Cor 11 and 14).

On the other hand, the understanding of office and sacrament was not yet as differentiated as it would later become. If on occasion it happened that in this time of clarification a woman "broke bread in remembrance of the death of the Lord" (?), this remained in any case, as far as social sensibilities were concerned, the exception and an "emergency solution." The normal case was—naturally—that the father of the house performed it and soon afterward an "elder," who probably offered the role to Paul, the "honored guest," if he was present. As we have said, this all remains in the dark for us, even if altogether there were no fixed "liturgical" customs; the Jewish Passover meal had long since developed a protocol for household ceremonies. In this the roles of father and mother were not interchangeable. Thus all that can be said is that in this realm as in the activity of proclamation, the generally prevailing norms for family and social life most likely also prevailed. A woman who provided hospitality had many administrative details to attend to; however, she did not become thereby the leader of the "assembly."

5. Sociological Influence and a Sense of Historical Proportion

In Judaism there were firmly established customs to the effect that women by themselves could not conduct an official worship service, but could only come together "for prayer," perhaps at a place for prayer (Acts 16:13), while a service in the synagogue required the presence of at least ten men. Thus, there was a traditional practice for deciding such questions and distinguishing clearly between different familial and community assemblies. We are then in the right to say also of the Christian communities that were establishing themselves: the more "public" and official an assembly was, the more clearly the leadership role of the male, as was generally true everywhere, would be emphasized.[348] To speak of "egalitarian community structures" is simply to perpetrate an anachronism. We may hope that people interacted in the Christian groups with greater openness, respect, and good will, but do not thereby have any reason for believing that they disregarded fundamental social norms. The latter were rather more an expression of mutual respect.[349] However, there was also friction and quarreling.

Is it seriously possible that, with great largeness of heart, the first community actually initiated a revolutionary change like ecclesiological-social equality between men and women, and then immediately abandoned it, so that it is never mentioned in the letters and had almost completely disappeared by the second generation, but may still be detected by us as characteristic of the first generation after exhaustive labors working on extremely scanty material? The fact that a woman, especially if she was from a higher social position, might from time to time exercise considerable *influence* does not yet prove that either in the public or in the familial sphere she took over the male role—even conceding that she might be superior to many men who happened to fill such "offices." Basically this is true even in our own day.

In this question it must be conceded that much depends on whether in the Pauline communities as in the Palestinian Church, there was a basic agreement on official structure, or whether and how far there was also a "charismatic" model which postulated a new gift of the Spirit for each kind of service, so that both men and women would be equally qualified for all functions and jobs. Thraede (101) adopts an extreme view here: "As long as there were no 'offices,' it makes no sense to say that 'women also' shared in them."[350] Without doubt the community life of the early

348. Cf. Klauck 34–36; for more details, see Atf III 2 (near the end).

349. See "Haustafeln und Ökonomik,"; cf. below, close to notes 416–418.

350. Thraede, 101; however, there was "official authority"; see above, close to note 331 and in what follows.

Church promoted a great vitality. Because of similar experiences of the Spirit, women were more powerfully integrated into the community's religious life than had been the case up to this point in either the Jewish or Hellenistic sphere. Within "God's family," certain rigidities and conventions were abandoned. The very fact that a woman could convert by herself shows that she could make up her own mind on matters of belief and had become more active. Certainly people were experimenting with new patterns of interaction, and thereby ran up against barriers. However, it would yet have to be expressly proved that this entailed a formal "exchange of roles." Mutual love leads to respect and acceptance of one another, not to rivalry.

The "equality" lies rather at a deeper level: in the personal encounter with Christ and with one another. It empowers the individual specifically to "occupy his or her own place" in the life of the community (1 Cor 12). In 1 Corinthians 14:33-36, a gentle suggestion of functional equality is rejected by Paul—as completely obvious. Is he then elsewhere in his letters supposed to be presuming much more radical revisions? Our method must be to move from those texts which are clear to those which are unclear, not the other way around. Even when the terms take on greater definition, we find in Paul an emphatic awareness of *his own* authority through his "apostolic commission," a sharing of *his* authority with others (Gal 4:14; 1 Thess 3:2; Phil 2:19-24; 2 Cor 7:7-16; 8:23); indeed, from the very beginning the Church in Jerusalem had—following the example of the Old Testament— "commissioned" certain tasks. To lay the responsibility for this ministerial tradition with "Luke" and the second generation cannot be accepted if we follow normal standards of critical historical research.

Although much did change and many borders shifted, still all this took place within the framework of the prevailing "social structures." In every century women have exercised a decisive influence upon what took place in society and in the Church, and in this process continually came up against restrictions imposed by their social "roles." However, a thoroughgoing transformation in such basic paradigms of behavior as gender roles cannot take place in a few years (and then be as quickly reversed), and also not in a single generation, as a look at contemporary history shows. Thus we should not confuse the freshness of the Christian beginning, which indeed pushed ahead into new territory, with a structural revolution. If the following centuries—especially after the Constantinian turn—did not carry the provocation that came from the New Testament decisively enough in a "Christian" direction, it remains true nonetheless that neither Jesus nor Paul, in their high esteem for and call to women, executed such a reversal of roles; however, they did point to a new direction that was open to further developments in society and in the Church, developments which in our own day have yet to be fully realized. We shall see that more clearly in part D.

Part B

The So-Called
Deutero-Pauline Writings

I. A One-Sided Subordination?:
Ephesians 5:15-33

In this pericope are found certainly the most comprehensive statements about marriage in the entire New Testament. Do they come from Paul himself? Although I personally am impressed by the arguments of those who defend a Pauline authorship for Ephesians,[351] in order not to prejudice the discussion I shall treat this passage among the "remaining" texts. This should round out our general picture. Thereby also its distance from the so-called main letters will diminish further.[352]

351. A. Vanhoye, "Personnalité de Paul et exégèse paulinienne," *L'Apôtre Paul,* A. Vanhoye (Leuven, 1986) 11ff.; A. van Roon, "The Authenticity of Ephesians," in: *Nov. Test. Suppl.* 39, Leiden 1974 (book review: M. Barth, "Die Einheit des Galater- und Epheserbriefes," in *ThZ* 32 [1976] 78–91); Baltensweiler, 218. Ollrogg advocates dating Col during Paul's lifetime, 219–242; similarly Witherington, 47ff.

352. I pursue the semantic and syntactic problems in a special monograph; see Atf VII; here I only bring forward the general thrust, mostly without citations.

1. To Become Filled with the Spirit:
Ephesians 5

"To be filled with the Spirit" is not merely a thought used to introduce the "household code paranesis" (5:21–6:9), but rather its supporting foundation; it returns in the concluding exhortation "at all times pray in the Spirit" (6:18), and thus constitutes an inclusion (whereby the last part rounds out the entire letter). What comes between them is an elaboration and specification of this basic Christian orientation. For that reason it is important to notice how verse 21 functions as a link with what follows. Verses 5:15–6:20 form a final interconnected part of the "paraklesis" beginning at 4:1, which after the exhortation to internal unity (4:1-16) proceeds to point out certain boundaries (4:17-5:14), following this finally, starting with 5:15, with a sequence of counsels formulated positively for the most part.[353] As a transition verse, 5:15 draws a consequence from our sharing in Christ's resurrection (5:14; 2:1-10). Thus resurrection and the reception of the Spirit have an internal connection. Since the structure of the passage is important, in our translation we will hold as far as possible to the Greek syntax, even if occasionally this makes for difficult reading.[354]

> 15a Pay close attention to how you live your lives,
>   b not like fools, but like the wise,
> 16a so that you *make use of the opportunity* (chance),
>   b for *the* days are evil.
> 17a For that reason do not act stupidly,
>   b rather understand what the Lord's will is (what pleases him) (!)

353. Occasional rejection of the contrary faults continues to serve as a contrast to the positive exhortations, while in Eph 4:17–5:14 it was rather the other way around; thus, the main accent has been transformed! "Do not become drunk with wine" in 5:18 is hardly a warning to drinkers (as if this were a particular danger in the community), but rather a contrasting image to being possessed by the Spirit.

354. For the breakdown into sense lines, I am indebted to Theobald; the exhortations begin at the left, explanations and justifications are indented, comparisons further. *Italics* indicate again our divergences, **bold** print those words which receive an emphasis from their position in the sentence.

18a and (so) do not become drunk with **wine**
      —*in which* unrestraint (disorder, perdition) lie—
  b rather become filled *with* (the) **Spirit,**
19a so that (thereby) you
      - converse among yourselves with psalms, hymns, and
        spiritual songs,
      - sing and chant psalms to the Lord with all your hearts,
20   - at all times give thanks to God (the) Father in the
        name of our Lord Jesus Christ,
21   - and submit *yourselves* to one another out of reverence
        for Christ,
22   wives to their husbands as to the Lord; (!)
23a   for (the) man *is* head (origin) of the woman,
  b   just as Christ (the Messiah) is head of the *assembly*
            (of humanity),
  c   *he himself* as savior of the body.
24a   *Yes in fact*
            just as *the assembly is subordinate* **to Christ (the
            Messiah),**
  b   in the same way altogether are the wives to the husbands.
25a You husbands, love your wives,
  b   just as Christ (the Messiah) has loved **the assembly**
        (humanity)
  c   and gave himself (delivered himself over) **for them**
        (in their place),
26a   so that they
  b   —after he had purified them
            through a washing with the word—
  c   **might be sanctified,**
27a   so as **to make glorious**—*he himself through himself*—
        the assembly,
  b   without a speck of dirt or a wrinkle or anything of
            that sort,
  c   rather (to the end) that thereby they be **holy and
            without reproach.**
28a As a *consequence,* husbands are *also* obliged to **love**
      their (own) wives like their (own) bodies.
  b   He who loves his wife loves himself;
29a   for no one in fact **hates** his own flesh,
  b   but rather nourishes and warms ("lavishes care
                and attention" upon) it,
  c   just as also Christ (the Messiah) toward
                the assembly (us, humanity);

30	for we (humans) are **members** of **his** body!
31a	"For that reason the man **leaves** father and mother
b	and joins himself with his wife,
c	and the two become one flesh."
32a	This *secret* (hidden reality) is *great; I am now speaking* of **Christ (the Messiah) and the assembly!**
33a	Yet (at the same time, alongside that) you
b	also as individuals: each should love his (own)
c	wife as himself, while, the wife should **reverence** the (her) husband.

Against Schnackenburg we find the structure proposed by Baltensweiler, which Lindemann has also accepted, to be correct:

Intro.	5:15-21:	"Spirit-filled Life in the Community"[355]
I A	5:22-24:	Exhortation to Wives
B	5:25-28a:	Exhortation to Husbands
C	5:28b-32:	Motivating the Husbands through an Explanation of "Self-Love"
Concl.	5:33	Final Exhortation to Husbands and Wives.[356]

In the course of this unfolding the motif of "fear of Christ" in 5:21 and 33 builds a kind of inclusion of the three main parts. We have indicated these passages by spacing them. Verse 21 constitutes a transition. Each of the three parts of I begins with a challenge/pronouncement; in A and C this is given a "natural" justification. Upon that follows, now introduced by an "as Christ also," a Christological justification, and finally a second challenge/pronouncement. In this regard part C has a special position; "The insertion is not only the high point, but also the main topic" (Baltensweiler). The accent is actually shifted strongly away from marriage parenesis to Christology, which Kähler shows by contrasting throughout "two series of dramatically different orders" alongside one another, which can be identified by "should" and "is" respectively; moreover, to the latter, which build the ecclesiological and soteriological "model," belong not only 22b, 23bc,

---

355. The heading comes from Schnackenburg; however, he closes with 5:20.

356. To this is added: II A 6:1-3: children; B 6:4: fathers; III A 6:5-8: slaves; B 6:9: masters; ending 6:10-20: exhortation to all (similar to the introduction).

24a, 25b-27, 29c, 30, and 32b,[357] but—as we shall see—also verses 31-32a.

To "examine carefully" one's lifestyle implies "wisdom" and "understanding" about those things which God delights in or finds good and beautiful, namely: that you become filled with the Spirit. This is implicitly contained in the expression "to take advantage of the opportunity." That is, not to "buy time" (how does one do that, actually? Perhaps through an intense activity?), but rather to take advantage of the favorable occasion. This expression, which has become proverbial, was originally borrowed from the realm of commerce. A person who goes shopping "examines carefully" (v. 15) what prices are being asked. But in this context *kairos* means something like "reduced prices" or "sale," so that the expression originally meant "Buy things cheap, or on sale."[358] To this corresponds: "for the days are evil." People have always complained about economic bad times, and thus about high prices. The expression has for a long time been used in an extended sense and means "seize the opportunity with both hands." However, in our case the "evil days" refer to the unsaved situation about which previously there had been so much discussion. An "astute" person is one who, in such circumstances, buys at the right place (Isa 55:1f.). Thus "God's special offer" is the Holy Spirit, with which God "now" intends to fill us (Eph 1:3, 13f.; 2:13, 18; 3:5)—if we come to appreciate the magnitude of God's offer!

The contrast of "drunk with wine" and "filled with the Spirit" gives rise to the impression that the author has noticed a striking similarity between their external phenomena (Acts 2:13; 1 Cor 12:2). Lest the impression should thereby arise that a person filled with the Spirit might lose control over him or herself and that "ecstasy" should be understood as a kind of "trance," in what follows the author shows clearly what the Spirit "pushes" us toward: not only to "songs of praise," but also to a continuous "thanksgiving for all"—thus, also for what is difficult—*and toward mutual submission.* Thus, being "filled with the Spirit" leads toward taking ourselves in hand and ordering our lives. Is

---

357. See the chart in Kähler, 107f., cf. 104 and 106.
358. For that reason ἐξ-αγοράζειν; for more details, see EuE 439f.

this an unexpected outcome? It fits with 6:14-18. However, the participial "submitting oneself" in verse 21 indicates that syntactically this clause is subordinate to the main verb "let yourselves be filled." This is one of the typical Christian exhortations to humility *(tapeinophrōsynē)* which we find not only in 4:2 and 5:2, but also in Philippians 2:3 and Romans 12:16, as well as in 1 Peter 5:5, and which run through the Gospels in the form of an exhortation to serve one another. This is not meant either to support or reject any preexisting social or hierarchical structure (cf. 1 Cor 12:28), but rather refers to the readiness to place *oneself* under others.

Still, verse 21—a typical transition verse—at the same time offers the catchword for the entire household code parenesis that now follows (until 6:9!), especially because verse 22 which follows does not have a predicate of its own in the best manuscripts, and is thus still subordinate to verse 21: "*submitting* yourselves to one another, ²²wives to their husbands as to the Lord." The reciprocal counsels now begin with the person who, in the ancient household *(oikos),* was in the subordinate position. Through this process, conventional standards of antique "household order" are accepted and given a new motivation through Christ. Apparently the author sees in this nothing that would offend anyone's sensibilities. Thus, he is not "opposing" a movement toward liberation (which probably did exist at that time), or a slave revolt, but is rather basing himself upon a general consensus among his readers, in that he here merely accents socially accepted norms.³⁵⁹ In the same way in 1 Corinthians 11 we also encountered the understanding, probably coming out of the Jewish tradition, that the husband was the "head" of the wife—as we now know, not "superior" or "Lord" ("dominator"), but "origin" or "source."³⁶⁰ It is the assertion of an essential organic relatedness, not of a power structure of domination.

However, some will object that the context expressly mentions "submission." This is indeed so, but this term is an addition not necessarily contained in the image of the head; here the latter

359. That would be parenesis in the true sense; see below, D IV 4. Cf. however, below, close to note 417.

360. On this see above, A VII 2; similar is Col 2:10. On the question of a (missing?) "social criticism," see below, D I 1 and 2.

provides only the foundation, it offers so to speak the fitting basis for the specific exhortation: *because* he is the origin, *therefore* be submissive. The latter is thus given a fundamental grounding, not from any arbitrary pronouncement; for anything living can only prosper if it observes the law of life given to it from the beginning. So even here, in this offensive notion (from our point of view) of self-submission, there lies hidden a reference to the "life of God." (4:18) or to the "fullness of the Spirit" (5:18).

In contrast to children and slaves (6:1, 5), "obedience" is not demanded of wives. This sometimes goes unnoticed. However, with all three groups the justification for the integration of oneself within a larger whole is given through a mention of "the Lord." Even here, however, there is a slight difference: For wives and children the phrase runs "as to the *Lord*"; for slaves it is "as to Christ [the Messiah]." The relation of slaves to their master is more distant than that between marriage partners, or that of children to their parents; this is why in v. 5 the somewhat more objective title of honor is used, and only in v. 7 converts to the more intimate "to the Lord." This is a detail, but it prepares us for the contrast to "Christ" in verse 23b.

2. The Messiah and Humanity

Indeed, the strong Christological foundation is the reason why in this instance the exhortation to the men (25-32) is longer than that to the women (22-24). In Colossians 3:19 (see below, #4), there will be a different foundation. In our presentation of the text we have indented the explanations and immediate basis for the imperative, and further set off the "comparative level" with a second indentation. But how does the author move from the relation in marriage to speak of the relation between "the Christ" and "the assembly"? What does he thereby intend? According to our research, he is not thinking of the relation between the (risen?) Christ and those (on earth?) who have already accepted his message (which we call "the Church"), but rather that between *the one who became human and humanity*. Such an interpretation alters certain perspectives on this passage and simultaneously on the entire Letter to the Ephesians.

The mutual relation of husband and wife is so fundamental that it concerns and touches everyone. Would not a restriction of the comparison to the assembly of believers here be strange? On the other hand one asks oneself, through which act does the "Church" "subordinate itself" to "Christ." This could only be a collective designation for the many steps by which individual people who are in the process of becoming believers, or believers themselves, come to the point of confessing Christ as their Lord and each freely submits himself or herself to him again and again. Otherwise "the assembly" would not only be a *metaphor* for the people of God—as we are familiar with this from the Old Testament: the virgin, the daughter of Sion—but almost a kind of mythological reality. Indeed, there is some speculation on this point; the development of this mythical discourse of the "Church as Bride" (sometimes thought of as preexistent) is given as one reason for a late dating of this letter. However, in general in the New Testament, *ekklēsia* does not yet have the specific meaning that we begin to find in the age of the Fathers.[361] In Ephesians "assembly" must be read in relation to the *qāhal jhwh;* however, the full assembly of the people of God is now widened to include *all* "peoples"! And *this* is the "assembly" to which Christ (the Messiah) joins himself.

Let us read Ephesians 5 in this sense from back to front: In 5:31f. the expression about "having left father and mother" is applied directly to "Christ." However, with whom does the descending one join himself, if not with all of humanity? Indeed, this union occurs *as a precondition* for our salvation. Only after he has made us members of *his* body[362]—at least that is the way the archaic thinking of the Letter to the Ephesians has it—does he "purify" us, that is, his body, whose "head" he is (5:23-27). To speak metaphorically: he does not first cleanse a body and then set himself as head over it (?!); rather, he joins himself with this (sinful) "wife," becomes thus "one flesh" with her, and *then* proceeds to wash *his own* body in the "bath of the word." (The image is thus not that of the bridegroom bathing the bride—which always seemed strange.) In this way he is both *the Savior* of his body and also its head, and thus the source or origin of its life (5:23). Moreover, he did not become this through the free agree-

---

361. On this, see above, A VII 3. More details in Atf III 2 and VII 5.

362. The Koine manuscripts and others add to 5:30: we are "from his flesh and bone" (plural: ἐκ τῶν ὀστεων—from his "bones").

ment and voluntary submission of the assembly; rather, he was *appointed to this by God.* Thus verse 24 should not be translated in the middle voice: "as the Church submits *itself* to Christ" (UT), but rather in the (frequently attested) sense of the present passive: "as the assembly *is subject* to Christ." Thus also in verse 24b there is no imperative to be supplied; instead, the indicative from 24a continues to control the thought: in the same way wives "are subject to" their husbands. In this way the entire verse 24 becomes a clarifying foundation for verse 23 and a *reason* for the exhortation in verse 22; moreover its second half is not some sort of repetition of this exhortation.

Seen in this perspective, from its very beginning Ephesians continuously presents these ten elements:

1. *God has*
2. made
3. the *Christ/Messiah*
4. to be the *head*
5. of the *body* =
6. *of the* assembly
7. that is, of *all humanity*
8. and through his *death*
9. *saved*
10. the *world/all reality.*

> "*He* unified all things in *Christ* as their *head*" (1:10) and "*gave him* to be the *head* over all in the *assembly,* which is *his body and* fullness" (1:22f.). To this "fullness" or completeness now belong *all* people: "For you who were once far off have now become *(been made) near* in the *blood* of *Christ*" (2:13); indeed, God has "*made the two of them into one*" (2:14) and "*fashioned*" the *two parts of humanity* "*into a single new human being in him,*" thus into *one* humanity (2:15). And Christ has "*reconciled to God both* (groups of humanity) in a *single body* through the *cross*" (2:16, etc.) We can now shed light on the Creator's household pattern for the world that had been kept hidden until then, that is, that "in *Christ* the *remaining peoples* make up a *co-body*" (with Israel) and "a *gift of God's grace*" (3:7-9), so that "through the *assembly,*" thus through a united humanity, "God's wisdom will become manifest to the nations" (3:10), "corresponding to what *he* has previously *ordained,* which in *Christ Jesus* he has now *carried out*" (3:11). Indeed, *all* fatherhood comes from God (3:15).

The foundations which God had laid through the incarnation and what transpired on the cross must of course be appropriated freely by humankind. Thus the entire letter *from its very beginning* lives in a tension between the indicative and the imperative, which we will attempt to elucidate through an examination of chapter four of Ephesians.

> Because God has done this, make efforts now on your own part to appropriate God's work and to become and to be "one body," etc., under the "one God and Father of all, who is over all and through all and in all" (4:6). However, the "upbuilding" (edification) of this body does not occur by the piecemeal addition of new members to a still unfinished body (?!—such a notion could be presented through the image of "building a house": 2:20-22); rather, "upbuilding" (edifying) (although this word is taken from house-building, it had long been understood in a figurative sense, and is here so used) of the *body* implies directly that those whom God has "given" to humanity, namely "apostles, prophets, etc," (4:11) are now on behalf of the "head" to equip[363] this "body," to which they already belong, so that the entire body may mature into an "organic growth in love" (4:12-16). Thus, according to the image presented here, the function of the "equipment stations" is not to *make* a body, but rather to guide a body *already on hand*—"all of us"—toward "complete human maturity" (4:13), to the extent that they "equip" the individual members from the head. This is the "salvation of acquisition," so to speak the "productive activity" that was announced as early as 1:14. For although they are already one body, they are still in a certain sense unsaved; they are still "the old humanity," who must put on "the *new* human being *fashioned* according to God" (4:22-24)—we are still "members of each other" (4:25). Since, "although once you were all darkness, now you are light in the Lord" (5:8); for that reason "arise from the dead, and Christ will give you light." We repeatedly come upon an imperative resting on the foundation of an indicative.

Is not everything now ready for the concrete specification of this in family life? The marriage partners should now express symbolically this relation between "head and body," since:

> "In the way the *assembly* (humanity) is *subordinated to Christ* (by God!), in the same way indeed (= in a true sense) are wives to their husbands" (5:24). This is a clarification of the *basis* for that exhortation, and indeed is so treated in what follows: Christ loved

---

363. Ἀφὴ τῆς ἐπιχωρηγίας = place of contact for supplying, furnishing, providing with something; see Ts 317.

humanity, offered himself on their behalf, purified, glorified, and sanctified them (5:25-27). For the assembled (collective) humanity is actually *his* body (5:30): indeed, in his incarnation he has become "one flesh" with it—this great, hidden reality which God now reveals to us (5:31f.; cf. 1:9f., 13, 17-20; 2:6; 3:3-5, 8-10; 4:20f.). It is as if the author wished to say: "Understand" finally what *God* has found good and offered us (5:15-17): the fullness of his Spirit!

Are not the consequences of this seemingly archaic form of presentation related to those that appear in the letter to the Romans? We can only draw out a few here for our section. There appears to be nothing gained for our inquiry with regard to the equal status of women. If, according to the traditional interpretation, it only said that the "husband is the head of his wife," now it is more clearly emphasized that she is also "subject" to him. Admittedly until now this was also the objective foundation for the command to "submit *herself* to her husband *as* to Christ (the Messiah)." This does not imply that the husband "is Christ" for her, or that he is the "intermediary to Christ"—of course the wife has direct contact with him, since her love for Christ is the specific motive for her submission to her husband; rather, that she should live out her familial position following the example of Christ, just as do the husband and the other groups. There is no suggestion that she is to be submissive and that the husband commands, but rather that she should *carry out in a Christ-like fashion* the social role of subordination that is prescribed for her.

In the imagery it is striking that "to become one flesh" is now so interpreted that the *wife* is the man's *body*. This means something more than only that "the two are one body." This is probably formulated to parallel the Christ-humanity relationship (v. 32). If "head" is understood as origin and organizing principle of the members, then the latter are not merely subjected to the head through "obedience"; rather, they are mutually bound together in an organic relationship: only together with the head can they come into their completion and maturity. Together they all build "the person." Of course, the comparison of marriage with the relation of "Christ and the assembly" remains an analogy which also contains many dissimilarities. For example, the husband is not the "savior" of his wife! The point of the comparison is the *essential organic relationship,* not a power relation of domination.[364]

3. Love of the Spouse as Love of Oneself

Corresponding the social order there is no discussion to the effect that *the husband* should "submit" himself to his wife—in spite of the general exhortation to mutual submission at 5:21. He is called to express this attitude in the form of love, and specifically as one who occupies a socially higher position. Still, *from this starting point* something is demanded from him that goes beyond pagan ethical expectations: a love that extends to self-donation—like that of Christ. This idea controls verses 25b-27. There the focal plane is not two independent persons; rather, the relation of Christ and the assembly is seen in terms of *the image of the body!* Christ offers himself for humankind, the head for the *body:* after he has cleansed it in the bath, he makes it beautiful so that it has no spots or wrinkles. Thus there is here no "displacement of the image" (Schnackenburg). Naturally what is said on the substantive level has an effect at the level of imagery, in the same way as the head is characterized as the "savior of its own body"; at the same time a bath as the cleansing of one's own body *is more natural at the level of imagination* than a beautifying of the bride by the bridegroom. Thus: on the objective level the discourse is about Christ and the assembly, on the level of imagery it is about the head and body (not: head and bride!); however, both of them are comparisons and models for husband and wife. Moreover, the question about marriage that was the point of departure does not penetrate the plane of imagery as much as has been previously thought.

From the self-surrender and concern of Christ *follows* the *moral obligation* of husbands *(opheilousin)* "to love their wives *as they do their own body*" (v. 28). Thus the discussion is here first, in its application to the question being dealt with, about two people confronting one another; however, this unity of husband and wife is also, as in 23a, and again in verse 31, seen under the *image* of "one body." Thus the idea of a "holy wedding" has vanished, while the notion that "the Christ" has joined himself with "the

364. Thus patriarchal models stand in the background; see below, D I 4.

assembly" into "one body" is now fully developed in 28b-32: love of one's own body is *love for oneself!* This is the next step in the thought process. By this the association of wife with the body is thought through to its conclusion. So also with regard to Christ in 5:25-27, the association was with "body" (and not with "bride"). By means of the general principle of natural self-love (any abnormal self-destructive tendency remains outside the field of vision of this passage), reference is made again, as in 23b and 25b through the "just as Christ," to the relation of Christ (the Messiah) to his body, to all humanity.

The quotation from Genesis 2:24 provides the grounds for holding that we humans are members of *his* body. With this quotation the author is thinking from the very outset of Christ the Messiah: *he* leaves "father and mother." This is not so much a more or less subtle reference to the fact that God also has maternal traits, but rather intends to emphasize first of all the descent of the "beloved one" (1:6), the "Son of God" (4:13), whom God in "generous compassion" (2:4) has given to all humanity as its new "head" (1:10, 22). The suggestion that the "assembly" is his "body" (1:22; 3:21; 5:23-27) is reinforced through the introduction of a new image: for just as husband and wife become "one flesh" in marriage, in the same way Christ (the Messiah) has become "one flesh" with humanity. Thus verse 32b is not some sort of belated "application" of this scriptural quotation to Christ, but rather the explanation of why the author quotes this verse *and what he meant by it in the first place:* "This secret (= this hidden reality)[365] is great; however *I* am speaking (in this connection) about Christ and the assembly." By this the author indicates that, as in verses 29c/30, so also in verses 31/32a he is still thinking of Christ and the "assembly," and thus in this connection is speaking of the union of Christ (the Messiah) with humanity, and is interpreting the scriptural quotation in this sense. He is thus not adducing an additional, belated "application" of

---

365. In our language "mystery" means a fundamental truth, thus something that transcends human powers of comprehension; μυστήριον, on the other hand, indicates that something is closed up or concealed. Through revelation it is made manifest and thereby understandable (Eph 1:9; 3:3, 4, 9; 6:19!). Here I contradict Schlier, 263, who sees here "events covering and uncovering themselves."

Genesis 2:24 to Christ, but rather presumes that the reader initially understands it in this sense. Thus "for this reason" really concludes verse 29c: *for this reason*—so that we may become members of his body (v. 30)—did Christ leave father and mother, etc. Thus the ambiguity of the word is intended from the very outset; in the postscript it is only clarified once more, not introduced for the first time. For that reason it does not read: "I *interpret it*," but rather: "*I am saying* (this) indeed about Christ, etc."—and am not speaking about Adam and Eve, nor about marriage, which otherwise the verse would be understood as referring to. Only in verse 33 is there a "practical application" to marriage.

And *for this reason,* because humanity is one flesh with him, *we are his members.* The topic of 28b-32 is indeed *self-love.* It thus must be explained how, in loving us, Christ loves *"himself,"* namely as his own members. Consequently, the recourse to the image of marriage is only a means to reach the concept of "one flesh." However, this does not primarily refer to the sexual act, as a Western reader might infer, but rather to personal and legal organic unity, which certainly does not exclude the marital union, but does not specifically refer to it.[366] The final intention is to motivate husbands to love their wives *as they love themselves* (vv. 28b/33a as an inclusion of this passage), in order to emphasize more clearly the love "of one's own *body*" (vv. 25-28a), while a wife is to love her husband "as her head" (thus also as her body!) (22-24; 33c).

This broadened vision of the *ekklēsia* opens up new perspectives. In what concerns the relation between man and woman, the discrepancy with the main letters becomes smaller. As in 1 Corinthians 11:2-12, the argument proceeds here as well from the image of the "head," which, through a reference to Genesis 2:21-24, describes the origin of woman. The fact that she is there called, not the man's "body" but rather his *doxa,* his glory or radiance, picks up the other topic, that is, that women seek to attract attention to themselves by "loosening their hair" (11:2, 10, 14f.), that is, they try to achieve independent "honor" for themselves. Although in this context "head" is not expressly continued in the image of "body," nevertheless both "*doxa*/glory" and "body"

366. On the biblical anthropology, cf. again below, C 3.

follow in Ephesians 5 in the series of *"unfoldings of the origin"* (the head). Here the two images merge. The catchword submission, which in the main letters only appears in 1 Corinthians 14:34, is in Ephesians 5:21 conditioned rather by the household code tradition. In 1 Corinthians 11 as well this natural background in ancient family law is not challenged. The two pronouncements thus do not constitute a contradiction, even though submission is not the topic in 1 Corinthians 11, but rather respect for the value of the woman, which Paul derives from her relationship with the man.

We must finally direct a short remark to the concluding sentence: "However each one[367] of you should love his wife as he loves himself." There is a slight contradiction with what went before: Christ, who has united himself with humanity as did Adam with his wife, loves the assembly *as his own body,* as his own flesh; in it he therefore loves himself! *However each one of you,* unlike Christ, who loves all universally, should "love your wives as yourselves." This is the simple conclusion from the passage verses 28b-32. It simultaneously sets up a framework and returns to the marriage exhortation that was the point of departure in verses 25a and 28.

It is often stated that here lie the most profound statements in the New Testament concerning Christian marriage. This is certainly correct, because here marital love is deeply anchored in our relationship with Christ. However, we have also seen that the point of the comparison is not so much the bridal relation between Christ and the Church, as it is his love for humanity "even unto death." Thereby one thing stands out clearly: the author establishes the relation of the marriage partners—and to that naturally belongs sexual union as well—unambiguously on the foundation of *love.* This implies no disparagement of the sexual, but rather a reattachment of it to its center and its taking on form from this core: an all-inclusive love emanating from God. Thus there is here also a redemption of physical love.

---

367. Πλήν also with Paul has no special meaning—such as "concluding a discussion," Schnackenburg, 262—but rather means (without ὅτι) "still, however, but"; cf. Ts 313; BDR 449.2. Schnackenburg and the UT suppress καί οἱ καθ' ἕνα!

The final verse segment is also about sincere love: if the woman treats her husband with reverence, this should be not out of insecurity or dependency, but rather from a mature freedom and sense of worth: "as to the Lord" (22!). The social understanding of proper roles touches only the external, unreflective framework, but this demand is rather about a spiritual disposition: the woman should shape her relationship to her husband out of her relationship to Christ, who does not oppress, but rather guides us into interior freedom and mature independence; not in a legalistic "fear" (Rom 8:15), not in a dependent anxiety, but in a reverence that is the expression of a mature love; a love that loses nothing, if it now assumes the place indicated for it in the existing order, but rather is able—something that is even expected of slaves—to recognize "the Lord" in its partner. This is without question an elevated ethic which can only be embraced and lived in the Holy Spirit, and which is anything but a passive compromise of oneself with the *status quo*. For how can the "war between the sexes" be overcome, except through a greater love? Otherwise there is no end to the chain reaction produced by pressure evoking counterpressure, etc. It is clearly stated that the man as well should operate from the same principle of love.

Similar passages can be found, not only in 1 Corinthians 13; Philippians 2; Romans 12:9-21; 13:8; 14:17–15:6 or in Galatians 5:22, but also in the texts about marriage in 1 Corinthians 7:1-5, 12-16, and 25-40 ("in the Lord"), as we have shown above. These texts are in no way inferior in profundity to the pronouncements in Ephesians 5, nor do the latter, by their discussion of "submission," take away anything from the freedom of the Spirit of these passages. The differences lie rather on the surface and are to be traced to the different topics and the sequence of thought. For that reason one should not exaggerate the importance of these differences, even if at this point the question of the Pauline authorship of Ephesians of course remains open.

4. Exhortation to the Men in the Letter to the Colossians

The parallel passage in Colossians 3:18 is similarly framed: on the basis of our salvation through Christ and our resurrection with him, again and again exhortations are pronounced, warnings in 3:5-11,[368] and starting with 3:12 positive challenges to accept peacefully what has already taken place. These lead from catchwords like compassion, forgiveness, love, and peace, the last of which is the "arbiter" in our hearts, and which decides and orders everything, toward the "rich" word of encouragement and toward the singing given by the Spirit, a communion in the power of the Lord Jesus up to the high point of the thanksgiving to the Father *(eucharistia).* A concrete expression of this basic attitude should be our ordinary lives, life in the *oikos:* "Wives, submit yourselves to your husbands, as is fitting in the Lord."

Doubtless, it is here presumed that the woman "is subject to the man" (cf. *hypandros*), by which are included not only the wives, but also *the other women in the household and in the community/society;*[369] for *every* woman has a *kyrios,* a man as legal representative, thus even grown sisters who may live in the house of their brother. In Ephesians 5:22, 28, 33, where the discussion is of marriage, "your own (husbands/wives)" is expressly added, while in Ephesians 5:24 the argument only says that "the" women "are subject to" their men; this is intended more generally. As a further point we should take notice of the reference to what is "fitting." This not only emphasizes that they are "subordinate," but simultaneously also that they should assume this position consciously as redeemed people thus neither in bondage and cowardly obsequiousness, nor in an aggressive way.[370] Everything must take place in the basic attitude that has already been clearly presented. Thus in the small addition "as is fitting [worthy, proper] *in the Lord,*" anything demeaning has been removed, because "the Lord" now indicates to each person what he or she should do in his or her situation.

The prevailing social order is fundamentally presumed without being challenged, and in this existing framework one can and should live as a Christian. This does not exclude, but rather directly incorporates, the possibility that under altered social relationships the same Lord might show us whether something

368. It is thus negatively expressed; the two participles in the aorist in 3:9f. refer specifically to the *presupposition* for the command *not* to lie.

369. Most likely similar to 1 Pet 3:7; cf. Atf IX.

370. Analogous—*mutatis mutandis*—to the parenesis of slaves in 3:22; cf. above, A III 3.

objectively different might then be "fitting." In such a situation it is always his peace—the reconciliation bestowed through him with both God and with our neighbor—that is the "arbiter," which is the literal way *brabeuein* in 3:15a should be translated.

The men are commanded, as in Ephesians 5:25, to love "the" women (here there is no "your own"). Sexual love for the wife must be integrated within a fundamental love for all people, one that takes on a special note in *each encounter between a man and a woman*. A man always conducts himself a bit differently with a woman than he does with a man, with a different style of courtesy and attention. He should do so with a specifically gendered reverence and esteem, with a care that, in its self-restraint, accords or creates for the woman a protected, anxiety-free space. Such characteristics will become all the more pronounced the more personal the encounter is. A relationship like that between man and woman based on Christ should leave its stamp upon one's entire life. It is deeper than any eroticism or sexuality, and must provide the basis for the latter.

Is it perhaps because the man's position is the "stronger" that he now—and only he—receives a negatively formulated exhortation, and thus a "warning"? "Do not be bitter against them," (thus Stier) not "cutting, prickly, sharp, hard, unpleasant, unbending, wounding, irritable, uncouth, brusque, unresponsive, violent, angry, contrary, cruel"—all these words are commonly used to translate *pikros!* A counsel like this comes from life experience; it touches primarily upon "male" offenses against women in general. Woman's "weapons" are of a somewhat different order; however, she is not the one who is here being warned, or before whom a mirror is being held up in which she may view herself. Is this due to a gentlemanly discretion on the part of the author, or rather to a Christian concern for the (socially and legally) "weaker partner" (1 Peter 3:7)? Whatever the cause, here there is certainly no (hidden?) oppressive mechanism at work.

In a similar way only fathers are then advised not to provoke their children, not to drive them to conflict or rebellion, so that those who find themselves in the weaker position do not become "disheartened," do not become "morose, listless, exhausted, anxiety-ridden" and—expressed in modern terms—in the extreme case, give up or become depressed. Finally it should again be mentioned that the word "obedience" appears only in connection with children and servants/slaves, while wives are expected—and with them the entire female gender—to *voluntarily* "subordinate *themselves* in a way worthy of Christ." This is the plain interpretation which is certainly quite compatible with the Paul of the genuine letters. What more there is to say on that account concerning the historical background or the integration in the household code tradition and the Hellenistic economic structure has been thoroughly presented by K. H. Müller.[371]

Finally, in Colossians 4:15 again a woman is named as the hostess of a "house assembly": "Greet Nympha and the community in her house" (UT). Here again it cannot be proved that she was the actual leader of the community.[372] It does not say "and her community," but "the assembly in her house." When the Jews in exile or in the Diaspora did not possess a specific meeting place, they met in private houses, and this custom was extended by the Christians. In the house of the wealthy Joachim "the Jews came together" *also* "to hold court" (Dan 13:4-6, 28, 49). There is no indication that the rich and influential Joachim was the "leader" of this "house assembly." He certainly did not act as judge, and in general appears to have been subordinate to the "elders." And anywhere in the Diaspora, if a rabbi was present, was he not the leader, or someone who would correspond to the "synogogue presider"?

On these grounds it is difficult to imagine that in a Jewish "popular assembly" a woman would occupy the leadership position. This further argues for the position that in a—perhaps somewhat freer—Hellenistic house a *Christian* assembly would also be led by a man, at least in Paul's sphere of influence, because specifically in his evangelistic "freedom" he remained thoroughly rooted in Judaism and was constantly concerned to

---

371. Cf. bibliography and below, close to note 416, as well as above, close to note 359; Müller's results (316–319), among others: "The ancient '*οἰκονομία*' prescribed in the first place for *a married couple* harmony according to the measure of wide-ranging reciprocity: husband and wife are exhorted to a mutual humanity, short of coming to the dismantling of the *patria potestas,* which was still held to be essential." Thus "in the Lord" is not a "more or less superficial 'regulation' of current social-ethical norms," but rather the "taking of an appropriate position" in favor of the social respect due to women.

372. Cf. above, A VII 4 towards the end and 5.

maintain unity with the Jewish-Christian communities (Rom 14:13, 20f.; 1 Cor 8:9; 9:18-23; 10:28; 2 Cor 6:3).

II. Woman in the Pastoral Letters— Improvement or Decline?

In order to round out our picture, we will include the other places in the Pauline literature where our topic is taken up: 1 Timothy 2:8-15; 3:2, 11f.; 4:3; 5:1-16; 2 Timothy 3:6-9; 4:19-21; Titus 1:6; 2:1-5. We group them according to theme. Although today there is a broad consensus that the Pastoral Letters were not written by Paul himself, new voices have been heard who speak on behalf of their authenticity, sometimes qualified through a "secretary" or "fragmentary" hypothesis.[401] The principal argument for the inauthenticity consists in the discrepancy between their content and that of the uncontested letters. However, one must ask whether we really find a different theology here.[402]

(1) Is there really present in the Pastoral Letters an "officially edited catechism" that in this form is unknown to Paul, and in which, in place of the variegated multiplicity of gifts and charisms we find rather a "group of officials"?

(2) Should in fact the "scriptural evidence of 1 Timothy 2:13-15 really be corrected by the Old Testament texts"?

(3) Is it true that it is virtually impossible to listen to 1 Timothy 2:9-11 alongside 1 Corinthians 11, and that in 1 Timothy 5:1 "marriage is not highly esteemed," since "in contrast to 1 Corin-

---

401. For a discussion and bibliography, see Lemaire; P. Rogers, "The Pastoral Epistles as Deuteropauline," *IrTQ* 45 (1978) 248–260. For historical reasons J. van Bruggen argues for authenticity; R. M. Lewis and H. Huizenga also assume this. Padgett defends the "secretary theory" (19) and refers continually in his article to "Paulus" as the inspiring author. Cf. further T. A. Robinson, Grayston and Herdan's " 'C' Quantity Formula and the Authorship of the Pastoral Epistles," *NTS* 30 (1984) 282–288.

402. In what follows we take up four points from the "summary" of Else Kähler, 168–171. The distinction between "charism and office" is a modern development that has nothing to do with Paul. On the other hand, it is not true at all that with Paul there are no indications of "office"; see my contribution ChuA 224–226 and "Sprachregelung." For similar reflections: v. Bruggen, 61f.

thians 7 it is here truly degraded into nothing more than a protection against immorality"—which some even claim to find also in 1 Corinthians 7:2-5?

(4) And is it true that in Titus 2:3 "the balance in exhortation that Ephesians 5 maintains is lost," so that "the woman is confined to her household role, while the husband is given almost an "official standing"?

One finds these or similar criticisms in many commentaries. But is it really true that "a completely different spirit breathes through these pages," one which is "neither biblical nor evangelical," so that we are confronted with an "either/or" situation?[403] Thus, we are in effect asking, as far as *their substance* is concerned, *how great the distance* is between the Pastoral Letters and the so-called authentic Pauline letters. In the process we leave aside the question concerning authorship. It is certainly legitimate to investigate first of all the inner unity of the New Testament Scriptures. A discrepancy may be assumed only if we discover incompatible pronouncements. In this our point of departure will be the modified understanding which we have formed from the "main letters." We will look for similarities, avenues of development, differences, or outright contradictions. These will later serve as elements for a historical appreciation of the Pastoral Letters, which we will for the present not define as either Pauline or post-Pauline.

1. Husband and Wife in Marriage and within the Family

Whoever its opponents may be—Hellenistic Gnostics or Jewish pre-Gnostics[404]—1 Timothy 4:3 expressly defends marriage:

> "Some will turn to deceitful spirits and the teachings of demons, to hypocritical liars who have seared their own consciences (or: whose own consciences have been seared), who hinder people from

403. Leenhardt, according to E. Kähler, 284, note 751; similarly Thraede, 109ff.

404. Padgett, 21: "precursor to Gnosticism arising from heterodox Judaism."

marrying,[405] (teachings, which say that) one should keep oneself from foods that God has made to be received with thanksgiving by those who believe and who have recognized the truth; indeed, these are **sanctified** through God's word and command.''

This is the same freedom of the Spirit as in 1 Corinthians 10:23-33[406] and a retrieval of respect for marriage, which we believe is in no way inferior to that of 1 Corinthians 7. The difference arises from the different situation: there it occurred in the course of an inquiry about abstinence; there was no doubt that marriage was fundamentally willed by God and that it was something good, and for that reason did not have to be emphasized. This conviction stood as something self-evident in the background also in 7:2-5 and 33-38, as we have seen.[407] Now, however, marriage is being attacked. The spiritual impulse to celibacy apparently found in Hellenistic dualism and asceticism a fertile soil, one which threatened to distort this drive. Padgett emphasizes (passim) that heretics should be seen as the background of the entire letter, and also for the many passages about women; Knoch feels the same way. As a matter of fact, the author presents a completely different side of himself than in 1 Corinthians 7.

And what about 1 Timothy 5:11-15? Can we agree with Else Kähler (162f.) that "there is no trace here of a high esteem for marriage''? For, in the face of all vices "the author sees only one protection: marriage! Thus from negative experiences he counsels remarriage.'' It is certainly true that the author here argues on the basis of unpleasant experiences (5:15: "for some have already turned away and followed Satan''). However, does that imply that the author "no matter what the situation says: woman is thus and thus (vv. 11-13); therefore, she must do such and

405. Not categorically: "they forbid marriage'' (UT), as if no one was permitted to marry, but rather: they hinder it, that is, they wish to make it difficult for their people. This could very well be an Essene influence on a (still young!) Christian community (cf. 1 Tim 1:6-9); it requires no explanation through "Gnosis.''

406. Knoch, 33: "What Paul said with regard to meat offered to idols (cf. 1 Cor 8:4-6; Rom 14:14: 'in itself nothing is unclean') is here extended to all foods.''

407. Incidentally, this is an indication that 1 Cor 7 does not argue against a tendency to disvalue the body.

such (vv. 14 and 15)''? As a matter of fact, he does not say that *all* are that way, but only that a danger exists: *"If* (!) they behave arrogantly against Christ, they wish to marry, whereby they then incur the reproach of having broken their earlier promise'' (5:11f.). Thus it is not the case that all the young widows are gossipy (etc.), but rather that this danger arises *if* they exploit their position as recognized "widows" in the community and "put on airs." One would expect that because of this danger (which cannot be denied and which apparently occurred in a few cases) one would have to carefully examine the young widows, etc. The simple specification of a minimum age of "sixty years" would seem to facilitate the decision; however, on the other hand, that appears to be a conventional criterion. Were there no Jewish precedents?

The somewhat brusque style would otherwise fit Paul well. One only has to think of 1 Corinthians 11:5f., 16, and 14:35f., or his polemic against the "super apostles" in 2 Corinthians 10-13. If the situation demands it, he can be decidedly sharp and occasionally exaggerate. We have to interpret such pronouncements according to the situation, and should not conclude to a fundamental disparagement of young widows, of women in general, or even of marriage, as if the latter were "only" a safeguard against certain vices. Indeed, it is a fact that the text would be more acceptable if it indeed did come from Paul, because its acerbity could then be explained through Paul's temperament, but if these sentences come from the pen of one of Paul's disciples, then they are possibly meant in a more deliberate and scornful way. We have to take into account that the author, who must have been superior to Timothy (who could that have been?) had specific cases in mind in that destination.[408] Perhaps he was even asked about them.

Still, how is the gruff command to remarry compatible with the statement "she is happier if she remains as she is" from 1

---

408. Padgett, 21, sees these young women as influenced by the "false teachers" who discourage marriage. He distinguishes them from "well-to-do women" who would financially support such teachers (1 Tim 6:3-10; 2 Tim 3:1-9). However, in this text, 5:1-16, that is not directly what is being spoken about. Even if such a teaching lies in the background, still in 5:11-15 nothing is made of it. They are indeed real, but general human weaknesses.

Corinthians 7:39? Is this not a blatant contradiction?[409] In 1 Corinthians it was a matter of young women who while still unmarried voluntarily expressed the wish to remain celibate; and if one had already proceeded for a time along *this path, if her fiancé should die,* she is encouraged *to remain* on this path. 1 Timothy 5:11-16 on the other hand is addressing the situation of a "widow," thus of a woman who up to now has lived a married life and is not accustomed to abstinence. Further, she is not asking if she may live by herself celibately, but is expressing the *desire* to be "accepted onto the rolls of the widows." According to 1 Corinthians 7, she would have to ask herself if she can take such a step with joy; otherwise she would be in the condition which Paul describes as that of "burning" (1 Cor 7:9; similarly Knoch; cf. also 7:6). On the other hand, in 1 Corinthians 7:8 one could sense a certain reserve on Paul's part with regard to widows and "single people." In 1 Timothy the concern is not so much with the new lifestyle of those concerned, but rather with the reception into a status that is associated with support of the widows by the community (5:9, 16!).[410] No such thing was under consideration in 1 Corinthians 7. Thus other motives might here come into play! A widow is "turned down" only in her request to be received and supported by the community; however, if she wishes to live a celibate life as a widow at her own expense, that is another matter entirely.

The somewhat brusque remark that those female applicants for the status of widow "should marry" should not be exaggerated into an apostolic command. Moreover, the inquiry here is on a different level than in 1 Corinthians 7; the accent is more that of an aid to decision-making for the leader ("counsel") than that of pastoral advice for those affected. Just as today a bishop may distinguish between these two forms of speech and avail himself of each as the situation warrants (he could say to a pas-

---

409. Schelkle, 86, says with an eye to Paul's "wish that all would be celibate like him": "the New Testament itself has moderated the rigor of Paul's position as—in a way closer to reality—it says (1 Tim 5:14): 'I desire that younger widows marry.'"

410. Knoch, 38, is of the opinion that the vow (πίστις) of the widow contained "an undivided dedication to the pastoral-religious service of the community they had taken on." In that case the idea of celibacy would be more like a consequence and not the principal motive. Specifically for that reason the author would be very cautious with "younger widows."

tor who inquires whether the community should support certain young widows: "they should marry," but to a woman who inquires of him personally about what lifestyle would be best for her, he might respond in a much more nuanced way); it would thus not constitute a contradiction if the same apostle wrote both texts—in different situations, however.

It is not thereby demonstrated that Paul is indeed the author of 1 Timothy; rather only that the contents of the two texts are no longer a reason for declaring the two letters to be incompatible. Neither is marriage disparaged in 1 Corinthians 7, as we have seen, nor in contrast to it does 1 Timothy introduce "a thoroughly positive position towards marriage";[411] rather, both texts apply the same basic principles to different situations. Thus there is no break with the early Paul, but rather a coherent development, one which extends down to the Apostolic Fathers: Ignatius, *Smyrn.* 13:1; *Pol.* 4:1; *Pol. Phld.* 4:2 and 3; 5:3; 6:1. Further, as Holtz correctly sees (123), "one should not speak here of a short-changing of the love commandment, because it does not enter into the discussion. The individual responsible for the community inquires (!) what should happen with the widows, what position they have in the priesthood of believers, what their relatives and the community owe them and they them." In this way the specific situation which the author is addressing is the principal key for unlocking each text.

The same is true for Titus 2:4f. Certainly "the tone is different than in Ephesians 5," but does this mean that the author basically does not feel it is also necessary to counsel the young husbands?[412] Why does he do this only in a general way (2:6)? One should pay attention to the structure: "You (singular) (!), however, teach what corresponds to sound doctrine: (!) *that* the older men should be sober . . ., that *likewise* the older women in their way of life should correspond to what is holy . . ., *so*

411. Kähler, 144; would that then constitute *simultaneously* an exaltation of marriage and a devaluation of the woman (see the beginning of this chapter)? But the author contradicts herself, since on p. 171 she writes that in the Pastoral Letters marriage is "not highly esteemed."

412. Cf. Kähler, 165 and 171. On the entire passage, see A. Padgett, "The Pauline Rationale for Submission: Biblical Feminism and the *hina* Clauses of Titus 2:1-10," *EvQ* 59 (1987) 39–52. On this also below, in what follows.

that they (!) may instruct the young. . . . However, encourage the young men to self-control in all things, and make yourself an example of this. . . ." Thus Titus is to present a standard to the older men and encourage the young men through his own words and example;[413] the young women, on the other hand, should be exhorted by the older women, not by Titus! Here apparently it is not so much a matter of preaching as of personal counseling, and there is a distance between the "young man" Titus and the "young women"; they are looked after by the older women. Is that the reason the author includes for the latter a longer list of suggestions, since these exhortations will only be communicated through others? Is he presuming, on the other hand, that because Titus is a man, he already knows what he has to say to the young men? The general counsel "to be calm and collected in all things" is further broadened through the "example" (2:7f.).

Finally, it is this text's intention "to shame the opponent." Is this someone definite, whom the author, however, will not identify? Is it the prosecutor and slanderer who lurks behind all human attacks (1 Tim 5:15), or does the singular stand for the unbelieving environment, "especially the circumcision party" (1:9-11)? In any case "one should refer the target of the *hina* clause (Titus 2:8) to the statements as a whole, including v. 2" (Holtz; cf. Padgett). All should take care not to disgrace Christ.

If the young women in 2:5b are especially intended by this reference, this is not because they had more need of it than the others, but rather because they are only exhorted "through an intermediary." However, perhaps there are also negative experiences here standing in the background which give the writer the occasion to emphasize this particularly. This no more intends a devaluation of women than the sharp phrasing in 1 Corinthians. Instead of declaring that 1 Corinthians 11:2-6 and 14:33b-36 were not writ-

413. Evidently because he is himself still a "younger man"; cf. 1 Tim 5:1-2. Knoch, 72, writes: "Paul's coworker of many years would not have needed such a detailed directive during Paul's lifetime." One would like to respond: did he perhaps require it *after* Paul's death? What "fictions" must one assume if these letters were written at a time when everyone knew that Timothy and Titus had either grown quite old or were already dead! *In this case* this would not be merely an occasional letter, but would have for its direct intention a widespread acceptance in this later period.

ten by Paul, one should draw attention to the fact that this and the other texts proceed from ethical norms that were universally accepted at the time, and in that sense are naturally conditioned by their times. In all these cases, it is not the author's goal to reform society, but rather that each person should conduct him- or herself properly according to his or her situation, for this is correct before God and does not bring the gospel into disrepute before outsiders.

One can establish the border between concepts conditioned by their times and standards valid for all times only after a protracted process of maturation in the course of history. The texts are open in this way to an educational process in which each generation must inquire precisely in what, given its situation, the public and individual good consists. However, *both* 1 Corinthians and Titus proceed from the, for them, self-evident foundation that the Christian wife should, in all freedom, integrate herself into the place accorded to her by the society of the time: in marriage "to be subject to her husband"⁴¹⁴ and to carry out properly her daily duties for her family (Titus 2:4f.; 1 Tim 5:8, 14). To dismiss this as "bourgeois Christianity" is to miss the main point; for the accent here does not fall on guaranteeing a comfortable, well-situated lifestyle, but the solidity of the everyday, in contrast to garrulousness and religiously camouflaged busyness (Titus 2:3-5; 1 Tim 5:4, 6, 8, 10, 13). It is never easy at any time to integrate religious experiences into the tasks of daily life. Still, for all that, this should not lead us to grow suspicious of religious ideas and thoughts, but rather to resolve to translate them into action, as in fact happens in the Pastoral Letters (1 Tim 5:8). Objectively speaking, this constitutes a development of thoughts which we have already met in 1 Corinthians 10:31 and Colossians 3:17.

In Titus 2:1–3:2 Dibelius sees a "Church order modeled on the household codes."⁴¹⁵ In comparison with Colossians 3:10 and Ephesians 6:1 ("Children, obey your parents"), what is striking is that here there is no talk of children. The latter are mentioned

---

414. Like Eph 5:22 ὑποτασσόμεναι, not "*obedient* to their husbands" (UT); cf. above, close to notes 360 and 371; but she *is* ὕπανδρος; see Rom 7:2; Eph 5:24.

415. According to Kähler, 144f.; similarly Baltensweiler, 214–217; K. Müller, 263–319.

only indirectly in Titus 2:4 and 1 Timothy 5:8, in that wives are encouraged to love and care for their children. However, if the fathers are not exhorted, as in Colossians 3:21, not to "intimidate your children," this means as little as the fact that husbands are not exhorted "not to be bitter or angry toward their wives" (Col 3:19). None of the lists of household commands is complete. The selection was at times random, at times conditioned by the local situation. Thus we read expressly only in Titus 2:5 and Colossians 3:18 that "wives should be subject to their husbands," that is, should voluntarily accept their position. If this command is not present in 1 Tim 5:14, one should not read too much into this absence. Objectively speaking it remains true here that the author is not proposing an entirely new ethic, but rather appropriates standards currently in place.

K. H. Müller has shown that the household codes in the New Testament do not derive from the "Stoic morality of duty," but rather from late Hellenistic "economy." These texts "on economy," that is, about the "household," attempted to find a middle ground between an incipient equality (liberalization) in the roles available for women on the one hand, and a patriarchal subordination on the other. Thus the household codes should not be seen in contrast to a common pagan ethic (something like Christian love in opposition to patriarchal oppression), but rather as "the expression of an (initially Jewish, later Christian) agreement with a moderate humanitarian position between the two extreme fronts that then confronted each other on the question of women."[416] Thus the acceptance of the pattern of the household codes would constitute an early Christian decision in favor of a middle path of social conventionality, for a moderately progressive behavior in social ethics. It does not, however, take a position toward an inner-Christian controversy over the direction to be taken, as though it were combating an exaggerated interpretation of Galatians 3:28.[417]

416. K. Müller, 284–289; cf. above 208; similarly Thraede, 119.

417. E. Schweizer, *Der Brief an die Kolosser* (EKK) (Zürich, 1976) 161. The supposition "of a wide-spread early Christian catechism, which would have contained such household codes" cannot be so easily dismissed. In any case, from this perspective there is no contradiction between the Pastorals and Eph/Col, and also no (longer) to Gal 3:28 (see below, D I 3) nor to 1 Cor 11, see above, A VII 2.

Thereby once again the difference between time-bound and God-given standards becomes clear: The New Testament authors take up current social norms, choose those which appear appropriate to their circumstances, and emphasize that, within this framework, the Christian must answer "before God" and "achieve his or her salvation" (Phil 2:12). Each age, like each individual person, must continually examine anew, as the social order transforms itself, and indeed through "spiritual discernment," what concretely God's will is. The ultimate norm is always that the human being can stand *before* God (Rom 14:4, 10, 12). The author of the Pastoral Letters[418] certainly believes that he has offered regulations that are valid before God for his time and situation, but he is far from dogmatizing their content for all times and places. It rather remains open[419] whether, under changed circumstances, a social order pleasing to God might look differently. Thus neither the conservative position as such, nor the progressive tendency as such, but rather the conscience that lies open before God is the place where here and now will be recognized what "indeed is pleasing to God."

2. The Term "The Husband of One Wife"

On one point, however, the Pastoral Letters appear to demand something completely new: that the person who holds office be "the husband of one wife" (1 Tim 3:2, 12; Titus 1:6) and a widow must have had "only one husband" (1 Tim 5:9). This certainly does not mean to imply that marriage is a *necessary precondition* for holding office; the examples of the celibate Jesus and Paul are too prominent for that. However, does the text intend to forbid a second marriage at least to clerics? There is a long and venerable tradition, which first developed only after this period, that specifies a single marriage as the ideal, and not only for clerics.[420]

---

418. K. Müller distinguishes clearly between the "household codes" in Eph/Col and the later "status codes" *(Ständetafeln)* of the Pastorals. However, the problem is similar, and in the historical classification I would be more cautious.

419. Even if he may not name it expressly; cf. below, D I 1 (3) and (4).

420. Cf. the commentaries as well as the two following notes, and below, close to notes 658f. Also Amphilochus, *Or. in occurs. Dom.* VII (PG 39:53C).

However, would this be the correct description? For indeed it is presumed, if a *widow* is described as "one man's wife," that he has already died; however, the talk concerning "supervisors, elders, and deacons" clearly does not have widowers primarily in mind. However, in this case the formulation is strange: should he *be* a man with one wife (thus not living in a second marriage), and *remain* so (that is, if his wife should die, not remarry)? The thought that he could become a widower, and then would not be allowed to remarry, seems peculiar, if at the same time such an obligation is set up as a *condition* for a still younger man being accepted into the office of elder. Then it should say that he must *remain* the husband of one wife. It seems equally strange if the author means to say that they may only *have been married* one time, that thus, should their first wife have died, they should not have entered into a second marriage, perhaps even before their conversion, and in any case before the question about the office of elder became acute for them. Or does he wish to emphasize that the candidates should not be divorced, or at least, if they are divorced, they should not have remarried (Holtz)?

Trummer joins with S. Lyonnet in reading this formula in the sense of leading a good married life.[421] German- and English-speaking people would do better to reverse the Greek sequence ("one wife's husband") to: "a husband of one wife"—as in the expression: "Beware the man of *one* book." According to Theodor of Mopsuestia this refers to a man who restricts himself to one woman and "confines to her nature's urges," not only in contrast to polygamy (which probably seldom occurred), but also to the conventional practice in their pagan environment of

---

421. P. Trummer, "Einehe nach den Pastoralbriefen," *Bib* 51 (1970) 471–494. On p. 489, note 2, T. refers to Stanislaus Lyonnet, "Unius uxoris vir," *VD* 45 (1967) 10, and on p. 472 to the New English Bible: "faithful to his one wife," as well as to Hanson's commentary. C. K. Barrett and N. Brox also agree, as does A. Lemaire, 32. The thesis is well grounded historically, by Lyonnet also through Jewish parallels. On this, see also Lyonnet, "Le Diacre dans l'église et le monde d'aujourd'hui," *Unam sanctum* 59 (1966) 272–278. Linguistically it does not require the detour through "the breadth of meaning of εἷς . . . from a numeral to the indefinite article" (Trummer, 481), since here certainly the numeral is intended, for otherwise the phrase "husband of a wife" would constitute a *demand* to marry.

consorting with *hetairae,* concubines, and prostitutes.[422] This is an understandable and thoroughly appropriate request. If only a single marriage was allowed, it would then in any case be strange that in 1 Timothy 5 "at the specification 'the wife of one man' (v. 9), there twice immediately follows a direct counsel to young widows to remarry" (v. 14) (Trummer, 480). For "this 'recommendation' to enter into a second marriage apparently does not mean that *henos andros gynē,* if she becomes a widow a second time and is dependent upon the church's care for the aged, would be excluded from care in the *viduat*" (Trummer, 480). Thus "the wife of one husband" only means that she was faithful to her (current) husband *as long as she had one,* a description which does not exclude the possibility of two marriages in succession. If on the other hand it was known that besides these she had had other relationships—people knew each other—she should be turned away. This interpretation makes more sense.

422. Similarly also Theodoret; see Trummer, 482f. Does not *univira,* which is frequently discovered on tomb inscriptions, indicate that they were *faithful* to their husband? For a discussion, see J. B. Frey. "La signification des Termes μόνανδρος et univira," *Recherches de Science Religieuse* 20 (1930) 48-60. There (49) the commentary by Fletwood (1691) on a pagan inscription is quoted, that a woman who died before her husband was praised as *univira.* This must certainly refer to marital fidelity. Otherwise one would have to assume that she married late and that it was noteworthy that she had not been married before. This sounds strange. Rather, it has for its practical meaning that she carried on with her (most probably first) husband until the end and was never unfaithful to him. Still, even if the word *also* refers to a widow's fidelity *after* the death of her husband (which sounds unusual as a tomb inscription, since such were normally put up by the surviving *husband*), it is to be noted that in 1 Tim 5:10 we do not find μόνανδρος, but rather: ἑνὸς ἀνδρὸς γυνή and μιᾶς γυναικὸς ἀνήρ, respectively (3:2, 12; Titus 1:6). If "once only" presumes that *de facto* she—probably in her youth—never had another, then the other interpretation only implies that she has been faithful to the one to whom she currently belongs. This question is not discussed by H. Funke, "Univira," *Jahrbuch für Antike und Christentum* 8/9 (1965/6) 183-188; rather *univira* is interpreted as obviously meaning "married only one time"—wholly apart from a partly inaccurate interpretation of Christian texts.

It should further be noticed that "supervisor" and "elder" probably refer to the same office,[423] and that thus here *episkopos* does not yet mean the "bishop" of the letters of Ignatius of Antioch, and certainly not the position of a contemporary diocesan bishop. It is thus expected of candidates for these offices that they are (and have been) faithful to their vows. It is one moral condition alongside many others, but certainly an important one. For this one does not require the supposed and strange joining of ascesis and libertinism in Gnosticism, which Trummer invokes (478f.), nor the statement that "because of the prominence he gives to eschatological expectations marriage still" (!) "occupied a secondary place in Paul's theology." We have interpreted 1 Corinthians 7 in a different fashion. Therefore it is not the case that "the post-Pauline literature had to go considerably beyond Paul in its pronouncements on marriage," as if now for the first time the value of Christian marriage had been fully discovered. We would then have in the Pastoral Letters an increase in the esteem for marriage. Is not rather what is new in Christianity the discovery of celibacy? It would be a curious roller-coaster ride if at first marriage were depreciated, and then raised in value. Rather, the demand for marital fidelity fits very well with 1 Corinthians 7:1-5 and the high esteem for marriage with the view of the main Pauline epistles.

3. Woman in the Community and in Public

In 2 Timothy 4:19-21, among those who send greetings, we again encounter "Prisca and Aquila" (in this sequence, as in Rom

---

423. Compare Titus 1:5 and 7: "Install elders—πρεσβυτέρους—. . . . For (!), the supervisor—ἐπίσκοπον—must be respectable." What follows now is not a repetition of vv. 5 and 6, but a continuation and explanation. And does the conjunction of ἐπίσκοπος and διάκονος in 1 Tim 3:1-13 imply that in their communities there were no "presbyters" or that here, as in Phil 1:1, they only had the name "supervisor"? Chief responsibility in the place, thus something corresponding to our office of bishop, fell upon Timothy himself, who, however, is rather to be understood as coworker of the "apostle" (whoever that might be). The terms are not yet firmly established. More on this, see ChuA 225. Cf. also G. Holtz, on the respective verses.

16:3 and Acts 18:18-26), along with a certain "Claudia." This fits with the picture of the female coworker that we have formed from Paul's main epistles.[424]

However, why is it said in 1 Timothy 3:11, in the middle of the instructions to the deacons: "Women must be equally[425] worthy of respect. . . ."? What is the meaning of "equally," and why is "Women" used without the article? If the wives of the deacons were intended, it would be better to have the article. Is he thinking rather of female deacons,[426] or of "women as unmarried female assistants"? After an examination of the first two possibilities, Lewis opts for the third.[427] However, in this he seems to press the text too far. It is indeed correct that it is a matter of "female helpers"; however, one cannot properly restrict the expression to any of the three named groups. Could not also the wives of the "supervisors" be included? So one should here translate it simply as "women" (as far as they are here involved),[428] and leave it open whether thereby the wives of those named, official "female deacons" (similar to Phoebe in Rom 16:1), or also "widows" are intended. The reference was at this time still open, and an unambiguous terminology had not yet firmly established itself.

The fact that already before the Pastoral Letters there is evidence of female deacons (Rom 16:1) and that the further development of this institution is well established, allows us to conclude

424. See above, A VII 4.

425. Ὡσαύτως in 3:8 and 11 picks up again δεῖ εἶναι of 3:2; similarly Titus 2:3, 6. Is it placing the women *alongside* deacons and elders, and not in dependency to them, as married women were?

426. Thus Knoch, 30; if it were "wives" according to him an "especially brusque transition" would be present, since the deacons were supposed to be "husbands of one wife" (3:12).

427. R. M. Lewis, "The 'Women' of 1 Tim 3:11," *Bibliotheca Sacra* 542 (1979) 167-175.

428. Stylistically a parallel to 1 Cor 7:39; see above A IV 3, with note 197: "a wife" (in the union being discussed) = the female portion of such a couple, or "a wife in this situation." Thus here: women = female persons in this context, thus those who have something to do with the mentioned tasks. "*The* women" (UT), on the other hand, creates a false impression, as if all women were intended.

that such things existed in the environs of the Pastoral Letters.[429] From these women it was expected that they "not be slanderers, but rather sober and reliable in all matters." Of course, such is expected of all Christians, be they male or female; if it is especially emphasized here, this is because it is a necessary precondition for a certain kind of service; something similar occurs with the "supervisors and deacons." These women have a special function within the community, whereas the general instruction for "the" women has already been given in 1 Timothy 2:9-10. For the rest, *more* exhortations are directed at the men in 1 Timothy 2:1-3:1 than toward the women—a good indication that, in the depiction of offices in chapter 3, the ultimate leaders were men.

Also in 1 Timothy 5:1-16 the concern is women in the community. At 5:1-2 Timothy himself is exhorted to speak "with the older women as with mothers, with the younger women as with sisters, with all reserve." This is more than a norm of respectability. It is consistent with the new solidarity in Christ, which was experienced and lived according to the model of family relationships.[430] With this greater intimacy—upon greeting, one exchanged a "holy kiss"—distance and reserve must also be relearned. Still, this reference alone should do away with the impression that in the Pastoral Letters women are no longer as highly esteemed as they are in the main Pauline epistles. Such a thesis could only be defended if one dismissed 1 Corinthians 11 or 14 as insertions (Thraede, 111f.).

However, the following passage shows that in this Christian family there were normal human problems which had to be resolved in a sober manner. This accounts for the objective tone.

---

429. G. Lohfink defends this interpretation, "Diakone," 395f., since it stands "in the middle of a list of offices." On the further development, see also Lohfink's reference to the two *ministrae* in the report of Pliny, above, note 343, as well as the image of the Church in the Syrian *Didascalia* (ca. 280), which compares the bishop with God the Father, the deacon with Christ, and the deaconess with the Holy Spirit (in Hebrew, a feminine), while the presbyters "only resemble the apostles." On the history, see A. Kalsbach, "Die altkirchliche Einrichtung der Diakonisse bis zu ihrem Erlöschen," *RQ*, 22, Supplementheft (Freiburg, 1926).

430. See above, A I 1; Knoch, 37: "not a patriarchal, but a brotherly authority."

1 Timothy 5:3-8 is written to show what an "authentic widow" in the community means. The talk here is not yet of official verification, but rather of the conduct that qualifies a woman as a Christian widow: that she is respected in her family and is supported by them as far as they are able (vv. 4, 8); that if she is alone, she places her hope in God (apparently also in what concerns her support); and that she spends her life in prayer. As a consequence, those women who do the opposite are not "true widows."[431] After this clarification of terms come the instructions in verse 9: a woman who satisfies these conditions and has passed her sixtieth year may be "officially received" into the "catalogue" of widows. Admittedly, besides this institution of widowhood there are also in the community many widows who are young or middle-aged who also are trying to live according to the same ideal, but who are not yet "officially" received.[432] Moreover, verse 9f. mentions even more and stronger criteria for acceptance. However, it is not clear from the text whether a "widow" undertakes

431. Ὄντως χήρα in 5:3, 5 apparently means the spiritual disposition, not their lack of being provided for. "Incorporation in a religious status group whose chief work consisted in the service of intercession and praise of God" (5:5, 11; Knoch, 38) seems to me over-precise. Yet one should still not conclude from the fact that such an "institution" existed that it could not already have been developed in Paul's time. There are Jewish precedents (Jdt 8:4) with a development toward voluntary celibacy (Kruse, 102), which was especially suggested for widows (Luke 2:36; 1 Cor 7:8, 39f.). Also, the manner of speaking in Acts 6:1 leads us to this conclusion, and one should not so easily suppose that in such historical details Luke was here engaging in back-dating. Kruse, 110–112, correctly reminds us of the wives and children whom the apostles left behind. Announcement and event are really "new," so that precisely at the start a new type may spring up relatively quickly, even if such would still undergo further development.

432. In 5:16 the thought is probably of a married woman who cares for widows among her relations (mother, aunts, sisters), not of a "believer" who is *herself* a widow, as Padgett (21) believes. Indeed, here the social provision stands in the foreground. Even more: "Perhaps widows lived together in the house of a well-to-do Christian woman, under the supervision of a woman (deaconess?)" (Haag, *Bibellexikon*). On the services they were to render: "While in the East deaconesses appeared, in the West it was more often widows. May we suppose the two offices were the same?" When Ignatius writes (*Smyrn.* 13:1): "I greet the households (οἴκους/families) of the brothers with wives and children—and the virgins who are called widows," these evi-

other work for the community besides "prayer," or whether she is only cared for; one can suspect the first only because of the negative contrary image given in 5:13.

We have already stated that the following verses 11-15 must be understood in relation to the situation: rejection only from inclusion into the lists, not necessarily also from celibacy; the sweeping injunction to marry then indeed applies only in view of the possible dangers.[433] That certain individuals may then still remain alone is not excluded; this belongs to the unspoken presuppositions, the "common sense" necessary for the interpretation of such a text. Certainly these arrangements are not written down as a formal law, but are rather to be adapted by a prudent conscience carefully weighing the data:[434] *normally* "they should marry"; nothing more is intended! For the rest, it is striking that the talk is not about "virgins"—which does not mean that this early movement had died away; rather, we must once more remind ourselves that all letters are occasional writings which do not treat systematically all the questions of community life.

That 2 Timothy 3:6f. contains no insult to the female sex should be sufficiently clear from the context. First are described general sins of "people in the last days," and in verse 6 it is indeed primarily *men—hoi enduontes—*"who sneak into houses and there draw certain women over to their side."[435] The broader context dramatically illustrates what kinds of things could develop under the cover of the community. The Christian brother- and sisterhood brought people into more intimate proximity than anywhere else in contemporary social life. This carried new dangers with it, if this intimacy lost its anchor in Christ. Since there were no "community centers" then, a life of Christian community could only be carried on in private houses ("house circles"). From this it should at least become clear that women in the Christian communities gave up many social protections and were thereby

---

dently have a certain coherence, and the terminology for such celibate women as a class in the community and in their service is not yet univocal; however, the thing itself has already existed for some time.

433. Cf. above, B II 1.

434. As Paul does abundantly in 1 Cor 7. The strong $\beta o\acute{\upsilon}\lambda o\mu\alpha\iota$ 5:14, we treat in researching 1 Tim 2:8: Atf VIII.

435. Like "Jannes and Jambres," Exod 7:8-12; cf. Knoch.

vulnerable to the danger of greater "public exposure."[436] The limits that are nonetheless urged correspond to contemporary sensibilities and do not constitute a particular disparagement of women in the Christian communities. On the contrary, Christianity worked more to soften than to rigidify such barriers, and thereby created precisely the difficulties that such texts as the Pastoral Letters are trying to resolve.

To conclude, let us return once more to Titus 2:3-5. Again, the topic primarily addressed is the conduct of older women in the community and in public. They should be "dignified in their behavior, neither slanderous nor given to drink." These are serious admonitions, and lead one to believe that substantial breaches of conduct had occurred. Thus we are all the more surprised to read further on: "They must be capable of teaching what is good, so that thereby they can encourage the young wives in their love for their husbands and children." As we saw above, the instruction of the young wives is the particular charge of the older women, not so much of the community leader such as the one to whom this letter is addressed. Naturally what is meant here is not instruction in the official "liturgy," but rather in the household sphere, but there also formation in the faith and the conduct that should flow from this—thus pastoral, and not merely domestic, education. Hence the prohibition contained in 1 Timothy 2:12 is at least relativized, since a woman can "teach" to that extent. However, the elucidation of this "most important text in this connection" (Kähler, 143), that brings together all the questions we have touched on requires a more profound investigation.[437]

4. "Keep Still and Be Quiet"?: 1 Timothy 2:8-15

If so far we have been able to make the statements from the Pastoral Letters comprehensible to some extent from the various situations they were addressing, in this difficult passage all the problems seem to appear together. For this reason exegetes have typically at this point given vent to their frustration, their dis-

436. On the difference between public and private roles: Love, "Roles," 54–57; cf. above, A VII 1 (towards the end).

437. See the monograph Atf VIII; in the following we again give only a summary.

pleasure, or their indignation. While the men are exhorted with a single, short sentence, women are the recipients of an extended moral sermon. Simple dress is prescribed for them, and they are positively forbidden to make themselves attractive. They should submit themselves peacefully and not get a notion of teaching or of giving any instruction to a man. And the justification? It is simply because Adam was created before Eve, while *she* allowed herself to be deceived before him, and then led him astray. However, if she does penance through giving birth to children, then she may also be saved. The last seems to be a case of "works-righteousness"; moreover, Thraede seems otherwise to be correct when he writes that here "the opposition to the traditional rights of female Christians in the community assembly, specifically 'praying' and 'prophesying' (1 Corinthians 11), is most clearly apparent." Must not an exegete lay down arms in light of this? The proposed translation we here present introduces substantial changes into verses 8, 9, and 15; but how should we treat verses 11-14?

> *1 Timothy 2:8–3:1a:* [8]Thus I desire that the men in every place pray, raising clean hands, without *vehemence* and *doubt;* [9]equally (I desire) that the women, with noble (appropriate) bearing *embellish* (adorn, bedeck) themselves with *tact* and *level-headedness,* not with braided hair or gold or pearls or expensive gowns, [10]but— which is fitting in women who have cultivated piety—with good deeds (through correct behavior).
> [11]A woman should **take instruction** in peace with complete (all) submission; [12]however, I do not allow that a woman **give instruction,** and also not that she dominate over a man (i.e., not with authority), but rather live in peace (in her social position in peace with the man). [13]For Adam was created (formed) first, then Eve. [14]And it was not Adam who was deceived; however, the woman, after she had allowed herself to be deceived, committed an offense, [15]but she (will) **should attain salvation** through *the* childbirth (the birth *of a* child). If *they remain* in trust (belief) and love and holiness with (under) tranquility, [3:1](thus) is **the word trustworthy!**

Structure: After the greeting (1:1f.), and the characterization of Timothy's task, specifically to combat false teachers (1:3-11), and a transitional expression of gratitude that Christ has deemed the author of the letter "reliable" *(pistos)* (1:12-14), v. 15 begins the actual body of the letter.

First Part 1:15–3:1a: "Salvation" through Christ
- for the author himself: 1:15c-17, with a doxology;
- for the one who receives the letter: 1:18-20, with a cautionary example;
- for the community and the world: 2:1-3:1a, which divides into
  (a) an exhortation to the community (2:1-3),
  (b) praise of the universal Savior, Christ (2:4-6),
  (c) a confirmation of his own universal mission (2:7) and
  (d) a development of the exhortation to prayer and godliness
     to men (2:8) and
     to women (2:9f.), as well as
  (e) a clarification of the place of women in the life of the community, with
     - a biblical justification (2:13-15a) and
     - a concluding promise (2:15b-3:1a), which simultaneously forms a larger inclusion (πιστός ὁ λόγος in 1:15a and 3:1a).

The location of the passage concerning women within the larger topic of salvation/redemption through Christ (1:15–3:1a) is significant. In the same way the immediately following episcopal and diaconal instructions (3:1b-13) are not presented as something on the plane of administrative "commands" or "rules and regulations for office holders" (thus Thraede, 109), but rather are viewed in their significance for salvation, which is strongly underlined through the concluding hymn to the "mystery of our religion." It concerns nothing less than the rescue of humanity through the unique mediator, Jesus Christ! *This is why* the men should pray with clean hands. This cleanliness is explained through the fact that when in prayer before God, they should *neither demand vehemently nor despair*. This language does not refer to quarrels among themselves, but rather concerns the purity and reverence of their relationship with God.

Also with regard to the "adornment" of women, the thought is about their relation to God. For they should not imagine that, in the cultivation of their piety, they can make any impression *upon God* through external embellishment, but only through upright behavior. Tactfulness and level-headedness, a sensitivity to what is becoming before God, should be their "adornment." That at the worship service they might possibly make either a good or a bad impression upon the men is at best a side issue. The stress is different in 1 Peter 3:1-6, where the "adornment" of good conduct is primarily appreciated in its effect upon the men, but then also from the point of view that it is also "precious before God" (v. 4).[438] As a matter of fact, the point of both texts is not to forbid pretty clothes and jewelry to women, but rather through a comparison with her attention to her appearance it is brought out that before God and human beings there is a deeper beauty that lies at a different level (cf. Ezek 16:13-15, 25; 28:12, 17). Thus, in analogy with the "clean hands" of the men, with the women what is primarily at issue is their relationship with God; for impure prayer is unprofitable. Starting with 2:11 the text indeed speaks of relations in the community, but under the aspect of engagement with God's word in Scripture and the extension of the good news. It is in this context that the questionable biblical argumentation occurs.

The instructions in 2:1-10 concern not *only* conduct *during the worship service,* but "in every place," thus also prayer and living before God *in ordinary, everyday existence.* And in a similar way there is a broader dimension attached to "learning and teaching," etc. (2:11f.). The fact that in a public assembly, in which customarily men and women were together, women should not "teach," corresponds to the general sensibility of the Hellenistic cultural world, intensified by the Jewish background of Christianity. For up to that time women were not even allowed to study the Torah, let alone to teach. Naturally, a woman was not forbidden to explain something to a man (or her husband) in the ordinary course of things, and thus to "instruct" him (Acts 18:26); it was only that, within the context of the community, a woman should not be a "teacher" to a man. Here probably the thought is primarily that she should not conduct any official baptismal catechesis for men, whether alone or "in a group." On the other hand, according to Titus 2:3, they *should* "instruct" the younger *women*—this probably concerns not only everyday matters but also baptismal catechesis and pastoral care, corresponding to the practice of the first centuries.

That a woman should not "*rule* over a man" is not a reprimand to the desire to dominate—this is never to be approved—

---

438. A detailed examination of 1 Pet 3:1-7 in: Atf IX. All the relevant passages from the New Testament letters are included.

but is analogous to the more fundamental command not to transgress the generally prescribed behavioral roles in social and community life. Therefore it is not the case that from now on "leadership role" in the community is forbidden her—although such may have been the convention under Paul—rather, the constraints seem to be older. The word *authentein* is rather vague and refers to everyday behavior. Because of the new freedom in mutual relationships, it probably happened more often that situations arose where a woman sensed that she was superior to men and held influence over them. Still, she should exercise her spiritual authority, in such things as prophetic service, within the context of the generally recognized social structures. These were, however, so shaped that basically a man is *kyrios* of a woman: he was the bearer of rights and responsible from the point of view of family law. Naturally this left its mark on the style of group and community life. Again: the author is inculcating norms that in themselves were generally accepted; in no sense is he here trying to dismantle violently what would have been common under Paul.

All this takes place within the framework of what we also found in 1 Corinthians 11 and 14, Ephesians 5, and the other statements in the Pastoral Letters;[439] however, we must again notice that the author is addressing a concrete situation and thus tailors his statements proportionately. There must have been women who overstepped the generally accepted norms, and these occasions may have influenced the concrete formulation, even though the statement in itself is universally valid. Under other circumstances, however, such an admonition would have been unnecessary. It in any case does not constitute a deliberate correction of an already accepted practice (coming down from the apostles). "Submission" and "peace" should be interpreted in connection with the valid community and social order, not in relation to marriage. Such statements come so naturally to the author that he would not even have understood our puzzlement. 1 Timothy is in no sense a polemical attack on emancipation—in that case, it would have looked very different—but verses 2:8-15 rather constitute *one*

439. Cf. especially above, A VII 1-3; B I 1 and B II 1; a more precise formulation and further evidence for our interpretation of 1 Tim 2 can be found in Atf VIII.

element in a community instruction. We must thus interpret the statement within its epistolary and sociological context.

The same holds true for the argumentation on the basis of creation and the Fall, which follows the contemporary pattern of Jewish Bible interpretation. Its intention is not to oppress women or to ascribe the guilt only to them; the purpose of this typological exegesis of the text is rather, as Padgett (27–29) emphasizes, to make understandable the specific threat to man and woman by means of their respective archetype. Both are in danger; the author is here in search of some—any—biblical evidence for a conviction which he already held for other reasons. It is not here being maintained that the woman is *more* endangered than the man; rather, the attempt is made here, from the *nature* of Eve's sin, to comprehend the *specific* threat to the woman. If it is said of Adam, "he was not tempted," then every Jew understood that this could only mean that he was not tempted *in the same way* (that is, *directly*) by the serpent, as was Eve. Ultimately both sinned and were judged independently, not one for the offense of the other. Thus, a Jew would not have heard this kind of typological exegesis in so selective a manner as a modern Western reader.

Historically, this particular passage has given rise to a sequence of unfortunate results because the time-bound material has not been sharply enough distinguished from the intent of the author. However, the intended moral message may be formulated as follows: "In the life of a community (not only at the worship service!), woman should occupy that place that in general is found appropriate, whether it be on the basis of universally valid criteria of value, or whether it be on the basis of the interpretation of certain biblical texts." However, this is not expressed abstractly, but immediately in a concrete fashion: in *our* particular social and community situation, the woman should "not teach or exercise authority over men."

The fact that women here receive a comparatively "long" admonition is certainly an indication that already at this time certain problems were found with this position, problems whose traces we perhaps only today are noticing. Still, once the basic openness of this section for further theological development is clarified, we will be prepared to accord again more uprightness to the biblical authors, and not attribute to them a misogyny and chauvinism where they were merely trying to pass on the good news of salvation to their age according to their limits and opportunities. Did they not perhaps give, from their total understanding of the mystery of Christ, a more appropriate response for their time than we—from our present stage of development—give them credit for? The more generously we grant these inspired authors the gift of discernment in the concrete application of the truths of salvation, the freer we will be to request from God such gifts for ourselves and for our own time. Hippolytus says in his Easter homily (59, SC 27:187): "Women were the first to see the Risen Jesus. Just as a woman was the first to introduce sin into the world, so was she the first to proclaim life to the world. Therefore they hear the holy voice: 'You women, rejoice,' whereby the initial sorrow was swallowed up in the joy of the Resurrection."

Finally, we have translated verse 15 differently. It is not through *giving birth to children* that women will be saved, but rather by *the* birth *of the Child,* specifically, of the Messiah, that (first of all) *Eve* will be saved! She is still the subject of the sentence. What is being referred to is not the process of birth as a human act, but rather *the Child who is born:* the Messiah. Thus verse 15a is an interpretation of the *promise* of Genesis 3:15 ("your offspring will crush the serpent's head"), not of the punishment pronounced at 3:16 ("under pain you shall bring forth children"). With this one stroke the problem of works-righteousness disappears from this text, and woman no longer has a *special* and extra path through penance to salvation. Rather, she will be saved through the *Child* whom *she* bears.

As far as its content is concerned, this interpretation fits with our analysis of 1 Corinthians 11:12 and, from this point of view, could be attributed to the same author (Paul). In his principal epistles, Paul does not yet speak of a "new Eve," alongside his "new Adam," and does not refer to the mother of the Messiah by name. However, the line is incipiently present in the phrase "born of a woman." It is thus not surprising that the author, where he speaks of the relation of husband and wife, does not remain with Adam and Eve, but looks forward from Adam to the Messiah, and from Eve to the mother of the "Christ." In both places, therefore, he is not stopping with the "order of creation," but complements this perspective with a view of the "new humanity in the image of the Creator" (cf. Col 3:10). For

1 Timothy 2:15a this means: in spite of the continuation of an apparently "misogynist" exegesis of Genesis 3, with whose help he supports what is for him a problem-free community order and in this is a child of his times, he does not allow "the woman" to remain subject to this reproach—conventional in Judaism— but rather also indicates her way and place in the events of salvation. Through the fact that the "Son" came into the world through a woman (Gal 4:4; 1 Cor 11:11f.), he wished to heal *this* wound of humankind. Feuillet comments on Genesis 3:15: "God gave the woman a *certain priority* in the history of salvation; she is the first to experience the divine promise of salvation." Ultimately, this passage is about Eve's "revenge against the serpent." For "the serpent is punished both by God and by the woman. The woman must be the one truly responsible for its destruction."[440] This also stands behind 1 Timothy 2:14/15a, and is applied in 15bf. There thus is one continuous line of development: Eve[441]—Mary—the women at the tomb—the women in the Church—summarized in Revelation 12. Admittedly, we have not yet come to a full realization of this saving act of God, not even within the Church.

After these typological statements (2:13-15a) about "woman" and at the same time "the" woman,[442] there then follows in the concluding sentence the application to Christian *women*. We thereby draw 2:15b and 3:1a together into one complex sentence: "*If* they[443] remain level-headed in trust, love, and holiness" (cf. 2:9), they will experience "the trustworthiness of the Word" (con-

440. Feuillet, "Sieg," 34 and 31. Cf. also LG 56.

441. Evdokimov, 174f.: "In the realm of religion, woman is the stronger sex"; thus "the temptation of Eve determines the religious principle of human nature. Once the most sensitive organ is affected, the rest follows of itself."

442. Feuillet, "Sieg," 31, correctly remarks that "it is not as if Eve is the type for Mary"; (just as little is Adam for Christ; cf. my contribution "Jesus Christus—die endgültige Offenbarung Gottes—Biblische Sicht," 55–57). It is rather the case that what we have here is a structural *parallel:* they may on occasion function as "types" for their *descendants.*

443. Now the plural; this indicates that the author has remained with his theme, "the conduct of Christian *women,*" and now draws the conclusion from the typological foundation. He illustrates in practice with "faith, love, and holiness" what he had intended with θεοσέβεια/devotion and ἡσυχία/peace in vv. 10 and 12.

cerning salvation through Christ: 1:15; 2:5, 15a). Thus even this most "offensive" text blossoms into a proclamation of salvation which did not shy away from the process of inculturation in its own time and thereby challenges us today to separate it from what is time-bound. And even if much still remains open, nevertheless some of the clefts between Paul's principal letters and the deutero-Pauline can be filled.

Part C

Toward a Biblical View
of the Human Person

The originality and specificity of different cultures shows up most clearly in their anthropologies, in the image they present of humanity. All words and concepts are indeed merely a perpetually renewed attempt to structure complex reality and thereby to render it comprehensible. The various languages or language families do not all analyze humanity the same way. Moreover, this can produce a whole series of misunderstandings as soon as these languages come into contact with one another. What does the Semite really understand by the words which we in the Western languages translate as body, soul, flesh, spirit, creator, or image? And why does Paul put "flesh" deliberately so close to "sin"? Does this indeed supply a justification for attributing to Paul a contempt for the body? In order to answer this question we shall first study the Greek and Semitic view of humanity in itself, and then examine its theological application to the events of revelation. In the space allowed us we cannot try for an exhaustive presentation of this topic, but must content ourselves with sketching these difficult topics in terms of some simple formulae.

1. Greek and Western Dualism

If there indeed exists in the Indo-Germanic languages, because of their common origin, a certain commonality in these basic questions, this is intensified by the fact that Western thinking is so powerfully stamped by Greek culture. Greek culture is based upon *the eye;* a basic grasp of a matter is referred to by preference as *theoria:* "sight" or "view." The analysis of humanity is also based upon what is visible. What of the human can be seen or perceived through the other senses is called *"sōma/body,"* while the *"psychē/soul"* is defined through the negation of the first: the soul is in-visible and not graspable; it cannot be spatially confined, is unfathomable, immortal, and immaterial. Thus, what is esteemed to be higher is not defined by its positive characteristics, but only through a negation of supposedly "lower" qualities. This introduces a considerable ambiguity.

Plato traces this duality back to our very origin. According to him, the soul, which descends from the realm of Ideas, is for a certain time bound in matter. Thus Plato depicts the three basic powers of the soul[451]—represented as a driver of a chariot with two horses—driving across the heavens, but because of the wilfulness of one horse, namely the "appetitive" nature of the soul, it gradually deviates from its proper path and is drawn downward. Thus, as both a punishment and a purification the soul must spend a certain time in the body. The word play involving *"sōma"* and *"sēma"* illustrates that the "body" is the "grave" of the soul. Salvation consists in the soul finally again "divesting" itself of the body; when, on the "island of the blessed," it attains the "vision" of the eternal "Ideas," it is forever happy.[452] Admittedly here Plato has to avail himself of spatial representations: *"eidos/Idea"* means "visible form." Aristotle, through his doctrine of form and matter (hylomorphism), tries to depict both elements together in the "substance" of human beings as a whole; however, ultimately through his positing of a *materia prima,* he retains a basic dualism. The body remains alien to the soul, and, as the principle of "multiplicity," matter remains a polar opposite to the "unity" which is the defining trait of the divine. The biblical notion of a "creation" of matter by God's "Spirit" (power) is foreign to the Greek outlook. So in the last analysis the latter remains dualistic.

---

451. Λογιστικόν, θυμοειδές, ἐπιθυμητικόν, roughly the "rational, emotional and appetitive," Plato, *Phaedrus* 247; cf. TDNT IX 610f.

452. Cf. Plato, *Cratylus* 400C 1f.

This division becomes especially clear in their view *(theoria)* of death: because the dead person no longer behaves as he or she did before, one says that the "life" or "soul" has departed. What remains behind is then a mere body, matter, a shell, which decomposes and ceases to exist, while the "soul" or "spirit" of the person (a spiritual substance?) continues living without the body. Thus death is a separation of the soul from the body. Since the ideal condition for the soul is thereby achieved, it is difficult for individuals of a Platonic orientation to perceive the doctrine of the resurrection of the body as "good" news and salvation. Its realization appears to them not only impossible, but also not even desirable, because perfection and completion are hindered by the body. It is difficult for them to understand the idea of a "transformation" of the body. We observe in 1 Corinthians 15:35-53 to what lengths Paul goes to make this notion comprehensible to the Greeks. It demands not only a willingness to believe in the power of God, but also a complete reversal in one's way of thinking.

2. The Integrated Thinking of the Semite

The Semite also attempts to analyze humanity, to "figure it out," and to express this in a variety of concepts. At the same time, and in contrast to the Greeks, in this endeavor this mentality to a certain extent "closes its eyes." It does not proceed from the "visible-invisible" opposition, but attends rather to basic conditions which it *experiences* and *feels* in itself. From this starting point it arrives at four fundamental words:

Nephesh[453]—*human beings as deficient.* When a human person considers itself, its first impression is one of compulsion and desire, the condition of being dependent on things and people; in short, mortals experience their poverty: hunger and thirst, a longing for presence and relationship, for help, and finally for a future and completion. The Semite does not characterize this primitive "desire" of humankind through an abstract category, but rather by an organ of the body, because we experience something of it in that organ: *nephesh—the throat!*

---

453. For content I depend upon Wolff, 25-95.

Bāśār—human beings in their frailty. The frequent experience that this basic desire is not satisfied repeatedly runs human beings up against a limit and makes them conscious of their weakness. To indicate this, the Semite says *bāśār—flesh.* Naturally the word first refers to the physiological reality of the flesh of animals and human beings, but also, as applied to humanity as such, is often used as a term for the human person as such, and specifically in the sense that human beings are frail, exposed to the predations of powers human and natural, weak, powerless, and mortal. The thought behind this is perhaps that it is precisely in the human *body* that *decay* becomes visible.[454] This is why in the Semitic reflection on the nature of humanity, "flesh" is the term used to register the basic experience of human weakness and powerlessness. It is not that a human being "has" flesh, rather a mortal "is" flesh. The word can also mean either kinship relation or humanity. Although *nephesh* is occasionally used in later texts of the Old Testament also for God, to refer to God's becoming aroused (Job 10:16), or to describe God's love or anger (Isa 1:14; Jer 12:7; 15:1; Amos 6:8), *bāśār* is never used with reference to God.

Rūach—human beings as empowered. The Semite experiences a third aspect of humanity: the experience of power and energy, of physical as well as psychological vitality. Again the Semite does not choose an abstract concept, but rather describes this condition concretely with *rūach—wind, air in movement, breath.* The fact that breath is the necessary source of vital power makes it for the Semite the image of an essential characteristic of humanity itself: vital power, feeling, personal energy, a dynamic relation to others.

Lēb—human beings as rational/sensible. Once again the Semites close their eyes and consider their "awareness" of themselves: "knowledge, insight, consciousness, thinking, understanding, know-how, and memory" lead without interruption to "conscience, intention, drives and decisions of the will," as well as the capacity to devote oneself to something. We in the West typi-

---

454. The heart "of flesh" in contrast to the heart "of stone" as a positive image for vitality in Ezek 11:19; 36:26; 2 Cor 3:3 is "simply unique": Wolff, 54.

cally reduce these to the basic powers of the intellect and will;[455] the Semite says *lēb—heart*. What is affective and sentimental, emotionalism and mood, what in our language we associate primarily with "heart¦," are only secondary overtones of this term. They more directly pertain to *nephesh* and especially to *rūach*. The location of reason in the "heart" may be partially explained by the fact that in the origins of the Semitic languages, functions which in our imagination are exercised by the brain were ascribed anatomically to the heart, especially "thinking and memory." This calls to mind our English expression "to know by heart." Physiologically the "heart" often indicates the whole chest and sometimes "the hidden center and depth of a person" is suggested. Thus the heart as a concept for the central vital organ becomes for the Semite the fundamental concept for what we indicate through "I" or the awareness a person has of him- or herself, and thus the center of relationship—that by which a human being is distinguished from an animal.

All four central anthropological concepts stand at times for the *entire* human being, and thus also for our word "person" in its various colors as needy, weak, strong, or self-aware. It is not the case that human beings are "made up of" these elements or are "put together" out of them, but rather *they are nephesh*/throat, *they are bāśār*/flesh, *rūach*/wind/breath, and *lēb*/heart. It thereby becomes apparent that all four basic conditions are characterized by a reference to bodily symbol; and all four make—when seen from the Greek perspective—a statement simultaneously about both "body and soul": *nephesh* refers to *both* physical *and* psychological appetites, *bāśār* to *both* physical *and* psychological weakness; *rūach* can mean *either* psychological or bodily power/vitality, and *lēb* includes the heart as the vital organ of the entire person; the phrase "to restore the heart" in Genesis 15:5 means "to strengthen oneself by eating a little bread."

Read in this fashion, basic biblical pronouncements sound a bit different: "YHWH God formed humanity out of the dust of

---

455. Incidentally we also understand intellect and will not as two distinct substances, but rather as two aspects or capacities of one "spiritual nature"; cf. Dihle, ψυχή κτλ., TDNT IX 612; however, see the entire article: 608–666.

the earth and blew into its nostrils the breath of life,[456] and thus humankind *became* a living *nephesh*/throat" (Gen 2:7). "You shall love YHWH your God with your whole *lēb*/heart and with your whole *nephesh*/throat and with all your strength" (Deut 6:5). "Create in me, God, a pure heart/*lēb* (thus a new, conscientious orientation for my life) and give me a new, enduring *rūach/spirit* (give me also the power for the corresponding patient execution of what I have conscientiously recognized)" (Ps 51:12). "All *bāśār*/flesh (every human being) is like grass" (poor, weak), but through the coming of God "the glory of the Lord reveals itself; all *bāśār*/flesh will look on it" (Isa 40:5f.).

It is always the *entire person* who, "with both body and soul," is regarded from different perspectives. For that reason it is customary to speak, in contrast to Greek dualism, of an integral or "holistic" image of humanity among the Semites. This becomes especially clear in their *images of death*. Death does not involve something like a split between *bāśār, nephesh,* and *rūach* (where would *lēb* be?), but rather implies that the entire person (in Greek terms: with body and soul) passes over into another condition. From now on it leads a shadow-existence; its home is the "grave" or *sheōl*/the underworld.[457] In the underworld knowledge is also darkened; there is nothing like a "spiritual soul" now "liberated" from the body. Of course, during the Hellenistic period this shadow existence is gradually mixed with the *psychē*/soul; however, originally *nephesh* and *rūach* move into the realm of death just as *bāśār* and *lēb* do. They are thus *changed* by death, and do not simply cease to exist. Ezekiel 18:4, 20: "Only the soul

---

456. Here we do not find *bāśār* and *rūach,* as if spirit and matter were mingled, but rather *hayyāh:* life, living soul; thereby the change to a living *nephesh* is described, thus: elevation (or alternatively, "transformation") of the dust into another quality. Cf. 1 Cor 15:43.

457. See Isa 14:4-22; Ps 88; Job 30:23; Eccl 3:19f. For more details, see Wolff, 152–176. Why did the Egyptians place food for their dead in the grave, and why did they construct such expensive pyramids for their Pharoahs, and why did they they mummify and anoint them? Evidently existence beyond the bounds of death had also a physical, bodily (if transformed) dimension for them. In Israel, as a matter of fact, graves were not particularly honored or venerated, not because the body no longer existed, but because the shadow existence of the "body *and* soul" was not something to celebrate.

(nephesh) that sins must die''; for the Greeks, it is unimaginable that a soul should die.

A final possibility to transgress these limits would be to say that the person is as a whole "whisked away" (Gen 5:24; 2 Kings 2:3, 5; Ps 49:16; 73:24, 26), and thus expressly "with body and soul" transported to the glory of God. "YHWH bestows death and life, casts down into the realm of death, and lifts out of it" (1 Sam 2:6; cf. Deut 32:39). Thus the gradually developing hope for a resurrection is described in such a way that "the dead" or "their bodies" arise (Isa 26:19; cf. Ps 22:12-30), and specifically to a final, definitive life or shame (Dan 12:2). This occurs not through a new union between an immaterially existing soul with the decayed body, but rather through a "transformation" of the dead (1 Cor 15:51-54), who "come forth from the grave" (John 5:28f.). Ultimately, indeed, death itself is "separation *from YHWH,*" and the overcoming of death is founded *in union with YHWH.* Those are theological categories; however, the anthropological perspective that lies behind it is holistic and not dualistic.[458]

3. The Theological Application of Anthropological Categories

In and through humanity's self-experience, moreover, the revelation of the Old and New Testament brings a further dimension to expression. In its relation to YHWH, humanity experiences its creator and itself as created, it encounters its Savior and acknowledges its own sin. In this area, as we have just done, Western thought would tend to work with abstract categories. Semites, on the other hand, prefer to speak concretely. At the same time, they have no other categories at their disposal for their experience of God than those they have developed to understand their

---

458. For more on this, especially with an eye to Paul, see Ts 49–68; 117–129; 144–153. It is significant that in the entire section "life and death" by Wolff, 150–176, the question of a "split" between body and soul never comes up. Everything suggests that death affects the entire person, but does not totally annihilate the person. For these people the dead continue to exist somehow, even for that period in the Old Testament before a belief in the resurrection developed.

own humanity. Thus, to describe the overpowering might of the self-revealing God, they reach back to the human experience of wind/breath/vital power, and bestow upon this divine reality the name: (the) *rūach* (feminine). Admittedly, this now refers to much more than human vitality. Later Christian theology will make the point that all our categories regarding God are only "analogically" valid: from one and the same point of view, God is both similar and dissimilar at the same time.

Before such divine might and holiness humanity experiences itself not only as a creature dependent upon God, but also as one who has failed in its relation to God and in its responsibility before God (Isa 6:5). This "sin," for which there are indeed other terms, refers to a fundamental weakness of humankind before God, and is therefore named "flesh"—alongside its basic meaning, now in a new theological, and specifically soteriological sense. Thus, soteriology or the doctrine of salvation bestows upon this anthropological term an additional new meaning. Beginnings of such a doctrine can be found already in Genesis 6:12; Deuteronomy 5:26; Isaiah 40:6; Psalm 65:3f. The Qumran writings speak of "sinful flesh" (*bāsār*—1 QM 12:12) or "flesh of unrighteousness" (1 QS 11:9). Paul falls directly in this tradition, in that for him "flesh" (also *bāsār*) very often refers to ethical vulnerability, weakness, egoism, and sin. As we saw, this implies no contempt for the body, but rather consists in the extension of a concrete manner of thinking (flesh = humanity in its frailty) onto a theological reality.

In this sense, "flesh" stands in pointed contrast to *rūach,* the new life force from God, in which humanity may now share,[459] and which therefore is now "proper" to humanity as well: *rūach* is the new existence from God (Jer 31:3; Joel 3:1; Rom 8:16). The opposition *rūach*/spirit and *bāsār*/flesh thereby comes to stand in practice for the unbridgeable opposition "God and the power

---

459. To that extent the spirit coming from God is a reality in itself that is *bestowed* upon the person. But then it is not something like a "part" of the person or a partial substance, but again a total aspect of the person, similar to the way a person "becomes" through God's act of creation in the anthropological sense *bāsār, nephesh,* and *rūach.* One should notice that *rūach* is feminine.

of sin,'' ''good and evil.''[460] The two terms, which on the anthropological level refer to the entire person from different points of view, and which thereby mutually complement one another, are applied, when transported into theology, to describe a (soteriological) ''dualism'' (or better, opposition) which is much more pronounced than the Greek (anthropological) dualism of soul and body. The other pairs of terms then follow in the wake of this opposition. Thus Paul does not employ *nephesh/psychē* to designate some sort of higher, indestructible essence of humanity, but rather to characterize its inability to receive God's gift (1 Cor 2:14; 15:44-49). The ''psychic'' and ''earthly'' person is one who is deaf to God and who is in need of salvation. ''Heart,'' on the other hand—in itself ambivalent (positive: 1 Thess 2:4; negative: Rom 1:24), stands rather on the side of *rūach*/spirit (2 Cor 5:12; cf. 1 Peter 3:4). However, with these translations we have anticipated a bit.

4. Greek and Semitic Thinking—Incommensurable

If up to now it has been possible with some effort to grasp the *content* intended by the Hebrew terms, we fall into complete confusion as soon as we attempt to *translate* one anthropological system into the *language* of the other.

Anthropological			Theological
HEBREW	**GREEK**	**ENGLISH**	
nephesh/throat	*psychē*	soul	psychic = human beings as
human beings			vulnerable to sin, incapable
as deficient			of God
bāśār/flesh	*sarx*	flesh	''fleshly'' = before God,
human beings	*(sōma)*	(bodies)	human beings as weak, sinful,
as weak			and *therefore* mortal
and powerless			
rūach/wind,	*pneuma*	spirit	spiritual = human beings as

460. The difference between the ''frail person'' and the ''person who shares in God'' (Closen, 170f.: Ps 8:5f.; 82:6f.) is an Old Testament image for the theological distinction between ''flesh'' and ''spirit.''

Anthropological			Theological
breath, human beings as empowered			penetrated by God's Spirit
lēb/heart human beings as reasonable	*cardia*	heart	human beings before God, in their knowledge and action, "conscience," "center."

One notices immediately: *psychē* captures scarcely anything of the appetitive aspect of *nephesh,* but rather introduces entirely new elements, especially in its distinction from "body." *Nephesh* and *bāśār* are related to one another and each embraces "body and soul"; in Greek, on the other hand, there is an unbridgeable chasm between them: a fundamental dualism. Indeed, the Greek word *pneuma* still has the double meaning wind/spirit (notice the word play at John 3:8), yet is understood anthropologically like *psychē* in the sense of an immaterial reality. However, our English word "spirit" has lost any association with a powerful physical "wind," but rather introduces the totally foreign element of rationality. "We cannot overestimate the distance from 'breath' to 'spirit' as the organ of knowledge, understanding, and judgment."[461] For in English we would rather associate the connotations indicated above of *lēb* with "spirit," while "heart" falls nearer to the vital experience of *rūach,* but is not able to carry the rational, intellectual, or "spiritual" baggage of *lēb.*

Finally, if one were to ask modern persons what is "more real," they would naturally point to flesh, to the material, graspable body, while "spirit" connotes to them something more insubstantial or "unreal," nonempirical. This would only precipitate a bemused shaking of the head from the biblical authors, for indeed *rūach*/spirit refers directly to one's vital power, next to which the "weak flesh" cannot stand comparison. The contrast becomes sharper in the theological application of these categories. It may well be the case that the Semites also wished to return to the "fleshpots of Egypt," because they could not exercise control over the divine "Spirit"; but then this is due to the total and unique

461. H. W. Wolff, 63.

transcendence of the divine, and not to any "unreality" of "spirit."

One particular basic Greek category does not exist in Hebrew: *sōma*/body—and that alone should cause us to sit up and take notice. In contrast to the four mentioned categories, *sōma* refers not only to an organ or part of the body, but to all the members together as a unity. For that reason it appears more suited to stand for "person," and in particular with fewer negative overtones than *sarx*/flesh. However, the break with Greek thinking becomes suddenly clear when, in the Greek (Septuagint) translation of Genesis 36:6, *nephesh* is translated by *sōma* (thus, soul with "body"). This is only understandable because in Hebrew both can mean "person"; in the Septuagint *sōma* stands for "back" fourteen times, fourteen times for three different words for "corpse," once for "skin" and in the plural once each for "babies" and for "soldiers/army" (collective). Twice it expresses *sheēr*/flesh as nourishment and twenty times *bāsār*/flesh. The last is especially common in the purity codes in Leviticus 14–19. Thus the translators see in *sōma* on the one hand a word for person; on the other hand they choose it where the body is meant, but where "flesh" is too harsh for Greek ears. For they translate *bāsār* a hundred and fifty times with *sarx*/flesh, and indeed both in the material-empirical sense and in the extended anthropological sense, also in the mentioned chapters of Leviticus. Thus it is no surprise that also in Paul *sōma* shifts back and forth, sometimes meaning "mortal humanity," and sometimes also "sinful humanity" (Rom 8:13). However, for that reason *sōma*/body for Paul naturally frequently has the anthropological, ethically value-neutral meaning of "body" or "person," and in the discussion about the resurrection or the "body of Christ" has positive theological connotations. Thus one should not simply equate *sōma*/body with *sarx*/flesh. As we see, no term is exactly congruent with the others in any respect.

What should we do? Some recent translators take the liberty of translating *sōma* sometimes with human being, *bāsār/sarx* in the corresponding places with sin or egoism, *rūach/pneuma* with divine power or might, *lēb/cardia* with reason, and *nephesh/psychē* variously according to the context. However, all five terms may occasionally be translated simply by "person" or a personal pronoun. Admittedly, thereby certain important connotations are underplayed, and completely new ones introduced. For that reason we cannot dispense with a so-called "literal" translation coming to us via the Greek, although the categories contained therein do not exactly correspond. There is almost always such a semantic difference with all the words of a foreign language; here, however, it is especially great. And since it is a matter of fundamental issues touching our life and belief, the consequences are especially serious. For that reason we cannot dispense with a "struggle with concepts." To this we must also add the fact that the contemporary conception of the human person, not least on the basis of new insights into psychosomatic connections, is leaning again toward a more integral or holistic view of the person. However, one should only be careful not to lose sight of the clear *soteriological* dualism, the opposition between good and evil; for then the kernel of the biblical proclamation would be betrayed. Humanity is sinful, and only through God's activity of uncovering and forgiving of sin can it be healed and sanctified, not through psychology alone.

It is obviously not our place to declare one anthropological system to be "true" and another "false"; each possesses its share of truth. However, we must attempt to understand the Hebraic system, because the proclamation of salvation has been passed on to us in this language, the message that lies behind the words and can be translated into every language. It is only that the Hebrew *words* for humanity can never be divided along the lines of body and soul in the Greek fashion, for each refers to the entire person under a particular aspect.

Thus our vision has been sharpened so as to understand the typical Pauline contrasting pairs. One should pay attention to whether Paul is using the corresponding words in a merely anthropological sense, one that is ethically value-neutral, or in a theological sense. This can be illustrated by the example of *sōma*/body, with the Semitic background of *bāśār:*

(1) BODY AS AN ANTHROPOLOGICAL CATEGORY,
   in the sense of
   (a) *totality* as a
      - personal pronoun or "in a personal fashion":
         2 Cor 10:10; Eph 5:28f.
      - biological unity of many members: 1 Cor 12:12-27

> – personal relationship: 1 Cor 6:19
> – humans as sexual beings: 1 Cor 6:13, 20; 7:4; Rom 4:19
> – a unity of several persons: 1 Cor 6:16 (Gen 2:24); Eph 5:28f. (the basis for the collective term "Body of Christ": 1 Cor 12:13)
>
> (b) *a specification and realization,* as
>
> – the (definitive) expression of the human essence, form, being, or one's own "nature": Rom 1:24; 1 Cor 6:18; 15:38; Phil 1:20
> – the thing itself (not a "shadow"): Col 2:17
> – place of the manifestation of human nature: 2 Cor 4:10f.
> – body (more Greek): 1 Cor 5:3 (13:3); 15:35, 37; 2 Cor 12:2f.
> – corpse: Matt 27:52, 58
> – (in contrast to the head = the remaining part of the body)
>   trunk: Eph 1:23; 4:16
>
> (c) *weak, powerless, mortal human,* as
>
> – *one* aspect of the human (next to body and soul): 1 Thess 5:23
> – transitory, secular existence: Rom 12:2; 1 Cor 15:44

Even if these pronouncements indicate an essential worth or its absence, they are still ethically value-neutral.

(2) BODY AS A THEOLOGICAL TERM

in the doctrine of salvation,

(a) *in the negative sense of:* the human as

> – an (ethically) sinful existence: Rom 6:6; 8:13: 1 Cor 9:27
> – vulnerable, able to be tempted by sin: Rom 6:12
> – mortal *as a consequence of sin:* Rom 6:12; 8:10
> – *hence* suffering, being tested: 2 Cor 4:10f.; 5:10
> – visible-temporal (contrast: invisible-eternal = new life), "the outer person" (contrast: the inner person): 2 Cor 4:16f.; 5:6-8
> – unredeemed existence (summarily, it passes over into the meaning of (1) c (above): Rom 8:23; 1 Cor 9:27
> Contrasting concepts: Lord/*kyrios,*
> spirit/*pneuma,* faith/*pistis,* hope/*elpis.*

(b) in the *positive sense* of "new existence," mostly with epithet
- the new being "in Christ" (in the present): 1 Cor 6:15, 19
- glorified body (of the resurrection): cf. 1 Cor 15:35
- body of Christ,
  as an individual: the historical body: cf. 1 Cor 11:24, 27
  as raised up: Phil 3:21
  corporate (ecclesiological): Rom 12:5; 1 Cor 10:17; 12:13
  sacramental (Eucharistic): 1 Cor 10:16; 11:24

Thus to the question: What does Paul mean by "body"?, there is no single or final answer; it all depends upon the context, and the answer must be derived by using this or a similar analytic grid.[462] Hence, a statement like "for Paul *sōma* as a whole has negative connotations" is misleading.[463] However much the

462. For that reason one should generally be warned against introducing modern philosophical categories into Paul. Bultmann, who has built an entire interpretation around this word (*Theology of the New Testament*, no. 17; cf. TDNT VII 1060–1074) emphasizes that the word is used in very different ways, but is nevertheless of the opinion that "on a number of occasions" σῶμα is the person "insofar as he can make himself as an object of his activity or experiences himself as the subject of an event, or its object. Thus he can be called σῶμα to the extent he has a relation to himself" (*Theology of the New Testament*, 195f.). Similarly Conzelmann, 133: "I am σῶμα (in contrast to 'stomach') to the extent that I am not a 'thing,' but rather conduct myself." However, the notion of a reflective consciousness would be rather expressed by the Semitic word *lēb*/heart. In the more recent philosophy this situation is no longer expressed through the opposition between body and soul/spirit, but body and mind, and is named "personhood": a human being's unique capacity to put himself or herself at a distance and relate to his or her self, the "ego." In his or her "body," the person would rather be an "object" for other persons, and for the powers of good and evil. However, according to 1 Thess 5:23, this is also true for soul and spirit. This is because the Semitic consciousness always grasps the person as a totality. Thus we must exercise caution with modern terms and theories, as difficult as such restraint may be; otherwise, we risk leaving Paul behind in our theorizing.

463. Biser, 69. Some statistics on σῶμα: in the NT it occurs 152 times; in the principal Pauline letters 74 times. Of these, about individual people: used neutrally 11 times, positively 18 times, negatively 11 times; about Christ's

human is seen as "in his corporality placed before this 'foreign realm' of his own existence,"[464] this is not caused by human corporality as such; rather, "body" is then already a soteriologically impregnated term for "unredeemed existence." The constant mixture of purely anthropological and soteriological pronouncements is fatal.

In a similar way with "flesh" we must distinguish whether it means "to live in the earthly world" (Phil 1:2; Eph 5:28f.), or whether it intends to contrast sinful existence with the new reality in the Spirit.[465] On the other hand, Paul does use "spirit" in a purely anthropological sense (1 Thess 5:23). Thus, when we have to do with a theological application of an (initially anthropological) term, we must pay attention to what it is placed in opposition to, for the term only takes on a specific meaning through this opposition. However, in all this they never take on the Greek duality, but rather refer to the soteriological opposition between good and evil, and thus never bespeak a disdain for matter or the body. To what extent they indicate a present or future eschatology must be investigated in each case. However, one has to expect that all the following pairs of opposed terms can indicate a present co-existence, even "earthly-heavenly" or "this age and the age to come."[466]

(3) Body	Spirit	1 Cor 5:3
creation	new creation	Rom 8:3, 19ff.; Gal 6:15
affliction	glory	2 Cor 4:17
mortal/dead	living	2 Cor 4:10ff.
the old person	the new person	cf. Eph 4:22ff.; Col 3:9f.
the outer person	the inner person	2 Cor 4:16; Rom 7:22

---

body: 25 times (mostly in 1 Cor; also in Eph 9 times); about the resurrection: 9 times (all in 1 Cor). Even if in certain cases it may be unclear whether the word has a positive or negative connotation, this survey further undermines the suggestion that Paul had a negative attitude toward the body. The author of Eph 5:28f. says expressly that "no one hates his own flesh."

464. Biser, 73.

465. Whether it be that thereby the ethical aspect, "good or evil" (Rom 8; Gal 5) is stronger, or more the aspect of "distress and glory" is in view (2 Cor 4:7-5, 10). More details in Ts 50–60.

466. A deeper exploration of these considerations occurs in Ts 49–60; 117–129.

visible	invisible	2 Cor 4:17f.
visible form	faith *(pistis)*	2 Cor 5:7[467]
earthly	heavenly	2 Cor 5:1f.
this age	the age to come	Rom 12:2; Eph 1:21
made by human hands	not made by hands	2 Cor 5:1; Col 2:11
body	Lord	2 Cor 5:5, 6
world	Lord	1 Cor 7:31-34
flesh	spirit	Gal 5:16f.; 1 Cor 6:16ff.
works of the flesh	fruit of the spirit	Rom 8:13: Gal 5:19-24
physical person	spiritual person	1 Cor 3:1
psychic person	spiritual person	1 Cor 2:13-15

Thus, persons are "fleshly" or "carnal" not when they lavish care upon their body (cf. Eph 5:29), but rather when they distance themselves from God. This, however, is primarily an affair of their "heart and spirit," not only (but still inclusive of) their body. And in the same way spiritual persons are not those who have turned their backs as far as possible on their material needs through ascesis, but rather those who, in their whole being, and thus in both mind and body, are filled and penetrated by God's Holy Spirit.[468] Such a person is not a pure spirit, but rather a "spiritual body" (cf. 1 Cor 15:44); their body (!) is "one spirit with the Lord" (1 Cor 6:17). This is a person who does everything that he or she does for the honor of God and "glorifies God in [the] body" (1 Cor 6:20). Otherwise expressed: these are persons who in the power of the Holy Spirit love God with all their *lēb*/heart and with their entire *nephesh*/throat, and with all their strength (Deut 6:5)—to which of course, employing Greek terms, their body also belongs.

467. This does not mean the opposition between the actual vision of perfection and present faith, but rather between the visible form of this world (εἶδος does not mean to look) and "trust" in Christ; see Ts 226-233.

468. Cf. 1 Thess 5:23, where *basar, næfæs* and *ruah* are anthropological realities. It would be disastrous to understand these, in the sense of the Western division of the person, as a "trichotomy." They are rather Semitic fundamental qualities that are conceived holistically (in Greek = embracing both body and soul) and that mutually "complement" one another. Thus, 1 Thess 5:23 means: "May your empowered, needy, and frail existence be preserved (= maintained) entirely (in all its elements) in the presence of our Lord Jesus Christ."

5. *Man and Woman as the Image of God*

Hardly any other scriptural statement can more help persons to come to terms with and appropriate their own nature, to integrate their sexuality, and to become totally themselves as Genesis 1:27, 31: "God created humanity in God's own image; as the image of God he created it, as man and woman he created *them*. And God saw that it was very good." "Image" here does not mean the same thing it means with paintings, photographs, or copies, that the one visible form is reconstituted in another concrete medium (for that reason the UT translation *Abbild* [= copy] is not as good), but rather that that which for us is invisible in any shape has expressed itself in a "form." This comes out in a unique way when, in Colossians 1:15 Jesus is called "the image of the invisible God": he is the visible expression of what in itself is "simply invisible"; in a wider sense, however, every person is a visible expression of the invisible nature of God, a created reference to the uncreated. When an artist brings forth his or her inner vision in a visible "image," he or she simultaneously makes something of his or her own essence visible. Thus, it is not only in spirit or "soul" that people resemble God; their body also is such a visible "image"; their whole being is fashioned in the image of God!

This is difficult for the Greeks to imagine, because for them everything material appears to be foreign to the divine essence. However, coming from the biblical thought-world, we should be more courageous. If God fashioned a body for humanity after God's own form, this does not mean that God possesses a visible (created) body, but rather that in God's nature God is the model for both soul *and body,* for the spirit *and the heart* of mortals. And when the Creator made matter, God did not create something totally "foreign" to God's self, but rather—in an analogical way—created something which was like God's own infinite nature. Even the so-called "spiritual side" of humanity is still infinitely distant from the transcendent nature of God, and the "body" to no less a degree takes its model from God.

We notice how we continually come up against juncture points; spirit, soul, and body have another feel, according to whether we understand them in a Greek or a Semitic sense. In any case the doctrine of creation in the "image" of God is not only a pronouncement about humanity, but also says something important about God. God is the model of everything which, as God's image, appears of positive value.[469] This is the reason that the Jews have less difficulty accepting the notions of creation and resurrection, of a new heaven and a new earth (Rev 21:1) than do the Greeks. And if the Bible stresses that "God is Spirit" (John 4:24), this should not be understood in opposition to matter, but only intends to emphasize that God is only life and power, that in God there is no weakness or inability. This therefore does not exclude the possibility that in God's nature God contains an uncreated, eternal, primordial reality for what we in the West call "body."

Such reflections explain the unembarrassed spontaneity with which the biblical authors repeatedly speak of God in an anthropomorphic manner, beginning with the Creator's "delight in strolling in the garden," through "YHWH's glory dwelling in his temple," down to the statement that "God will live in their midst," that God intends to be the temple and light of the Holy City, and the Lamb will be their light (Rev 21:3, 22). Why should the infinite distance between the eternal God and the human psyche be fundamentally different from the equally infinite distance between God and the human body? If a human being is a totality, then it is also as a totality that he or she is an "image" of the uncreated God, and the body is not something of lesser value; if humanity indeed receives in the "taking on of flesh" *(incarnatio)* by God's Son its highest worth, then in Christ it is

---

469. The Scholastic distinction between *perfectio simplex* and *perfectio mixta* attempts to grapple with this problem, but appears to me not to have caught the essential point! *Everything* in humanity is a "limited" reality, even our "spiritual aspect"; however, every limited reality has its unlimited model in God, matter just as much as the (limited) human spirit. There are perhaps inklings of this in the talk about "God's spirit-body" in Tertullian, *adv. Prax.* VII 8f. (CSL II 1166f.): "Qui in effigie Dei constitutus non rapinam existimavit esse se aequalem Deo. In qua effigie Dei? Utique in aliqua, non tamen in nulla. Quis enim negabit Deum corpus esse, etsi Deus spiritus est? Spiritus enim corpus sui generis in sua effigie. Sed et si invisibilia illa quaecumque sunt, habent apud deum et suum corpus et suam formam, per quae soli Deo visibilia sunt, quanto magis quod ex ipsius substantia emissum est sine substantia non erit." For other places, see G. Claessom, *Index Tertullianeus* (Paris, 1974), under "corpus."

"made new after the pattern of the one who created [it]" (Col 3:10), and at the final resurrection human beings will be "transformed" in their physical *bodies* (1 Cor 15:51-54).

This last catchword leads us now to the question concerning man and woman. For God created "them" *as man and woman* in God's own image. Thus in essence God is not only masculine; indeed, God is not at all "masculine," for God is neither man nor woman (these are limited categories), but rather God is the eternal, unlimited *model* for humanity, and for the feminine as much as for the masculine. Though we may call God Father—analogically—God is just as much our Mother (Ps 131:2; Isa 49:15; 66:12f.). Here we are certainly confronting the limits of the scriptural pronouncements which—to a certain extent unreflectively and as a matter of course—picked up the given speech and imagistic resources of their culture and through these sought to formulate theological statements through them. With the transformation of social ideas and progress in the development of theological teaching, such forms of expression must naturally be recast, appropriately modified, and filled out. Moreover, Genesis 1:27, 31 is clear concerning the mutuality between man and woman, that *together* they reflect the divine nature, not as though it were transmitted to one only through the other.

Also, the second (and older) creation account (Gen 2:21-25) should not be interpreted as meaning that the woman possesses only "a mediated image of the divine."[470] On the contrary, and as Jewish commentators have stressed down to the present day, the unity and equal standing of the two are emphasized: "Bone of my bone and flesh of my flesh." However, affixed to this it is said specifically of the man that he "leaves father and mother and joins himself with his wife," although as a social reality it is the woman who leaves her parents and joins the family of her husband. Why this esteem for woman? Why not: "and she is joined to him"? Is it perhaps that, appreciated psychologically, it is rather the woman who is the "fixed pole"?

---

470. Delling, 107; Niederwimmer. To the extent that here a subordination of the woman is expressed in imagistic material, one could rather say that in Gen 1:27, that is, the later priestly creation account, the accent is more clearly placed upon equality. Is this intended as a theological correction of the Yahwist account (Gen 2:24)? Wolff's excellent presentation, 243–258,

Moreover, if "the two become one flesh," there is obviously no suggestion of sin introduced here—this account occurs *before* that of the Fall into sin—but in a purely anthropological sense, that is, one that is ethically neutral, simply means "to become one [corporate] body, one unified life." Admittedly, and in accord with a patriarchal culture, the man is named first. However, to what extent does this sequence imply an order of value? "They were not ashamed before one another" indicates an equal standing. Certainly there is, when seen from the New Testament, an order and structure in the threefold nature of God. However, it would be inappropriate if one sought to attribute the masculine to the Father and the feminine to the Son or to the divine *rūach* (which linguistically is feminine). It is rather the case that all three divine "persons" (to use this later Greek terminology) are concurrently the model for both man *and* woman[471]; that is, each unifies in itself "masculine and feminine" in a divine way. The "Incarnation of the Son" takes place, to the extent that he is human, in a masculine shape, but in itself the Second Person, in whom and through whom all was created (1 Cor 8:6; Col 1:15f.), unites in itself the original model of each.[472] The original authors of Scripture may have been hardly aware of such considerations; however, their pronouncements are, in their theological dimension, open to such a development.

The Bible clearly teaches that the war between the sexes and the traditional domination by the male is a consequence of sin

---

clearly demonstrates the fundamentally positive attitude toward sexuality and love relationships in the Old Testament. The book by Haag-Elliger, on the other hand, offers much more extensive evidence, but must be used critically, distinguishing between objective information and the theoretical bias of the authors (see my review in *ThPh* 62 [1987] 265f.). How this concerns the Pauline texts the reader may determine through a comparison with the relevant passages of the present work.

471. Plato attempts to represent the original unity through the myth of androgynous humanity (*Symposium* 14–16); however, he never suggests that this is prefigured in the divine ἕν (One). In the absolute Idea there is for him no sexual analogy. How long have we Christians remained caught up in this? To distance ourselves as far as possible from polytheism, we tried to empty our image of God of any notion of gender—which, because of the image of God as "Father," could not entirely succeed.

472. 1 Cor 11:12c; cf. above, A VII 2; further, below, D II 4 and 5.

(Gen 3:16). *Into this* situation there is sent the promise of salvation, the "protoevangelium." Why is not the "hostility" set up between the serpent and *the man?* It is *her* offspring who will tread upon the serpent's head. Throughout the entire story the woman is fully responsible beside the man,[473] and equal responsibility presupposes equal worth.

Admittedly, when one blames the other for what has happened, and finally both blame God (Gen 3), this shows that their relationship is disturbed. "All have sinned; no one is righteous, no, not even one" (Rom 3:12). And since they cannot rescue themselves, the "Son, born of a woman," enters the realm of sin (Gal 4:4), in order to make them into "new people." However, humankind is renewed "after the image of the creator" (Col 3:10), and this means that the relation between man and woman is also redeemed,[474] and specifically that the man no longer dominates, but rather serves, and the woman for her part does not boast over the man. Only a person who, with Paul, recognizes the human need for salvation[475] and the futility of every attempt to achieve such through oneself will find in Christ the path to life, and through being a child of God a way to redeemed sexuality and redeemed partnership.

473. Cf. above, B II 4; further below, D I 4 and D III 1.

474. Cf. above, A VII 2 and below, D I 4.

475. The area of sexuality also shares in salvation. "Israel was not blind to dangerous disturbances to the love relationship"—despite, or better, precisely because of its esteem for this gift from God, H. W. Wolff, 253–258. On the correlation between sexuality and one's relationship with God, see above note 68; A V 1-3; notes 255, 258, 259 and 284, as well as more below, C 5; D II 4; notes 604f.; 619 and D III 3 (5).

Part D

God of the Past and of the Future— Perspectives

We have dug deep furrows, plowed new territory, and discovered new, rich soil. It is the first task of exegesis to clarify the original meaning of the scriptural text. Under this imperative in part A we have carefully examined every passage in the principal Pauline letters in which sexuality, the relation between the sexes, and continence are discussed—almost all located in 1 Corinthians; in part B we studied those in the remaining Pauline corpus, and in part C we examined the Hebrew view of human nature. Revisions at a fundamental level have brought about a profound alteration in the picture. Our proposed interpretations of controversial passages have mutually supported one another, apparent contradictions have been smoothed out, and difficulties removed,[501] even with regard to the so-called deutero-Pauline letters.

In what follows we will not attempt to build the various statements into a system; however, now that we have become witnesses in a new way to discussions between the apostle and his communities, it is the common task of the theological disciplines to integrate any insights won thereby within the totality of contemporary

501. One may appreciate how "problematic" the exegesis of 1 Cor 7 was more clearly after the fact, if one now reads the summary by Bornkamm: 212–216, and 183f.

theological thinking. In this enterprise the exegete should remain a partner in the discussion. We have already offered a summary of 1 Corinthians 7; in what follows, several exegetical and pastoral consequences will be drawn from a systematic point of view.

I. The Divine Kingship and Human Society

Let us begin with the anthropological-sociological realm. For this we may start with Galatians 3:28—a text which many readers certainly up until now have been expecting. Many commentators, and not only those of a feminist slant, regard this as the highpoint of Pauline anthropology and regret that the apostle never elsewhere—before or after—regained it, specifically his point that all people are equal or at least have equal rights. Then the attempt is made to measure Paul's other statements against this one and to chastise them more or less accordingly. However, does the New Testament so contradict itself? Was Paul really such a broken or confused personality?[502] Did his own personal development, and that of primitive theology, really develop in such leaps, and produce such declines? The results of a thoroughgoing investigation of Galatians 3:28, which we will present under no. 3 below, will show that human differences do not substantiate a particular claim for "being in Christ" ("there the distinction of male and female does not matter," etc.); on the other hand, the various national, social, and anthropological distinctions are not thereby removed. So once again here we meet the same principle we encountered in 1 Corinthians 11 and 12, that is, "equal immediacy to God, coexistent with differentiation between one another." At the same time, with this the complex question concerning the social relevance of the Christian proclamation is not yet answered.

1. Six Hermeneutical Principles

After a clarification of the original contextual meaning of the Pauline statements, the question for all these texts remains: what

502. Betz, 331, 340: Paul's standpoints "cannot always be harmonized."

if any claim can they make upon us today, or with what hermeneutical key may we unlock their respective significance for Christian life in contemporary society? How may the original meaning of such texts, which as inspired Scripture have a normative character, be maintained under our changed situation, without being fundamentalistically misunderstood? Here we are not inquiring into the political-social implications of something "purely religious"; it is rather a matter of how salvation in our world takes shape ("Incarnation"), or how the "Word" may seize people and world both synchronically and diachronically. What differences should we pay attention to?

(1) *God's acting within a human person* should be distinguished from *human relationships.* This said, however, the first should not be understood incorrectly in a purely spiritual or individualistic fashion, for it always relates to the entire person with all his or her social relationships; nor should the second be misunderstood in a purely social (secular or profane) sense, for ultimately all inter-human relationships must be carried out in the Holy Spirit.[503] In what concerns the action of God, the parables of the unmerciful servant, the talents, and the workers in the vineyard (Matt 18:23-35; 20:1-16; 25:14-30) make clear that God does not simply treat people as "equal," but rather "according to their capabilities" and "according to their deeds," just as God forgives one a greater guilt than another. The formal object is not that all people are "equal," but rather that they are all redeemed, they are in the house of the same Father and in "many mansions." In such a state of multifaceted salvation, each discovers his or her full redemption, and the question why others are other or are handled differently no longer even arises. It is rather the case that everyone lovingly accepts every another as unique (1 Cor 12). On the other hand, when persons no longer see themselves to be supported by God in their uniqueness, they give in to the compulsion not to tolerate anyone being "over them." However, the rhetoric of the Enlightenment and the "equality" of the French Revolution are not part of the Bible's vocabulary. As important as "equality before the law" is, the value of the person is ulti-

---

503. Corresponding to the twofold command of love. On the anthropology, cf. what we said above, C 3, about "spirit."

mately protected through the reverence called for by the image of the divinity. Contemporary emphasis on equality falls short of this.

(2) Besides, we must distinguish between, on the one hand, the *direct statements* that a text makes, and the *theological consequences* that one may draw from these, as for example: if God has bestowed upon us all—in various ways—life in Christ, then we must nurture this life within us by respecting its presence in others and reverencing them in their entire humanity with all their social relationships, without any form of oppression or force. These are necessary "conclusions" from the situations addressed in Galatians 3:27f. and 1 Corinthians 12, among others; they are not explicitly stated there, but must be *logically concluded* from them. In the reality described this is certainly already suggested, but in the order of reflection is it a *conclusion*.

(3) Further, the difference between the *announcement of the reign of God* and its *various forms of presentation* should be observed. "God's Word in human words" is forced to make use always of limited, one-sided, and time-conditioned concepts and images. Exegesis involves uncovering, beneath the changes in conditions and times, in thought and value systems the unchangeable message, and continually to retranslate the latter appropriately. With regard to Genesis 1–11, it took decades before the compatibility between revelation and modern science could be worked out and formulated. Since the message about creation is transmitted in the Bible in the language of the contemporary picture of the world, it is to be expected that its statements concerning humanity would also be expressed in a time-conditioned anthropology and sociology, whether this be already in Genesis 1–11, or whether it be in the New Testament. Perhaps we must now take more serious notice of the fact that the revelation concerning humanity was brought to expression with the materials of a patriarchally structured society. If so, then what therein is conditioned by its time of composition, and what remains valid? In the past we have run up against such questions on numerous occasions.

(4) *God's salvation* indeed always involves the *whole person;* however, it is disclosed and appropriated by the person only in a step-by-step process. This is not restricted to what goes on in-

side a person, but also includes the environment; indeed, often salvation takes its beginning in the center of the person—Mark 2:3-12: first there is forgiveness of sins, then healing—but it may also begin with external factors—Luke 17:12-19: first, a healing as a way to invite belief, with the danger that the conversion thereby intended might still not succeed. The objection to a split between spiritual and social needs correctly observes that we may not finally divide in two what ultimately makes up a totality in humanity. However, it does on occasion overlook the fact that God is a God of history, who leads God's people step by step. The heart of the proclamation is the call to conversion of heart and to reconciliation with God; this message has to shape the Church/humanity as a whole in the course of its history more and more, in ever new situations and in spite of all its brokenness, in an always-newly-to-be-redeemed generation, similar to the way the seed of salvation in individual people must penetrate their modes of behavior more and more in a maturing process that often does not progress in a linear pattern. Just as God works on a person, now from within, now from without, just as Jesus proclaimed the kingdom of God through both word and deed (from his subordination to his parents, the work of his hands, his acceptance of the marginalized, up to the remarkable signs that we like to call "miracles" to distinguish them from his other works), in the same way preaching and lifestyle, social and political service naturally belong together; *both* of them are Christian only if they came from the Holy Spirit. And in the exercise of the redeeming service of the Church in the world, the service of ecclesiastical officialdom in the world (as representative of the Church as a whole), and the service to the world by the laity must further be distinguished.

In concrete cases it is certainly not easy to verify the individual steps, as clear and unambiguous as the distinction between concepts may be. As limiting positions we may say that Jesus did not allow himself to be made a king, and did not come in order to render superfluous all the hospitals in the world (as much as this will certainly be the case at the end of time; however, in God's kingdom on earth healings have a "sign" character); on the other hand, that the activity of the Holy Spirit is never purely interior, but rather constantly strives to take on integrated shape in this world, and specifically in accord with its indwelling dynamic. The processes of this spiritual growth can only be begun, maintained, and completed by the Spirit of God. So everything depends on whether humanity or the Church in all of its dealings is proceeding according to this standard.

The applications to the details of our everyday existence are certainly multiple and various; however, the basic structure remains: Christian responsibility for the world is part of our responsibility before God; as a further consequence, the gift of salvation in Christ must unfold gradually into all the areas of human life, especially into those that touch inter-human relationships; this divine activity of salvation can begin in an "interior" or "exterior" fashion, and the individual steps in this process will never come to a final stage. In watchful attentiveness to the guidance of the Spirit, it is a matter of "integrating" all the areas of life within the various impulses toward redemption and liberation, so that more and more the "entire" life is transformed "spiritually," or, so to speak, from the "reign of God *and* society" into "the reign of God *within* society." One should notice: it is not that the spiritual impulses are to be integrated into our lives (as if we were free to select according to our nature what is appropriate for us), but rather it is this world/our life that is to be integrated within what comes from God, and thereby become a "unity." What is human is healed by the divine, not the other way around.

(5) It thus comes down to the Christian personality whether social progress, or "the struggle for faith and justice" are going to be a way of real Christian life, or alternatively "works" of human contrivance and ideology. Even if in this the *integrity of the human orders and sciences* should be respected, these must ultimately be integrated within the salvific activity of God in this world and must accordingly be *"relativized,"* as we saw above.[504] Here the borders have been frequently violated, in that the relatively(!) independent laws of political, social, and economic processes have been exaggerated; on the other side, the normative power of the order of salvation may be applied in an inappropriate literalness or immediacy, with the result that the proper

504. See above, A III 1-4; A IV 2 and 3; A VII 1; A VII 5 and B I 1. Cf. Schuster, 182f., with reference to GS 36, 43, 59.

laws of the order of creation are not integrated, but ignored. Besides, it is not easy to say what may be sinful in the basic anthropological structure of man and woman, community and society, and is therefore in need of salvation, and what was set down by God in God's "creation," and therefore should be "preserved." What is decisive is that the person in whole essence, with heart and mind, with body and soul, with senses and power of abstraction, be open to God (Deut 6:5); persons must recognize that God may make use of every area of creation in order to bring to bear upon them God's saving activity; thus a human being can search for and discover "God in all things." However, *God's free self-gift* always remains *the center* of God's saving activity and an incomprehensible mystery of God's gracious choice. It requires considerable reverence and patience, attention and humility, not to anticipate God, and thereby ultimately to conduct ourselves in an independent and autonomous fashion.

(6) Once we have clarified the issues of revelation and salvation, we must conclude with a note about a *law of interior structure within Christian existence.* Just as one and the same Spirit of Pentecost may work in both a gentle breath and in a storm, in visions and everyday observations, in the power of patience and in the fire of enthusiasm, in proclamation and in service, in word and in deed, contemplation and action, a person must be prepared for all these forms of its activity, so as to be able to recognize and be receptive to the ones presented to him or her. The task of finding the balance in the tension that results thereby is the job of Christianity and of humanity as a whole. Thus, the alternatives are not Christian engagement in the social order *versus* piety;[505] these concepts are rather from the very beginning *only two foci* within one and the same indivisible Christian life—if you will, something like *the two foci* of an ellipse.

Is this not the best way to understand the enduring tension between distancing oneself *from* the world and contributing to the

---

505. Mary and Martha are not presented as examples *of this!* In Luke 10:38-42, Martha is not scolded because she "is working," but rather because she is motivated not by what she hears, but by busyness; and this is not a *redeemed* way of acting. On the other hand, in all the alternatives mentioned here there is always intended a reaction/response to God's invitation. In the "kingdom of God," the initiative always lies with God.

shape of the world? Each is a fundamental constituent of Christianity, if it is a form of listening and compliance directed toward God. Piety can easily pass over into self-approval, and religiously inspired social activity into self-fulfillment or "doing it oneself." However, if both are filled with God's Spirit, we in the Church rightly recognize various and diverse "vocations," the contribution of the "charismatic renewal" and those of more "conservative" movements as well. Persons must keep the entire community before their eyes, and yet carry out their respective activity with the accent which is *distinctively* their own.

Does not even the form of the earthly Jesus in this sense stand under a necessarily *limited* "vocation" as a consequence of his being human? While he is certainly, in his basic behavior, normative for all people, the concrete pattern of his life cannot simply be copied by others. If he renounces a particular form of political activity which would have made him king, he does not necessarly do this because he is fundamentally opposed to all political involvement, but rather because *this* political action in *this* situation did not come from the Spirit, and because the Father had not chosen for *him* the path of an earthly king. In other contexts, such as the feeding of the five thousand and the healing of the sick, his lifestyle was marked by a powerful intervention and involvement in the world. Naturally Jesus' manner of conducting himself does not exclude the possibility that Israel's kings—such as "David his father"—were chosen by God and that among those who followed Jesus there could have been those legitimately called to political activity. This also means that, as politically active, they could and should have recourse to the sword when confronted with the evildoer (Rom 13:3f.), even if in another context, and with regard to his own mission, Jesus says "Whoever lives by the sword (that is, uses it on his or her own initiative, without it having been 'given from above') will die by the sword."

Of course God remains Lord *of the entire* human realm, and indeed, in the form of the Savior, presents us with the way of the Cross, that is, the path of powerlessness and of the death of our unredeemed existence as the door to salvation. What must in any case come about, namely the observance on humankind's part of God's will and command, can only be learned in a fallen world by following the one who has been crucified. To that extent every person must pass through this door, this particular "focus" of Christian existence, in order to learn (as the second focus) how to live a redeemed life; he or she must become like Jesus in his dying, in order to be taken up into his prophetic Word and his transforming resurrection. In a certain sense all Christians bear the form of *both* the earthly *and* the exalted Jesus in themselves; in a certain sense his "immortal life" must become manifest in our "mortal flesh"; and in us the "old" age is always *coexistent* with the "new age (or: 'eon')." Thus one could trace back every aspect of Christian existence that has been mentioned finally—in good Pauline fashion—to Jesus' death and resurrection and measure them thereby.[506]

In order to discuss the anthropological and social relevance of our Pauline texts, we have now established six criteria, namely the distinction between

(1) *God's activity* toward humanity, and humankind's *inter-human relationships;*

(2) the *direct statements* that a text makes, and the *logical consequences* which may be drawn from them;

(3) the revealed *truth,* and the *social imagery* through which it is transmitted;

(4) the *integrally oriented divine activity of salvation,* and its *gradually progressing* integration of all the areas of God's people's life into the new force field of this Spirit of Pentecost;

(5) the relative *independence and autonomy of the created or "human" order,* and the *ultimate normativity of God's gift of Godself in grace,*

(6) so that ultimately within our Christian existence itself and behind all opposed foci, we learn to recognize our *participation in his death and in his resurrected life.*

Thus equipped let us take up a few basic questions concerning the Pauline texts we have examined up to now.

---

506. 2 Cor 4:7-6, 10; more on this in Ts *(passim);* further Rom 4:25; Phil 3:10f. As an example here 2 Cor 13:2-4 (Ts 92, 351): "Christ is not weak with regard to you, but strong among you; if he was crucified out of weakness, still he *lives* out of God's power. We also are now weak (are now retiring, mild) among you, but will with him out of God's power *live* (appear more energetic) with regard to you."

2. Socially Conservative?

In our discussions of 1 Corinthians 11 and 14, it was difficult to suppress the question why Paul did not make use of the opportunity to help women in their social ascent—if in 11:11f. he indeed announces a new mutual dependency in Christ. Is he so weak a fighter for the recognized truth that he bends before the dictate of what is socially *aischron* ("unseemly")? Instead of placing himself on the women's side or at least insisting upon what is theirs by right, he appears to accept the current standards and to use them as weapons to enforce "peace and order." Rather than being a protagonist for women, does he instead become their oppressor? Although it may be concealed at this point, in the interpretation of 1 Corinthians 7:17-24 which has been common down to the present, it appears to be not only incontrovertible, but also unbearable: how could he advise a slave against accepting liberation? Is he on the side of the slaveholders? Moreover, even if—according to our new interpretation—he approves of the acceptance of liberation, there remains the clause: "do not bother yourself about it" (7:21), which indeed makes us sense a lack of concern for the liberation of slaves.[507] And in 7:29-31 Paul appears, from beginning to end, to discourage a *deeper* interest in the world; for not only the "as if," but also the "in a certain manner not having" hardly prompts us toward a profound transformation of the world.

One would like to inquire: does Paul not then see the injustice in the social structures and patterns? Is the "Apostle to the Gentiles" thinking so unpolitically and individualistically that he does not notice that evil powers are at work in these structures, powers which can only be overcome through Christ? Or is he so fatalistic that he is resigned to letting everything in this area simply run its course? Does "salvation" stop at that point? Is the horizon of his field of vision so limited? In these decades revolutionary movements among his people were not unknown, and in the Roman/Hellenistic thought-world, there were impulses for the emancipation of women.[508] What has he made of the liberating message of Jesus?

507. However, cf. above, A III 3.
508. Cf. Hauke, 335-338; Thraede, 106; opposing tendencies Thraede, 111-114.

How would Paul respond to such a charge? "Who is weak, and I am not weak; who takes offense, and I am not inflamed?" (2 Cor 11:29). If he, who in the tanning of leathers worked side by side with slaves, truly became "all things to all people" (1 Cor 9:22), if he "weeps with those who are weeping" (Rom 12:15), opposed Peter to his face, carried through the confrontation with the Jews and the Jewish-Christians and gave deposition before the High Counsel and the emperor, then we cannot say that in such matters he is weak of heart, or is paralyzed by a false modesty, nor is he the prisoner of individualistic categories.

In the questions about letting down one's hair and keeping quiet in the so-called "community assemblies," only the importance of the position which these things take on in the concrete life of the community makes the decisiveness of the apostle comprehensible. In the way that these practices were carried out he evidently observed a distraction from what is essential to the good news, and a provocative element introduced into the solidarity maintained with the other Christian communities.[509] Beyond that, however, this is to be attributed to his effort not to give unnecessary "offense" to the Jews (1 Cor 10:32). Thus, he attempts until the very end to gain access among them (Rom 9–11) because the gospel is precisely the fulfillment of the promises made to them (cf. Acts 13:1 passim; 18:19f.; 28:17f.). Paul does not intend to found a new sect that will distinguish itself immediately through its behavior; rather, he intends to announce the expanded "new Israel," through which the "peoples"—together with the remaining branches of Israel—may be grafted onto the trunk that is ultimately the "Christ from the Jews" (Rom 11:17). From the perspective of such a program, the question concerning the social, political, and also "ecclesiastical-political" "equal rights of women" (which is never expressed in such words) takes on a different importance, although Paul not only leaves room for its

---

509. Cf. above, A III 3. The unity between the Gentile Christian and Jewish-Christian communities, especially with Jerusalem, is a central concern with Paul. K. Berger has developed this concern through the example of the offerings which, analogous to the charity through which "God-fearers" (of non-Jewish peoples) expressed their tie with the people of Israel, should now be understood as a sign of unity with the Jerusalem community: "Almosen für Israel," *NTS* 23 (1977) 180–204; cf. Luke 7:5; Acts 10:2; 24:17.

development, but even lays the foundation for it. We must, of course, be willing to admit that with this Paul more correctly appraises the contemporary *spiritual* condition of the Church than we can today reconstruct it through various suppositions.

The fact that Paul considers such questions to be of secondary importance must have something to do with his relationship to Christ and his commission, as in the case of the relative value of marriage and celibacy. In a Pauline formulation, Matthew 6:33 means: place the kingship of God in the first position; however, this "kingdom of God does not consist in eating and drinking, not in male priority or the subordination of women, neither in marriage or celibacy, neither in freedom nor the condition of a slave, neither in riches or poverty, neither in human wisdom or a lack of education, neither in human life nor in death, but in the peace and joy that come from the Holy Spirit."[510] Paul determinedly resists the temptation to see the kingdom of God in anything "that is not Jesus Christ" (Rom 15:18); positively expressed: nothing and no one can hinder a person from being a Christian and living in the discipleship of Christ (following Rom 8:36). This posture makes us free in the truth, because we are thereby completely independent from everything that is not the Lord.

"Let the dead bury the dead" (Luke 9:60), or in Pauline terms "it is no longer I who live" (Gal 2:20), and "I know among you nothing besides Jesus, and him crucified" and resurrected (1 Cor 2:2), first of all opens up a path into the interior, into the heart of humankind, where alone conversion and salvation can take place, even if it is "a stumbling block for the Jews and foolishness for the Greeks" (1 Cor 1:23). The actual struggle for the apostle consists in alerting the Corinthians that with these concerns (not only the question about the behavior of women), they are dragging secondary matters into the foreground, and thereby thwarting their own salvation. Only if a person "leaves everything else radically behind, in order to obtain Christ" (Phil 3:7, 13), thus "dies to the world,"[511] only then will one have entered even now into the life of the resurrected Jesus (Phil 3:10-14).

---

510. Cf. Rom 14:17; 8:35-39; 1 Cor 1:20, 26; 2 Cor 6:6-10; Gal 3:28; Phil 1:20-24; 4:11-13, etc.

511. This is the way Gal 6:14 should be translated; similarly Rom 7:4. See above, A I 5 and Atf V 1.

Just as Jesus declined to allow himself to be misused as a political Messiah—so to speak, to lead the Israelites for a second time out of Egypt into a new Jewish kingdom—but rather became through his death and resurrection the authentic Savior of *all* people, in the same way Paul realizes that it is not his principal task to challenge fundamentally the antique social order, but rather to begin operating in a "new covenant" at a much deeper level: there where alone humanity is in a position to receive salvation. From this perspective, indeed, the criteria of this world are far more radically called into question. So as not to distract people from their authentic salvation or to set them upon a false trail, on which they would again quickly remain stuck in superficial details and miss the true gospel (Gal 1:6f.), he must propel them through this experience of death, in which they first of all must give up their religious, social, private, and political desires, which are all in the first instance penetrated with egoism; this means realizing first of all that all these concerns are in the hands of God (Phil 4:6), and not to keep a firm hold on them even on the pretext of love of neighbor. Christ himself will then bestow tasks upon his disciples, not in a narrow subjectivism, but taking us into every social and political realm, "each, as the Spirit leads them."

Paul realizes that this is the only way in which a person can achieve that resurrection, that new life in the Spirit, which cannot be the product of any human activity, but which is pure gift—*charis, charisma, klēsis.* At this point, however, the divine power takes over our entire life. And because it is resurrected life, it also grasps our "body"; more than that, it seeks to transform everything, including the social structure and political power relationships. This is very clearly present in Paul in his teaching about the *sōma.* There God as such becomes the instigator of salvation, the guarantor of righteousness within humankind, the defender of peace and social well-being—all in the spirit of the prophets. It is, however, God's Holy Spirit who then carries this out through the medium of humankind; further, only in the Spirit's name can the disciples achieve this, whether it be healing the sick or ruling a state.

One could persist with the reproach that Paul did not follow the Spirit consistently enough, the Spirit who indeed wishes to penetrate all things. However, was his commission really of the type we imagine? Should not we go for lessons to *him,* and ask whether we have today correctly understood our own commission? Here there are different opinions. In any case, the sequence cannot be reversed; as long as a believer construes righteousness as a "demand" (and indeed most often on others), the believer is attempting to bring it about by some human device—thus, in any event, as a species of self-justification. However, it can only be lived as received *from above,* and thus from the center outward. It is not the case that the state may pass no laws that make demands upon people, for that is what it means to be a "state." When acting "in the name of Christ," a person must walk down a different path: that of salvation as God's gift. From God the person receives a new capacity to deal with differences in a different way; one learns simply to accept them as a point of departure (the "acceptance of oneself"), and receives an interior disposition of readiness to endure and diminish tensions, in that he or she is in service to the others and is attentive to maintaining their freedom.[512] However, precisely for this reason it is important to respect the relatively independent laws and processes of the anthropological, social, and political orders. Therein lies the foundation for a *distinction* (not necessarily a "separation") between Church and state, and we can see the error of conceiving "Christendom" in some way as "God's kingdom on earth." "A theology of politics" should also not be misconstrued in this direction; for Jesus specifically renounced the realization of his "kingdom" through political means; and further, in Israel, the state was a concession to the weakness of humanity (1 Sam 8). Efforts to anticipate a "paradise on earth" do not succeed; in a world that has fallen into sin, the kingdom of God can only again and again be received anew as gift.

Thus once more Christians must confront the question of belief: if they observe that their efforts are not bringing about what they had hoped for, and this means finally: if they notice that God does not immediately send down the visible salvation that humans have petitioned, they must then resist the temptation to

---

512. It is different with the state which as such in this sinful world possesses its own autonomy, which neither Jesus nor Paul fundamentally disturb (John 19:11; Rom 13:1-7), and this in spite of the fact that these "institutions" (1 Pet 2:13) still stand in need of redemption.

attempt to bring about righteousness through their own efforts. They will often not realize where the obstacles lie, but they will be forced to admit that the effects of divine redemption only appear symbolically, here and there, like the miracles in the life of Jesus. Even he did not succeed in transforming his people as a whole, either in their relations with God or in the political-social order. For that reason the disciple is asked simply to endure this *aporia;* on the one hand, to recognize that God wills to redeem and to take up in the resurrection the entire life of humanity—only God can do this—and on the other hand in proclaiming this divine intention, to face our limits, and then to have to ask again: "Lord, what keeps you from coming here and now?" In other words, it will be decisive which actual, concrete task a Christian receives, and what tools he or she uses, whether political or also theological ideologies, with which one attempts to gain control of situations and people; whether it be with the moral indignation of those who are not prepared to endure injustice themselves but rather remove the oppressor, or with the obedience of the one who called injustice by its true name and at the same time endured a condemnation unto death, so as to overcome it from within, from the side of God. Unless they undergo death with Christ, humans at the end will be—even if all social structures are transformed—still unredeemed.

Today as well we must have the freedom and the courage to say to a believer (not to one who is still standing at the door): "If you have been called as a slave,[513] then make freeing yourself from this condition no longer your major concern." Only then may a Christian correctly receive the counsel: "If, however, you have the opportunity to become free, take advantage of it"—namely, in the power which has grown in you in virtue of your liberation in Christ. Further, do it "rather" (7:21), that is, not with a grim determination, as if your genuine salvation depended upon it, but rather with an inner freedom and distance that teaches you equilibrium and that relativizes all goods by setting them in relation to that which is essential. Finally, everything comes down to the question whether we Christians trust that God is more concerned about justice in the world than we are. God knows the

513. Not: called *into* slavery, but rather taken up while in the situation of external dependency as a son/daughter of God. See above, after note 105.

best way to help people, but at the same time also how little they can be helped—since God refuses to interfere with their freedom. It is indeed not easy to place oneself on the side of this ineffectual divinity, but Paul lived it, taught it, and endured it. A theology of liberation that takes its starting point in such a position will repeatedly testify to the experience that the divine activity reaches down to humankind's concrete needs, fashions new people, and on this basis transforms society. People who live this way will recognize with surprise how God is active through them and through many other people, and how God "liberates" those who are saved for the full utilization of their talents. Thus no one has to worry about his or her rights, because God has taken them in trust; one does not need to cling to them desperately, as if salvation consisted in them.

As long as 1 Corinthians 7:20-24 was interpreted as saying that, in any and every eventuality, a Christian should maintain his or her social position, it admittedly could appear as if this position was being identified with salvation, and also if one did not place the supposed question of the veil and the command about keeping quiet in their proper relativity. However, Paul immediately places them in relation to one's "vocation," as the authentic criterion. Thus, Paul does not have anything *against* professional, social, or economic advancement; it is only that he is rather *for* the proper prioritizing of values.

Thereby, the charge of "social conservatism" which Schulz[514] has leveled against the apostle Paul, is refuted at its root. It is removed, not only from verse 21, but from the entire seventh chapter. However, the exhortation in verse 23, "do not become slaves to any human being," returns in a different form in Ephesians 6:5ff. and Colossians 3:22ff. Schulz twists the thrust of these household codes *(Haustafeln)* and what, in his opinion, is the rigoristic Church structure of *Frühkatholizismus* in which Paul "has been understood only too well," into its opposite, when he writes: "The unconditional obedience which the Christian slave owes to his earthly master, presented as a quasi-metaphysical status, is due in reality and truth to the heavenly Lord. Thereby permanent worth is accorded to the social order, without . . .

---

514. Siegfried Schulz, 243 and *passim;* cf. above, close to note 113.

even the smallest criticism being lodged from the side of the gospel."[515]

This is to stand the real situation on its head, for in Ephesians and Colossians the talk is explicitly about a liberated obedience and a relativizing of the authority of the earthly master.[516] It is not the permanent value of the social order that is promulgated, but rather the much greater value of individual people, who, even in an external condition of slavery, may become "free" (1 Cor 7:21-23). Paul deeply appreciated the value of earthly life; precisely in chapter 7 he has once again defended marriage, specifically against an exaggerated religious enthusiasm and against spiritualism. However, he also knows about sin and the divine offer of salvation, which charts out a different course.

The proper ordering of these components arises from the fact that *salvation* does not come about through social reform, but rather comes only from the death and resurrection of Jesus, through our participation in his death and his new life, while our efforts on behalf of human *well-being* must be an objective consequence of this.[517] Thus it is a matter of establishing the proper priorities. It is not the alternative between the spiritual and the worldly orders that is hereby addressed, but rather that between an attitude of "works righteousness" and dependence on God. Only then do the *two* foci mentioned in our sixth fundamental point of Christian existence—death and resurrection "in Christ," the renunciation of life and the fashioning of life—become distinguishable. It may well be that the God of history in the Church *at first* emphasized more the reality of dying with Christ (three hundred years of persecution), before the effects of the resur-

---

515. Schulz, 192 and 213; cf. 204-210.

516. Cf. Ts 425-429; further, see above, note 115, and below, note 542.

517. Therefore, it does not release us from social responsibility, but rather demands it—according to the time (cf. Rom 12-15; 1 Cor 8 and 9; 2 Cor 8:13f.). For the rest, O. v. Nell-Breuning has replied sufficiently to S. Schulz: "Kirche und soziale Frage," *StdZ* 98 (1973) 122f. Since it has long become clear in the areas of science and philosophy that the Scriptures do not invade the autonomy of these orders but rather respect their pronouncements, this insight should pose no further problems for questions of social theory. Cf. EuE 119; P. Stuhlmacher, "Historisch unangemessen," *EK* 1972, 297-299.

rection could become more strongly perceptible in their world, when the Constantinian revolution created more possibilities for fashioning the world. Today we also realize how quickly such a "Christian" shaping of the world can again become unchristian. Only too quickly what is unredeemed in humankind mixes itself in and takes control, and is capable of disfiguring every kind of spiritual activity. At that point humankind must enter once again into a school of dying and renunciation in order to be rescued. We are not here supporting some sort of power structure, but only saying that we should be forewarned against a certain naiveté, as if the process of salvation—of the individual as well as of humanity—were transparent or could be carried out exclusively from our side, or that all supposedly "Christian" activities in the world were thereby and by that fact already "spiritual."

With this we encounter the priorities God has set up and which often enough run counter to ones we have chosen. According to our own ideas should God have chosen different points of emphasis in the primitive Church and in the inspired Scriptures?

3. Is Galatians 3:28 the Magna Carta for Equal Rights for All?

Just as this text does not constitute a cry to slaves to rise up in liberation, nor an appeal against nationalism, so its intention is also not to establish equal rights for men and women. One could indeed claim that Galatians constitutes in many ways a high point in Paul's teaching about salvation; thus it would come as no surprise if there were also a pearl to be discovered regarding the war between the sexes. However, any such expectations we might have are not realized in the actual text. Of course, this has an ethnic, social, and anthropological background, but the explicit purpose of Galatians 3:28 is to stress the gratuitous character of our salvation in Christ, which depends upon no human claim or merit. Let us summarize briefly the results of our own analysis, which leads us to view Gal 3:15–4:7 as an interconnected argument which we have called an "argument for the Christological inheritance."[518] The central verses circle around the key concept of "one":

518. Atf I.

^{3:16}The promises were made to **Abraham** and **to his seed.** It does not read "and to his **seeds**," in the plural, but rather, so to speak, the individual (in the singular): "and **your** seed"; this is Christ (the Messiah). . . .

¹⁹The Law was added to this, and specifically until "the seed" should come, about whom the promises had been spoken. It was arranged by angels, through the hand of an intermediary. However, there is no such thing as an *"intermediary between one";* and God is indeed "one". . . .

²⁶Namely, you are **all** God's "sons" through *your "trusting" in Jesus Christ,* ²⁷for all of you who have been baptized in Christ have put on Christ (the Messiah).

²⁸*It has no importance* ("there is nothing in it") if you are a "Jew" *and not* a "Greek"; *it does not matter if you are a* "slave" *and not* "free"; *it has no importance whether you are* "male" *or* "female"; for **all** of you are **"one"** in Jesus the Christ.

Christ is the "one" seed of Abraham, who receives his inheritance from God not through an intermediary, for he is indeed "one" with him, that is: the *one God;* thus between "Father and Son" (4:4-6) no intermediary is necessary or thinkable. But since *we* through baptism become, so to speak, "identical" with Christ, we are now "one in him" (not "the same"), that is, *this* "one seed" that receives the inheritance from God without intermediary. As a consequence, the Law in the sense used above has no importance for us. Thus the singular "one" becomes for Paul a conceptual bridge leading from the "one seed" through the "one God," to the "one" that each person has become through baptism; whether Greek or Jew, by taking on his person he has, so to speak, "become Christ" = the *one* seed. Being male or female is irrelevant to this process; neither has any advantage for "being in Christ."

Thus "one" says nothing concerning the type of relationship that exists *between* men and women, but only something about the relationship to God we have in Christ, specifically to be "one" *with Christ* and thereby in him an "immediate" recipient of the promises. Ethnic, social, and class distinctions are not immediately canceled thereby—but also not ratified. However, they are not the explicit theme of this passage, and hence also not their revolutionary transformation. Their receptivity for modification is rather a presupposition of the section; an *actual* change, however, must be drawn out as an *interior consequence* of the situation that we are all one in Christ. Equality in social position is a social and political *consequence* that can and should be drawn at their appropriate time (our second principle). Galatians 3:28 itself defends neither ecclesiological nor social equality, nor an equality of rights and duties for all, but rather makes clear within the context of the ancient social order that such differences, even if they continue, do not interfere with a direct and immediate access to God in Christ.

On the basis of these results of our analysis, a dialogue should now be undertaken with various recent works, some of them operating from the perspective of feminist theology, that have interpreted this text to a greater or lesser extent in the direction of proclaiming a social or ecclesial equality of man and woman.[519] In contrast to the exhaustive commentaries we have produced in chronological sequence in the course of our thorough examination,[520] the quite varied positions of these monographs will now be arranged thematically. Without abandoning the question concerning the biblical foundation for equal rights, we shall attempt to approach the desired goal by another route.

(1) It is indeed true that Galatians 3:28c is through its adjectives "deliberately referred to the wording in the creation account" (Thyen, 109f.), but it is not therefore the case, as Stendahl states (32), that "thereby the *most fundamental distinction within God's creation,* that *between male and female, is overthrown,*" as if humankind were now, "beyond this distinction," the perfect image of God. Is this perhaps said out of the conviction that God is neither male nor female? However, the Creator-God is the model for them both! Further, the redeemed human person is simply a *higher or more complete* "image" *of this same God;* otherwise the "new creation" would not constitute the completion, but rather the overthrow and destruction of the "equal image" in man and woman so much emphasized in Genesis. Thyen considers the possibility that *creation* (which after all was "very

---

519. These are, in chronological order, the works of K. Stendahl, K. Thraede, H. Thyen, H. Paulsen, H. D. Betz, G. Dautzenberg (on Gal), E. Schüssler Fiorenza, and H. Ringeling (TRE), which each includes a further bibliography.

520. Cf. Atf I 5.

good") is equated with the "former age" (the "old aeon") and the "Law," whose "end" is Christ. However, these are three different categories: it is not the case that the creation itself is the "former age"; on the contrary, it fell into this through sin. If we are to use the term "the old creation" (Thyen, 109) (Paul does not use this expression), it can only refer to our existence as sinners, not, however, to creation itself. Moreover, the latter was not "canceled" or destroyed through Christ, but rather "freed" through salvation (Rom 8:20-23); further, the *holy Torah,* which begins with the account of creation and contains, besides the Ten Commandments, also the story of Abraham, is *fulfilled* as a "promise" through the "Good News" (Gal 3), and does not become *in this sense* an "old" covenant. The "Messiah" is indeed the "end" of the pattern of Law given and response demanded, for through him "faith has come."[521] However, on the other hand this constitutes the "fulfillment" of the Law (Gal 5:14; Rom 10:4; 13:8f.; cf. Matt 5:17-20; 7:10-25), and indeed the "fulfillment or apex of the aeons" (1 Cor 10:11), namely "when the times were fulfilled" (Gal 4:4). Further on (125) Thyen says correctly: "The notion that through Christ the Old Testament might somehow have been replaced or no longer be valid is completely foreign to the apostle. Exactly the reverse is the case! Paul says expressly and emphatically that the Law which through sin has become darkened and through the flesh robbed of its energy has now through Christ been restored to its brightness and power."

(2) The contrast between *"the order of creation"* and *"the order of salvation"*—not to be found thus distinguished in the New Testament—means, as Schüssler Fiorenza correctly emphasizes (206), neither that in both orders women occupy a subordinate position, nor that this is so only for the order of creation, but that the equality of rights in the order of salvation will come into effect only in the world to come. The question is rather whether "equality of rights in the order of salvation" is really the prin-

---

521. Cf. Atf I 2, notes on 3:22f. The legal penalty ("if you do not do this, you must die") is *as such* the "curse" that is overcome through Christ (Gal 3:12f.; Rom 10:4-6), since the person who has been marked by his spirit now lives in "faith." Thus it is not that since no one could fulfill the law anyway, they were forgiven.

cipal issue. Is Paul here really wrestling over the "social equality of the saved"? One may not find with Stendahl (32), behind the "household codes of both 1 Corinthians 11 and 14," the order of creation, but in Galatians 3:28, on the other hand, "a transcendence [of these] in Christ." In all these passages it is indeed behavior *in the community* that is being referred to! We have shown that in 1 Corinthians 11 the thinking explicitly concerns *both* orders (11:3, 11f.) which, however, are set in relationship to one another in that "being in the Lord" does not eclipse or nullify the "being from Adam," but rather completes, heals, and sanctifies it. Ringeling goes so far as to say that "For himself Paul recognizes a dualism between the 'spiritual and the sexual.' "[522] But in that case how could spouses undertake a marriage "in the Lord" (1 Cor 7:7, 39) or love one another "as the Lord" and "as the Lord loves" (Eph 5:22, 25, 29)?

We should not seek, therefore, to resolve the perceived difficulty as if the order of salvation totally superseded the order of nature. This problem is reduced by our interpretation of Galatians 3:28, since now the talk in neither order is about equality among them, but rather that the human and (let us say) creation-based human preconditions (such as male and female) do not provide a title for "being in Christ." Here it is not the relations among themselves that are being considered, but rather each member in itself on both levels. According to Galatians 6:15, circumcision, etc. does not provide a sufficient ground for "boasting." Also, such have never been the categories here discussed; that is why one cannot say: "They have *lost* all significance for salvation before God" (Mussner, 264), which Dautzenberg also rejects (195). Moreover, the "former age" and "sin" naturally were never viewed as a "work for salvation"; the only reason such thoughts are not here corrected is that they are absurd from the outset.

The serious issue which lies beneath the difference between the order of nature and that of salvation may be formulated rather following our fourth principle in such a way that the new existence (the "garment of Christ") gradually purifies, renews, and indeed also exceeds "according to the model of the Creator" every behavioral mode of male and female creation *that has become*

522. Ringeling, 433; cf. above, C 3 and 4; further, A V 2 and 3.

infected by sin.[523] This certainly means that (no longer) should the man "dominate" the woman (he "should" never have done it, it was a consequence of sin: Gen 3:16). They here become for the first time all that they were intended to be: man and woman in their differentiation. Whether and in what sense this new existence besides that also implies an *equality* must be determined in other ways, perhaps from their being brothers and sisters in Christ. However, such expressions cannot be found in our text, and much less so any suggestion of a cancellation of the order of creation.[524] In this context the point is certainly not that a *sinful* nature provides no basis for boasting (just as it is not that being a Jew is itself sinful), but rather that being male or female *as such* is not what makes a "Christian." However, it is also not necessary or a title to salvation, because we become first through faith "Abraham's seed" in the true sense. And of the notion that it is "better" to be a Jew than to be a Greek, there is also no suggestion.

(3) The distinction *"equal before God"*—*"not equal in this world,"* that is, in the "social-political sense," also does not resolve the problem before us. Although it is often mentioned in the same breath with the previous distinction, strictly speaking it lies at a different level. Stendahl (34) restricts the *coram Deo* even more narrowly to the "personal salvation" of the individual. Several authors feel that Galatians 3:28 is really referring to the relation to God. However, this is not achieved by fencing it off or opposing it to our inter-human relationships (our principle 1); rather, from start to finish the context speaks *only* about the way in which the person (in the first place considered individually) achieves salvation, and verse 3:28 about what this salvation consists in; it leaves open the manner in which this plays itself out in our inter-human behavior! It does not mention it, but also does not exclude it. So while it is indeed correct that "before God" male and female may not introduce their advantages into consideration, still in their relationships with one another they may

523. This could be derived from Gal 6:15; 2 Cor 5:17; 5:2-9 (see Ts 167-244), or Rom 5:12-21 and Rom 12; cf. Col 3:10.

524. While it is not mentioned that within the creation there is an order and sequence, this was taken as obvious by the people of antiquity.

naturally also not stress their "social standing." The issue is thus not about either the order of nature or the order of salvation, but rather the mutual relationship between God's activity of salvation toward humanity and our inter-human relationships. As for what concerns the second, from our text, which discusses explicitly only the first, one could draw a logical consequence (principle 2). About "equality," however, nothing is said, but rather that in our mutual dealings each should occupy the position that *God has indicated* to him or her—one would almost like to say, following Genesis 1: "each according to his or her kind." The text does not say how this place is to be determined. In any case, the various places are clearly not equal, but rather different.

(4) According to Paulsen (94), "Galatians 3:28 does not project a social program, but rather has a preliminary character," and is "a piece of *anticipatory eschatology* under the conditions of this world (Lührmann)." Thraede (103) on the other hand defends Stendahl's thesis (35) that "Galatians 3:28 anticipates what was possible *at that time,*" as an "acceptable idea." Paul is not thinking of the eschaton, but rather of the "revolutions of the new age," in which "equality had been brought about as a matter of fact," although perhaps in a manner that Paul could hardly imagine.[525] The reference frequently made to Mark 12:25 *par.* is, however, not conclusive, if only because nothing is said there about those resurrected having no gender, but rather that they "do not marry," and thus do not produce any more offspring, for indeed they no longer experience death; they are like angels, and this means that specifically as "offspring of God" they are "offspring of the resurrection" (Luke 20:36). Besides that, "as a rule it was not the *cancellation* of sexuality which Judaism awaited as salvation, but rather its redemption" (Thyen, 139). And naturally, as Schüssler Fiorenza emphasizes (218), Paul does not see salvation consisting in "women becoming like men."

Whether an inner-historical or a meta-historical future—both would be a "music of the future" that would fit badly with the present "there is neither male nor female"; the fit is equally bad

525. Cf. what was said apropos of the first principle, above, D I 1; on what follows, see below, D V 1, towards the end.

with "it does not count." According to our results the *eni* does not describe interpersonal relations but rather provides a condition under which the individuals have "put on Christ." That is to say: they put on not plurality, but "singularity," and thereby they belong to God not in virtue of their own distinctive style or merits. Thus the thesis about any kind of anticipation of a future condition collapses.

Dautzenberg (188–196) had challenged this thesis already on the basis of a comparison of verse 28c with the first two pairs of opposites verse 28a/b and the apocryphal tradition; however, he was of the opinion that here we had to do with "an overcoming or reconciliation of the oppositions *in the present*": "[It is] the articulation of the primitive Christian community's experience, and not a hope." However, since "these differences were everywhere still in place," Paul could only be speaking about the "breaking up of the assigned distribution of roles," namely, in an "undifferentiated participation in Christ." What is correct in this is that, in spite of various previous conditions, all belong to the "One" and "are" that one; however, the statement does not say that this belonging is "undifferentiated" (cf. only "trunk" and "branches"), nor that it either implies or demands "equality" in our relationship with one another (cf. a "body with many members").

(5) Building on the work of Meeks, Schüssler Fiorenza sharply distinguishes this passage as a *"pre-Pauline baptismal formula"* (208–220), especially underlining the self-contained character of verses 3:26-28, which, however, may now contain some Pauline "additions." Working independently almost at the same time on the same material, Dautzenberg concludes rather that the "sentence built up from negations (v. 28a-c) could only make sense within a larger context/syntagma" (183). Specifically, the "third member does not necessarily belong to this series"; at the most a "certain pre-existence" may be suspected," and specifically "coming from a tradition that arose in the experience of the missionary communities" (200–204). According to Schüssler Fiorenza (210–213), verse 28c does not say that in Christ there is no more male and female, but rather that "patriarchal marriage . . . is no longer constitutive of the new community in Christ." For that reason the separation of the genders and sex-based roles must be

done away with. However, where is there anything about another conception of marriage? And was a "patriarchal" marriage, as a "domination based on sexual divisions" (213) indeed "constitutive" of Jewish society? Madeleine Boucher has shown that "it was first in Judaism that equality rose to consciousness": "It may be that the contrast between the Jew's subordination of women and the Christian's new interest in their equality has been too sharply drawn, indeed, that such a contrast never existed."[526]

Besides the difficulty of bringing such a dismantling of patriarchal structures into accord with 1 Corinthians 11 and the household codes, Schüssler Fiorenza is surprised that Paul "explicitly refers to Galatians 3:28 in 1 Cor 12:13" and in 1 Corinthians 7:17-24 (218f.). (Does she believe that 1 Corinthians was written later?) But there indeed it is not a question of overthrowing differences, but rather specifically of their acceptance, and thus of a reconciled *unity out of different parts* ("each according as he or she is called"; "members of one body"), not of equality. In sum, the thesis founders once again on the fact that *eni* does not describe a condition that would be proclaimed over newly baptized persons, but at the most could (in advance!) clarify the "preconditions" for admission to baptism, namely that faith, and not a human entitlement, is decisive. However, here the issue is not faith as a personal precondition for baptism, but rather it is *by God* that, through the "faith of Christ" we as "sons" *have been* made into the "one seed/son," and thereby *are* inheritors of the promise. Thus, this is not a catechesis *before* baptism, but at the most after it. Further, in this context Paul is writing this sentence not to people newly baptized, but rather to people who *long after* having been baptized suddenly raise the question about circumcision. To these he says: "The differences are indeed (still!) 'there,' however they 'accomplish nothing'; at the beginning of your Christian existence they had no importance; why at this point do you wish to attribute to them any significance for salvation?"

Thus the verse in its present form (with *eni*, without *eti*) is certainly not (as Betz agrees) a "baptismal formula," even if during baptism the instruction may well have concerned the identifica-

---

526. Boucher, 52 and 55. She quotes among others *Sed El* 7: "Whether Jew or non-Jew (Gentile), man or woman, manservant or maidservant—God will hear [their prayer]" (53).

tion with the one Christ or the "oneness of all in Christ" (cf. 1 Cor 12:13). However, at no time was the "overthrow of all distinctions" and the "equality of all" proclaimed. Besides that, it is important to notice, as Thyen reminds us (128f.), that in the matter of adult baptism, Paul is not thinking in terms of a Hellenistic "mystery cult," but rather of the "word that they themselves at their baptism and through their baptism have given" (cf. 1 Peter 3:21). They have thereby put on Christ; they have not, however, thereby confessed any "equality" among themselves (extending into their civil status). That would be reading too much into the words and the action. Since ecclesial and civil equality would have been something revolutionary, they would have left traces behind on a wider front, and would not only be preserved in a single "key sentence." However, as we have seen, it is not even contained in this.

(6) *The mutual belonging together* of different types naturally brings consequences with it, and this is the kernel of truth in the contemporary discussion which we should pay careful attention to. We are aware of the extent to which the common path to salvation in Christ altered the *relationship between Jewish and Hellenistic Christians* not only from Ephesians 2 and 3, but directly from Galatians itself. Admittedly the "boundary line," the "dividing wall that Christ has thrown down," is not simply the "Law," but rather the "enmity" (Eph 2:14, 15), and God has not thereby simply set aside "Israel's glory and faith."[527] Can we imagine that in the pre-Pauline Hellenistic communities, alongside the difficult regulations of the apostolic council, a catchword concerning the full "equality" between Greeks and Jews developed and was put through; and that Paul, who in 1 and 2 Corinthians exerts himself strenuously on behalf of unity between the communities of Jewish and Gentile Christians, would here produce it as a battle cry against the Jews (without being able to maintain it)? H. Thyen (129) is probably closer to the truth when he says concerning the "empirical Israel" that Paul "never contested the special position Israel had received through God's election and guidance ahead of all other people" (Rom 2:3, 9-11), and that Galatians 2:15 "must be taken quite seriously": we Jews are "not

527. Stendahl, 32; on Eph 2:15, see EuE 107, note 204.

sinners from the world of pagans." "Anyone who would understand what Paul means," Thyen continues, "when he says that neither being a Jew nor being a pagan (better: 'being a Greek') has any relevance 'in Christ' (Gal 5:6)" (why not also a reference to v. 3:28?) "should not simply confuse 'in Christ' with 'since Christ' and maintain that since Jesus' crucifixion the Jews have become a people just like any other people." The relativization of the two (also 1 Cor 7:18f.) does not at all imply an equalization! However, on this basis Paul naturally supports a good social solidarity and their *"oneness"* in the body of Christ. Thus it is correct to say that, as a *consequence* of identification with Christ, social barriers are broken down.

(7) "We must also be prepared for a similarly differentiated perspective by the apostle with regard to the relation of *slaves* and *free persons*" (Thyen, 137). Reference is freqently made to the fact that otherwise Paul accepts the institution of slavery and does not fundamentally challenge it, even though in Philemon he intervenes in favor of liberation,[528] as he does, as we have seen, in 1 Corinthians 7:21! The "mutual approach" of both free and slaves in 7:22f. certainly presupposes the same human dignity in both (although this is not expressly stated); however, this does not yet imply that the gospel declares slavery in the social sense as abrogated or advocates that it should be overcome through political means. Certainly the gospel contains principles that lead finally to this result; however, the kerygma is not immediately a social-political proclamation—something that could be the program for a political party—but rather breaks into human history as God's message with the claim, *in virtue of our relationship with God,* to transform humankind's entire life.

---

528. Stendahl, 33: "His appeal takes place within the accepted structure of slavery and of Philemon's rights over Onesimus." Cf. also Dautzenberg, 184f. According to P. Lampe, "Keine Sklavenflucht des Onesimus," *ZNW* 76 (1985) 135ff., from the very beginning it was only a matter of financial damages that Onesimus had caused his master, on account of which he turned to Paul as an intermediary. One should notice that in *this* case Paul does not simply condone the "offense" of the slave. Naturally he remains confined within the understanding of rights which prevailed during his time, but he would certainly seek to protect a slave who was being tortured by his master from such injustice.

However, the God of history leaves this transformation to a development lying within human historicity and propelled by God's Spirit. Even if the idea of a full equality of all people had been generated by ancient philosophers, it would indeed be an anachronism in biblical thinking, surprising in Paul, and in this context out of place. Thus we "should not precipitously interpret Galatians 3:28 in the sense of modern movements toward emancipation as the isolated key sentence of the apostle" (Thyen, 113). What remains is that free persons and slaves, masters and slaves each in their own way, should acknowledge the "Lord," whereby a new impulse is given to reflect anew upon the (equal) personal worth lying within the essence of humanity, and its consequences.[529] Here concretely a stone is set rolling, a process is set in motion; but everything must happen according to the laws of historical development, as we have seen in the preceding section (D I 2).

(8) The (supposedly) "totally new thing of the '*no longer male and female*'" (Thyen, 113) has already, together with v. 28a and b, been characterized by Stendahl (32f.) as a "breakthrough," which, however, stands "in tension with those biblical passages—Pauline or non-Pauline—that retain the subordinate position of women" (one should continue: . . . and which are not fundamentally suspicious about ethnic and social distinctions). First, it is not correct simply to describe this subordination as the "order of creation" (Stendahl 32f.); at the very least Judaism was also awaiting with salvation "a liberation from the curse that since Genesis 3 had burdened sexuality with the pangs of birth, the domination of the husband over his wife, the difficulty of work, infertility, etc." (Thyen, 139). On the other hand the demand for equality naturally runs up against physiological limits; for that reason Schüssler Fiorenza (211) and Dautzenberg (197) also talk only about a breakthrough of changeable "roles." The simple statement "there are no such differences" would admittedly go beyond this; on this ground some criticize Paul, even occasionally discerning an "androgynous figure of Christ" in Paul's thinking (Meeks; Betz, 347). If, on the other hand, *eni* means "it counts for nothing," in that case gender differences are neither denied

---

529. Rengstorf is clear in this direction: δοῦλος, TDNT II 273–277.

nor placed in any specific relation to one another, but rather considered in their "significance" for being a Christian: they are no basis for "boasting" (Gal 6:14), and the statement is no longer something "completely new."

In passing we may note that "neither the Old Testament nor the Jewish tradition regarded the distinction between male and female as having any significance for salvation" (Dautzenberg, 95). From the identification with the same Savior there naturally arises a new respect for one another which in the New Testament gradually takes on shape and which is open for further developments. The "equal value of every person" becomes visible in this, without these words ever being used. As powerful as is the inbreaking of salvation in Christ, still Paul shows only the next step for the development of mutual conduct (which still is quite difficult), but does not usher in a social "breakthrough." Thraede's statement (103) that Paul "is basically not interested in social structures" sounds a bit negative to our ears; however, it remains true that he does not normally think in such categories[530] and in no sense "overturns the legal and social barriers in the community," as Dautzenberg believes (202). We should guard ourselves against any kind of theological "nostalgia" that embellishes our origins (Stendahl, 36). The priority goes to love for one another, out of which at the appropriate time social and structural consequences can and should develop. Thus, in the discussion of Galatians 3:28 the term "equality" can never be taken directly from the text, but only as a consequence which must yet be determined more precisely.

(9) As should be clear, the various tensions and contradictions between Galatians 3 and 1 Corinthians 11 or 14, but also with Colossians, the Pastoral Letters, and 1 Peter, which have given rise to very different theories, thereby evaporate.[531] The individual pronouncements remain, though addressed to various situations, still within the conventional thinking of their time and are consistent with one another. We no longer have to have recourse

---

530. See again the previous note.

531. Cf. Dautzenberg, "Zu Gal 3," 198–200; Schüssler Fiorenza 216–220, Ringeling.

to the invocation of a Pauline "interim ethic,"[532] in order to resolve "contradictions" within Paul or in the New Testament (Ringeling, 433f.). Also, the further development does not take place within the odd breaks and tensions which some purport to have discovered, and we do not have to make use of the suggestion that Galatians 3:28 quickly lost its efficacy (cf. Dautzenberg, 203). It is indeed rather surprising that, after the first two pairs of opposites, Paul still adds "male and female"; this can be explained through the customary triad and does not indicate a particular emancipatory intent. It should rather be emphasized that being male offers no specific advantage for our being saved in Christ (and neither does "being female").

(10) An "equality" is only indirectly contained to the extent that both parties can *not* introduce their perduring differences: male is not stronger and female is not weaker, "slave" is not worth less and "free person" is not more powerful, "Jew" is not nearer and "Greek" is not further away; in short, the one adds nothing to being-in-Christ, and the other detracts nothing from it. The two poles are "equal" in the sense that they both "mean" nothing; thus, this is a *negative equality*. It says nothing more. As a *consequence,* however, it is possible for us to say: because the apparent differences have been trivialized under this decisive perspective, one may the more easily alter or put up with them. Admittedly, this is not the thrust of Galatians 3; however, if we pose this question to the text in conjunction with our interpretation of 1 Corinthians 7:17-24, we may conclude: if you were a slave when you were called—*mē soi meletō*—don't concern yourself with it. Accept what for the moment cannot be avoided and the fact that it has happened, as something hidden in God and do not rebel against it (Job), but rather make the best of it—to which also belongs making use of the chance to be set free. Applied to our case: if you were a man when you were called, do not gloat about it; if you were a woman when you were called, do not interpret your weaker legal position as any detriment to your salvation. Learn to entrust these matters also to God's care,

---

532. We have already refuted this in conjunction with the hypothesis of the "expectation of the imminent second coming"; see above, close to note 160; cf. below, D V 1.

and yet make the best of your situation. This way the door remains open; and should the possibility develop for you to occupy a position of greater responsibility, take advantage of it—first in your personal situation, but then also for the benefit of other women and in society generally!

All this remains possible and falls easily into the tradition of Pauline thinking, even if Paul did not direct his thoughts to the problem in this context. At the same time we notice with such statements that on this topic a great deal more remains to be said. The intent of Galatians 3, moreover, was to demonstrate the uselessness of circumcision; it thus was preoccupied with the first member of this triad. Neither being a "Jew" nor a "Greek" adds anything to our salvation in Christ, but also it does no harm (1 Cor 7:19). Anyone who attempts to introduce such considerations alongside Christ, so to speak on the same level with him, underappreciates Christ and "shoves God's grace to one side" (Gal 2:21). The mentioned differences—naturally existing—"contribute nothing" to our being-in-Christ. Here we are back once again to a negative equality—which does not mean that Paul does not continue to remain consciously a Jew (Rom 9) and hardly propounds any overall sameness with the Greeks. However, from the two groups he forms in the *ekklēsia* a new community in which every believer has a full and complete share in Christ (the "one").

4. The Male as "Head/Source"?
The Female as "Brilliance/Glory"?

Penetration into the categories of ancient human thought requires a strenuous revolution in our thinking. All too easily unrecognized assumptions are introduced into our words that formed no part of their original meaning. This is the reason we go forward with small steps, attempting to justify each one. Up to now the question has remained open whether from the *oneness* with Christ also a "positive" *equality* of all those who belong to him could be concluded, and this not only from Galatians 3:28, but also even more clearly from Philippians 2:3 or 1 Corinthians 12, as well as Ephesians 1:10; 2:13–3:6; 4:1-5. To determine this we must take up once again the catchwords "head" and "subordination" and follow the considerations introduced above with regard to 1 Corinthians 11 and Ephesians 5 to their end.

(1) "The man is head of the woman" does not mean, as we have seen before, that he has priority over her, but rather strikes at a deeper anthropological level: he is joined to her in an *organic unity*. The internal structure of this organism is conceived in such a way that the man becomes the "head" = the source, while the woman becomes his "radiance, his brilliance, his glory."[533] However, in this allocation does not the man receive the more important role? In a contemporary perspective we would prefer to say: two who in their nature are essentially mutually related can only be conceived and exist as a pair. As image of God, only together, at the same time, and equally immediately could they have been created; thus, neither comes "before" the other. Is it then simply an ancient (clumsy, perhaps colloquial) way of envisaging things, to place them thus one after the other?

If the Genesis accounts are stamped with the patriarchal thinking of their time, then we should correctly distinguish the revelation concerning humankind from this manner of presenting it, that is, from the "material" (our third principle). However, how should we appropriate the theological message in our own categories? At the very least it remains true that both partners are created by God specifically in their differentiation, and for that reason should not attempt to become "like the other." However, does the correlative structure necessarily given with these differences imply that God intended an order of precedence? The first account of creation provides no indication of this,[534] and the account of the Fall makes clear that the "domination" by the man

---

533. Gen 2:23f.: "Bone from my bone; taken from the man; one flesh." Feuillet, *Sieg,* 26f.: "1 Cor 11:7 has often been improperly understood." It implies "that she is his glory, about which he should be proud." Gen 2:18 says "literally: 'a help-mate which God himself provided for his people,' and if in Gen 2:33 Adam gives a name to his spouse, the emphasis does not lie on the lordship that he may exercise over her, but rather on the intimate bond and the similarity of persons that is indicated through the similar sounds of the names *(ish–shā)*."

534. Many see in P a kind of correction to the Yahwist creation account (Gen 2); see Boucher 52. However, J shows through Gen 3 that he also understands his own "second" creation account as a partnership.

is a consequence of sin.[535] However, even had the hagiographer expressed himself in terms of an original "love-patriarchalism,"[536] the question remains whether this would belong to his theological intent and thus also to the content of revelation. It appears to me that the idea of "source"—taken up again in the image of the head—does not necessarily indicate superior status or legal precedence. Does this way of speaking then only reflect the fact that man is "physically stronger" and that in the act of generation he appears to be more the "originator"—without suggesting anything about superiority? The existence of matrilinear cultures[537] should already serve as a warning to us not to characterize this as "against the order of creation." What belongs to the content of authentic revelation is not established by a single person or a single argument, but only through the consensus of believers, which the theologians must continually test and consult. What the exegete may contribute to this process is to warn us against improper interpolations into the text, and to alert us to the limits of what the text actually says.

The first limit seems to me to consist in this, that Scripture does not sanction any particular social structure, not even when it is presumed to be "self-evident" (our third principle). Another limit seems to be that between the sexes there is a difference that God intended. A third would be that the structure that goes along with this does not necessarily imply a priority in rank. However, it does certainly imply a "mutual adaptedness." How does this appear? Who can say how far the so-called masculine and feminine "behavioral models" that have evolved in the course of

535. Not "he *should*," but "he *will* have dominion over you." N. Lohfink interpreted the primitive text as a personal conversation: "You will desire your husband *if* he dominates you." The punishment would then consist in the fact that *she herself* hangs onto the "dominating" husband and thereby surrenders her self-worth. Salvation would then mean liberation from such masochistic obedience and dependency.

536. Troeltsch, quoted by Thraede, 120.

537. Matrilinear means that "the children are only related to the family of their mother." Even there admittedly, according to Hauke (96), we may not assume an authentic matriarchy as a substitute for "male domination," and there never was a "matriarchy" (Hauke, 94–99); cf. also Evdokimov, 176–181. Still, that person is a Jew who has a Jewish *mother!*

human development, and which are now "imposed on" people extend, and to what extent they correspond to the fundamental structure bestowed by the Creator? In our nature's fallen condition, moreover, we must always anticipate a certain degree of alienation and decline from the ideal. On the other hand, it is not as if God first formed a "general human being," and then added to this person one set of gender characteristics and to another the other;[538] rather, each person is thoroughly penetrated and stamped by his or her gender. If, apart from physical externals, all remaining sexual differences were purely cultural and could be changed, then—apart from this remarkable dichotomy—the fact that male and female are equally made in God's image would remain strangely superficial.

Are not paternalistic and "maternalistic" cultures[539] alike simply different attempts to concretize the mutual accommodation of the sexes, with all the limitations and liability to mistakes that afflict every human operation? It is thus not so easy to specify what belongs to the inexpressible natures of man and woman, and where the socially developed roles begin (Lehmann). Could perhaps the image of "head and brilliance" capture something of the bisexual polarity or accommodation which we should not too hastily overlook? Although it is not in itself a "revealed truth," still we should attend carefully to the human experience concentrated in such a statement, and, in an age of a multicultural theology, not indignantly turn up our noses at it as something antiquated. Revelation has considered it as at least suitable "material."

We cannot in this work attempt to analyze the anthropological accommodation; however, the metaphor purified of misapprehensions should make us attentive to structures that perhaps lie deeper. In what ways does the author of Genesis, or Paul in 1 Corinthians 11, conceive the original relationship between man and woman? Each of them indeed had then a non-interchangeable role to play, without—in the original status—a problem of (in)equality arising, because the two of them were thoroughly

---

538. This would be perhaps the fourth of the models presented by Lehmann, 484f.; cf. also J. Splett, *Der Mensch ist Person* (Frankfurt/M 1978) 112–120.

539. Hauke, 96.

embedded in the love and worship of the Creator. If we take the creation seriously as creation, and omit its misuse through sin, could not the images of head/source and brilliance[540]/glory/unfolding/highpoint constitute a model of considerable beauty, in which both—in the purified "new creation" stamped by the Spirit of Pentecost—understand their *relationship to each other* in a new way, without any suggestion of superiority or derogation being introduced, and neither one making excessive demands either on themselves or on the other?[541]

To what extent can such an "ideal" become an actual norm of society? Indeed, it can only be lived out of an experience of God. Without this total reflex it will be continually misused (even by Christians). Admittedly, terms like head and glory have many negative connotations, and the suspicion quickly arises that still here acquired valuations continue to play a role. On the other hand it is equally possible that within modern conceptions of equality criteria are at work which do not derive from divine inspiration, but have their basis in human prejudices. How, then, may we come to terms with this "difference"?

(2) As soon as anthropological principles are used to resolve ordinary problems of behavior and are absorbed into legal language, reductions and misinterpretations are scarcely avoidable. As a consequence we must take into account that, in the conclusions which Paul draws from this, he allows elements to enter which derive from his socially conditioned appreciation of human roles. Thus in 1 Corinthians 11, following a common rabbinical form of argument involving wordplay, he produces, from the male's being the "head," an argument that the female should not dishonor her "head" by loosening her hair. What irritates us about this is primarily the circumstance that in the ranking the male appears to stand closer to God than does the female. However, that is primarily because of the nature of the paradigm. One could just

540. Not a reflection or copy (German: *Abglanz*); see above, A VII 2; similar Feuillet, *Sieg*, 26.
541. "Woman should have the right to be of equal worth and be human in a different way than the male" (Arlene Swidler, 233). The sexes should encounter one another in "a love which leads the other toward maturity, which neither oppresses nor glorifies the other" (Elisabeth Moltmann, 89).

as well argue—by posing the question differently—the other way around, that the man should not disgrace his wife through unseemly conduct, because thereby he dishonors his *doxa,* his brilliance and his glory. However, in the case before us the central question is how men and women should treat their "head." To conclude from this chain of argumentation that Paul—contrary to Genesis 1 and the whole Jewish tradition—suddenly intends here to accord women an equality as image of God only as mediated *through* the male (Delling), is to go astray. Still, we cannot escape the suspicion that his ways of thinking and accent are stamped by the *legal* precedence of the male, which seems self-evidently given in his environment. This would then be another instance of a time-conditioned "mental furnishing" that it would be unfair to burden the anthropological "head-glory model" with, and which should certainly not be described as a doctrine of revelation concerning the nature of humankind.

In Ephesians 5:22f., this model appears to take on an obvious patriarchal coloring, where the male's being the head is invoked to justify a *subordination* of the woman. We have however learned to distinguish between an image itself and the use to which it is put in an argument. Here it runs: She should accept a lower position, *for* the male is her "source." Herein lies an authentic progress in thought, a conclusion, whereas it would be a pure tautology to say: she should take a lower position, for the male is her superior = is placed above her. Moreover, it was said just before that *the two* should freely subordinate themselves to one another. However, it still remains true that the author names only the conduct of the woman "submission." It would not have fit in with the legal sensibility of the time to speak of the (voluntary) "subordination of men," just as in Ephesians 6 "obedience" is only demanded of children and slaves (this term was not used with regard to women), and in 1 Peter 2/3 also, "subordination" is always expected only from the socially weaker side, while parents, masters, and heads of families, as recognized authorities, are reminded of their responsibility before God. In the same way with a husband it is always the love of a person who before the law is set over his wife—just as Christ is set over the community—and from this (superior) position bends down. The author does not question the assumption that the husband is legally responsible for the wife, that he is her *kyrios.*

If a certain model of society exists in Paul's Bible—our "Old Testament"—it is accepted by the author, and by Paul, unreflectively, *but that does not mean that it represents the content of revelation and is thus laid down definitively for all time.* Just as little as with kingship (although it was established by God) is a form of leadership here set up that is intended to endure for all ages. Admittedly, people have frequently misinterpreted the Bible in this (literal or fundamentalistic) sense. Still, the theological content consists only in the statement that God called a particular person and that he (she) should now be respected accordingly (Prov 24:21; Qoh 8:2; Rom 13).

In any case Paul and the other biblical authors are convinced that in all these time-bound conditions, the Christian can and should practice love. This is the principle out of which all Christian "liberation" must take its origin. Therewith is first of all every misuse of a given order renounced, whether it take the form of oppression on one hand or submissiveness on the other.[542] Through the Bible certainly nothing that is wrong is sanctioned. Reversing this, we may conclude: to the extent that today in our social structures we recognize institutionalized injustice, this cannot in former times have been justified through the inspired word of God. This is a further support for our thesis that a given social structure as such is never made legitimate through the words of revelation. The factual alterations during the three-thousand-year-old Jewish-Christian development of belief also show that the "people of God" ultimately have not understood revelation in this fashion, even if individual representatives or even entire generations may have supported particular structures by invoking the Bible. The consensus over centuries is different. Moreover, one cannot so easily reproach the New Testament that it was not critical enough of social structures. Jesus is highly alert to any injustice; however, he approaches these at a different level and sets up *different priorities,* so that first of all *salvation* may be embraced *as salvation.*

For the rest, we may not simply discredit the ancient patriarchal household as a "structure of domination." Wives and children were not treated by the head of the household as slaves, but were respected as equals. In spite of her legal dependency, woman

542. 1 Cor 7:22f.; cf. above note 115 and note 516.

occupied a position of respect. When in 1 Peter 3 it says that the husband should "honor" his wife, this only expresses outright what was universally considered proper, even if it was not written down as "law." "Subordination" in the social structure should not be taken as something degrading. Without this no state can exist. Modern industrial society has developed considerable "hierarchies" (even if the word does not exactly fit). Even if it is continually misused, a particular system of legal super- and subordination does not fundamentally contradict the notion of human dignity. Also we still presume today that such are compatible with the "freedom and equality of all people in dignity and rights" (Article 1 in the United Nations' *Declaration of Human Rights*). It is of course true that the ancient world did not produce such a proposition in this form, and from first to last distinguished between Greeks and barbarians, free persons and slaves; however, in his relation to his "equal" wife, a husband was probably aware in general of what today we would call the "dignity and worth of the human person." This was not first discovered only in modern times. So even in a patriarchal social order a high degree of mutual respect, of easy exchange free of intimidation could be experienced. And on the other hand, in a society modeled on partnership, a considerable degree of power manipulation and oppression can be carried on, so that the "war between the sexes" continues under the mantle of "equal rights."

In any case what is new today is a different manner of dividing the roles, a different manner of interacting with one another, especially a legal guarantee of personal dignity and the "equal rights of man and woman" (Preamble to the U.N. *Declaration of Human Rights*). Is this profound transformation in social structures, which is by no means complete in all societies, in fundamental agreement with the Bible? We would again overtax the Bible if we expected it to "document" all of these steps. However, it may be demonstrated that they do not stand in contradiction to it; even more, they correspond to its general thrust, even if they were often not actively advanced and pursued by people in the churches. As a matter of fact, it is primarily a matter of social and political developments, and here much is said about the secularization of Christian ideas.[543]

543. Beinert, Maria 2: "During the Enlightenment the Churches overlooked

We should not too easily accept the excuse that indeed—as in the New Testament itself—the Church's commission does not consist in changing social relationships. For to the extent that Christians (not actually "the Church," for then it becomes secularized) shaped social life, they were and continue to be, almost as a proof of the authenticity of their belief, under obligation to raise these questions, just as were the people of the Old Covenant. Indeed, the prophets did speak up in similar situations! In this respect the relevant Pauline passages have admittedly had a disastrous effect throughout history, probably in the first instance because—besides the semantic misunderstandings—the theological content and the socially determined "material" through which the former was transmitted were not sufficiently distinguished. Such tendencies to fundamentalism continue into the present day.

The actual ethical-theological statement of the apostle is probably: "accept the position appropriate to you under the contemporary circumstances." This, no matter how simple it sounds, is the hard core that we can apply, in this abstract form, in a variety of new situations. It requires a clear eye to distinguish in every situation what should be encouraged, what should be corrected, and what should be tolerated. The proportions must add up. We must believe Paul capable of making such a discernment for his own situation. However, a consequence can result for us from the same principle that seems to contradict what he says. Just as at that time it followed from the fundamental principle that a woman should behave in a way that accorded with the general sensibility and the community order, that in council sessions she should keep quiet, today, on the other hand, it would follow that

---

the fact that Christianity itself sought liberation from unjust compulsion—the biblical catchword 'law.' 'It is precisely the tragedy of modern times that the liberating impulses of Christianity were often forced to set themselves against the established institutions of Christianity, and succeeded despite their hindrance' (H. Blumenberg). This is true for the institution of slavery, the Jewish question, and the question of human rights. This is also true for the rights of women." However, one should at least mention John Chrysostom who in *Hom. 4 in Gen.* (MG 54:593-598; cf. Ritter, 88) emphasizes that "sin introduced three forms of slavery: the subjugation of women under men instead of the originally intended 'help,' slavery, and the power-politics of nations." We are thus almost back again to the well-known triad.

she should take part;[544] in the same way from the basic principle "Accept the appropriate place for yourself under the contemporary circumstances," today in view of the equality of rights would follow: let all persons voluntarily subordinate themselves in Christ to one another: the husband to his wife, and the wife to her husband (this is a spiritual invitation, not a legal command). Make use of your "equal rights" in society in responsibility before God, for you will have to give an account of whether you shoved your responsibility off on your neighbor, whether you oppressed or outwitted him, or whether you helped her.

(3) However, with what right can we say that the development of *"equal social rights"* lies within the *"general thrust"* of the *biblical message?* Here we are not hoping to discover in the Bible social programs which we may transfer to our own situation; rather, we are looking for whatever basis there might be in it for a new "equality." We find here first of all the foundational struggle against sin and injustice which must be taken up anew by each generation, as well as the appeal to love, which does not cheat one's neighbor, but rather treats the neighbor "as the Lord."[545] The "image of the Creator" becomes clearer as we "are conformed to the image of his Son" (Rom 8:29). And though, in accord with ancient thinking about order, in the body of Christ there must be an assignment of various services and functions, 1 Corinthians 12 cautions lest anyone be treated badly, for all belong to the "one" body and are led by "the same Spirit" (Phil 2 and Eph). In virtue of being brothers and sisters in the one Lord, in which now Jews and Gentiles, slaves and free persons have been equally received, a *directionality is indicated* which leads logically (thus as a "consequence," now from Gal 3:28) to an *equal status of man and woman in society and before the law.* How could we deny equal dignity and equal rights to Christ in the other?

Admittedly, we must be careful now not to fall into the other extreme. If Christ identifies himself with every person, this does not mean that that person simply becomes identical with Christ.

544. See above, A VII 3.
545. Expressed in the Synoptics: ". . . then you have done it to me" (Matt 25:40). By the way, equality in the image of Christ is an argument that Chrysostom enlists against the institution of slavery; cf. above, note 543.

These kinds of statements must always be read within the context of the brokenness of human existence. And here probably lies the fundamental reason why the Bible does not directly challenge the existing social structures and does not immediately deliver a finished model for a new humanity. The God of history continually meets humans where they stand, and begins there a process of development with them. Paul indeed does not dismantle slavery; however, he reminds slaves of their dignity in Christ, and masters of their responsibility before God. Paul has no intention of putting women under a yoke or inculcating an attitude of timid subjection in them, but rather desires that they occupy their place in a spirit of freedom in Christ. If the two social partners meet one another "in Christ," they will one day begin to notice at which points their "legal positions" might be unjust. And if married Christians can see Christ in their partner, they will not misuse a physical or mental superiority, nor the privileges that society may have given them, in order to oppress the other; this is the counsel of the letter to the Ephesians. If they live this out consistently, they will continually notice how they should regulate their behavior toward one another.

The fact that it has taken so long—and is still taking a long time—for the sense of an equal status before the law for women to evolve in the so-called "Christian West" certainly has something to do with the necessary slowness of such profound transformations; however, it is also and at the same time the history of sin, of sin even among Christians, who have here wrongly invoked Ephesians 5 as if it said that the husband should stand over the woman. The spiritual counsel to women in Ephesians 5 to accept their position in society under the contemporary circumstances has been frequently misused by men as a way to perpetuate such a situation. However, what Paul intended to say was that, in the light of Christ, both partners should be ready to serve one another and thereby *to place themselves* voluntarily under the other and "to regard the other as standing over themselves" (Phil 2:2-8) in freedom and love. If one partner exploits the other's humility to his or her own advantage, this is a sin, in fact the same sin that was practiced against Jesus when he was cast aside.

Although it is correct that a legal code should provide protection against every form of injustice—which is the specific job of the state—the decisive point still remains people's basic attitude, on the basis of which such norms must be continually "relativized" anew, that is, continually placed in relation to Jesus Christ. There, in our salvation through his Spirit, lies the source of life. And if humankind does not heed this call, all its other efforts, whether they be for liberation or the preservation of the status quo, are disfigured. For the salvation of humankind is decided in Christ. Under the guidance of the Spirit Christianity must certainly exert itself further in its life and reflection to discover whether in the metaphor of head/source and glory/highpoint (it is an image!), indications of essential anthropological characteristics are not contained. They are certainly not contained in it in the sense that a patriarchal or hierarchical social structure is there set down firmly for all times. A person who encounters the Lord in the other will find "in the Lord" a standard that cannot be imprisoned within any "law."

(4) Our reflections have shown us that even our talk about equality runs up against a barrier. The question of the nature of man and woman goes deeper than this and cannot ultimately be solved in such categories. The application of 1 Corinthians 7:21 to other situations is not indeed exhausted by saying: "If you were a woman when called, don't complain about it." Rather, it must run: "If you were created as a woman, this does not first of all indicate a lack (at least not in Paul's eyes), but is rather something positive, a unique way of being like God, that is entrusted only to you. (To that extent the triad is dissimilar.) Thus, conceive God as fully endorsing your nature. Do not measure yourself against the man, but rather against your ultimate source itself. Only on this basis will you, as the various members of the body, be able to accept yourself spontaneously in gratitude and joy." It is similar for the man: "Do not be proud or self-assured, but also not unsure with regard to women; realize that your nature is a gift from God and that you may rest in God full of gratitude."[546] Equality thus does not mean the pressure or compulsion to be like someone else, but rather that each person, in what is distinctive and unique in each, may be fully him- or herself with the other. What each one needs is the space of freedom and worth in which everything that God has placed within him or her can

---

546. On the psychological aspect, cf. Lehmann; Beinert; E. Moltmann, "Menschwerden"; R. Rohr, *The Wild Man/Der wilde Mann,* Munich, 1986.

come to its full unfolding. Whenever someone deprives a person of this space or unfairly constricts it, that is unjust.

But how can women win such free space? On the social and political levels, certainly also through the "struggle" that is appropriate to this area of life. Viewed from her personally, however, this struggle should be a consequence of her own salvation in Christ. For salvation begins at the point where Christ refuses to answer force with force. Indeed, he saw injustice and called it by its correct name, and yet overcame it by laying it in the hands of his Father. Is this perhaps a reason why frequently women, as people discriminated against, have a deeper understanding for the way of Jesus? In any case he followed the path of love and had to find out how the Father himself would transform everything. Does it not frequently enough happen that through such treatment a man is in fact bowled over and reduced to silence, that is, embarrassed and "routed" (1 Peter 3:1f.)? And correspondingly the man must learn to sacrifice himself for the woman, as Christ did for the assembly. Again, through such a reflection on Christ the woman will not lose herself through her "struggle" (even within the Church).[547] Once she has accepted herself and her initial situation positively before God and from God, she also obtains the power, at the right moment and with her own "weapons," to set limits to men where they are practicing injustice. It is the struggle of a humanly mature and redeemed humanity that both men and women in equal measure must continually learn anew.

Thus, at the end what has become of our ideal of "equality"? This depends in part on how uniform we picture grace to be. With all the variety and individuality that should be even more pronounced in the order of salvation than in the order of creation,

547. This is intended in the sense which C. Halkes formulates: "I hope that, on the basis of the Bible and theology, we may uncover a Mary who is a powerful, prophetic, and critical figure, who calls us forth to liberation, but who can at the same time be humanly close to us, attentive and full of concern, because she is not greedily striving after power, but rather represents one aspect of eschatological existence, in that in her protest she does not demand but rather points out, does not scold but reveals, does not narrowmindedly push through her own view but remains open, participating in that fullness of Being to which she is attached in a unique way" (quoted according to Beinert, "Maria," 13).

there is among those who have been saved no jealousy, since each one is content with his or her own portion, and all respect God's gifts in the others. Under the influence of one's personal relationship with God, this differentiation becomes not only acceptable, but even a reason for marveling, thanksgiving, and joy. The ideal of equality becomes more and relativized, with the effect that we will not so readily dismiss the anthropology of the biblical narrator.

Are then people at least equal in their relationship with God? Verses 7 and 17-24 from 1 Corinthians 7 speak of each one "according to his or her own call," and Matthew 20:9-16—where all the workers receive "one denarius"—creates the impression that this wage does not have the same effect in everyone. In fact, "equality" does not seem to be a biblical category at all.[548]

Is it perhaps possible that the ancient world had a deeper understanding of humanity in that by justice it understood, not "the same thing for everybody," but rather "to each person his or her own," perhaps also with the knowledge that, in view of the factual variety in people, "equality" would very soon overburden some and unfairly favor others? If, however, we wish to approach the Bible as modern people with this concept, then we should speak of "equal worth as persons," of equal entitlement, equal standing, or equal value (LG 32), which belongs equally to men and women, along with people of every class and physical and ethnic variation; of equality before the law and finally before the judgment seat of God—although this last image can easily become problematic if God is pictured as being "equally severe" on everyone. Ultimately we would have to say that God loves each person in a different way, and nobody gets shortchanged in the process. Only in this unique divine devotion can the problem of the *de facto* differentiation between people ultimately be resolved; in a manner of speaking, God loves each one of us best.

---

548. The only reference in the New Testament is Acts 11:17: God gave the same gift to all the peoples that God gave to the Jews: ἴσην δωρεάν. Further, see Phil 2:6; John 5:8.

II. Man and Woman within the
Priestly People of God

From the one salvation bestowed in Christ the community of believers gradually learns how to deal more justly with one another—and this should also have its effect in the larger society (at its appropriate time). This, at least, is the task of the saved in an unsaved world. Occasionally the relationships among Christians may well be characterized by a greater respect than are relations outside this community. Structurally seen, however, is it not today rather the reverse, specifically that in the civic and social sphere women may attain a proportionally greater independence and responsibility than within the Church? This is also true, even if we abstract from the limits imposed by our understanding of the sacraments and by canon law. If we are indeed able to trace social developments toward equality of rights back to positive Pauline foundations, this should be even more evident in the ecclesial sphere. Thus, after having considered the matter in its social anthropology, we now wish to examine ecclesiological anthropology. Against both the contemporary and biblical background, how does the actual behavior of men and women in the Church appear today?

If through our interpretation of the ancient head-glory model the differences in rank have been somewhat softened, it is still true that Paul remains the prisoner of the subordination model characteristic of his time. We can only show that he does not reinforce it to the extent that is often imagined, but rather lives out and promulgates an opposing tendency. In this he admittedly shows his limitations and remains bound within the conceptual models of his time. Still, it must be said that his actual theme is not "woman within the family and society," but rather woman within the community of those being saved. But should he not here have used other standards, as well as cultivated the possibility of establishing new ones? In practice women were now experiencing greater esteem and respect for their dignity ("sisters in Christ"), and were sharing in new tasks in community prayer, in prophecy, and in evangelization. This has its foundation in the common gift of the Holy Spirit to both man and woman. But still it was true that these tasks were assigned or entrusted to women by men, and then only within a sphere perceived to be "proper." Does this not constitute a pure capitulation to convention?

The issue of priesthood for women and the existence of a clergy in general is only the tip of the iceberg. It is rather necessary to ask in a larger sense about the received "roles" in our communities—recognizing the dangers both of clericalism as well as that of a female "devotion" toward persons holding orders. Do the examples of conduct on the different levels of Church life correspond to Jesus' Spirit? Are they a consistent extension from the "starting points" Paul provides and that suited his contemporary practice and circumstances? The Church (leadership's) concern to avoid a precipitous and immature step might explain a certain degree of caution; however, the same Pauline principle of appropriateness also forbids us from ignoring a question like that once it has come up. It must be addressed seriously, without prejudice or fear, both before God and the Church.

What then follows from our "oneness in Christ" and the "equal status and equal dignity of men and women if we recognize a single humanity shaped in different ways" (Lehmann, 485)? What follows from this for the spiritual communication of man and woman in the areas of pedagogy and spirituality, family and society, in the service of the word in proclamation and teaching (women such as Teresa of Avila as "Doctors of the Church"), in diaconal service (deaconesses?), leadership of the community, and presiding at liturgy?[551] Let us attempt to draw out the consequences, under fourteen aspects, from the Pauline perspective we have gained.

---

551. Cf. Rahner, 299f. As representatives for many others we here mention the works by W. Beinert, E. Gutting, Catharina J. M. Halkes, M. Hauke (these contain a more extended bibliography), F. Kamphaus, K. Lehmann, Elisabeth and Jürgen Moltmann, H.v.d. Meer, K. Rahner ("Priestertum"), Rosemary Ruether, Elisabeth Schüssler Fiorenza, Edith Stein, and Arlene Swidler, (for all of which see the bibliography) as well as the Roman documents *Inter Insigniores* and *Mulieres Dignitatem*. We further mention P. Gordan, ed., *Gott schuf den Menschen als Mann und Frau. Die Vorlesungen der Salzburger Hochschulwochen 1988* (Graz, 1989); F. Kamphaus, *Frauen in der Kirche, Hirtenwort und Anregungen,* (Bischöfl. Ordinariat Limburg, 1989); C. F. Parvey, ed., *Ordination of Women in Ecumenical Perspective,* Faith and Order Paper 105 (Geneva, 1980) 75–94: bibliography.

1. The Historical Aspect

The attempt to demonstrate that for Paul women could bear authority, in the sense of the "ordained" leadership of a community, did not succeed because of a lack of evidence (see above A VII 4 and 5; B II 3). Since the entire society was thoroughly stamped with a patriarchal character,[552] the Christian communities were modeled, as concerns their fundamental standards, on the community order coming to them from Judaism (1 Cor 11:16; 14:34-36); and there would have to be clear evidence of such a revolutionary situation. The burden of proof is on those who uphold the thesis. In cases of doubt our method must be to try to understand the problematic statements within the context of the contemporary sociological environment, for which sections of 1 Corinthians 11 and 14, which are more concrete on this point, are ideally suited. Thus, all we could conclude from the scanty data was ultimately that women were only active as "coworkers" (along with men) (A VII 4). However, at the same time it should be noticed that the function of male authority figures only gradually began to emerge. The lack of clarity thus more concerns the distinction between "persons in office" and other believers; because this is not yet so clear conceptually, so also the borderline for women is more open (house communities, presiders at the breaking of the bread). One may nowadays observe a similar actual exercise of leadership by women in communities where the Spirit is breaking out anew,[553] and with many of the great women in Church history. The traditional division of roles is perhaps thereby *challenged,* however not actually consciously overthrown in its basic structures.[554] For that considerably more extensive processes are required.

552. Hauke's question mark behind this word reflects a too euphoric view of how accommodating to women the Greek world was (334–338). Admittedly, we are still probably male-centered; how can we change this? What does the mutual relatedness of different kinds of people look like?

553. "In many Christian base-communities of Latin-America, female leadership is taken for granted," Moltmann, 90f. In the "Community of the Lion of Judah and the Slaughtered Lamb" (now: "Community of the Beatitudes"), which comes out of the charismatic renewal, women are also "shepherdesses" over communities made up of men, women, and families.

554. History frequently repeats itself, beginning with the New Testament; however, are we going once again to have the same division of roles?

Certainly Jesus "broke through taboos in his encounters with women," "in his cures or his signs of the forgiveness of sins he made no distinction between men and women," he accepted "women among his disciples—a highly offensive behavior,"[555] so that they went around with him; however, he reached a certain limit when he called only men to be among "the Twelve," in analogy to the twelve "tribal patriarchs" of Israel. Thus Karl Rahner's conclusion is on target, that "in their concrete cultural and social milieu, Jesus and the apostles could not conceive of installing women as leaders of communities (without undertaking what would then have been impossible to carry out)," since such a state of affairs "in their situation could not even emerge as a serious possibility" (298). Our question is: Is this the only reason? We must hold ourselves to the provable "facts." If the facts were of this sort, this argument would actually make it easier to say that the exclusion of women from orders was due to *the view of humanity that prevailed at that time*. Otherwise one would have to ask oneself: If at the beginning there had actually been a possibility for the development of female leadership in the communities through God's initiative, then why—in spite of external circumstances—did the Holy Spirit not make use of it? For as a matter of fact, socially speaking, the early Christians were not a minority bent upon conforming at all costs to the larger society.

2. The Sociological Aspect and Cultural History

But what happens when the situations and circumstances become different? According to the principle of appropriateness that Paul frequently expounds, a different style of conduct would then be possible and in certain situations necessary. In this case, how far would Paul go? The question comes down to determining why Jesus and the apostles drew a line at the mentioned borders. Was it only out of consideration for the cultural and social situation, or because they really felt it would be inappropriate and as not corresponding to the nature of their service, to transfer it to women? Now mind you, *they* would have had to "transfer" it— that is, it first lay in their own hands, that is, in male hands.

---

555. R. Schnackenburg, "Die sittliche Botschaft des Neuen Testaments," HThK, Suppl. 1 (Freiburg, 1986) 146f.

Does some kind of divine purpose then stand behind this? Does it belong to the *essence* of the Church Jesus established, does it have the status of a revealed doctrine, that a woman cannot exercise this office? Direct statements to this effect are conspicuously absent in the New Testament; only on the basis of the Old Testament is it unthinkable.

Now we must freely admit that an *argumentum e silentio* is no justification for a thesis; in this case it also does not have to be proved that revelation either allows or forbids it, but only that it says "nothing" (expressly) about it. So we return to the question of how a behavior should be interpreted. And then the burden of proof falls upon those who are of the opinion that the restriction of office exclusively to men must be viewed as "divine law." Of course, this could have occurred under the guidance of the Spirit; but did the Spirit guide them to this because *under these circumstances* it was unsuitable, or because it was *fundamentally against* it? Why is there no express indication concerning motivation? And since the Church continues to stand under the guidance of the Spirit, it may clarify this further at a later date and "lead it into all truth."

On the level of argumentation the relevant Vatican declaration *Inter insigniores* (IV, p. 105f.) says that no one can "prove that this way of acting resulted *only* from social and cultural reasons." Karl Rahner responds (298): "Anytime cultural and social reasons are put forward for the refusal to employ women as leaders of the community (a special eucharistic privilege [for men] is especially difficult to justify from the New Testament), then it would have to be clearly demonstrated that these reasons *are insufficient* to explain the comportment of Jesus and his apostles." Admittedly, even if they are sufficient according to our logic, there could be other motives lying concealed behind them. However, the burden of proof lies on the one who claims more, in that one cannot point out a revealed word of Scripture to support this. Thus the Vatican declaration also confirmed that for the exclusion of women there was "no direct evidence of the sort that is immediately apparent."

Besides this, the text from the Congregation for the Faith allows the principle to stand that among Paul's regulations there are some that we would have to regard today as untenable (106);

however, these are said to be items of minor importance. If such a statement is indeed justified (in itself it is questionable), it becomes very difficult to say under what circumstances and for which people some things are of "minor importance" (106). Once the door is opened to abrogating "inspired" instructions, then all that remains is the choice—with regard to important and unimportant things alike—either to call inspiration itself into question (who decides which things are "important"?), or to describe such directives as *conditioned by the situation they were addressing.* There are then commands for a specific time or situation, just as from the time of Abraham to the communities of the Book of Revelation, many orders or instructions were given to individual people or to groups which were only valid for them and which cannot simply be extended and applied to all people at all times (bring me an animal for sacrifice; move into this land; the "law" is for a time: Galatians 3; bring me my cloak); this belongs to the nature of a historical word. The contents are indeed very much "inspired," but are uttered with reference to a specific situation.

Admittedly, what is time-conditioned and what is universally valid are not easy to distinguish; at the same time the Church has always been conscious of the need and the competence to do this, on the basis of the "assistance of the Holy Spirit." On the level of the argumentation, according to our results several of the Pauline justifications for the Vatican explanation would no longer be valid. On the one hand the norm of conduct remains in effect today that neither men nor women while speaking or praying in public may loosen their hair and behave coquettishly (1 Cor 11), whereas the "remaining quiet" "in assembly" (1 Cor 14) was not said, as in 1 Timothy 2:12, "with reference to the office of teaching in the assembly," but rather keeping silent during a council meeting, in which they nonetheless were allowed to be present. Certainly this is no longer valid today. The arguments of all three texts are based on what is "proper." It is therefore correct that, with changed circumstances, specific regulations can be revised; however, the line runs not between those that are "important" and those that are "unimportant"; it must rather be able to be shown that in the meantime the circumstances have changed, that the specific rules were thus given only "in consideration of the circumstances in effect" (1 Cor 7:26), and therefore their pronouncements were conditioned both by the times and the situation.

If one considers how cautiously Paul argues in 1 Corinthians 7, one will indeed be surprised at the high value placed on his equally situation-specific concrete regulations. The question may and should continually be asked, what trans-temporal, universally valid principle stands "behind" them? The test question is not: Is this a "command from the Lord"? A divine instruction may also be given with a view to a specific circumstance. Thus the question is not whether this is a matter of "divine or human law," but rather whether it is universally, or only particularly, valid. In the absence of such distinctions the Bible quickly becomes inhuman (and thereby also ungodly)—or irrelevant. "For truth is proposed and expressed in a variety of ways, depending on whether a text is history of one kind or another, or whether its form is that of prophecy, poetry, or some other type of speech" (DV 12).

Thus the question whether the exclusive commission of men with Church leadership was itself time-conditioned today stands —as a consequence of these results—in question within the community of believers. Could we not today include *women* among the deacons (again) and among the "elders" *(presbyterae)* (for the first time)? In parish councils up to being the "presider," today this is no longer a problem, and in exclusively women's communities there has always been authentic leadership authority all the way up to abbesses.[556] In saying this we are conscious of the fact that the biblical *presbyteros* is not simply identical with the later, more precisely sacramentally qualified "priest," and that our contemporary objective specification (definition) of "ordained priesthood" is capable of being changed. Does it not lie thoroughly within the hand of the *ekklēsia* with its office of leadership to specify how participation in the teaching, priestly, and pastoral roles of Christ shall be divided? We shall come back to this.

---

556. However, the noteworthy construction of the word "abbess" (= she-father) indicates the androcentric orientation.

3. The Ontological Aspect

However, is there perhaps a difference between man and woman based upon their *nature* that would deny women the possibility of representing God by occupying a leadership position? Hauke refers to "a greater similarity of the male to God on the level of *representation* that is founded in his 'eccentric' disposition that is oriented toward 'leadership' " (343). This ability to surpass existing reality which "corresponds to the essence of the male character," is a "clear symbol for the divine transcendence" (138f.). "In our imaging of God the greater importance lies with transcendence rather than immanence." This would be the explanation for "the primacy of male symbolism in the imaging of God" (172f.).

Here an attempt is made, from a starting point in philosophy and the history of religion, to explain the constraints on representation in leadership positions. But is this classification accurate? Must not one say rather that transcendent and immanent aspects in the divine image may also be represented in the male-female polarity, but in such a way that men and women contain them *both,* and simply accentuate them differently; however, on that basis neither one is "less similar" to God in what is specific to him- or herself than the other. Or is perhaps the Holy Spirit less "divine" than the Father? Besides that, the greatest caution must be exercised so that philosophical speculations do not become the basis for theological argumentation. At the most they may be used as aids for explication. Even if we could say philosophically exactly what belongs to the "essence" of man and woman,[557] still no obligatory conclusion could be drawn from that as to how God, in the sharing of God's self, would make use of this "essential form" to render God's self transparent. Thus any consideration of this type is not decisive.

4. The Theological Aspect

Long before the incarnation of the Second Person of the Trinity, God revealed God's self as "father." Is it then not more in keeping with this truth if the official "representation" of God

557. But who can do this? Cf. Splett, 149–156.

is carried out by *men?* But here again a question must be asked: which is conditioned by which? Does God show God's self as father because in the nature of God, God is ultimately masculine, or is it that within a culture penetrated by patriarchal symbols, God chooses to reveal God's self more powerfully by using male symbols, so as to be understood and accepted by such people, especially the decision-makers? What does the authentic "image of God" look like?

If God created humankind as male and female after God's own image, God's very self must be the original model for both. When one examines the revelatory texts more carefully, one notices that YHWH always remains at a significant distance, grammatically indicated indeed by the masculine form, but never specified more narrowly in essence as "male." Is this because YHWH desires not to appear as excessively masculine, or as not *only* masculine (Exod 33; but Dan 7? Rev 4?)? The image of God in the Old Testament is more open than one suspects, open indeed for a self-revelation as "Father, Son, and Spirit" to take place in the fullness of time (Gal 4:4-7); it is tied irrevocably neither to one gender nor to one person. Otherwise the Law, the Prophets, and the Writings would be a poor introduction to YHWH's revelation in the Christ Messiah.[558]

Is it possible within the three-person image of God to assign gender-specific functions, such as to designate the First Person as masculine? Would it then be appropriate to refer the feminine to the Second Person (in its receptive capacity) or perhaps to the Holy Spirit,[559] who since Genesis 1:2 reveals a maternal aspect of God? J. Moltmann reminds us of an "old, forgotten tradition which accords a maternal office to the Holy Spirit. Those Christian communities which later would be excommunicated from the larger and male Church as 'Gnostics,' were able to speak of the Spirit as the Mother of Jesus and the Mother of those born again. The Ethiopian depictions of the Trinity show the Spirit as a mother. Further, the Greek Fathers often saw in the original

558. In "Jesus Christus—die endgültige Offenbarung Gottes—Biblische Sicht," 45–55, I have described in more detail the various "stages of self-revelation" of the threefold, Trinitarian God; cf. further above, note 475.

559. The feminine *rûach* means vitality, life force, not intellect; see above, C 2 and 3; Hauke, 284–291.

family—Adam, Eve, and Seth—the image of the God who is three in one, which presumes that the Holy Spirit is feminine and the original model for motherhood.''[560]

Certainly there is much truth in this, but it should not be understood as saying that sexual differentiation in God could be parceled out in this fashion among the three persons; this already becomes clear in the unclarity about how and in what sequence one should distinguish the "Second and Third Persons." Where would the feminine be? A "child" is not a third sex, and within the Godhead the Spirit is not the "mother of the Son." J. Moltmann then goes a step further and discovers that "the certainly very difficult and abstract development of the doctrine of the Trinity within the Christian conception of God prepared the way for the overcoming of the dominating male divinity."

Actually, such abstract talk about the transcendent God can preserve possibilities of the mystery that further unfold themselves in the course of history. God is neither male nor female, but rather the model for both. This cannot be limited to the divine "essence," but must become apparent also in the divine Persons. If within humanity a person's "casting" as male or female is final and decisive, this does not exclude a person's having something of both (and necessarily, to be a complete human being). Admittedly we should inquire here what is "specifically male" or "specifically female." Would not such a supposed concept already contain what first has to be demonstrated? Each person contains the fullness of humanity. With what right do we characterize one element as male and another as female? We may thus conclude that the divine Persons are characterized not by limitation, but rather by a harmony between the masculine and feminine which they carry within themselves as a model for all that is. In this sense the First Person would be simultaneously Mother and Father, the Second Person Son and Daughter, and the Third Person the (male-female) power of life. These analogies are put forward with the greatest caution.[561] Do they not cast a little more light upon the

---

560. J. Moltmann, 86f.; cf. however, Hauke, 286–292.

561. According to Hauke, 231f., in the Father the masculine has integrated the feminine, but the two are not on the same level. However, in that case one would also have to say that in the Holy Spirit the feminine integrates the masculine. So that would apply to both cases.

background of Genesis 1:27; Romans 8:29; Colossians 3:10; Ephesians 1, and the Johannine writings, so as to guide us admittedly again into a still deeper mystery?

The anthropological analogue to this theology would be: each human being as a "person" should first of all be seen in their independence and as such as *immediately* an image of God. "The woman is not primarily defined through her relationship (to the man), but rather in herself; the male already develops his self-understanding without reference to the female." Further, "the woman was not simply created as directed toward the man, but rather toward God," an "original idea of the Creator."[562] If this statement surprises, it is nonetheless a consequence of biblical pronouncements, including those of 1 Cor 11:9: woman was created "because of" man, that is, in his regard as an appropriate correlate, but created *immediately* by God *after God's own image,* and not as though through the "mediation" of the male. Otherwise that passage would say "in the image of the man."[563]

Moreover, if we follow this line of thought to its conclusion— since our images of God and humanity always correspond—this means that we must fundamentally rethink both "images" in such a way that male and female are seen on both levels (in analogy) as standing in equality, mutual relatedness, and harmony (1 Cor 11:11f.). The fact that a distinction then can and should be drawn in our thinking between the "source" and the "manifestation" no more diminishes the "essential equality" between male and female than does the difference between the three Persons of the Trinity—which, as was shown, lies on a different level. The Person who became *fully* human has said "The Father is greater than I." About the "Son" who is of the same nature as the "Father," one may at most say: "He is in his person the receptive one."[564] He is not, for that reason, however, diminished or less, but rather is the Father's equal in nature! In the same way men and women must rediscover each other's essence in God to be fundamentally equal and equally original.

---

562. Lehmann, 481 and 486.

563. Thus it was objectively correct to interpret διὰ with the accusative as causal; see above, before note 310; Atf II 4.

564. Thereby to be receptive should not simply be equated with "female."

To conclude, there remains the question why God, in God's historical revelation, elected to go the way of a man. Or perhaps we should ask why God chose to *begin* with an epiphany in a male form? Is the reason that, in these matters, there exists a natural "sequence"? However, could this then still not have been arranged, as in the event of creation itself, to have taken place *simultaneously?* Or is the reason that God took into account the patriarchal mindset of the recipients of this revelation—since otherwise they would not have understood? Then there would only remain the question: still, why did God allow history to take this androcentric direction? Does not Genesis 3:16 say that male domination is a consequence of sin? Would it then be a sign of God's humility and ever-pursuant love that God sought entrance into humanity even in its fallen state, that God deigned to rescue and meet it where it was? In that case, would then the pronounced "male" paradigms of revelation not be explained to a large extent by their "sociocultural" and sinful circumstances?[565]

If we examine things carefully, we will notice that in the central texts of revelation the feminine is never suppressed; it belongs, admittedly in a hidden way, to the complete image of God.[566] And does not something in Jesus's cry of *Abba* resonate with this? It is said to be an affectionate or familiar term; perhaps less that of a small child to its father than one which, in the term *Abba* simultaneously addresses something both male and female (analogously). If the one-sided exaggerations of patriarchalism are overcome, is this not also a process of salvation?[567] Would it not be

565. Adam's son Seth is similar "to him," because he is a son; would a daughter then be similar to the mother? However, that is not what is being said. In Gen 5:1-3, UT translates the Hebrew *adam* sometimes with *human person,* sometimes with "Adam," and similarly also the Septuagint in Gen 2. The word thus stands *simultaneously* for both! In his language, unfortunately Closen also (182f.) remains male-centered in the interpretation of Gen 5 and 6.

566. Yahweh's fight against fertility cults does not intend to repress the feminine (there are indeed masculine variants), but rather the "foreign gods," such as the bull, "the calf." For an introduction into the literature on this, see Beinert, Halkes, and Lehmann. On issues in the history of religions, cf. also Atf VIII 2.

567. Arlene Swidler clearly names the until-now unredeemed condition, and reveals many wounds—as a means toward healing them.

possible that today, at this point of the history of the Church, God may show God's self to us more completely—which would correspond to the deepest intention of God's revelation and would also be a forward step in our understanding of the faith? There remains an interior "order" to gender aspects. How does this interior order limit the imitation in human life of the divine life, and how does it structure it? We here leave this question open.

5. The Christological Aspect

The Messiah was a male. (This does not mean, as we have seen, that the Second Person of the Trinity should be described as "male.") May we conclude from this that it was more appropriate to the divine nature to become human as a male? Or does this again reflect a concession to human limitations? Is this *all* it is? How could we say this? In his created human nature the Second Person of the Trinity is indeed "a man," but in such a way that at the same time he embraces all of humanity in himself,[568] that we *all* become *equally* conformed to the image of the "Son," that under the expression "his brothers" women are also meant to be included, and we all together constitute "the Christ" (Rom 8:29; 1 Cor 12:12, 27). Does he include women as "second-class citizens," as if they were people less akin to himself? Every baptized person shares in Christ's priestly, prophetic, and royal offices (thus also in a certain sense in the responsibility for leadership). Also, it is the same Christ whom we encounter in *every* human being. Thus Jesus the "God-human" is—if we may so speak—simultaneously "God-man" and "God-woman," that is, in his God-human-ness, he is at the same time the form of identity of both men and women. This is the fundamental reason why all people, women as well as men, but especially the members of his body, "represent" him.

According to the metaphorical language of Ephesians, Christ as head is *distinguished from* his "body." However, to the extent that his position may be represented within the historical corpus, there are also—to borrow again the inclusive picture from 1 Corinthians—within this historical *ekklēsia* certain members who may represent the head (1 Cor 12:27f.: first, etc.). And here lies

568. Cf. our notes to 1 Cor 11:3 in Atf III 6, as well as what follows.

our central question: is it absolutely necessary, appropriate, or at the very least a positive command of God that *this* manner of representing the head may only be carried out by men? The general position that the second divine person may not be represented through a woman we have just refuted, in that Christ is indeed present in everyone. However, is an "official" representation by women perhaps less appropriate to his *human* nature? One could say: God has indeed chosen the male form in which to become human; it behooves us now in all respect to adjust our participation in this office to God's choice. However, thereby virtually every form of representation of Christ by women would be again thrown into suspicion, and the question would immediately arise, why do we make the cut-off point here, and not earlier? We would then return to certain historical forms of Church life which for a long time kept women at a greater distance from certain forms of ecclesiastical life than today. The borders have been moved in the meantime. However, if against such a redrawing of the borders once again the argument of the male sex of the Savior may not be brought out, is Jesus' maleness still adequate as a response to the challenge of the "last" border, that of the "ordained priesthood"?

From the point of view of theological anthropology, there is no foundation for the latter's limitation to males. It would then have to be the express will of God revealing God's self. However, at least in the Scriptures there is nowhere any indication that God intended *fundamentally* to *exclude* women from this office. It is simply that, as a matter of fact, only men were called. Admittedly, not every revealed doctrine has to be expressly formulated in Scripture. We again have to face the question of whether Jesus and the apostles acted this way *because of the social circumstances.* At the very least no other reason is ever articulated or even referred to indirectly to explain why only men could represent the "male" Christ. "Who hears you, hears me" (Luke 10:16; cf. Matt 10:40) is not intended unconditionally only for male disciples; and if among the seventy-two "other disciples" there were perhaps no women, then we should ask if this was not perhaps due to the fact that it would have seemed unfitting for two women to set out as independent itinerant missionaries ("this will not do"). However, when Paul states that he "speaks in the place of Christ" (2 Cor 5:20; 13:3), it is not so easy to say that he would not also grant such claims to his female coworkers. Admittedly, the final responsibility, and thereby the "highest" form of representation, was as a matter of fact occupied only by men.

Thus, where should the line be drawn, and why? Again we come up against the sociocultural argument. The Vatican declaration provides reasons for this from the "analogy of the faith," which it does not intend to present as a "strict proof" (*Inter Insigniores,* 108-113). On this question K. Lehmann (208) writes: "The simple fact that Jesus was a man" does not make it "unambiguously clear that a person who, as commissioned by Christ and to that extent (but also for no other reason) is acting *'in persona Christi,'* must represent this specifically by *being a male.*" Thus, from this point of view the question still remains open.

6. The Typological Aspect

Without attempting to justify it, I here understand by "type" in the strict sense the idea of a "first one," through whom all those who "come after" have been *stamped;*[569] only in a wider sense does it mean model. The first one is present in Christ insofar as he is described as the head or source, as the "first born of many brothers" (and sisters), after whom we have been "formed," the "beginning/first of those who have fallen asleep,"[570] and especially as the "second Adam" (Rom 5/6; 1 Cor 15). In contrast to the previous argument, here it is not so much a matter of the step from Eternal Son to human being, but of the relation of the man Jesus to all people. Within this inter-human process of salvation there arises a sort of familial unity, the man Jesus becomes the type or "stamp" of all who would be saved, whether they be men or women. It is thus difficult to see from this point of view where a line could be drawn so that some could be stamped "differently." In any case the concept would not be suited for a special "stamp" of an office reserved exclusively for men. And Adam in a similar way is also a "type" for all of his descendants,

569. More details in "Jesus Christus—die endgültige Offenbarung Gottes— Biblische Sicht," 55–57; similarly Padgett, "Wealthy," 27–29. More below, note 575.

570. 1 Cor 15:20; cf. Heb 12:2: beginning and perfecter of our belief and especially "brothers = children," Heb 2:10-17.

that is, for all men and women—Adam, "through whom sin entered the world." Thus in Romans 5:12f. Adam is seen not as "male," but rather as the "original human," with no special guilt ascribed to him simply insofar as he is a male (here he stands inclusively for "Adam and Eve"). And thus also in the "many," all his male and female descendants are infected through *him*.

In 1 Corinthians 11:3, on the other hand, Paul distinguishes the sexes. This begins with the fact that he names Christ as "head (only) of the man," in contrast to the woman. Is he then not also head of the woman, or is this only as transmitted through the man? Here, however, Paul is juxtaposing two perspectives: in 11:3a he is considering man as such; in 11:3b he is regarding the relationship between the sexes, with both passages bound together by the catchword "head," although it is used in different senses. Just as the man is prefigured in Adam and the woman in Eve, so now also the man finds his pattern in Christ; the woman, however, is referred to that woman who bore the Messiah. Thus there here stand *as models,* parallel to Adam and Eve, *two* people at the "new beginning," who each have the same function for their sex: here we should not say "stamp," but rather the original presentation of a new way of existing and behaving. Only here do gender-*specific* relations to the beginning become important for the men and women who will come later.

Significantly, it is precisely these passages that are frequently invoked to justify the differentiated position of women in the community. Totally apart from the fact that, according to our interpretation, with the phrase "wishing to make an impression with their head," Paul is reprimanding *both* sexes; this difference has nothing to do with the notion that women are less able to represent the *sōtēr*/Savior than men (for example because only the latter, like Christ, were "heads"), but rather with the fact that, in his reprimand, the same misconduct on their part receives another explanation. We would have gladly heard: "You women should be ashamed if you are making a spectacle of yourselves with your 'head,' for your 'head' is Christ." But Paul's thinking takes place in anthropological categories. This shows first that he is regarding the question on the level of social behavior; on the other hand that, although he extracts a reason from the order of creation and salvation, for him it is a matter of propriety and social custom. By contrast, when it is a matter of our *salvation* in Christ, then neither "male nor female" is of any account (Gal 3:28). We now see how the two texts fit seamlessly together. However, the question of how women conduct themselves with regard to the "first woman" in the new order leads us to the next point.

7. The Mariological Aspect

The woman who bore the Messiah (1 Cor 11:12; Gal 4:4; 1 Tim 2:15) is named *alongside* him in 1 Corinthians, as he had placed himself *under* her. To that extent the behavior of the Messiah to her becomes the model for the conduct of every man toward a woman: disposed to receive life from her. Thereby the enduring characteristic he has received from creation, that of "being the head/source," is complemented through the *reception* of life through the mediation of the woman. The woman, on the other hand, recognizes her deeper essence in the mother of the Messiah. No longer is she only the brilliance/glory of the man, but rather each woman should also be a transmitter of life *for him* (the thought here is not of common children, nor of their relation to their own mother). Although the individual "child" of his mother, the Messiah still remains here the model for all men, and as such stands beneath and *alongside* this "woman." God thus heals the wound caused by the misuse of power by the (first) man through the humility of the new man, and indicates, through a reference to his mother/partner, the essence of the redeemed relationship between the sexes: "In the Lord, woman is not without man, and man is not without woman" (1 Cor 11:11, consciously at the generic level in Greek, without the article). As a reason, verse 12 says: regard the two original pairs and notice how the *whole thing* comes from *God*. In the same way is the (second) pair, who establish a new beginning *for all of humanity,* as much a model for *all* persons (see Eph 5) as was the first pair. Through their conduct all people *are already* in a fundamentally new relationship to one another, even if this is only first grasped by the faithful.

What significance does this have for a woman "within the body of Christ"? Through this she receives a new dignity, something like a new commission ("office"): to be an original transmittor of life[571] to, and indeed for, the one who is her "head." In which forms can and should she carry out this service? In ways different from a man? The latter's status as "head" is justified in this model by the fundamental relation between Adam and Eve, that is, in the creation; the new mediation of life, on the contrary, is grounded "in the Lord." Of course, Jesus' mother bestowed on him physical, and not divine life, but still in the Spirit (she "conceived through the Holy Spirit"). Thus we may not parcel out the orders of creation and salvation between the two pairs (at the very least, the second pair remain also descendants from Adam and Eve, and therefore within the order of creation), but rather we should more cautiously say that through the birth of the Messiah from a woman, a foundation and aptitude was created for what would be completed in the death and resurrection of Jesus (who, in this sense, is a type for everyone) together with the sending of the Spirit. Thus the woman is certainly no less suited for the service of salvation than is man; to what extent in this enterprise does she have a function that is specific to her gender?

Two lines of thought open up at this point; one would take as its starting point the notion that men and women may be characterized as such as possessing a distinctive form of service for salvation: the male symbolizes the source, while woman represents the mediation of life. Admittedly this would be a specifically Marian-female service of salvation for *every* Christian woman not touching on the distinction between hierarchy and laity but rather preceding such a distinction at the fundamental level of gender-specific formation of life "in the Lord." Should such a distinction be represented at the level of ecclesial "offices"? Should there be a division between male and female "offices"? Such a distinction is at least conceivable—though it has barely been developed in the Church.[572]

571. Elisabeth Moltmann, *passim*. About Mary, Evdokimov (234) says: "For the Virgin her office as woman begins at the moment of the annunciation; it grows as a model towards the cross and sinks its root there." More Evdokimov, 233–247.

572. Evdokimov's thought indeed proceeds in this direction: 236–239. Admittedly one would then have to ask to what extent such a female "office" would be part of the symbolic-hierarchical office, or would perhaps constitute a different genus.

The other possible direction of thought—the way *existentially* male and female are related to one another each in their own way "in the Lord"—would correspond, also on the level of representation, to a set of gender-specific functions. For that reason only a man could *represent* Christ as head (now no longer as "second man" in contrast to the "second woman," but rather as the Savior, that is, as the shape of their identity for *everyone*). Still, this entire analogical argumentation can be criticized. There is a common platform on which *everyone* represents the Christ: in their baptisms men and women have "put on Christ" (Gal 3:27), and thus both of them make Christ visible to the world. Why on the level of offices should representation be denied to women? The response that Jesus did not entrust the same service to his mother and his women disciples as he did to the twelve apostles takes us no further than did the sociocultural argument: why did he not do this? Because in itself it was not appropriate for them, or because of the reigning (patriarchal) social order? One may no longer invoke the man's being the "head," for in the new order woman does not come out of the side of the man, but rather man proceeds from the womb of the woman. Thus on the level of our new life she has an authentic *originating* function. Why she should be less suited to "represent" the Savior is not apparent. If she should do this in a fundamentally different way, we would again be back with the previous thought model, and there would be far-reaching consequences from the Pauline starting point. Such a splitting of offices would then be more problematic than an opening of the one office to women. In any case the example of Mary cannot so easily be used to justify a limitation of the possibilities of representing Christ. Thus the question remains open.

If *beyond that,* Marian piety in the practice of the Church *de facto* constitutes a "substitute" (this is more than being simply transparent) for a female element that is lacking in the traditional imaging of God, this must be interpreted as the expression of the yearning of the people of God, a signal of the *sensus fidelium,* which has missed the female features in the image of God! However, it is at times an improper form, because it surreptitiously attempts to attribute to the Savior's mother a quasi-divine stature.[573] On the other hand, as the model new human pair, the

---

573. LG 66f.; Lehmann, 485; cf. 483; Beinert, "Maria," 9, 14, 24, with bibliographical references.

Messiah and his mother may properly serve as the model of the relation between the sexes, and Mary may correctly be called the *first* in the communion of saints, of the saved, to the extent that she stands in a mutual relationship with her Son. She thus stands on the pinnacle of all *men and* women, in her independence, as her "own person," not defined through her relation to a man, but rather as a created work directly facing her creator, who in full responsibility for herself delivers her "yes." By that indeed she does not yet become a "type,"[574] but she does become a "model," and indeed for men, too! For response and self-surrender are not something specifically female, but—with reference to God—something specifically *human*. To that extent each person, whether male or female, discovers his or her true self in Christ as the one who has become fully human, and in Mary as the one who answers "yes" to him.

8. The Symbolic Aspect

In our last reflections various lines of thought seemed to intersect, and we must in the future pay close attention to see on what level the discussion is taking place. Our question is about the extent to which representation should be assigned along gender-specific lines and to what extent it transcends sexual differences. To the latter belongs the existential level, on which every person—whether man or woman—carries within themselves both the christological and the mariological components (making present the identification of God with humanity as well as the fundamental "yes" of those to be saved to God's offer of salvation). But how does this become concretized on the level of signs and symbols?

Here in the area of creatures there are classifications that are not interchangeable,[575] and neither man nor woman should try to take over the symbolism that is assigned to the other sex. A

574. In our strong sense of the word; see above, D II 6; thus, not something like "Ur-mother" or female mold for all of humanity, who would then be her "descendants" (this remains, since it lies at the deeper level, the way of being and acting unique to the incarnate "Savior"). Substantially similar: Beinert, "Impulse" (= ULF 139-168), although he interprets the term "typological" differently; see Beinert, "Maria," 23.

575. On this theme see E. Schmid, *Symbol der Taube. Das Ewig-Weibliche.* Visp, 1975. Also Evdokimov, 235–239.

presupposition to all this is the acceptance of oneself growing out of the sense of having been saved, without any envy or jealousy over what is specific to the other sex, so that neither stands under a hidden pressure to imitate the other or to do something "like" the other. Here our body symbolism offers important suggestions; this is indeed made up not only of an accidental difference of organs, but rather constitutes a unified indication of the fundamental constitution of men and women, down to the deepest levels of their natures. While on the existential level everything is "created" in Christ, male and female included, these created natures are yet disposed to "manifest" this each in its own way.

For our investigation this means that in a certain sense man and woman symbolically represent the relationship between God God and God's work of salvation as bridegroom and bride. Speaking in a Trinitarian language one could say that they each in their own way reflect the two "processions" of the Second and Third Persons. Does there exist within creation any stronger image for God's love than the unity in love between a man and a woman? In this sense both bride and bridegroom are images of God's salvific action in the world; this has to be distinguished from the Old Testament image of the marriage covenant between YHWH and the people. Would it then be the specific task of the woman to be the transparent window for the activity of the divine *rūach?* Does it have something to do with the comparative neglect of the Spirit in the Western Church that the feminine dimension has been ecclesiologically so weakly developed?

In that case there would arise before the question about participation in the (up until now predominantly masculine) "offices" the question of the development of a specifically female symbolism. The catchwords "virgin–bride–mother" do not yet cover all that needs to be said; they have to be complemented or so broadly interpreted that personal self-appropriation, Marian responsibility for the whole (the "yes" to God above everything else), the spiritual transmission of life, the prophetic proclamation of salvation and correction as well as the redeeming transformation of this world (and perhaps still other elements?) come to have their full effect. Are we not still very far from an appropriate realization of these goals, and indeed often because, on the one hand, clerical fear of women runs up against an obsequious dependency on the other hand, and the two mutually reinforce one another? What, concretely, does "a life-transmitting function with regard to men" in the spiritual realm mean? How can it be represented symbolically? Would there not be, independent of the question concerning participation in "sacramental" office (about that, more later), in any case a feminine-Marian service to be discovered and developed within the Church, one that cannot be restricted to the traditional role of the religious sister, but which rather ties together and more efficiently implements the many new directions that have opened up?

Just as woman is fully responsible in the family and in society and carries her full load (often picking up the load in the face of the male's failure to do so), so she also has in the transmission and organization of the *new* life a competence that far exceeds what is structurally possible for her within the Church. This concerns not only the area of pastoral care and diaconal service, but also those of proclamation and liturgy, the prophetic-missionary impulse, and responsible leadership—even before it touches on the issue of representation in orders. All of this may be developed and guided by a physical-spiritual female symbolism that has been redeemed and shaped by the Spirit of God.

With reference to the two divine "missions" for the salvation of humanity, it would then not be a matter of indifference whether the Second Person of the Trinity took on human form as a man or woman; rather, it constitutes an indication that he comes as a bridegroom, so that creation may understand itself as the bride and allow itself to be filled with the Holy Spirit. In the refraction of this in human symbolism, this means: as the redeemed man represents in a specific way the mission of the Son, so is the redeemed woman a representative in a specific way of the mission of the Holy Spirit. However, since this fits all men and women, the question of representation in orders is still not yet decided. Admittedly it is here and only here, on the basis of this symbolism, that one could find convenient reasons for limiting orders to males. But one should reflect on the fact that orders are also an "official" representation of the sending of the Spirit. The two missions of the Trinity do not allow themselves to be divided in the establishment of ecclesiological offices. And further, on the basic level these two assignments are indeed only accents that do not permit a total assignment of the two divine missions to men and women. Does this not have something to do with the fact that, in their transcendence, each of the divine Persons constitutes a model for *both* male and female? Thus in the categorical presentation it is not the case that the one divine Person should be assigned only to the one sex, and the other only to the other.[576]

9. The Sacramental Aspect

In another and unique sense "sacramental" representation should be assigned to the level of symbols. This is not biblical terminology; however, the intended matter must be evaluated according to the Scriptures. An exclusion of women cannot be part of the essence of the sacraments as such, since with baptism (admittedly until now only in "emergencies") and in the administration of the sacrament of marriage a woman acts *in persona Christi*. It thus would have to be part of what was distinctive to *certain* sacraments if a woman could not do likewise with them or if a man was deemed at least more suitable to officiate at them.

576. The line from Evdokimov: "The question of the ordination of women receives its answer through the order of the charisms" (237). "Before all gifts of grace, to bring Christ to life in the souls of human beings is most appropriate to woman" (247). "If parishes are not always an illuminating center for their communities, this is also because women have been refused the possibility of engaging in responsible collaboration with men to erect living cells in the body of the community. She is not admitted, but is only employed about externals. However, an authentic spiritual situation cannot be brought about by mere practical considerations, but only through respect for the inner dignity of the office" (280). At the same time E. does observe a limit: "Ordained priesthood is a function of male witness. . . . Woman's service lies not in functions, but in her being, her nature. The ordained priesthood does not belong to her charisms; that would betray her essence. The revelation of the holiness of Being is represented by the woman. In her essence which is bound to the Holy Spirit, the saving comforter, the woman is the sheltering and enlivening one. It is Christ who celebrates the heavenly liturgy; however, at the pinnacle of the common priesthood remains the *Theotokos*. For she expresses in a way unique to her nature the kingdom of God." More Evdokimov, 273–295. However, are not the charisms or vocations divided in a different way? Here one discerns the questionable tendency to limit "charisms" through natural qualities, or to simply reduce them to natural gifts; see below, close to notes 752 and 753.

Next to the actual passing on of the leadership role (the Twelve, elders, etc.), the laying on of hands for the reception of the Spirit (Acts 8) and the anointing of the sick (James 5) appear to have been matters for those possessing authority in the early Church; and all these were in fact men. The same was probably true for presiding at the eucharistic celebration and forgiving sins. Even further, the baptism (of adults) at the beginning was hardly at all administered by women. From the second century we learn of deaconesses who during baptism, which was administered by full immersion, carried out specific duties for the women, while the one who actually performed the baptism was a (male) office-holder (Hauke, 434f.).

With marriage it is naturally different, even if its finalization soon becomes bound to the *episkopos* (Ignatius, *Pol.* 5:2). Did this take place in "God's family" in analogy with the fact that contracting a marriage was a matter of "family law"? Spiritual reasons were supplied for tying it to the bishop: "This is fitting, so that the marriage be according to the Lord and not according to lust." On the whole it soon becomes apparent that the fundamental ("legal") acts in the life of the community are tied to the authority figures. Was it different in the very early years? This is hardly likely, even if here and there there may have been unclear situations or occasions of crossing borders. For both Jew and Greek the (patriarchal) pattern of conceiving society was in the very blood. Thus, does the noninclusion of women rest on the fact that in sacramental actions the representation of the salvation-bringing Christ could or should only be carried out by men, or on the fact that *de facto* the authority figures were—without question—all men?[577] And was this so because Jesus and his apostles either "could not dismantle within their own communities the prevailing privilege granted to men in that society for precisely these sociological considerations, or even because, in spite of the insight that had broken through with them . . . concerning women's equal status," they simply did not wish to challenge it (Rahner, 297), or did they rather do so on the basis

---

577. We must keep in mind that sacramental representation and the occupation of a leadership position are not the same thing, so that the notion of women as dispensers of the sacraments would present fewer problems. Cf. also the following note.

of divine instruction? As we have said, a direct indication on this matter is not available to us. We nowhere find a reflection on this topic or positive reasons supplied from God's will; it is simply treated this way as a matter of fact.

1 Corinthians 11 does not raise *this* question, and 1 Corinthians 14 argues against allowing women to speak on the basis of "shamefulness" and because "it has always been the case that women were not permitted to do this." To that extent, there also the "law" stands for human *tradition*. The evaluation of baptism in 1 Corinthians 1:13-17 is interesting. Evidently there arose through baptism a certain personal connection, which Paul avoids. Thus, who normally performed the baptism? Also the "female coworkers" of Paul? May we here proceed on the basis of the Jewish practice of women's *mikvah* and the baptism of proselytes? There it was women who led women into the bath. (Even this took place admittedly under the male authority of the community leadership.) In any case, it was Christian women who introduced other women to the faith. Thus we here again come up against a lack of clarity, perhaps an open border that remains open down to the present day on the question of baptism (are not ancient traditions at work here?), which, however, because of the "male officeholder" remained closed. With what justification? Once again we bump up against the sociocultural situation.

It is thus difficult to draw a line, in what concerns a leadership function in the authentic sense, to determine where according to our categories the "sacramental" representation of Christ begins or leaves off, and from the administration of which sacraments a woman is excluded. Because of the generally altered situation of women, the borders have also shifted in the Church, so that in principle, at least, women should take on greater responsibility. To what extent is the authentic sacramental function, which today is combined with the leadership role,[578] exempt from this? Does the christological representation in *certain* sacramental performances encounter a limitation in the feminine personality, perhaps in its different symbolism? The existential and spiritual representation in a strongly witnessing life can naturally go much

---

578. One recalls, however, the distinction between sacrament and authority in the office of auxiliary bishops.

deeper than an "objective" presentation in an "official" performance. To what extent do these two levels correspond to one another?

Seen from the point of view of conformity to Christ, it is difficult to draw any distinction unless you see it in terms of the socio-ecclesiological function of "office." Does the masculinity of the occupant really belong to the "substance" *of this* sacrament as established by Christ, as the Vatican document (*Inter Insignores,* 107f.) would have it? It would really depend on whether the former is actually a "natural symbol" for this sacrament. This is indeed the case in the sacrament of marriage, where being male and female belongs to the *materia* of the sacrament. But does this hold true for the service of leadership, for presiding at the Eucharist, for the forgiveness of sins, the passing on of the Spirit, or the anointing of the sick (*Inter Insigniores,* 107–110)? Must the occupants of these offices also have to imitate Christ in his masculinity? More fundamental is the (typological) being-both-God-and-human of the one who "is the uncontested firstborn of the entire human race of men and women" (*Inter Insignores,* 110). The invocation of Galatians 3:28 in this context could, according to our results, mean: as concerns our *participation in Christ,* being male or female is without significance. On the level of grace, of the *res sacramenti,* this is indeed conceded. Is it different on the level of symbols, *in genere signi?* Does symbolism then suffer (111)? Doubtless these questions cannot be resolved in a purely argumentative fashion. Many women experience on the basis of their feminine symbolism an interior barrier to the occupation of an "office." However, to what extent is this to be explained by the fact that, up until now their only experience of "officeholders" has been masculine?

10. The Ecclesiological Aspect

The Roman document further states that through the "character" of ordination (thus on the level of signs) "Christ himself, the founder of the covenant, bridegroom and head of the Church, in the exercise of his saving work" is represented (111), and from that concludes that at least for the sake of an inherent appropriateness this may only be bestowed on men. Admittedly, "head" here is not used in exactly the same sense as in the apostolic letters. As regards 1 Corinthians 11, we saw that this term does not refer to the aspect of leadership, responsibility, or authority (that would be *kyrios*/Lord). And if in Ephesians 5 the term "head" is used as a *justification* for subordination (not to designate the relationship of subordination itself!), then in what follows under this image it is not the legal, so-to-speak "official" structure that the author has in mind, but rather the fact that as the "head of the assembly," Christ is its "Savior," the one who "offers himself on its behalf." As his *doxa*/radiance (1 Cor 11:7), it would be the woman who is the "representation" or (perhaps better) manifestation of this head.

Admittedly, in this context "representation" poses the question of who can represent whom. If in this sense "head" is applied to the male, this should not be extended to Ephesians 4. For there the "assembly" or "the body" and the head (which there refers exclusively to Christ) are complementary realities. However, within the (remainder of the) "body," the apostles, etc., are not some sort of representatives of the "head," but rather "points of contact, which provide the body with what it needs."[579] The latter do indeed occupy a special position with regard to the other members, but *here* this does not fall under the image of the head—a fact that certainly does not exclude the possibility that one could also use this image in another context for the correspondence of "leadership role of Christ" with "person in office." Correspondingly one would have to differentiate if one is saying that the priestly office also represents the "assembly," and that a woman would certainly be suitable for this. At the very least one cannot argue *directly* on the basis of Ephesians 4.

Again the question comes up: and who then is suited to the special "service work for the building up of the body of Christ"? As in 1 Corinthians, so also in Ephesians 4:11, after the apostles there follow immediately the "prophets." Does the author here intend (and similarly in 2:20) to deliberately separate male prophets from the many female prophets? To what extent "evangelists" (shepherds perhaps less so) also includes women is difficult to say, as there could also be women included among the "deacons" in Philippians 1:1. And where is the border between

579. Thus Eph 4:16, often improperly translated with "joints": Ts 317f.

the Spirit-based "teaching" (1 Cor 14:26, similar to a prophetic statement) and the official "teachers"? Not everyone who once passes on a teaching is already for that reason a "teacher." If the first, as a special gift of the Spirit, is certainly also available to women, the latter at that time—obviously!—was only an issue for men; and wherever this border is crossed, reprimands ensue (1 Tim 2:12). Something similar is true with regard to "public" speaking by women in the "assemblies" authorized to make decisions (1 Cor 14:35). This occasionally comes up but arouses so much opposition and is perceived to be so "unseemly" that it is finally not permitted, either by the community order or by the apostle. Both events illustrate that the borders are becoming more open, but that the dynamic soon runs up against an apparently insurmountable obstacle. Does this rest on a specific divine command, or should it be traced back again to the sociocultural dimension?

In an ancient assembly or "life community" of men and women, the final official responsibility could only reside with the men. Was this the reason the just-mentioned probings for an expansion for woman's competence were not seized and taken up? If texts refer to an office (1 Cor 12:28: first . . ., second . . ., third; Eph 4), they take no notice of this border ("no women"). The simplest explanation seems to be: because the restriction to men took place not in principle, but only as a matter of empirical fact, in a certain way "self-evidently," for reasons which need have had nothing to do with the theological sphere. Biblical foundations for a fundamental restriction of certain offices within the *ekklēsia* to men thus do not appear to be provided by the Pauline texts.

11. The Traditional Aspect

As a matter of fact, the practice of the early Church, which *de facto* always reserved the leadership functions for men— perhaps after initial explorations, which one should still not regard as a fundamental breakthrough against the prevailing social constraints—this practice was taken up and continuously preserved almost unanimously by the entire tradition[580]—until in our

---

580. Cf. *Inter Insigniores,* 101. Significantly, however, the prophetic service did not enter into the "office," which was soon more sharply circum-

own days the question is breaking out across a wider front. Was it never an issue between these two periods? The tendency lying behind 1 Corinthians 14 and 1 Timothy 2 shows that at the beginning an attempt was made to call into question not male authority as such, but rather here and there the empirical limits in the distribution of talents[581]—which revealingly was never reproached by invoking a formal commission by God or Christ. References to "various heretics, especially gnostic sects in the first centuries,[582] to Epiphanius,"[583] the aggressiveness and the "invalid arguments of the Church Fathers and theologians of the Middle Ages," who "massively denigrated women,"[584] to the sisters of St. Bridget in the Middle Ages, among whom—something unheard of at the time—a woman could have authority even

scribed (and that probably because of the different nature of this service; cf. "Sprachregelung," 32), and this constitutes a challenge to the development, at the very least an indication of the relativity = relatedness of the later limitation of functions concretized in the *ordo.*

581. This stands behind 1 Cor 11 at least to the extent that, in accordance with the universal social practice, such misbehavior by a woman was perceived as more striking and would perhaps receive a sharper reprimand.

582. *Inter Insigniores,* 101; see the quotation from Moltmann, above note 560; cf. Hauke, 101f.

583. Epiphanius (fourth century) reports in *Panarion* 49:2, 5/GS 31:243, concerning the Quintillianists: "Often seven virgins (therefore dressed in white) bearing candles enter an assembly in order to prophesy to the people. Manifesting a certain sort of enthusiasm, they lead the people present astray and bring it about that they all begin to weep, as if they had led them into a sorrowful mood of penance; in doing so they pour out tears and through a specific gesticulation lament the mode of life of humanity. Both elders *(presbyteroi)* and overseers *(episkopoi)* among them are women; and also the rest (probably: women who occupy the other functions); to indicate that this makes no difference, they cite: 'In Christ (is) neither male nor female' " (without a predicate: interestingly, *eni* is left out; is this where the modern misunderstanding in the sense of "there is" began? This would fit into the evolution of the language; see Atf X 4 end). It is hardly likely that this was an assembly made up exclusively of women; rather, there were probably *also* women who occupied such offices.

584. Rahner, 298f. There is material, e.g., in Annette Kuhn ed., *Die Frau im Mittelalter* I and II (Düsseldorf, 1983/4). V. d. Meer's "researches in historical theology" chart a path through the ages; and also the work of Hauke, with conclusions that downplay the problem.

over the male branch of a monastery, and to the deep sighs of Catherine of Siena and Teresa of Avila, to Zinzendorf's pneumatology, down to the wishes of Thérèse of Lisieux and the questions of Edith Stein,[585] demonstrate at least that the distribution of roles in the Church was not so unquestioningly accepted as God's directive by those affected by it as some think. Moreover, women had little opportunity to express themselves, at least not in writing, so as to leave a record. If in spite of such initiatives nothing changed, this is undoubtedly first to be explained by the fact that in the general society as well a woman's role was similarly dependent, and that an (often unconscious) androcentric interpretation of the Scriptures together with exegetical misunderstandings (see Paul) encouraged this.

The argument that in the Christian Churches which in recent decades have begun to ordain women, the participation of women nonetheless still remains small[586] misses the point. On the one hand the social environment has not yet been sufficiently altered; on the other one suspects that ordained women would give priestly service a different look and that over time it would take on different emphases. Do we not have a similar problem with the question of ordaining married men *(viri probati)?* If at the beginning the Church gradually diversified participation in the office of the "Twelve," and this diversification continued over the course of time (for example, "minor orders," "auxiliary bishops"), would it not lie within the Church's competence to divide the tasks in a new way, taking into account a person's competence, vocation, education, social position, and perhaps also gender, without thereby disturbing the essence of priesthood? Or, to take up the alternative line of thinking, should we perhaps uncover and develop a genuine feminine "office" that would be self-sufficient in its Marian-maternal symbolism and the equal of the male office, without detracting from the characteristic male form of representation? How would one then distribute the different tasks?

Even where there is not a question of ordaining women, the distribution of roles within the Church has to be seriously re-

585. For more details, see Gutting, 28–37, 100f.; on Zinzendorf, see Moltmann, 86f.; on Thérèse of Lisieux, also the impressive quotation in Beinert, "Maria," 25, etc.

586. Hauke, 99–102.

examined. Are the examples of clerical ineptness and the many, mostly unintentional examples of narrow-mindedness not an ongoing signal that here "something is not right," that male clerics are demanding too much of themselves—and perhaps also overestimating themselves? Does there not lie hidden behind this unresolved problem something unredeemed, and indeed not only at the moral, but also at the doctrinal level? The proper alignment of men and women within the Church thus remains an open question and—at least today—an open wound. We require patience, certainly, but also the courage of truthfulness.

Our inquiry is purposely not restricted to the question of woman priests. However, in the theological discussion, this issue is the "tip of the iceberg" of the problems and constitutes at least an orientation point which has bearing on all other questions and responses. Thus the invocation by the Vatican document of the "unbroken tradition of the Church" should be closely examined to see if this restriction of office to males is a transmission of a "divine revelation" (valid for all situations), or a "human tradition."[587] In the first case any violation would be *by that very fact* (not necessarily a formal) "heresy," that is, a distortion or denial of the truths of the faith; with a human tradition or also a temporally conditioned divine instruction on the other hand, it must be said that "even the fact they may be unchallenged and taken as self-evident for long periods of time offers no guarantee of their truth" (Rahner, 293). For the possibility exists of development in both dogma and teaching.

12. The Dogmatic Aspect

Now our investigation concerning the position of women in the Church will focus on woman's ordination as the matter most easily addressed. "Dogmatically" in the strict sense, the question is still open. The first "official" statement on this issue was the aforementioned declaration by the Congregation of the Faith in 1976, *Inter Insigniores.* It is the "first," because "the practice that had

587. Rahner, 293: "The (Vatican) Instruction naturally insinuates the first, but does not make this transparently clear." Again here we must remember that divine regulations can also be specific to a situation and thereby valid only for a certain time; see above, D II 2, and below, D VI 4.

been unchallenged heretofore had not called forth any more precise or thoroughgoing reflection" (Rahner, 293). Is this then a sign that the exclusion of women from the priesthood belongs to the self-evident deposit of faith, or rather that we stand now at a new step in the development of doctrine? With due respect to the authority of the Vatican congregation we should add that this statement "is in no way a definitive decision; it is in fundamentally reformable."[588]

The genuine question in all this is whether the long and (almost) "unbroken practice of the Church (and the teaching implicitly contained in this) really is based on an authentic divine revelation" (Rahner, 296). To what extent is there really in the Church's practice an "implicit teaching" to the effect that women *may* not be ordained? As for what concerns Scripture as a source, that could at best be contained only indirectly and implicitly in Jesus' and the apostles' manner of operating. There is no express teaching on this topic,[589] as we have seen and as the document also admits (103). It quotes Innocent III to the effect that "the Lord, although Mary was more worthy and excellent than all the apostles, nevertheless entrusted the keys of the kingdom of heaven not to her, but rather to them."[590] It would be odd if someone

588. Rahner, 293. Hauke judges differently, although not regarding the Instruction, but rather the "Church's tradition, which rejected the opposed thesis generally as 'heresy' " (472–474). However, it is striking that the Roman Instruction never points to such decisions of the ecclesiastical teaching authority. The apostolic letter of John Paul II, *Ordinatio Sacerdotalis* (Pentecost, 1994), strengthens the disciplinary force of the prohibition of women's ordination, but offers no new supporting arguments. According to the commentary of Cardinal Ratzinger, this prohibition seems not to be a decision *ex cathedra*.

589. Also not in 1 Cor 14:37f.; according to Hauke, 471, these verses "had the same structure as a conciliar or papal anathema." The more important question concerns what they are in reference to. In any case they concern the *entire* chapter (originally specifically not the "insertion" 14:33b-36; see Atf III 4) and obviously intend these statements within the context of the meaning that a responsible hermeneutic discovers therein. To that in this case belongs especially a reference to what people *then* would have found proper, etc. Cf. again our results above, A VII 3.

590. *Inter Insigniores*, 2 (103); according to v. d. Meer, 15f., this quotation can already be found in Epiphanius: *Adv. Haer.*, 79/GCS 37:477. On this matter, see again above, D II 7.

tried to draw the conclusion from this that the men were fundamentally less worthy, and therefore they were chosen. As for
Mary, in a unique way she stands beside Jesus as "the woman,"
and in this sense is existentially much more deeply involved in
his work than through sacramental representation. In this sense
she is more available to serve as the primeval type for a specifically
feminine "office" in the Church. The reason other women were
not entrusted with "office" certainly had just as little to do with
any purported (un-)worthiness. Did they, as women, really appear less suited for this work in an essential sense, or was it only
because of the general social position of women? The results of
the exegetical and systematic reflections we have carried out so
far lead us progressively closer to the edges of the sociocultural
argument. According to Karl Rahner "the conclusion is undeni-
able: the contemporary cultural and social milieu suffices to explain the conduct of Jesus and his apostles in which they did and
must conduct themselves as they did, without their practice taking on a normative value for all times, even when and to the
extent that this cultural and social milieu has changed" (Rahner,
299). This argument naturally does not suffice by itself to decide
the question; it must be brought before the whole Church according to the usual rules that apply to the development of doctrine.
Moreover, the latter must be considered within the context of the
Church's actual life; we will conclude by examining this in its
psychological and spiritual dimensions.

13. The Psychological Aspect

Without doubt, with our question we are probing into a very
sensitive area. We have already seen with Paul how changes in
traditions like circumcision and Jewish practice, recognized social modes of behavior or appropriate conduct during prophetic
speech, can irritate many people because such changes call into
question at a very deep level standards and customs we have become accustomed to. We know from our recent experience what
strong emotions can be unleashed by liturgical changes. New spiritual movements encounter the same response as soon as they
conduct the worship service "differently" (in a completely orthodox way) and begin to live out their beliefs. The interactions

between men and women, regulated by many diverse conventions and "roles," are an especially sensitive area. Not only the "sexual revolution," but also the behavior modes of young people, constantly changing from generation to generation, constitute a reliably inflammable topic. These points are so delicate because substantial values are here on the line, and the "conservatives" have a hard time seeing how and to what extent these values are protected by other people's "progressive" ways of behaving. All this reaches a peak of intensity if the question concerns how God should be worshipped. Here the highest values are at stake. For that reason the clarification procedure that we have in process, and to which we are obligated before God, must be carried out with great respect before God and all.

Respect also includes truthfulness. For that reason the psychological dimension of this process must be clearly understood. We cannot here enter deeply or in detail into this process, but would only like to indicate that, for example, with the question about women priests (and similarly with that of the ordination of married men), often the answer has been already decided before the matter has even been seriously taken up. However, such preferences or prejudgments succeed only in blocking dialogue. Most common opinions about what is typically masculine and typically feminine often contain a kernel of truth, but in practice are more a product of convention and our own projections than we care to admit.[591] On the other hand, "aggressive" positions are also often very much motivated by feeling. The most important thing is to recognize objectively as a common good everything that goes into making up a human being, even if this may be differently accented by the different sexes. The men cannot, for example, delegate the capacity and obligation to accommodation and self-surrender to women, and the women cannot delegate all initiative and power to resistance to men. The particular capacities a woman may have can only show themselves fully if she has the opportunity to develop them, such as by taking on responsibility

591. As an introduction to these questions: Beinert, Gutting, 94–104, Halkes, Lehmann, Swidler, as well as Edith Stein, *Eine Frau ist nicht nur eine Frau,* ed. v. H. Gerl. Lucia Scherzberg, *Sünde und Gnade in der Feministischen Theologie* (Mainz, 1991), refers on p. 241 to "pneumatology as the horizon of feminist theology."

and authority in political, scientific, or business life. Rather than saying "They simply do not fit into this 'men's world,'" we should hope that they would introduce different criteria and change the style in these spheres of life. Indeed, the whole point is that this should not remain a "man's world"! Thus, as seen from the point of view of psychological structure, the field is certainly more open than we believe. When we succeed in creating the widest possible room for both, then it will be all the easier for each in a relaxed fashion to find the task that is most appropriate for him or her.

These universal human rules also apply within the Church. Certainly there would be new problems if a woman exercised the priesthood or also a "feminine office" in the community. But is this problem not often exaggerated? Has the increased participation of women in recent decades really brought more problems? Has it not also resolved many problems? No one may suggest that thereby an erotic element has been or is being introduced into the worship service. To what extent does the notion of a "Church predominantly populated by women, but led by men" play a role in this? In both cases the problem can only be overcome through a redeemed differentiation so that all participants are continually reorienting themselves towards God. Paul certainly has no sexual taboo regarding spiritual services, nor indeed one that would affect women only. A person must be *redeemed* in his or her sexuality; but this holds true for male and female alike in equal measure.

Why should not women, after a pastoral visit to a person in a hospital, be able to dispense absolution for sins, celebrate the Eucharist, and anoint the sick? What is "offensive" is that today these are things that a female pastoral worker visiting the sick may not do. And as regards families and communities: in our culture today, the old *pater familias* has gone the way of the dinosaurs. In such circumstances what would stand in the way of a woman presiding? What would Paul say today? According to the principle of what is "appropriate," it follows that, if there is nothing else against it, in these changed conditions she should be allowed to do it, even if she would do it less publicly and more in small circles. How much spiritual good could women transmit! Dare we stand in their way?

Simply to raise these questions does not mean that we are proposing an unambiguous answer. However, if they are not candidly posed and treated in a fair manner, we risk being trapped in the quicksand of repression, protest, and polemic. In the process the discussion should also take up the fact that—with or without orders—a new and somehow "official" status must somehow be found through which women may manifest more clearly how the "Spirit becomes Church"[592] and how they manifest the divine *rūach*. Psychologically, because of their generally greater integration, immediacy, and capacity for relationships, women bring with them gifts that could clarify in a new way Jesus' devotion, his compassion, and his humanity.[593] Since as a matter of fact they already do this in myriad ways through their lives and their service to the body of Christ, the only question that remains is whether there is anything in divine revelation, and thus not merely psychological, sociological, or cultural reasons limiting the tasks that may be assigned to them.

Those who bear the highest responsibility in the Church as hierarchically constituted certainly represent Christ in a special way; what they represent, however, is not his maleness, but rather Christ "as human," the one and only God-become-human who, as the head (source) incorporates all humankind within himself and who in the universal priesthood offers everyone a share in his nature and service. Does reverence before his choice to insert himself into our history as a man require that, in contrast to the many other ways of representing him open to both sexes, *this* specific form should be reserved exclusively to men? This question must ultimately be submitted to the *sensus fidelium* of God's people.

14. The Spiritual Aspect

In conclusion we listen once again to Paul's continual counsel "to live in the Spirit" and to approach every question not with

592. Cf. LG 8; for an interpretation of this, see P. Knauer, *Der Glaube kommt vom Hören* (Freiburg, 1991) 156, and *Unseren Glauben verstehen* (Würzburg, 1991) 96f.

593. Cf. the contributions by Beinert (14), Lehmann, Moltmann, and Swidler.

a merely human wisdom, but with a love and knowledge filled with the Spirit. In the Spirit we should "test all things so as to preserve the good" (1 Thess 5:21). Paul counts on the effective presence of God's Spirit to all members of the community, especially in difficult decisions (1 Cor 7:40; 11:13; 14:37). So it will not be the isolated theologian, but rather the "sense of the faith of the entire people of God" together with the "teachers" and "shepherds" (cf. LG 12) that will receive wisdom from God, if they "bring their problems with gratitude before him" (Phil 4:6). This is not just a pious platitude; God's Spirit is the only teacher who can preserve us from error. However, the Spirit's effectiveness is the greater the more purely people are oriented toward God and the better the mutually dependent members of the body are communicating with one another: men with women, professors of theology with those with practical experience, those on the "cutting edge" with those who know the tradition well, the shepherds with the prophets (Eph 2:20), those who bear authority with the rest of the faithful, the local Churches with one another and with the central office of leadership, but also those Churches and ecclesial communities which are separated from one another, all of whose members have become "justified by faith through baptism and . . . incorporated into Christ'" (UR 3).

Only if we make use of all the Spirit's instruments given by God, including those elements of the truth which have been preserved for centuries by the various "separated communities," and do not neglect the dialogue with the Orthodox, that is, only if we exploit these diverse sources of theological insight *(loci theologici)* will we be capable of hearing God's response. Thus, everything that takes place within the ecumenical world should be tested before God, and not lightly pushed to one side, since "whatever is wrought by the grace of the Holy Spirit in the hearts of our separated brethren can contribute to our own edification" (UR 4). It is therefore incumbent on us to distinguish between fidelity to the recognized truth and a theological arrogance that does not allow itself to be challenged. When does a protest arise from a new listening to the Spirit, and when from what "we have always already known," without asking ourselves before God how far someone else's opinion might be true? The ecumenical movement in recent decades has given rise to astounding developments. Does not this process occasionally come up against unnecessary obstacles, simply because our spiritual attentiveness is so poor?

The request for a response from the Spirit to a question we lay before the Spirit is clearly only genuine if we have not from the very beginning already decided our position, but rather are ready and disposed for a conversion, for a revolution in our thinking. We have nothing to fear because it is the Spirit of God who is leading the Church; however, we must indeed attend to the Spirit in every manner in which the Spirit chooses to lead. With such a spiritual communication no one will be able to maintain that he or she alone has the Spirit, but rather each will do his or her share according to their task and function in listening to the others and in their own testing by the Spirit. This is the way this exegetical study should be understood as well. Out of such processes grew—beyond all human limitation—the Second Vatican Council; in this way we should also hope for clarity from God in these questions.

Is there not a decisive signal that many women feel a call to service in the Church that is being denied them—not because they are personally unsuited to it, but simply because they are women? And is not the Spirit also speaking through the fact that today many women are experiencing an interior call to priestly service, even if this is partly conditioned by the fact that there is currently no alternative in the form of a fully authorized feminine "office"? It may well be that such pressure often indeed has a high degree of resentment mixed up with it; who can endure indefinitely a sharply felt rejection with equanimity? And if sometimes—with both men and women, clerics and lay persons—immature notions and mixed motives, impatience and stubbornness also come to the fore, in a sound process of maturation, all such emotions should be allowed to reach the surface in order to be overcome. On the other hand, is it not clear that in the majority of cases women's sense of rejection cannot be accounted for by christological or sacramental explanations, but simply by psychological, social, and unspiritual motives? It is our duty to carry all these lapses and weaknesses before God and thereby to diminish these tensions. This principle applies not only in the life of each individual, but equally in that of the Church as a whole. All this must not turn our gaze from the authentic vocations which are present among us.

The process of spiritual discernment in which all of Christianity is involved over this question must be confronted and borne relentlessly. And since it regards women, women especially must be allowed to bring forward their experiences and their points of view. Ultimately, however, it is not only a question about "women," but equally about "men," which can only be answered if both of them place themselves in question anew before God and realign their relationships to one another "in equal dignity and unqualified equal standing. Any theologian who does not begin by renouncing across the board the category of 'subordination' (specifically, a subordination of woman to man given by nature) cannot be a credible defender of another answer" (Lehmann, 485). For only in this manner will the way be opened up for a "subordination *to one another*" (Eph 3:21; Phil 2:3) in freedom and love, to an acceptance of the structure of human living in common given us by God at different times, whether this be through the order of creation, the order of salvation, or the prevailing historical situation, whether it be unchangeable or time-conditioned, whether it can be altered given a different environment or whether, at least for the moment, it "cannot be changed without an immoral use of power" (Rahner, 296). However, the marks of the Spirit are "love, joy, and the freedom of the children of God" (Rom 8:21; 14:17). If on the contrary, and in spite of good spiritual disposition, a lack of freedom, sorrow, paralysis, and anxiety are in evidence, one has to ask oneself whether such a burden is really imposed by God. This is true both in the individual's life as well as in that of the community,[594] regarding this and all the questions provoking controversy within the Church.

Would not Paul here tell us once again: "Each one, as he or she is called by God. So test carefully where the Spirit is luring each person, and then attempt to communicate this to one another in the proper manner and to make room for the Spirit's call." These final reflections perhaps confirm once more that Paul himself never posed such a fundamental question, and also that in Galatians 3:28 he did not "anticipate" it. Women as the authority figures of ultimate responsibility in an assembly of both

594. Thus one should also apply the "rules for spiritual discernment" to community processes within the Church: Ignatius of Loyola, *Spiritual Exercises*, nos. 313–336. Text with commentary also in DGJ 45–94. Further aids and criteria for this can be found in "Der Geist macht lebendig," *Jesus ist der Herr*, ed. N. Baumert (Münsterschwarzach, 1987) 20–34.

men and women—that would have been something so new that he would have pursued this question directly and "in the Spirit." Would he not rather have justified and explained his position for the surprised "little ones" and "weak," and not simply mentioned it in a single dependent clause, and otherwise blocked it through an occasional brusque remark? As a matter of fact, such a radical change would have required greater effort—and indeed also in the remainder of the New Testament—than just the short formula: "Now there is no more male and female." If in the face of the completely new inquiries concerning celibacy Paul undertakes a surprisingly detailed dialogue with his communities, would he not have done as much in this other case? Perhaps in this case he would also have chosen to close with the humanly so disarming support for his "opinion": "And indeed I believe that I also possess the holy Spirit." In any case, in his responses to *this* question he certainly mentions no divine instruction coming from revelation.

III. Salvation and Sexuality

After having looked at the social and ecclesiological dimension involved in being a man or a woman, we now inquire into development and maturity in sexuality, both in our individual personal lives and in our interpersonal relations. In this process we will bring to the texts contemporary questions which Paul did not pose in such psychological differentiation. Still, he is speaking about the whole human person; as instruments of divine revelation his words may be able to respond to new questions with new answers. We will again distinguish in what Paul says between what is directly addressed to the situation he was confronted with and what is implicitly contained or simultaneously communicated together with this, or may be concluded from this as a logical deduction.[601]

601. Cf. above, D I 1, 2. For material and an expanded bibliography on the following, see Delling and Oepke, the relevant article in RAC; further, Häring, *Frei;* Beinert, "Impulse" (= ULF 139–168); Bachl; Schuster; Rotter.

1. Living Out of the Newness of the Spirit

Although trained in the Law as a Pharisee, Paul is certainly thinking not casuistically in terms of limits—what one may or may not do—but rather in terms of the new relationship with God which he has found in "faith of Christ." What effects does this new way of "being human" have in our sexual life? Since salvation works its transforming stages into all areas—forgives sins, heals wounds, and bestows new powers—the life of a believer stands under a different emblem than that of an "unbeliever." Not only does he or she see the order of creation in a new light (Rom 1:19; 3:21-26; 5:20), but also recognizes in the Spirit what God has gifted us with in Christ (Rom 8:32; 1 Cor 2:12). Moreover, with each one's personal call to be a Christian either in marriage or in celibacy, powers are also promised that will enable that person—and only that person—to persevere in that course (1 Cor 10:13).

Thus the obligatory rules of conduct for Christians are not only contained in a "law of nature," but rather the latter must now be read anew in the light of a "new creation"; moreover, both the laws that may be recognized from human nature as well as the universal commands of revelation—such as to "live in Christ," "to worship God in the Spirit"[602]—are, as regards their concrete application, referred to the light of the Holy Spirit, which the Christian may continually look for from God in each new situation. For just as "nature" has already given each indi-

---

602. Can these be deduced from nature? To that extent the thesis would be problematic that revelation adds nothing "materially" to naturally evident ethical norms, but has a *purely* maieutic function (cf. Schuster, 189). Apart from the fact that concrete "nature" is always fallen nature, the "self-revelation of God" opens up possibilities of conduct and interaction of a different order that not only purify, but also transcend, the "natural." This pertains not only to particular paths of mystical devotion, the surrender of one's own life in the service of love or as a witness to faith, but it must also be something that penetrates and transforms one's entire life. In addition, something lies within the personal calling by the Spirit to be a Christian that cannot be deduced from any premises, something which is only valid for this person, but *can be normative for him or her,* such as a prophetic calling or a vocation to either marriage or celibacy; cf. below, D VI 1 towards the end, and D VI 6.

vidual his or her own gifts and tasks, in the same way the unique self-communication of God to each person shapes him or her own individual form of Christian personality. "Christian living" thus does not consist in mechanically carrying out prescribed actions, but rather in continually new decision making and acting out of a relationship of faith, a "living in the presence of God" in which the general rules as well as the concrete circumstances and graces are newly illuminated each time by the Spirit.

For Paul living "out of faith" *(pistis)* is what is specific and distinctive of Christian life, a faith that should not become encrusted back into "law." What does the distinction consist in? A legal mind asks: "What do I have to do? What may I do (or not do)?" A faith-filled mentality, on the other hand, asks: "What would you like?"[603] Paul continually directs his appeals to people who have put on Christ and who, as adults, have received and experienced the Spirit; "Those outside, God will judge" (1 Cor 5:13). Thus all Christian "criteria" presuppose first of all mature "Christians"; certainly one's whole nature should be integrated in the carrying out of a fundamental decision, but precisely as a nature either already redeemed or yet-to-be-redeemed. The ultimate criterion, in terms of which everything else in reevaluated, lies in the living relationship with Christ, as we have seen with regard to 1 Corinthians 7:29-32. Only in this way may the Sermon on the Mount and 1 Corinthians 13 be lived; but in this way also they become livable, in that the Christian, in spite of many faults, continually aligns him- or herself on Christ.

Each person's individual, concrete "call" (1 Cor 7:17-24) has as its basis and framework the universal ground rules which are not canceled in favor of our personal relation to Christ, but rather are precisely the criterion for the latter's authenticity. As regards sexuality, this means primarily that human beings, in conformity with their nature, are oriented toward a personal "thou." "It is not good for the human being to be alone" is admittedly valid not only to justify the marital bond, but analogously for all social relationships and also for each person's relationship with Christ; for those who have remained celibate for the sake of the kingdom, this takes on a special quality. Love of God and love of the neighbor cannot be separated, and for each person love is

603. Cf. 1 Cor 7:32-35; see above, A IV 2; further, Atf I 4.

qualified by gender. For that reason it is necessary for each person's living and loving to appropriate and integrate his or her own sexual situation. Integration in the area of sexuality means redemption from all egoism and the penetration of the entire erotic sphere with the love produced by the Spirit. This is a lifelong process. It begins again and again with an effort to "set in relationship" all sexual yearning and any disappointment in such, ultimately and fundamentally in relationship with God.[604]

Thus for believers there is not only the alternative "immediate satisfaction or repression," but rather primarily a positive "working through" of the problem before God: the "acceptance" of one's sexual condition from God the Creator and the acknowledgement of oneself as the "image of God"; revealing all one's thoughts, desires, fantasies again and again to God in complete trust, in the knowledge that God "understands" them all. Thus, instead of becoming a prisoner to desire or falling helplessly into such, the human being rises to something higher.[605] Whenever God in Christ in this way becomes continually in a new way the fundamental "other," the ultimate personal "Thou" of a person, there slowly develops the freedom not to take advantage either of oneself or another person, but rather to proceed only in harmony with God—either in giving back, that is, renunciation, if fulfillment is not possible, or in action, if God provides us someone to love. In marriage too this process must also be continually pursued. (One will be able to do this more easily in marriage to the extent that before marriage one already practiced it.) Does not all this stand behind the words: "The Lord for the

---

604. Beinert, "Impulse," 75 (= ULF 148): "As part of the whole person, one's sexuality is also related to God. Both men and women discover in God their final fulfillment, including that dimension in which as sexual beings they are attracted to one another." Similarly Rotter, 175f., with a striking quotation from R. M. Rilke: "Why are we left in the lurch, there at the root of all life? . . . Why have they (in this twilight of Christianity) made sexuality homeless, instead of celebrating it as the festival of our responsibility? And why does our attachment to God not spring precisely from this root?"

605. Could not one say that all moral norms are always "open" to something higher or to the center of creation? For indeed they exist to serve each person's unique relationship with God, and should thus protect and support this.

body and the body for the Lord"—and "the body is a temple of the Holy Spirit" (1 Cor 6)?

Many people fail to break through to such a level of faith, either because their relation with Christ is not vital or personal enough (such a situation can be the occasion to open oneself at a deeper level), or because a profound mistrust of God keeps them from it, caused perhaps by childhood experiences or an inadequate image of God; or perhaps they are prevented from building up such a positive image of sexuality by negative experiences. Ultimately these are all consequences of original (or humankind's) sin (Rom 5:12-14). In such a situation, without abandoning moral standards, one's center of effort, the next step, will have to lie more in the area of faith, of one's relationship with Christ. Only then will it become possible to introduce order into one's psychological drives, which in their unredeemed condition carry the internal tendency to split off and become independent. Without a continually renewed reference to one's spiritual center, the standards set up in the name of the gospel become incomprehensible, appear impossible to achieve, or lead to the attempt at a rigoristic piety bent on human effort ("works righteousness"), which is always condemned to failure, even if at first it appears to yield high moral "achievements." Whatever is not sustained by God's grace, itself cannot carry any load. Aberrations in one's relationship with God always show up in one's relations with one's fellow humans, either in permissiveness or in rigidity. There is only *one* love, and everything depends on its purity (1 Cor 13). However, this is a gift from God, and only the person who can accept forgiveness receives it.

One might object: is this not all a bit ideal? Are not things different in reality? Even the early Christians were not perfect, and Paul was well aware of human weakness. He nevertheless speaks about the new life as a transforming energy which he has experienced and which he takes for granted as known to his readers. Besides that, his frequent talk of "growth" and "becoming abundant" shows that he was well aware that such life within us is in its beginning stages. And yet it remains the standard and source of power. Thus the "severity" of a fault is also measured by its distance from this center; it depends upon the extent to which something we do damages our relation to Christ, whether it takes place out of faith in God or in our own autonomy, or to what extent it runs counter to graces already bestowed, for which the "weight" of the object-matter is certainly one index.

Because sexuality is a form in which love expresses itself, it is important; but once grouped under this heading, sexual misconduct shows the same scale of seriousness as do other sins against love. Many take place due to inner need; this need is particularly felt by young people who, on the one hand, have heard the gospel proclamation but who, on the other hand, may live in an environment which knows nothing of the love of Christ and which conducts itself autonomously with sexuality in a terrifying way. Paul gives us a compass to take with us on our way: "Do everything in such a way that from it Christ's glory shines out" (1 Cor 10:31). Should not the positive statement that "the earth belongs to the Lord," that humankind has been made "very good," and that Christ is with us in all things, be heard *before* all particular instructions? It is striking that beyond this Paul refrains from specifying our basic attitudes any further, and does not go into any matters of detail. This shows the breadth of the Pauline spirit, where narrow minds all too quickly try to promulgate a "God of order" (cf. 1 Cor 14:33, 40) through overly extensive prescriptions.

It is only against the background of salvation that a person first becomes aware of how deeply he or she is embroiled in egoism and sin. This is why revelation first leads us to a full acknowledgement of sin. If we occasionally in our Western languages speak about the "rent" caused by original sin which runs through human nature, and if we try to express what we mean by the discrepancy between "head" and "heart," the biblical distinction between "spirit" and "flesh" refers more to the difference between what is not at our disposal ("breath," "wind": John 3:8), and the tangible, manipulable nature of human beings.[606] If the place of the "spirit" is the heart, and thus the center, then the place of the "flesh" is the periphery, the outside of the bodily region. It is not that the skin and senses were something evil, but to the extent that the two principles can be "localized," the Semite

---

606. It constitutes one of history's tragedies that this would be frequently enough misunderstood in the Greek world in the sense of an anthropological dualism (body–soul). The Semitic mind intends by this no hostility towards the body. Cf. above, C 3 and 4.

chooses these sections of the body. Indeed, even biologically speaking, they have different functions.

From the soteriological point of view, "flesh" does not stand for physical love, but rather for that *disordered* desire ("covetousness": Rom 7:7f.) of humankind, which shows itself among other ways also in our sexual drives, and that indeed in a specific way. To the extent that it makes itself apparent in the form of demands and pressures, it is a signal of human resistance, of a lack of integration in the human personality. In this case our sensuality moves to the center of our interest, and the person bases his or her decisions upon it—some say on emotions. And to that extent sexual disorder is in a specially visible way a symptom of our psychological-spiritual waywardness. Have not modern Westerners, in quest of liberation from a hidebound and prudish Victorian sensibility, been in danger now for some time of careening into the opposite danger, to the extent that they have naively entrusted themselves to their inherent, spontaneous (but unredeemed) "feelings" and are thereby in danger of sliding into another form of disintegration? Perhaps there lies within the Semitic-biblical soteriological dualism between "spirit/heart" on the one hand and "flesh/psyche" on the other, indeed, a valid physiological starting point. For if one asks where the center of a person's attention is at a certain time, it makes a difference whether it is the "heart" (the Semite *thinks* with his heart!) or the genital area.

This does not mean that sensual feelings and sexuality should be suppressed, but only that they should be kept in their proper place. If the genital area becomes the dominant part of the body and the place where decisions are made, the person becomes unhinged. Sexuality then takes on a false priority. Rather than being the foundation and ground of life, it takes over the leadership and causes untold damage. In the end the uncontrolled "drives" lead to libertinism instead of freedom, brutality in place of strength, mechanical performance instead of a personal encounter between the sexes, drug experiences in place of an experience of the Spirit, terror instead of constructive criticism, war in place of dialogue, orgies instead of festivals, the occult in place of mysticism, and finally satanism instead of the worship of God. And must we not admit that in countless discotheques and so-called concerts, "power" is "transmitted" specifically toward the lower area of the body in order to focus it into the center of attention and activity, and thus to arouse rather than to integrate people sexually? Variations are continually being devised so as to provide more "spice," but the overall sense is one of dreariness.

Into this contemporary situation Paul speaks the gospel of liberation from the slavery of sin and of death, the struggle of the spirit against the "flesh" (Gal 5). It is not a matter of casting the body into suspicion, but rather of pursuing an inner alignment of the various zones of the body, which are symbolic for the various functions of an integrated personality, in which the foot neither can nor tries to be the hand and the ear does not try to be the eye, but where also the head does not say to the feet: "I don't need you" (1 Cor 12). The attacks of evil are not only concealed behind the active, aggressive "passions" (often attributed to the "masculine" aspect of a person), but equally behind the passive and depressive emotions (frequently described as "feminine"). Paul then speaks of the sinful *pathēmata,* the sinful suffering of a person.[607] The latter is often overlooked in the Church's preaching, for the active sins are more evident. However, both of them disturb the clarity of moral vision; the person falls into confusion without noticing it. In the apparent full possession of one's mental faculties, one can be or become blind precisely in one's spiritual center. "Blessed are the pure of heart, for they shall see God" (Matt 5:8). Only on the foundation of a total dedication to God will a person be able to recognize and follow the way of God appropriate for him- or herself.

2. The Place and Limits of Sexual Life

Our individual conscience is oriented toward what has been commanded and forbidden by God, as this has been communicated to us primarily in the Scriptures. There the fundamental assumption is: (negative) prohibitions point out a limit that one should never cross, (positive) commands, on the other hand, obligate us to do something, *to the extent that this is possible.* But does this not introduce a "legalistic" element into our moral action, in that the most one can do with prohibitions is to "observe" them? And yet this would constitute a false under-

607. Cf. Atf V 1, on Rom 7:5; Ts 271–273; see also above, note 535.

standing of God's moral order. This *always* has the character of a given norm and does not allow humankind to decide whether something is good or evil, but rather simply informs humankind unilaterally that one thing simply *is* good and something else simply *is* bad (forbidden). The difference lies in a person's subjective disposition: a "slave" sees himself or herself as *burdened* under the weight of the law, the "son" on the other hand sees the father and does his will as a free exercise of love (Gal 4 and 5); one sees the rule, the other sees the person. The content is the same for both; but what for one seems impossible to achieve appears to the other within his or her competence (Rom 8:4f.). While it is true that both the Old and New Testaments, and especially Paul's letters, offer us numerous examples of rules, salvation consists in our being able to view them with the eyes of a son or daughter. Correspondingly, our preaching must pay attention that these do not come across to our congregations like rules (which, as a consequence, raise up slaves); rather, we should so present the Father to them that they become capable in faith of doing good. Scripture provides no rules for those who are unconverted, but rather first preaches Jesus as Lord and Savior, and only then begins to draw out consequences for our conduct. From this point of view, what if any consequences relating to our sexual behavior may be drawn from Paul's letters?

(1) The appropriate place for the sexual union of man and woman is *marriage*.[608] If this is true in the Old Covenant, all the more so in the New. In that engagement already signified a decisive legal bond, it is understandable that sexual relations between an engaged couple were not universally condemned by Jewish teachers.[609] But does it not still constitute a transgression?[610] For the early Christians it appeared self-evident that sexual relations outside of marriage do not correspond to God's will. The fact that already in the Old Testament in this area there were different degrees of punishment shows that all transgressions in this

608. Cf. above, A VI 1 and Atf VI 9.

609. Cf. below, note 612; above, around note 254; Atf IV 5, note 30; to the extent that sexual relations were forbidden as a means to establish a marriage, they were also after such an encounter not allowed until the marriage.

610. Cf. Häring's reflections, *Frei,* 525–529.

area were not found to be equally reprehensible, least of all, probably, relations between an engaged couple. However, from that it does not follow that "premarital relations"[611] were "allowed" in the Bible.[612] Such a development certainly does not follow the radicalizing tendency of the ethics of the Sermon on the Mount.

There still remains the question of whether this biblical criterion was no more than the acceptance of a temporally conditioned social value—comparable to the prohibition against women speaking in "decision-making assemblies" or the requirement for them to subordinate themselves within a patriarchal society. If the principle of permanent validity stands behind this: "to live in one's social position in an appropriate manner for the Lord," then one could here raise the question: under our altered modes of conduct, what does it mean today for people "to belong to one another"? Must it necessarily be in the institution of marriage? Is not a private bond sufficient? And how absolute must it be to correspond to what the Bible means by "marriage"?[613] Since the marriage of a Christian must be contracted "in the Lord," Christians are no longer free to attempt a union apart from this standard, independently of whether they call it a sacrament or not. Thus they must ask God: Does this union please You? Does it lead me closer to You? Do You bless our being together? Subjectively perhaps some Christians engage in an extra- or premarital sexual act in this sense and think that they there discover love,

611. By that is meant that the serious intention to marriage is present, which should then be distinguished from other "extramarital" relations. Besides that, one should keep in mind that engagement in our culture connotes less obligation than it did in the ancient world; cf. above, note 149 and EuE 174–177.

612. Jesus' "attitude toward the sexual area" is not adequately captured by "indifference," neither did he see "nothing immoral" in the "companionship of a (lay or married) man with a lay woman": Haag and Elliger, 90. Str.-B. III 343: "Rabbi Eliezer (ca. 90) said: 'A single man who has intercourse with a single woman without the intention of marrying her, makes her into a whore' (here we have the view that extra-marital cohabitation is equivalent to whoredom)." C. Locher, *Die Ehre einer Frau in Israel,* Orbis Biblicus et Orientalis 70, (Göttingen, 1986) 236f., discusses the "abundant testimony to the high value placed upon a woman's virginity" before marriage in the ancient Middle East.

613. On this, consult Häring's reflections, *Frei,* 526f.

liberation, and even a deepening of their relationship with Christ. However, objectively the question remains whether this feeling really derives from the nature of the deed or rather perhaps from the "good faith" of an (erroneous) conscience *(bona fide)*. For would such a free union be willing to accept the claim that to the phrase "What God has joined together," there should also belong "let no one put asunder"? In that case such a contract would be practically equivalent to entering into marriage. In the event, however, that it implied rejection of the Church's "formal requirements," it would be a question of ecclesiology.

To argue that this mode of conduct is "not so bad" would be to disregard the One whom we reverence as the Lord. Even if, because of certain circumstances, a mode of conduct may indeed be "forgivable," because people have reached their practical limits, it does not thereby become "good," but must still be "forgiven." However, a genuine experience of God's mercy is not compatible with a halfhearted apology. The authentic relation to Christ would thereby in itself be cheapened and no longer function as a standard of personal conduct. On the other hand, persons who acknowledge their failure to Christ receive from him the power, in spite of their "sin," to honor God's standard. Thus not only any formal violation of marriage, but every sexual act which takes place outside of marriage is to a varying degree (!) a *moichāsthai*[614]—a union that in itself is not proper, because at least objectively it does not take place under God's direction and with God's blessing.

(2) However, if the act itself is not in full union with God or even if one has sinned only in one's heart (Matt 5:28), then everything else that accompanies the act—*thoughts, desires, and expressions*—is affected.[615] While fantasies and desires may suddenly come upon someone, these should still be distinguished from an inner acceptance. In this sense the rule applies: not to "do" anything interiorly that fundamentally one should not and would not do exteriorly (Matt 5:28). Wishes and dreams for the future, on the other hand, one should "lay open before God" (Phil 4:6); all the more easily will they be protected against tension and ex-

614. In the sense of "blemish, dishonor"; see above, A VI 1.
615. On "shame," see above, close to notes 284–288.

perience the saving power of Christ that frees us from the pressure to carry them out immediately. At the end of such processes and struggles stands again and again the greater "Thou" of God, so that one's sexuality (true renunciation of which presupposes acceptance) becomes in fact the door to a deeper contact with God. The person, on the other hand, who does not make such efforts, who expects nothing from God and remains imprisoned within his or her own ego or does not accept God's offer of forgiveness, runs a good chance of considering God's commands as exceeding the human capacity to carry them out. However, is this not the case because they themselves (whether out of their own guilt or incapacity) have not yet accepted the crucial presupposition, namely, a relationship with Christ that penetrates every feature of their existence?

The inner purity and integrity achieved in Christ will express itself in corresponding talk and modes of conduct, so that as a matter of fact "unclean sexual relations[616] and every sort of impurity or greed will not even be named" any more than obscene, silly, and vulgar talk" (Eph 5:3). For this only shows that a person still has not attained a redeemed relationship with his or her sexuality. Here we are not speaking about prudery and also not of an apparently pious front, but of a simple objectivity and reverence. Chastity does not consist simply in "sexual continence and self-control, including speech and thought," as the dictionary *(Das Neue Brockhaus)* defines it, but rather in an ordered human relation to sexuality, whether it be in the activity or the renunciation of it; it consists in a mature harmony between the outward signs and interior love at each of the steps, in the "appropriateness" of physical signs of affection, in spiritual freedom from compulsive drives. The "purity of heart" that Jesus called blessed is thus not some sort of innocent childhood condition which most people later lose, but rather a virtue which only grows in a mature personality, even if it parallels one's stages of development.[617] However, interior freedom and harmony are possible for (fallen) humanity (only) "in the Holy Spirit," as the latter is bestowed upon us through Christ. Our analysis of texts has demonstrated this in exemplary fashion with regard to Paul himself.

---

616. Πορνεία in this sense: see above, A VI 1, and Atf VI 5.
617. More on this in Häring, *Frei* II, 476f.

This high ideal may discourage some, in that, in spite of many attempts, up until now they have not attained it. But the answer is not to lower the standard—there is no cheap Christianity—or to compromise. It is rather the case that knowledge of this goal provides us with the incentive to remain on this path; at the same time it continually gives us back our sense of worth, when after a defeat we ask God for forgiveness. Paul is well aware of this daily battle, as his numerous appeals show. Just as in other areas it is self-evident that people acknowledge that they are not yet perfect, in the same way it should not disturb anyone too much if they have to declare: "I am not yet entirely chaste." In this virtue as well there are many stages. Already on this account one should be hesitant before one designates an offense against chastity on the basis of its object (the "matter") as in itself "objectively mortally sinful." And yet it remains a moral lapse. This is the sense in which the warnings of Ephesians 5:4 about "obscene, silly, and vulgar talk" should be understood. According to context this could take in the entire scale of this form of misconduct,[618] from a serious offense to a momentary lack of control. As with Romans 13:13, so also Galatians 5:19—and similarly Ephesians 4:19; 5:3; Colossians 3:5—the *category as such* is what is intended, which, like "quarrels, dissensions, factions, etc." cover both minor and major cases.[619] And yet it remains true that *there is no case* in which one is "allowed" to do it.

618. Cf. Rom 1:24, 27; 1 Thess 4:7 with Rom 6:19; 1 Cor 13:5; 2 Cor 12:21; 1 Thess 2:3.

619. There is an obligation at all stages; however, whether it is a "major" offense or not is determined in all areas by a consideration of the seriousness of the object *(gravitas materiae),* the subjective freedom of those involved, and the strength of their moral commitment. Depending on the extent a person has encountered Christ, these matters take on a different weight, since an improper exercise of our capacity to love damages at a correspondingly deeper level our love relationship with God. However, it is not convincing to say that in the matter of sexuality, the uniqueness of this area already establishes by itself the "serious nature" of any offense *(in mandato sexto nulla parvitas materiae),* and that only extenuating circumstances would save such from constituting a mortal sin. Why do we make an exception here from the normal variability of the "object"? It seems more proper, in analogy with the other virtues, to start with chastity also from the question if and to what extent thoughts and deeds seek to "objectify" oneself

(3) What does this mean for the way the *individual handles his or her own sexuality?* There are here various steps in our perception and appropriation of its truth, steps which are necessary as a presupposition for a free decision either to use or renounce sexual activity. Ultimately it comes down to the ability to rejoice over a gift, without having therefore to "use" it (immediately). The fine line between a receptive and active attitude, between existing and coveting, can only be maintained by focusing on the One who in sexuality shows and entrusts to us an image of the divine creative nature. Here it is important to attain a concrete understanding of theological truths. Some Christians are uncomfortable in viewing themselves in this way before God, either because they believe it is inappropriate, or because they fear the arousal and fascination that could go along with this. And yet we should not attempt to cover up or remove sexuality through prayers, but rather, in an intimate colloquy with God, attempt to unlock the meaning of our sexuality, so that we may be able either to use or to "leave" it in accordance with God's intention. "The body for the Lord, and the Lord for the body" (1 Cor 6:13).

However, if this "leaving" is not successful, and if especially young people cannot overcome the temptation toward masturbation, how should this be judged? One cannot say simply that self-gratification is "always condemned in the New Testament whenever the topics of 'impurity, shamelessness' and other offenses against chastity and celibacy are discussed."[620] This is of course impossible, simply because the Bible nowhere explicitly

---

or other people. Granted, a person is not divisible into parts; however, not every kind of sexual impulse "implicates" the entire person. On the other hand, an awareness of one's sexual capacity and relationships is proper and it can be necessary to occupy oneself with this, even if one has not yet reached interior clarity or has not yet attained the capacity to observe external limits. In that case, developmentally conditioned difficulties and habits, or an affective imbalance, would no longer automatically fall under the suspicion of being "serious sin." Similar views in Häring, *Frei,* 476–478.

620. Congregation for the Faith, "Response to Various Questions on Sexual Ethics" 9, of 12 December 1975 (see AAS *sub dato*). We have demonstrated above, A VI 1, as well as in Atf V 4 and VI, that these forms of behavior are nowhere specifically castigated in the text.

takes up this topic.[621] That of course does not mean that the Bible condones self-gratification; however, the scriptural response will have to be more nuanced. In any case Paul is not warning against cultic uncleanness, like Deuteronomy 23:11; and the wording is so loose in Leviticus 15:16f. that one could not confine it to a nocturnal emission, quite apart from the fact that at night the line indicating fully conscious behavior fluctuates. The fact that Scripture nowhere mentions individual sexual arousal or satisfaction either with regard to men or women appears to have nothing to do with any taboo, for other sexual activities are referred to clearly by name. Masturbation, of course, has been recognized in every culture.

We must therefore stay with our position that the Bible does not directly reprimand this conduct.[622] Whether this could at least be included in the New Testament under "uncleanness" in a wider sense, and whether this includes also youthful masturbation or only that of adults cannot be demonstrated exegetically—but also admittedly not excluded. We are thus justified, in attempting to set up an inclusive ethics of sexuality, in reflecting on this matter; for there are a good number of detailed cases that are not discussed in the Scriptures. Thus, if one takes one's premises from some place else one should be careful, when drawing consequences, to always keep this biblical situation before one's eyes, lest some "unnecessary burdens" be laid upon people. Between

621. Not even Rom 1:24 (above, A VI 2) or 1 Cor 5:9 (above, A VI 3 with A VI 1; "weakling" does not mean this, but rather in a special sense the passive, "feminine" role in a homosexual relationship. The term "onanism" is improperly applied to Gen 38:9; but there the offense is a disrespect for the brother and his wife (see below, after note 639), not a supposed "wasting" of seed, or such like. The biblical concordance by Luegs (Regensburg, 1923) remarks under "Onanism": "authentic O.: see Onan; inauthentic O., see whoredom." The latter is defined: "Every type of carnal offense, the satisfaction of carnal lust" (!), "carnal mixing *(Vermischung)*" (?!). Not one of the texts offered as evidence speaks about masturbation. This is a complete confusion of language! The dates given by Haag and Elliger, 111–112, on the history of the problem should be used with circumspection, but are informative.

622. As we saw above, A VI 1, it could only resonate in the words ἀκαθαρσία and ἀσέλγεια remain such a semantic expansion has not been demonstrated for πορν-.

a male's nocturnal emission while asleep and a deliberate self-arousal, for either men or women, there are many stages. Where does the fault begin? In any event, it does not lie in "wasting one's seed," as was for a long time maintained,[623] but should probably be placed earlier, where what is taking place does not happen as a stage of development and not as a result of inner tension or need,[624] but rather where the person "disposes" over him- or herself in an autonomous way.[625] The moral value derives primarily from the motive, not only from the behavior "in itself." In the concrete each individual must discover the answer before God.

Moral theology will have to rethink this question on the basis of the spiritually discerning *sensus fidelium.* Will we not have to start from the fact that sexuality by its very nature should always orient a person toward a personal "Thou"? If the person becomes fixed upon him- or herself, something is not right. Since this can already begin through experiences in childhood and adolescence, there is probably no age at whch individual sexual self-satisfaction ca be called indifferent.[626] This problem leads a person continually to a point where he or she must think "beyond themselves," must "transcend" themselves—and if not (yet) toward another human being, then certainly always toward God. This is certainly the most natural way in which a young person learns to deal with arousal and orgasm without tension. In any case, this should be the goal. It may be a long way towards it, but it is one that is not paved over simply with "mortal sins." In that sexuality intimately involves a person's capacity to love, one cannot treat its physical fulfillment as a merely biological event, like eating and drinking (cf. 1 Cor 6:12-20, although eating naturally also stands

623. From rabbinic Judaism down to the beginning of the nineteenth century; Häring, *Frei* II, 501, 530; Haag and Elliger, 112f.

624. Do we even have a sin here? Häring, *Frei* II, 531f., distinguishes "need" and "intentional" onanism. "Galen, the greatest medical authority of the ancient world, justified for medicinal reasons a necessary masturbation to alleviate tension." On the whole matter see Häring, *Frei* II, 529–533.

625. Cf. again above, note 62.

626. Δέφομαι and *masturbari* only have currency in the popular idiom and appear to have a decidedly negative connotation (to knead until soft; *manu stuprare = perpetrare stuprum*/a dishonor); the very construction of the words indicates that people did not view the practice indifferently.

in need of spiritual integration); one must shape it much more forcefully according to the personal relationship. It is precisely at this point that individuals realize that they are never finished and in no case can be "content with themselves," but in an abiding openness of their body as "sign" must always be on the way toward the (greater) "Thou." If God touches a person in his or her deepest regions, God then intends that everything in that person be oriented toward God's self. In that case sin ("isolation") consists in the fact that the individual then nevertheless does something without God.

Persons who honestly exert themselves and do what lies within their powers at the time (without a perfectionistic scrupulosity), may be assured that, in a case where they are unsuccessful, there is no "mortal" sin. And should the tension become *too* great (an upright conscience can acknowledge this before God), and persons have not consciously worked themselves into a powerful state of arousal, it cannot be a mortal sin if they release the tension. What is sinful lies rather in what is unredeemed in persons and in their nature. At the same time it remains true that the person should work at finding some other way to handle this circumstance.[627] This is no question for married people, but it is valid for everyone else. Moreover, each must leave the final judgment to God here, so as not to come to rest in self-righteousness, but rather "in that justification that comes from God" (Phil 3:9). In the final analysis we are never sure, in any of our deeds, to what extent unredeemed motives may still be insinuating themselves. Thus sexual acts are fundamentally not structured any differently than our other acts; nevertheless, in them the deepest powers of human love become particularly visible.

(4) In contrast to self-gratification, *homosexuality* and *lesbian love* are mentioned several times by Paul by name and condemned (1 Cor 6:9—active and passive; 1 Tim 1:10). In this context the expression "against nature" also appears (Rom 1:26f.). The con-

---

627. Thus one could extend to this matter what Häring, *Frei* II, 509, writes with regard to the African practice of polygamy: "The Church should present a single marriage with pastoral delicacy and yet firmness" (here we would change that to: the avoidance of masturbation) "as a normative ideal, all the time imitating God's patient pedagogy in dealing with Israel."

temporary tendency to explain such inclinations as "natural" and genetic is by no means shared by all professionals.[628] In any case, another notion of "nature" is functioning here than the one that Paul is using. Moreover, one would have to know which among the various types of homosexuality were the occasion for Paul to classify it this way. He knows of no such condition as that of a constitutional homosexual; he presumes as self-evident that it is not morally as it should be. On the other hand, it is not his intention to crush a person's interior need with a simple prohibition. At the same time this experienced spiritual counselor sees in this form of behavior the signal of a more profound need.[629] We cannot get past the fact that the purpose of the biblical author is to call sexual relations between members of the same sex not "good"—without saying anything about the subjective guilt of concrete individuals. There are indeed many people who with their own "natural" powers cannot resist this kind of tendency. On the other hand there are people who have been so transformed by God's Spirit that they have recognized this as misconduct and can even (possibly in spite of a lingering inclination—as with alcoholics) "give it up."[630]

Whichever way individuals have to go in order to open themselves to Jesus' saving Spirit and to come to a deep interior healing can only be answered individually, for the "nature" of each person, just like God's grace in his or her life, has its own history. As with other faults, here as well one will have to try and try again. Nevertheless, "the demands of the law can be carried out in the Spirit." This is what Paul writes in Romans 8:4 in re-

628. Thus, e.g., G.J.M. van den Aartweg, *Das Drama des gewöhnlichen Homosexuellen* (Neuhausen-Stuttgart: Hänssler, 1985). The Dutch psychologist explains homosexuality largely out of a "compulsion to self-pity" which leads to an "immature form of human sexuality" (Introduction).

629. With reference to Rom 1, see above, A VI 2; Häring, *Frei,* 533f., emphasizes that homosexuality as a whole (not each individual case) "is an epiphenomenon that should be appreciated as part of the larger alienation of humankind from God."

630. This is primarily a personal experience born out of pastoral care; similarly Häring, *Frei,* 535. V. d. Aartweg, see above, note 628 (book jacket), finds in his (not easy) therapy "an escape from circling around oneself, from loneliness, depression, interior turmoil, restlessness, and jealousy" towards "an emotionally mature personality with a fully developed sexuality."

sponse to the sexual aberrations named in Romans 1. The scriptural message is not that humans can change such deep-seated modes of conduct on their own power, but indeed rather that God's grace is up to it. Admittedly this presupposes that persons themselves acknowledge their fault before God, and out of this encounter with God experience a power which liberates them for an even greater love.

(5) Finally, sexual faults can also show up *in religious dress,* all the way from temple prostitution down to subtle forms of impure devotion. The experience of God's proximity and love can, since its purpose is indeed to transform and reshape the entire person, also set the sexual faculties into motion as well. What comes to the fore there is what is unredeemed in persons who, on the one hand, must still go through a process of purification and integration, until they can "love God with all their powers," but who on the other hand can also misuse this grace. In that case the intimacy with God experienced in prayer is answered in an impure fashion, without the appropriate inner and outer reverence, clarity, and discipline. But this would mean ultimately "to know Christ according to the flesh."[631] This kind of (un-)spiritual unchastity has many levels, and early stages which can take the form of awkward, bombastic or importunate "religious" conduct, or also in saccharine, "kitschy" pictures and songs.

The right proportion of closeness and distance must also be learned anew with regard to people. Mutual spiritual experiences can bind men and women deeply with one another in new ways; however, they attain a mature balance in their relationships neither through repression nor through living out their (apparently) spiritual inclinations, but rather through a continually new letting-go and receptivity, acceptance and renunciation,[632] because thereby at the same time their human relationships are also purified. The entire activity of the Spirit indeed takes form in the human subject, and sensual, spiritual, and religious drives are only slowly

631. In contrast to 2 Cor 5:16, where this expression indicates that Paul had persecuted Christ. See further, G. Delling, "Geschlechtsverkehr," RAC 812f. and 822.

632. Here reference is being made to 2 Cor 5:14; see below, "Conclusion" (at the end of the book). Further, see above, note 475.

"integrated" by God's Spirit, and thus fused into a "whole," until the divine love penetrates everything.

Ignatius of Loyola in his *Exercises,* after the fundamental principles for discernment, presents a second group of rules that alert us to more subtle distinctions. Because it is "characteristic of the evil angel to take on the form of an angel of light" (2 Cor 11:14), even with "pious" inclinations one must be circumspect. Here also "flesh" becomes a symbol for unredeemed ("religious") passions.[633] It perhaps begins with special "sweet experiences," sometimes long periods of consolation that are an imitation of the clear joy of God. Under some circumstances they may lead to a subtle search for religious satisfaction, with a tendency to open our entire emotional world, including sexuality, to such (supposedly spiritual) consolations, until it may end by going as far as pseudoreligious sexual contacts.[634] The root in this case is not an (unredeemed) sexuality alone, but at the same time an imitation of spiritual experience ("spiritual deception"). Through more careful attention one recognizes that these consolations begin with the (for the most part external) senses, whereas God touches the "heart," goes "in and out of it as in [God's] own house," and from there works through the entire person. Here on the other hand, the center of (religious!) attention lies more on the periphery, or in the stomach or genital region. Monks of the Eastern Church have drawn our attention to the fact that, when at prayer, the ideal center of attention is the heart, while every "attention below the region of the heart," anywhere "in the renal or intestinal area," is dangerous and can indicate or lead to deceptions.

By this we intend to say nothing against a healthy awareness of one's body, but rather that the mentioned areas should not become the *religious* or *"spiritual"* center, assume the leadership, or become in some sense the locus of our search for salvation.[635] Thereby it again becomes understandable why Paul characterizes the opposition between divine influences and those that act against the latter as "spirit and flesh." In their wider effects one recog-

633. Gal 3:3; cf. again above, close to note 627.

634. Is this at the root of temple prostitution? Cf. above, note 208.

635. More on this within the context of the Ignatian rules for discernment in DGJ 67–94, esp. 84f. This puts in question oriental methods of meditation and the "New Age" movement.

nizes these kinds of subtle deception in the typical "religious" faults of pious exaggeration: rigorism instead of faith, fanaticism in place of consistency, delusive light as opposed to clear illumination, a hectic rushing around instead of peace, haranguing in place of giving witness and information, high-pressure persuasion instead of calm conviction, manipulation instead of attractive radiance, cajoling rather than a brotherly or sisterly directness, violence in place of strength, rigidity instead of flexibility, monologue where there should be dialogue, a splintering into sects where there should be integration, heresy instead of an inclusive ("catholic") outlook; and behind everything, pride, disguising itself as humility.

Just as in the classical religious vows chastity stands between poverty and obedience, in the same way aberration in the spiritual life often contains a moment of sexual disintegration, whether in the direction of license or rigorism. The susceptibility to spiritual imitations is not directly an openness to sexual temptations, but it indicates that also in the "fundamental" area of human relationships and sexuality something has not yet been integrated; for human structural weaknesses reappear at different levels. One's maleness or femaleness plays a role in every area of human activity, especially where personal relationships are at stake, and for that reason disturbances show up again at all other levels. Sexual misconduct shows simultaneously that something is not right in the spiritual realm, just as on the other hand an unredeemed sexuality seeks to establish its supremacy over the religious.

In summation, we have seen that the Bible gives few concrete descriptions of sexual violations—it presumes people are aware of them—but rather directs its attention to the person's disposition. That is the center from which the diverse individual modes of behavior are to be personally formed by every individual (Deut 30:1-16). According to 1 Corinthians 7:17-24 the motivating power lies in each person's calling, not in a narrow casuistry. An ethics consisting of nothing but prohibitions does not lead to moral maturity; the most this can achieve is to wake us up to our responsibility before the One who gave his life for us (Gal 2:20f.). The human is healed through the divine, not the other way around. This process of the salvation of humankind cost Jesus his life, and requires of us in turn a dying to the "old person." An authentic "miracle" must take place, until in a progressive "resurrection" all human dispositions and drives, sensitivities and longings are transformed through the Holy Spirit, and sexuality is liberated in its depths to assume its true nature: a sign and symbol for what is greatest in humankind—its capacity to love.

3. The Marital Act

If the act of sexual surrender has its authentic place in marriage, one may ask *how* it should be carried out by married people. If in 1 Corinthians 7:1-5 Paul speaks about an occasional abstinence,[636] this is not because such would be the stronger thing to do there, or because marital relations in themselves disturb prayer. Rather, in the highest form of abstinence it seems to be the case that the individual at this time becomes filled or moved or drawn by God's love (this can also be painful), so that he or she feels the need to attend to this love as far as possible; an intense sexual attention to their partner at this point would distract them from this. We saw, however, to what extent Paul "relativizes" this in his answers, how he places the many individual aspects in relation to one another, and this above all else: he insists that the partner must be able and willing to "act in symphony" with this option for abstinence. We also saw that "avoiding fornication," that is, relations between a married person and an outsider, is not mentioned as a reason for contracting a marriage, but rather—in a deliberate curbing of "pious exaggeration"—as a motive for the maintenance of regular marital relations in an existing marriage.

From the argument that the partners *belong* to one another—neither one should "steal" what is the other's—it is clear that Paul sees the reason for sexual relations as lying not only in the production of offspring, but also in the union of the partners. In the questions concerning celibacy also the consideration of offspring never comes up. Thus 1 Corinthians 7:1-5 contains more motivation for sexual relations than just "conceiving children and

636. Cf. above, A II 3. On Jewish models, see Delling, "Geschlechtsverkehr," 819f.; Philo rejects passionate sexual relations even within marriage: Delling, 820.

a remedy for sexual desire,"[637] and in connection with our discussion of 1 Corinthians 6 it becomes clear that one cannot find the slightest devaluation of sex in Paul, but rather the opposite: he knows from experience that this important area of human physicality, and therewith of the human person, can and should be entirely filled and thoroughly penetrated by God's Spirit.[638]

Without question the full form of the sexual act is attained if it is simultaneously the expressive display of the personal love that is distinctive to marriage (an actualization of the "yes" or "I do," etc.) and the generation of a child. While the first should never be absent, the second is not present as a "natural necessity," since as a matter of fact there often is no fertilization due to "natural" causes. While contraception and abortion have indeed been traditional topics, in the development of marriage ethics the theme of "birth control" has only taken on sharp contours since the population explosion in the last century; and only since the middle of this century have teaching authorities recognized that married people may *consciously* avoid conception by practicing "rhythm." As a matter of fact the majority of theologians and believers who are affected by this question are today of the opinion that other means of birth control could be morally permissible within a marriage.[639] What does Scripture say on this topic?

637. *Remedium concupiscentiae,* as the classical expression for this "secondary purpose" is called. D. R. Cartlidge, 221, quotes Scroggs: "Paul . . . implies that the purpose of sex is mutual enjoyment rather than procreation." Fitzer, 27: "The commands (to sexual relations) in 7:2-5 are unmistakable." But his thesis that the marital union "also serves simultaneously to avoid idol worship, because for Paul πορνεία in itself constitutes idol worship, cannot be maintained; see Atf V 2.

638. This is something our researches have amply demonstrated; cf. e.g., above, A V 1-3. On the contrary, Bornkamm, 214, speaks of "what appears to us today as the purely negative reduction through which Paul views marriage. One searches in vain through the detailed discussions of 1 Cor 7 for a positive appreciation of the love between the sexes or the richness of human experience in marriage and the family." He overlooks the fact that marriage is not the subject of this section. Delling is much sharper: "Stellung," 55-97: "Ch. 2: Hostility to Marriage."

639. On the history and discussion of this problem, see, besides Häring, *Frei* II 490-505; W. Bulst, "Fundamentaltheologische Überlegungen zu 'Humanae vitae,' " and G. Kaufmann, "Humanae vitae in der Sicht des

As far as I can see, only in one spot does Scripture speak about birth control: "As often as Onan went to his (dead) brother's wife (whom he had to marry as the brother-in-law), he let his seed fall upon the earth and spoil, so as to deny his brother offspring" (Gen 38:9). This is condemned as an offense against the love for a brother, not on the basis of his "wasting his seed." However, the reference makes us suspect that this (easy) method was also otherwise used if one wanted to avoid conceiving a child. Indeed, mostly what we hear concerns the desire for offspring; however, there have always been numerous situations where—properly or improperly—people wished to avoid having a child.[640] Why is this never characterized in the Bible as "not permitted"? It cannot be included under *moicheia* and *porneia,* as we have seen. Apparently what here is much more decisive is what this means as between the two parties (Gen 38:9). The fact that a husband should not approach his wife during the time of her menstrual flow (Lev 15:24, 33; 18:19) is not a defense against wasting his seed, but rather is part of their notion of ritual purity. Thus there is no avoiding the conclusion: the Scriptures say nothing about birth control.

If a man experienced an orgasm unintentionally without sexual union, that made the man cultically unclean, but received no moral reproach in the Old Testament; for Christians the cultic aspect falls away. Still, how far may married people go, in love play, if they do not wish sexual intercourse? According to the rule of double effect, one may "allow" an unintended but foreseeable possible consequence for correspondingly important reasons. Then where is the limit in the exchange of affections? Leviticus 15:18

Arztes," *Orientierung* 32 (1968) 165–172. There are also references to discussions with not-yet-finally-decided, but still "authentic" statements by the "ordinary" teaching authority.

640. Thus, e.g., prostitutes; and how did engaged couples behave (see above, note 609)? Did they always "risk" conceiving a child? For more, see E. Lesky, "Empfängnis," RAC IV 1251f., 1254. One sees clearly how only in the Roman-Hellenistic milieu with its hostility to sexuality was contraception (to be distinguished from abortion) prohibited among Christians, and indeed with an immediate invocation of the "fruitfulness which God intended for nature" (Caesarius of Arles). Unfortunately I have not discovered any Jewish testimony. Haag and Elliger, 113, refer in another context to the "command to conceive posterity" and the motif of "wasting seed."

probably does not have sexual intercourse in mind, but rather a seminal emission without sexual union while either asleep or awake.[641] If the orgasm was not sought, according to the classical moral rules it has no guilt attendant to it. However if, because of the time chosen, an act may be intended that will be unfruitful because of this circumstance, the question may be asked if this does not also apply to other forms, such as withdrawal or the use of birth control devices.[642]

More important in any case is the manner in which the sexual encounter is integrated in the entire relationship between the partners (cf. GS 50f.). Is not a limitation or control (not a transforming intervention) for the sake of this larger goal as much justified as in other natural processes? "Objectively," nothing else takes place than what happens on the infertile days.[643] But the partners must be in agreement! Thus the factors that determine the significance, as well as the possible sources of fault, fall more strongly on the entire mode of conduct and on the sensibility during the sexual relation itself. It is *in the love between the two people* that the authentic values come into play, while the physical act is always a limited "expression" for this. If the full form of the act is not, for various reasons, possible, could not an at least partial form still be justified and helpful? In all its forms, the act requires a cultivation of love, and should never simply be "used."

In any case Scripture does not address the nature of the act, but rather speaks always in personal categories, which one could summarize thus: Do not desire one another without belonging to one another! Whether in thoughts or in the external act, whether in the full or restricted form, the question is always put whether the sexual encounter corresponds to the personal bond. The sin

641. Haag and Elliger, 111: "Probably premature ejaculation during marital foreplay." The commentaries stress that even coitus also rendered one cultically unclean. However, is this what is intended in this context? In any case these regulations also applied to those situations which did not reach coitus.

642. More details in Häring, *Frei* II, 498–502.

643. One must clarify in each case whether a "pill" or preparation prevents the fertilization or the implantation of an already fertilized egg. The latter is almost equivalent to abortion, and, like the coil, morally not permitted. In all these cases the responsibility also falls upon the man.

of the "sons of God" in Genesis 6:1-4 consisted in that *men*[644] "took women as they pleased," thus capriciously, without a bond, and that children were then born from a dishonorable union—in contrast to the previously listed genealogical trees. In Genesis 20:1-18 intercourse has indeed not yet taken place, but the fact that Abimelech has abducted Sarah is already a serious offense. Nevertheless, it took place "with a clean heart" (v. 5f.). So ultimately it comes down to one's fundamental attitude. Just as the value of an industrious wife lies in the fact that "the heart of her husband trusts in her" (Prov 31:11), in the same way a relation with a stranger is rejected primarily because thereby her heart will be turned away from her husband (cf. Prov 2:17; 5:17; 6:34). This aspect is especially clear in the transferred meaning that the heart of the people of Israel has turned from JHWH (Hos 2:15; 4:1 etc.). For that reason the sin consists not only in the sexual act, but rather already in the willing "desire" (Exod 20:17; cf. Matt 5:28).

Everything depends therefore upon the personal relationship, and married people must determine their behavior from this. Since, as we have seen, even with regard to the physiological actions the borders are blurred and take on different moral significance according to the situation and the intention, we must beware of any mechanical approach, as if by drawing an external border we could capture the interior attitude: "You may go this far, but no farther. . . ."; rather also in marriage one must first ask: "Where is your heart while doing that?" This falls not only in the line of thought of Matthew 5:28, but also of the entire Sermon on the Mount. From a pure conscience no one is dispensed; and from that perspective the "objective" boundaries look different and, if need be, should be "relativized." For what appears to be "given by nature" in the marital act can still be done from a false (perhaps self-righteous, rigoristic) motivation, and if in that area something is shaped and cultivated in freedom by people, this must not come from egoistical motives. Thus, for our question an important source of theological knowledge is the

---

644. Not "angels"; see above, note 258. It would be strange if *humankind* had to bear a penalty for the *angels'* sin (Gen 6:5ff.). In any case, it is not women who are here considered guilty! Also, it is not said that the giants proceeded from *this* union with the "sons of God"!

judgment of conscience of many affected Christians who from their situation recognize in the Spirit that the "nature of the act" in itself is morally more open than an abstract understanding believes it can deduce.

From a study of the historical material,[645] we can again and again observe the gulf between the integrated Semitic way of thinking and the Hellenistic-Roman dualism, a split which became sharper after the second century and which within Christianity reached a first highpoint under Augustine. For with him at the very latest is sexual pleasure itself regarded as impermissible, something which is only tolerated for the sake of generation, but which is in itself something to be avoided. Is this attitude not still present today? We saw in chapter and verse how Paul has been misinterpreted by the Greek-Western mentality. Have we yet entirely understood the original biblical truth?

Haag and Elliger (88) certainly go too far when they assert that the Song of Songs is "uniquely concerned with the joy that two young people have in one another, and with the indulgence between two unmarried people who have no intention of contracting a marriage." Such an endorsement of free love is not consistent with the other biblical texts, nor is it adequate to this particular text. "The one whom my soul loves," etc., refers neither to a short-term love nor to any "indulgence," and the "bringing into the mother's chamber" (Song of Songs 8:2) indicates unambiguously an intention to marry. Anything else would be a serious violation of social norms throughout the Orient![646] Thus many commentaries on the Song of Songs speak correctly in terms of "bridal state." However, at *that* point it is true that the legal aspect retreats significantly behind the personal level, and the physical relationship is not burdened with trepidations. The text shows the interior freedom of people who are sure of their personal love and fidelity, which *then at the same time* can also become an image for our love bond with God. The problem for our time is that, through an over-hasty fixation on the act, the culture of the erotic and of the attraction of the heart are neglected.

Also the phrase that "the two become one flesh" is in the West usually restricted to the notion of sexual union. But the latter is

645. See the pertinent articles by Delling and Oepke; more above, Part C.
646. Cf. just above, note 612, and Splett's position, 134–142.

usually rendered by the phrase "joining himself with his wife."[647] "One flesh" on the other hand is almost like "one nature,"[648] and indicates a personal union founded on persevering *commitment*. This is also the way Jesus argues (Mark 10:8f. par.). Not because occasionally they unite themselves physically, but because they *are* permanently *one* body/flesh, no one may put them asunder. This now leads us to the question of divorce. However, preachers will have to learn not to burden the forms of sexual union, which indeed is a constant learning process, with excessively detailed instructions but rather—like the Bible—to restrict themselves to fostering and requiring an ethical stance of human love and fidelity. However, this kind of "purity of heart" only comes to maturity in the course of a loving response to the God who is faithful to the covenant.

IV. The "Indissolubility" of Marriage?

Anyone who looks for a teaching on Christian marriage in our texts will be disappointed. They speak only indirectly to this topic: 1 Thessalonians 4:3-8 about courtship; 1 Corinthians 6:12-20 places relations with a prostitute not, as one would expect, in contrast to marriage, but with the loving relationship with the Lord (is temple prostitution here *also* in the background?); 1 Corinthians 7 considers marriage only from the narrow perspective posed by the inquiry concerning abstinence. This is a consequence of the question that was asked, and does not represent a fundamental imbalance. Moreover, verses 7:28-34 specifically, which are often trotted out in support of celibacy, have marriage in view throughout, since they are addressed to those inquirers who, after an initial attempt at abstinence, end up marrying. First Corinthians 7:35, however, asks where one could "without excessive effort be good in their relationship with the Lord,"[651] and holds

647. Thus, not Gen 2:24c, but 24b; similar 1 Cor 6:16f; 7:2.

648. See above, C 4 (1)a and (2)b, as well as C 5.

651. Cf. above, A IV 3. Baltensweiler interprets the verse in a similar way (173f., 260), but from it develops a highly unconventional interpretation of 32-34, which is that if a person is busy about the world, he serves God indirectly, etc. But where is this in the text? Other commentaries and appar-

that, according to the circumstances, this is thoroughly possible in both conditions of life.

It thereby appeared that specifically through a relativization—"in a certain way not having"—marriage is sanctified, takes place "in the Lord," and thereby becomes liberated to its true nature. To that extent it is also legitimate for the tradition to extract as presuppositions from 7:29-32 standards which should be applied to *every* Christian marriage. The spiritual integration of the "new person" means a growing unity with his or her own sexuality, brings an interior freedom and relaxation with it, and offers the appropriate foundation for an unbreakable marital fidelity. The capacity for marriage is indeed a *charism,* a gift from God (1 Cor 7:7).[652] Then what does the New Testament have to say about the indissolubility of marriage?

1. Summary and Questions

According to our extensive study of this question (Atf VI), *moicheia* does not mean "adultery," but rather defilement, and in the *logia* about divorce, *apolelymenē* refers not to a woman sent away, but rather to a woman who has *separated herself* from her husband (= Mark 10:12; thus the Synoptics all use the active voice). However, the "adultery clause" refers to incest, and thus to an impermissible marriage between closely-related persons. The texts should be translated thus:

> Mark 10:11f.: Anyone who dismisses his wife and marries another *defiles her (the new wife!);* and if a woman, after she has left her husband, marries another, *she defiles him* (the new husband).
>
> Luke 16:18: Anyone who dismisses his wife and marries another *defiles* (carries out with this new wife a dishonorable sexual union);

---

ently also the UT see in 7:35 only a recommendation of celibacy; with Conzelmann this is not clearly discernible, but to be suspected.

652. Baltensweiler sees in the "high estimate of marriage in Paul's eyes . . . new understandings opening up that will culminate finally in the pronouncements of the letter to the Ephesians." As a matter of fact, there is no great abyss between Ephesians and the principal letters on this point, as is often assumed; however, many maintain this, such as Bonhöffer, *Epiktet,* 330; cf. EuE 242. Further references: Ts 263 with note 488; further above, note 1; A IV 2 (beginning); Atf VII (towards the end).

and whoever marries a woman who has *separated herself* from her husband, *defiles.*

Matthew 5:32: Anyone who dismisses his wife—except on grounds of *incest* (that is, because this wife was too nearly related to him)—*brings it about that she is defiled* (is guilty should others sin with her). And anyone who marries a woman who *has separated herself* (from her husband), *defiles.*

Matthew 19:9: Anyone who dismisses his wife—except on grounds of *incest*—and marries another, *defiles.*

Matthew 5:28: Anyone who looks on a woman with lust has already *defiled* her in his heart.

From these interpretations of the text far-reaching *consequences* result and are summarized as follows.

(1) The wording of the sixth commandment is basic: "Thou shalt have no dishonorable sexual relations," that is, neither sexual relations contrary to marriage nor any relations at all outside of a bond. Although in its English form "Thou shalt not commit adultery," one could easily construe this as a prohibition against divorce, the text says nothing directly about this. Otherwise texts like Deuteronomy 24:1-4 and Sirach 25:26, and the Jewish divorce practice would stand in *formal* contradiction with this command. Thus Jesus is also not criticizing this practice by invoking the sixth commandment. Leviticus 21:7, however, forbids at least priests from marrying "women whom their husbands have rejected"; Sirach 7:26 (LXX) and Malachi 2:16 reject divorce generally: "Do not dismiss your wife and do not be unfaithful." Thus divorce was never a matter of indifference, but rather always carried a stain with it; that is the reason there were so many discussions about when it could nevertheless be "allowed."

(2) Jesus carries this line of prohibition to a consistent conclusion while invoking the Genesis account of human creation: "You should not separate what God has joined together." In his argument with the Pharisees in Mark 10:2-9, he lets stand this general rejection of divorce.[653] In this the new marital bond should be

---

653. On the terminology, cf. above, A VI 1. The combination of this controversy dialogue with the saying ("logion") on divorce in Matt 19:9 may be secondary; this is also Schürmann's position, "Verbindlichkeit," 109f., 113f. It is remarkable that only here, that is, in the dispute with the "hard-

distinguished from the previous (!) act of separation. Separation in itself is forbidden, but the condition of *moicheia*/defilement only develops with a new marriage or simply with sexual relations (Matt 5:32b). From the meaning of the words, one would have to say in English: Anyone who separates "is breaking the existing bond of a marriage" but they only "defile" if they then join with somebody new; they then debase both themselves and their new partner. Our notion of "adultery" still has more disgrace about it than does separation, since, for example, one frequently understands an "adulterous affair" in such a way that one's marriage is not necessarily ended because of it.

(3) The reason why such a new union (of the two new partners) is "soiling," lies in the fact that one of the two has *on their own initiative* and thereby in responsible fashion dissolved their former marriage, whether they be man or woman. *Chōrizesthai* (to separate *oneself* from) and *aphienai* in 1 Corinthians 7:11f. and their variants in the Synoptics reflect in the process the different legal status of men and women, without, however, excusing the woman, in the case where she is the initiating party, of moral guilt. Concerning the "validity" of the new union, which indeed Mark 10:11 *par.* characterizes as "contracting a marriage," so far nothing has been said.

(4) On the *innocently separated party*[654]—whether they have been "cast off/abandoned" by an unbeliever or by a Christian—no burden is placed. In that in all the passages no statement is made concerning their further rights and duties, the presumption in favor of the universally accepted conviction that he or she was free to remarry remains undisturbed, so that on this point neither Jesus nor Paul intended to preach anything "new." Other-

---

hearted men," the second half of the statement is left out; otherwise, Jesus always also speaks to the woman's conscience. He does this—according to our interpretation—not only in Mark 10:12, but also in Luke 16:18 and Matt 5:32.

654. Jesus' sayings on this matter in the Synoptics presume that the guilt lies clearly on one side, specifically on the person who dismisses the other. This is legal discourse. What proportion of responsibility the other may have on the psychological level is a distinct question; that topic does not come under consideration here. See Atf VI 6 and 9.

wise they would have had to say so. They would have to have presumed that their audience was of the opinion that an innocently separated party could marry again.[655]

(5) Paul understands Jesus' command not to dissolve a marriage as only applying in its absolute form to *believers,* so that an unbeliever is not bound to the same extent; in their case the foundation, the necessary belief and acceptance of Jesus as the Lord, is not present. Paul even goes so far as to state that in a mixed marriage even the Christian party is not bound to the Lord's word to the same extent as they would be if they were married to a believer, although *he,* Paul, *advises* that person to remain with such a marriage. For the grounds of a possible separation on the part of the Christian partner we must reflect further.

(6) If the limits of binding obligation are set on the one hand by the desire of the unbelieving partner to separate, on the other hand this obligation is also open *to God,* for what God has joined together God can also pull apart, either through death or by calling somebody out of a marriage (Luke 18:29). There are also other implications in 1 Corinthians 7:10f., which we will consider in the following section.

(7) The question remains whether the *guilty party after a genuine conversion* not only may receive forgiveness for the sin they have committed of sending their spouse away, but at the same time may again receive the moral permission to marry; and if he or she is not able to achieve this through a restoration of the first marriage, whether then under certain conditions before God—"in the Lord"—they may enter into a second. This question is never formulated in the text in so many words, but from the entire thrust of the New Testament the answer would probably be yes.

Let us inquire then into the moral, pastoral, and legal consequences of these results. These are always tied to the judgment coming from the Spirit-led community of believers, especially

---

655. The Fathers repeatedly inquire about guilt for this reason; see Delling, *Ehescheidung,* 714–717. This comes from the Jewish tradition; see R. Neudecker, *Frührabbinisches Scheidungsrecht* (Rome, 1982); review of this by R. Sebott, *ThPh* 59 (1984) 582f.

where they go beyond data that can be firmly estabished exegetically, as in points 6 and 7. What does the history of the Church and its pastoral experience down to the present have to say?

2. The Historical Reception

The way the Christians of the first centuries understood these texts may be determined by a study of their practice and their controversies. Ignatius (*Pol.* 5:2) counsels married people to mutual love, those living deliberately alone to humility, and those who marry to do so "with the consent of the bishop, that the marriage be according to the Lord and not according to lust."[656] The *First Letter of Clement* carries exhortations in the style of household codes (1:3; 21:6) and speaks about the fact that during the persecution of Christians, marriages were destroyed through jealousy (6:3). A reference to *divorce* is found for the first time in the *Shepherd of Hermas* (Man. IV 1:6, 11; GCS 48:26f.); if the wife is unfaithful the husband is *required* (!) to dismiss her (invoking Matthew 5:32); at the same time, however, out of consideration for the possibility that she may repent, her husband is forbidden from contracting a second marriage. Still, these rigorous demands on both sides do not constitute the general practice. Stockmeier[657] clearly shows that at about the time of Tertullian the situation was "still largely unclarified," and that various Fathers even down to Augustine fought repeatedly against a widespread Church practice, according to which the "local ecclesial officials in the community have authorized divorces along with second marriages," frequently after an appropriate time for penance. This practice permitted a new marriage both in the case of licentiousness on the part of the wife as well as for other "serious reasons."

Origen,[658] the Synod of Arles, Basil, Chrysostom, Ambrose, and others adopt a more restrictive attitude with regard to this

656. For the text, see above, note 178.

657. P. Stockmeier, "Scheidung und Wiederverheiratung in der alten Kirche," *ThQ* 151 (1971) 39–51. There is a collection of similar material in Delling, "Ehescheidung."

658. Delling, "Ehescheidung," 714, believes that "already" Origen observed "that even during the life of their first husband, a second marriage

practice, but it is not simply condemned by them. Epiphanius of Salamis (fourth century: *Haer.* 59:4, 9/GCS 31L368f.) is still of the opinion that someone innocently separated who "enters into a further marriage, is not accused by God's word nor excluded from the Church and the common life, even if the divorce results from another cause than adultery (by the woman)." People thus wrestled for a long time with the question, especially whether a person innocently separated was still bound, until finally Jerome (*Epist.* 55/CSEL 54:494f.) "also refused those innocently separated—in the case of adultery—a second marriage."

Augustine at first calls a dissolution of a marriage like this a "forgivable error," but later turns against Pollentius "who allowed the husband, if the wife committed adultery, to remarry, but advised the wife against it," because by his understanding in any event the "bond of marriage" still existed. Thus through his teaching on the sacramental bond of marriage *(vinculum),* Augustine here (for the first time!) introduces into the Western Church a category which appears to no longer allow the possibility of remarriage. Moreover, the entire discussion is gradually overshadowed by an ever more stringent demand for *a single* marriage, against which the Council of Nicaea protected the possibility of a second marriage—admittedly "only after an appropriate period of penance has been established" (Stockmeier, 50 and 47). In the meantime also the Pastoral Letters were read evidently in this sense.[659]

While the West became visibly stricter, a persistent tradition seems to have maintained itself in the East down to the present

---

was permitted to divorced women by the Church," but that Origen, like Clement of Alexandria, "still" considered this as not in accord with the Scriptures. But could it not be the other way around, that they *already,* in the sense of *no longer,* considered it in accord with the Scriptures, although Church practice retained older memories? Is it really accurate to say that gradually society became "stricter with women, and more lax with men" (Delling, "Ehescheidung," 714)?

659. Specifically with reference to a single marriage, which we rejected above, B II 2. Cf. Haacker, "Ehescheidung und Wiederverheiratung im NT," *ThQ* 151 (1971) 37f. For Stockmeier it remains questionable whether the "penitential period" before a second marriage was intended (only) for widows and widowers or (also/only?) for divorced persons.

day which—even against an invocation of the written word, as it was later interpreted—permitted at least to someone innocently separated the possibility of remarriage.[660] Even if the contemporary justification in the Eastern Church is based on a broader interpretation of the adultery clause, since indeed the one who departs breaks the fidelity, still in light of our results and further studies[661] it is to be asked whether in this case the "oral tradition" is not nearer to Jesus' intention than later Christian scriptural scholarship.

Could this not be a sign that in the first decades (centuries?) many readers understood these passages differently, perhaps in the sense that we have suggested, and that *for that reason* this tradition possessed such a remarkable capacity to endure? Moreover, the Roman practice on annulments shows a steady recognition of new justifications and "exceptions." Pastoral care and insistence on the word of Scripture as one understands it here enter into a tragic conflict with one another.[662] How would it be, if the Scriptures may indeed be understood differently?

660. Similarly Gansewinkel, "Ehescheidung," 199, note 18; cf. further Gnilka, 170. Trilling, 405f., refers for the Church practice of the early centuries to the "meanwhile forgotten speech by the Melchite patriarchal vicar in Egypt, Elias Zoghby, on Sept 29, 1965, at the Second Vatican Council," in J. David, T. Schmalz, *Wie unauflöslich ist die Ehe?* (Aschaffenburg, 1969) 332–334, with a further bibliography on this question in Wetzel, 42–93.

661. For more details, see Chersones, 337–351. He quotes Bonsirven (340): "If we turn to the East, we have the impression that the direction has changed: the insertion *'nisi fornicationis causa'* seems to be viewed as determining the general regulation; as a consequence the other texts from the gospels and from Paul must be understood according to this exception." In fact: because *all* of them declare a second marriage to be a sin only for the guilty parties. This would thus require a further investigation.

662. See the rich material on this in J. Neumann, 1–22; further, A. Müller, 301–305. Individual attempts by exegetes to move ahead here: Schürmann, "Marginalien," 422f., asks whether the gospel "did not indeed set up a rather tolerant early Christian practice with reference to marriage." "It is striking: nowhere in the New Testament writings (or perhaps in 1 Cor 5:11?) is there mention of how community members were treated or should be treated if they had not followed—either before or after their baptism—Jesus' prohibition against divorce or Paul's interpretations of this. . . . Were second marriages tolerated more or less silently? . . . The pastoral practice of the early communities cannot have been uniform." Now, if the early genera-

3. Law and the Norm of Conscience

Today all exegetes emphasize in one way or another that Jesus did not intend to set himself up as a lawgiver promulgating some new form of "marriage statutes." This is accurate; but then, how are his words about divorce intended? People have tried to resolve the resulting problem through a distinction between "ideal and judicially-binding law" (Schürmann, 415; 417f.), "pronouncement and declaratory legal statement" (Fitzmyer, 204; A. Müller, 301), especially since it has been frequently noticed that this "Word of the Lord sounds strangely 'lawlike' within the 'gospel' " (Schürmann, 420; Trilling, 394). However, is not every commandment an "ideal" command, to the extent that we always fall short of it? Kirchschläger sees in the redactional shifts of accent in the New Testament authors a "tension between fidelity to the apostolic proclamation and fidelity to the responsibility for the individual person" (88), between "fundamental principles and personal concern" (91f.). One would like to ask: did Jesus not always have the second in each pair in mind? Whether it helps to say that Jesus' commands should not be understood in a "static, deontological sense," in that it permits things "not as concessions in the style of Moses," but "analogous exceptions,"[663] may be doubted. J. Blank (361) tries to resolve it through appeals "which bring it home to the individual to undertake the ways and means to bring it about in one's own unique fashion—one, however, that is not legally specifiable beforehand." Furger (29) attempts it with a "balancing of goods" that does not allow "ethical norms to freeze deontologically into unbreakable legal statutes, but rather preserves them as teleologically open." Schüller distinguishes even more clearly between unconditioned and conditioned ethical principles.[664] Thus the

---

tions read the texts in the sense mentioned above, then many problems which we have with the historical material would disappear, for one would then presume that in the early Church's interpretation a second marriage would be "sinful" only for the guilty party, while the innocent would be free to remarry.

663. Schürmann, "Marginalien," 414 and *passim;* Gnilka, 170; Fitzmyer, "Divorce," 224f.

664. See below, 404f.; Schüller, "Problematik," 2-4; on the application to creation, Schüller, "Problematik," 18-23.

command to love (cf. Furger, 28–31) must be continually retranslated in light of new circumstances. In this sense the crux in our inquiry seems to be the norm of conscience: "If you have said 'yes,' you should not from your side desire or strive for a separation," or in sum: you should not injure the marital fidelity. This applies, so to speak, "unconditionally." However, under what conditions external to yourself (whether it be through your partner's decision, through objective limits on both sides, or through God's call), *you may become* freed from this, is another question. And I would like to add that this central principle can only be applied correctly in the light of the "Spirit who distinguishes."

Every norm of conscience is naturally valid for the entirety of human affairs, and as such allows for no "moderating additions," even if for a violation there may be "extenuating circumstances." However, the notion that a person *should* not separate is still somewhat different from the idea of an objective and ontically conceived, *separately existing and enduring* "bond of marriage," that then becomes confused with "sacramental" or concretized as *ius divinum.*[665] Cannot the "divine law" behind every command be restored by forgiveness? If this is not possible for marriage in the legal code, the latter must be reconceived (Trilling, 392f.).

As a matter of fact, the crux of the matter seems to lie in the notion of an "indissoluble bond of marriage." This notion only arose because the Western Church translated *apolelymenēn* by *dimissam,*[666] and thereby came to the conviction that even the innocent party was still "bound," that, despite their being released, the "tie" had not been destroyed. But what happens if this foundation collapses? Chersones (339), a theologian of the Eastern Church, argues correctly: "Indissoluble refers to something 'that cannot be dissolved.' If this is to be applied to marriage, this adjective would have to have the meaning that on the basis of an inner, essential character, absolutely nothing could impair the marital bond, as long as both partners were alive. If Jesus indeed

665. On this, Trilling, 400–406; Gansewinkel, "Ehescheidung," 201; Schüller, "Problematik," 22f.

666. Thus interpreted as a passive—"the dismissed person"—not as an active middle, which Gansewinkel strongly underlines, 196, and in "Weisungen," 16. Cf. above, D IV 2.

clearly and distinctly teaches that marriage *should* not be dissolved, this does not mean that it *cannot* be dissolved."

Still further: the command presumes that a person "can" do it, similar to: "Thou shalt not kill." This means: if one partner "offends" against the other, that is, cuts the marriage bond, that partner sins. However, the marriage bond is then indeed severed! The text does not say: "the person is then not really released." Certainly there remains an obligation, according to the possibilities, of making restitution; but what happens if a restoration is not possible, especially for the innocent party? Would not the same rules of what is morally possible and appropriate apply here as in other areas? Expressed in a different way: does not this Western notion of the marriage bond lead us down a false trail, intensified by the talk of sacrament? Is this not perhaps the deeper reason for Luther's objection to the sacramental status of marriage? Expressed in Catholic terms: Can one not sin against a sacrament in such a way that its effectiveness ceases? Cannot one sin against the forgiveness of confession, or against the Eucharist? The fact that, unlike baptism and orders, marriage does not stamp the individual with an "indelible mark" is already indicated by the admonition that "young widows may marry" (1 Tim 5:14).

What would happen if it were possible for people to actually destroy or tear up this "marriage bond"? In that case the "bond" would consist on the one hand in the mutual free relationship of fidelity, on the other hand in the fact that God *demands* such fidelity from the partners as a moral response, but does not, however, *force* such through an ontic reality independent of human freedom. *And what happens if God as Lord of marriage dissolves it through another calling?* Does God somehow "destroy" this "marriage bond"? Or how should we conceive such a release from duty? Does it take place even while the marriage bond continues to exist? And what happens at the *death* of one of the partners? In his *Retractationes,* Augustine calls this matter an "extraordinarily obscure question" (Chersones, 342).

Is not the intended reality better expressed through personal categories that indeed indicate a reality, but one which is constituted through a free consent of the will by the partners sanctioned by God, and which thereby "comes into being" and "passes away"? A person who perseveres in this situation does so because he or she holds firm to God's command and not simply because he or she "is not able to do anything else." "It is the violation of the command that breaks the bond; the act of divorce merely acknowledges this and gives a confirmation before the law." And the other way around: "According to the Orthodox view the ties that bind a married couple cannot be maintained simply through legal compulsion" (Chersones, 342–348). "The goal of the Sermon on the Mount," however, is an "upright and undivided heart" (Lövestam, 28).

How difficult it is to maintain the thesis of a marriage bond enduring in itself can be seen in the cases where even in the interpretation prevailing up to now a separation has been possible. What does it mean to say that a marriage between two unbaptized persons, or between a Christian and a non-Christian, can be dissolved? In these cases is there no "bond of marriage"? Who severs it? Is it perhaps not so strong because the sacramental status is not present, or at least is not as fully present?[667] On the other hand, how can it be explained that even a sacramental marriage, if it has not been consummated, may be dissolved? Is there even in this case no "sacramental" bond? And what about the case of the *dissolution of marriage through religious vows?* The other partner then really has no more "rights" over the former partner. What, finally, is behind the fact that Paul considers a "marriage with an unbeliever" (1 Cor 7:12-16) to be dissolvable, and that he nevertheless advises the person to remain in it? The latter would in any case be more in keeping with the vocation of a Christian and the sign of a greater love than if one separates out of a selfish concern for one's own salvation (7:15f.). Still, even this must be a tie "in the Lord," for otherwise Paul could not counsel one to stay in it. Then how should we consider its "sacramental status"?

The answer probably lies rather in the fact that a Christian brings along in his or her conscience a different order of values than an unbeliever and brings his or her concrete marriage into relation with them, and thereby "relativizes" it (1 Cor 7:29ff.; 35). If the non-Christian partner does not accept this, the obligation of the Christian reaches a limit. In fact, even if the former were ready for a common life, the Christian is not bound to this partner "through a word of the Lord," but rather only in virtue

667. More on this in A. Müller, 301, 303; Schüller, "Problematik," 18f.

of a piece of Paul's advice! Why is this "bond" so loose? The objective deficiency probably consists in the fact that the Christian cannot communicate with the partner about what is most important to him or her.

Paul and the later Church have understood Jesus' words *as fully binding only for a Christian couple,* while in a mixed marriage the final unity "in the Lord" is not present. Thus there can indeed be cases where the Christian feels "in the Spirit" the power and the commission to remain together with this unbaptized partner, but there are also sufficient cases where the other indeed would be ready to build a home together, but the one who (after the marriage!) has converted to Christ has experienced such a different development that they see themselves considerably hindered in the practice of their faith by their previous partner. Most probably for that reason in what follows Paul immediately relativizes his counsel to remain in such a marriage (7:17-24): "*But,* let each one do as *God* calls him or her" (not as I advise). This is the ultimate criterion.[668] Thus as far as *God* is concerned, in principle in such a relationship a door would be open—which admittedly should not be taken as an alibi for convenience, but rather should only be used under the guidance of God's Spirit. Hence the repeated weighing of the possibilities by the apostle in 1 Corinthians 7: what weight has his own advice (7:25, 40), what weight has the "Lord's command," what weight has one's actual call, which may perhaps be stronger than the general command of the Lord not to separate?

Thus the tie with one's partner is completely dependent upon when and how God binds two people together. From this position it becomes understandable that Jesus' clear command, "Thou shalt not separate," is, *in this form,* a command *for his disciples,* that is, for people who follow him. "The proclamation of God's original plan through Jesus changes the situation only for those who believe in him and give themselves over to his grace" (Häring, 511). It is true that it is a matter of an "original plan" that is applicable *for all;* however the *obligation* deriving from Jesus only applies to those who accept him as Lord. Here the contemporary problematic of "premarital counseling" and the capacity of many engaged couples for a sacramental union becomes strikingly clear.

668. Cf. above, A II 5.

If divorce is not prohibited to an unbeliever in this unconditional way, it is not because he or she does not stand within God's
plan of creation, but rather because God *first* awaits *belief* from
them before God will impose on them this demand in its unconditional form. This is analogous to the concession made by
Moses "because of the hardness of their heart." And one cannot
object here: "but Jesus was indeed speaking to Jews (thus not
yet to 'Christians') and based his command on creation, which
is valid for all."[669] The question is indeed not what is laid down
in the order of creation, but rather who, under what circumstances, and to what extent, can and should recognize and follow these obligations. "But I say unto you"—this key phrase that
runs through the Sermon on the Mount constitutes a clear allegiance to Jesus' person: "If you cast yourself upon my word, you
will find therein a means to carry it out."

The universal demand consists in this, that everyone should accept Jesus' word; however, the specific consequences fall only
upon those who have placed themselves on this foundation. As
Paul says, "The psychic person cannot understand this" (1 Cor
2:14f.). And if Paul himself testifies to the fact that he and the
young Church did not apply the prohibition against divorce in
its full weight to Christians in a mixed marriage (1 Cor 7:12-15),
then this shows us to what extent he and the early Church started
from "living in Christ," and not from the restoration of a "law
of nature" (A. Müller, 301f.). In fact, it is only in the power of
the Spirit that a person can be steadfastly faithful. This alone
makes it "reasonable" for God to expect them to be able to cope
positively with the difficulties of an entire life lived together, and
for that reason to demand constancy "unconditionally." Thus
God does this only in return for the promise of God's help in
Christ. Thus as long as the two of them really live from faith,
God expects that neither of them will give in to the temptation

669. Murphy-O'Connor's criticism; cf. above, note 55. In agreement with
us: Schürmann, "Verbindlichkeit," 110–114; 117f. This article also shows
the difficulties and inconsistencies of the received interpretation: that the
"circumstances could mitigate Jesus' prohibition against divorce" (112–114)
and that Paul would permit an act which is "materially in itself wrong" (116),
so that one could choose something that was *intrinsece malum* as the lesser
of two evils (107, 114f., 118f.). Who could be satisfied with this?

to become unfaithful. If they abandon this foundation, then admittedly everything collapses.

Thus we have clearly distinguished between the prohibition to separate oneself from one's partner (Mark 10:9; Matt 19:6) and the casuistic statutes (that really are not "laws"[670]) in which Jesus *applies* this principle. Strictly speaking, these are indeed in no sense "divorce" sayings; the logia speak about the *consequence* of a divorce that *has already taken place*. Jesus thereby emphasizes the command: "Thou shalt not dismiss him or her," but he does this by saying: "if you have done this and then marry, *in that case* your new marriage is a sexual sin"—not because the bonds of marriage still perdure, but rather "because on the basis of your violating the prohibition against separation, you are not in order," or: "since you *yourself* have broken your marriage by separating, you may not now swear marital fidelity to another partner." That is the reason why the new sexual union is a defiling act. This shows once more that *moicheuein* has nothing to do with the validity (or invalidity) of the new marriage, but rather concerns its moral foundation. Such a marriage cannot be ratified by the Church simply because *it is sinful,* not because the first marriage is still in effect.

The condition of *moicheia* is essentially independent of the question concerning legal "validity." Chersones (350) emphasizes that "in the first centuries the Church never expressed itself about the validity of marriages," not even "in the canons" (344), because the legal order was the concern of the state. However, this means that it regarded divorce as legally binding, thus as a real divorce, and on this basis put together grounds for moral standards which according to its conviction enabled someone who had been divorced to marry again: if the guilt lay unambiguously on the side of the other partner, in cases like adultery, etc., or when *bona gratia* grounds were present, like impotence, disappearance, profession of religious vows, difference of religion. Thus we already have here a "marital law" that begins in practice from the proposition that the possibility of remarrying should not fundamentally be denied to someone who through no fault of their own

---

670. Cf. G. Lohfink, "Ehescheidung," 212–216; instead of "legal statute," it appears rather to be a "wisdom counsel"; for more details, see Atf VI 7 and 8.

has been divorced. The implementation varies, sometimes with generous adaptations.

4. Is the Dam Breaking: Or: "Where Will This Lead?"

It is the task of an ecclesial marriage law to objectify and to support those norms of conscience given by God. It must ultimately always serve our spiritual discernment before God, especially by preserving conscience from incorrect judgments. Paul the Pharisee is thoroughly at home with legal thinking and continually surprises us with his positive evaluations of the "law's demands" (Rom 7:12; 8:4; 13:8-10); he himself has nothing to object against the Church as "lawgiver," since he himself in given circumstances could deliver extremely concrete stipulations. However, everything must take place "in the Spirit," "in faith" (Rom 8:4; 14:23), not "in a *legal fashion.*" Thus it is already accurate to say that Paul "does not understand the Lord's words against divorce in a legal fashion" (Baltensweiler, 263), that is, as a simple demand without provision of the necessary strength or as a temptation to autonomous works-righteousness.

> Baltensweiler's conclusion (263) on this question reveals once again the questionable nature of his textual interpretation, when he says that Paul "in principle rejects divorce" (1 Cor 7:10f.), but that he "still as a matter of fact permits it in a 'mixed marriage' (1 Cor 7:15)." Is Paul then inconsistent? Do we not have to understand this "principle" in a different sense? It is noteworthy, as B. immediately goes on to point out, that the "prohibition of a second marriage (after a divorce) is only understandable against the background of the contemporary sociological community structure." But, this structure acknowledged no such prohibition! Does this sentence mean that the prohibition which Jesus made did not apply "in principle," but rather would change with alterations in the structure? Here the logic and justification are missing. One could understand it if B. sought to explain the prohibition against remarrying as a legal custom of the early community—one which Baltensweiler then would relativize; for previously (262) he had made a distinction between "Jesus' original demand that a marriage should not be dissolved" and the "development in the first communities, which interpreted this demand in the sense of a marital law" and then "ultimately (!) saw the sin no longer in the di-

vorce by itself, but rather in the remarriage.'' One cannot discover why suddenly the one should be legally binding, but not the statement ''that a marriage may not be dissolved.'' This distinction which he postulates in the Synoptic tradition itself is not convincing.

It is equally not clear that 1 Corinthians 7:11a has in mind only someone ''who was divorced *before* their entrance into the community.'' B. indeed later gives as a reason for the possibility of divorce in a mixed marriage the fact that ''the non-Christian party remains behind in the old era.'' Then this would also apply to a pagan from whom a Christian had already separated before conversion! Finally, it seems strange that Paul's ''nonlegalistic understanding'' should consist in the fact that he ''adapts'' the Lord's words, and assumes the freedom ''to permit a divorce under the conditions named above *because there is a means to prevent a descent into chaos:* the prohibition against remarrying (1 Cor 7:11).'' Would such a prohibition then not indeed be a ''legalistic'' implementation, since it attempted to prop up and reinforce a moral demand with legal stipulations and moral weight? Based on such support, may one then weaken a moral demand?

On the other hand, an ecclesial law is meant for the redeemed on the basis of grace. The limits which according to our results it would have to set would be: to the extent that someone is responsible for the breakup of a marriage, he or she cannot in this condition before God enter into a new marriage; but to the extent that they are not guilty for the separation, they retain such a possibility. The common failures in living together should be distinguished from this. If a just person ''seven times a day falls and rises again'' (Prov 24:16), this is then no reason for their partner to ''dismiss'' them. In practice, however, these often cannot be so easily distinguished.

Thus the solution to our problematic would not consist in choosing between ''law'' and ''conscience,'' but rather in giving the law—as it is here interpreted and as it is practiced in the Orthodox Church—a new formulation of the norms binding for conscience, on the basis of a new understanding of the Scriptures and the conscience of the Church. Certainly in such a case so much would change and begin moving that some could fear that everything was becoming unhinged. However, when viewed in the sober light of day, the marriage law has long been incapable of dealing with the actual problems of the faithful. Are not many who, caught in a moral dilemma, are formally in "violation" because of having been divorced and remarried also a sign that many people, despite honest efforts, are overburdened and/or feel there is a discrepancy between the Church's marital law and their personal life before God?[671] On the basis of pastoral care the entire organism of the Church feels that here through many cases of hardship an unbearable tension has arisen which is often experienced as a contradiction between God's "command" and God's "mercy." However, what kind of "command" would this be? Because people believed themselves bound to the literal word of Scripture, often the "law" could only with effort and sometimes with considerably complicated and humanly humiliating means (such as the conditions for annulments), here and there provide a little help, but still had to maintain the fundamental position that somebody innocently divorced may not remarry. However, is not the true answer which lies hidden behind these various gestures at a solution now rising to the surface, and in a simpler form?

The central core of the problematic concerning divorce is thus transferred from Church law to pastoral concern, or better expressed: pastoral counselors can perceive their task differently if they have a different law behind them. The number of questions which suddenly open up cannot even be sketched here. However, it should be said that the effort required for a clarification of conscience with a responsible pastoral counselor (pastor, confessor) and with regard to questions of public concern also in consultation with an appropriate pastoral committee (perhaps in place of a "marriage tribunal") should not discourage anyone from providing this kind of pastoral help for the clarification of decisions of conscience.

671. Everyone is aware of enough cases among those they know; here reference is made only to the moving, almost shocking appeal by B. Häring, *Ausweglos?* (Freiburg, 1989); further to the books by Brunsman, David-Schmalz, Heimerl, Kirchschläger, Wetzel, and Steininger (see the bibliography), as well as to J. Neumann, who at the end (22) asks, "whether the 'bonds of marriage' really may be considered as independent of personal relationships and one's actual living situation. Neither from natural law *alone,* nor as a sacrament *alone,* is the 'bond of marriage' indissoluble. The viability of such a legal fiction thus becomes questionable." Cf. A. Müller, 301–305.

5. *"Pastoral Care" or*
Spiritual Counseling for Married People

What does it mean concretely, in the complexity of life, to hold firmly in purity to Jesus' command: "Thou shalt not *on your own initiative* separate or work toward a separation"? Kirchschläger (94) speaks about "a sphere of coping" for everybody who "wrestles with the *kerygma* and its demands." So we stand before the question of how the Church should require, protect, and support this type of judgment by conscience through specific stipulations—not in the style of civil laws, which under prescribed circumstances compel a given mode of conduct, but rather as pastoral aids whereby a person may be liberated to behave in a responsible fashion before God. And we must reflect anew how a decision arrived at in conscience may take effect in the "outer forum."

If it is true that the innocent party may remarry and, under conditions to be clarified, an "objective bond of marriage" ceases to exist, then ultimately the question must come up whether the guilty party may not also at some point become free of his or her guilt. For a conversion the Church's old institution of a time of penance would be something to reconsider. This always entails at least: a request for forgiveness before God and as far as possible from the offended party, and, at least on the side of the guilty party, an interior reconciliation with the other; whether or not the other accepts this lies admittedly beyond the control of the guilty party. What would be appropriate under different circumstances and what presuppositions would have to be fulfilled before a divorced person would be permitted a new marriage, or before the already existing second marriage would be accepted by the Church, cannot even be suggested here. One will notice all the more clearly in this that such a "process" may only be carried out with Christians who are living out their faith, while on the contrary many people who are Christian in name only would be rendered uncertain by this. However, such events could confront many people anew with the living, demanding word of God and could also contribute to a clarification of their faith. Perhaps we are too little aware of how the easily manageable categories of "baptized—not baptized," "validly married or not" lead to simplifications which are ultimately not useful to the faith.

However, participation in the sacraments, where a person is standing and acting in genuine repentance before God, should no longer be forbidden.[672]

Finally one should consider that often people on both sides, and in spite of good will, reach such a limit that the marriage "breaks apart" without either one of them actively "breaking" it. People who are psychologically sick can become a torture to one another; but also a progressive alienation even with "healthy" people frequently exceeds the capacity of those affected to cope with it. In this situation, is there not also a limit to endurance, beyond which one cannot expect married people to live together? It can also happen that one tortures the other and at the same time will not let the other go; does the tortured partner then have the right to leave, even though from a purely legal point of view the initiative for the divorce then stems from him or her? In that case, however, the sick or malicious behavior of the partner was the actual cause. The many limit-situations cannot be decided on paper. Still, the pastoral counselor requires a framework in order to offer such people appropriate help. At what point do we come to the "objective limits" of something like a "higher power" that approximates an incurable illness, and releases the partner from continuing in the marriage? While in the Eastern Church impotence is already a ground for divorce, in the West often even more elementary rights are not recognized. Of course there can be people who in the Spirit receive a heroic power and can continue down such a path with their partner in peace before God. For those, however, who fall apart under such pressures—"for them have we no blessing"?[673]

How would Paul act with such people? He would certainly speak to them differently than in 1 Corinthians 7:10f. For it is not his intention to use the Lord's words "like a stick" (1 Cor 4:21) to somehow beat Christian partners back together again. Is he not extraordinarily sensitive to people's current situation?

672. Indeed, because the "objective bonds of marriage" no longer exist. On this topic and for a bibliography, see R. Puza, *Katholisches Kirchenrecht* UTB 1395 (Heidelberg, 1986) 355–364. Cf. Schüller, "Problematik," 22.

673. Similarly Gansewinkel, "Weisungen" with reference to W. Kasper, *Zur Theologie der christlichen Ehe* (Mainz, 1978) 66: "what is humanly possible" as a limit, etc.

Do we not sense specifically in 1 Corinthians 7 a great breadth and flexibility, such that the callings to marriage as well as to celibacy do not constitute a final value, but are viewed rather in their *relativity* and relatedness? Has not the often strained comparison made in Ephesians 5 led us frequently into a "theological overloading" of marriage? There certainly exists an analogy between marriage and the relationship between Christ and the "assembly." But as we have seen, this text does not justify a mystification of the "Church"; besides that, *ekklēsia* now means humanity. Beyond the similarity, one should not forget how great also the differences are: the relation of Christ to humanity vastly exceeds the relationship of man to woman; the image of the "body of Christ" may not be extended to marriage, since indeed the two of them become "one flesh," but the woman never in the marriage becomes "the body" of the man, and the man is not the savior of the woman. Thus, in the midst of all the encouraging similarity, there is also a strong dissimilarity. It confers a false mystification and sacralization upon marriage and also on the marital act which no longer respects the latter's relativity.[674] In all these questions, in any case, Paul would differentiate and not oversimplify.

6. The "Privilege of the Faith"

Not the least evidence for the relativity and dissolvability of marriages is the fact that both in Scripture (Luke 18:29) and in the Church's practice there are continually new applications of separation or divorce *in favorem fidei*. This alone makes any talk about an absolute, objective "indissolvability" appear questionable. This does not mean that one command would contradict another, but rather proceeds from the hierarchy of values, down to the extreme case: *contumelia creatoris solvit ius matrimonii circam eum, qui relinquitur*—disdain for the Creator dissolves the marriage law for someone who is abandoned (DS 768). One can certainly also apply the principle of the privilege of the faith in many of the cases mentioned in the previous section. In the cases we must now consider, however, this principle says that God wills the indestructible fidelity of the spouses to one another, but that

674. Cf. Rotter, 177f.

the latter must once again be measured against their personal fidelity to God. And on this basis God can also call them out of it. This occurs not only in extraordinary callings like that of Nicolas von der Flüe, but also in the course of everyday struggles and growth.

We have explained the dissolvability of a mixed marriage up until now by the fact that an unbeliever could not formally be obligated by a command from Jesus. But then why, if the unbeliever is prepared to remain with spouse, is it not *then* sanctioned through the Lord's word (1 Cor 7:12-14)? Does not this lesser degree of union also have its basis in the fact that the one partner's relation to Christ could experience a development which the other might oppose, or also that the believer would be hindered in this, due to excessive consideration for the partner? Admittedly, Paul first of all counsels for continuance, because he interprets the supposed "danger" as a chance to win the partner for Christ. However, if it is not, as in the context of 1 Corinthians 7, *only a matter of a desire for abstinence,* but rather of the whole practice of the faith, would Paul then not indeed decide *in favorem fidei,* in analogy with 7:35: "according to where you, without excessive strain, may be close to the Lord"? For then the tension referred to would not arise from *human incompatibility,* but rather because of the faith and different styles of life. If it becomes too exhausting, practically speaking the hierarchy of values could suggest a separation; the objective possibility is available in any case.

And what does Paul think about *entering* into such a "mixed marriage"? He brings a certain awareness of the problem of mixed marriages out of his Pharisaic training. He also sees their practical difficulties, to the point where they could even justify a divorce. From this, and from his style of circumspect and balanced reflection one may conclude that Paul would never indiscriminately advise in favor of such a union (7:39). On the other hand, a marriage with a non-Christian in no way contradicts the essence of being a Christian, even if Paul could probably more easily recommend the *continuation* of such an *already existing* marriage than the entering into such (which, however, for 7:40 does not mean that the new partner must be a Christian). To this must be added the fact that the few Christians in Corinth often had almost no choice, while as their numbers grew, the possibility of a marriage with a partner who was a believer became greater. These are factors which should be considered in any personal decision, *but which should never lead to any discrimination or suspicion with regard to a mixed marriage,* and if not toward one with an "unbeliever," then all the less toward one with a *Christian* of another denomination. Thus the "each according to" of 1 Corinthians 7:17-24 certainly applies here as well: not a legalistic rigidity, but rather a responsible attention both to God's call and to the circumstances to which the individual must then respond before God.

Admittedly the principle of the privilege of the faith is not easy to apply in practice.[675] It is all too easy to fall into the temptation to misuse it as an alibi. However, it appears to stand also behind 1 Corinthians 7:10f. Here Paul is certainly not considering that someone has violently torn themselves loose from their partner. This would be unjust, and would receive a different commentary from him. Thus this constitutes a further ground for believing that here it is a matter of people who came with a particular spiritual concern, and that in this at least no gross injuries were under discussion. Only such could have been the object of an *inquiry,* while an answer to the basic question about divorce (specifically because of human incompatibility) and on the other hand a reprimand by Paul because of adultery would have taken a different form (cf. 1 Cor 5). Thus it should be noticed that in 1 Corinthians 7 the word choice is colored by the motivation of abstinence. And to the extent that the Christian partner was also able to share in this motivation, and was not just the passive object of a divorce, he is also obligated to remain unmarried (in analogy to 7:39). This would more easily explain why Paul can say: "She should unite herself again with him."

Finally, one must also recognize this principle behind the counsel in 1 Corinthians 7:2-5. Here again the final criterion is the "calling" of the individual. Paul has no intention of setting up a fundamental prohibition forbidding married people from practicing continence *permanently* within their marriage. As he believes an engaged couple capable of it (since they live this way

675. On fundamental as well as practical questions, see Schüller, "Problematik," 19–22. Especially: it is rather a "concession to human 'weakness'" than a "privilege."

from the beginning, this is practically the same thing as happened when at a later time two people entered into a "Josephite" marriage), he does not rule out (in spite of 7:3-5) the possibility that others could live this way as a married couple. In fact, he can and will not fundamentally forbid people who agree to it before God to live continently. One may thus conclude from this part of his answer that the examples in the inquiry were somewhat more problematic and that he probably sensed generally a certain spiritual immaturity in the community as a whole. Thus as a community he gives them "milk" to drink (1 Cor 3:1), in other words only the more general framework, so that some do not improperly apply the finer distinctions.[676] However, this does not rule out that Paul would also have granted further possibilities to some in a pastoral discussion—if he had recognized that God was leading them in a certain direction.

To conclude, there remains the question of when someone should be called an "unbeliever." Being a believer or unbeliever is not with Paul the same thing as being baptized or unbaptized, but rather refers to the actual life in the faith of people who have opted to become Christians as adults. Whether among the unbelievers there might also be some who have slipped back from Christianity into unbelief can be neither refuted nor demonstrated. While at the start of Christianity there were only a few, today there are many who were baptized as children without ever having ratified their status as Christians. Are they not in practice equivalent to these "unbelievers"? The facts of a purely formal baptism or of having had one's marriage blessed in a church do not by themselves make people Christians. If both partners have begun in this fashion, and then one converts seriously, psychologically they are in the same situation as those described in 1 Corinthians 7:12-16, and not those described in 7:10.

---

676. We again recall Ignatius of Loyola, according to whom the rules for discernment of the "second week" should not be presented to a person "who is not yet experienced in spiritual matters, and if he is tempted in an obvious and vulgar way," and specifically because "they involve more elevated and subtle material than such a person could appreciate." *Spiritual Exercises,* no. 9; cf. no. 18, 150ff., 314–336, 349f. Two experienced pastoral counselors are speaking here.

And how much of a difference does it make if already before the marriage the two of them had achieved clarity about their different standpoints? It could be that the "believer" put pressure on the unbeliever, but also that the "unbeliever" at first was prepared to be tolerant, but then in practice did not maintain this, or perhaps only later turned away from the faith. Admittedly the borders here become more blurred, since one can never say exactly at which point someone is or is not a believer. In any case the bare fact of having been baptized as a child is too small a basis for us to evaluate a person according to the norms intended for disciples. Where one cannot legally clarify a situation, there always remains then a sphere of ambiguity in which the individual must scrutinize him- or herself before God and allow him- or herself to be examined.

Kirchschläger (94) refers to the contemporary "forgetfulness of God's lordship" and thus inquires about the capacity of many couples to receive the sacraments. For many, would not a personal renewal of their baptism have to take place before they could be capable of entering into the sacrament of marriage? Even if the minimal amount of belief necessary is difficult to determine, it is still true that without belief the administration and reception of the sacrament (the couple administer it to one another) do not take place. Are not for this reason alone many weddings "sealed by the Church" in fact "invalid," or at the least "not sacramental," and therefore simply natural unions? In this way the spectrum of marriages that can be dissolved becomes ever more various, broader, and more confusing. Does not this state of affairs confirm once again in its own way the result which we first extracted from the New Testament on semantic grounds: that marriage is not in itself "indissolvable"; rather, one *should* not dissolve it! It is guaranteed through the moral virtue of fidelity and the divine command that stands behind it. Further, one cannot ascertain its presence through an external act alone, but rather may only view the latter as a sacrament if it takes place in a context where there is belief.

Finally, a summary overview of the results:

1. No sexual intercourse outside of marriage.
2. Jesus' command is: "Thou shalt not separate" (initiate separation).

3. The "active," i.e., guilty partner through a new marriage "defiles" the second partner; but there is nothing said about a continuation of a "bond of marriage" from the first marriage nor about invalidity of the second marriage.
4. Jesus' demand addresses only believers in this absolute way.
5. God can separate what God has joined.
6. The person who is divorced without being responsible for this separation is free to remarry.
7. The "guilty" party (see 3 above) may experience conversion and receive forgiveness. Wouldn't he or she be able—under certain circumstances—to remarry validly?

V. Celibacy and Its Motive

Paul provides no comprehensive teaching either about marriage or about celibacy. For example, 1 Corinthians 7 does not consider the concrete lifestyles of those who, as disciples of Jesus, wished to live celibate lives, but rather gives only, in response to specific questions, an aid for decision-making by pointing out the limits and the opportunities for a spiritually motivated practice of continence. The latter may also be used temporarily by married people; insofar as it can also be applied to the single life, Paul is thinking not only of unmarried people, but also of those permanently engaged, about whom he speaks in 7:25-40, widows and widowers (7:38), and probably also those "separated," whom Paul refers to at 7:11 and 15. Baltensweiler (264) is "uncertain" about this reference at 7:11. Further, we should think of those who, because of a special call from Jesus, "leave wife and children," and finally people who indeed cohabit in a legal marriage but who from the very beginning intended no sexual union.[701] Paul is not considering these last two groups but, as we have seen, he also does not exclude them.

The manner in which this celibate lifestyle outside of marriage is carried out has transformed itself today into a variety of lifestyles. Even before there was in the Church the state of widows

---

701. This was probably the intention of Mary and Joseph (Kruse, 96f.; cf. also Num 30:2-16), which quickly led to numerous imitations in the early Church, and later was called a "Josephite marriage" (EuE 323).

and virgins,[702] simultaneously with that of unmarried apostles and itinerant preachers, some people were called to a celibate life in the context of their everyday world. What began with Jesus' pre-Easter call away from family bonds, in the preaching of the apostle now touched not only those who accompanied him as (male or female) itinerant missionaries, but also others, who were bound to the Resurrected One in such a way that they experienced the desire for celibacy but remained in their environment. Paul did not (yet) consider the possibility that in the communities where these callings were generally recognized, such people would (already) constitute a distinct "state." If the "widows" in the Pastoral Letters were still really widows, already Ignatius greets "the virgins who are called widows" (*Smyrn.* 13:1). Here, apparently, a distinct state seems to have been created.

Only with the development of monasticism, the female religious orders, and the institution of priestly celibacy does the unmarried Christian lifestyle become more and more identified with these forms. At the same time, they are only *one,* although an especially visible and structured form of this divine call to either continence or the single life of which Paul speaks. It must today be more strongly acknowledged that many men and women living alone, among them the widowed and separated, are also deliberately pursuing a path of continence "for the Lord," and that the ethos of such callings is in no way secondary to that of the religious orders, even if some have not chosen this path from the very beginning, but rather were gradually led to understanding their life with God in this fashion.[703] The same thing holds true for many couples, whether they are abstinent on a temporary or permanent basis, just as it is for individual married people who, out of consideration for their partner (as in the case of an illness) are obliged and willing to live continently.

702. Whether as prophetesses, as so-called *syneisacte,* or as their own group within the community; cf. EuE 318–324; 422; further Luke 2:36f.; Acts 21:9; 1 Tim 5:3-16. Kruse's early dating within the primitive Jerusalem community of such groups is not overly convincing, at least in the numbers he suggests; however, the consideration of what became of the wives and children the apostles "left behind" is worthy of thought (109–112). For more material see Kruse, 112–116.

703. Although many people still silently choose this way, the early Church development and already the fact that in Corinth these questions were agi-

The fact that such a life, lived in the power of the Spirit, can become at the same time a source of moral and spiritual strength that is precious to the human community and as important to the life of the Church as healthy, believing families, is part of the mystery that the Apostle Paul experienced, not only in his own life, but also in the early communities. As an occasional writing, 1 Corinthians 7 is a particular witness to this, as a conversation with some people who would like to have their calling recognized; however, this chapter contains no complete or systematic presentation.

1. An Eschatological Motive?

We have to extract what moved these people toward celibacy indirectly from the texts. In the more recent literature the eschatological motive is said to have been the most important. But here we have clearly recognized that an "imminent expectation" has completely disappeared from 1 Corinthians 7,[704] and indeed the text is "privative," in that there is no discussion at all of a return of the Lord or of a projected time for it; also, Paul cannot have expected the Lord's return in the immediate future, for he counsels those who "are burning" to marry, gives those who wish to marry help toward their life together in family and profession, considers that, after a common decision a bride remains bound

---

tating the community as a community show that this gift, like all charisms, implied a relation to the community/church, whether it be to the local community, to an ecclesial group or spiritual fellowship, to pastoral help by laypersons or priests, etc. Since the start of so-called "secular institutes," a growing interest in new, authentic paths of spiritual celibacy can be observed within the Church, often similar in their origin to those in Corinth. In the charismatic renewal in the U.S.A., one hears of being "single for the Lord." Cf. further, F. Wulf, C. Bamberg, A. Schulz, *Nachfolge als Zeichen* (Würzburg, 1978), *Kommentarbeiträge zum Beschluß der Gemeinsamen Synode der Bistümer in der Bundesrepublik Deutschland über die Orden und andere geistliche Gemeinschaften*, 72–75 (O. Knoch); further, 143–163; 194ff.; 293ff. One can sense the same concern throughout the entire ecumenical world; cf. Lydia Präger, *Frei für Gott und die Menschen, Evangelische Bruder- und Schwesternschaften der Gegenwart in Selbstdarstellungen* (Stuttgart, 1964).

704. Cf. above, close to notes 146 and 160; on 1 Cor 15 a dissertation is in progress.

to her fiancé "as long as this man lives," and gives instructions for the period thereafter. Paul's formulation does not give the impression that he believes the fiancé will experience a sudden death in his early years, but still he says that the woman afterwards is free to marry again.

Thus the only indication of time in this chapter is the fact that Paul is reckoning with at least the possibility of a longer time period for the early Church. Beyond that it is certain *that* he believes history will come to an end,[705] and thus acknowledges an expectation of the end. Because the various eschatological-sounding statements in his letters mutually support and interpret one another, the exegesis of individual passages should restrict itself to stating only what may be unambiguously extracted from the text lying in front of us. So it is certain: Paul is not counseling celibacy in this chapter because he expects the end to arrive soon, and neither because it will demand all of our strength nor because this life is "no longer worth the effort" and therefore one should neglect the world and marriage.

However, "eschatology" can also abstract from the question about how long or short the time may be, and then simply mean that we stand "in the expectation of the Lord," even though *the time remains uncertain;* Schürmann describes this fittingly as "permanent expectation."[706] Finally, our glance may turn aside from the future to orient itself on the present. Then "eschatological" simply means that already now "the fulfillment of the ages" has come upon us (1 Cor 10:11). For with Jesus' resurrection already something (!) of the fulfilled eon has broken into our worldly time, so that through our participation in his resurrected life we live already to a certain extent beyond the limit of death and to that extent in the (post-Easter) eschaton ("realized eschatology"). Still, this is only a beginning, and even this we have "in hope"; this means that we possess it in concealed form and we are not sure about what we have reached, nor are we free from danger (Rom 8:24f.; Phil 3:12; 1 Cor 9:27; 2 Cor 1:10f.; 2:11). Given together with this is the fact that this new life is

705. Cf. 1 Thess 4:13-18; 1 Cor 15; EuE 193; 208–210; 242–245; Ts 264f.

706. H. Schürmann, "Eschatologie und Liebesdienst in der Verkündigung Jesu," *Vom Messias zum Christus,* ed. K. Schubert (Vienna, 1964) 226f.; note 39. On the "coexistence" of old and new ages, see Ts 461 (Index).

subject to a steady growth, so that we must look for a "hidden" and continually repeated coming of the Lord (Gal 1:16; 2:2, 20; 3:4f., 23ff.; 5:5f.; 2 Cor 4:16; 5:2-10; cf. Col 3:3). However, because this takes place invisibly, there will come a day when its present form will end, and the coming of the Lord will be "revealed." In this way, realized and future eschatologies are not opposed as contraries, but rather involve one another.

In this sense the Pauline "eschatology" obviously stands in the background of 1 Corinthians 7. But what is its connection with celibacy? Our new existence is what is determinative for *every* Christian. This general category is described by Paul through various images and concepts: to be born of the Spirit, to be dead and resurrected with Christ, the interior person, the new person, the house from heaven, the first fruits of the Spirit, or simply *pneuma*/Spirit, indestructible, overflowing glory (2 Cor 4:17; 5:2-5), the treasure in an earthen vessel (2 Cor 4:7), eternal life as *charisma* (Rom 6:23), among others. A special group are those images that bring this new reality to expression through a personal relationship: the Christian as the slave and servant of the Lord, as the Father's "son" and Christ's brother, temple of the Holy Spirit. "Kingdom of God" refers to the fact that God is the king of my life; it means a *relationship,* as Christoph Wrembek has ably demonstrated.

Also in this sequence belongs the fact that husband and wife are one body, that the person "is one Spirit" with Christ, is devoted to him in "chastity" like a "pure virgin" (2 Cor 11:2f.) and a faithful wife (Rom 7:4). This means that persons cleave to the Lord with their whole essence, with body and Spirit (1 Cor 6:13-20; 7:23) and therefore must be oriented toward pleasing the Lord in all the areas of their life.

When persons experience this relationship to the Lord in such a way that with regard to their capacity for sexual devotion they find their satisfaction in the Lord and require no other form of expression through a relationship to a partner, they have the charism of celibacy.[707] This style of life is thus a special way *to*

---

707. Baltensweiler, 264, on Matt 19:10ff.: "Unsuitability for marriage for the sake of the kingdom of God does not mean simply celibacy as a sacrifice and renunciation, but rather declares that joy over the kingdom of God can be so great that beside it everything else becomes unimportant, even the

manifest the (inclusive or common) vocation to being a Christian in this world. That is the reason Paul can use it in this case as a symbol for all, in that he also suggests to married people, as regards their relationship to Christ, to orient themselves by the lifestyle of the celibates: to so conduct themselves for the Lord as if not married, "in a certain way celibate." As a matter of fact, objectively speaking, this is an eschatological = ultimate dimension, and to that extent celibacy has a special affinity to the eschaton. However, in itself it is not "eschatological," but only on the basis of the universal nature of Christian existence, which it *manifests.*

Thus one must be careful in the use of this term not to designate celibacy *in contrast* to marriage as eschatological, but rather in *union* with it. For from 1 Corinthians 7:7, 17-24 and Ephesians 5 one could equally well argue that the charism of *marriage,* the capacity and the commissioning for an unbreakable communion in love, is an eschatological sign, because *Christian* marriage as such (later this will be called "sacramental" marriage) *manifests the totality and indestructibility of the love between the Savior and humanity.* For that very reason in individual cases it can function as a rival to the call to celibacy (7:9, 10f., 12, 28, 35f.). And thereby it is for its own part a *sign* for basic attitudes which the celibate Christians can indeed learn from the married, since they themselves do not manifest it in this fashion, but rather live it only analogously (or if you will: they also should live "in a certain way as if married" = in an indestructible love and faithfulness to God *and* humanity). In other words, if Paul were spe-

---

state of marriage." In order to avoid any suspicion of a disparagement of Christian marriage, in place of "can be so great," I would prefer to say: "can be of a type," and in place of "unimportant," "that one may even forsake precious goods such as marriage" (Matt 13:44). This does not exclude the aspects of "sacrifice and renunciation" (Luke 18:28f.; 22:28-30). For Paul, sacrifice, renunciation, and struggle are fundamental categories for the Christian life (Rom 12:1; Phil 1:30; 2:17); this also in response to Kruse, above, note 190. But this is different from being coerced by moral pressure. Besides 7:39, this also comes indirectly to expression in the fact that, in 7:29-34 Paul "encourages" those putting the question. However, the hallmark of an authentic charism is a "certain lightness"—"peace and joy in the Holy Spirit" (Rom 14, 17).

cifically concerned to defend marriage against an excessively high valuation of the celibate state (because people would be seeing the value in the lifestyle itself, rather than in the personal relationship), he could certainly argue the other way around—as many preachers do today—and on the basis of marriage make clear to the celibate: just as spouses love one another in the Lord, in the same way should you also, in your own fashion, mature into a full love for the Lord *and for other people.* This can be a society, a community, the Church, or any other group or friendship. The accent in 7:25-40 indeed depends on the situation; Paul has in mind those who are skeptical about celibacy, and he does not attribute to it any absolute worth.

Thus the so-called "eschatological reservation" *(eschatologischer Vorbehalt)* is in fact a *soteriological reservation.* It proceeds neither from the "not yet," nor from the fact that this world "is passing," which ultimately leads to pessimism. The grounding is not: "everything is going down hill," but rather: "everything is still infected with evil, and for that reason we need distance." In *every* human action we must be conscious of the worldly aspect and for that reason maintain *everywhere* a final distance—thus with the lifestyle of marriage *as well as with the celibate lifestyle.* The latter is subject to its own dangers and does not by itself guarantee holiness or salvation. We have attempted to capture this with the notion of "relativization." Admittedly, this kind of reflection only builds the background and goes beyond the direct statements of the text. The term "eschatological," which does not appear in the text, is normally introduced in interpretations in the form of the imminent expectation and even in more profound studies[708] is usually not separated from the temporal dimension. Still, the reservation should be understood in the context of a theology of salvation.

> From this point of view Neuhäusler's remarks (54f.) are questionable: those called to celibacy have "through the fact that they have heard this call to some extent ended the further continuation of history; they have anticipated their own future." Not by the fact of hearing, but only by their response; but as a matter of fact such an "anticipation" applies in the same way to everyone who

708. See Baltensweiler, 167–172 and 264.

responds to a call from God, including those who respond to a call to marriage! N.: "The celibacy of those called to remain unmarried has erased the future; it is their decision for celibacy which has, in fact, replaced this future." But the same is true for every life of love and fidelity in marriage which is lived out in the Lord (ὡς μή—in a certain sense not having). The "future" lies in the existential dimension of devotion to the Lord, not at the level of signs. Besides that, such a "decision" always takes place "in hope"; it still looks to a "future" of ultimate security, like every other decision by a Christian. N.: "The celibates already stand existentially in the future. They are and remain celibate because in the future eschaton there will be neither marrying nor giving in marriage. Such an anticipation of the future distinguishes their spiritual effectiveness." However, the first is true of every believer, while the second confuses different levels.

The Lord's words "they will not marry" (Mark 12:25 *parallel*) are said in explanation of the resurrection, and indeed they apply to married people (!); they are not an explanation of celibacy on earth. "Eschatologically" one could argue equally that people who have failed to find a partner in this life, will in heaven discover precisely the kind of human companionship for which they have always longed—of course on a different level, as will also those who have been married. In both cases a transcending must take place. That is the reason it is illegitimate to declare the heavenly "being like the angels" as a continuation of earthly celibacy. To those who are resurrected (and that is who we are talking about) no possibility of a (deeper) communion with those whom they loved on earth is denied, but only the possibility of generating new life—in the same way as they are no longer subject to death.

Earthly celibacy on the other hand ought to manifest symbolically in a distinctive manner *one* aspect of the *present* nature of all Christians (namely belonging entirely to God), while marriage illustrates another aspect of this same nature (a steadfast fidelity to God and to humankind). On the other hand, both lifestyles already manifest each in its own way something of our *future* saved condition: our final communion in love with the incarnate Son of God. In that completion naturally *both* forms must be transcended. Still, for the immediate exegesis of 1 Corinthians 7 such references reach too far, because the motif of future existence is not present anywhere in the chapter, even according to the understanding of the text that has prevailed up to now, and according to our results the question of "now" and "later" no longer belongs to this field of association at all. A final reason one should also not overstress the eschatological motif is that there already existed celibacy for God in Israel and even among the "nations" (Kruse, 102ff.).

2. "Service" for the Lord?

The central motive for celibacy lies in one's personal love for the Lord, not in any "service" for him, just as marriage ultimately also has for its primary meaning not any transcendent "purpose" it may serve, but rather the unique, mutual care and fidelity of the two spouses for one another. In 1 Corinthians 7:32-34, such a "desire to please the other" is unambiguously the point of comparison between marriage and the relation with Christ. However, most often in more recent interpretations it is service for the Lord that has been placed in the foreground. But "concern for the things of the Lord" (UT) does mean in fact consent to the *"Lord's desires, so as to be pleasing to him"* (32), and verse 35 does not speak about "uninterrupted service" (UT) or of "putting oneself at the Lord's disposition" (Schlatter), but rather that, like a disciple or a lover, one can remain effortlessly sitting at his feet. Similarly, "to be holy in body and spirit" is also a personal category: *to belong to him, to be filled with his Spirit, to be present to him.* Certainly the fact that one may then serve him through one's activity, and that particularly within his community, is frequently a consequence of this (if it is *he* who commissions it), but this is not thematized at all here.[709]

---

709. Kruse, 105f., takes his point of departure in the "care for the *affairs of the Lord*" makes it equal to "care for the kingdom of God," and characterizes it as a "pragmatic motivation": a human being can "not easily serve two masters, the kingdom of God and one's own family. . . . For a person of active disposition like Paul such a motive—leaving aside the question of whether it is the highest or strongest motive for the renunciation of marriage—would be especially attractive, and the (sensually oriented) Corinthians were evidently not responsive to higher reasons." But renunciation of marriage "for the sake of the reign of God" means precisely in the places referred to (Matt 19:12; Luke 18:29), not a particular *service;* "to desire to

According to our results, Baltensweiler's statement that Paul prizes celibacy in virtue of its function in the life of the community can no longer be sustained.[710] Attention is on the personal relationship and the *joy* that results from it, for this "being with him" *guards against distress.* This is the second accent in this passage, while "working" for the Lord is certainly a recurring Pauline theme (1 Cor 15:10, etc.), but is here not indicated.[711] Paul is entirely preoccupied here with safeguarding the authenticity and purity of the personal relationship with the *kyrios* and with humankind. Also the word *charisma* does not with Paul have the connotation of "service," and even today should not be used

---

be pleasing to the Lord" indicates something that Paul not only lives himself, but recommends to all *these inquirers* (not all the Corinthians are being addressed here), and is something completely different from activism; the being divided "between two masters," however, brings back to life the old misunderstanding of 7:34: "A person who would love both God and his or her spouse at the same time, would be divided" (Kruse, 105)! This misses the point of the text. Admittedly, Kruse at least concedes that there are "hints" that the motive of "pleasing God" lies behind this, and that this is one of "the most basic *theologumena* for Paul"; but this motif stands *at the center* of the entire passage.

710. Baltensweiler, 264: "Paul regards his own celibacy . . . as a gift of grace, by which he means, however, not celibacy itself, but the possibility opened up for him through his celibacy to achieve more for God than would otherwise be allowed him." But where does this stand in the text? Paul is speaking to people who remain with their families. We shall see that precisely celibacy itself is the gift of grace; however, the concept of charism neither means a higher or lesser good before God nor a moral good. This does not contradict what was said above, note 703; cf. further above, A IV 3 towards the end.

711. Even with the "widows" such a moment is not associated; see above, around note 80 and 197f. In 1 Tim 5:14-16 as well, personal devotion to Christ is regarded as primary, and is not subordinated to service to the community; see above, B II 3. One must distinguish this from the fact that in 1 Tim, as a motive for acceptance into the *list* of widows, provision perhaps stands in the foreground. J. Coppens, "L'Appel Paulinien à la virginité," *EThL* 50 (1974) 278, rightly criticizes Legrand, "Saint Paul et célibat," by stating that ἀρέσκειν indicates primarily a matter of "affectivity and attention," but then sets as equally important beside it "the service of Christ" and "apostolic engagement." Indeed, according to our interpretation of 7:32b and 35, nothing of this lies in the text.

to indicate such.[712] If according to our contemporary understanding a full explication of "celibacy for the Lord" would have to include service to humankind, still the primary accent always falls on the personal relationship. The "contemplative" lifestyle thus does not have to be tediously justified, but is rather the essential foundation on the basis of which any active lifestyle must be developed. Thus "service" in the Church can never be the central motive for celibacy, for otherwise the personal relationship, which is here the primary concern, would be compromised and its meaning for worship as the center of Christian life would be lost.

This also serves to illustrate more clearly that what is distinctive to celibacy is not that one has no earthly cares and rather expends oneself in ecclesial service, either missionary or charitable; not even in the fact that "one has more time for God and religious exercises" and thus can attend religious services. Here Paul is thinking of none of this—since at his time celibates remained in their profession and family circle—but rather of the manner and form in which, in all that he or she does, a person devotes him- or herself to God. And here one realm is opened to the celibate which he or she can consecrate to God in a special way, namely, the disposal of the sexual powers, which a married person should consecrate to God in another fashion, namely, "*in a certain way* not having." The distinction between the two thus does not lie in whether they love God or not, but rather in the manner in which one and the same love for God—God is integrally the primary "Thou" of every person—takes shape. It is thus a matter of a quality of the heart, a posture which may be carried through in every form of activity, but which is realized in different ways. For that very reason Paul can indeed identify the specific charism of continence as a model for all Christians insofar as it is characterized by "in a certain way not." This would not be possible if specific external exercises were connected with it. The difference also does not lie in the fact that the one group loves Christ "more" than the other because they belong to him in an "undivided" way and "do more for him," but rather in

712. For justification, see ChuA and "Sprachregelung" as well as below, D VI 1.

the fact that both of them realize and manifest *the same complete, undivided devotion in different lifestyles.*

And this is the only difference. Only for that reason can Paul relativize the two lifestyles and go so far as to hold open the door, or even to encourage, in a genuine spiritual sense, marriage to someone who experiences within him- or herself an inclination to celibacy. In both cases a Christian may, according to what circumstances suggest to him or her, be entirely with the Lord (7:35). Although this passage is most often read as if Paul were devaluing marriage, his concern, especially in 7:25-40, is rather to defend the value of celibacy. Taking as his point of departure the self-evident value of marriage, his desire is first of all to fashion a legitimate position for celibacy, and he then adds that marriage obviously retains its worth. But even this is already a background problem, since the primary intention of his statements in 7:28-37 is simply to explain to married people how the "advantage" of the celibates can also become a protection for them in times of distress.

3. *"Better"—or Easier?*

Here we have only mentioned the specific reason which, for Paul, bestows a *preference* on celibacy: it is good for those who have a calling to it, and *for them* is advantageous. On the other hand, according to him the central motive of love applies equally to both (7:35) and for that reason does not distinguish the two states of life. Here, where the actual difference is mentioned, the language becomes very simple, almost sober and profane:[713] "If you *can* live celibately, *you* have it easier"! We are first surprised, since renouncing marriage appears to us the more difficult. However, Paul is not speaking universally, but only intends to give those who experience a call to celibacy an encouragement in their

---

713. Kruse, 105, believes "that thereby Paul did not hit on the highest motives. For thereby celibacy would be the more comfortable, carefree life." And since Paul probably did not feel "that this reason fitted well with his otherwise more rigorous demands," he "quickly tacked on an explanation: '(understand me correctly here), I mean this, that the time is short.' " Who is supposed to be convinced by this? Besides that, K. concedes that Paul considered celibacy the "easier" way; cf. above, note 190.

decision (if you can . . .), and is not thinking here of the natural, *but of the spiritual person:* persons who experience their freedom in Christ and on that basis feel the possibility within themselves to shape their life with Christ as the sole partner, notice then more clearly how much human bonds can "make demands" upon people—simply because, in the brokenness of our condition after original sin we are perpetually in danger of binding ourselves to one another or of remaining dependent upon creatures, rather than binding ourselves through and with the creature to God. To this extent the person discovers in his or her relation to Christ that Christ has a different way and bestows a much deeper communion and freedom. Such a person notices that in general it is "best" with Christ, but also that on the other hand the world "draws" him or her. Thus they *would* suffer *more,* should *they* marry, from this tension, distress, and constriction (*anagkē*— 1 Cor 7:26), which before they did not perceive with such intensity.

It is thus not about the economic cares that marriage brings with it, also not about the number of tasks in marriage or celibacy—Paul as a missionary had "done more work than all the apostles" and had great demands made upon him through his double calling (1 Cor 15:10; 2 Cor 11)—but rather about the *type* of claim that people and things make on the one concerned, a claim upon his or her person, and at the same time how he or she deals with these claims. Persons who are filled in their heart with Christ feel these claims more intensely, and *in that respect* Paul would like to protect those who did sense an invitation to celibacy in themselves (1 Cor 7:28df., 37f.). For such people celibacy is thus "easier": not for the old, but *for the "new person";* and indeed for the person who has a possibility of following this call. On the other hand, for a person who "burns," celibacy would be "difficult" for the new person, and for that reason he or she should marry. Why God gives to one this charism and to another, another, is not explained. This remains the mystery of God's "distribution" (7:17; cf. 12:7, 11, 28-30; Rom 12:3). In any case, each is directed back to *his or her* call.

One of the most important results of our research is that, according to Paul, celibacy is not necessarily morally the better or more perfect state. Only a superficial understanding could come to this opinion, which nevertheless is very widespread, as if a person would already be a "better" Christian simply by the fact that he or she lives under religious vows. In dogmatic and spiritual theology it was always well understood that the worth of individual persons did not depend upon what position they occupied, but upon *how* they filled *their* place. However, regarded in itself, the celibate seemed indeed to have chosen what was "objectively" better.[714] If you will: in comparison with the married person, the celibate seemed to have received five talents, the other only two. Even if in both cases the talents were doubled and the proportions remained the same, the celibate still seemed to have the greater value. But one may no longer argue this way on the basis of 1 Corinthians 7, for *kreisson* does not lie on the level of value, either subjective or objective, but rather in the area of degree of difficulty. Moreover, the suggestion that for God the more difficult is always the more valuable is a further error that sometimes sneaks in here; in any case, here the more difficult is marriage—and thus this whole construction comes falling down.

> Kruse's statements (108) conceal with great effort the mentality of a (in Catholic circles still rampant) piety based upon good works, right through his concluding sentence: "Celibacy without renunciation or sacrifice would be worthless." Certainly the "credibility of a conviction also depends upon the engagement of its represen-

714. According to Augustine, for this there will be given "in eternal life . . . an especially brilliant glory, that will not be shared in by all who long for eternal life, but only by some. For this, it is not enough to be free from sin. Rather, one must make a vow to the Savior that, although one may omit it without sinning, still merits praise if it is promised and fulfilled. . . . Virginity will have preference," and those who live in the discipleship of perpetual continence "will give to the lofty value of their condition the precedence over marriage, without, however, condemning marriage as evil." This is hardly Paul's world! In an underhand manner, what "for me is better" has been transformed into something "better in itself," with not only a qualitatively different, but also a greater heavenly "glory," which one can only achieve through a particular "work." Has Augustine completely freed himself from Pelagianism here? The incorrect analysis of 1 Cor 7:38 has led to an unfortunate twist in the teaching concerning virginity, which has not been overcome even today. Augustine, *De virg.* 14 and 18, see PL 40:402, 404f.; selection and translation in the Liturgy of the Hours, Tuesday, sixth week in year 1; Basil is different; see below, note 721.

tatives," but if Paul refers in his lists of sufferings to his "deprivations," he does not do so in order to persuade us of the "value" of the life he has led, but rather in order to show that *God* is at work in him (2 Cor 4:7; 6:2ff.). K: In his invitation to follow the way of the Cross, Jesus "was probably thinking primarily of his renunciation of marriage, for he could scarcely have expected his sacrifice unto death generally of others." It is worthy of note that death indeed is common to everyone; the call to celibacy, however, is not. Luke 14:26 only teaches that persons must be prepared to place spouse and life behind God (whether married or not) and to give them up if such is demanded of them, but not to get rid of them on their own. Should they in some sense take away their own life? Obviously it is not said that the "renunciation of marriage" would be "comfortable and easy," but still the traditional talk of a "little martyrdom" is misinterpreted when Kruse writes: "The renunciation of marriage is worth more before God the more it is a sharing in the crucifixion of his Son." It is true that it derives its value through our oneness with Christ, but not necessarily through a higher degree of self-deprivation and pain.

Such an unchristian mystification of suffering (which is entirely different from a love for the Crucified One and a readiness for compassion with Christ) grows from a piety based on good works that appears in other places. Kruse (105): "I maintain that, apart from extreme and clear cases of unsuitability, everyone" (meaning apparently not every Christian, but rather every priest or candidate for the priesthood) "may assume about himself that he possesses the charism (of celibacy), or at least the possibility of acquiring it through prayer, self-discipline, the cultivation of higher interests, etc. If someone develops a neurosis over this" (in Paul: *pyrose,* 1 Cor 7:9), "this is indeed a sign that he does not have this charism, but not that he has never had it." Obviously a person has to cooperate with any charism offered to him or her, but here Kruse embroils himself in a contradiction with the theology of grace he also defends. Nevertheless, he gives clear expression to what many Catholics quietly believe. We have discovered, however, that Paul is of a different opinion.

If according to the widespread interpretation celibacy is "objectively better," then marriage would automatically appear second best to someone standing before a choice between the two. However, for Paul it depends upon the call and the individuals' situation whether *for them* marriage or celibacy would be *kreis-*

son/more advantageous (7:9, 38). Thus, neither one is in itself the better path to salvation nor in itself more pleasing to God (in spite of 7:32-35), but rather only receives a value with regard to the individual person. Only from that perspective can either one or the other become *for them* the particular way in which they are "more pleasing" to God. Thus for many, marriage may be a path to a sober appropriation of their gifts and recognition of their limits (7:8) and of the greater love (1 Cor 7:27a, 36: cf. 13:3) in which, as a consequence, *this* person is *more* pleasing to the Lord (7:35), whereas for such people the choice for celibacy could mean a flight from self-confrontation and responsibility, or a presumption, as the choice for general abstinence would represent for some married couples (7:2-5, 8).[715]

4. Paul and the Council of Trent

But does not our interpretation contradict the Council of Trent? There it says in canon 10 of the Decree on Marriage (DS 1810): "If someone says that the state of marriage is preferable to that of virginity or of the celibate man *(caelibatus),* and that it is not better and happier *(melius ac beatius)* to persevere in virginity or (as a man) in celibacy than to be bound in marriage (cf. Matt 19:11s; 1 Cor 7:25s, 38, 40), let him be anathema." One should notice that here *caelibatus* does not mean the Church law concerning the celibacy of priests (the previous canon addresses that, but not under this category), but rather simply the state of a man who is unmarried (whether in a monastery, as a priest, or simply as single), parallel to feminine *virginitas;* naturally, in both cases with the condition "for the sake of the kingdom of heaven." For the sake of simplicity in what follows we shall refer to both cases as "virginity."

Here two positions are rejected: (1) that the state of marriage is preferable, and (2) that to remain in virginity is not better and

---

715. The command given in Mark 10:21 *par.* is framed in an individual manner: "One thing is still lacking *in you*" and "if *you* would be perfect," leave everything and follow me. To another who would follow him, Jesus says: "Go to your house and family" (Mark 5:19). Does he thereby bar this person—in spite of his desire—from the path to perfection? Cf. Kruse, note 39.

happier than to marry. Thus in the second part of the quotation it is not the *state* of virginity that is elevated above or declared to be better than marriage, but rather it is two different ways of life that are compared: it is better to remain in virginity than to marry. The first thing we must do is to ask whether this statement of the teaching authority contradicts what we have said. One should take note of the fact that the reference to the four passages from Scripture belongs as well to the canon, and thus should be used to interpret and understand its statements.

The canon is certainly meant to be in harmony with the cited passages and does not intend to set itself *above* the Scriptures. On the other hand, it makes no statement concerning the authentic interpretation of these verses, but rather declares that these verses are valid. From the original text it is now clear that Paul does not intend these sentences in a general sense, but rather is addressing them to people who have such a call. One should also presume this implicitly for the council, for the council fathers did not intend to say either that celibacy would be better for every person (such has never been either the teaching or the practice of the Church, and would also contradict 1 Cor 7:9), nor that a person should choose this as a way of spiritual life without a call from God (1 Cor 7:7, 17-24, as well as the general interpretation). With that this statement is relativized, "set into relation" with the personal trajectories of individual people. Even if in fact some council fathers may have been of the opinion that celibacy generally is the better condition, still, the text of the council does not say this. If one asks why it might be better and happier, the texts themselves refer to the mentioned passages from Scripture; however, if it is asked whether these modes of conduct are "better and happier" for those affected *because they have such a personal call,* then following the reflections given above the answer must be "yes."

We still have to clarify whether the deep respect shown to virginity/celibacy by the council is partly based on the belief that objectively it is the "better" of the two. Here we would have to ask whether *melius* indicates an ethical, an ontological, or some other type of superiority, perhaps according to the degree of difficulty. Since the statement is only talking about the mode of behavior, it says only that *for the appropriate people* this *mode of behavior* is "better"; but that evaluation is not made about the state as such or in the abstract. However, ultimately "better" must be interpreted in line with the meaning of the passages cited from the Scriptures. For obviously the council's intent is to strengthen, and not to modify, the Scriptures. Thus, if, as the original text shows, *melius* should be understood not in the sense of *beltion* (that would be morally better), but of *kreisson* (stronger, more advantageous: "better and happier"), and it can be shown exegetically that this intends no higher moral ranking of this mode of behavior in itself, then this is also the background and foundation of this canon—even if the council fathers and many interpreters may have understood it differently. For the *norma normans,* on which they here moreover expressly base themselves, remains the Scriptures. Vatican II says apropos of this topic (LG 42), and basing itself on 1 Corinthians 7:32-34, that with virginity one may "*more easily* devote [oneself] to God alone with undivided heart."

The orientation of each specific act to the divine other, however, now allows room even for a moral evaluation of celibacy. Even though Paul in connection with 1 Corinthians 7 also means to say that the person who remains celibate avoids the "extra distress due to the flesh," which for him or her is "more advantageous," still the thought behind the mixed form of the conditional sentence at 7:28 remains that *on his own* Paul will not say that someone who, although initially desiring a celibate life nevertheless finally married, has sinned. Ultimately Paul refers such persons in 7:7, 17-24 directly to their calling from God: "From the outside I neither can nor will say that in that case you have sinned." As with all the apostolic counsels in this chapter, such a person is still referred to his or her own conscience. On the other hand it is thoroughly conceivable that someone might receive so clear a call to celibacy that this becomes morally binding on such a one.

The balancing of many factors that goes on in this chapter shows that there can be a greater or lesser obligation, and that ultimately each person alone must recognize this for him- or herself before God. Thus it is thoroughly possible that in the concrete it could happen not only that, in choosing celibacy, someone might do something that was *more* pleasing to God, but that, by choosing marriage, he or she might be taking a step that would *not* be pleasing to God (and the other way around). In each case this depends upon the individual and is not based on the nature of celibacy as such. So it is not: "Choose celibacy because in itself it is the better," but rather: "*If* you feel called and stand a good chance of carrying it out, *then* examine your conscience to see if you are allowed to refuse this invitation." Quite a few vocations to religious life in fact follow a course like that. It is thus not a matter of the choice of an "objectively better" "object," but rather of a "subjectively obligating" call—this one this way, that one that way. The decision is not subject to general rules and can only be clarified within the encounter of the individual person with God. We call this discernment of spirits. The only presupposition is that celibacy for the sake of the kingdom of heaven is "in itself" something good.

Certainly one must often, according to circumstances, choose what is objectively the lesser good (for example, when sick, one must remain in bed instead of attending Sunday Mass), but it is exceedingly questionable whether this framework fits our case. Kruse justifies his statement that "the state of marriage is (objectively) a lesser charism" through reference to 1 Corinthians 7:7: "Each one has his or her charism, in this or that way."[716] But such cannot be extracted from this verse. Thus for Kruse the justification (107) remains: "If a person *(ceteris paribus)* could love God equally 'with the whole heart' either by marriage or by the renunciation of marriage, then any commendation of celibacy would rest upon a major error." However, Paul "commends" celibacy in neither so absolute or objective a fashion as has sometimes been maintained. And does the value of something commended consist in the fact that it is "better" than something else? On this point Pia Gyger remarks: "It is not a matter of a *greater,* but of a *different kind* of availability" (654); indeed, each type has its own particular call as its foundation. Kruse's error consists in this, that as a matter of fact there *is* no "under otherwise equal circumstances," because what is paramount is the concrete relationship with God that is particular in every case, with

---

716. Kruse, 104; Zmijewski, 67, concludes on the basis of the redactional development of Matt 19:10 that "the charism of celibacy is greater than marriage," something which, however, does not follow. For even if celibacy is the goal of the entire pericope, this does not imply a lower estimate of marriage.

the result that it is always an individual who stands before the question where *he* or *she* in the concrete circumstances can and should love God "with the whole heart"; this can—objectively speaking—for many be celibacy, *but for others marriage.*

To the extent that, in spite of a good spiritual disposition, some persons have not reached sufficient clarity in a proper decision process about where their call lies, they would be in a position to love God equally "with their whole heart" in one way or in the other. This fits Paul's measured response. Such a situation should not lead us to conclude that persons in this inquiry have received no call and guidance from God, as if God had forgotten them; it could also indicate that the individual concerned has not yet penetrated clearly enough into the spiritual level. Nevertheless, the rule applies: "In cases of doubt, choose the 'normal,' " that is, marriage. While celibacy requires a *positive, distinguishing* clarity, the call to marriage may more commonly be presumed.

The fact that many Christians simply stumble into marriage because they never learned to reach a decision before God does not prove that they could not, with the appropriate disposition, have recognized their "calling" to it. Thus, before one counsels certain young people whom one considers suitable to consider a "spiritual call," one should rather exert oneself to suggest to *all* young Christians to come to their life decision *before God,* and to expect a "calling" *either* to celibacy *or* to marriage. As a matter of fact, many are afraid to enter into such a process because they believe that any intensive reflection will force them to conclude that they should remain celibate. This secret prejudice already indicates how little marriage is regarded equally as a call from God, and also *how great the suspicion against God is,* that God would lead persons down a path that they (unreflectively) would experience from the beginning as making excessive demands upon them.

However, all this may be partly initiated through the insight that "obviously" celibacy is "objectively" better, with the result that, if one truly desires to love God "with one's whole heart," ultimately only this way remains open. For "through his or her renunciation itself, an unmarried person is more pleasing to the Lord than a married person" (Kruse, 106). Thus it often happens that even people who have put themselves through such a process of discernment and have then opted for marriage come out of it with a "guilty conscience" for having chosen what is supposedly only the "second best." Also sometimes people hold it against God that God only bestowed upon them the "objectively lesser" call, while perhaps others out of a false ambition held fast to the "ideal" of celibacy and sometimes only too late come to the realization that it was their own ambition, and not God's call, that prompted them to choose the way of celibacy. Of course spiritual doctrine has always known that all must ultimately be content with the grace God has chosen to give them. However, as long as it was believed—often primarily on the basis of 1 Corinthians 7—that the "state of perfection" had to be defended as the objectively better, married folk had no choice but to be satisfied with the sense of occupying a second rank.[717]

Still, what pertains to the rank order of God's gifts of grace can be found in 1 Corinthians 12. Admittedly there are—from the human point of view—more or less "respectable" members; however, they all receive the same honor and experience the same reality.[718] Certainly they are different; however their objective or subjective higher and lower worth are known only to God who "bestows on each what God thinks good" (1 Cor 12:7, 11). As soon as one charism begins to compare itself, let alone place itself over another—naturally only "objectively"—it has betrayed its nature,[719] or at least posed the wrong question (Mark 9:33-37 *par.*; Rom 12:3; John 21:21f.). *All* Christians are called to perfection (Matt 5:48; LG 39-42), and it is possible in *every* state of life. The only limits are subjective: *"for me,"* more precisely through the natural presuppositions and because of one's own individual call, which admittedly leaves room for a certain lati-

---

717. The Synod of Gangra, 343, says: "If someone defames the condition of marriage and criticizes the wife who lives with her husband in marriage, even if she believes and is pious, and finds fault with her as if she could not enter the kingdom of God, let them be excommunicated. If someone lives unmarried and continent, in the sense that he refuses marriage out of contempt for it and not because of the beauty and holiness of virginity, let him be excommunicated. If someone who remains unmarried for the sake of the Lord, flaunts his or her state over the condition of those who are married, let him be excommunicated." (Quoted from P. Ketter, "Zu 1 Cor 7:28," *Herders Bibelkommentar* XIV [Freiburg, 1937].)

718. Cf. above, A VI 5; EuE 482-485; ChuA 210f.

719. For more details on this, see "Sprachregelung," 31-33.

tude of response, as we saw. The advantage of celibates lies in the fact that (for the inner person) they have it "easier." Further, the fact that Paul recommends continence to young people also on this basis highlights his *spiritual profile* with a markedly sympathetic light.

But the notion of according either a moral or theological "higher value" to celibacy in itself is thereby definitively banished. And in case someone should be shocked or frightened by this, they will, if they look on Christ, experience a liberation like Paul, who became free of the pressure of legalistic piety and experienced his worth solely in trusting God. However, if something within us fights against this, because indeed we have chosen "what is better,"[720] ultimately we will stop before God's grace and learn to rejoice again over the fact that we *all* live equally out of God's grace and that God in no sense has "favorites," but rather leads each one of us ever further along the path that is perfect "for him or her." How many people who are seeking and are "called" suffer under the secret fear that they "must" choose the path of celibacy, because it is supposedly the "better." But the development of love is constricted by this, for ultimately one should only choose this path "in order to please God." In the concrete this means that celibacy would "for me" be the "better" way to God, just as "for another" marriage would be better. This is precisely what the German Synod has stated: "The basic commission of religious life does not constitute in itself a higher way of being a Christian than the universal Christian calling" (Orden 2, 1, 4).

720. Martin Luther wrote in 1521 (*De votis monasticis,* Weimarer Ausgabe 8:604) that one should not regard vows as a path to justification, holiness, and forgiveness of sins, but should approach this state of life in order "to exercise love, to serve the Highest One, to meditate on the word of God, in the same way someone else chooses farming or a craft." And yet, "how many take vows in this spirit? Most people believe that taking a vow is something supererogatory, of utmost perfection, to which nothing else is similar or equal!" Perhaps there were more people than Luther believed who practiced the vows not as described here but in a proper manner; but the danger addressed here (cf. above, note 178) is continually encouraged by a teaching of an "objectively better" status.

5. *"State of Perfection" and "Evangelical Counsels"?*

Thereby the traditional talk of a "state of perfection" and the "evangelical counsels" becomes more problematic. Certainly a person who has experienced a call to continence has the obligation to cultivate those opportunities given to him or her to become a disciple of Jesus; further, a violation of this must be evaluated differently than if he or she had *not* received such a call. Still, does such a person have a "greater" obligation to perfection than any other? Just as talk by those outside about the "state of perfection" of people in religious life can be distorted into an alibi to excuse themselves from the demands properly made upon themselves, in the same way for religious such talk can run the risk of leading them to make excessive demands upon themselves or of having an exaggerated notion of their condition.[721] The gospel calls *every* person to be "perfect" (= whole and undivided) "like the Father in heaven" (Matt 5:48). Even if some receive an especially clear summons to discipleship, this does not mean that a "two-class" system has been set up, as if less were expected or demanded of the others. For "all who believe in Christ, of whatever condition or state they may be, are called to the fullness of Christian life and the perfection of love."[722]

This clarification by the council has still not penetrated the language used to discuss the vocation to celibacy. Moreover, the council avoids—apparently deliberately—the term "state of perfection" (cf. LG 5–6) which in the tradition is indeed applied not only to religious life but also to the bishops. If by that is meant that their obligation to strive toward perfection (and this would

721. This is something Ignatius of Loyola was already warning about; see above, note 178. One may observe a gradual differentiation in Basil: letter 207:4 (BDK II, vol. 46, p. 46ff. and 233). One should notice that the distinction of monks from the multitude takes place through the more perfect fulfillment of the commandments (common to all), not at the level of the counsels (that distinguish them). And Cyprian, *De habitu virginum* 22, invokes the parable of the sower: The martyrs receive hundredfold, virgins sixtyfold, and the remaining Christians thirtyfold. This unfortunately set the pattern for the future. Is not the contemporary crisis in the orders a call for a purification from such hidden biases?

722. LG 40; cf. LG 11 and 42. In a similar direction, Bishop F. X. Eder, "Von der Berufung, die allen gilt," *Anzeiger für die Seelsorge* 6 (1991) 237f.

then mean: to fulfill the universal "commands and instructions of the gospel" and to be faithful to their individual call) is especially serious, then there would be a kernel of truth in this; however, it should *never* be understood as if the way to perfection was open only to them, or as if only *they* were obligated to follow it! Such is rather a right and duty of every Christian. Thus we should be glad that this expression is used less and less.

From these considerations one could draw the conclusion that in that case "it should be possible for everyone to live according to the evangelical counsels."[723] Here we must clearly distinguish the question of content from the question about terminology. We have seen that the Pauline letters provide no basis for speaking about a "state of the counsels," for *gnōmē* in 1 Corinthians 7:25 and 40 means "opinion"; in terms of content, however, Paul "counsels" according to the circumstances, one toward marriage, another toward celibacy, this one to persevere in a marriage, another to separate, one toward being set free, others to the inner acceptance of their social dependency—each one as an individual! One of the most important "circumstances" in this is that all the statements in this chapter are addressed to people for whom continence has become a subject of inquiry in their spiritual life. With all his suggestions, though, Paul ultimately directs these people to the call of God within them, which means, however, to the "counsel" that God gives them.

While the Vatican Council avoids the term "state of perfection," it does speak together with the entire tradition of the "exercise of the so-called counsels" (at least they say "so-called"!) in the "state of life under the counsels" (LG 39, 47). What is referred to here is the renunciation of private property, marriage, and self-disposal within the framework of an ecclesiastically protected community and way of life (LG 43–46). Moreover, a renunciation of marriage entered into outside such conditions, for the sake of the kingdom of heaven, is also included under this. There is agreement over the fact that this must be grounded in the charism of a corresponding calling. The only question is whether one can describe such a call as a "counsel" directed to a single individual, in contrast to the "commands" which are addressed

---

723. Thus Pia Gyger on the German Catholic congress *(Katholikentag),* p. 644.

to everyone. Since later we will have something to say about degrees of obligation, here we will only make some comments about terminology: if "counsel" means a renunciation of the aforementioned goods lived out according to a legal code, then it is certainly restricted to individuals (Matt 19:21: "If *you* would be perfect . . ."). If, on the other hand, one is thinking of the attitudes of poverty, chastity, and obedience, then of course every Christian is obliged to live them.

Pia Gyger uses these terms in the latter sense and defines virginity as "the total surrender to the divine Trinity in Jesus Christ," to which, accordingly, "every person is called" (651). This corresponds to the "in a certain way not having" of 1 Corinthians 7:29f., through which Paul does indeed expand celibacy "in a certain sense" to include also married people. From this Gyger distinguishes *chastity* "as respect and attention to the dignity of people from their deepest center," as well as *abstinence* as "either the temporary or permanent renunciation of sexual activity; it can be voluntary or—conditioned through a situation of either interior or exterior necessity—involuntary, and either with or without the entire dedication of one's life to God" (653). It thus refers to a biological fact (like "continence" in 1 Corinthians 7:5!). While total surrender and chastity as spiritual attitudes should be common to all, Christians differ according to whether they practice these in a marital union or through abstinence.

The traditional language would refer only to the latter as an "evangelical counsel." In this, however, there obviously lies a witness for everyone, so that Bishop Kamphaus can say: "The evangelical counsels, as voices of the gospel in the areas of possessions, power, and sexuality, wish to call us to mindfulness" that these fundamental human drives can be misused (642f.). We find here again the universal invitation which "concerns everyone." For "purity of heart and a non-manipulative freedom between husband and wife do not come about automatically" (Kamphaus, 642f.). Thus, to the extent that the "counsels" contain something that touches every Christian, they would exclude nobody, but rather be something which unites all Christians.[724]

724. German synod, *Orden* 2.1.3: "Every Christian vocation derives its vitality from what have been called the evangelical counsels. The kernel of these consists in the fact that a person lets go of earthly securities and fulfill-

Otherwise, how could those who live according to the "counsels" function as a "symbol" for all? Indeed, according to Kamphaus (642), "the 'more interiorly' people are bound to God, the freer they also are for relations with other people, with the other sex. Along the narrow path between sexual attachment to another person (which for married people is the authentic Christian path) and an anxiety-ridden love of God that for God's sake prefers to reject in a panic the very approach of an erotic or sexual urge, there opens up—in different ways according to God's grace—a space for this falling in love with God which unlocks and frees us as men and women, even for relations of genuine love (without sexuality). For love between persons is more than sexuality; it is, thanks to God's love for us, a love which transcends death. It is particular to the evangelical counsel of celibacy to give witness to such love."

In conclusion, there yet remains the question whether *objectively speaking* this way of celibacy can correctly be described as a "counsel." For what degree of moral obligation does such an invitation from God bring with it?

VI. Toward a Hermeneutic of Apostolic Recommendations

The strong attachment that each person has to his or her own call will lead some to pose the question: Does Christian life not then become very subjective? Now, at the very least one of the "subjects" in this relationship is simultaneously the most "objective" of standards, and the other subject is the human being in his or her specificity derived from creation and salvation, as well as in his or her conscience before God—thus, not the subject conceived in any fashion you like. It is precisely the gospel message that this personal relation to God is not open to general access, but rather protects the individual, just as also it alone imposes a total obligation on him or her. It is here that a person

---

ments for the sake of Christ and his message and to respond to his call, in order to grasp the 'one thing necessary' (cf. Luke 10:42). In its most explicit form, this takes place through the acceptance of poverty, chastity, and obedience." Thus, the "counsels" may be lived by all, if in a "less explicit" way.

finally finds his or her "place," discovers peace and security (1 Cor 1:6, 8; 3:11; 2 Cor 1:21; 5:5, 10). Thus our final question will be, in what fashion does a divine call bind persons, and with what sort of obligation can and should persons bind themselves to it?

1. "Charism" and "Vocation"

Ernst Käsemann speaks of a parallel between *charisma* and *klēsis*/vocation in 1 Corinthians 7:7, 17-24 and argues on this basis that the central statement of this chapter belongs to Paul's doctrine of charisms.[751] Charisma*s* are the "manifestation and concretion" of the one "charism of God" (Rom 5:15-17; 6:23). Since Paul found this term only in the general sense of gift or favor, we may examine how slowly under his hands it was transformed into a technical term. Thus there could exist a certain difference between its mention in Romans 5 and 6, where it is only used in the singular, and its other applications, which allow a plurality. In the first case *charisma* is identical with *charis* as fundamental divine love; in the second case *charisma* and *charismata* have the meaning of specific gifts of grace, "concretions" (Rom 1:11; 11:29; 12:6; 1 Cor 1:7; 7:7; 12:4ff., 31). This would be more or less the difference between grace and gift, between life itself and its functions, between being in Christ and individual activities, between the "gift" which the Spirit itself is and the "gifts" of the Spirit, or as we prefer to say today, between grace and gift of grace. Thus Käseman's position.

In a series of investigations I have showed that *charisma* in Paul is not yet a technical term, but rather still has only the meaning of a (divine) *gift,* while the elements "of a talent / given individually / by the Holy Spirit," and with it the leap from gift to endowment/ability are only more or less discernible after a thousand years. Still, it took until the seventeenth century until, by being tied together with the Scholastic idea of the *gratia gratis data,* further elements were added, like a talent given "that is event/not for one's own salvation / for service to the salvation of others

---

751. Käsemann, "Amt," 114, refers correctly to a similar equation in Rom 11:29; on the following, Käsemann, "Amt," 109-120.

/ for building up the community.''[752] I define as a technical term nowadays: "Charism is an ability or capacity proceeding from God's grace, in each case specially bestowed freely and spontaneously by God for life and service in the Church and the world," and distinguish this from the biblical (almost exclusively Pauline) term, which means simply "gift," without any connotation of "service." It thus becomes clear that celibacy does not derive any sense of service for God from the term *charisma*. Due to the fact that these semantic displacements were not sufficiently clarified in the past, numerous problems of both language and content developed in both Pauline exegesis and modern systematic reflection.

If the divine activity stands at the center of a notion of charism with this dual nature, it can encompass all dimensions of humanity. To that extent every human ability, every good activity, can become "charismatic," that is, supported by grace. But thereby it is not the human deed itself that becomes a "charism," such as speaking or helping, but rather it becomes the place of God's salvific activity. In Scholastic terminology, nature is perfected through grace, but it does not itself become grace. Even though the two orders may penetrate one another, they still remain distinct orders in their origin and essence, proceeding in different ways from God. This means that charism may never be defined in terms of a natural capacity, "from below," so to speak, as in "a charism is a capacity given to a person in their creation, insofar as this is embraced by the Holy Spirit,"[753] but rather the other way around: a charism is the *effect of the Spirit* (this is the central notion) that empowers persons to conduct themselves in a new way, and thereby also uses and informs their natural talents.

As difficult as it may be in the concrete to distinguish this from a "purely human" behavior, it is still important that this distinction be made at the theoretical level. In practice it consists in the difference between unredeemed and redeemed modes of behavior. Admittedly the person is still the active subject, but now with a different "direction and empowerment through grace." In the performance of miracles this becomes especially apparent; how-

---

752. Summarized in "Sprachregelung"; further, above, note 79.

753. Thus, among others, Bittlinger; see "Sprachregelung," 39f.; on the following, see Bittlinger, 39–44 and "Fremdwort," 409.

ever, it constitutes the basic structure of all spiritual life, for example, every act of the "supernatural virtues." Otherwise unspectacular actions would be in their end effect "purely natural," the special nature and norms of the new life would not be preserved, and finally the natural would become the criterion for the possibilities of the spirit. God's saving acts would be restricted by the current limitations of people.

Exactly this would be the case if in 1 Corinthians 7:17-24, *klēsis* on the one hand referred to a person's previous calling or state, and on the other hand were identical with *charisma*. To return to Käseman's presentation, it is here that one detects a clear break in his line of thought (114f.): after he has in fact described "charisms as the gifts of the victorious Christ," he writes: "Then we would also have to count as charisms the things mentioned in connection (with 7:17), namely, the existence of the circumcised and the uncircumcised, of slave as well as free. We are forced all the more to such a conclusion by the fact that, in verse 7, marriage and virginity are presented as charisms," and further, according to Galatians 3:28, "we may add being a man or a woman to this list." Käseman discerns a certain "rhetoric" at work here, but still believes that one must "take the words seriously."[754] His intention is ultimately to say that all these "modes of conduct" are not "as such or from the outset charismatic, but could become so." Although objectively speaking this may be true, the path that leads to this is questionable. Käsemann believes himself bound to it by the usual interpretation of the text. However, since it has now become clear that the middle term *klēsis* does not mean "occupation," but rather "God's call," it is no longer necessary or possible to count circumcision or being a slave or marriage among the gifts "of the victorious Christ"—*and just as little virginity or being free according to the civil code!* Seen in themselves they are all natural realities, they are "nothing" in comparison to the call/gift (7:19; Phil 3:8)—including celibacy. Strictly speaking, they are not themselves "charisms," but rather places where a gift from God can express itself.

With that it is clear that also in 1 Corinthians 7:7 neither marriage nor celibacy is described as *charisma*/gift, but rather primar-

754. For a further discussion of its definition and those that follow it, see "Fremdwort," 412; "Sprachregelung," 35-37.

ily the individual, personal relation to Christ, on the basis of which alone the person can recognize his or her concrete vocation and only then reach a decision: "I would be in agreement if everyone would be like me," but not, however, if they would take me as their standard; for *"each one has a specific gift of grace from God,"* that is, they have received a standard *within themselves,* according to which they should make their decisions. It is not that one is born to be a married person or indeed made by God into a married person, and just as little into a celibate for the Lord; rather, these people *ask* how they should decide.[755] The charism is thus not the condition of either married or celibate life, but rather the graced existence, the spiritual invitation, if you will, in this case also the "capacity" *for the one or the other:* "this one this way, that one the other way."

So it has once again become clear on the basis of systematic reflections that here *klēsis* cannot mean "condition" or "state" (not ecclesially and certainly not occupationally), and that *charism* refers not only to the possibility of celibacy, but also that of marriage,[756] specifically as an invitation and empowerment given within the order of grace that must indeed be something different from simply the natural condition for marriage, which every healthy person already possesses, and also something different from the legally binding status of being already married. Such gifts arise rather from the unpredictable, ever-new spring of the Spirit's working, and are freely and spontaneously given "because they do not exist on the simple empirical plane, but only in the activity of *agape*" (Käsemann). To that extent the "gifts" mentioned in 1 Corinthians 7 in fact come closer to what we today call "charisms": individual vocations which the Spirit distributes "as the Spirit will," and which are thus distinct from redeeming "grace," which God never withholds from a believer. No one can

---

755. Cf. ChuA 209. When Kruse, 104f., complains that the term "capability" no longer contains "an active connotation," he is overlooking the active element that lies in the *use* of the charism (concerning the degree of obligation of which we are now speaking); however, the gift of grace itself does not include the human activity, nor does it compel the latter (1 Cor 14:32). In fact, one can "waste" it (Kruse, 104f.)

756. Cf. above, A II 4 and A III 2 and 3. The explanation of "condition/status" given by the commentaries very often is slippery.

have a claim upon a specific charism; and despite their differences, no one is disadvantaged, but rather each one experiences "in his or her own measure" that God fully loves them and can fully use them. This is a mystery which only God understands.

These "gifts of grace" indeed often have a certain correspondence with purely natural talents, but they cannot be derived from them, and on the other hand often cut across such conditions: "God has chosen what the world considered weak" (1 Cor 1:27). They are integrated as parts within a whole, the body of Christ, and for that reason only mature in this framework. As forms of the actual living of this body they encompass and penetrate all its functions, from the gifts of prayer and liturgical worship to preaching and witness before the world and service within the world, from the variety of human lifestyles (such as marriage, celibacy, occupation) to miraculous powers and the simplest deeds. They are not restricted to service for the salvation of others, in that in Paul the gift of tongues also belongs to them: it is primarily carried out in private, and also in the community is primarily for the praise of God. It is similar with a life of celibacy, whose first meaning it is to be present to the Lord in one's own personal way.

Charisms are not given without conditions; rather, as a call they carry with themselves an obligation. For this reason the question again arises whether the category of "counsel" captures the seriousness and gravity of charism in general, but especially of *this* charism. For charisms determine the unique function of each Christian as a member in the body of Christ; they must then, even if they seem to have a certain duration, be received ever anew and continually responded to as a gift of God that is not under our control.

2. Freedom and Vows

How do persons *behave* toward such calls or charisms? They do not coerce the individual, but are rather an appeal to his or her freedom and open up for the first time the offer of a sphere of freedom in which he or she may say "yes." As we have seen in 1 Corinthians 7 itself, the "spiritual impulses" are often not so unambiguous as in the conversion of the apostle himself, and in any case require some time for their clarification and maturation. It is into such a situation that Paul is sending his helps for decision-making. In the style which he uses to speak to these people one recognizes his assessment and esteem for God's gifts, as well as his respect for the situation and conscience of the individual. After he has presented his view with much concern, twice under the specific qualification that this represents *only his own view,* there comes the *ei mē*/but (7:17), which once again relativizes everything he has said. Whether in an individual case an even longer abstinence or even a separation of married people might be more appropriate, they must ultimately judge for themselves before God; just as whether continence is really possible for the engaged, on which subject he twice declares that he is here only sharing with them his "opinion" (not "counsel").

Paul thus releases believers, after he has guided them with the help of his arguments, into a confrontation with their own individual "calling." The fact that at the end he emphasizes that "I also have God's Spirit," shows how much he realizes that others may well place the accents differently[757]—*also* "in the Spirit." Here he is speaking out of *his own* experience, and about how *he* has experienced celibacy. Thus the contemporary reader should also be ready to receive these aspects of his pastoral presentation with the relativity in which they were initially delivered. To the extent that there is an assessment of a concrete situation in the text, it reflects the considered judgment of a pastoral counselor who certainly is being led by the Spirit, but does not on that account lay down absolute norms of belief, even if his own "opinion" has more weight than empirical "material." Jesus speaks in a more measured way than the impulsive Paul. All the more so can we then take the text as an ingenuous witness of a person who "glowed in the Spirit" and who knew something about the essential laws of the spiritual life. Under the influence of the Spirit many things in fact become light and easy that from the outside appear difficult.

Once the interaction of a divine call and a human response has been addressed, the question must be raised whether the human response to a charism is given always only episodically and in an ever-new fashion, or whether there could also exist therein bind-

757. Phil 3:15: "if you judge something differently"; see EuE 539f.

ing structures. Just as our "yes" to God takes on in baptism an obligatory form, in the same way the vocation to marriage also leads into a secure structure, that indeed was already laid out in creation, but that now in Christ becomes clarified, strengthened, and secured, since it now, as an *unbreakable bond,* presents symbolically something of the redeeming fidelity of God ("as Christ has offered himself"—Eph 5:25f.). Is something similar true of celibacy? To put the question differently: does it contradict the nature of the call to celibacy that the human response may perhaps bind itself fast through a vow?

First of all, nowhere in 1 Corinthians 7 is Paul being questioned about the possibility of a vow, and thus he nowhere answers it. At the same time he takes into account that those posing the question would like to make a fundamental decision, but also that such a decision should mature through a considerable period of time and may throughout that period be rescinded, if for example someone notices that he "is burning," or that their engaged partner is *hyperakmos,* that is, that their desire for marriage is very strong. Neither of these conditions is a function of youth, but on the contrary may surface after quite some time. Thus Paul is presupposing that, even if those asking the question "desire" celibacy, they are still not as fixed on this path as one would be by entering into a marriage. But it does not follow from this that Paul fundamentally rejects the possibility of a vow in this realm. He thinks the Jewish practice of a vow in lesser matters (Deut 23:22) is permissible also in Christian existence (Acts 18:18; 21:24), and naturally acknowledges the practice of a temporary or also permanent vow of abstinence.[758] In our text he is at least assuming that those concerned will at some point come to a basic decision, and thus will not daily question their option for celibacy: "be like me" (7:7), "remain like me" (8), "stay with your respective calling" (7:20, 24), "remain firm in your hearts" (37), as well as the fact that through such a (common) decision, an engaged person is then no longer free for another (39).

This regulation remains in the sphere of a personal spiritual decision, without a legal foundation. However, it will shortly be transformed into an institute for widows and virgins. This de-

758. Cf. Num 30:2-16. "Limited to one or two weeks," Delling, "Geschlechtsverkehr," 819. Cf. also 1 Cor 7:5; see above, note 64.

velopment is primarily guided by the principle of remaining with
that wherein one finds peace before God. To that also belongs:
not in the name of Jesus to disappoint someone who already
through engagement has a certain right, and also not to place
excessive demands upon oneself. The call to abstinence "proceeds
with caution, with respect for those who are involved," neither
hurting those who are called nor the others who are affected. One
almost has the impression that Paul is being overly cautious, for
sometimes Jesus' call does appear as a clear demand. However, in
this connection Paul evidently wishes to avoid any taint of
rigorism—something that again suggests to us that those raising
these questions seemed to him to be in danger in this regard. Also
here it is only a matter of abstinence; a fundamentally different
form of life is not under discussion. Thereby it appears that this
text has another *Sitz im Leben* than other calls to discipleship in
the Gospels or even Paul's call itself (Luke 9:57-62; Gal 1:16;
Phil 3).[759]

Thus the question whether someone should strengthen/consoli-
date their response to a recognized call finally through a promise
or a vow must be clarified by the same principle: "according to
the way God has called him or her." Only such a personal encounter with God can supply the reason for someone to bind themselves in this fashion, with an inner joy and lightness (= spiritual
power) and with the desire to commit themselves to vows as a
sign of his or her loving devotion. Corresponding to this foundation, the obligation is of a different type than that of the institution of marriage. The community/Church can indeed create the
possibility and prepare a space for them to do this, but not more
than that. In the same way a dispensation from such a vow should
be handled differently from the dissolution of a marriage. Both
are obligations before God. However, the moral command which

---

759. If Kruse, 103f., from the eunuch-logion ("they have made themselves into eunuchs") for disciples attempts to derive "a promise to God
(or to Jesus)," than it is overstated (indeed, Matt 19:12 is not directly applied to the Twelve) and the same applies to his assumption that in the early
community "celibates were in the majority" (111), even if, in agreement with
him, I suspect "that after Jesus' resurrection the apostles did not return again
to their families and households" (110), but rather continued the new patterns of life. Cf. above, note 702.

Jesus reestablishes, "Thou shalt not separate" is anchored in creation, while a "vow" is something freely established by human beings. One should note the difference between a calling and a vow. Indeed, some spiritual communities live without vows. However, *if* a vow is to be made, it is made to God (Deut 23:22; Num 30:6, 9, 13).

Thus the question arises whether under certain circumstances God releases a person again from such a "contract." One thinks of the Church's practice of a commutation of vows. Where for an individual the line should be drawn between careless action and coercion or moral pressure cannot be answered generally. As to Paul's position, one may only say that even the option for a vow should not mean that individuals lose the character of their charism or their gift. If indeed this attitude is fundamentally lost, this can lead to paralysis and hypocrisy.[760] It is thus a question of spiritual discernment when and where the legal obligation of a vow has the effect of supporting a spiritual decision. If it has not been interiorly accepted, but rather enforced because of external pressure—whether this be through inappropriate universal standards or an improper application of a proper standard—then it has not been true to its purpose. It then becomes unspiritual and certainly no longer corresponds to that respect for the conscience of the individual that we noticed in 1 Corinthians 7.

In any event the ecclesial community must conscientiously oversee the administration of vows. For example, it can happen that the maintenance of a vow may also be enforced legally when the individual has interiorly renounced it. The reason does not have to be an interior deterioration; it may also lie in the fact that the one affected has reached the conviction that he or she made a wrong decision and thus basically never lived out what is spiritually intended by such an obligation to God (somewhat analogous to a deficiency in one's capacity or intention to marry). And here again the reason may be either a personal immaturity or that, through a one-sided theology, spiritual narrowness, or an unsound asceticism, one received false criteria by which to make a decision, such as the opinion that "in itself" celibacy is the more perfect, or that what is more difficult is always better. Then the question must be asked: were one's personal relation to Christ,

760. Cf. again above, note 178.

as well as joy and peace in the Holy Spirit, the central criteria for the decision, or did objective reasons and utilitarian considerations predominate (a better opportunity for service)? Are young people who today are confronting this question sufficiently clear that "in itself" marriage can be just as good a means of dedication and total discipleship to Jesus? Before such an alternative, a genuine spiritual recognition as to which one is preferable for me, and by which way *I* may be more pleasing to God, may mature in far greater interior freedom.

It often happens that people who are considering such a decision also feel pressure from expectations emanating from their environment, to such an extent that they no longer experience the spiritual freedom of choice to acknowledge interior aversion or to strike out in peace along another path. The verdict that one has "not persevered," however, makes the path toward the correction of a wrong decision especially difficult for many; such a narrow-minded judgment by many Christians who consider themselves pious has nothing in common with the interior freedom that we found in 1 Corinthians 7. In such an environment it is more difficult even to remain *in freedom* with a decision that one has firmly established through vows. Even if one would *no longer decide the same way,* one must still have been able to accept them, precisely because *celibacy and marriage do not represent absolute values,* but are only two presentations of the same mystery. We thereby open up a new path to the declaration of the Council of Trent according to which, together with a vow, God also gives the strength to maintain it (DS 1809).

Nevertheless, the fact that today comparatively many Christians are not able to carry out or maintain their vows raises a question not only about the individuals concerned, but at the same time a question concerning the general climate in the Church, which evidently encouraged wrong decisions and provided too little spiritual freshness and freedom to the forms of celibate life. Just like an individual, so also a community and the Church as a whole can overtax itself. In that case there would then prevail a spirit of rigorism, and no longer the Holy Spirit.

On the other hand, Paul would certainly not treat cavalierly a vow of celibacy, but rather earnestly inquire of the person: "How seriously do you take God and the word you have given to God?"—just as Jesus asks Peter: "Do you love me?" And this is the other question that must be raised within the contemporary climate in the Church: are we really prepared to put God first and to carry out authentically our dedication to God? If such can be lived out in convincing fashion by married Christian people, could this not be an incentive to celibates to proceed in fidelity along their own path as well?

3. Priestly Celibacy

Thereby the question is raised to what extent the tying of priesthood to celibacy in the contemporary Church corresponds to the concrete guidance of the Holy Spirit. As in the life of an individual, so also in that of the Church as a whole, spiritual joy and peace are telling indications of whether a decision agrees with the concrete call of God for this time. In this endeavor both the reaction itself of those affected, as well as the judgment of the faithful, the *sensus fidelium,* should be treated as sources of insight. It is thus a matter of carrying through a process of spiritual discernment in the Church, not simply of particular opinions forcing themselves through, whether they be of a progressive or a traditional stamp. Those occupying positions of spiritual authority must in addition make sure that they honestly foster this process, and not, because of their position, simply "impose" *their own* view and thereby transform themselves into "rulers and masters over the belief" of their fellow Christians (2 Cor 1:24). Only if all are prepared for a new conversion will they be able to hear correctly what the Spirit is saying today to the communities.

The Second Vatican Council does not speak with a single voice on this matter; on the one hand it speaks of the "precious gift of divine grace . . . [of] virginity, or celibacy . . . [that] has always been held in particular honor by the Church as being a sign of charity and stimulus towards it" (*eximium donum supremaque probatio caritatis*—LG 42); on the other hand, of the "law of celibacy [which] must remain in effect" (LG 29). More pointedly OT 10: "students who, according to the holy and fixed laws of their own rite, follow the revered tradition of priestly celibacy should be very carefully trained for this state." Is not this language already suspicious? Certainly a charism must be protected and built up, but that is something different from taking on oneself "a fixed law" and a "revered tradition," especially when in the same breath it is said that they should recognize "the superiority (!) of virginity consecrated to Christ." It would be more appropriate to say: they should examine themselves to see whether *for them* God has intended celibacy to have "superiority," so that thereby *they* will be more pleasing to God. The recognition of such a personal call is, however, made the more difficult if it is presupposed as a requirement for the priesthood. A "legal solution" of this question runs the constant danger of demanding, rather than fostering, a charism (from the person? from God?). As long as there were sufficient vocations to celibacy, it seemed suited to function as a principle of selection; perhaps too little attention was devoted to the question whether it ran contrary to the person's individual call and reduced the dimension of personal relationship to the dimension of a "work." Furthermore, one must question with what right other callings, which are also from God, were suppressed. I am thinking in comparison of the lively, dynamic callings in many free Churches. What has the law of celibacy *not* allowed to come to fruition?[761]

Thus, if today many young people feel a call to the priesthood, but not to celibacy, it should be seriously considered whether this is not a working of God's grace.[762] If on the other hand many candidates force themselves at great effort to accept celibacy as a necessary price *out of their love for the priestly vocation,* this should give grounds for concern. For the more clearly one acknowledges and esteems the value of abstinence for the sake of the kingdom of God, the more clearly one must see that this should only arise from an inner joy and special kind of *love for God as God's self.* Otherwise precisely one's personal relation to God and other people will be intolerably burdened, and this can lead to serious spiritual damage.

---

761. Evdokimov, 240, finds it "highly significant that at the First Ecumenical Council (of Nicea), the most ascetical wing wished to establish priestly celibacy under the pretext that the celebration of the sacred Liturgy and of the Eucharist was incompatible with married life. It was Bishop Paphnutius, himself a monk and one of the most severe ascetics, who brought about the decision of the council that commanded priests to be married."

762. To this the voices of women must be added, such as Thérèse of Lisieux or Edith Stein; cf. above, close to note 585. Similarly Vogels, see bibliography.

One should not say: "No one *has* to be a priest." The individual's sense of responsibility is here underappreciated, if on the one hand he experiences a clear call to place his life entirely in the service of the proclamation of the gospel, but does not perceive the other calling, and is candid about acknowledging it. Is God's call really leading him into a kind of schizophrenia, or is it rather that the Church, if such cases become comparatively numerous, should ask itself whether this does not consitute a sign of the times? At the very least it should review its standards and criteria before God. Is it legitimate to keep many from "fashioning their lives as God directs them" (7:17), especially if at the same time there is an objective dearth in the communities and the faithful quite justifiably are expecting people who will "administer the divine mysteries"? Do the practice and witness of the entire remainder of Christendom, including that coming down in the Eastern Church from its very beginning, then have so little weight that for a part of the Roman Catholic Church the question of "married priests" is not open for discussion? It is not only individuals who may be afflicted with a false and (un-)spiritual certitude.

Even if those affected—communities who have no priest, and those called—attempt to bear honorably what is thereby laid upon their backs, the question remains whether this indeed comes from God in the sense of the individual's personal call and the community's guidance. And do not also many priests who in a moral dilemma have given up their priesthood bear part of the burden of the Church community? They are and remain members of the body of Christ with a specific commission, and often enough they contribute through their suffering, if they accept it as their share in Christ's Cross, to the whole Church's recognition and acceptance of the clarification process described here. On the other hand, if the faithful do not take the plight of their brothers and sisters seriously, they then do not take themselves seriously.

The entire Church must thus reexamine its criteria and exert itself strenuously to remove all force as well as moral or legal pressure from the pursuit of spiritual goals, and must give up any false guarantees. A person in a position of authority discerns the activity of the Holy Spirit beyond the Scriptures and the teaching of the Church not only in his or her own person, but just as much by attending to the many faithful who "also have the Holy Spirit" (to adapt 1 Cor 7:40). And instead of saying: "if there are currently so few vocations to the celibate priesthood, we must then pray God to give us more again," it would indeed be more appropriate, honest, and thereby also spiritual to first ask which vocations God *as a matter of fact has already given* and how we have received them. The best preparation for future gifts is always to accept and use thankfully what one has already been given. Is this only valid for individual spiritual counseling? Only if the Church as a whole follows this criterion will the prayer for vocations to a celibate life be properly based. It can then be placed alongside the prayer for Christian families, and beyond that also the prayer for the corresponding charism for priests and also for teachers, doctors, politicians, social workers, those responsible for science, technology, the economy, and indeed for Christian men and women.

In 1 Corinthians 7 we found no support at all for tying a person or a service to celibacy outside of this type of call itself. From this one cannot fashion any argument against an institution tying celibacy and priesthood together, but also indeed none *for* such. Moreover, it may be demonstrated that *any* kind of pressure stands in contradiction to the Pauline outlook. This is all the more apparent in the results of our studies of 7:6f., 16, 20, 24-40. This makes it all the more painful to hear such arguments as: the Church is easier to lead with a celibate priesthood, that such a clergy is a better guarantee of unity, that economically it is easier to maintain and easier to deploy, as well as having more time for service. Such pragmatic considerations, but also presumed numerical projections in one case or the other,[763] or appeals like "the communities want to have the priest undistracted (all to themselves?)" are basically shameful because they are out of place.

Such secondary motivations serve to frustrate and distort the specific nature of personal dedication as it is present in celibacy.

763. On the question of priesthood, the German synod, *Dienste und Ämter* 5.4.6, sets as the most important element "the Church's pastoral care." In this regard one should keep in mind that the tasks that are today part of the priesthood could be parceled out in different ways, so that the celebrations of reconciliation and the Eucharist at least might be more accessible and leadership tasks could be discharged by various parties. In this we are thinking not only of the situation in Latin America, but the danger that many pastors in Europe are running of being overextended and turned into bureaucratic functionaries.

As a matter of fact, in this inner forum of one's relation with God, nothing else has a right to play a role. Does there not sometimes lie hidden behind all this the temptation to protect the gospel by some other means than the gospel itself? And if this is also combined with the notion that celibacy "in itself" is the better and more perfect state, we then are dealing precisely with that temptation against which Paul was fighting in 1 Corinthians 7: the tendency to regard abstinence or celibacy as a means of salvation, and not to look at it in relation to each person's own calling (7:7, 17).

4. Apostolic Directives and Conscience

With that we come finally to the question of what degree of obligation attaches to the individual *recommendations of the apostle* and to *God's call.* Baltensweiler finds in 1 Corinthians 7 a fivefold progression in "seriousness of Paul's instructions" (188): "*thelō*—I would like" (according to our results: I agree); "*legō*—a statement; *gnōmē*—opinion*" (as in our interpretation!); "*diatassomai*—his own prescription; *parangellō*—order, the Lord's 'command.' "

Schürmann[764] distinguishes generally in Paul between "transcendentally" and "categorially" oriented values and directives. The first "articulate in their fashion basically the demand of loving total self-dedication," the latter "make concrete demands which relate to particular areas of life or particular actions and which—in varying degrees—also impose an enduring obligation." Among the latter one may distinguish "spiritual" (Gal 5:16) from (in the narrow sense) "moral" directives, among which moreover many "are formulated in a very general and abstract way (for example, righteousness, willingness to work)," while others "add up to specific norms for action." Among the latter he lists: 1 Corinthians 11:2-16 (now: do not let down your hair), 7:21-24 ("remain a slave"; more correctly: "prefer" to be set free, but do not fall apart if this is impossible), 11:2-16 with 14:33b-36 (subordination), "three cases that are generalized and repeatedly paraded out in support of the thesis that all of Paul's values and

764. Schürmann, "Wertungen," 241–258 and 265; similarly Schürmann, "Verbindlichkeit," 107f.

recommendations, at least the concrete norms for action and individual instructions of a particular type, are historically relative, can be dismissed in advance as conditioned by their times, and therefore non-binding and subject to hermeneutical challenge." The investigation that follows leads him to the conclusion that: "The more concrete the values and recommendations become *materialiter,* the more should their universally binding nature be questioned."[765] There are two questions raised here: that concerning the area of applicability, and that concerning the weight of a recommendation. In the process we should pay attention not only to the theological question of "correctness," but also to that of the transmission from one subject to another.

W. Wolbert approaches 1 Corinthians 7 (18-20, 24, 39) from the point of view of a moral theologian. He makes a formal distinction between parenesis and normative ethics. "Parenesis includes the forms of ethical speech that urge a moral command or prohibition, that either counsel one toward a form of behavior recognized as morally required or warn one against one recognized as morally reprehensible, that either condone or disapprove of a deed already done according to its moral worth, either praise or reprove the person concerned, in all of which it is presupposed that both the subject and the person addressed concur in their judgment about the action at hand." Thus, it is a matter here of strengthening a "moral *good*" that is already appreciated as such. "On the other hand, normative ethics is the effort to *discover* by some process of reasoning what the correct behavior might be in the current situation." Its purpose is therefore to remove uncertainty in our knowledge. One of the few Pauline

765. Rahner, "Priestertum" 296f., demonstrates that a "practical maxim of conduct" can stand "in objective contradiction" to "universal and fundamental moral principles," without this being noticed or being able to be changed. Indeed, if particular presuppositions "may only be changed through an immoral use of force, the opposing concrete maxim may be morally obligating." In everyday life, the question would be whether something has to be done now or not. One thinks of specific modes of conduct within the family, or in religious obedience: it can here be the case that in the "concrete," God desires something from me that "in itself" God would not impose. However, God "desires" that I accept my situation of being historically conditioned. God did not "desire" the Jews to condemn the Son; however, God *did desire* that Jesus accept the unjust judgment.

examples of the latter would be parts of 1 Corinthians 7: 1-16, 32-40 (where Paul is answering specific questions), next to the parenetic sections 7:17-24 and 29-31.[766] However, are there not many texts in Paul in which he does not simply presume certain moral norms as recognized, but which on the other hand he does not attempt to justify with arguments; he simply "presents" and to that extent "transmits" them (as in 7:17a)? One need not invent a third category to handle this type, but simply take parenesis in a wider sense: the "presentation" of immediately comprehensible norms and/or the "urging" of recognized moral norms.

The two distinctions introduced by Schürmann and Wolbert do not coincide, for both transcendental and categorial values, both general and specific norms can contain a justification for their moral correctness[767] and/or a reminder/appeal to their goodness, even if the transcendental directives are to be found *more* in a parenetic situation and the categorial directives "should be assigned more to a normative ethic." To that extent these categories are helpful only for grasping more sharply the specific intention shaping a text. As formal structures, they provide no information on the obligatory status of a demand, but only that with categorial values it is more likely that under different circumstances the formulation of the directive must also change. It thus contains at most more elements of uncertainty. However, "other things being equal—*ceteris paribus*—a Pauline recommendation, like every other moral judgment, is valid "for all time." For that reason, Wolbert refines the abovementioned rule of thumb of Schürmann: "A concrete judgment, if it is correct, is just as obligatory in itself as a universal judgment." Only, "the more in detail a directive describes a given situation, the more,

766. Wolbert, 77, 92f.; 106f.; 115; 121; 126; 131; 133f. 1 Cor 6:12-20, on the other hand, is not only paranesis (Wolbert, 60–63), but unambiguously "normative." See above, A V 1-3.

767. Wolbert, 204f., speaks of the morally correct only in categorial directives *(kategoriale Weisungen)*. We must understand this as meaning that it only becomes fully clear in the concrete what, for example, fidelity or mercy means in the here and now. And Schnackenburg, "Argumentation," 35, emphasizes that an authentic ethical foundation for the New Testament directives is also contained in the specific New Testament paraclesis. But still, by what criteria would one recognize such a "foundation"? On these questions see also my review of Wolbert, *ThPh* 57 (1982) 284–286.

in the application of this directive to a new situation, must the relevant factors be taken properly into account when fashioning a new judgment,'' and corresponding to this, if the situation warrants, ''a decision may be reached that deviates from the wording of the directive.''

Schüller reminds us of the well-known ''two types of ethical principles: on the one hand those which would still be valid under all conceivable circumstances, and from which accordingly no exception is allowed; and on the other hand, principles which under normal circumstances, that is, in the normal course of affairs, are valid.'' More precisely: ''The first principles are valid independently of any type of contingent conditions'' (e.g., ''always treat people fairly''; ''love God with your whole heart''; love of neighbor as being ''well intentioned and disposed toward him or her''); principles of the second type are valid ''only under a specific contingent condition concerning which, however, one may add that in most cases this is fulfilled.'' It can however happen that a higher value competes with the second type of principle, and then the priority must be given to the higher value. Schüller's ''hypothesis'' runs: ''Every ethical norm that concerns what we must do and what we may leave undone with regard to our fellow humans and our environment, can only be a particular application of this *universal rule of priority.*[768] Thereby ''what we must do'' refers respectively to the *concrete application* of basic attitudes like wishing others well, and so on, from which naturally one is never exempt.

Thereby the point of our questioning becomes indeed more sharply delineated. Most difficulties in coming to a decision and in the ''passing on'' of norms of conduct in other areas of culture derive from the fact ''that the contingent conditions under which a moral judgment is valid are not sufficiently appreciated.'' Such should be suspected especially if the ''application to a new type of situation leads to results that disturb our spontaneous moral consciousness, or perhaps even lead to feelings of anger.'' If this ''hypothesis'' is valid, it would have far-reaching consequences, for example, for the question of divorce, consequences which, moreover, converge with our results.

---

768. Schüller, ''Problematik,'' 2 and 4; on ''divorce,'' 18–23.

Furthermore, this distinction helps us not only to understand what Paul is saying in 1 Corinthians 7:10-16, but in the entire seventh chapter generally, and elsewhere. For herein we have more precisely expressed what we suggested by the "principle lying behind" 1 Corinthians 14 and 11.[769] Thus the obligatory status of a directive is not less simply because it is formulated concretely, but rather primarily because the presuppositions under which it has validity have changed.[770] The difference may depend upon whether a value occupies a central or a peripheral position[771]; however, it can also stem from the fact that the person giving the advice does not understand the circumstances precisely enough to be able to make a final judgment. The latter is the case at several points in 1 Corinthians 7. In the process, fundamental (= universal) statements and their concrete application continually overlap:

> 7:1-2: It is indeed correct that restraint is becoming to a man— but then be careful about the danger of improper relations!

> 7:3-5: You belong to one another—however, abstinence may be practiced if you are in agreement about it, for a specific time, and for the purpose of prayer.

> 7:8-9: In itself, such is good for you—but if they are burning, then not.

> 7:10-11: They should not separate from a spouse who is a believer (this is the Lord's will; especially strong certainty)—but if they do, then do not marry again.

> 7:12-14: In itself, *they* should attempt to remain together with a spouse who is an unbeliever—but under the assumption that this is all right with the partner.

> 7:15-16: In principle, God intends unity (= that you strive for such)—however, if the *nonbeliever* will not have it, then *he* may leave.

> 7:27-28: If you detect an impulse toward abstinence, remain engaged or, in the event that you have already broken off the

769. Cf. above, around notes 117f. and after note 322.

770. In that case one could speak with Baltensweiler of a differentiated "weight" to directives; see above, the beginning of this chapter. However, Baltensweiler intends this probably more about the variable emphasis which Paul himself gives to his instructions.

771. We saw an example of this kind of "comparing" by Paul himself in Phil 3:16: EuE 539. Cf. again above, D II 2.

engagement, do not seek another woman—but if you marry . . .
(that is: if you can, remain alone; and yet I do not know your
call and circumstances).

7:36-37: If the bride has a strong desire, you have an *obligation*
to marry her—however, if she is agreeable to abstinence, follow
the wish of your two hearts.

7:39-40: She is free to marry—however, if she remains (or can
remain) unmarried, she will be better off.

The second half of each sentence gives a limitation or a condition for the validity of the universal first statement, and the concrete decision is always left to the individual; and by "decision"
is meant in the first place the *judgment* about what has priority
in each case. To that extent these sections should be addressed
as aids to decision-making. They constitute a recommendation
or a counsel, and never say directly or immediately what the
individual should do. It is different in 1 Corinthians 6:12-20;
11:2-16; 14:33-35, where a specific action (of central or marginal
nature) is either forbidden or commanded without naming a
condition—which presumes, according to our reflections, that the
respective conditions are widely and sufficiently recognized. First
Corinthians 7:10 appears to constitute a kind of exception. But
what does this consist in? Not in the "absolute validity of a formula," but rather: (1) As an historical saying of Jesus, the universal statement has a particular authority; but 7:3 and 15 also speak
about divine commands. (2) The demand also contains, despite
apparent exceptions, a negative restriction: do not on your own
initiative seek to separate—but if it has happened, repent and be
reconciled. In that is revealed so to speak the "hard core" of the
prohibition against divorce. Finally it may be said of all adaptations (and thus for the second members in our presentation) that
God always shows an individual how the respective universal formula should be applied in their own situation. The apostle merely
offers a support for this and marks out limits in each case.[772]

772. It should become clear on the basis of Schüller's formulation that
this does not encourage a "situation-ethic bottleneck" (Furger), because the
decision respectively rests upon objectively given presuppositions. Similarly
Furger, 24–26; Schnackenburg, "Argumentation," 40–45. For the rest, the
distinction between universal and charismatic vocation should be kept in mind
here (see the following).

For this reason between the particular directives stand the universal statements that name the highest or final criteria in each case: "to each, as God enables them" (7:7, 17, 20, 24), "in all things to be pleasing to the Lord" ("not" or "in a certain way not" having: 7:29-34), "noble practices and temperament" as well as "relatively easy communion with the Lord" (7:35). On this basis rite/cult, social position, abstinence within marriage, married or celibate, engaged or single, become "relative."

Thus, next to the variable weight of the matter, the degree of obligation in our context is not determined so much through a formal index—"a formulation of the divine will through a historical word of the Lord or through an apostolic kerygma"—but rather by the fact that Paul does not know precisely the relevant circumstances and also cannot know them in all their details. Here he recognizes the irreplaceable autonomy of the judgment of conscience by the individual, to which as an apostle he extends help and criteria, but whose results he does not presume to determine. For this reason, to these questions he can and will offer only "recommendations," nothing more. However, as we have seen, these "counsels" in 1 Corinthians 7 have a quite varied content, and can in no way be reduced to a "recommendation of celibacy."

Thus the theological concept of so-called "evangelical counsels" does not belong among the various types of Pauline advice or "opinion"—among which a valid counsel to celibacy in certain circumstances is only one among many—but rather in that space in which the individual in his or her conscience knows him- or herself to be called by God. But after our reading of 1 Corinthians 7, what sort of meaning could such a concept have? The ambiguity returns in that Paul presupposes that God calls people in different ways and thus "counsels" one person to celibacy, another toward marriage. If a person who has a "call" to marriage[773] were nonetheless to choose celibacy (perhaps because it was supposedly the "higher"), that person would thereby abandon the status of the "counsel" (given to him or her), and *vice versa.* Admittedly, along with the terminology a whole system of concepts would collapse, since traditionally by "evangelical coun-

---

773. 1 Cor 7:7, 17-24; thus, not on the basis of a personal or external necessity (7:9, 36), but rather as an authentically spiritual, "charismatic" calling.

sels" we mean the lifestyles of celibacy or religious vows. Concepts have their own history, which one can not simply do away with; however, we should at least notice that the path from 1 Corinthians 7 to this terminology was possible only through some misunderstandings, and for that reason we should avoid this expression as much as possible.

5. "A Supererogatory Act"?

Here there is much to say: May one place the "call" to marriage so easily on an equal footing with the "call" to celibacy? Is the degree of obligation to follow the call perhaps less in the second case?[774] May not the tradition use the term "counsel" to express *this* aspect? In any event we can discover no grounds for this in 1 Corinthians 7, since indeed each should follow "his or her own call." However, such a call becomes "binding" for individuals to the extent that they recognize with certainty that this *is God's will for them*. In this process, the necessary or sufficient degree of "moral certainty" that an individual should reach may be extremely varied. In practice it is helpful to refer to the insight that, in cases of doubt, the exception—that is, celibacy—requires a greater certainty than the "rule" of marriage. Moreover, where uncertainty remains, the obligatory status is reduced *for this reason,* not because the subject of this decision could not be obligating *from its very nature*. For in that case, how could one draw a line between this and the contents of other decisions? For example, are there acts involving love of neighbor which, *by their very nature,* God could never make binding upon the individual conscience?

---

774. Strictly speaking, one should compare the "obligation to (this) marriage" and the "obligation to follow this call (to religious life)." However, the question is not posed this way; also not whether the vowed state is more binding, but only whether a person should follow the call to celibacy *or not.* If a "status in the commandments" is placed in the scales against this, then it is not marriage that is the counterweight, but rather the indispensable moral commands (among which for a Christian, in contrast to a Jew, there is no longer a "duty" to marry). Thus with the "status of counsels" it is not taken sufficiently seriously that a Christian who will be married also needs a "call" to marriage, since he or she should marry "in the Lord."

Some may object, however, that Paul himself says: "If you marry, you do not sin" (7:28), and this *even though you detect a certain inclination towards celibacy,* as precisely our own interpretation has made clear. Thus it would never be a sin if a person evades a personal invitation of the Lord to the celibate life, but marries instead; and consequently this is only a "counsel," and "not a command" (7:25). Really never? Even the traditional spiritual doctrine held that there can be cases in which a person in conscience is obligated to a celibate lifestyle. Is it then for such people more than a "counsel"? It is likely that the real problem lies deeper. Thus Schüller (Rat, 205) writes that many "Catholic moral theologians, precisely in the name and interests of freedom, believe they should intercede for the ethical categories of the merely advised and permitted. However, one can no longer pursue such a goal as soon as one realizes that it is precisely the unconditional moral demand by which a person is transported into the freedom of decision, and that consequently the freedom of the human will is interiorly constituted by its relation to this moral demand—which indeed for this reason should be defined as freedom for moral obedience, or freedom for moral freedom." Freedom is thus an interior moment of *every* genuine call from God, whether it be through a universal command or through a personal calling.

We are here penetrating more deeply into the real substance of the supposed "command—counsel" opposition. On the one hand there are moral principles intended for everyone, among which some are valid "under all circumstances," others under specific conditions; but then indeed "under the same circumstances they are equally valid for all." On the other hand there are personal callings that cannot at the outset be deduced or extracted from one's circumstances (although one must take these into account—for example, one's suitability for a certain lifestyle), but that instead could be different for different people under objectively the "same" conditions. This is indeeed what is specific and unique to those callings that "the Spirit distributes at will," and that we today call "charismatic."[775] Only in this way can the

---

775. Does ethics not perhaps too often keep its eye on the universally valid moral requirements, and dismiss prematurely whatever is personal as a "counsel"?

"radicality" of Matthew 8:21 *par.* be understood. "Let the dead bury their dead" is a call to a specific person in a specific situation, not a general command to the living never to bury their deceased relatives. If you will, it is a "charismatic" call to discipleship, not unlike the call to the rich young man (Matt 19:21 *par.*). Something like this cannot be universalized; for that reason it is also not true that everyone who would be perfect should actually sell everything they own. However, for those called, it may be that, in the course of a weighing of goods, the concrete "claim of belief on the value of discipleship," that is, in a specific manner, will have the priority (Furger, 27). Whether this will be a moral demand, and thus the "concrete will of God for the individual," depends not so much on its content, but rather on the type of call. In this way a "charismatic vocation," which is always individual, *may well also be* morally binding.

If many Christians do not experience marriage as a spiritual vocation, this is probably due to the fact that they have not consciously penetrated with the corresponding impulse into that (often implicit) space of spiritual reality, partially because it has not been opened up for them properly. And the fact that vocations to religious life are often answered in inner freedom and moral obedience is due to the fact that such impulses receive a serious spiritual examination, not because the object of such choice necessarily suits the subject's fancy. Certainly there are many decisions in which a Christian receives no clearly perceptible guidance through a "call." However, any persons who seek to clarify pressing questions "in the Lord" will recognize that they should follow whatever *insight* they are given, and that in this way they finally recognize HIM in the *ordo bonorum,* and this means: they judge morally.

> Such "everyday" recognition may naturally not only be a logical conclusion (which Wolbert very strongly emphasizes), but rather is often a type of existential intuition. It is also not only a *natural* moral awareness that is *in principle* accessible to *all people,* and that neither formally, since it is only possible under the light of the Spirit, nor materially, as if out of the new relation to God no new moral imperatives could develop, such as missionary or charismatic commissions. Here I would like to join Schürmann ("Wertungen," 268 and *passim*) in registering doubts concerning a tendency within moral theology that places "the accent dispropor-

tionately on the side of rational recognition." "Paul would certainly have been surprised if someone had said to him that a naturally reasonable morality was hermeneutically the only legitimate and binding horizon within which to understand his counsels and directives." But this would be a separate topic. Illumination through grace follows its own laws. It does indeed always lead to an illumination of the understanding (even if frequently it does not begin there, but rather in a person's unconscious), but rationally grounded argumentation is *only one* form of knowledge which, moreover, can never fully reflect the light bestowed on an individual, and cannot deduce charismatic vocations. Karl Rahner speaks of a "logic of the existential recognition of the charismatic divine impulses."[776]

Many decisions or completed weddings and ordinations remain uncertain in their status because the person affected has never advanced to the point of a full basic decision that consists *in that specific case* in a "total surrender" (Schürmann). Admittedly there is here always a "remainder." We have explained an "unconditional moral demand" primarily through "such a genuine call from God." Is this not an extension of the term? Are there not "invitations" from God, a gentle calling, that do not immediately present themselves with the character of an obligation? Here we are indeed once again on the Pauline border between "law" and "belief/faith." The law makes its demands "unconditionally," an invitation to love carries with it no sanction. However, is it for that reason less "unconditioned"? I would rather say that because of its defenselessness it makes an even stronger moral claim. And this is especially true for the basic moral demand to love God with one's whole heart. This "demand" first makes itself really felt when it comes forth as the inviting call that reveals itself in the loving surrender of God's self. The category of "command" is not sufficient for this reality. If one experiences oneself touched or enticed by this love of God, he or she then enters the very center of morality, to the extent that if such do not respond at this level, their "guilt" can be even greater. For perhaps they are then refusing a "vocation" that has for its content something of a very individual nature and which could never be

776. K. Rahner, "Charisma," *LThK,* end, with reference to his article by the same name in F. Wulf, *Ignatius von Loyola* (Würzburg, 1956) 345–405. See above, D III 1.

demanded of everyone, as the "Ten Commandments" can be. If he or she declines here, they could be thereby robbing the Church or the world of an important vocation. Thus one cannot set up strict borders, as if there were specific contents that in themselves determine whether something was a "counsel" or "above and beyond what is required by duty." Here, rather, the saying applies: "To whom much has been given, from them much will be demanded" (Luke 12:47f.), or in Pauline language: "Each according to his or her own measure."

With that we would be back once again to the principle that neither marriage nor celibacy "in itself" is better, but rather "one of them could be better for me, and the other could be better for you." It is self-evident that besides this, within the many goods of human existence, there is often a freedom of choice, and a person may decide between various goods. This is true not only when the goods in question are "not moral" or pre-moral goods, but is also partially a matter of the extent to which God transforms the objective goods for the individual subjectively into a place of God's calling, and this means a personal encounter with God's self; expressed differently, it depends upon how "indifferent" they remain for the person. To learn a mathematical theorem is in itself morally indifferent; however, in the concrete it may be morally demanded. Thus, where one person might properly "select" one among other objects, another may perhaps have no "choice," since for them in certain acts their relationship to God is at stake. In such a case, values that "in themselves are not commanded" might become *for them* "unconditional moral demands," or we should rather say, "the inviting revelation of the love of God," which they cannot reject without guilt. By stressing the distinction between counsel and command, do we not tempt some to complacency and apply pressure to others, which then frequently entails a covert pride for the one, and a permanent inferiority complex for the other?

Thus Schüller's "reservations concerning the ethical categories of counsel and of supererogatory good works"⁷⁷⁷ should be

---

777. Schüller, "Rat," 197, 203f. and index VIII; Schüller, "Problematik," 9; Müller, *Gesetz und Freiheit* (Düsseldorf, 1966) 61–75. I discovered a first indication of such thinking in the *Shepherd of Hermas, Sim.* 5:33: "If you do something above and beyond the Lord's command, you will win

underscored from both the pastoral and exegetical perspectives, and from the exegetical also because the objection just formulated on the basis of 1 Corinthians 7:28 rests in fact upon an erroneous understanding of the text. For Paul does not say generally: "Any person who, in spite of another calling, marries, does not sin," but rather: "However, if *you,* in *your* situation, should then come to the decision to marry (naturally after having considered your situation before God), *then I will not say* that you have sinned!" We here see how significant the grammatical idiosyncrasies of this "mixed form of a hypothetical condition" were.[778] As so often happens in this chapter, Paul again makes clear that he neither can nor will make any statement concerning this matter, but rather that the decision remains with individuals "in accord with their calling"; nor does he immediately thereafter revoke this principle.

However, this statement is only indirectly contained in 1 Corinthians 7:28. Indeed, Paul is not inquiring about motives; his goal is something different. He steers toward *thlipsis* and intends to distinguish this "distress" from "sin" (the missing *men*): I do not say "sin" (for that you must examine yourselves before God), but rather "distress due to the flesh" (which admittedly is a consequence of sin working itself out in the "world"). Paul thus leaves the ethical question open and does not say that the vocation to celibacy "cannot bind under pain of sin." In 7:36 on the other hand he describes a case so unambiguously where a moral obligation to marriage does exist *(opheilei)* that he can say directly: such a person *does not sin* (in the indicative) namely against a "vocation" to celibacy. This at least allows us to surmise that he *also* considers it possible for one to sin against such a call to celibacy; in any case, however, he anticipates such a question from those making the inquiry.

From these results we can refine Schüller's "Remarks on 1 Corinthians 7" ("Rat," 208): not only from v. 9 but from the entire structure of the chapter it has now become clear that Paul "does not hold that a celibate life is from *every* point of view

---

for yourself abundant reward." However, there is as yet no notion of a "higher calling" or a "divine counsel." Neither one is present in Scripture—although both are present in Augustine; see above, note 714.

778. Cf. above, note 154.

better than married life and for this reason is to be preferred in all circumstances. . . . It may be that (some) have to make their decision from standpoints from which marriage must be held to be the better form of life.'' Thereby ''one is given to understand, at least by way of inclusion, that, in a choice between different forms of conduct, one has set up only one criterion of judgment among other (possibly) equally relevant value criteria, in any case not the criterion that could provide the decisive factor to every conceivable choice,'' that is, ''according to the categories of good and bad.'' This means: by such criteria alone a choice would not yet be morally qualified, or its value ''before God'' would thereby not yet be established.

Here is said in different words what we expressed through the ''relativity'' of different forms of life, since in themselves they are not efficacious for salvation, and since celibacy, even for the sake of the kingdom of heaven, is not already in itself objectively better. However, we could go further and say: this ''better'' about which Schüller is speaking, Paul does not even have in mind in the concrete individual case as an ethical judgment, as if it would be morally better for these concerned to remain celibate; rather *kreisson* and *kalon* there only refer to greater facility and avoidance of distress. Nevertheless, Paul intimates that such may well at some time involve a moral decision for the individual when he says: ''Each, as God calls him or her.'' The claim that such a charismatic call can never in an individual case have binding power, could now hardly be seriously maintained, and in any case could never be demonstrated.

6. The Degree of Obligation

Paul is a pragmatic person. Here he reflects no philosophical or theological categories, nor does he develop an ascetical system of ''counsels and commands,'' but rather proceeds phenomenologically and describes events in the spiritual life—a performance which nevertheless stands up to systematic examination. He is aware that there exists a kind of call which a person should not evade (Gal 1:16; 2:9; 1 Cor 9:16), although the person retains the possibility of doing so. Paul is also aware that in practice a person often disposes over a considerable area of free response, in which only slowly a decision may grow to maturity. Thus, if Paul warns one and encourages another to attempt the path of celibacy, this is because behind this lies Paul's conviction that often persons only discover while on the way how God is leading them (Phil 1:6; 3:15f.; John 8:31), but that on the other hand individuals will come to sufficient clarity, if in trust *(pistis)* they carry out such steps as are possible for them.

This also corresponds to the way God bestows charisms: persons can and should make their own efforts to receive them (1 Cor 14:1, 12-20, 39). Especially our interpretations of *"thelō/ I agree"* (25), "rather use" (21), "to give one's opinion" (25), "bound" (27: engaged), "care for" (28d), "without anxiety" (32), "according to their usefulness" (35), and the "freedom with regard to the wishes of your own heart" (37) show how large a person's freedom to maneuver is, and how a person can only come to clarity ultimately through personal encounter with the Lord (7:17, 20, 24). That this is no legalistic demand,[779] but rather an encounter in trust and love in which the person seeks to "please" the Lord and as far as possible "to be with the Lord without great struggle" (32-35), freed from any false pressure or compulsion created by a so-called vocation, also applies to this command. For this is also the way universal moral demands are presented in the New Testament. Wherever they suppress or constrict people, this atmosphere is destroyed, and therewith the plane of love, of an "unconditional promise of salvation," and of the gratuitous gift of grace that a person can accept in freedom, is lost. For it is characteristic of the unmistakable charismatic vocation, which demands "totally" of a person, to have this spiritual freedom as its characteristic mark, a freedom that is still fully compatible with enormous effort by the "outer person" (Gal 5:1, 13; 2 Cor 4:16).

How an individual should treat a call which he or she experiences as a clear demand, as a mild invitation, or simply as a possibility, requires other criteria and cannot be directly resolved through the category of "counsel." A superficial Christian could seek in the doctrine of counsels an excuse for evading the total surrender that nonetheless is being asked of him or her. A concern to distinguish between counsel and command must admit-

779. For example, to earn for oneself thereby a better place in heaven; cf. again above, note 777.

tedly fight off any tendency toward rigorism.[780] This would have to occur in some other fashion, but it must be in a way that does not spare or postpone for the individual a direct confrontation with a personal call, but which rather guides him or her toward such. For it is not only the question of celibacy that is being debated, but rather every individual vocation, the concrete shape of all areas of one's life, as well as the conflict between the realm of conscience and ecclesial jurisdiction.[781] In continuity with the apostolic recommendations, the rationale for any ecclesiastical legislation can only consist in supplying help and support for a deeper spiritual reflection and for fidelity to the truth as recognized.

It may be that, from the standpoint of ecclesial order, many decisions may appear to fall in a "border area." From God's point of view, however, there are no "border areas," but rather always the individual person who has to come to a decision within the framework of one's own circumstances, and to the latter belong also ecclesial regulations and advice; a person who, however, before God is not simply delivered over to these "laws," but rather preserves an ultimate uniqueness and immediacy. The fact that this freedom of conscience can be misused, and often is misused, alters nothing in the fact that it is a gift from God to humanity, and for that reason must be respected by the community of the faithful. Expressed in Pauline language, ultimately what is decisive is not "being judged by you (the community!) or by a human court"; rather, "the one who judges me is the Lord" (following 1 Cor 4:4).

The one who is writing this knows full well that the community has to make judgments concerning its own members (1 Cor 5:3f., 13). At the same time, such a verdict touches only "the body,"[782] it achieves an order of the "outer person" (should we not say for the external order: the *external forum*?), while it is God alone who "searches hearts" (1 Thess 2:4). The human attempt to bring these two orders as far as possible into coincidence, which means in practice to shape the external regulations to ac-

---

780. Schüller, "Rat," 197; on the misuse of ethical norms, see Schüller, "Problematik," 12f.

781. Cf. in the context of the question of divorce, above, D IV 3-5.

782. Cf. above, A VI 3.

cord as far as possible with universal moral principles and also the radically individual judgments of conscience, is legitimate, but can become a danger if it is exaggerated. It is true that Christians have the task of keeping this discrepancy as small as possible, so as neither to impose inappropriate burdens nor to leave individuals struggling with their decisions without the corresponding helps, nor to hem them in improperly; however, these two realities can never in this world be brought into full alignment. Otherwise morality becomes either mired down in regulations or trivialized by arbitrariness. Therefore the tension between these two poles belongs to the very life of the Church, in such a way that the external ordinance derives its life from the energetic conscientiousness of individuals, so that Paul, after all his recommendations, ultimately refers the individual to God.

Thus the degree of obligation does not derive from the object under consideration, but rather from the "seriousness" of a reality, which may be determined from the degree of clarity and from the power of the spiritual call that is received, from the personal conditions and the external situation (if you will, the spiritual inclination, suitability, as well as confirmation through circumstances and competent advisors/representatives of the Church). In conjunction with these factors judgments have to ripen and be taken in all areas of Christian life, even down into social and political matters (7:21f.). Because of the tendency of external regulations to harden and resist change, this realm of free maneuver, in which individuals may follow their conscience without anxiety or pressure, and can bring this decision to a conclusion, must continually be recreated in the Church. Any attempt to establish or safeguard belief or morality through pressure ultimately produces the opposite result because it smothers the heart of the Church, the personal responsibility before God. The two poles require one another; neither stands by itself or rests upon the other; rather, each must remain open. Canon law (as the community decision) as well as the individual conscience must remain flexible and alert to the ever-new working of the Spirit, who alone supports and guarantees them (LG 8). Thus ultimately the Church is a mystery of faith.

Therefore we should distinguish:
(1) between *unconditionally* valid norms of conscience that per-

mit no exceptions, and *conditionally valid ethical rules of behavior* (the first are primarily basic attitudes, e.g., to maintain marital fidelity, while the latter concern particular concrete actions, such as choosing a condition of life);

(2) not between a "command" to be a Christian directed to everyone, and a "counsel" to perfect discipleship intended only for a few, but rather between the *universal vocation to total dedication,* and the *charismatic vocation* to live out this complete dedication *according to the art and manner bestowed on each,* such as in marriage or in celibacy. Therein "charismatic" should be understood in the specific contemporary sense that also includes all the "simpler" charisms.

(3) The question about the intensity or the *degree of obligation* of such a vocation is something different. Both types can be either *very clear or only extremely vague and unclear.* Basically a rejection of God's will is always sinful. However, from what point and to what degree the individual is guilty *(formaliter)* depends primarily on the clarity and the unconditionality of the call. This path is often prepared by many indications and gentle invitations. What is decisive is how far the individual encounters the living God (expressly or anonymously) in his or her respective concrete appeal. Ultimately each person must request and receive a recognition of his or her obligation and guilt from God. While it is true that the basic obligation, namely, "to believe," has the greatest weight, still, a charismatic vocation, whether to marriage or to celibacy, is not something with which we do as we like, but is rather an obligating commission (think of Jonah!) and not merely a "counsel" or possible object of choice.

(4) An important and necessary *help toward clarification* in such decisions of conscience, whether it be to the faith in general or to its particular charismatic expression, is the *community of the faithful with the pastoral office.* Besides the proclamation of the Good News directed to everyone in various ways by witness, brotherly and sisterly fellowship, pastoral direction with spiritual discernment, through canon law and the authoritative decision of its officers, it has to protect and foster its members' *personal relationship with God* and the formation of their consciences. It is also important for the salvation of all humanity, even those outside the Church, how this is lived out.

Paul shows in 1 Corinthians 7 in exemplary fashion how the individual's conscience and apostolic authority, as well as the building up of conscience within the community, make up a living dialogue, and how precisely the Church comes into being through this interaction. Through the results of our translations the refinement of the apostle, whereby he steps back in favor of an encounter of the Lord with the community, has become clear. Paul believes the individual capable of recognizing what the Lord communicates to him or her, and thereby of discovering the one who never presents himself as a rival to earthly values or to human love, but to whom *every* Christian can and should give full, undivided love, whether this be by "having no partner," or whether it be by "in a certain way not having"—ὡς μὴ ἔχων γυναῖκα.

Conclusion

Paul—Open to God's New Ways

Fatigued perhaps by our long and twisting journey, we may now look back upon a transformed landscape. The interior world of the Apostle Paul is spiritually broader and more profound than its conventional presentation. Also in the area of sexuality he is the messenger of the Spirit and the apostle of freedom, bound by the love of Christ.

This basic feature of his nature shines through in 2 Corinthians 5:13f. After he has expatiated eloquently on God's glory and power in his own weakness, his conclusion: "If we were outside of ourselves (it was) for God, or if we are *moderate and level-headed* (it is) for you; for our love *for Christ* holds us together," gives us the correct attitude and teaches us modesty:[791] There are two agencies that move the process of human spiritual maturation forward: on the one hand the *dynamic* of the Spirit, which by keeping its gaze upon God opens new paths and occasionally sweeps people along with it (this is a kind of *ekstasis*). On the other hand there is the love *for* Christ, that is, for the community (2 Cor 4:5; 1 Cor 12:12, 27); that means Paul pays attention to people's historical limitations and is careful not to pass over any developmental step. In all this, it is not as if love has to rein

---

791. Similarly Eph 5:21; cf. above, B I 1. Thus not: "the love of Christ presses us (forward)" (UT). Also in Phil 1:23, συνέχομαι is more passive: "I become pressured = cornered."

in the Holy Spirit; what we have is a twofold work of the same Spirit, experienced by unredeemed humans as tension in unity. For God's Spirit that is poured out upon us spontaneously a-wakens powers in people that must first be purified so that they may not misuse or distort what is divine (2 Cor 12:1-10). However, the purifying power is a "love that holds together" (2 Cor 5:14), which the same Spirit bestows: reverence before the laws of growth of nature and grace. Only in this way can individuals be liberated to their true essence—although admittedly still in the brokenness that characterizes our earthly existence.

This tension is experienced especially clearly in the domain of sexuality. Here also it is true that the Holy Spirit liberates powers of love in people; the Spirit does not suppress sexuality. The Holy Spirit leads toward an integrated personal love that is specifically not under any compulsion to act itself out. Out of this there develops marital and celibate chastity in equal manner. A rigoristic suppression, like a careless attitude or obsession, are signs that other forces are at work here, whether it be human immaturity or the power of evil, perhaps in the form of a sophisticated spiritual deception. For devaluation and overestimation of sexuality both come down to the same mistake, for in both cases a person remains by him- or herself and does not progress toward the ordering center of a loving relationship. A redeemed love, on the other hand, keeps everything in its own place, or better: it allocates to each thing its place. For Paul at any rate sexuality is entirely taken up in the process of salvation, without either a puritanical constriction or a libertine abandon. In the holistic encounter with the divine "Thou" become human, persons are instead liberated to their capacity for relation and expression, and empowered either to make use of this faculty or to leave it—"as it may please the Lord." For Paul, therefore, a healthy spirituality and a healthy sexuality stand in a mutual relationship.

If we regard the history of the influence of these texts from this perspective, and the struggle of Christianity to discover a redeemed form for sexuality, we sometimes find the accent placed on one side, sometimes on the other. We should guard ourselves against judging or condemning previous centuries, but may be thankful that we can now liberate many of the Pauline statements from the interpretations laid upon them. Precisely thereby it becomes clear that we gain access to this spiritual freedom only through the *Pascha* door of the death of the old person and the resurrection of the new.

Not only the individual alone, but the entire Church must endure this painful process of maturation. In which direction is the Spirit guiding it today? In addition to a respectful attitude toward the vocations of both marriage and celibacy (one that is free of anxiety and free from any secret pressure, but at the same time is prepared to appear strange to the world), we must above all rethink the relation of the sexes within the community. Paul's apparent hostility towards women has been revealed as a complete misunderstanding. On the contrary, he is a man with a great sympathy and understanding, and within Judaism stands with those who plead for woman's equal rank. Admittedly, he remains constrained within the ancient model of society, and is attempting to find what is appropriate under these circumstances. However, precisely for this reason he would today counsel us toward what our altered circumstances, respect for one another, as well as a distinguished high-mindedness suggest to us. And just as one can find in his statements no foundation for a law of celibacy, but rather an admonition toward an integrated and unburdened love (1 Cor 7:35), in the same way he provides no theological reasoning against equality for men and women. After a consideration of the uniqueness of his style of argumentation it becomes clear instead that the door is open not only to a greater responsibility for women within the Church, but also, as far as he is concerned, for women also advancing to the priesthood—although he never directly considered this question.

Admittedly this does not yet decide the questions which today stand before us, and it remains an open question where the freedom to which Paul entrusts us is leading us, for he himself emphatically refers us to a process of spiritual discernment. For this, however, the same laws apply for the Church as a whole as for the individual. Where gloominess, narrowness, and tension reign, stiffness and a spirit of we-have-to-get-through-this, protest and revolt, there God's Spirit has not yet spread its light. Rather, the Christian community as a whole must trust that, in these questions as well, it is being led by the Spirit, even if this be often through a painful growth process. We should be able to raise all questions without fear—overcoming our narrowness. God's answer, however, then consists in "peace and joy in the Holy Spirit," who ultimately in a conciliar process will point the way toward a substantial consensus and new interior unity among the Christian people. Our new view of the Pauline letters may contribute toward such, for *this* Paul opens up new possibilities.

Bibliography

Books and articles which are mentioned only once are cited in the respective footnotes. See also Schwertner, above, footnote 9; similarly for the authors of antiquity.

Bachl, G. *Der beschädigte Eros. Frau und Mann im Christentum.* Freiburg, 1989.

Balch, D. L. "Backgrounds of 1 Cor 7: Sayings of the Lord in Q; Moses as an Ascetic *ΘΕΙΟΣ ΑΝΗΡ* in 2 Cor 3" *NTS* 18 (1972) 351–364.

———. 1 Cor 7, 32–35 and Stoic Debates about Marriage, Anxiety, and Distraction." *JBL* 102 (1983) 429–439.

Baltensweiler, H. "Die Ehebruchsklauseln bei Matthäus. To Matth. 5, 32; 19, 9." *ThZ* 15 (1959) 340–356.

———. *Die Ehe im Neuen Testament.* Zürich, 1967.

Balz, H. and G. Schneider, eds. *Exegetisches Wörterbuch zum Neuen Testament I-III.* Stuttgart, 1980–1983.

Barret, C. K. *A Commentary on the First Epistle of the Corinthians.* London, 1971.

Bauer, W. *Wörterbuch zum Neuen Testament. 6. völlig neu bearbeitete Auflage, herausgegeben von K. und B. Aland.* Berlin, 1988.

Baumert, N. "Zur Begriffsgeschichte von χάρισμα im griechischen Sprachraum." *ThPh* 65 (1990) 79–100.

———. "Charisma und Amt bei Paulus." *L'Apôtre Paul.* Ed. A. Vanhoye. Leuven (1986) 203–228.

———. "Charisma—Versuch einer Sprachregelung." *ThPh* 66 (1991) 21–48.

———. *Ehelosigkeit und Ehe im Herrn. Eine Neuinterpretation von 1 Kor 7* (fzb 47). Würzburg, 1984.

———. "Das Fremdwort 'Charisma' in der westlichen Theologie." *ThPh* 65 (1990) 395–415.

479

_____. *Gaben des Geistes Jesu. Das Charismatische in der Kirche.* Graz, 1986.

_____. *Dem Geist Jesu folgen.* Münsterschwarzach, 1988.

_____. "Geistliche Gastfreundschaft (1 Petr 4, 7-11)." *Weite des Herzens, Weite des Lebens.* Eds. A. Bilgri and M. Langner. FS O. Lechner. Regensburg, 1989.

_____. "Die Gnadengaben in der Kirche." *GuL* 51 (1978) 245-260.

_____. "Impulse zur charismatischen Erneuerung unserer Gemeinden." *Gottes Volk, Bibel und Liturgie im Leben der Gemeinde.* Lesejahr A 1. Stuttgart, 1986.

_____. "Jesus Christus—die endgültige Offenbarung Gottes—Biblische Sicht." *Ist Christus der einzige Weg zum Heil?* Eds. K. Müller and W. Prawdzik. Nettetal, 1991.

_____. "Zur Semantik von χάρισμα bei den frühen Vätern." *ThPh* 63 (1988) 60-78.

_____. Täglich sterben und auferstehen. Der Literalsinn von 2 Kor 4, 12-5/110 (StANT 34). München, 1973.

_____. "Zur 'Unterscheidung der Geister.' " *ZKTh* 111 (1989) 183-195.

Beinert, W. "Maria in der Feministischen Theologie." *Catholica* 42 (1988) 1-27.

_____. "Die Impulse der Mariologie für die Theologische Anthropologie (I und II)." *Anzeiger für die Seelsorge* 98 (1989) 74-76 and 156-159.

_____. *Unsere Liebe Frau und die Frauen.* Freiburg, 1989.

Betz, H. D. *Der Galaterbrief. Ein Kommentar zum Brief des Apostels Paulus an die Gemeinden in Galatien. Aus dem Amerikanischen übersetzt und für die deutsche Ausgabe redaktionell bearbeitet von Sybille Ann (Hermeneia Kommentar).* München, 1988. English: *Galatians.* Philadelphia: Fortress Press, 1979.

Biser, E. *Der Zeuge. Eine Paulusbefragung.* Graz, 1981.

Blank, J. "Zum Problem 'Ethischer Normen' im Neuen Testament." *Concilium* 3 (1967) 356-363.

Blass, F. and A. Debrunner. *Grammatik des neutestamentlichen Griechisch.* Bearbeitet von F. Rehkopf. Göttingen, ¹¹1979.

Bornkamm, G. *Paulus.* Stuttgart, 1969.

Boucher, M. "Some Unexplored Parallels to 1 Cor 11, 11-12 and Gal 3, 28: The NT on the Role of Women." *CBQ* 31 (1969) 50-58.

Brooten, B. J. "Zur Debatte über das Scheidungsrecht der jüdischen Frau." *EvTh* 43 (1983) 466-478.

_____. "Konnten Frauen im alten Judentum die Scheidung betreiben? Überlegungen zu Mk 10, 11-12 und 1 Kor 7, 10-11." *EvTh* 42 (1982) 65-80.

Brox, N. *Der erste Petrusbrief* (EKK 21). Zürich, 1979.

Bruggen, J. v. *Die geschichtliche Einordnung der Pastoralbriefe*. Brockhaustal, 1981.

Bruns, B. " 'Die Frau hat über ihren Leib nicht die Verfügungsgewalt, sondern der Mann . . .' Zur Herkunft und Bedeutung der Formulierung in 1 Kor 7, 4." *MThZ* 33 (1982) 177–194.

Brunsman, B. . . . *das darf der Mensch nicht trennen? Neue Hoffnung für geschiedene Katholiken*. Zürich, 1986.

Bultmann, R. *Der zweite Brief an die Korinther* (KEK 6). Göttingen, 1976.

Cartlidge, D. R. "1 Corinthians 7 as a Foundation for a Christian Sex Ethic." *The Journal of Religion* 55 (1975) 220–234.

Chersones, P. v. "Ehescheidung in der Theologie und im Kirchenrecht der Orthodoxen Kirche (Orthodox)." *Wie unauflöslich ist die Ehe*. Eds. S. David and Schmalz.

Closen, G. E. *Die Sünde der "Söhne Gottes" Gen 6, 1-4. Ein Beitrag zur Theologie der Genesis* (Scripta Pontificii Instituti Biblici). Rome, 1931.

Collins, R. F. "The Unity of Paul's Paraenesis in 1 Thess 4, 3-8. 1 Cor 7, 1-7, a significant Parallel." *NTS* 29 (1983) 420–429.

Conzelmann, H. *Der erste Brief an die Korinther* (KEK 5). Göttingen, 1969.

Cornely, R. *Commentarius in S. Pauli Apostoli Epistolas. Vol. II: Prior Epistola ad Corinthios* (Cursus Scripturae Sacrae NT). Paris, 1909.

Countryman, L. W. *Dirt, Greed and Sex. Sexual Ethics in the New Testament and Their Implications for Today*. London, 1988.

Dautzenberg, G. " 'Da ist nicht männlich und weiblich' Zur Interpretation von Gal 3, 28." *Kairos* 24 (1982) 181–206.

_____. Ed. *Die Frau im Urchristentum* (QD 95). Freiburg, 1983.

_____. *Urchristliche Prophetie. Ihre Erforschung, ihre Voraussetzungen im Judentum und ihre Struktur im ersten Korintherbrief* (BWANT 6/4). Stuttgart, 1975.

_____. "Zur Stellung der Frauen in den paulinischen Gemeinden." Ed. G. Dautzenberg. *Die Frau im Urchristentum*.

David, J. and F. Schmalz, eds. *Wie unauflöslich ist die Ehe? Eine Dokumentation*. Aschaffenburg, 1969.

Delling, G. "Ehebruch." RAC.

_____. "Ehegesetze." RAC.

_____. "Eheleben." RAC.

_____. "Ehescheidung." RAC.

_____. "Eheschließung." RAC.

_____. *Paulus' Stellung zu Frau und Ehe*. Stuttgart, 1931.

Denzinger, H. and A. Schönmetzer. *Enchiridion Symbolorum Definitionum et Declarationum de Rebus Fidei et Morum.* Freiburg, ³²1963.

Dibelius, M. *Die Pastoralbriefe. Neu bearbeitet von H. Conzelmann (Handbuch zum Neuen Testament* 13). Tübingen, ³1955.

Ebach, J. "Frau II. Altes Testament." *TRE* 11:422-424.

Eichholz, G. *Die Theologie des Paulus im Umriß.* Neukirchen-Vluyn, 1972, 278-283.

Einheitsübersetzung: Die Bibel, Altes und Neues Testament, Einheitsübersetzung. Stuttgart, 1980.

Evdokimov, P. *Die Frau und das Heil der Welt.* Moers, 1989.

Fascher, E. "Der erste Brief des Paulus an die Korinther, I. Teil." *Theologischer Hand-kommentar zum Neuen Testament* 7/1. Berlin, 1975.

Feuillet, A. "Der Sieg der Frau nach dem Protoevangelium." *Communio* 7 (1978) 26-35.

Fitzer, G. πορνεία, πορνεύω. *EWNT* III, 328-333.

Fitzmyer, J. A. "The Matthean Divorce Texts and some new Palestinian Evidence." *TS* 37 (1976) 197-226.

―――. "Glory Reflected on the Face of Christ (2 Cor 3, 7-4, 6) and a Palestinian Jewish Motif." *TS* 42 (1981) 630-644.

―――. "A Feature of Qumran Angelology and the Angels of 1 Cor 11, 10." *NTS* 4 (1957/58) 48-58.

Fuchs, E. "Die Herrschaft Christi. Zur Auslegung von 1 Kor 6, 12-20." *Neues Testament und christliche Existenz.* FS für H. Braun. Eds. H. D. Betz and L. Schottroff. Tübingen, 1973.

Furger, F. "Ethische Argumentation und neutestamentliche Aussagen." *Ethik.* Ed. s.K. Kertelge. Pp. 13-49.

Gansewinkel, A. v. "Ehescheidung und Wiederheirat in neutestamentlicher und moraltheologischer Sicht." *Theologie und Glaube* 76 (1986) 193-211.

―――. "Sind Weisungen Christi, sind ethische Normen der Bibel über alle Zeiten hinweg unverändert gültig?" *Anzeiger für die Seelsorge* 100 (1991) 16-18.

Gerstenberger, E. S. and W. Schrage. *Frau und Mann.* Stuttgart, 1980.

Gnilka, J. *Das Matthäusevangelium.* Teil I und II (HThK 1, 1 und 1, 2). Freiburg, 1986 and 1989.

Gössmann, E. "Glanz und Last der Tradition. Ein theologiegeschichtlicher Durchblick." *Mann und Frau.* Ed. Th. Schneider. Pp. 25-52.

Gutting, E. *Offensive gegen den Patriarchalismus. Für eine menschlichere Welt, (Frauenforum).* Freiburg, ²1987.

Gyger, P.-M. "Kurzvortrag ohne Titel im Forum mit Gesprächskreisen . . . damit ihr das Leben in Fülle habt!" *Dein Reich komme,*

89. Dt. Katholikentag Aachen 10.-14. September 1986. Dokumentation Teil I. Paderborn, 1987, 643-655.

Haag, H., ed. *Bibellexikon*. Einsiedeln, 1956.

Haag, H. and K. Elliger. *"Stört nicht die Liebe." Die Diskriminierung der Sexualität—ein Verrat an der Bibel*. Freiburg, ²1986.

Hainz, J., ed. *Münchener Neues Testament*. Studienübersetzung, Düsseldorf, 1988.

Halkes, C. J. M. *Gott hat nicht nur starke Söhne. Grundzüge einer feministischen Theologie*. Gütersloh, 1980 (Evangelische Verlagsanstalt Berlin, 1988).

Häring, B. *Frei in Christus. Moraltheologie für die Praxis des christlichen Lebens. Bd II: Der Weg des Menschen zur Wahrheit und Liebe*. Freiburg, 1980.

_____. *Ausweglos? Zur Pastoral bei Scheidung und Wiederverheiratung. Ein Plädoyer*. Freiburg, 1989.

Hauke, M. *Die Problematik um das Frauenpriestertum vor dem Hintergrund der Schöpfungs- u. Erlösungsordnung* (KKS 46). Paderborn, 1982.

Heiler, F. *Die Frau in den Religionen der Menschheit* (Theologische Bibliothek Töpelmann 33). Berlin, 1977.

Heimerl, H., ed. *Verheiratet und doch nicht verheiratet? (Theologie Konkret)*. Wien, 1970.

Heine, S. *Frauen der frühen Christenheit. Zur historischen Kritik einer feministischen Theologie*. Göttingen, ²1987.

Höfer, J. and K. Rahner, eds. *Lexikon für Theologie und Kirche I-XI*. Freiburg, ²1957-67.

Holtz, G. "Die Pastoralbriefe." *(Theologischer Handkommentar zum NT 13)*. Berlin, 1965.

Huizenga, H. "Women, Salvation, and the Birth of Christ; A Reexamination of 1 Timothy 2, 15." *SBT* 12 (1982) 17-26.

Ignatius v. Loyola. *Geistliche Übungen und erläuternde Texte*. Übersetzt und erklärt von P. Knauer. Leipzig, 1978. English: *Spiritual Exercises*.

Inter Insigniores, Declaratio circa quaestionem admissionis mulierum ad sacerdotium ministeriale. AAS 76:98-116.

Johannes Paul II. *Mulieris Dignitatem. Apostolisches Schreiben über die Würde und Berufung der Frau anläßlich des Marianischen Jahres* (Verlautbarungen des Apostolischen Stuhles 86). Bonn, 1988.

Kähler, E. *Die Frau in den Paulinischen Briefen, unter besonderer Berücksichtigung des Begriffes der Unterordnung*. Zürich, 1960.

Kalsbach, A. *Die altkirchliche Einrichtung der Diakonissen bis zu ihrem Erlöschen* (Röm. Quartalschrift Supplement 22). Freiburg, 1926.

Kamphaus, F. Die evangelischen Räte als befreiende Einladung heute.

Dein Reich komme, 89. Dt. Katholikentag Aachen 10.-14. September 1986. Dokumentation Teil I. Paderborn, 1987, 635-643.

_____. *Frauen in der Kirche. Schwestern im Glauben. Hirtenwort und Anregung zu Verkündigung und Glaubensgespräch in der österlichen Bußzeit.* Limburg, 1989.

Käsemann, E. Amt und Gemeinde im Neuen Testament. *Exegetische Versuche und Besinnungen I.* Ed. E. Käsemann. Göttingen, ²1960, 109-134.

Kertelge, K., ed. *Ethik im Neuen Testament* (QD 102). Freiburg, 1984.

Kirchschläger, W. *Ehe und Ehescheidung im Neuen Testament. Überlegungen und Anfragen zur Praxis der Kirche.* Wien, 1987. (Besprechung von N. Baumert in *Theologische Revue* 86 [1990] 295-296).

_____. "Kurzfassung." *Diakonia* 19 (1988) 305-316.

Kittel, G., ed. *Theologisches Wörterbuch zum Neuen Testament I-X.* Stuttgart, 1933-1979.

Klauck, H. J. *Hausgemeinde und Hauskirche im frühen Christentum.* Stuttgart, 1981.

Klausner, Th., ed. *Reallexikon für Antike und Christentum I-XI.* Stuttgart, 1950-1981.

Knoch, O. *1. und 2. Timotheusbrief. Titusbrief* (*NEB* 14). Würzburg, 1988.

Kruse, G. and G. Müller, eds. *Theologische Realenzyklopädie.* Berlin, 1977 ff.

Kruse, H. "Eheverzicht im Neuen Testament und in der Frühkirche." *Forum Kath. Theologie* 1 (1985) 94-116.

Küchler, M. *Schweigen, Schmuck und Schleier. Drei neutestamentliche Vorschriften zur Verdrängung der Frauen auf dem Hintergrund einer frauenfeindlichen Exegese des AT im antiken Judentum* (Novum Testamentum et Orbis Antiquus 1). Göttingen, 1986.

Kühner, R. and B. Gerth. *Ausführliche Grammatik der griechischen Sprache.* Satzlehre I-II. Hannover, ³1898; Nachdruck, 1966.

Lamsa, G. M. *Old Testament Light. A Scriptural Commentary Based on the Aramaic of the Ancient Peshitta Text.* St. Petersburg Beach, 1964.

Lang, F. *Die Briefe an die Korinther* (NTD 7). Göttingen, 1986.

Lehmann, K. "Das Bild der Frau. Versuch einer anthropologisch-theologischen Standortbestimmung." *Herder Korrespondenz* 41 (1987) 479-487.

Lemaire, A. "Pastoral Epistles: Redaction and Theology." *Biblical Theological Bulletin* 2 (1972) 25-41.

Lewis, R. M. "The 'Women' of 1 Timothy 3, 11." *Bibliotheca Sacra* 542 (1979) 167-175.

Liddell, H. G. and R. Scott, eds. *A Greek—English Lexicon.* Oxford,

⁹1966. A Supplement. Oxford, 1968.

Lietzmann, H. "An die Korinther I-II" (*Handbuch z. NT* 9). Tübingen, ³1933; Lietzmann/Kümmel, ⁴1949.

Lindemann, A. "Der Epheserbrief" (*Zürcher Bibelkommentare* 8). Zürich, 1985.

Lohfink, G. "Weibliche Diakone im Neuen Testament." *Diakonia* 11 (1980) 385–400.

———. "Jesus und die Ehescheidung. Zur Gattung und Sprachintention von Mt 5, 32." *Biblische Randbemerkungen. Schülerfestschrift für R. Schnackenburg.* Eds. H. Merklein and J. Lange. Würzburg, ²1974, 207–217.

Love, S. L. "Women's Roles in Certain Second Testament Passages: a Macrosociological View." *Biblical Theological Bulletin* 17 (1987) 50–59.

Lövestam, E. "Die funktionale Bedeutung der synoptischen Jesusworte über Ehescheidung und Wiederheirat." SNTU 2, Linz 1976, 19–28.

Malina, B. "Does Porneia Mean Fornication?" *NovTest* 14 (1972) 10–17.

Meer, H. v. d. *Priestertum der Frau? Eine theologiegeschichtliche Untersuchung* (QD 42). Freiburg, 1969.

Menge, H. and O. Güthling, O. *Enzyklopädisches Wörterbuch der griechischen und deutschen Sprache I.* Berlin, ¹⁸1964.

Merklein, H. " 'Es ist gut für den Menschen, eine Frau nicht anzufassen.' Paulus und die Sexualität nach 1 Kor 7," Dautzenberg, *Frau,* 225–253.

Metzler, K. *Der griechische Begriff des Verzeihens* (WUNT 2. Reihe Bd. 44). Tübingen, 1991.

Migne, J. P. *Patrologiae Cursus completus, Series Graeca* (PG), *Series Latina* (PL). Paris, 1857 ff.

Moiser, J. "A Reassessment of Paul's View of Marriage with Reference to 1 Cor 7." *JSNT* 18 (1983) 103–122.

Moltmann, E. and J. "Menschwerden in einer neuen Gemeinschaft von Frauen und Männern." *EvTh* 42 (1982) 80–92.

Müller, A. "Für eine Neuorientierung der katholischen Ehelehre." *Diakonia* 19 (1988) 300–316.

Müller, K. "Die Haustafel des Kolosserbriefes und das antike Frauenthema. Eine kritische Rückschau auf alte Ergebnisse." *Die Frau im Urchristentum.* Ed. G. Dautzenberg. Pp. 263–319.

Munier, Ch. *Ehe und Ehelosigkeit in der Alten Kirche (1.-3. Jahrhundert)* (Traditio Christiana 6). Frankfurt, 1987 (Texte und Übersetzungen).

Murphy-O'Connor, J. "The Divorced Woman in 1 Cor 7, 10-11." *JBL* 100 (1981) 601–606.

Mußner, F. Der Galaterbrief (HThK 9). Freiburg, 1977.

Neidhart, W. "Das paulinische Verständnis der Liebe und die Sexualität. Pastoraltheologische Überlegungen." *ThZ* 40 (1984) 245–256.

Nestle, E. and K. Aland. *Novum Testamentum Graece.* 26. neu bearbeitete Auflage. Stuttgart, 1979.

Nestle, E. *Novum Testamentum Graece et Latine.* Stuttgart, ¹⁶1954.

Neuhäusler, E. "Ruf Gottes und Stand des Christen (1 Kor 7, 17-24)." *Bz NF* 3 (1959) 43–60.

Neumann, J. "Unauflösliches Eheband? Eine Anfrage zum kanonischen Eherecht." *ThQ* 151 (1971) 1–22.

Niederwimmer, K. *Askese und Mysterium. Über Ehe, Ehescheidung und Eheverzicht in den Anfängen des christlichen Glaubens* (FRLANT 113). Göttingen, 1975.

Oepke, A. Der Brief des Paulus an die Galater, bearbeitet von J. Rohde (Theologischer Handkommentar zum NT 9). Berlin, ³1973.

———. "Ehe I." RAC.

Ollrog, W.-H. *Paulus und seine Mitarbeiter.* Neukirchen-Vluyn, 1979.

Padgett, A. "Paul on Women in the Church. The Contradictions of Coiffure in 1 Corinthians 11:2-16." *JSNT* 20 (1984) 69–86.

Paul VI, Declaratio "Inter insigniores" vom 15. Okt. 1976, in: AAS 76 (1976) 98–116.

Paulsen, H. "Einheit und Freiheit der Söhne Gottes—Gal 3, 26-29." *ZNW* 71 (1980) 74–95.

Pesch, Römerbrief. (NEB 6). Würzburg, 1983.

Rahner, K. "Priestertum der Frau?." *Stimmen der Zeit* 195 (1977) 291–301.

Ringeling, H. "Frau IV: Neues Testament." TRE 11:431-436.

Ritter, A. M. *Charisma im Verständnis des Joannes Chrysostomos und seiner Zeit. Ein Beitrag zur Erforschung der griechisch-orientalischen Ekklesiologie in der Frühzeit der Reichskirche* (Forschungen z. Kirchen- und Dogmengeschichte 25). Göttingen, 1972.

Rotter, H. "Theologie der Geschlechtlichkeit." *TPQ* 125 (1977) 173–179.

Ruether, Rosemary R. "Frauenkirche. Neuentstehende feministische liturgische Gemeinschaften." *Concilium* 22 (1986) 275–280.

Saffrey, H. D. "Aphrodite à Corinthe. Réflexions sur une Idée Recue." *RB* 92 (1985) 359–374.

Schelkle, K. H. " 'Denn wie das Weib aus dem Mann ist, so auch der Mann aus dem Weib' (1 Kor 11, 12). Zur Gleichberechtigung der Frau im Neuen Testament." *Diakonia* (1984) 85–90.

Schiwy, G. *Weg ins Neue Testament. Kommentar und Material, III Paulusbriefe.* Würzburg, 1968.

Schlatter, A. Die Korintherbriefe (Erläuterungen zum Neuen Testament 6). Stuttgart, 1962.

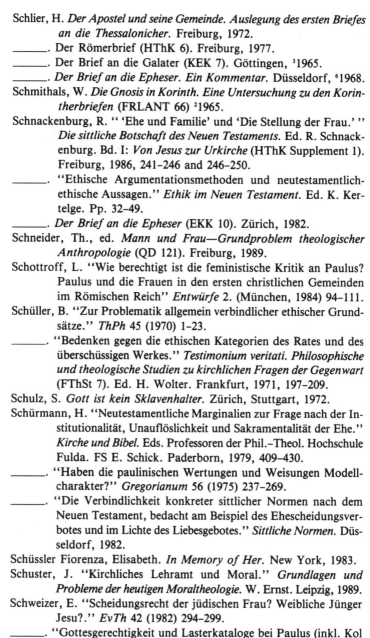

Schlier, H. *Der Apostel und seine Gemeinde. Auslegung des ersten Briefes an die Thessalonicher.* Freiburg, 1972.

———. *Der Römerbrief* (HThK 6). Freiburg, 1977.

———. *Der Brief an die Galater* (KEK 7). Göttingen, ³1965.

———. *Der Brief an die Epheser. Ein Kommentar.* Düsseldorf, ⁶1968.

Schmithals, W. *Die Gnosis in Korinth. Eine Untersuchung zu den Korintherbriefen* (FRLANT 66) ²1965.

Schnackenburg, R. " 'Ehe und Familie' und 'Die Stellung der Frau.' " *Die sittliche Botschaft des Neuen Testaments.* Ed. R. Schnackenburg. Bd. I: *Von Jesus zur Urkirche* (HThK Supplement 1). Freiburg, 1986, 241–246 and 246–250.

———. "Ethische Argumentationsmethoden und neutestamentlichethische Aussagen." *Ethik im Neuen Testament.* Ed. K. Kertelge. Pp. 32–49.

———. *Der Brief an die Epheser* (EKK 10). Zürich, 1982.

Schneider, Th., ed. *Mann und Frau—Grundproblem theologischer Anthropologie* (QD 121). Freiburg, 1989.

Schottroff, L. "Wie berechtigt ist die feministische Kritik an Paulus? Paulus und die Frauen in den ersten christlichen Gemeinden im Römischen Reich" *Entwürfe* 2. (München, 1984) 94–111.

Schüller, B. "Zur Problematik allgemein verbindlicher ethischer Grundsätze." *ThPh* 45 (1970) 1–23.

———. "Bedenken gegen die ethischen Kategorien des Rates und des überschüssigen Werkes." *Testimonium veritati. Philosophische und theologische Studien zu kirchlichen Fragen der Gegenwart* (FThSt 7). Ed. H. Wolter. Frankfurt, 1971, 197–209.

Schulz, S. *Gott ist kein Sklavenhalter.* Zürich, Stuttgart, 1972.

Schürmann, H. "Neutestamentliche Marginalien zur Frage nach der Institutionalität, Unauflöslichkeit und Sakramentalität der Ehe." *Kirche und Bibel.* Eds. Professoren der Phil.-Theol. Hochschule Fulda. FS E. Schick. Paderborn, 1979, 409–430.

———. "Haben die paulinischen Wertungen und Weisungen Modellcharakter?" *Gregorianum* 56 (1975) 237–269.

———. "Die Verbindlichkeit konkreter sittlicher Normen nach dem Neuen Testament, bedacht am Beispiel des Ehescheidungsverbotes und im Lichte des Liebesgebotes." *Sittliche Normen.* Düsseldorf, 1982.

Schüssler Fiorenza, Elisabeth. *In Memory of Her.* New York, 1983.

Schuster, J. "Kirchliches Lehramt und Moral." *Grundlagen und Probleme der heutigen Moraltheologie.* W. Ernst. Leipzig, 1989.

Schweizer, E. "Scheidungsrecht der jüdischen Frau? Weibliche Jünger Jesu?." *EvTh* 42 (1982) 294–299.

———. "Gottesgerechtigkeit und Lasterkataloge bei Paulus (inkl. Kol und Eph)." *Rechtfertigung.* FS Käsemann. Tübingen, 1976, 461–477.

Steininger, V. *Auflösbarkeit unauflöslicher Ehen.* Graz, 1968.

Scroggs, R. "Paul and the Eschatological Woman." *Journal of the American Academy of Religion* 40 (1972) 283–303.

Sickenberger, J. *Die beiden Briefe des heiligen Apostels Paulus an die Korinther und sein Brief an die Römer* (Die Heilige Schrift des Neuen Testaments 6). Bonn, ³1923.

Splett, J. *Freiheits-Erfahrung. Vergegenwärtigungen christlicher Anthropo-theologie.* Frankfurt, 1986.

Staab, K. *Pauluskommentare aus der griechischen Kirche. Aus Katenen-Handschriften gesammelt und herausgegeben* (NTA 15). Münster, 1933.

Stendahl, K. *The Bible and the Role of Women. A Case Study in Hermeneutics* (Biblical Series 15). Philadelphia, 1966.

Strack, H. L. and P. Billerbeck. *Kommentar zum Neuen Testament aus Talmud und Midrasch* I–IV. München, ⁴1965.

Swidler, A. "Die Frau in einer vom Vatergott bestimmten Religion." *Concilium* 17 (1981) 228–234.

Theissen, G. *Psychologische Aspekte paulinischer Theologie* (FRLANT 131). Göttingen, 1983.

Theobald, M. "Heilige Hochzeit. Motive des Mythos im Horizont von Eph 5, 21-33." *Metaphorik und Mythos im Neuen Testament* (QD 126). Ed. K. Kertelge. Freiburg, 1990.

Thraede, K. "Ärger mit der Freiheit. Die Bedeutung von Frauen in Theorie und Praxis der alten Kirche." *"Freunde in Christus werden . . ." Die Beziehung von Mann und Frau als Frage an Theologie und Kirche* (Kennzeichen 1). Gelnhausen, 1977, 35–169.

Thyen, H. "'. . . nicht mehr männlich und weiblich . . .' Eine Studie zu Galater 3, 28." *Als Mann und Frau geschaffen. Exegetische Studien zur Rolle der Frau* (Kennzeichen 2). Eds. F. Crüsemann and H. Thyen. Gelnhausen, 1978, 107–201.

Trilling, W. "Ehe und Ehescheidung im Neuen Testament." *Theologie und Glaube* 74 (1984) 390–406.

Trompf, G. W. "On Attitudes toward Women in Paul and Paulinistic Literature: 1 Corinthians 11, 1-16 and its Context." *CBQ* 42 (1980) 196–215.

Trummer, P. "Einehe nach den Pastoralbriefen. Zum Verständnis der Termini μιᾶς γυναικὸς ἀνήρ und ἑνὸς ἀνδρὸς γυνή." *Bib* 51 (1970) 471–484.

Vogels, H.-J. *Pflichtzölibat. Eine kritische Untersuchung.* München, 1978.

Weiser, Alfons. "Die Rolle der Frau in der urchristlichen Mission." Frau.

Weiß, B. *Die paulinischen Briefe und der Hebräerbrief im berichtigten Text. Mit kurzen Erläuterungen zum Handgebrauch bei der Schriftlektüre.* Leipzig, ²1902.

Weiß, J. *Der erste Korintherbrief* (KEK 5). Göttingen, 1910.

Wendland, H. D. *Die Briefe an die Korinther* (NTD 7). Göttingen, ¹²1968.

Wetzel, N., ed. *Die öffentlichen Sünder oder soll die Kirche Ehen scheiden?"* Mainz, 1970.

Wibbing, S. *Die Tugend und Lasterkataloge im Neuen Testament unter besonderer Berücksichtigung der Qumran-Texte* (BZNW 25). Berlin, 1959.

Wilckens, U. *Das Neue Testament. Übersetzt und kommentiert.* Hamburg, 1970.

Witherington, B. *Women in the Earliest Churches* (SNTS monograph series 59). Cambridge, 1988.

Wolbert, W. *Ethische Argumentation und Paränese in 1 Kor 7.* Düsseldorf, 1981.

Wolff, H. W. *Anthropologie des Alten Testaments.* München, 1973.

Wrembek, Chr. "Der Heilige Geist und das Reich Gottes. Neue Gedanken zu einem alten Thema." *GuL* 64 (1991) 167-183.

Zmijewski, J. "Neutestamentliche Weisungen für Ehe und Familie." SNTU 9, Linz 1984, 31-78.

Subject Index

Scripture Index

This index lists the pertinent Scripture quotations discussed in this book. It is not a complete list of Scripture citations referred to throughout the text.

497